CRIMINAL JUSTICE 91/92

Fifteenth Edition

Annual Editions

A Library of Information from the Public Press

Editor

John J. Sullivan
Mercy College, Dobbs Ferry, New York

John J. Sullivan, professor and former chairman of the Department of Law, Criminal Justice, and Safety Administration at Mercy College, received his B.S. in 1949 from Manhattan College and his J.D. in 1956 from St. John's Law School. He was formerly captain and director of the Legal Division of the New York City Police Department.

Editor

Joseph L. Victor
Mercy College, Dobbs Ferry, New York

Joseph L. Victor is professor and chairman of the Department of Law, Criminal Justice, and Safety Administration at Mercy College, and coordinator of Criminal Justice Graduate Study at the Westchester Campus of Long Island University. Professor Victor has extensive field experience in criminal justice agencies, counseling, and administering human service programs. He earned his B.A. and M.A. at Seton Hall University, and his Doctorate of Education at Fairleigh Dickinson University.

Cover illustration by Mike Eagle

The Dushkin Publishing Group, Inc.
Sluice Dock, Guilford, Connecticut 06437

The Annual Editions Series

Annual Editions is a series of over fifty volumes designed to provide the reader with convenient, low-cost access to a wide range of current, carefully selected articles from some of the most important magazines, newspapers, and journals published today. Annual Editions are updated on an annual basis through a continuous monitoring of over 200 periodical sources. All Annual Editions have a number of features designed to make them particularly useful, including topic guides, annotated tables of contents, unit overviews, and indexes. For the teacher using Annual Editions in the classroom, an Instructor's Resource Guide with test questions is available for each volume.

VOLUMES AVAILABLE

Africa
Aging
American Government
American History, Pre-Civil War
American History, Post-Civil War
Anthropology
Biology
Business and Management
Business Ethics
Canadian Politics
China
Comparative Politics
Computers in Education
Computers in Business
Computers in Society
Criminal Justice
Drugs, Society, and Behavior
Early Childhood Education
Economics
Educating Exceptional Children
Education
Educational Psychology
Environment
Geography
Global Issues
Health
Human Development
Human Resources
Human Sexuality

Latin America
Macroeconomics
Management
Marketing
Marriage and Family
Microeconomics
Middle East and the Islamic World
Money and Banking
Nutrition
Personal Growth and Behavior
Psychology
Public Administration
Race and Ethnic Relations
Social Problems
Sociology
Soviet Union and Eastern Europe
State and Local Government
Third World
Urban Society
Violence and Terrorism
Western Civilization,
  Pre-Reformation
Western Civilization,
  Post-Reformation
Western Europe
World History, Pre-Modern
World History, Modern
World Politics

Library of Congress Cataloging in Publication Data
Main entry under title: Annual editions: Criminal justice. 1991/92.
    1. Criminal Justice, Administration of—United States—Addresses, essays, lectures.
I. Sullivan, John J., *comp.* II. Victor, Joseph L., *comp.* III. Title: Criminal justice.
HV 8138.A67   364.973.05   LC 77-640116
ISBN: 1-56134-016-2

Fifteenth Edition

Manufactured by The Banta Company, Harrisonburg, Virginia 22801

To the Reader

In publishing ANNUAL EDITIONS we recognize the enormous role played by the magazines, newspapers, and journals of the *public press* in providing current, first-rate educational information in a broad spectrum of interest areas. Within the articles, the best scientists, practitioners, researchers, and commentators draw issues into new perspective as accepted theories and viewpoints are called into account by new events, recent discoveries change old facts, and fresh debate breaks out over important controversies.

Many of the articles resulting from this enormous editorial effort are appropriate for students, researchers, and professionals seeking accurate, current material to help bridge the gap between principles and theories and the real world. These articles, however, become more useful for study when those of lasting value are carefully *collected, organized, indexed,* and *reproduced* in a *low-cost format*, which provides easy and permanent access when the material is needed. That is the role played by *Annual Editions*. Under the direction of each volume's *Editor*, who is an expert in the subject area, and with the guidance of an *Advisory Board*, we seek each year to provide in each *ANNUAL EDITION* a current, well-balanced, carefully selected collection of the best of the public press for your study and enjoyment. We think you'll find this volume useful, and we hope you'll take a moment to let us know what you think.

During the 1970s, criminal justice emerged as an appealing, vital, and unique academic discipline. It emphasizes the professional development of students who plan careers in the field, and attracts those who want to know more about a complex social problem and how this country deals with it. Criminal justice incorporates a vast range of knowledge from a number of specialties, including law, history, and the behavioral and social sciences. Each specialty contributes to our fuller understanding of criminal behavior and of society's attitudes toward deviance.

In view of the fact that the criminal justice system is in a constant state of flux, and because the study of criminal justice covers such a broad spectrum, today's students must be aware of a variety of subjects and topics. Standard textbooks and traditional anthologies cannot keep pace with the changes as quickly as they occur. In fact, many such sources are already out of date the day they are published. *Annual Editions: Criminal Justice 91/92* strives to maintain currency in matters of concern by providing up-to-date commentaries, articles, reports, and statistics from the most recent literature in the criminal justice field.

This volume contains units concerning crime and justice in America, victimology, the police, the judicial system, juvenile justice, and punishment and corrections. The articles in these units were selected because they are informative as well as provocative. The selections are timely and useful in their treatment of ethics, punishment, juveniles, courts, and other related topics.

Included in this volume are a number of features designed to make it useful for students, researchers, and professionals in the criminal justice field. These include a topic guide, for locating articles on specific subjects; the table of contents abstracts, which summarize each article and feature key concepts in bold italics; and a comprehensive bibliography, glossary, and index. In addition, each unit is preceded by an overview which provides a background for informed reading of the articles, emphasizes critical issues, and presents challenge questions.

We would like to know what you think of the selections contained in this edition. Please fill out the article rating form on the last page and let us know your opinions. We change or retain many of the articles based on the comments we receive from you, the user. Help us to improve this anthology—annually.

John J. Sullivan

John J. Sullivan

Joseph L. Victor

Joseph L. Victor
Editors

Contents

Unit 1

Crime and Justice in America

Eight selections focus on the overall structure of the criminal justice system in the United States. The current scope of crime in America is reviewed; topics such as criminal behavior, drugs, and organized crime are discussed.

The concepts in bold italics are developed in the article. For further expansion please refer to the Topic Guide, the Index, and the Glossary.

Unit 2

Victimology

Six articles discuss the impact of crime on the victim. Topics include the rights of crime victims, the consequences of family violence, and the legal complications of AIDS testing in rape cases.

Unit 3

Police

Seven selections examine the role of the police officer. Some of the topics discussed include police response to crime, utilization of policewomen, and managing police corruption.

Unit 4

The Judicial System

Eight selections discuss the process by which the accused are moved through the judicial system. Prosecutors, courts, the jury process, and judicial ethics are reviewed.

The concepts in bold italics are developed in the article. For further expansion please refer to the Topic Guide, the Index, and the Glossary.

Unit 5

Juvenile Justice

Five selections review the juvenile justice system. The topics include effective ways to respond to violent juvenile crime, juvenile detention, female delinquency, and the impact of teenage addiction.

The concepts in bold italics are developed in the article. For further expansion please refer to the Topic Guide, the Index, and the Glossary.

Unit 6

Punishment and Corrections

Ten selections focus on the current state of America's penal system, and the effects of sentencing, probation, overcrowding, and capital punishment on criminals.

The concepts in bold italics are developed in the article. For further expansion please refer to the Topic Guide, the Index, and the Glossary.

The concepts in bold italics are developed in the article. For further expansion please refer to the Topic Guide, the Index, and the Glossary.

Charts and Graphs

The concepts in bold italics are developed in the article. For further expansion please refer to the Topic Guide, the Index, and the Glossary.

Topic Guide

This topic guide suggests how the selections in this book relate to topics of traditional concern to students and professionals involved with the study of criminal justice. It can be very useful in locating articles that relate to each other for reading and research. The guide is arranged alphabetically according to topic. Articles may, of course, treat topics that do not appear in the topic guide. In turn, entries in the topic guide do not necessarily constitute a comprehensive listing of all the contents of each selection.

TOPIC AREA	TREATED IN:	TOPIC AREA	TREATED IN:
Abortion	21. Abortion Protesters and the Police	**Criminal Behavior**	3. Are Criminals Made or Born?
AIDS	12. AIDS and Rape 40. AIDS in Prison	**Criminal Justice**	1. Overview of the Criminal Justice System 2. What Is Crime? 23. Public Defenders 24. Prosecutor as a "Minister of Justice"
Attorneys	23. Public Defenders 24. Prosecutor as a "Minister of Justice" 27. Convicting the Innocent		
		Death Penalty	44. 'This Man Has Expired'
Battered Families	11. Battered Families 43. Family Violence Program at Bedford Hills	**Defense Counsel**	26. Public Defenders
		Delinquency	*See* Juveniles
Beccaria, Cesare	41. Of Crimes and Punishment	**Discrimination**	17. Women On the Move?
Children	*See* Juveniles	**Drugs**	14. Prostitutes and Addicts: Special Victims of Rape 20. Police Hard Pressed in Drug War 34. Teenage Addiction
Constitutional Rights	26. Myth of the General Right to Bail 27. Convicting the Innocent 28. When Criminal Rights Go Wrong 29. Defendants Lose As Police Power Is Broadened		
		Ethics	24. Prosecutor as "Minister of Justice"
		Family Violence	11. Battered Families 43. Family Violence Program at Bedford Hills
Corrections	35. Sentencing and Corrections 36. Women in Jail 38. Under Arrest—At Home 40. AIDS in Prison 41. Of Crimes and Punishment 42. Turn the Jailhouse Into a Schoolhouse		
		Fear of Crime	9. Fear of Crime
		House Arrest	38. Under Arrest—At Home
Courts	22. Judicial Process 23. Public Defenders 24. Prosecutor as a "Minister of Justice" 26. Myth of the General Right to Bail	**Jails**	36. Women in Jail 42. Turn the Jailhouse Into a Schoolhouse
		Judges	22. Judicial Process
Crime	1. Overview of the Criminal Justice System 2. What Is Crime? 3. Are Criminals Made or Born? 4. Number of Killings Soar in Big Cities 6. New Strategies to Fight Crime	**Juveniles**	30. Handling of Juvenile Crime 31. Evolution of the Juvenile Justice System 32. Girls' Crime and Woman's Place 33. Juvenile Crime: Who Is Responsible? 34. Teenage Addiction
Crime Victims	*See* Victimology		

TOPIC AREA	TREATED IN:	TOPIC AREA	TREATED IN:
Law Enforcement	*See* Police	**Public Defender**	23. Public Defenders
Mafia	*See* Organized Crime	**Punishment**	*See* Corrections
Narcotics	*See* Drugs	**RICO**	7. RICO: A Racketeering Law Run Amok
Organized Crime	5. New Faces of Organized Crime	**Sentencing**	35. Sentencing and Corrections 41. Of Crimes and Punishment
Parole	39. Difficult Clients, Large Caseloads Plague Probation, Parole Agencies	**Sex Offenders**	12. AIDS and Rape
Police	15. Police Response to Crime 16. Police in the United States 17. Women On the Move? 18. Making Neighborhoods Safe 19. Community Policing 20. Police, Hard Pressed in Drug War Are Turning to Preventive Efforts 21. Abortion Protesters and the Police	**Victimology**	9. Fear of Crime 10. Implementation of Victims' Rights 11. Battered Families 12. AIDS and Rape 13. Can a Marriage Survive Tragedy? 14. Prostitutes and Addicts: Special Victims of Rape
Prisons	40. AIDS in Prison	**Women**	11. Battered Families 17. Women On the Move? 36. Women in Jail: Unequal Justice 37. Status and Performance of Female Corrections Officers in Men's Prisons 43. Family Violence Program at Bedford Hills
Probation	38. Under Arrest—At Home 39. Difficult Clients, Large Caseloads Plague Probation, Parole Agencies		
Prosecution	22. Judicial Process 24. Prosecutor as a "Minister of Justice"		
Prostitutes	14. Prostitutes and Addicts: Special Victims of Rape		

Crime and Justice in America

Crime continues to be a major problem in the United States. Court dockets are full, our prisons are over-crowded, the probation and parole caseloads are over-whelming, and our police are being urged to do more. The bulging prison population places a heavy strain on the economy of the community.

Crime is a complex problem that defies simple explanations or solutions. While the more familiar crimes of murder, rape, and assault are still with us, drugs are an ever-increasing scourge, and international crime is an issue to be dealt with.

The articles presented in this section are intended to serve as a foundation for the materials that are presented in subsequent sections. "An Overview of the Criminal Justice System" charts the sequence of events in the administration of justice. "What Is Crime?" offers definitions and characteristics of the most common serious crimes.

Why do people commit crimes? In spite of the best efforts of experts, human behavior is still not fully understood. Although there is much diversity of opinion as to the causative factors of criminal behavior, the article "Are Criminals Made or Born?" is presented to stimulate discussion and thought.

Murder is on the rise in the United States, and the article "Number of Killings Soars In Big Cities Across U.S." indicates that the increase in drug trafficking and in the availability of weapons to the young are contributing factors.

Is the Mafia or La Cosa Nostra, as we once knew it, on the wane only to be replaced by a new and even more vicious group of organized criminals? "New Faces of Organized Crime" discusses the new criminal organizations arising in the United States. "RICO: A Racketeering Law Run Amok" presents a critical look at the new Federal law designed to stem the illegal activities of organized crime.

Traditional methods of fighting crime are no longer effective in fighting violent crime and "New Strategies to Fight Crime Go Far Beyond Stiffer Terms and More Cells" discusses new efforts being utilized. It is difficult to determine from which side terrorist activity may originate. In "Radical Right vs. Radical Left" the composition and characteristics of these diverse groups are analyzed.

Looking Ahead: Challenge Questions

What is crime?

What is the sequence of events in the criminal justice system?

Is the RICO law being abused by the Federal government?

An Overview of the Criminal Justice System

The response to crime is a complex process that involves citizens as well as many agencies, levels, and branches of government

The private sector initiates the response to crime

This first response may come from any part of the private sector: individuals, families, neighborhood associations, business, industry, agriculture, educational institutions, the news media, or any other private service to the public.

It involves crime prevention as well as participation in the criminal justice process once a crime has been committed. Private crime prevention is more than providing private security or burglar alarms or participating in neighborhood watch. It also includes a commitment to stop criminal behavior by not engaging in it or condoning it when it is committed by others.

Citizens take part directly in the criminal justice process by reporting crime to the police, by being a reliable participant (for example, witness, juror) in a criminal proceeding, and by accepting the disposition of the system as just or reasonable. As voters and taxpayers, citizens also participate in criminal justice through the policymaking process that affects how the criminal justice process operates, the resources available to it, and its goals and objectives. At every stage of the process, from the original formulation of objectives to the decision about where to locate jails and prisons and to the reintegration of inmates into society, the private sector has a role to play. Without such involvement, the criminal justice process cannot serve the citizens it is intended to protect.

The government responds to crime through the criminal justice system

We apprehend, try, and punish offenders by means of a loose confederation of agencies at all levels of government. Our American system of justice has evolved from the English

common law into a complex series of procedures and decisions. There is no single criminal justice system in this country. We have many systems that are similar, but individually unique.

Criminal cases may be handled differently in different jurisdictions, but court

decisions based on the due process guarantees of the U.S. Constitution require that specific steps be taken in the administration of criminal justice.

The description of the criminal and juvenile justice systems that follows portrays the most common sequence of events

What is the sequence of events in the criminal justice system?

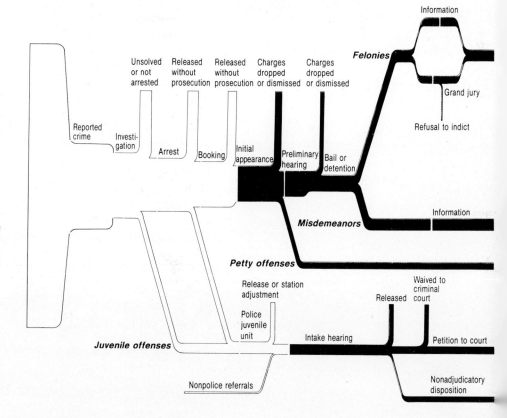

Note: This chart gives a simplified view of caseflow through the criminal justice system. Procedures vary among jurisdictions. The weights of the lines are not intended to show the actual size of caseloads.

From *Report to the Nation on Crime and Justice,* Bureau of Justice Statistics, U.S. Department of Justice, March 1988, pp. 56-60.

in the response to serious criminal behavior.

Entry into the system

The justice system does not respond to most crime because so much crime is not discovered or reported to the police. Law enforcement agencies learn about crime from the reports of citizens, from discovery by a police officer in the field, or from investigative and intelligence work.

Once a law enforcement agency has established that a crime has been com-

Prosecution and pretrial services

After an arrest, law enforcement agencies present information about the case and about the accused to the prosecutor, who will decide if formal charges will be filed with the court. If no charges are filed, the accused must be released. The prosecutor can also drop charges after making efforts to prosecute (*nolle prosequi*).

A suspect charged with a crime must be taken before a judge or magistrate

nation of guilt and assessment of a penalty may also occur at this stage.

In some jurisdictions, a pretrial-release decision is made at the initial appearance, but this decision may occur at other hearings or may be changed at another time during the process. Pretrial release and bail were traditionally intended to ensure appearance at trial. However, many jurisdictions permit pretrial detention of defendants accused of serious offenses and deemed to be dangerous to prevent them from committing crimes in the pretrial period. The court may decide to release the accused on his/her own recognizance, into the custody of a third party, on the promise of satisfying certain conditions, or after the posting of a financial bond.

In many jurisdictions, the initial appearance may be followed by a preliminary hearing. The main function of this hearing is to discover if there is probable cause to believe that the accused committed a known crime within the jurisdiction of the court. If the judge does not find probable cause, the case is dismissed; however, if the judge or magistrate finds probable cause for such a belief, or the accused waives his or her right to a preliminary hearing, the case may be bound over to a grand jury.

A *grand jury* hears evidence against the accused presented by the prosecutor and decides if there is sufficient evidence to cause the accused to be brought to trial. If the grand jury finds sufficient evidence, it submits to the court an indictment (a written statement of the essential facts of the offense charged against the accused). Where the grand jury system is used, the grand jury may also investigate criminal activity generally and issue indictments called grand jury originals that initiate criminal cases.

Misdemeanor cases and some felony cases proceed by the issuance of an *information* (a formal, written accusation submitted to the court by a prosecutor). *In some jurisdictions*, indictments *may be* required in felony cases. However, the accused may choose to waive a grand jury indictment and, instead, accept service of an information for the crime.

Adjudication

Once an indictment or information has been filed with the trial court, the accused is scheduled for arraignment. At the arraignment, the accused is informed of the charges, advised of the

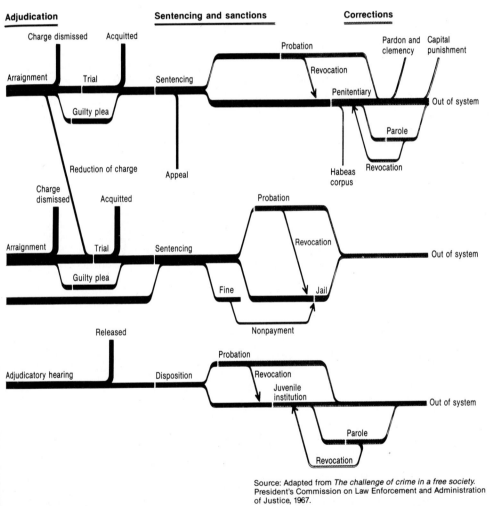

Source: Adapted from *The challenge of crime in a free society.* President's Commission on Law Enforcement and Administration of Justice, 1967.

mitted, a suspect must be identified and apprehended for the case to proceed through the system. Sometimes, a suspect is apprehended at the scene; however, identification of a suspect sometimes requires an extensive investigation. Often, no one is identified or apprehended.

without unnecessary delay. At the initial appearance, the judge or magistrate informs the accused of the charges and decides whether there is probable cause to detain the accused person. Often, the defense counsel is also assigned at the initial appearance. If the offense is not very serious, the determi-

rights of criminal defendants, and asked to enter a plea to the charges. Sometimes, a plea of guilty is the result of negotiations between the prosecutor and the defendant, with the defendant entering a guilty plea in expectation of reduced charges or a lenient sentence.

If the accused pleads guilty or pleads *nolo contendere* (accepts penalty without admitting guilt), the judge may accept or reject the plea. If the plea is accepted, no trial is held and the offender is sentenced at this proceeding or at a later date. The plea may be rejected if, for example, the judge believes that the accused may have been coerced. If this occurs, the case may proceed to trial.

If the accused pleads not guilty or not guilty by reason of insanity, a date is set for the trial. A person accused of a serious crime is guaranteed a trial by jury. However, the accused may ask for a bench trial where the judge, rather than a jury, serves as the finder of fact. In both instances the prosecution and defense present evidence by questioning witnesses while the judge decides on issues of law. The trial results in acquittal or conviction on the original charges or on lesser included offenses.

After the trial a defendant may request appellate review of the conviction or sentence. In many criminal cases, appeals of a conviction are a matter of right; all States with the death penalty provide for automatic appeal of cases involving a death sentence. However, under some circumstances and in some jurisdictions, appeals may be subject to the discretion of the appellate court and may be granted only on acceptance of a defendant's petition for a *writ of certiorari*. Prisoners may also appeal their sentences through civil rights petitions and writs of habeas corpus where they claim unlawful detention.

Sentencing and sanctions

After a guilty verdict or guilty plea, sentence is imposed. In most cases the judge decides on the sentence, but in some States, the sentence is decided by the jury, particularly for capital offenses such as murder.

In arriving at an appropriate sentence, a sentencing hearing may be held at which evidence of aggravating or mitigating circumstances will be considered. In assessing the circumstances surrounding a convicted person's criminal behavior, courts often rely on presentence investigations by probation

agencies or other designated authorities. Courts may also consider victim impact statements.

The sentencing choices that may be available to judges and juries include one or more of the following:
• the death penalty
• incarceration in a prison, jail, or other confinement facility
• probation—allowing the convicted person to remain at liberty but subject to certain conditions and restrictions
• fines—primarily applied as penalties in minor offenses
• restitution—which requires the offender to provide financial compensation to the victim.

In many States, State law mandates that persons convicted of certain types of offenses serve a prison term.

Most States permit the judge to set the sentence length within certain limits, but some States have determinate sentencing laws that stipulate a specific sentence length, which must be served and cannot be altered by a parole board.

Corrections

Offenders sentenced to incarceration usually serve time in a local jail or a State prison. Offenders sentenced to less than 1 year generally go to jail; those sentenced to more than 1 year go to prison. Persons admitted to a State prison system may be held in prisons with varying levels of custody or in a community correctional facility.

A prisoner may become eligible for parole after serving a specific part of his or her sentence. Parole is the conditional release of a prisoner before the prisoner's full sentence has been served. The decision to grant parole is made by an authority such as a parole board, which has power to grant or revoke parole or to discharge a parolee altogether. The way parole decisions are made varies widely among jurisdictions.

Offenders may also be required to serve out their full sentences prior to release (expiration of term). Those sentenced under determinate sentencing laws can be released only after they have served their full sentence (mandatory release) less any "goodtime" received while in prison. Inmates get such credits against their sentences automatically or by earning it through participation in programs.

If an offender has an outstanding charge or sentence in another State, a

detainer is used to ensure that when released from prison he or she will be transferred to the other State.

If released by a parole board decision or by mandatory release, the releasee will be under the supervision of a parole officer in the community for the balance of his or her unexpired sentence. This supervision is governed by specific conditions of release, and the releasee may be returned to prison for violations of such conditions.

The juvenile justice system

The processing of juvenile offenders is not entirely dissimilar to adult criminal processing, but there are crucial differences in the procedures. Many juveniles are referred to juvenile courts by law enforcement officers, but many others are referred by school officials, social services agencies, neighbors, and even parents, for behavior or conditions that are determined to require intervention by the formal system for social control.

When juveniles are referred to the juvenile courts, their *intake* departments, or prosecuting attorneys, determine whether sufficient grounds exist to warrant filing a petition that requests an *adjudicatory hearing* or a request to transfer jurisdiction to criminal court. In some States and at the Federal level prosecutors under certain circumstances may file criminal charges against juveniles directly in criminal courts.

The court with jurisdiction over juvenile matters may reject the petition or the juveniles may be diverted to other agencies or programs in lieu of further court processing. Examples of diversion programs include individual or group counseling or referral to educational and recreational programs.

If a petition for an adjudicatory hearing is accepted, the juvenile may be brought before a court quite unlike the court with jurisdiction over adult offenders. In disposing of cases juvenile courts usually have far more discretion than adult courts. In addition to such options as probation, commitment to correctional institutions, restitution, or fines, State laws grant juvenile courts the power to order removal of children from their homes to foster homes or treatment facilities. Juvenile courts also may order participation in special programs aimed at shoplifting prevention, drug counseling, or driver education. They also may order referral to criminal court for trial as adults.

Despite the considerable discretion associated with juvenile court proceedings, juveniles are afforded many of the due-process safeguards associated with adult criminal trials. Sixteen States permit the use of juries in juvenile courts; however, in light of the U.S. Supreme Court's holding that juries are not essential to juvenile hearings, most States do not make provisions for juries in juvenile courts.

The response to crime is founded in the intergovernmental structure of the United States

Under our form of government, each State and the Federal Government has its own criminal justice system. All systems must respect the rights of individuals set forth in court interpretation of the U.S. Constitution and defined in case law.

State constitutions and laws define the criminal justice system within each State and delegate the authority and responsibility for criminal justice to various jurisdictions, officials, and institutions. State laws also define criminal behavior and groups of children or acts under jurisdiction of the juvenile courts.

Municipalities and counties further define their criminal justice systems through local ordinances that proscribe additional illegal behavior and establish the local agencies responsible for criminal justice processing that were not established by the State.

Congress also has established a criminal justice system at the Federal level to respond to Federal crimes such as bank robbery, kidnaping, and transporting stolen goods across State lines.

The response to crime is mainly a State and local function

Very few crimes are under exclusive Federal jurisdiction. The responsibility to respond to most crime rests with the State and local governments. Police protection is primarily a function of cities and towns. Corrections is primarily a function of State governments. More than three-fifths of all justice personnel are employed at the local level.

	Percent of criminal justice employment by level of government		
	Local	State	Federal
Police	77%	15%	8%
Judicial (courts only)	60	32	8
Prosecution and legal services	58	26	17
Public defense	47	50	3
Corrections	35	61	4
Total	62%	31%	8%

Source: *Justice expenditure and employment, 1985,* BJS Bulletin, March 1987.

Discretion is exercised throughout the criminal justice system

Discretion is "an authority conferred by law to act in certain conditions or situations in accordance with an official's or an official agency's own considered judgment and conscience."[1] Discretion is exercised throughout the government. It is a part of decisionmaking in all government systems from mental health to education, as well as criminal justice.

Concerning crime and justice, legislative bodies have recognized that they cannot anticipate the range of circumstances surrounding each crime, anticipate local mores, and enact laws that clearly encompass all conduct that is criminal and all that is not.[2] Therefore, persons charged with the day-to-day response to crime are expected to exercise their own judgment within *limits* set by law. Basically, they must decide—
• whether to take action

• where the situation fits in the scheme of law, rules, and precedent
• which official response is appropriate.

To ensure that discretion is exercised responsibly, government authority is often delegated to professionals. Professionalism requires a minimum level of training and orientation, which guides officials in making decisions. The professionalism of policing discussed later in this chapter is due largely to the desire to ensure the proper exercise of police discretion.

The limits of discretion vary from State to State and locality to locality. For example, some State judges have wide discretion in the type of sentence they may impose. In recent years other States have sought to limit the judges' discretion in sentencing by passing mandatory sentencing laws that require prison sentences for certain offenses.

Who exercises discretion?

These criminal justice officials...	...must often decide whether or not or how to—
Police	Enforce specific laws Investigate specific crimes Search people, vicinities, buildings Arrest or detain people
Prosecutors	File charges or petitions for adjudication Seek indictments Drop cases Reduce charges
Judges or magistrates	Set bail or conditions for release Accept pleas Determine delinquency Dismiss charges Impose sentence Revoke probation
Correctional officials	Assign to type of correctional facility Award privileges Punish for disciplinary infractions
Paroling authority	Determine date and conditions of parole Revoke parole

1. CRIME AND JUSTICE IN AMERICA

More than one agency has jurisdiction over some criminal events

The response to most criminal actions is usually begun by local police who react to violation of State law. If a suspect is apprehended, he or she is prosecuted locally and may be confined in a local jail or State prison. In such cases, only one agency has jurisdiction at each stage in the process.

However, some criminal events because of their characteristics and location may come under the jurisdiction of more than one agency. For example, such overlapping occurs within States when local police, county sheriffs, and State police are all empowered to enforce State laws on State highways.

Congress has provided for Federal jurisdiction over crimes that—
• materially affect interstate commerce
• occur on Federal land
• involve large and probably interstate criminal organizations or conspiracies
• are offenses of national importance, such as the assassination of the President.[3]

Bank robbery and many drug offenses are examples of crimes for which the States and the Federal Government both have jurisdiction. In cases of dual jurisdiction, an investigation and a prosecution may be undertaken by all authorized agencies, but only one level of government usually pursues a case. For example, a study of FBI bank robbery investigations during 1978 and 1979 found that of those cases cleared—

• 36% were solved by the FBI alone
• 25% were solved by a joint effort of the FBI and State and local police
• 40% were solved by the State and local police acting alone.

In response to dual jurisdiction and to promote more effective coordination, Law Enforcement Coordinating Committees have been established throughout the country and include all relevant Federal and local agencies.

Within States the response to crime also varies from one locality to another

The response differs because of statutory and structural differences and differences in how discretion is exercised. Local criminal justice policies and programs change in response to local attitudes and needs. For example, the prosecutor in one locality may concentrate on particular types of offenses that plague the local community while the prosecutor in another locality may concentrate on career criminals.

The response to crime also varies on a case-by-case basis

No two cases are exactly alike. At each stage of the criminal justice process officials must make decisions that take into account the varying factors of each case. Two similar cases may have very different results because of various factors, including differences in witness cooperation and physical evidence, the availability of resources to investigate and prosecute the case, the quality of the lawyers involved, and the age and prior criminal history of the suspects.

Differences in local laws, agencies, resources, standards, and procedures result in varying responses in each jurisdiction

The outcomes of arrests for serious cases vary among the States as shown by Offender-based Transaction Statistics from nine States:

	% of arrests for serious crimes that result in . . .		
	Prosecution	Conviction	Incarceration
Virginia	100%	61%	55%
Nebraska	99	68	39
New York	97	67	31
Utah	97	79	9
Virgin Islands	95	55	35
Minnesota	89	69	48
Pennsylvania	85	56	24
California	78	61	45
Ohio	77	50	21

Source: Disaggregated data used in *Tracking offenders: White-collar crime*, BJS Special Report, November 1986.

Some of this variation can be explained by differences among States. For example, the degree of discretion in deciding whether to prosecute differs from State to State; some States do not allow any police or prosecutor discretion; others allow police discretion but not prosecutor discretion and vice versa.

What is crime?

Crimes are defined by law

In this report we define crime as all behaviors and acts for which a society provides formally sanctioned punishment. In the United States what is criminal is specified in the written law, primarily State statutes. What is included in the definition of crime varies among Federal, State, and local jurisdictions.

Criminologists devote a great deal of attention to defining crime in both general and specific terms. This definitional process is the first step toward the goal of obtaining accurate crime statistics.

To provide additional perspectives on crime it is sometimes viewed in ways other than in the standard legal definitions. Such alternatives define crime in terms of the type of victim (child abuse), the type of offender (white-collar crime), the object of the crime (property crime), or the method of criminal activity (organized crime). Such definitions usually cover one or more of the standard legal definitions. For example, organized crime may include fraud, extortion, assault, or homicide.

What is considered criminal by society changes over time

Some types of events such as murder, robbery, and burglary have been defined as crimes for centuries. Such crimes are part of the common law definition of crime. Other types of conduct traditionally have not been viewed as crimes. As social values and mores change, society has codified some conduct as criminal while decriminalizing other conduct. The recent movement toward increased "criminalization" of drunk driving is an example of such change.

New technology also results in new types of conduct not anticipated by the law. Changes in the law may be needed to define and sanction these types of conduct. For example, the introduction of computers has added to the criminal codes in many States so that acts such as the destruction of programs or data could be defined as crimes.

What are the characteristics of some serious crimes?

Crime	Definition	Facts
Homicide	Causing the death of another person without legal justification or excuse, including UCR crimes of murder and nonnegligent manslaughter and negligent manslaughter.	• Murder and nonnegligent manslaughter occur less often than other violent UCR Index crimes. • 58% of the known murderers were relatives or acquaintances of the victim. • 20% of all murders in 1985 occurred or were suspected to have occurred as the result of some felonious activity.
Rape	Unlawful sexual intercourse with a female, by force or without legal or factual consent.	• Most rapes involve a lone offender and a lone victim. • About 32% of the rapes recorded by NCS in 1985 were committed in or near the victim's home. • 73% of the rapes occurred at night, between 6 p.m. and 6 a.m. • 58% of the victims of rape in 1985 were under 25 years old.
Robbery	The unlawful taking or attempted taking of property that is in the immediate possession of another, by force or threat of force.	• Robbery is the violent crime that most often involves more than one offender (in almost half of all cases in 1985). • About half of all robberies reported by NCS in 1985 involved the use of a weapon.
Assault	Unlawful intentional inflicting, or attempted inflicting, of injury upon the person of another. Aggravated assault is the unlawful intentional inflicting of serious bodily injury or unlawful threat or attempt to inflict bodily injury or death by means of a deadly or dangerous weapon with or without actual infliction of injury. Simple assault is the unlawful intentional inflicting of less than serious bodily injury without a deadly or dangerous weapon or an attempt or threat to inflict bodily injury without a deadly or dangerous weapon.	• Simple assault occurs more frequently than aggravated assault. • Most assaults involve one victim and one offender.

(continued on next page)

What are some other common crimes in the United States?

Drug abuse violations—Offenses relating to growing, manufacturing, making, possessing, using, selling, or distributing narcotic and dangerous nonnarcotic drugs. A distinction is made between possession and sale/manufacturing.

Sex offenses—In current statistical usage, the name of a broad category of varying content, usually consisting of all offenses having a sexual element except for forcible rape and commercial sex offenses, which are defined separately.

Fraud offenses—The crime type comprising offenses sharing the elements of practice of deceit or intentional misrepresentation of fact, with the intent of unlawfully depriving a person of his or her property or legal rights.

Drunkenness—Public intoxication, except "driving under the influence."

Disturbing the peace—Unlawful interruption of the peace, quiet, or order of a community, including offenses called "disorderly conduct," "vagrancy," "loitering," "unlawful assembly," and "riot."

Driving under the influence—Driving or operating any vehicle or common carrier while drunk or under the influence of liquor or drugs.

From *Report to the Nation on Crime and Justice,* Bureau of Justice Statistics, U.S. Department of Justice, March 1988, pp. 2-3, 8-9.

1. CRIME AND JUSTICE IN AMERICA

Liquor law offenses—State or local liquor law violations, except drunkenness and driving under the influence. Federal violations are excluded.

Gambling—Unlawful staking or wagering of money or other thing of value on a game of chance or on an uncertain event.

Kidnaping—Transportation or confine-

Weapons offenses, bribery, escape, and tax law violations, for example, are included in this category.

How do violent crimes differ from property crimes?

The outcome of a criminal event determines if it is a property crime or a violent crime. Violent crime refers to events such as homicide, rape, and assault

households (property crimes, including household larceny).

How do felonies differ from misdemeanors?

Criminal offenses are also classified according to how they are handled by the criminal justice system. Most jurisdictions recognize two classes of offenses: felonies and misdemeanors.

Felonies are not distinguished from misdemeanors in the same way in all jurisdictions, but most States define felonies as offenses punishable by a year or more in a State prison. The most serious crimes are never "misdemeanors" and the most minor offenses are never "felonies."

What are the characteristics of some serious crimes?

Crime	Definition	Facts
Burglary	Unlawful entry of any fixed structure, vehicle, or vessel used for regular residence, industry, or business, with or without force, with the intent to commit a felony or larceny.	• Residential property was targeted in 2 out of every 3 reported burglaries; nonresidential property accounted for the remaining third. • In 1985, 42% of all residential burglaries occurred without forced entry. • About 37% of the no-force burglaries were known to have occurred during the day between 6 a.m. and 6 p.m.
Larceny-theft	Unlawful taking or attempted taking of property other than a motor vehicle from the possession of another, by stealth, without force and without deceit, with intent to permanently deprive the owner of the property.	• Less than 5% of all personal larcenies involve contact between the victim and offender. • Pocket picking and purse snatching most frequently occur inside nonresidential buildings or on street locations. • Unlike most other crimes, pocket picking and purse snatching affect the elderly about as much as other age groups.
Motor vehicle theft	Unlawful taking or attempted taking of a self-propelled road vehicle owned by another, with the intent of depriving him or her of it, permanently or temporarily.	• Motor vehicle theft is relatively well reported to the police. In 1985 89% of all completed thefts were reported. • The stolen property is more likely to be recovered in this crime than in other property crimes.
Arson	The intentional damaging or destruction or attempted damaging or destruction by means of fire or explosion of property without the consent of the owner, or of one's own property or that of another by fire or explosives with or without the intent to defraud.	• Single-family residences were the most frequent targets of arson. • 16% of all structures where arson occurred were not in use.

Sources: BJS *Dictionary of criminal justice data terminology*, 2nd edition, 1981.
BJS *Criminal victimization in the U.S., 1985.* FBI *Crime in the United States 1985.*

ment of a person without authority of law and without his or her consent, or without the consent of his or her guardian, if a minor.

Vandalism—Destroying or damaging, or attempting to destroy or damage, the property of another without his or her consent, or public property, except by burning, which is arson.

Public order offenses—Violations of the peace or order of the community or threats to the public health through unacceptable public conduct, interference with governmental authority, or violation of civil rights or liberties.

that may result in injury to a person. Robbery is also considered a violent crime because it involves the use or threat of force against a person.

Property crimes are unlawful acts with the intent of gaining property but which do not involve the use or threat of force against an individual. Larceny and motor vehicle theft are examples of property crimes.

In the National Crime Survey a distinction is also made between crimes against persons (violent crimes and personal larceny) and crimes against

What is organized crime?

Although organized crime has been considered a problem throughout the century, no universally accepted definition of the term has been established. The President's Commission on Organized Crime, for example, defines the criminal group involved in organized crime as "a continuing, structured collectivity of persons who utilize criminality, violence, and a willingness to corrupt in order to gain and maintain power and profit."

Some characteristics of organized crime are generally cited:
• **Organizational continuity:** Organized crime groups ensure that they can survive the death or imprisonment of their leaders and can vary the nature of their activities to take advantage of changing criminal opportunities.
• **Hierarchical structure:** All organized crime groups are headed by a single leader and structured into a series of subordinate ranks, although they may vary in the rigidity of their hierarchy. Nationwide organizations may be composed of multiple separate chapters or "families," each unit generally headed by its own leader who is supported by the group's hierarchy of command. Intergroup disputes, joint ventures, and new membership are generally reviewed by a board composed of the leaders of the most powerful individual chapters. For example, La Cosa Nostra currently is estimated to include 24 individual "families" all under the general authority of a "National Commission" comprised of an estimated nine bosses.
• **Restricted membership:** Members must be formally accepted by the group after a demonstration of loyalty and a willingness to commit criminal acts. Membership may be limited by race or common background and generally

Organized crime includes many traditional crimes as well as offenses such as racketeering

involves a lifetime commitment to the group, which can be enforced through violent group actions.

• **Criminality/violence/power:** Power and control are key organized crime goals and may be obtained through criminal activity of one type or in multiple activities. Criminal activity may be designed directly to generate "income" or to support the group's power through bribery, violence, and intimidation. Violence is used to maintain group loyalty and to intimidate outsiders and is a threat underlying all group activity. Specific violent criminal acts include, for example, murder, kidnaping, arson, robbery, and bombings.

• **Legitimate business involvement:** Legitimate businesses are used to "launder" illegal funds or stolen merchandise. For example, illegal profits from drug sales can be claimed as legitimate profits of a noncriminal business whose accounting records have been appropriately adjusted. Legitimate business involvement also elevates the social status of organized crime figures.

• **Use of specialists:** Outside specialists, such as pilots, chemists, and arsonists, provide services under contract to organized crime groups on an intermittent or regular basis.

Organized crime groups often are protected by corrupt officials in the government and private sector

Such officials include inspectors who overlook violations, accountants who conceal assets, financial officers who fail to report major cash transactions, law enforcement officers who provide enforcement activity information to drug traffickers, and attorneys who have government witnesses intimidated to change their testimony. The public also supports organized crime by sometimes knowingly or unknowingly purchasing illegal goods and "hot" merchandise.

Organized crime groups are involved in many different activities

In addition to its well known involvement in illegal drugs, organized crime is also involved in prostitution, gambling, and loan sharking operations and has been shown to have infiltrated legitimate industries such as construction, waste removal, wholesale and retail distribution of goods, hotel and restaurant operations, liquor sales, motor vehicle repairs, real estate, and banking.

How much does organized crime cost?

A recent survey for the President's Commission on Organized Crime estimates that 1986 net income from organized crime activity ranged between $26.8 billion (a low estimate) and $67.7 billion (the high estimate).

The indirect costs of organized crime affect all consumers through increased consumer prices. Kickbacks, protection payments, increased labor and material costs, and lack of competition in industries controlled by organized crime all increase consumer costs. Unpaid taxes on illegal activities result in higher tax burdens for legal wage earners.

Racketeer Influenced and Corrupt Organization (RICO) statutes are key tools in the fight against organized crime

The Federal RICO statute was enacted in 1970 and was amended most recently in 1986. Unlike other existing statutes that address individual criminal acts such as murder or robbery, the RICO statute was specifically designed to target the overall and continuing operations of organized crime organizations. Specifically, the act prohibits the use of racketeering activities or profits to acquire, conduct, or maintain the business of an existing organization or "enterprise." Racketeering activities are defined to include any act or threat involving murder, kidnaping, gambling, arson, robbery, bribery, extortion, dealing in narcotic or dangerous drugs, fraud, and other crimes. The act also provides for forfeiture of illegally obtained gains and interests in enterprises.

Twenty-three States had enacted RICO statutes by 1986. Most of them are very similar to the Federal statute.

The government also has other tools to fight organized crime, including witness protection programs, electronic surveillance procedures, and immunity statutes.

There is much debate about how to define "white-collar" crime

Reiss and Biderman define it as violations of law "that involve the use of a violator's position of significant power, influence or trust ... for the purpose of illegal gain, or to commit an illegal act for personal or organizational gain." Another researcher, Sutherland, defines white-collar crime as "a crime committed by a person of respectability and high social status in the course of his occupation." Edelhertz defines it as "an illegal act or series of illegal acts committed by nonphysical means and by concealment or guile to obtain money or property, to avoid the payment or loss of money or property, or to obtain business or personal advantage."

Although specific definitions vary, the term is generally construed to include business-related crimes, abuse of political office, some (but not all) aspects of organized crime, and the newly emerging areas of high-technology crime. White-collar crimes often involve deception of a gullible victim and generally occur where an individual's job, power, or personal influence provide the access and opportunity to abuse lawful procedures for unlawful gain.

Specific white-collar crimes include embezzlement, bribery, fraud (including procurement fraud, stock fraud, fraud in government programs, and investment and other "schemes"), theft of services, theft of trade secrets, tax evasion, and obstruction of justice.

Unlike violent crimes, white-collar crimes do not necessarily cause injury to identifiable persons

White-collar crime instead can cause loss to society in general as in cases of tax evasion, for example. For this reason, white-collar crimes, unlike violent crimes, may not always be detected and are more difficult to investigate.

Little data are available on the extent of white-collar crime

Measuring white-collar crime presents special problems:

• **No uniform definitions** exist that define either the overall scope of white-collar crime or individual criminal acts.

• **Wide variations** in commercial recordkeeping procedures make it difficult to collect and classify data on the loss.

• **Uncertainty over the legal status** of financial and technical transactions complicates the classification of data.

White-collar crime refers to a group of nonviolent crimes that generally involve deception or abuse of power

• **Computer technology** can conceal losses resulting from computer crimes.
• **Crimes may not be reported** to protect consumer confidence.

Almost three-fourths of the white-collar crimes prosecuted at the State level resulted in convictions

A study of 8 States and the Virgin Islands found that 12% of the white-collar crime cases that originated with an arrest and for which dispositions were reported in 1983 were not prosecuted. The study defined white-collar crimes as forgery/counterfeiting, fraud, and embezzlement.

Prosecution rates for white-collar crimes were similar to those for violent crimes (murder, rape, robbery, kidnaping, and assault), property crimes (stolen vehicles, burglary, and arson), and public order crimes (drug and weapons offenses and commercial vice). Because the study focused on white-collar crime cases that were reported through the criminal justice system, the sample does not take into account the large number of white-collar crimes that were not discovered, not reported to authorities, or did not result in an arrest.

The study also found the conviction rate for cases prosecuted to be about 74%, slightly higher than for violent crimes (66%) and public order crimes (67%) and about the same as for property crimes (76%).

About 60% of the persons convicted for white-collar crime vs. about 67% of those convicted for violent crimes were sentenced to prison. Eighteen percent of white-collar offenders sentenced to prison were sentenced to more than 1 year (about the same as persons convicted of public order offense) vs. 39% of violent offenders.

ARE CRIMINALS MADE OR BORN?

Evidence indicates that both biological and sociological factors play roles.

**Richard J. Herrnstein and
James Q. Wilson**

*Richard J. Herrnstein is a professor of psychology
and James Q. Wilson a professor of government at
Harvard.*

A revolution in our understanding of crime is quietly overthrowing some established doctrines. Until recently, criminologists looked for the causes of crime almost entirely in the offenders' social circumstances. There seemed to be no shortage of circumstances to blame: weakened, chaotic or broken families, ineffective schools, antisocial gangs, racism, poverty, unemployment. Criminologists took seriously, more so than many other students of social behavior, the famous dictum of the French sociologist Emile Durkheim: Social facts must have social explanations. The sociological theory of crime had the unquestioned support of prominent editorialists, commentators, politicians and most thoughtful people.

Today, many learned journals and scholarly works draw a different picture. Sociological factors have not been abandoned, but increasingly it is becoming clear to many scholars that crime is the outcome of an interaction between social factors and certain biological factors, particularly for the offenders who, by repeated crimes, have made public places dangerous. The idea is still controversial, but increasingly, to the old question "Are criminals born or made?" the answer seems to be: both. The causes of crime lie in a combination of predisposing biological traits channeled by social circumstance into criminal behavior. The traits alone do not inevitably lead to crime; the circumstances do not make criminals of everyone; but together they create a population responsible for a large fraction of America's problem of crime in the streets.

Evidence that criminal behavior has deeper roots than social circumstances has always been right at hand, but social science has, until recent years, overlooked its implications. As far as the records show, crime everywhere and throughout history is disproportionately a young man's pursuit. Whether men are 20 or more times as likely to be arrested as women, as is the case in Malawi or Brunei, or only four to six times as likely, as in the United States or France, the sex difference in crime statistics is universal. Similarly, 18-year-olds may sometimes be four times as likely to be criminal as 40-year-olds, while at other times only twice as likely. In the United States, more than half of all arrests for serious property crimes are of 20-year-olds or younger. Nowhere have older persons been as criminal as younger ones.

It is easy to imagine purely social explanations for the effects of age and sex on crime. Boys in many societies are trained by their parents and the society itself to play more roughly and aggressively than girls. Boys are expected to fight back, not to cry,

Intelligence and temperament have heritable bases and influence behavior.

and to play to win. Likewise, boys in many cultures are denied adult responsibilities, kept in a state of prolonged dependence and confined too long in schools that many of them find unrewarding. For a long time, these factors were thought to be the whole story.

Ultimately, however, the very universality of the age and sex differences in crime have alerted some social scientists to the implausibility of a theory that does not look beyond the accidents of particular societies. If cultures as different as Japan's and Sweden's, England's and Mexico's, have sex and age differences in crime, then perhaps we should have suspected from the start that there was something more fundamental going on than parents happening to decide to raise their boys and girls differently. What is it about boys, girls and their parents, in societies of all sorts, that leads them to emphasize, rather than overcome, sex differences? Moreover, even if we believed that every society has arbitrarily decided to inculcate aggressiveness in males, there would still be the greater criminality among *young* males to explain. After all, in some cultures, young boys are not denied adult responsibilities but are kept out of school, put to work tilling the land and made to accept obligations to the society.

But it is no longer necessary to approach questions about the sources of criminal behavior merely with argument and supposition. There is evidence. Much crime, it is agreed, has an aggressive component, and Eleanor Emmons Maccoby, a professor of psychology at Stanford University, and Carol Nagy Jacklin, a psychologist now at the University of Southern California, after reviewing the evidence on sex differences in aggression, concluded that it has a foundation that is at least in part biological. Only that conclusion can be drawn, they said, from data that show that the average man is more aggressive than the average woman in all known

societies, that the sex difference is present in infancy well before evidence of sex-role socialization by adults, that similar sex differences turn up in many of our biological relatives—monkeys and apes. Human aggression has been directly tied to sex hormones, particularly male sex hormones, in experiments on athletes engaging in competitive sports and on prisoners known for violent or domineering behavior. No single line of evidence is decisive and each can be challenged, but all together they convinced Drs. Maccoby and Jacklin, as well as most specialists on the biology of sex differences, that the sexual conventions that assign males the aggressive roles have biological roots.

That is also the conclusion of most researchers about the developmental forces that make adolescence and young adulthood a time of risk for criminal and other nonconventional behavior. This is when powerful new drives awaken, leading to frustrations that foster behavior unchecked by the internalized prohibitions of adulthood. The result is usually just youthful rowdiness, but, in a minority of cases, it passes over the line into crime.

The most compelling evidence of biological factors for criminality comes from two studies—one of twins, the other of adopted boys. Since the 1920's it has been understood that twins may develop from a single fertilized egg, resulting in identical genetic endowments—identical twins—or from a pair of separately fertilized eggs that have about half their genes in common—fraternal twins. A standard procedure for estimating how important genes are to a trait is to compare the similarity between identical twins with that between fraternal twins. When identical twins are clearly more similar in a trait than fraternal twins, the trait probably has high heritability.

There have been about a dozen studies of criminality using twins. More than 1,500 pairs of twins have been studied in the

United States, the Scandinavian countries, Japan, West Germany, Britain and elsewhere, and the result is qualitatively the same everywhere. Identical twins are more likely to have similar criminal records than fraternal twins. For example, the late Karl O. Christiansen, a Danish criminologist, using the Danish Twin Register, searched police, court and prison records for entries regarding twins born in a certain region of Denmark between 1881 and 1910. When an identical twin had a criminal record, Christiansen found, his or her co-twin was more than twice as likely to have one also than when a fraternal twin had a criminal record.

In the United States, a similar result has recently been reported by David Rowe, a psychologist at the University of Oklahoma, using questionnaires instead of official records to measure criminality. Twins in high school in almost all the school districts of Ohio received questionnaires by mail, with a promise of confidentiality as well as a small payment if the questionnaires were filled out and returned. The twins were asked about their activities, including their delinquent behavior, about their friends and about their co-twins. The identical twins were more similar in delinquency than the fraternal twins. In addition, the twins who shared more activities with each other were no more likely to be similar in delinquency than those who shared fewer activities.

No single method of inquiry should be regarded as conclusive. But essentially the same results are found in studies of adopted children. The idea behind such studies is to find a sample of children adopted early in life, cases in which the criminal histories of both adopting and biological parents are known. Then, as the children grow up, researchers can discover how predictive of their criminality are the family histories of their adopting and biological parents. Recent studies show that the biological family his-

tory contributes substantially to the adoptees' likelihood of breaking the law.

For example, Sarnoff Mednick, a psychologist at the University of Southern California, and his associates in the United States and Denmark have followed a sample of several thousand boys adopted in Denmark between 1927 and 1947. Boys with criminal biological parents and noncriminal adopting parents were more likely to have criminal records than those with noncriminal biological parents and criminal adopting parents. The more criminal convictions a boy's natural parents had, the greater the risk of criminality for boys being raised by adopting parents who had no records. The risk was unrelated to whether the boy or his adopting parents knew about the natural parents' criminal records, whether the natural parents committed their crimes before or after the boy was given up for adoption, or whether the boy was adopted immediately after birth or a year or two later. The results of this study have been confirmed in Swedish and American samples of adopted children.

Because of studies like these, many sociologists and criminologists now accept the existence of genetic factors contributing to criminality. When there is disagreement, it is about how large the genetic contribution to crime is and about how the criminality of biological parents is transmitted to their children.

Both the twin and adoption studies show that genetic contributions are not alone responsible for crime — there is, for example, some increase in criminality among boys if their adopted fathers are criminal even when their biological parents are not, and not every co-twin of a criminal identical twin becomes criminal himself. Although it appears, on average, to be substantial, the

precise size of the genetic contribution to crime is probably unknowable, particularly since the measures of criminality itself are now so crude.

We have a bit more to go on with respect to the link that transmits a predisposition toward crime from parents to children. No one believes there are "crime genes," but there are two major attributes that have, to some degree, a heritable base and that appear to influence criminal behavior. These are intelligence and temperament. Hundreds of studies have found that the more genes people share, the more likely they are to resemble each other intellectually and temperamentally.

Starting with studies in the 1930's, the average offender in broad samples has consistently scored 91 to 93 on I.Q. tests for which the general population's average is 100. The typical offender does worse on the verbal items of intelligence tests than on the nonverbal items but is usually below average on both.

Criminologists have long known about the correlation between criminal behavior and I.Q., but many of them have discounted it for various reasons. Some have suggested that the correlation can be explained away by the association between low socioeconomic status and crime, on the one hand, and that between low I.Q. and low socioeconomic status, on the other. These criminologists say it is low socioeconomic status, rather than low I.Q., that fosters crime. Others have questioned whether I.Q. tests really measure intelligence for the populations that are at greater risk for breaking the law. The low scores of offenders, the argument goes, betray a culturally deprived background or alienation from our society's values rather than low intelligence. Finally, it is often noted that the offenders in some studies have been caught for their crimes. Perhaps the ones who got away have higher I.Q.s.

But these objections have proved to be less telling than they once seemed to be. There are, for example, many poor law-abiding people living in deprived environments, and one of their more salient characteristics is that they have higher I.Q. scores than those in the same environment who break the law.

Then, too, it is a common misconception that I.Q. tests are invalid for people from disadvantaged backgrounds. If what is implied by this criticism is that scores predict academic potential or job performance differently for different groups, then the criticism is wrong. A comprehensive recent survey sponsored by the National Academy of Sciences concluded that "tests predict about as well for one group as for another." And that some highly intelligent criminals may well be good at eluding capture is fully consistent with the belief that offenders, in general, have lower scores than nonoffenders.

If I.Q. and criminality are linked, what may explain the link? There are several possibilities. One is that low scores on I.Q. tests signify greater difficulty in grasping the likely consequences of action or in learning the meaning and significance of moral codes. Another is that low scores, especially on the verbal component of the tests, mean trouble in school, which leads to frustration, thence to resentment, anger and delinquency. Still another is that persons who are not as skillful as others in expressing themselves verbally may find it more rewarding to express themselves in ways in which they will do better, such as physical threat or force.

For some repeat offenders, the predisposition to criminality may be more a matter of temperament than intelligence. Impulsiveness, insensitivity to social mores, a lack of deep and enduring emotional attachments to others and an appetite for danger are among the temperamental characteristics of high-rate offenders. Temperament is, to a degree, heritable, though not as much so as intelligence. All parents know that their children, shortly after birth, begin to exhibit certain characteristic ways of behaving — they are placid or fussy, shy or bold. Some of the traits endure, among them aggressiveness and hyperactivity, although they change in form as the child develops. As the child grows up, these traits, among others, may gradually unfold into a disposition toward unconventional, defiant or antisocial behavior.

Lee Robins, a sociologist at Washington University School of Medicine in St. Louis, reconstructed 30 years of the lives of more than 500 children who were patients in the 1920's at a child guidance clinic in St. Louis. She was interested in the early precursors of chronic sociopathy, a condition of antisocial personality that often includes criminal behavior as one of its symptoms. Adult sociopaths in her sample who did not suffer from psychosis, mental retardation or addiction, were, without exception, antisocial before they were 18. More than half of the male sociopaths had serious symptoms before they were 11. The main childhood precursors were truancy, poor school performance, theft, running away, recklessness, slovenliness, impulsiveness and guiltlessness. The more symptoms in childhood, the greater the risk of sociopathy in adulthood.

Other studies confirm and extend Dr. Robins's conclusions. For example, two psychologists, John J. Conger of the University of Colorado and Wilbur Miller of Drake University in Des Moines, searching back over the histories of a sample of delinquent boys in Denver, found that "by the end of the third grade, future delinquents were already seen by their teachers as more poorly adapted than their classmates. They appeared to have less regard for the rights and feelings of their peers; less awareness of the need to accept responsibility for their obligations, both as individuals and as members of a group, and poorer attitudes toward authority."

Traits that foreshadow serious, recurrent criminal behavior have been traced all the way back to behavior patterns such as hyperactivity and unusual fussiness, and neurological signs such as atypical brain waves or reflexes. In at least a minority of cases, these are detectable in the first few years of life. Some of the characteristics are sex-linked. There is evidence that newborn females are more likely than newborn males to smile, to cling to their mothers, to be receptive to touching and talking, to be sensitive to certain stimuli, such as being touched by a cloth, and to have less upper-body strength. Mothers certainly treat girls and boys differently, but the differences are not simply a matter of the mother's choice — female babies are more responsive than male babies to precisely the kind of treatment that is regarded as "feminine." When adults are asked to play with infants, they play with them in ways they think are appropriate to the infants' sexes. But there is also some evidence that when the sex of the infant is concealed, the behavior of the adults is influenced by the conduct of the child.

Premature infants or those born with low birth weights have a special problem. These children are vulnerable to any adverse circumstances in their environment — including child abuse — that may foster crime. Although nurturing parents can compensate for adversity, cold or inconsistent parents may exacerbate it. Prematurity and low birth weight may result from poor prenatal care, a bad diet or excessive use of alcohol or drugs. Whether the bad care is due to poverty, ignorance or anything else, here we see criminality arising from biological, though not necessarily genetic, factors. It is now known that these babies are more likely than normal babies to be the victims of child abuse.

We do not mean to blame child abuse on the victim by saying that premature and low-birth-weight infants are more difficult to care for and thus place a great strain on the parents. But unless parents are emotionally prepared for the task of caring for such children, they may vent their frustration at the infant's unresponsiveness by hitting or neglecting it. Whatever it is in parent and child that leads to prematurity or low birth weight is compounded by the subsequent interaction between them. Similarly, children with low I.Q.s may have difficulty in understanding rules, but if their parents also have poor verbal skills, they may have difficulty in communicating rules, and so each party to the conflict exacerbates the defects of the other.

THE STATEMENT that biology plays a role in explaining human behavior, especially criminal behavior, sometimes elicits a powerful political or ideological reaction. Fearful that what is being proposed is a crude biological determinism, some critics deny the evidence while others wish the evidence to be confined to scientific journals. Scientists who have merely proposed studying the possible effects of chromosomal abnormalities on behavior have been ruthlessly attacked by other scientists, as have those who have made public the voluminous data showing the heritability of intelligence and temperament.

Some people worry that any claim that biological factors influence criminality is tantamount to saying that the higher crime rate of black compared to white Amer-

icans has a genetic basis. But no responsible work in the field leads to any such conclusion. The data show that of all the reasons people vary in their crime rates, race is far less important than age, sex, intelligence and the other individual factors that vary within races. Any study of the causes of crime must therefore first consider the individual factors. Differences among races may have many explanations, most of them having nothing to do with biology.

The intense reaction to the study of biological factors in crime, we believe, is utterly misguided. In fact, these discoveries, far from implying that "criminals are born" and should be locked up forever, suggest new and imaginative ways of reducing criminality by benign treatment. The opportunity we have is precisely analogous to that which we had when the biological bases of other disorders were established. Mental as well as physical illness — alcoholism, learning disabilities of various sorts, and perhaps even susceptibilities to drug addiction — now seem to have genetic components. In each case, new understanding energized the search for treatment and gave it new direction. Now we know that many forms of depression can be successfully treated with drugs; in time we may learn the same of Alzheimer's disease. Alcoholics are helped when they understand that some persons, because of their predisposition toward addiction to alcohol, should probably never consume it at all. A chemical treatment of the predisposition is a realistic possibility. Certain types of slow learners can already be helped by special programs. In time, others will be also.

Crime, admittedly, may be a more difficult program. So many different acts are criminal that it is only with considerable poetic license that we can speak of "criminality" at all. The bank teller who embezzles $500 to pay off a gambling debt is not engaging in the same behavior as a person who takes $500 from a liquor store at the point of a gun or one who causes $500 worth of damage by drunkenly driving his car into a parked vehicle. Moreover, crime, unlike alcoholism or dyslexia, exposes a person to the formal condemnation of society and the possibility of imprisonment. We naturally and rightly worry about treating all "criminals" alike, or stigmatizing persons whom we think might become criminal by placing them in special programs designed to prevent criminality.

But these problems are not insurmountable barriers to better ways of thinking about crime prevention. Though criminals are of all sorts, we know that a very small fraction of all young males commit so large a fraction of serious street crime that we can properly blame these chronic offenders for most such crime. We also know that chronic offenders typically begin their misconduct at an early age. Early family and preschool programs may be far better repositories for the crime-prevention dollar than rehabilitation programs aimed — usually futilely — at the 19- or 20-year-old veteran offender. Prevention programs risk stigmatizing children, but this may be less of a risk than is neglect. If stigma were a problem to be avoided at all costs, we would have to dismantle most special-needs education programs.

Having said all this, we must acknowledge that there

is at present little hard evidence that we know how to inhibit the development of delinquent tendencies in children. There are some leads, such as family training programs of the sort pioneered at the Oregon Social Learning Center, where parents are taught how to use small rewards and penalties to alter the behavior of misbehaving children. There is also evidence from David Weikart and Lawrence Schweinhart of the High/Scope Educational Research Foundation at Ypsilanti, Mich., that preschool education programs akin to Project Head Start may reduce later deliquency. There is nothing yet to build a national policy on, but there are ideas worth exploring by carefully repeating and refining these pioneering experimental efforts.

Above all, there is a case for redirecting research into the causes of crime in ways that take into account the interaction of biological and social factors. Some scholars, such as the criminologist Marvin E. Wolfgang and his colleagues at the University of Pennsylvania, are already exploring these issues by analyzing social and biological information from large groups as they age from infancy to adulthood and linking the data to criminal behavior. But much more needs to be done.

It took years of patiently following the life histories of many men and women to establish the linkages between smoking or diet and disease; it will also take years to unravel the complex and subtle ways in which intelligence, temperament, hormonal levels and other traits combine with family circumstances and later experiences in school and elsewhere to produce human character.

Number of Killings Soars In Big Cities Across U.S.

Michael deCourcy Hinds

Special to The New York Times

PHILADELPHIA, July 17—After an alarming increase last year, homicide rates have continued to soar this year, and experts attribute the rise to an increase in drug disputes, deadlier weapons and a tendency among more young people to start careers in crime with a gun.

Although the Federal Government has not compiled nationwide statistics on killings in the first half of 1990, police departments in more than a dozen major cities report increases ranging from 10 percent to more than 50 percent over the first six months of 1989.

New York City, for instance, which set a record in 1989 with 1,905 killings, reported a 22 percent increase in the homicide rate in the first three months of 1990, or 45 percent when the 87 arson deaths at the Happy Land Social Club are included.

'Going Through the Roof'

In Boston the rate has increased 56 percent on top of a 5 percent increase for all of 1989. Here in Philadelphia murders this year are up 19 percent, after a 21 percent increase in 1989. And in Milwaukee, killings are up 25 percent after a 35 percent increase for all of last year.

The statistics have alarmed the police and prosecutors across the country, some of whom describe the situation in dark terms. "Our homicide rate is going through the roof," said Ronald D. Castille, the Philadelphia District Attorney. "Three weekends ago, 11 people were killed in a 48-hour period."

"What's causing most of the increase," he said, "is the ready availability of powerful handguns and the effects of drugs on human beings."

Crime specialists and gun-control advocates say the ban on assault rifles that was included in the crime bill that the Senate passed last week would have no immediate effect on the murder rate even if it was immediately enacted. They say too many people already have the weapons.

22 Cities Surveyed

In a *New York Times* survey of 22 major cities around the country, all but five reported increases in homicides in the first half of 1990 over the same period in 1989. Their reports suggest that the nation's murder rate, after dipping in the mid-80's, is continuing a strong upsurge and the number of victims may even surpass the record year of 1980 when 23,040 people were slain.

Among the 22 cities, Chicago recorded a 14 percent increase so far this year after a 12 percent increase in 1989; in June alone, the city had a record-breaking 83 killings. Seattle reported a 75 percent increase this year after the rate fell 32 percent in 1989.

But in Washington, which for the past two years has led the nation in homicides, the murder rate increased only 1 percent, after an 18 percent rise in 1989.

The increases across the country reflect a generally worsening crime situation, statistics from the Federal Bureau of Investigation show. Last year, the bureau reported that violent crimes increased nationwide by 5 percent and homicides by 4 percent, while in cities with populations over one million violent crime increased by 6 percent and homicides rose by 7 percent, the steepest increases for those cities since 1985.

In five cities surveyed, murder rates are lower now than in 1989: Atlanta, Cleveland, Miami, Portland, Ore., and Tucson, Ariz. Of those, only Miami also had a decline last year.

Pessimism About Improvement

Willie L. Williams, Commissioner of Police in Philadelphia, said rigorous gun control would help curb the number of killings in his city, which reached 489 last year. And while he strongly supports the Senate move to ban semiautomatic assault weapons, he said he thought it would have no immediate effect on the homicide rate. "There are so many of these weapons around," he said, adding that Philadelphia police confiscate assault weapons in about half of their drug raids.

Others are even less optimistic about the effect of the Senate's approval of a ban, which the House has yet to vote on. "Expecting a ban on assault rifles to bring down the homicide rate is a bit like banning high-powered sports cars from highways as a way to bring down the highway fatality rate," said James Q. Wilson, professor of public policy at the University of California at Los Angeles. Most homicides are committed with ordinary handguns, he said.

Across the country murder rates have increased steadily over the past several years. After reaching a peak of 10.2 killings per 100,000 population in 1980, the rate fell to 7.9 per 100,000 in 1984 and 1985, a decline that officials attribute to the drop in numbers of people in their teens and 20's. It has since begun rebounding, reaching 8.4 in 1988, the last year for which the F.B.I. has figures broken down in that way.

Inner Cities Hit Hardest

Criminologists say the steep increase in homicides appears to be statistically significant. "Most year-to-year fluctuations tend to be random, but the bigger the increase the more important it is and the more it sounds like a real trend," said Lawrence W. Sherman, professor of criminology at the University of Maryland who is president of the Crime Control Institute, a nonprofit research organization.

Murder rates are primarily escalating in impoverished inner cities with large minority populations and heavy drug use, said M. Dwayne Smith, an associate professor of sociology at Tulane University. Most of those slain continue to be young and black, as are the killers. In 1987, for example, there were 26.9 black victims and 4.6 white victims for each 100,000 people. "But what this profile doesn't show," he added, "is that many of these victims are just poor folks who happened to be in the wrong place at the wrong time."

In Seattle, which usually has 50 to 60 killings a year, no one knows why the number dropped to 38 last year or why it snapped back in the first six months of this year, said Mark D. Amundson, a spokesman for the Police Department.

In Boston, Joseph V. Saia, chief of detectives for the Police Department, said domestic disputes and turf battles over drugs were primarily responsible for the 78 killings in the first half of 1990, a large increase from the 50 killings in the same period last year. Mr. Saia said it was handguns that were turning more arguments into killings.

In Los Angeles 452 people were slain in the first half of this year as against 418 in the same period last year. Lieut. Fred Nixon of the Los Angeles Police Department estimated that more than half of the killings were drug-related and said gang killings accounted for 158 deaths so far this year,

up from 150 in the same period last year.

"We have had a few more multiple homicides, where three or four people were killed at once," he said. "Sometimes these are drive-bys, sometimes just execution-style murders, which, of course, suggests drug-trafficking."

Drugs, Alcohol and Relatives

Police often report an increase in drug-related killings, but criminologists like Leonard D. Savitz say there is little research to support it. "It's

---

Handguns and drugs prove a lethal mix on the street.

---

fashionable for the police and the media to talk about drug murders," said Dr. Savitz, a professor of sociology at Temple University, "but I suspect that drug-related murders were fairly prevalent in the past as well."

In Dallas, the police do not break out the numbers of drug-related homicides, but they say 30 percent of the homicide victims this year had drugs or alcohol or both in their blood, as did 14 percent of the suspected killers. There have been 189 killings in the city this year, as against 157 in the first six months of last year. About 10 percent of this year's victims were related to the killers, and 32 percent were acquainted with the killer. Sixty percent of the homicides were committed with handguns, and other firearms were responsible for an additional 17 percent.

Police in Chicago and Atlanta said murder weapons have become more powerful and killers, more youthful. "We're getting many more younger people, and we're seeing a lot more semiautomatic weapons," said Capt. Calvin A. Wardlaw, commander of Atlanta Police Department's homicide squad.

John J. Townsend, chief of detectives for the Chicago Police Department, said: "People used to use Saturday night specials, which were cheap and small and didn't do as much damage as these big guns are doing. More people are dying from their wounds because a semiautomatic or a 357 magnum really tears up the body."

Impact of Vietnam War

In 1988 there were 660 killings in Chicago. Last year, the number rose to 742, including 29 child-abuse homicides, seven accidents and two mercy killings. The police attributed about 22 percent of the killings to domestic disputes and 24 percent to drugs, though the police did not break down which drugs were involved.

Professor Sherman said there is a very strong relationship between the availability of weapons, as measured by indicators like sales and confiscations by the police, and annual fluctuations in the homicide rate. "The number of assaults don't vary much, but the means of destruction do," he said.

Improved medical techniques, learned on the battlefields of Vietnam, may have contributed to decline in homicides in the mid-1980's, Professor Sherman said, but the homicide toll is rising again because emergency medicine is no match for the firepower of a semiautomatic gun.

"The number of bullets these guns fire, the speed they travel and the damage they do is driving the homicide rate up," he said, citing reports from Washington and Oakland, Calif., that the number of gunshot wounds per victim has increased dramatically since 1985.

Handguns are used in nearly half of all homicides; about one quarter of American households have handguns, and in those homes there are 3.2 handguns on average. Some cities, like Chicago, New York and Washington, have stringent regulations on handguns, but they have been undermined by the lack of restrictions elsewhere.

The National Rifle Association says such regulations are counterproductive. "Washington has had a 160 percent increase in homicides since banning the handgun in 1977," said Dr. Paul H. Blackman, research coordinator for the association. "The ban has been totally ineffective except in protecting criminals from law-abiding citizens who might have been able to shoot back."

But Carl T. Bogus, a Philadelphia lawyer and a director of the Center to Prevent Handgun Violence, an advocacy group based in Washington, said law-abiding citizens rarely use handguns to protect themselves. No more than about 2 percent of killings nationally are considered justifiable, he said.

NEW FACES OF ORGANIZED CRIME

THE GROWTH OF DRUG-RELATED CRIMINAL EMPIRES

EDWIN J. DELATTRE

Edwin J. Delattre is the Olin Scholar in Applied Ethics and a professor of education at Boston University. His latest book is Character and Cops: Ethics in Policing.

PERSISTENT APPLICATION OF RICO (the Racketeer Influenced and Corrupt Organizations Statute) is unraveling the criminal empire of La Cosa Nostra in the United States. Yet today, an array of nontraditional organizations distinct from La Cosa Nostra is involved in unprecedented levels of organized crime, ranging from highly sophisticated narcotics trafficking and money laundering to targeted and shockingly indiscriminate street violence. We are being diverted from combating the pernicious activities of these groups by a misguided debate over the legalization of drugs.

These new crime groups now generate immense criminal profits in the United States. Some of them—white-supremacist outlaw motorcycle gangs, black street gangs originally mainly in Los Angeles (now also in Chicago and New York), and Hispanic gangs—are largely home-grown. Others, including Asian organized crime, Colombian drug trafficking organizations, and Jamaican posses, spring from foreign-based criminal organizations. Newly powerful organized crime now constitutes an enormous, malevolent presence in America.

Criminal organizations perpetrate many kinds of crimes: narcotics trafficking, money laundering, smuggling weapons and aliens, contract murder, kidnapping, counterfeiting identification documents, burglary, robbery, auto theft, gambling, loan sharking, extortion, arson, medical insurance and welfare fraud, bank fraud, prostitution, pornography, infiltrating private industry, and corrupting public institutions. Their drug-related activity poses a serious threat, not only to the adult population who use drugs, but also to children involved as their agents.

Outlaw Motorcycle Gangs

Four white-supremacist outlaw motorcycle gangs—the Hell's Angels from California, the Outlaws from Illinois, the Pagans from Maryland, and the Bandidos from Texas—have approximately 152 chapters throughout the United States and parts of Canada. Their 3,000 members, plus many more thousands of associ-

Reprinted from *The American Enterprise*, May/June 1990, pp. 38-45.

ate members, traffic in amphetamines ("speed") and weapons; they also specialize in contract murder, arson, extortion, and prostitution. They can be expected to play a major part in the new methamphetamine ("ice") traffic in the United States.

They use gang-associated women—whom they treat as property—to infiltrate telephone companies, government offices, and police departments. The gangs fortify their facilities with electronic surveillance equipment and heavy weaponry, and they routinely conceal poisonous snakes where police would search in any raid.

The "big four," however, do not begin to tell the story of organized crime by outlaw motorcycle gangs in America. There are over 500 other known motorcycle gangs in the United States that engage in similar criminal activities, many of which have been associated with La Cosa Nostra.

Asian Organized Crime

At least five distinct Asian cartels traffic in drugs in the United States, fueling the belief among some law enforcement officials that Asian organized crime could become America's most intractable crime problem. As many as 50 Chinese triads (political and criminal organizations dating from the seventeenth century identifying themselves by a triangular emblem) have organized criminal tongs and street gangs such as the Ping On, United Bamboo, and Ghost Shadows in American cities. Gangs based in Hong Kong and Taiwan (the Big Circle Gang, for one) also operate in the United States. These Chinese criminal organizations traffic primarily in heroin, and they run large gambling, extortion, and prostitution rackets. Some of them exercise great power over the Chinese entertainment industry in the United States.

By 1984, the President's Commission on Organized Crime had gathered evidence of Chinese group criminal activity in 26 cities from every major region of the United States. It also heard testimony describing the savagery of the triads, whose heroin smuggling tactics have been known to include murdering babies, storing drugs inside the corpses, and having women carry them across national borders pretending to nurse them.

Japan's Yakuza crime syndicate is well-anchored here as well, with heavy involvement in smuggling weapons to Japan, narcotics, gambling, management of foreign criminal investments in American corporations, and control of the North American Japanese tourist industry. Through the purchase of American businesses and real estate, the Yakuza launders huge sums of money. Yakuza members are described by Japanese law enforcement officials as "Boryokudan," or violent ones.

With a worldwide roster of over 100,000 members, the Yakuza resembles La Cosa Nostra in its structure. Its power in the United States may grow as ice is pushed into the drug subculture. Ice, a Japanese product, was legal in Japan until 1952 and is still the drug of choice for many Japanese users. There are now 130,000 ice addicts in South Korea, and the drug has already hit Hawaii very hard. It became available on the streets in both California and New York City in 1989.

Ethnic Viet Ching (Chinese-Vietnamese) and Vietnamese criminal gangs have made their way into the United States since the collapse of South Vietnam. Noted particularly for property crimes and exceptional levels of violence in all their criminal activities, Viet-

FEDERAL AUTHORITIES ESTIMATE THAT $87 BILLION IN COCAINE PROFITS WERE LAUNDERED IN 1988, COMPARED TO $34 BILLION IN MARIJUANA AND $10 BILLION IN HEROIN.

namese gangs operate in as many as 13 states coast to coast and are unusually mobile. One ranking police official told the Commission on Organized Crime that Vietnamese criminal organizations threaten to "make the Mafia look like a fraternity of wimps."

But Asian organized crime is not unique in its range of activities or in the routine acts of savagery by which it terrorizes victims and prospective witnesses in criminal prosecutions and eliminates criminal competition.

Colombian Cartels

The most grievous of all the organized crime developments in the 1980s relate directly to cocaine traffic. It is the demand in the United States for cocaine and for its even more dangerous derivative, "crack," that has emboldened the Colombian cartels and their drug-trafficking subsidiaries in the United States, the Jamaican posses, and the Los Angeles-based drug-dealing street gangs—the Crips and the Bloods. Federal authorities estimate that $87 billion in cocaine profits were laundered in 1988, compared to $34 billion in marijuana and $10 billion in heroin.

Colombian drug traffickers control cocaine production and wholesaling worldwide. The Medellin and Cali cartels dominate, and through a wholesale marketing and smuggling network that employs thousands of people, they distribute roughly 80 percent of the cocaine consumed in the United States including that which is converted to crack. No American city, suburb, or rural area is beyond their reach.

The wealth and power of the cartels has enabled them to cause governmental instability and terrorize entire populations. They can corrupt morally weak public servants anywhere in the world. In the United States, the Colombian traffickers employ Cuban Mariel-boat-lift criminals and Colombians illegally here for extortion and murder.

So sophisticated are the cartels that logistics involved in shipment and distribution of drugs, accounting, and movement of money are all managed with state-of-the-art technology. Cartel money laundering seems to be expanding in the United States to include more extensive real estate holdings, the construction of shopping malls and banks, and control of large import-export firms under covert Colombian ownership.

But technological and management sophistication is no guarantor of civility. The cartels are implicated in close to 1,000 murders in Colombia alone, including the killing of at least 596 national police officers. Even their tactics of bribery are extortionate: they offer "gold or lead"—"Take the money or make your wife a widow." Colombian traffickers in the United States not only murder anyone they can reach who opposes or betrays them, they also murder entire families as a message to employees and competitors alike, and they maintain a code of silence by the threat of reprisal against family members still in Colombia.

Jamaican Posses

Jamaican posses may be the greatest beneficiaries of the demand for crack in the United States. Originally formed as strong-arm political street gangs in Kingston, Jamaica, the posses have spread. It is now estimated that there are more than 40 posses with at least 10,000 members in Jamaica, Great Britain, and the United States. Incredibly brutal (some of their members were trained by Cuban guerrilla warfare specialists), the posses have been implicated in over 2,000 drug-related murders since 1985.

The power of the posses in the United States is such that they not only buy and fortify "crack houses" as bases for the retail distribution of drugs, they also buy other houses for wholesale distribution of crack to their own retail outlets, with local black juveniles running the supplies. Sometimes they buy whole sections of neighborhoods in order to shelter their operating facilities. By these methods, they control almost half the crack market in America.

Though many in the top leadership of the posses are Jamaican nationals who have been legal residents of the United States for years, most of the rank and file are illegal aliens. They are provided with false identification documents and can change locations and identities virtually at will, both within the United States and abroad.

This advantage against law enforcement penetration is increased by two other dimensions of posse operations. First, the posses' record of reprisal when betrayed makes police efforts to enlist informants and to persuade witnesses to testify against them extremely difficult, just as in the case of the Colombian traffickers. Second, the posses communicate in a corrupted dialect with French roots that complicates law-enforcement infiltration and poses a language barrier to gathering evidence similar to problems encountered in investigating Asian organized crime.

Los Angeles-Based Gangs

By 1989, the United States had become home to more than 100,000 street gangs with a combined membership of over 1 million youths and adults. Los Angeles County alone is the base for some 750 of these gangs, with a total membership of roughly 70,000.

Law enforcement officials in the Los Angeles area estimate that long-standing Hispanic gangs have about 30,000 members. These "Home Boys" ("cholos") are known for heroin trafficking, high levels of deadly violence in defense of neighborhood turf, and more recently for crack sales, primarily to black users.

But the most dramatic change in Los Angeles crime organizations in the 1980s took place within the black gangs. With a total of 15,000-20,000 members, these gangs are no longer neighborhood street gangs. Their entry into the crack trade has enabled them to expand violent criminal operations into every area of the country, and they have been directly linked to crack distribution in 46 states. They may market as much as one-third of all the crack sold in America, after purchasing cocaine wholesale from Colombian traffickers.

The most infamous of these gangs are the Crips and the Bloods. Each of these is a rough association of smaller gangs; by 1988, there were 189 distinct "sets" of Crips and 72 Bloods. Though these two super-factions are endlessly at war with each other, they also fight among themselves, and they account for most of the 1,026 gang-related killings in Los Angeles County since the beginning of 1988. An uncertain number of the victims—estimates run as high as 50 percent—were innocent bystanders.

A particularly heinous practice of the LA-based Crips and Bloods, like many similar gangs in Chicago, is their active recruitment of children, sometimes only seven or eight years old, as new members. The gangs recruit them by a combination of terror and seduction. They threaten reprisals for refusing to join, while they promise the rewards of wealth, sex, thrills, mutual loyalty, and the safety of numbers. The children who are forced, or drawn, into the gangs are known as "wanna-bes" or "baby gangsters." They serve in a variety of criminal roles: some act as lookouts and carry drugs and guns to older members; some commit burglaries, particularly to steal weapons. These children, along with older juvenile gang members, are largely immune to criminal sanction. If they are apprehended in criminal acts, police often have no choice but to release them to the custody of their parents—many of whom exercise no parental control in any situation.

Indeed, it is the extent to which organized criminal groups are staking claim to the next generation of our nation's children by selling them drugs and by recruiting them into gangs that is the most serious of all their threats. They would remorselessly condemn the young to lives as blighted by ignorance and cruelty as their own—barren, corrupt, violent, and often short. This attack on the hopes, possibilities, and aspirations of the young violates the future, and its viciousness proves that legalization of narcotics promises no relief from the ravages of drugs or from organized crime itself. This is the irreducible element in current disputes about the merits of narcotics legalization.

Against Narcotics Legalization

Demand for illegal narcotics and criminally diverted prescription drugs is directly responsible for the strength of the criminal groups in the United States described above. Demand has promoted drug trafficking and nourished criminal empires. As drugs become more widely available, consumption tends to become contagious: users who can easily obtain drugs give them to friends, encourage use by companions, and belittle peers who do not use.

America has suffered for years through this cycle of demand that both increases supply and fuels greater demand. For too many of those years, we ineffectively opposed rising levels of drug consumption by concentrating primarily on hurling police into a breach they could not possibly close by themselves.

THE EXTENT TO WHICH ORGANIZED CRIMINAL GROUPS ARE STAKING CLAIM TO THE NEXT GENERATION OF OUR NATION'S CHILDREN ... IS THE MOST SERIOUS OF ALL THEIR THREATS.

Only recently have combined public and private-sector initiatives in law enforcement (as applied to both drug traffickers and users), education and prevention, treatment research, employee-assistance programs to combat substance abuse, and encouragement of public contempt for drug use begun to gain headway in making drugs unfashionable. The most powerful message we can get across to Americans, including children, is that drugs are not evil because they are illegal, they are illegal because they are evil. And they are evil because they destroy lives, happiness, and decency.

The latest survey of the National Institute on Drug Abuse shows that drug consumption has declined by 37 percent since 1985, and cocaine use has been cut in half in the United States. Yet, according to a recent State Department report, the increase in worldwide drug production and the criminality associated with it has been dramatic. Opium production is up 187 percent since 1985, coca 143 percent, and marijuana 502 percent. In this climate, legalization would further exacerbate our drug problems. Many advocates of legalization admit that drug consumption would rise—perhaps dramatically—under legalization. The progress we have made against drug consumption and dependency would be erased.

The victims of legalization would include countless children. First, if drugs were legal, an even greater number of women, including teenagers, could be expected to use them during pregnancy. Many of the infants who survived drug exposure would suffer severe lifelong mental and physical disabilities.

Second, legalization would have little power to make inroads into the adult black market. But if it did, organized crime would market drugs more intensively among youths and children.

As we have seen since the end of Prohibition, criminal organizations like La Cosa Nostra do not fade away just because substances are legalized. They must be unraveled by prudent modifications in antiracketeering and other laws and by unrelenting and extended application of those laws. The higher the stakes in money and power, the more these efforts will be evaded. The present organized crime groups will not be driven from drug trafficking and the rest of their criminal enterprises by narcotics laws. Legalize some drugs, and they will undersell the legal distributors with higher potency versions, market illegal drugs, and introduce new drugs. Legalize drugs for adults, and organized crime will sell to children by persuading them that what is all right for grownups is all right for them. This is the basic lesson their past and present treatment of children has already taught.

Priorities

Critical questions of law, policy, and ethics are being obscured by the debate over legalization. We could serve the interests of the public much more effectively by asking how to combat nontraditional organized crime and its causes and effects.

What should we do to prevent organized crime from thwarting investigations by using the Freedom of Information Act to identify and take reprisal against informants? How should we modify juvenile courts and law to handle juvenile involvement in organized crime drug trafficking, violence, and intimidation? How shall we intervene to prevent gang recruitment of children? What should we do about the collapse of the social and cultural order associated with gang-related crime and violence? Which kinds of neighborhood drug treatment and recovery programs should we publicize and provide with financial support? How should we combat urban gang tyranny? How shall we modify bail and probation standards to safeguard the public?

All of these questions, and many more like them, are of inestimably greater importance than the question of whether we should legalize drugs. They demand answers. By contrast, legalization debates trivialize our gravest problems. Quick-fix "remedies" like legalization are irrelevant to facing and controlling the worst effects of human frailty as they reveal themselves in drug consumption and of human depravity and viciousness as they reveal themselves in organized crime.

New Strategies to Fight Crime Go Far Beyond Stiffer Terms and More Cells

Andrew H. Malcolm

Faced with the growth of violent crime and the political pressures of even faster-growing citizen fears about crime, the nation's police, prosecutors, wardens and researchers are designing an array of new strategies that are already beginning to reshape American criminal justice.

Despite today's tight government budgets, a surprising amount of experimentation and quiet change are under way: In McAllen, Tex., police officers are stationed in neighborhood trailers and encouraged to build community contacts even by helping teen-agers with homework. In suburban Maryland a county prosecutor is completely reorganizing his office to more closely match the crime patterns and local concerns of nearby police districts.

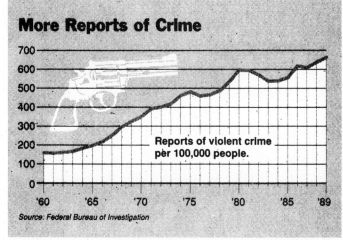

More Reports of Crime

Reports of violent crime per 100,000 people.

Source: Federal Bureau of Investigation

The New York Times

Different Sanctions

Some prosecutors and researchers are suggesting greater use of sanctions short of formal incarceration, although they lack the political appeal of outright imprisonment. Combined with speedier trials, such sanctions are aimed at increasing the certainty of some punishment for wrongdoers and a sense of justice for their victims.

The problems that emerge in such a transition can be as big as the cynicism and detachment that many rank-and-file officers in New York City feel about a new anti-crime program announced by Mayor David N. Dinkins that is to put more police officers on foot patrol. If fully financed, the expansion of New York's community policing experiment to department-wide policy will be by far the nation's largest use of the new philosophy.

As always there is an obvious risk of corruption, law-enforcement experts say. But police corruption was not exactly snuffed out by the abandonment of the old beat-cop system 60 years ago, they say, adding that keeping the status quo is worse because officers will remain isolated as overworked crime responders rather than innovative crime solvers. Additionally, community police will be only one of many government agencies combating crime and its root causes.

Warnings of Urban Upheavals

Many researchers warn that without significant changes in popular thinking and in the criminal justice system, the country faces the likelihood of widespread urban disturbances like those of the 1960's, which were also marked by increasing crime rates.

Indeed, the term "quiet riot" is now used to describe the mounting outbreaks of random urban violence like drive-by shootings, the New York subway slaying of a Utah tourist defending his mother and racial confrontations like those in Howard Beach and Bensonhurst and scattered vigilantism.

To most experts the country's major crime problems, with their frightening randomness and senseless violence, reflect the simultaneous decay of vital urban institutions like schools, transportation and health care, and even the nuclear family, especially in the inner cities. These accumulating ills are compounded by drugs, the availability of high-powered firearms, the pervasiveness of violence in the entertainment media and many years of policy and spending neglect.

"The trend is overwhelming and the evidence inescapable," said William L. Tafoya, a Federal Bureau of Investigation agent charged with studying the future. "When frustration levels reach a certain point, criminals, their victims and those afraid of becoming victims do things they wouldn't otherwise consider. But it's hard in the United States of today to sell expensive solutions in advance of disaster."

Social Problems Reflected

Herman Goldstein, a law professor at the University of Wisconsin, said: "So many people throw up their hands in dismay at the colossal scale of our crime problems. But the criminal justice system is just a concentrated stew of all our larger social problems. And it's time that mainstream America began displaying as much concern about filling up our prisons as filling up our landfills."

But politicians and voters seem unwilling to address these larger issues, especially if the suggested cures seem to carry large price tags with no guarantees. They prefer instead to concentrate on more immediate symptoms and dramatic, seemingly simple solutions like hiring more police officers, despite those sizable costs and the unmentioned impact on courts and jails of their additional arrests.

"We need a much broader approach than more of the same," said Mark Kleiman, a lecturer at Harvard's Kennedy School of Government. "When politicians say 'Let's hire 5,000 more police!' everybody cheers. Say, 'Let's hire 5,000 probation officers and create cost-effective alternatives to prison!' and everybody yawns."

Michael Smith, president of the Vera Institute of Justice, a nonprofit New York organization that researches crime issues, said: "We do need more cops. But the question is what do you have them do to be more effective, not just more of the same, which hasn't worked. That requires some serious thinking."

The Philosophy
Doctoring Problem At the Source

Much of the emerging new thinking centers on community or problem-solving policing, a philosophical shift away from seeing the police as mere responders to repetitious service calls—"prisoners of 911," as one criminologist put it. A police officer acting as a community problem solver notes patterns of crime in his or her assigned territory and uses innovation and imagination to find solutions that prevent crime.

"Do you keep pulling drowning people from the river?" asked Prof. Dennis Rosenbaum of the University of Illinois at Chicago. "Or do you go upstream to find out why so many are falling in in the first place?"

Thus, for instance, instead of simply responding to frequent purse-snatchings at a bus stop, an officer might work with transit officials and merchants to move the bus stop away from the vacant lot that provides the thieves' hiding place.

Then the officer might help organize neighborhood youths into a basketball team that puts the overgrown space to more constructive use. Not coincidentally,

such officers also discover that residents, who would never flag down a passing patrol car to chat, are more willing to help solve crimes by passing on information to a familiar officer with a demonstrated stake in the area.

'Redeploying Existing Resources'

"Police can't do it alone," said Darrel Stephens, executive director of the Police Executive Research Forum, an organization of big-city police chiefs. "But they can be vital coordinators, organizing tenants for self-protection one block at a time, befriending youths, alerting other city agencies. Pretty soon, they know who the troublemakers are.

"They see the patterns, that 10 percent of the addresses produce 60 percent of police calls, for instance. Or 10 percent of the criminals do 50 percent of the crime. It can simply be a question of redeploying existing resources."

Some 300 of the nation's 16,000 law-enforcement agencies have formally adopted this new philosophy.

Spirit of Innovation

But community policing is less a set strategy than a spirit of innovation that is not always easy to transplant into the traditional military organization and philosophy of large police departments. While many officers are stimulated by the new challenge, others are intimidated, deriding it as "hand-holding."

While mayors and police chiefs may like the idea of community policing, the practical reality may be something else. For example, police officers helping organize vocal neighborhood groups will not respond immediately to the non-emergency 911 summons of an influential voter. And traditional measurements of an officer's activity—arrests made, tickets written, felons convicted—do not reward preventive work like purse-snatchings avoided or juvenile delinquents redirected.

Prosecutors Taking Part

Now, this new philosophy of customized law enforcement is being applied to prosecutors. This month Andrew Sonner, the State's Attorney in Maryland's Montgomery County, reorganized his office into five units corresponding to geographic police districts. The goal is for each unit's seven prosecutors to develop close contacts with their area's police officers, civic groups, teachers and neighborhood associations to discern the patterns and concerns about crime.

The prosecutors will be paid bonuses not by their conviction rates but by the quantity and quality of their community contacts, like the number of community meetings attended. "I don't want my people just processing cases," said Mr. Sonner, who has held office since 1970 and is unopposed for re-election next month, "I want them solving community problems."

As an example, he cited vandalism like graffiti by loitering youths. Although research shows these activities are precursors of serious neighborhood decay, arrests and prosecutions of such offenses have a very low priority for the standard busy police officer or prosecutor.

In a community where graffiti vandalism is a big concern, Mr. Sonner said, "we would work with police to solve the crimes and have some well-publicized prosecutions. And just so the judge got the community's message, I might show up personally and we'd see that a fair number of residents did, too. The community gains back a sense of control and safety and who knows how many more serious cases we avoid over time."

'Informal Social Controls'

In the coming months related experiments will be started in Lansing, Mich., Aurora, Colo., Fort Pierce, Fla. and Norfolk, Va., by Michigan State University's School of Criminal Justice. Robert Trojanowicz, the school's director, said: "We're after the other Yuppie—the young urban predator. The goal is to bring back a system of informal social controls because the police can't do it all. We want to blend high tech with high touch."

The experiments will involve decentralized "neighborhood network centers" where local beat officers will coordinate the work of their counterparts in varied agencies like public and mental health, foster care, welfare, school truancy and even building code inspectors.

Each worker will focus on the same case, devising strategy, hounding landlords to maintain buildings and evicting drug dealers, for instance, or steering troubled parents into drug treatment and their children into temporary foster care. "We want to use the formal criminal justice system as a last resort the way neighborhoods used to," Mr. Trojanowicz said.

In McAllen, Tex., Chief Alexjandro Longoria has opened mini-police stations in troubled neighborhoods, and officers and residents are encouraged to mingle at all hours. The idea is to give officers a personal familiarity and stake in the neighborhood and encourage residents to see the officers less as outsiders serving daily shifts.

The Punishments
Options Better Than Prisons

Fueled by new laws, longer sentences and an impatient public and judiciary, state prisons now house nearly 700,000 inmates, almost 6 percent more than a year ago. Federal institutions hold 60,000 prisoners.

Nearly every state prison system is pushed beyond capacity, requiring early releases, more cells or both. In the last two years prison construction worth $8.4 billion was authorized. For instance, New York State, which had about 32,000 inmates in 44 prisons just six years ago, now has 55,000 in 63 prisons, and 6,000 more beds in the works.

With no sign that the flow of prisoners will let up and 37 states now under some court order to control prison overcrowding, interest is growing in alternative sanctions with teeth for appropriate cases, freeing expensive prison care for the worse offenders.

Random Imprisonment

Mr. Kleiman noted: "We have several hundred thousand convicts, not necessarily the worst, locked up in cages, watched 24 hours a day and consuming 90 percent of our corrections budgets. And we have several times more serious offenders suffering no real inconvenience whatsoever."

And even those in custody may get the wrong impression. "We nab a kid for selling dope," said Michael A. Chernovetz, warden of the Community Correctional Center in Bridgeport, Conn. "He should do a few months' time. But we're really crowded. He's not violent. It's his first or second known offense. So he's out early.

"We had no money to train him. All we did was process him, feed him well, treat him medically at taxpayers' expense and protect him from his enemies on the street for a few weeks. Can you blame him for thinking, 'Hey, if they're not taking this seriously, why should I?' "

"Right now," said Barry Krisberg, president of the National Council on Crime and Delinquency, "we can give criminals an aspirin or a lobotomy. We need more steps in the middle to make some kind of punishment more certain."

Getting Tough and Tougher

"We're babying criminals," added Neil Behan, chief of the Baltimore County police force. "We need to get tough on some and tougher on others."

Reuben Greenberg, the police chief in Charleston, S.C., put it more bluntly: "We've got to get back to holding people responsible for their actions. A guy who pulls a gun in a bank is responsible, not his granddaddy's slavemaster, not the landlord who used lead paint and not his father for leaving home. Most kids from broken homes don't become criminals."

Chief Greenberg, who is widely sought for advice on his tough street-crime patrol program, suggests punishing first offenders swiftly and surely, though not necessarily harshly. "We're giving too many people 10 chances," he said. "By the 10th crime, it's too late to teach a different life to someone who lives only for right now. How fast would you learn to get your hand off a hot burner if it took a year to feel the pain?"

Prosecutor Shifts Focus

As the prosecutor in Marion County, Ind., which includes Indianapolis, Steven Goldsmith is responsible for determining how much emphasis to place on each case, like the severity of the punishment. He is shifting his office's focus.

"Of course," he said, "we're always going to have

Central Park jogger cases that require severe punishment. But we need to get away from a system of mindless prosecutions in a system out of resources. I could get my conviction rates up to 99 percent, which is great on Election Day. But prison terms may have less impact on crime over time than alternative, less expensive customized arrangements."

He sees his job as coordinating many social institutions to design such arrangements according to the needs of each criminal case. "We need prisons to give teeth to our intermediate punishments," he said. "But maybe we get a kid and his mother to sign a contract with all of us. He'll go to school, stay out of trouble, submit to drug tests and counseling. We'll help him find a job to pay restitution. We won't arrest him as long as he complies. And we'll enforce it."

In some cases Mr. Goldsmith has even hired Boy Scout troops to take juvenile delinquents to camp for exposure to a different kind of life. In Maryland, Mr. Sonner jails some youths for an hour, as a warning. He sends some youths to "Dutch uncles" who provide personal guidance.

Other law-enforcement officials use electronic monitors to enforce strict house arrests or invest in more officers for strict probation programs, sometimes involving daily visits.

Mr. Kleiman noted, "There is no limit to the kinds of programs possible to make people wish they had not done a crime without society having to pay expensive room and board for each one."

The Fears
Losing Faith And Courage

Even if comprehensive social and crime programs began this afternoon, the experts agree that crime would continue growing for the foreseeable future.

"Part of it is simply demographic," said John A. Conley, chairman of the criminal justice department at the State University of New York at Buffalo. "We go through cycles of crime, which are tied in part to how many people are in their teens and 20's, the most crime-prone age."

In the 1960's, when the nation experienced its last major crime wave, the school-age population went from 44 million to 52 million before drifting into a 15-year decline. In 1985, the year before the national spread of crack began raising crime rates, the school-age population began climbing again, past 45 million, and is expected to peak at 50 million in the year 2000.

'Vulnerability Nerve'

Professors Conley and Rosenbaum see some classic features in the current national concern about crime. "We also experience cycles of fear of crime," said Professor Conley. "Fear lags behind the crime rate until some catalytic crime like the rape-beating of the Central Park jogger or the murder of the Utah tourist in New York strikes our vulnerability nerve and takes on a magnified life of its own."

Professor Rosenbaum added, "People generally feel invulnerable; many still don't wear seat belts. And then that illusion is punctured by one person's mugging, which is described 50 different frightening ways by the victim's friends, or by a major crime which is magnified through today's instantaneous media."

Some police departments, including Chief Behan's in Baltimore County, have created special units to combat fear of crime, a self-fulfilling fear if it causes residents to shun public areas and thus leave the streets to criminals. These units teach self-protection tactics to citizens' groups and may even devote hours to spreading the news of a prominent purse-snatcher's capture.

But many experts and police officers have larger worries. They are afraid that the desperation and frustration accompanying poverty are contributing greatly to violence within cities, and that these emotions will erupt into larger-scale disturbances soon, in what the Rev. Jesse Jackson has called the "imploding" of black neighborhoods.

"Ghetto violence has been going on a long time," said Kathleen Daly, an associate professor of sociology at Yale University. "It's only when it breaks out to strike whites that it becomes a crime wave."

'Fed Up and Overloaded'

Professor Trojanowicz worries about racial groups falling into mutual recriminations fueled by ignorance and fear. "Both sides are getting fed up and overloaded," he said, "and everyone starts looking out less for the community and more for themselves. In the middle are the police, who can be seen as enforcers of the status quo unless they develop their own community links."

"As a society," warned Yale Kamisar, a professor at the University of Michigan Law School, "we must beware when we lose such confidence in our institutions and social structures. We can happily give up our decency and larger civil rights in the desperate search for political panaceas.

"We already willingly empty our pockets to board an airplane. High schools search students with metal detectors. Police patrol with computer profiles of likely criminals and search passengers' bags on city buses. It's not a large leap then in the good fight against crime to close off certain neighborhoods altogether."

There are also fears of vigilantism, as in Detroit, where a crowd burned two reputed crack houses.

Few experts are optimistic that society will suddenly focus on these problems.

"The problem," Mr. Kleiman said, "is that the costs of solving our basic problems will come in the short term while the advantages would come only after the end of every current officeholder's term of office. So it's in no one's political interest to force us to start paying the price now."

RICO
A Racketeering Law Run Amok

". . . The flood of civil RICO [Racketeer Influenced and Corrupt Organizations Act] cases has become a torrent. Virtually every kind of controversy, from the most common to the truly bizarre, has come to serve as the basis for litigation under this statute."

Rick Boucher

Rep. Boucher (D.-Va.) is Assistant Majority Whip and a member of the Crime Subcommittee of the Judiciary Committee.

IMAGINE a law that allows warring spouses to sue each other as "racketeers" and seek more than three times their actual monetary claim in divorce or child custody battles. Imagine the same law being invoked in disputes between church members, landlords and tenants, and family members fighting over the family business.

Imagine the same claims of "racketeering" and demands for multiple damages being asserted against Walter Mondale in a dispute over politics, against anti-abortion demonstrators by advocates of pro-choice, by opponents of U.S. foreign policy in the Middle East against the CIA, by industries against striking unions, by a target of a successful FBI "sting" operation against the Bureau and the individual agents.

If your imagination is stretched to the limits by my suggestions, consider how a law Congress created in the early 1970's to fight organized crime has become the weapon of choice between warring parties in every type of dispute you can conceive of.

Throughout the 1950's and 1960's, our leaders searched for new methods to combat the scourge of organized crime and its harmful effects upon American society, including its ability to drive companies out of business through threats and other criminal activities, as well as through the power of the money it obtained through illicit activities. Congress' answer to this problem, in part, was to enact the RICO (Rackeeteer Influenced and Corrupt Organizations) statute in 1970. It specifically crafted the law to protect legitimate businesses from "infiltration" by organized crime groups and from injury to their businesses by the Mob. In RICO, Congress armed Federal prosecutors with the ability to seek long prison terms, substantial fines, and the forfeiture of a racketeer's interest in legitimate or criminal enterprises.

Before its passage, almost as an afterthought, Congress added to the statute the right of private individuals to sue organized, professional criminals. Perhaps to create an additional incentive for private parties injured by organized crime's activities to bring suit against such fearsome defendants, it provided that a successful plaintiff would be entitled to recover three times actual damages plus costs incurred in bringing the case, including attorneys' fees.

At first, this new power went virtually unnoticed by government prosecutors and private individuals. Few RICO cases were brought in the early years. In the late 1970's, however, RICO began to live up to its promise as a weapon in the government's arsenal. Federal prosecutors began using the statute to bring cases against mobsters who long had evaded justice. In addition, Federal prosecutors began using RICO against other types of hard-core criminals, such as drug rings and terrorist groups. The severe criminal penalties the law provided, along with its innovative forfeiture provisions, proved effective in the government's war against crime. Some of the biggest organized crime cases of the last decade have been prosecuted under RICO.

During the same time period, civil RICO cases virtually were unheard of in the courts. One study has shown that only nine civil RICO decisions were reported before 1980. Over the next five years, however, as plaintiffs' lawyers discovered the lure of treble damages and attorney's fees that civil RICO provided, the situation changed dramatically. As a result, the filing of civil RICO cases exploded between 1980 and 1984.

Unfortunately, this spurt of legal action was not created by hordes of courageous citizens suing mobsters for their ill-gotten gains. In fact, through 1984, only nine percent of the civil RICO cases involved allegations of illegal activity of a type generally associated with professional criminals.

Instead, clever attorneys had figured out that RICO was worded broadly by Congress in order to give Federal prosecutors a wide net for catching hard-core criminals. That broad language allows almost any type of ordinary civil or commercial dispute to be transformed into a "racketeering case," complete with enormous damage awards and the smear of the "racketeering" label. The threat that such charges pose to honest businesses and professionals—whose livelihood depends on their reputations—is enormous. Smart attorneys soon recognized that many defendants in civil RICO cases are willing to settle quickly, rather than face the disastrous implications of being involved in such a suit, regardless of its validity. Supreme Court Justice Thurgood Marshall recognized the ironic result of this use of the "racketeering" laws: "Many a prudent defendant, facing ruinous exposure, will decide to settle even a case with no merit. It is thus not surprising that civil RICO has been used for extortive purposes, giving rise to the very evils that it was designed to combat."

Efforts by some Federal courts to limit civil RICO were rejected by the Supreme Court in 1985. A bare five-to-four majority of the Supreme Court held that, although the statute was being used in areas far afield from organized crime, it could not be restricted in its civil form so as to exclude ordinary commercial disputes. Although the Court acknowledged that, "in its private civil version, RICO is evolving into something quite different from the original concept of its enactors," it said the solution lay with Congress, not the courts.

Since that decision, the flood of civil RICO cases has become a torrent. Virtually every kind of controversy, from the most common to the truly bizarre, has come to serve as the basis for litigation under this statute. The instances mentioned in the opening of this article are real-life examples of civil RICO cases.

While those bizarre lawsuits illustrate the abuse this statute invites, the most serious threat it poses is in ordinary, everyday commercial and business litigation. Much of this has been handled for decades, if not centuries, in local, rather than Federal, courts or under carefully crafted statutes or legal doctrines. Civil RICO blows a gaping hole through those standards and threatens to overwhelm the Federal courts with lawsuits better handled in state courts and under well-established legal doctrines. The result is a rising chorus of responsible observers of the legal system urging Congress to reform civil RICO. Recently, William Rehnquist, the Chief Justice of the Supreme Court, joined that chorus: "Virtually everyone who has addressed the question agrees that civil RICO is now being used in ways that Congress never intended when it enacted the statute in 1970. Most of the civil suits filed under the statute have nothing to do with organized crime. They are garden-variety civil fraud cases of the type traditionally litigated in state courts."

Reforming RICO

To rectify these severe problems, a diverse and broad range of labor, business, and public-interest organizations have banded together to urge Congress to reform the civil RICO statute. This group includes the AFL-CIO; American Bar Association; American Civil Liberties Union; National Association of Manufacturers; representatives of the accounting profession and of the securities, banking, and insurance industries; and the U.S. Chamber of Commerce.

Sen. Dennis DeConcini (D.-Ariz.) and I, among others, have responded to these concerns by introducing legislation that would rein in the abuse of the civil RICO statute in an effective, but balanced, way. The heart of our approach allows most plaintiffs bringing civil RICO suits to collect for actual damages that they can prove, but would eliminate their right to treble damages. It is the lure of this windfall damage recovery that has spurred much of the abusive litigation involving civil RICO, and its elimination should cut these lawsuits back significantly, particularly in routine commercial cases.

At the same time, our proposal recognizes that there are certain circumstances where the recovery of multiple damages is appropriate. Victims harmed by a defendant who has been convicted of a felony related to a RICO charge, certain units of government, and victims of violent RICO violations would continue to recover automatic treble damages. In addition, many consumers harmed in connection with a purchase for personal or household use or investment would be able to collect up to treble damages in particularly egregious cases, as would the victims of the insider trading that has undermined the faith in the integrity of Wall Street and our financial markets.

Our legislation also would make other changes to the civil RICO statute to help cure other past abuses. The result would be a statute that is more geared toward Congress' original purpose in enacting RICO—penalizing the real racketeers and aiding, not victimizing, legitimate businesses and professionals.

Those raising their voices in opposition to reforming civil RICO are ignoring or unduly discounting the harmful and harassing effect of civil RICO in its present form. They argue, for instance, that there is no real problem because courts can dismiss "frivolous" RICO cases. However, the problem with this law is not frivolous cases that courts can throw out, but those they feel compelled to allow to proceed because of the statute's broad language. The recent refusal of a Federal court to dismiss Eastern Airlines' $1,500,000,000 racketeering suit against its unions is a prime example of a claim that Congress never intended to create, but which a court found that the statute supports. The Eastern example is not isolated, illustrating that innocent defendants may have to pay hundreds of thousands of dollars in legal fees to extract themselves from an inappropriate civil RICO suit.

Other opponents of reform assert that defrauded consumers can find a meaningful remedy only in the statute's treble damage provision. This concern already has been addressed to a great extent by the provisions in the legislation Sen. DeConcini and I have introduced, which will protect the ability of consumers to continue to collect multiple damages in egregious cases. In addition, those bringing civil RICO claims have many other legal remedies under other state and Federal laws which provide for punitive damages in cases of egregious misconduct. To continue on the current course, as the opponents of reform suggest, would allow the continued displacement of well-thought-out laws and remedies without a significant counterbalancing benefit.

Much is at stake in the effort to reform the statute—reputations of legitimate businesses and professionals; protection of our most important civil liberties; the ability of companies to engage in business without the fear that they will be bankrupted by a ruinous civil RICO suit; and the integrity of the state and Federal court systems and their ability to administer timely and effective justice for all of America's citizens. Congress intended civil RICO to protect legitimate businesses and individuals, not to make them its victims. The time has come for Congress to fix this statute before more Americans suffer under a law that clearly is unjust, unbalanced, and unfair.

RADICAL RIGHT
vs.
RADICAL LEFT

Terrorist Theory and Threat

THOMAS STRENTZ, Ph.D.,
Supervisory Special Agent (Retired),
Behavioral Science Unit, FBI Academy,
Quantico, Virginia

Mental health can be conceptualized as a wheel, with normal people at the hub and the seriously disabled at the rim. Those who seek violent solutions to domestic social or political problems in a democracy, where peaceful procedures for orderly change are abundant, can be considered to have moved along the spokes of the wheel away from the large hub of normality and toward the thin rim of pathology.

During this examination of political philosophies, it is very important to remember that, while the Democratic party in the United States has a leftist orientation and the Republican party is more to the right, left-wing and right-wing terrorist groups represent outrageous and illegal expressions of these diverse and legitimate political perspectives. Because of their violent opposition to constitutional democracies, extreme left-wing (or communist/socialist) and radical right-wing (or fascist/Nazi) terrorists share some personal characteristics. However, there are several significant socioeconomic, psychosexual, educational and religious differences between terrorist groups.

I do not suggest that individual terrorists are suffering from an identifiable mental illness. However, if investigators are aware of the elements of some mental disorders and the fundamental differences between left- and right-wing political philosophies, then the personalities, thought processes, patterns of social interaction, educational levels, group dynamics and sexual preferences of those they will be investigating will be better understood.[1]

Though these social deviants may not be specifically described in the psychiatric literature, as a general rule, the more democratic, open and free the society, the more one sees evidence of psychological pathology in its violent domestic dissenters. When a political or social system has adequately provided for dissenting views and orderly change, violence perpetrated by its adversaries tells one more about the aberrant personalities of these antagonists than about the alleged intransigence of the system.

As situations change and stress develops, healthy people adapt their behavior to deal with the new demands. Psychological adaptiveness is a gradient to which *unhealthy* personalities do *not* respond.[2] When new challenges are encountered, the psychologically infirm may become less flexible and resort to rigid responses that usually make matters worse. The greater the demand for different or adaptive behavior, the more intransigent they become. Thus, when dealing with those whose stress responses are maladaptive, we frequently see behavior patterns that are predictable and lend themselves to manipulation by others.[3]

After examining terrorist group activities and looking at the personalities of several domestic terrorists, it becomes clear that predictive generalizations can be made on the overall structure and functioning of these aberrant organizations.

Sociological and Sexual Differences

Generally, radical left-wing groups consist of persons who are single, separated or divorced. Many are involved in a subconscious conflict with their parents and terrorist group membership provides them with an expression for this

rebellion.[4] Others seek to complete the revolution they believe their parents began.[5] Their ages tend to be clustered in the twenties and early forties.

On the other hand, radical right-wing groups frequently include entire families and, in that sense, are like cults. It is rare to find a female leader on the right. Perhaps this is because the Bible speaks of the man as the head of the house and commands the woman to be obedient to her husband.

On the left, gender or sexual preference does not exclude one from a leadership role. One explanation for this is the more liberal attitude of the left toward women and their rights on a variety of issues from abortion to voting. Overt homosexuality is quite acceptable on the left and is not a bar to leadership.

On the right, a reactionary and rigid orientation toward respective roles of men and women in our society is especially strong. Homosexuality is an abhorrence on the right and may result in expulsion.

Psychological Considerations

There are other psychological differences, as well. Marxist groups engage in protracted sessions of self-criticism, while the right spends its time reinforcing its self-image as genuine, dedicated and God-like people. This develops from the basic difference of the right wanting to maintain, or return to, the wonderfulness of the establishment and the left wanting a revolution to rectify the world's many imperfections and inequalities. In other words, left-wing groups deny the authority of the establishment, while radicals on the right deny the legitimacy of the opposition.[6]

Reprinted from the *Police Chief* magazine, Vol. LVII, No. 8, August 1990, pp. 70-75. Copyright © 1990 by The International Association of Chiefs of Police, Inc., 1110 North Glebe Road, Suite 200, Arlington, Virginia, 22201. Further reproduction without express written permission from IACP is strictly prohibited.

The three personality types seen with some degree of regularity in both left- and right-wing domestic terrorist groups are

1. The leader—a person of high dedication; a theoretician with a strong personality. This person has a pattern of social interaction and psychological reasoning that is similar to what many psychologists have labeled as a paranoid personality disorder. In left-wing groups, this person can be male or a female; on the right, it is almost always a male.

2. The activist-operator—a male with an antisocial personality. Frequently an ex-convict, this action-oriented person gives the group its criminal orientation, which brings it into conflict with the law.

3. The idealist—frequently a university dropout on the left or a youthful family member or drifter on the right. Each exhibits an empty life style and a penchant for searching for the meaning of life. Both men and women are found in this role. They are the guilt-ridden hitchhikers who thumb a ride on every cause from communism to Christianity, needing a Marx or a Christ to worship and die for. They are the mortal enemy of the status quo and insist on sacrificing themselves for an impossible dream.[7]

Educational Differences

Those on the left tend to be better educated. They join a particular group because of some deep personal conviction or unresolved psychological problem. They are more likely than right-wing radicals to understand and believe in the group's goals. In the course of their college education, they have read revolutionary rhetoric and many think that the poor and other minorities are being exploited. As a result of their youth, they are better able to pay the price of incarceration for their political and criminal acts. Many seem to revel in the martyr's role.

Conversely, while one may find an articulate, university-educated leader on the right, the rank and file are usually high school dropouts from blue collar families. Many were attracted to the terrorist group because of its scapegoating rhetoric and emotional—rather than intellectual—appeal. Some have characterized them as street corner racists who lack a depth of conviction.[8] Due to their general lack of education and limited employment skills, they are more susceptible to economic reversals; they tend to be the last hired and the first fired. It is always comforting to believe that problems are due to forces beyond one's control. Some experiencing social, psychological or economic distress are very vulnerable to charismatic leaders who mix religion, anti-semitism, revisionist history and a pet economic theory to provide quick and simple fixes to complex social and economic problems.

Preparatory Criminal Activity

Those on the right tend to be impulsive. Once a target for their criminal activity has been identified, they usually complete the felony with considerably less planning than one sees on the left. The Symbionese Liberation Army (SLA) tended to plan its felonies meticulously. Its members took pictures, made diagrams, studied maps and tirelessly surveilled their targets.[9] Most right-wing terrorists seem to enjoy the planning phase more than the actual operation. The overt criminal act is almost anti-climactic.

Arrest and Conviction Differences

A recent research project has developed information that tends to confirm the tendencies toward impulsive criminal activity by the right and meticulous planning by the left. The research was based on over 500 people who were identified as domestic terrorists in American newspaper articles—212 from left-wing groups, 279 from the radical right and 26 whose political affiliation was difficult to determine. Among the leftist groups represented were the SLA, the May 19th Communist Organization, the Black Liberation Army, Puerto Rican independence groups and several other communist organizations. On the right were the American Nazi Party, the National Socialist White Peoples Party, the Ku Klux Klan, the Aryan Nations, the Covenant, Sword and the Arm of the Lord, the Order and others.

A search of FBI files resulted in the location of over 300 cases. Some cases contained many names, while others contained only one. There were duplications in the listings of names in several files. A review of these names and their group affiliations revealed approximately 50 left-wing convictions, over 100 right-wing convictions and several other convictions of individuals who belong to such groups as the Jewish Defense League, which is neither left nor right in its political orientation.

When the individual arrest records were reviewed, it was found that the majority of the arrests of those on the left were for such offenses as trespassing, failure to obtain a parade permit, disorderly conduct and other violations associated with the political demonstrations that were common in the late 1960s and early '70s. There was also a sprinkling of felony arrests for bombing, bank robbery and hijacking.

This is not to suggest that the left is nonviolent, however. The October 20, 1981, armored car robbery in Nyack, New York, which left two police officers and one armored car employee dead, provides evidence of their violence.[10] The SLA shootout in Los Angeles also attests to leftists' capacity for violence.[11]

The arrest records for those on the right provide a stark contrast to the left-wing misdemeanor arrests. Although members of right-wing groups engaged in very few armed confrontations with law enforcement,[12] they have used a submachine gun to murder an unarmed radio personality in Denver, attacked and killed several unarmed left-wing demonstrators in Greensboro, North Carolina, and murdered unarmed fellow radicals. When an armed confrontation did develop between the right wing and law enforcement, the terrorists usually surrendered or died under conditions that suggested the possibility of suicide.

The study also indicated that right-wing terrorists tended to be more forthcoming in police interviews than those on the left. Thus, when one person on the right was arrested, a series of other arrests soon followed. Frequently, those arrested provided names to match the physical evidence recovered by law enforcement at the scene of a successful but poorly planned criminal escapade.[13]

Multiple arrests of left-wing terrorists were the result of information developed from investigations or after the serving of search warrants on their safe houses. These places of hiding and planning generally revealed lists of associates, names of places to be bombed, a wealth of fingerprints, correspondence with other groups and data that led to more and more individuals and groups. Leftist arrests were usually the result of very intensive investigations, while those on the right were more commonly attributed to the good interviewing techniques used by arresting officers.

Attitude Toward Law Enforcement

The left, which generally views law enforcement as the willing tool of the oppressive regime, has planted bombs targeting police officers, law enforcement buildings and vehicles with some success. The right, on the other hand, tends to see law enforcement as the misguided instrument of the government and there is no record of the right planting bombs to kill police.

Those on the right tend to have more respect for, and may even admire, law enforcement officers. Their penchant for dressing up in military and police-type uniforms provides some evidence of this. One could argue that they desperately want to be part of what they perceive as the inner circle, ruling class or power structure. However, their lack of education, lower social class and highly mobile life style preclude this. Therefore, when given the opportunity to implicate their associates in felonies, thus cooperating with a representative of the establishment they subconsciously admire, they are much more likely to do so than are those on the left.

Level of Sophistication

The sophistication of terrorist groups can be gauged by looking at the types of crimes they plan and perpetrate. These acts fall into two broad categories. While both provide publicity for their cause, one cluster involves intimidation by violence while the other entails monetary returns. When considering the number of people needed and training required, those acts that result in uncontrolled violence like bombing and shooting are frequently the crimes of a less sophisticated group. Obviously, a higher level of competence is required to commit acts that are monetarily motivated—armed robbery, kidnapping or other violations that include a ransom demand. Theoretically, those "groups" that only bomb or shoot may be comprised of only one person. On the other hand, the ability to successfully hijack an airplane or kidnap and hold victims for ransom requires several well-trained people and a lot of planning.

There have been two political kidnapping cases in the United States. One was the abduction of Patricia Campbell Hearst by the left-wing SLA. The other involved a right-wing group called the Army of God, which abducted two doctors who operated an abortion clinic in the Midwest. While the left has hijacked airplanes and the right has not, both groups have robbed armored cars and banks, and neither has engaged in burglaries. Both have shot at people and bombed buildings. The right has engaged in short-lived and not very professional counterfeiting operations in the Northwest. It is apparent that there is very little difference between the types of criminal acts generally perpetrated by domestic terrorist groups on either end of the political spectrum.

Radical Group Conferences

Both groups try to achieve some sort of solidarity with similarly oriented political organizations. When the left conducts a conference, the meetings are held at a major hotel in a large metropolitan area and feature delegates from many nations who arrive by air. The larger meetings usually focus on global strategies, presented by a guest speaker in a plenary session that is supplemented

Characteristic	Right Wing	Left Wing
Radical political orientation	Nazi/fascist	Communist/socialist
View of government	Perfect—retain or revive	Perfectible—replace
View of government opposition	Illegitimate	Honorable
Desire for social change	None/reactionary	Revolutionary
Social class	Lower/middle	Lower/middle/upper
Leadership	Male-dominated	Egalitarian
Sex roles	Established/rigid	Unspecified
Marital status	Married	Single/divorced/separated
Group dynamics	Families/cults	Single co-equals
Age	16-76	25-45
Education—members	High school	University
Education—leaders	High school/university	University
Religion	Fundamental/Protestant	Agnostic/atheistic
Criminal planning	Impulsive	Meticulous

with break-out groups. These conferences provide a cover for their clandestine gatherings. Sometimes travel costs for such meetings are paid by leftist or revolutionary governments like Libya or Cuba. There is evidence that these governments have assisted left-wing domestic groups with training, refuge and generous funding. In return, domestic left-wing groups provide money from their bank and armored car robberies to organizations overseas.

When the right engages in such conferences, most of the attendees are from the United States and the meetings are held in remote rural retreats. Members arrive in pick-up trucks with travel trailers and their families in tow. Their sessions feature survival lectures, firearms training, prayer sessions and war games in the woods. The conference closes with a family barbecue. Participants rarely travel internationally and receive no support from foreign governments. A right-wing group member who recently won a large amount of money became less active in the organization and was eventually evicted from the group when he refused to share any of his new-found wealth. Yet there are other members of the radical right who are very philanthropic, dividing their booty from large robberies with some who share their political or religious views.[14]

Geographic Considerations

There is a noticeable geographic di-

chotomy of domestic terrorist groups. Left-wing groups are concentrated in the East and in urban areas, while right-wing groups are more commonly found in rural areas. The right-wing racial hate groups that abound in New York, Chicago, Los Angeles and other cities constitute the main exception to this rule of thumb.

Religion

Because of the strong communist influence, domestic left-wing groups tend to be atheistic or agnostic. The right incorporates religion into its political beliefs. Right-wing terrorists are radical fundamentalists who seek to justify their political activity and anti-semitic beliefs with quotes from the scriptures. They attribute their successes and failures to the will of God, and consider those who oppose them to be either disciples of the devil or members of an inferior race whose extinction is sanctioned by their interpretation of the Bible.

The Next 10 Years

Left-wing domestic violence has been on the wane for many years. With the democratization of Eastern Europe and failing communist economies around the world, it is anticipated that most domestic leftist groups will remain dormant. However, Middle Eastern-sponsored domestic groups will probably remain active, as will those that seek independence for Puerto Rico and those that espouse racial or ethnic issues.

The domestic right wing has been dealt a serious blow in recent years and many of its members are now in jail. However, as we approach the next century, it can be anticipated that radical religious prophets predicting the end of the world will abound in the United States. Of course, most people looking to the year 2000 with the expectation of fundamental religious or social change are not religious radicals, just as most people who disagreed with the U.S. policy in Vietnam did not join terrorist groups or violate the law. Yet it was from this discontented portion of our population that violent radical groups drew their members.

A close parallel exists between the teachings of today's charismatic leaders and those of several historical religious cults. Many developed in Europe during the final decade of the Dark Ages, at the end of the 10th century and at other significant times in history when a mathematical interpretation of the Bible provided the date for the end of the world.[15] One thing that may serve to make these groups more dangerous in the future than they have been to date is their belief that they must now migrate to our western mountains to escape the earthquakes, economic collapse, nuclear war and other catastrophes their prophets predict for the 1990s. This will bring them into the region of the United States that presently houses the leaderless and sympathetic remnants of the religiously oriented radical right wing.[16]

Conclusion

The right-wing and left-wing domestic terrorist groups active in the United States seek violent solutions to resolve social and political differences when peaceful avenues of resolution are available. Thus, their actions tell us more about them as people than about the systems they seek to revolutionize. Although similar personalities are seen in both groups, the individuals' reasons for joining, their economic backgrounds, their level of education and their social status all thrust these comparable personalities into very diverse settings. Consequently, law enforcement must develop a solid understanding of their idiosyncrasies and adapt its strategies accordingly in order to successfully investigate these aberrant organizations.

[1]T. Strentz, "Terrorist Organizational Profile," *Behavioral and Quantitative Perspectives on Terrorism*, Y. Alexander and J.M. Gleason, eds. (New York, NY: Pergamon Press, 1981), pp. 86-104.
[2]T. Millon, *Disorders of Personality* (New York, John Wiley & Sons, 1981).
[3]R. Ault, personal interview, Behavioral Science Unit, FBI Academy, Quantico, Virginia, January 16, 1990.
[4]B. Salert, *Revolutions and Revolutionaries: Four Theories* (New York, NY: Elsevier Scientific Publishing Co., 1976).
[5]M. Decter, *Liberal Parents, Radical Children* (New York, NY: Coward, McCann & Geoghegan, 1975).
[6]J. Conley, personal interview, Behavioral Science Unit, FBI Academy, Quantico, Virginia, January 17, 1990.
[7]E. Hoffer, *The True Believer* (New York, NY: Harper & Row, 1952).
[8]K. Flynn and G. Gerhardt, *The Silent Brotherhood: Inside America's Racist Underground* (New York, NY: Free Press, 1989).
[9]P. Hearst, personal interview, Hearst Corporation Headquarters, New York, New York, February 15, 1990.
[10]E. Frankfort, *Kathy Boudin and the Dance of Death* (New York, NY: Stein & Day, 1984).
[11]P. Hearst, *Every Secret Thing* (New York, NY: Doubleday & Co., 1982).
[12]Flynn and Gerhardt.
[13]*Ibid.*
[14]*Ibid.*
[15]N. Cohn, *The Pursuit of the Millenium* (Fairlawn, NJ: Essential Books, 1957); R. Niebuhr, "Millenium Fever: As the Year 2000 Draws Near, Guru Ma, Among Others, Says Head for the Hills," *Wall Street Journal*, December 4, 1989, p. 1; and A.A. Vasiliev, "Medieval Ideas of the End of the World: West and East," *Byzantion*, 16 Fascicle 2 1942-43, pp. 462-502.
[16]Niebuhr.

Victimology

The crime victim, traditionally the forgotten person in the criminal justice system, is now the center of attention for those who want to change the system. Indeed, historians might call the 1980s the decade in which a move was finally made toward acknowledging victims of crime as central characters in the criminal event, worthy of compassion and concern.

From 1981 to 1990 Presidents Reagan and Bush have proclaimed a National Victims of Crime Week annually with a view to focusing attention on the problems and concerns of crime victims. In December 1982 the President's Task Force on Victims of Crime published a 144-page report on the treatment of crime victims throughout the country. This publication contained 68 recommendations for addressing the problems of victims. While studying the experiences of crime victims, the task force recognized that family violence is often more complex in its causes and solutions than crime committed by unknown perpetrators.

Victims of crime have also been the subject of legislation during the 1980s. For example, the 1982 Omnibus Victim and Witness Protection Act requires the use of victim impact statements at sentencing in federal criminal cases, and provides for greater protection of federal victims and witnesses from intimidation. The Comprehensive Crime Control Act and the Victims of Crime Act of 1984 authorize federal funding for state victim compensation and victim assistance programs.

Comprehensive legislation that protects the interests of the victim has been enacted in more than 35 states. State victim compensation programs have continued to expand—43 states and the District of Columbia now have these programs—as have victim assistance services in the community. Thus, recent developments have been supportive of the crime victim.

The articles in this unit provide sharper focus on some key issues. From the lead essay, "The Fear of Crime," we learn that the fear of being victimized is pervasive among people, including some who have never been victims of crime. This article addresses the effects of crime on its victims.

Andrew Karmen's essay, "The Implementation of Victims' Rights: A Challenge for Criminal Justice Professionals," maintains that how criminal justice agents respond to victims' demands will resolve many controversies and generate new ones. The tragedy of family violence is the focus of "Battered Families: Voices of the Abused; Voices of the Abusers."

Groups that have grappled with the issue of testing sex offenders for AIDS have only been able to come up with incomplete rationales for their positions. Read "AIDS and Rape" to see why this is so. "Can a Marriage Survive Tragedy?" is the title of the next article. The author maintains that many relationships are destroyed after victimization. The unit closes with "Prostitutes and Addicts: Special Victims of Rape."

Looking Ahead: Challenge Questions

Is the fear of crime realistic?

What life-style changes might you consider to avoid becoming victimized?

Are you familiar with victim service programs in your area?

How does crime affect the victim's psyche?

The Fear of Crime

The fear of crime affects many people, including some who have never been victims of crime

How do crime rates compare with the rates of other life events?

Events	Rate per 1,000 adults per year*
Accidental injury, all circumstances	242
Accidental injury at home	79
Personal theft	72
Accidental injury at work	58
Violent victimization	31
Assault (aggravated and simple)	24
Injury in motor vehicle accident	17
Death, all causes	11
Victimization with injury	10
Serious (aggravated) assault	9
Robbery	6
Heart disease death	4
Cancer death	2
Rape (women only)	2
Accidental death, all circumstances	.5
Pneumonia/influenza death	.3
Motor vehicle accident death	.2
Suicide	.2
Injury from fire	.1
Homicide/legal intervention death	.1
Death from fire	.03

These rates approximate your chances of becoming a victim of these events. More precise estimates can be derived by taking account of such factors as your age, sex, race, place of residence, and lifestyle. Findings are based on 1982–84 data, but there is little variation in rates from year to year.

*These rates exclude children from the calculations (those under age 12–17, depending on the series). Fire injury/death data are based on the total population, because no age-specific data are available in this series.

Sources: Current estimates from the National Health Interview Survey: United States, 1982, National Center for Health Statistics. "Advance report of final mortality statistics, 1983," Monthly Vital Statistics Report, National Center for Health Statistics. Estimates of the population of the United States, by age, sex, and race: 1980 to 1984, U.S. Bureau of the Census. The 1984 Fire Almanac, National Fire Protection Association. Criminal victimization 1984, BJS Bulletin, October 1985.

The chance of being a violent crime victim, with or without injury, is greater than that of being hurt in a traffic accident

The rates of some violent crimes are higher than those of some other serious life events. For example, the risk of being the victim of a violent crime is higher than the risk of death from cancer or injury or death from a fire. Still, a person is much more likely to die from natural causes than as a result of a criminal victimization.

About a third of the people in the United States feel very safe in their neighborhoods

The fear of crime cannot be measured precisely because the kinds of fears people express vary depending on the specific questions asked. Nevertheless, asking them about the likelihood of crime in their homes and neighborhoods yields a good assessment of how safe they feel in their own immediate environment.

In the Victimization Risk Survey, a 1984 supplement to the National Crime Survey, most people said that they felt at least fairly safe in their homes and neighborhoods. Yet, the people who said that they felt "fairly safe" may have been signaling some concern about crime. Based on a "very safe" response, a little more than 4 in 10 people felt entirely safe in their homes and about 1 in 3 felt totally safe in their neighborhoods—
• homeowners felt safer than renters
• people living in nonmetropolitan areas felt safer than those living in cities
• families with incomes of $50,000 or more were most likely to report their neighborhoods were very safe from crime.

The Victimization Risk Survey found that—
• 9 in 10 persons felt very or fairly safe in their places of work
• few persons—about 1 in 10—felt in danger of being a victim of a crime by a fellow employee, but persons working in places that employ more than 50 people were more likely to express fear of possible victimization.

The groups at the highest risk of becoming victims are not the ones who express the greatest fear of crime

Females and the elderly generally express a greater fear of crime than do people in groups who face a much greater risk. The Reactions to Crime project found that such impressions are related to the content of information about crime. Such information tends to emphasize stories about elderly and female victims. These stories may influence women and the elderly in judging the seriousness of their own condition. Perhaps groups such as females and the elderly reduce their risk of victimization by constricting their activities to reduce their exposure to danger. This behavior would account, at least in part, for their high levels of fear and their low levels of victimization.

Relatives, friends, and neighbors who hear about a crime become as fearful as the victim

When one household in a neighborhood is affected by a crime, the entire neighborhood may feel more vulnerable. This suggests that people who have not been victimized personally may be strongly affected when they hear about how others have been victimized. The Reactions to Crime project found that

From Report to the Nation on Crime and Justice, Bureau of Justice Statistics, U.S. Department of Justice, March 1988, pp. 24-25.

How does crime affect its victims?

indirect reaction to crime is often very strong.

$13 billion was lost from personal and household crimes in 1985

The direct cash and property losses from personal robberies, personal and household larcenies, household burglaries, and privately owned motor vehicle theft in 1985 was slightly more than $13 billion. This NCS finding probably underestimates the amount covered by insurance because the claims of many respondents had not been settled at the time of the NCS interview.

UCR data show that in 1985 losses from reported robberies, burglaries, and larceny/theft surpassed $5.9 billion. Among the many economic consequences of crime are lost productivity from victims' absence from work, medical care, and the cost of security measures taken to deter crime.

Other costs of crime include the economic costs of the underground economy, lowered property values, and pain and suffering of victims, their families, friends, and neighbors.

The economic impact of crime differs for different groups

The cost of crime is borne by all segments of society, but to different degrees. A study on the economic cost of crime using NCS data for 1981 shows that the dollar loss from crimes involving money, property loss, or destruction of property rises with income.

• Median losses were higher for households with incomes of $15,000 or more than for households with incomes of

less than $7,500 from burglary ($200 vs. $100) and from motor vehicle theft ($2,000 vs. $700).

• Median losses from personal crimes were higher for blacks ($58) than for whites ($43).
• Median losses from household crimes were higher for blacks ($90) than for whites ($60).
• More than 93% of the total loss from crime was in crimes without victim-offender contact (such as burglary, theft without contact, and motor vehicle theft).

Many victims or members of their families lose time from work

Along with injuries suffered, victims or other members of their household may have lost time from work because of a violent crime. Lost worktime was reported in 15% of rapes and 7% of assaults (11% of aggravated assaults, 6% of simple assaults).

Violent crimes killed 19,000 and injured 1.7 million in 1985

NCS data for 1985 show that of all rape,

robbery, and assault victims—
• 30% were injured
• 15% required some kind of medical attention
• 8% required hospital care.

The likelihood of injury was—
• greater for females than males even when rape was excluded from the analysis
• about the same for whites and blacks
• greater for persons from lower than from higher income households.

Who is injured seriously enough to require medical attention?

An analysis of NCS data for 1973–82 found that—
• Female victims are more likely than male victims to be injured, but they have about the same likelihood of requiring medical attention (13% of female vs. 12% of male victims).
• Blacks are more likely than whites to require medical attention when injured in violent crimes; 16% of black violent crime victims and 16% of the victims of all other racial groups required medical attention, while 11% of white victims required such care.

How seriously a victim is injured varies by type of crime

	Percent of all violent victimizations requiring:			Median stay for those hospitalized overnight
	Medical attention	Treatment in hospital emergency room	Overnight hospital stay	
Rape	24%	14%	3%	4 days
Robbery	15	7	2	5
Assault	11	5	1	5
Aggravated	18	9	3	5
Simple	7	3	—	2

—less than .5%

Source: BJS National Crime Survey, 1973–82.

THE IMPLEMENTATION OF VICTIMS' RIGHTS: A CHALLENGE FOR CRIMINAL JUSTICE PROFESSIONALS

Andrew Karmen

The victories of the victims' rights movement have led to the enactment of many pledges of fair treatment and of opportunities to participate in the criminal justice process. Evaluations are now needed to determine whether criminal justice officials and agencies are implementing these recently gained rights in good faith. Such evaluations could help to clarify continuing concerns, such as whether the system can ever be reformed to operate in the best interests of victims, how the observance of victims' rights can be guaranteed, whether all victims can be treated fairly, and how often victims might opt for non-punitive resolutions of their conflicts with offenders.

INTRODUCTION

The struggle to gain formal, legal rights has been a powerful moving force throughout history. The concept of "rights" suggests both an escape from oppression and exploitation plus an achievement of independence and autonomy. A number of social movements seeking freedom, liberation, empowerment, equality, and justice have sought greater rights for their constituencies. The most well-known include civil rights, workers' rights, students' rights, children's rights, women's rights, gay rights' and prisoners' rights movements. The victims' rights movement of the late 1970s and 1980s falls within this tradition. The underlying objective of the victims' rights movement is to assure that certain standards of fair treatment towards victims are adopted and respected as their cases are processed within the criminal justice system.

The criminal justice system is a branch of the government that routinely comes under scathing criticism from many different quarters. Conservative advocates of "law and order" find fault with its alleged permissiveness. Liberal proponents of procedural egalitarianism decry the system's apparent discriminatory inequities. Radical activists denounce the system's suspected role as an instrument of ruling class domination. Crime victims, the system's supposed "clients," "consumers," or "beneficiaries", complain that standard procedures fail on a most basic level to deliver "justice".

In recent years, the victims' movement has won a number of impressive victories in its struggle for formal rights within the criminal justice process. Some of these rights have been enacted by statutes passed on the municipal, county, and state level, often as part of a legislative package called a "Victim's Bill of Rights." Others have been derived from case law based on court decisions. In some jurisdictions, certain police chiefs, district attorneys, or judges have taken it upon themselves to grant victims certain privileges and prerogatives not required by law or precedent. (For the full scope of proposals and recent gains, see the President's Task Force, 1982; NOVA, 1988; and Stark and Goldstein, 1985).

The rights that victims have fought for - and won - have become so numerous and complex, and vary so dramatically from place to place that they need to be categorized or classified. One way to group them is by the stage or phase in the criminal justice process at which these standards of fair treatment ought to be implemented. For example, some rights of victims must be respected by the police, while others should be observed by prosecutors, judges, corrections officials, or parole boards. But a better way of grouping these new rights is by asking "At whose expense were they gained?" Given the conflicts between individuals, groups, and classes, the rights gained by one side strengthen their position vis-a-vis their real or potential adversaries. Some recently enacted rights of victims clearly were secured to the detriment of "offenders" - or more accurately: suspects, defendants, and prisoners. For example, under the so-called "Son of Sam" statutes, victims in most states are enabled to lay claim to any royalties and fees paid by movie producers or media outlets to convicts who profit from their notoriety by selling the rights to their "inside story". But other rights, such as the right "to be informed" - an obligation on the part of police departments and prosecutors' offices to keep victims posted of any progress and developments in their cases - come at the expense of the privileges and conveniences of criminal justice officials and the budgets of their agencies. The most widely enacted rights of this kind are listed Part A of Chart One. A third group of rights that empower victims to directly participate to some degree in the criminal justice decision-making process, such as allocation before sentencing, may come at the expense of "offenders" or "officials", depending upon what victims seek as they exercise their new chance to have some input (see Karmen, 1990). The most common statutes of this sort are listed in Part B of Chart One.

CHART ONE: PART A

Informational Rights Gained At The Expense of Criminal Justice Agencies and Officials

---

1) To be read one's "rights": to reimbursement of losses - from state compensation funds, court ordered offender restitution, insurance coverage, civil lawsuits, or tax deductions; to referrals - to counseling programs, self-help support

From *Issues in Justice*, Chapter 4, pp. 46-57, edited with contributions by Roslyn Muraskin, 1990. Reprinted by permission of Wyndham Hall Press, Inc., Bristol, IN.

groups, shelters for battered women, rape crisis centers, and other types of assistance; and to be told of one's obligations - to attend line-ups, appear in court, be cross-examined under oath, and to be publicly identified and the subject of media coverage.

2) To be informed of the wherabouts of the (accused) offender: at large; or in custody (jail or prison); escaped from confinement; or released back to the community (on bail, or due to dropped and dismissed charges, or because of acquittal after a trial, or out on appeal, probation, furlough, parole, or after an expired sentence).

3) To be kept posted about key decisions: arrests, the granting of bail, rulings at evidentiary hearings, negotiated pleas, verdicts at trials, sentences, and parole board deliberations.

4) To receive assistance in the form of intercession by an official in behalf of a victim with an employer or creditor; advance notification and facilitation of court appearances; and expeditious return of recovered stolen property.

CHART ONE: PART B

Participatory Rights Gained At The Expense Either of Offenders (Suspects/Defendants/Convicts) or Agencies and Officials

---

1) To be consulted when the terms and conditions of bail are being determined (as a protection against harassment and reprisals for cooperating with the prosecution).

2) To be consulted about the offers made during plea negotiations.

3) To be permitted to submit a victim impact statement, detailing how the crime caused physical, emotional, and/or financial harm, as part of the pre-sentence report, and to submit a statement of opinion suggesting remedies, for the judge's consideration.

4) To be permitted to exercise allocation rights in person, in court, detailing the harm caused by the offender and suggesting an appropriate remedy, before the judge imposes a sentence.

5) To be permitted to bring to the attention of the parole board, either in writing or in person, information about the harm caused by the offender and an opinion about an appropriate remedy.

Source: Karmen, 1990.

Now that a sufficient amount of time has passed since the enactment of these rights, a growing body of data is accumulating about their implementation - or lack of observance - and evaluations are underway (for example, see NIJ, 1989). In fact, legislation introduced before Congress in 1989 called upon the Department of Justice to conduct an annual evaluation of the extent of compliance of federal agencies with the provisions of the Victim and Witness Protection Act of 1982 and the Victims of Crime Act of 1984 ("Bi-partisan Victim Rights Bill," 1989). Thus, it is time to anticipate how the results of these evaluations of pledges about fair treatment might be compiled and interpreted to answer some classical questions that persist within the disciplines of criminal justice, criminology, and victimology.

The findings of evaluation studies, as they accumulate, might either undermine or else lend support to some long-standing suspicions and criticisms about the ways that the criminal justice system operates. It seems worthwhile to hypothesize and speculate about what researchers might discover. If the findings consistently fall into certain patterns, well-grounded answers will emerge for the following questions:

Whose interests are primarily served by the routine operations of the criminal justice system?

The idealistic answer to this question is that the system primarily serves the interests of the whole society in general, and crime victims in particular. Of course, there are many other legitimate sources of input into the decision-making process, and victims are just one of many interested parties. But if indeed victims are truly the clients, customers, consumers, and beneficiaries of a system ostensibly set up to deliver justice to them, then evidence should accumulate that officials and agencies concede their right to participate in the decision-making process. Evaluations should show that victims feel satisfied that their needs and wants were taken into account by decision-makers, even if their requests did not prevail; and that although they were not always "catered to" or "handled with care", they were treated with dignity, respect, and fundamental fairness.

The skeptical, more sociological answer to this question is that a displacement of goals occurs within bureaucratic settings. Unofficial goals, such as minimizing collective effort and maximizing individual and group rewards might be substituted for the official goals of dispensing justice, aiding victims, and serving the public interest. In the context of criminal justice agencies, the hidden agenda behind many official actions might be to dispose of cases in a manner that lightens workloads, covers up mistakes, and curries political favors (McDonald, 1979). Since criminal justice professionals are not directly accountable to victims, either legally or organizationally, they can be inclined to view victims as a resource to be drawn upon, as needed, in the pursuit of objectives such as maintaining high levels of productivity in case processing, and in achieving smooth coordination with other components of the system (Ziegenhagen, 1977). When minor inconveniences to insiders (such as prosecutors, defense attorneys, judges, probation officers, and parole board members) have to be balanced against major inconveniences to outsiders (victims, defendants, witnesses, jurors), insider interests prevail (Ash, 1972). For instance, the courtroom work group of insiders develops a consensus about the "going rate" of appropriate penalties for particular crimes at a given time and place. This work group composed primarily of prosecutors, defense attorneys, and judges tends to resist attempts by outsiders and reformers to alter the penalty structure and disrupt their assembly line processing of cases (Walker, 1989). To the extent that the courtroom workgroup is successful in maintaining their standard operating procedures, victims will find their attempts to influence sentencing (or bail determinations, or plea negotiations, or parole deliberations) an exercise in futility. Their efforts to become involved in the decision-making process will be rebuffed as an intrusion, interference, and a threat to jealously guarded and highly prized professional discretionary authority (see Ranish and Shichor, 1985).

Some preliminary evidence already supports this prediction of "more of the same." Researchers who evaluated the use by victims of their right (since 1982) to allocation in felony cases in California confirmed its ineffectiveness. Plea negotiations which resulted in dismissals of all felony charges or in an understanding of what the sentence would be eliminated the chance for many victims to have any meaningful say in determining the outcomes of their cases. Determinate sentencing laws further eroded victim input. In many cases, officials failed to inform victims of their rights; some of the remaining eligible victims forfeited their chance to appear because of a belief that their appearance before the judge would make no difference in shaping a sentence that was already decided. Of those who exercised their opportunity for allocation, a considerable number felt their recommendations were not heeded. In the opinion of the majority of probation officers and judges, and about half of the prosecutors surveyed, the personal appearances by victims were "minimally, or not at all effective" (Villmoare and Neto, 1987). Similar findings about the difficulty victims have experienced in trying to influence the decision-making process appeared in evaluations of "structured" plea negotiation experiments. Victims who were permitted to attend the negotiation conferences tended to conclude that their presence and the statements they made had no impact on case disposition (Heinz and Kerstetter, 1979; Villmoare and Neto, 1987).

Are some victims more equal than others?

Evaluations might uncover great disparities in the way victims are treated by officials and agencies. A relatively small percentage of privileged people harmed by street criminals might enjoy "first class," "red carpet," or "VIP" treatment - their rights are scrupulously observed - while socially disadvantaged persons experience mistreatment as "second-class complainants." Such a blatant double-standard of justice is not supposed to develop because it violates official doctrines and constitutional guarantees subsumed under the clause "Equal protection under the law", and the pledge, "And justice for all." But many previous studies of case processing indicate that victim characteristics can influence outcomes like decisions to arrest, prosecute, convict, and severely punish offenders (see Myers, 1977; Myers and Hagan, 1979; Paternoster, 1984; Farrell and Swigert, 1986; and Karmen, 1990).

What if evaluations demonstrate that certain categories of victims are more likely to be informed by officials and are more likely to exercise their participatory rights, with demonstrably favorable results? Will the discriminatory treatment in the implementation of informational rights - and especially participatory rights - be correlated with victim characteristics such as race/ethnicity; gender; age; and social class (financial standing; educational attainment; occupational status; reputation in the community)? To state the matter bluntly, will victims drawn from the "right" backgrounds receive better service from the criminal justice system than the vast bulk of underprivileged people routinely preyed upon by street criminals?

Of course, the evaluations might uncover differential treatment on the basis of other factors, as well, which could stimulate considerable debate between officials and victims advocates. For example, should assault victims with "unsavory" backgrounds, such as street gang members, drug abusers, gamblers, and prostitutes be granted the same privileges concerning information and participation as totally innocent, law-abiding victims drawn from other walks of life? If they receive perfunctory responses when they turn to the system for help, would it be justifiable because they are assumed to be offenders in other incidents? Should surrogates and advocates who represent victimized children, and should survivors of murder victims exercise the same rights as direct victims?

What happens when criminal justice professionals violate the rights of crime victims?

The evaluations might expose a thorny problem. What recourse do victims have when their informational and participatory rights are violated? Anticipating the possibility that agencies and officials might fail to inform and involve victims as promised, legislators in many states crafted into their "Victims' Bills of Rights" clauses stating that "nothing in this statute shall be construed as creating a cause of action against the state, a county, municipality, or any of its agents." However, under the separation of powers doctrine, judges might direct officials and agencies to honor their commitments and could authorize injunctive relief for victims who file lawsuits (Stark and Goldstein, 1985). If evaluations turn up widespread non-compliance, additional remedies will be demanded.

Besides inadequate mechanisms for enforcement, evaluations might highlight another related problem: the absence of clear lines of responsibility for implementation. Several different officials and agencies might be held accountable for respecting victims rights. For example, the duty of notifying complainants who served as witnesses for the prosecution of their right to allocation before sentencing might fall to the police, the district attorney's office, the probation department, or a clerk in the office of court administration. All sorts of unanticipated complications might come to light. For example, how many attempts to contact the victim must be made (by phone or mail or in person) before the responsible official can declare that a good faith effort was undertaken to inform and involve the victim in plea negotiations, sentencing recommendations, or parole board deliberations?

Are victims invariably punitive toward offenders?

It is anticipated from common stereotypes, widespread assumptions, and some survey findings (see Hernon and Forst, 1984) that the vast majority of victims will use their newly gained influence to press for the most punitive sanctions permitted under the law. But a significant proportion (how often and under what circumstances?) might argue against lengthy confinement of convicts if alternatives are available. Those victims who do not seek the system's help to exact revenge might expect criminal justice professionals to treat and rehabilitate the persons who harmed them, especially if the offenders are former friends, acquaintances, or relatives. Other victims might place a higher priority on being reimbursed through offender restitution as a condition of probation and parole. Some preliminary reports indicate that when victims are given a full range of options, a significant fraction favor restitution, rehabilitation, and reconciliation over retribution (see Galaway, 1985; Villmoare and Neto, 1987; and Umbreit, 1989).

In conclusion, it is clear that the implementation of victims' rights poses a challenge to criminal justice professionals, especially police administrators, district attorneys, probation officers, judges, corrections officials, and parole board members. How they respond, as revealed by evaluation research, to the demands by victims for fair treatment will resolve many controversies and provoke new ones.

REFERENCES

Ash, M. 1972. "On witnesses: A radical critique of criminal court procedures." Notre Dame Lawyer, 48 (December), pp. 386-425.

"Bi-partisan victim rights bill introduced in U.S. Congress." 1989. NOVA Newsletter 13, 3, pp. 1, 5.

Farrell, R. and Swigert, V. 1986. "Adjudication in homicide:

An interpretive analysis of the effects of defendant and victim social characteristics." Journal of Research in Crime and Delinquency 23, 4 (November), pp. 349-369.

Galaway, B. 1985. "Victim participation in the penal-correction process." Victimology 10, 1, pp. 617-629.

Hernon, J. and Forst, B. 1984. NIJ Research in brief: The criminal justice response to victim harm. Washington, D.C.: U.S. Department of Justice.

Heinz. A. and Kerstetter, W. 1979. "Pretrial settlement conference: Evaluation of a reform in plea bargaining." Law and Society Review, 13, 2, pp. 349-366.

Karmen, A. 1990. Crime Victims: An introduction to victimology. Second edition. Pacific Grove, Ca.: Brooks/Cole.

McDonald, W. 1979. "The prosecutor's domain." In W. McDonald (Ed.), The prosecutor (pp. 15-52). Beverly Hills, Ca.: Sage.

Myers, M. 1977. The effects of victim characteristics on the prosecution, conviction, and sentencing of criminal defendants. Ann Arbor, Mi.: University Microfilms.

_____ and Hagan, J. 1979. "Private and public trouble: Prosecutors and the allocation of court resources." Social Problems, 26, 4, pp. 439-451.

National Institute of Justice (NIJ). 1989. Research in action: The courts- current federal research. Washington, D.C.: U.S. Department of Justice.

National Organization for Victim Assistance (NOVA). 1988. Victim rights and services: A legislative directory - 1987. Washington, D.C.: Author.

Paternoster, R. 1984. "Prosecutorial discretion in requesting the death penalty: A case of victim based racial discrimination." Law and Society Review, 18, 437-478.

President's Task Force on Victims of Crime. 1982. Final Report. Washington, D.C.: U.S. Government Printing Office.

Ranish, D. and Shichor, D. 1985. "The victim's role in the penal process: Recent developments in California." Federal Probation (March), pp. 50-56.

Stark, J. and Goldstein, H. 1985. The rights of crime victims. Chicago: Southern Illinois University Press.

Umbreit, M. 1989. "Violent offenders and their victims." In M. Wright and B. Galaway (Eds.), Mediation and criminal justice: Victims, offenders, and community (pp. 99-112). Newbury Park, Ca.: Sage.

Villmoare, E. and Neto, V. 1987. NIJ Research in brief: Victim appearances at sentencing under California's victims' bill of rights. Washington, D.C.: U.S. Department of Justice.

Walker, S. 1989. Sense and nonsense about crime: A policy guide. (Second edition). Pacific Grove, Ca.: Brooks/Cole.

Ziegenhagen, E. 1977. Victims, crime, and social control. New York: Praeger.

BATTERED FAMILIES
VOICES OF THE ABUSED

Mistreated wives tell their stories of physical threat

By Ellen Steese
Staff writer of The Christian Science Monitor

Boston

At the request of the women interviewed for this story, their names have been changed, and some details have been altered to protect anonymity.

Battered wives in shelters are invisible refugees in our midst, fleeing a war declared on them alone.

Many are in hiding, innocent prisoners on the lam. You meet them in basements with no name on the door, in quiet, incurious, residential neighborhoods. The sorts of places where a succession of exhausted-looking wives and their children can come and go unremarked.

Routine information is oddly absent. It's an act of supreme trust to give someone your full name—and unthinkable to tell anyone where you live.

But if you listen carefully enough and stay long enough, you find in these shelters the story of women emerging from the shadow of secret violence into a world that, if not free of fears, is at least a safe haven from physical abuse.

Cathy is short, cute, a little plump, and she has a sensible, understanding, reassuring air, like a nurse, which she is. Life is peaceful now. She is about to receive an advanced nursing degree. She is safe and divorced, with full custody of her seven-year-old daughter. This is the calm after a storm.

Her relationship with her ex-husband started out like a fairy tale, with no dark shadows. "I thought I was so ugly, and how could I get a man as tall and dark and handsome as George?" Cathy says.

They had a very romantic courtship, with flowers and dinners out: "He treated me like a queen."

Then, a month before the wedding, he pushed her. "I thought it was because of the tension of the marriage," she continues. He said it would never happen again.

He always said it would never happen again. Her life became a round of slaps and punches—always below the neck, so the bruises would be out of sight. Sometimes once a week. Sometimes every day. Sometimes there'd be a respite of two weeks.

Her job as a nurse supported the family (he had 18 jobs in seven years, she says), but that was no guarantee of independence: "He told me when to go to sleep and when not to go to sleep. . . ."

Cathy was always tiptoeing around, not knowing what was going to set him off. Her home was like a concentration camp for one. One terrifying day she was forced to sit in a chair, without doing anything, for 12 hours, while he got drunk and said things like "I'm going to break your . . . head and then tear you to pieces."

"I used to wait for the beating. It seemed like an *eternity*," Cathy comments. She thought things would be better after Janey was born, but then she says, "I was torn between being a mother and surviving."

One evening, because Janey was crying, her husband knocked Cathy down and held a butcher knife at her throat. Missing a tooth and with a concussion, she ran into the January night in her nightgown and slippers, the several miles to her father's house.

In situations like this a person has to make instant, terrifying decisions. Asked if she felt comfortable leaving Janey behind, Cathy says her husband had never injured her. She feels now that leaving the baby saved her own life. To get her child back, however, she had to return to the marriage.

Her father-in-law had been a batterer, too. So when Cathy asked her mother-in-law for help, she said, "You'll just have to get used to it."

Cathy evokes these dark memories as we sit in a plain but warm and comfortable room. It has the feeling of a refuge.

In the other room, her daughter, Janey, and a friend are industriously playing house. There is a vigorous debate about whether some imaginary pork chops had, or had not, already been cooked. But in between the girls' housewifely comments you hear prattling references to foster parents, jail, police.

"He stay in jail so long," one little voice says.

Why did Cathy stay? Because afterward there would be a 'honeymoon" period, she says.

"They're so sorry for what they've done. They're going to kill themselves if you leave. You want so much to believe it's not going to happen again."

Another problem: Her husband threatened to kill members of her family if she left: "I always thought I was protecting them by staying." And he threatened her with loss of custody of her daughter. Cathy says it was a happy moment when the judge at her divorce trial said, " 'Nobody has the right to hurt anybody, and yes, that baby is yours.' "

The neighbors would hear her screams and call the police, and then she would be blamed for the disturbance and beaten again.

"People think we like it, and that's why we put up with it. We're afraid he'll come after the person [who intervenes]," she says. "You show me the person who likes to get beaten. I think that's a myth that needs to be stopped."

Cathy also says that other women should be alert, rather than thinking nothing like this could ever happen to them. She emphasizes that she had come from a loving family, and that she had been confident as a teen-ager.

Once, at 16, she saw a friend being

What statistics and shelters say about battered women

Advocates commonly quote a Bureau of Justice Statistics figure that a woman is beaten in the United States every 15 seconds. That is based on figures for the number of reported beatings that took place between 1978 and 1982.

The National Coalition Against Domestic Violence (NCADV) estimates that somewhere between 2 and 6 million women are battered each year.

(To put this in perspective, according to the Bureau of the Census in Washington, there are 97.3 million women 15 and older in the US, of which 58 million are married and living with spouse, married but spouse absent, or a partner in an unmarried couple with no other adult in the household.)

Getting out of the marriage or relationship does not guarantee protection. According to Bureau of Justice Statistics figures, in three-fourths of spouse-on-spouse assaults, the victim was divorced or separated at the time of the incident.

Battering tends to escalate over time, and homicide is sometimes the culmination. In 1986, 40 percent of all female homicide victims were killed by relatives or boyfriends.

Many statistics are based on a fairly small sample, but these still provide some interesting clues to the whole picture of domestic violence.

Women who murdered their husbands were often battered women. Accordingly to a study in Cook County (Chicago),Ill., 40 percent of the women who committed homicides were battered women who killed their batterer.

A five-year study at Yale-New Haven Hospital concluded that 40 percent of all injury-related visits to the hospital by women were the result of battering. The study also disclosed that battering was a major precipitating factor in cases of female alcoholism and drug abuse, child abuse, attempted suicide, and situational disorders.

The children are victims, too. Not only is child abuse more likely in homes where the wife is battered, but also, children are very often witnesses to the battering. The NCADV estimates that, of these children, 60 percent of the boys will grow up to be batterers, and 50 percent of the girls will grow up to be battered women. The NCADV also estimates that in one-quarter of violent families, the wife is attacked while pregnant.

One study showed that three-fourths of all battered women reported that their abuser was not violent in public, and that they were not believed when they reported instances of brutality.

Advocates insist that emotional abuse is as devastating as physical abuse. Among the behaviors considered abusive are ridiculing a woman's beliefs or women as a group, criticizing and shouting, attempting to control, and refusal to work or to share money.

Other characteristics of a batterer include extreme suspiciousness and possessiveness, poor self-image, strongly traditional ideas about men's and women's roles, and a tendency to isolate a woman from her family or friends.

It is commonly thought that battering is largely a problem in poorer neighborhoods, but advocates insist that the problem extends across the social spectrum.

"Any woman, rich or poor, black, white, or Latina [or otherwise], could be a battered woman," says Alba Baerga, who is on the staff of Casa Myrna Vazquez shelter in Boston. Upper-class or upper-middle-class women are less likely to *report* abuse, however.

All over the US, there are shelters offering help to women who are battered. The National Coalition Against Domestic Violence, in Washington, D.C., has a toll-free hotline, 800-333-SAFE. Women who call there can get information on shelters and programs near them.

Shelters also share information. A shelter in one state, for instance, will refer a woman fleeing for her life to a shelter in other state. Some shelters in Boston offer transitional housing. And there is a long-established network in Massachusetts of "safe homes"—homes in the community that take in battered women. This is not common in most parts of the country, according to the NCADV.

Not all women who come to a shelter leave the batterer. "Some have been in shelters before," Ms. Baerga says.

"Some come for half an hour and decide to give another chance to the relationship. Some come determined to be independent, to find an apartment. Our main goal is to provide a safe place where they can make their own decision."

Katrina Pope, on the staff of Elizabeth Stone House, concurs. "We aren't here to say you can't go back. We're here to provide as many resources as possible, and to say there are possibilities in your life, there are options. No one deserves to be beaten."

One of the main obstacles to putting a stop to battering is that women want to deny that there is a problem.

"Some of them are strong enough to say 'Yes, I am a battered woman.' Some of them are very open about it," says Baerga. "Others are there for two months—and don't even remember they were in the shelter. It can take your whole life and you still never admit you were [battered].

"The way we measure success here: Only one phone call might be a success. It might take the woman her whole life to make that phone call." —E. S.

slapped, and she thought at the time she would never allow anyone to treat her that way. She continues, "And look what happened to me. . . ."

The keynote of domestic violence is confusion. What is unclear is what love is, how it is properly expressed, how you recognize it, or its absence.

"You're practically *mesmerized,*" Cathy says.

But physical violence is not the only battering that women fear. "Emotional abuse is just as damaging," says Katrina Pope, from the staff of Elizabeth Stone House, in Boston. This is supported even by women with stories of attempted strangulation and broken bones.

Viola is a small, confident woman who tells her story in a pizza parlor. For her, it was a relationship that degenerated slowly, taking with it her self-respect. She stopped bathing and combing her hair—but saw to it that the children were fed and the rent paid.

Her family stopped coming; "He created an atmosphere where my family wouldn't come to visit. . . . I was so depressed." A friend pointed out the change in her: "And this is when I began to see some light."

Like many of the women, Viola says drugs were a large part of the problem, causing a complete personality change.

On one occasion, after she had taunted him, her husband started to strangle her and knocked her to the floor. She told him "You can't deal with the truth—knocking someone down to shut them up."

Unlike many women, who stay to ever-intensifying physical abuse, that was the end for Viola. "Some people stay in a cage forever. They believe they're powerless," she continues.

The question you ask after meeting Sarah is, Where did she learn about love? Abused as a child, she lived for 10 years with a man who among other injuries, fractured her skull nine times.

"I was used to it because that's how it was when I grew up. I would get beaten for leaving toys on the floor or for not doing the dishes right," she says.

Mostly Sarah's injuries came from interposing her 5-foot-2 self between her 6-foot-4 husband and one of the children.

"When you're looking at a two-year-old getting a beating for leaving a toy on the floor, you have to put a stop to it," Sarah comments, firmly.

"The abuse started even before we got married. I was cooking supper one day, and he didn't like what I was cooking. He threw me up against the wall and broke a kneecap." Asked if she had been concerned about marrying a man who

had broken her kneecap, she paused. "I had *doubts,*" she said hesitantly.

But it was his hitting the children that finally made Sarah leave. One boy lost several teeth. She says, "If you raise your hand, he will duck automatically. He was afraid of moving out of the shelter. He felt 'safe'—that's the word he used to use. 'I feel safe here.' "

His teachers have commented on the seven-year-old's improvement in the nine weeks since they left home.

Now it's a triumph that her children will go off into the living room to play by themselves. "All the people around them are showing them love. I think that's what's bringing them out of it."

Sarah is not optimistic or ecstatic, however, about being free for the first time in 10 years. Asked why not, she said simply, "He hasn't found me yet."

The question you want to ask, over and over, is, Why don't you leave? One of many reasons is that it's hard to leave someone who won't be left.

Stephanie met Danny when she was 16 and moved in with him. She realized this was a major mistake when he held her over the porch edge of the third-story apartment and threatened to throw her over if she ever left him.

The offhand way she tells her terrible story shows you the happy-looking young woman still ought to have been going to school and giggling with her friends. Now in her early 20s, Stephanie has spent the last seven years fighting off a nightmare of rape and harassment, by herself.

"After a while, you get used to it. It's like a way of life." Danny said he didn't mean it, so Stephanie took him back, and

then he left her when she was three months pregnant. But he didn't leave for good. After the birth he came back with a knife and gun, threatening to kill the little girl.

According to Stephanie, he told the Department of Social Services that she was abusing the child, and she was put on probation for three months. "He said, 'Now you have to be nice to me and do what I say.' That's when the rapes started."

According to her, Danny would throw rocks in the window and come sit in her apartment with a gun. He called her 100 times a day. He would threaten to get visitation rights and cut the daughter to pieces. He would have her electricity and phone shut off. And when she was out, he would try to drag her into his car.

As a result Stephanie stayed in her apartment most of the time.

"I used to call the police, and they wouldn't come. I'd say, 'he's outside!' and they'd say, 'Call us when he comes to the door. This isn't "Hawaii 5-0." ' I stopped calling the police."

Meeting an advocate from a shelter— she didn't even know of their existence— made the difference for Stephanie. Now she has an apartment, a job, and a car. "I started dating late last year," she says.

Stephanie is gradually relaxing her precautions. She doesn't, for instance, keep a butcher knife under the bed anymore. She no longer pursues her ritual of checking the closets and windows to make sure Danny isn't lurking somewhere. But freedom won and freedom felt are two different matters. Now she says, she just checks under the bed.

VOICES OF THE ABUSERS

Husbands who have mistreated wives discuss need for help

Ellen Steese
Staff writer of The Christian Science Monitor

Cambridge, Mass.
At the request of the men interviewed for this story, their names have been changed. The counselors' names are their own.

We think of the family as a bulwark against the world. But there is a down side to this: It sometimes makes people feel that whatever happens within the

family, short of murder, is private—a personal, not a legal, matter.

In this context, while smacking your next-door neighbor would be reasonable cause for assault charges, doing the same to your wife can seem like a family argument that just got a little out of control.

"Many men we see—it just never occurred to them that what they do is against the law," comments David Adams of Emerge, an 11-year-old counseling service for men who batter, in Cambridge, Mass. So, he says, you often get very respectable people—"doctors, lawyers, ministers"—battering their wives.

"So often, men have the attitude that what they do in private should not count . . . that they should only be judged according to their public behavior."

A common image of a batterer is a man who cannot control his temper, who lashes out in frustration. But Mr. Adams says that at Emerge, battering is thought of as a deliberate strategy, a way of maintaining control.

Some batterers are so violent that this behavior spills over into all areas of their lives. But for many, home is the one place they can express violence without being punished for it.

Thus, batterers "are able to have the

last word in arguments," he remarks.

"They are able to secure compliance on the part of the woman. They are able to not deal with her grievances. The woman is perpetually on the defensive. She's always dealing with *his* grievances."

Adams points out that "every husband gets angry at times, but if once a month or twice a year you get violent, your anger has more weight."

Don Conway-Long, of Raven, a men's counseling service in St. Louis, uses words such as "choose" and "choice" a lot to discuss the actions of batterers.

He says that there are men who have witnessed battering as children—a very common prelude to becoming batterers themselves—who *choose* not to. He points out that there are men who had terrible experiences in Vietnam, who again *choose* not to become batterers.

Many men choose violence against women as a way of releasing anger, he comments.

"We live in a culture that permits us to make that choice and supports that choice . . . that provides ways for men to show they have dominance over women."

There are groups all over the country that offer counseling. Unfortunately, batterers seldom perceive themselves to be in need of these services.

Mr. Conway-Long estimates that they reach "about 1 percent" of all the men who need help.

Many men come to Emerge because they are required to by the courts, "rather than genuinely seeing that they have a problem. Internal motivation often doesn't develop until later," says Mr. Adams.

"The men we see are very susceptible to which way the law leans. If the law is taking a laissez-faire approach, it's much easier for the men to minimize or deny their violence.

"If the law is imposing clear sanctions, then battering men take it more seriously. They see it not just as a domestic affair, but as a crime against the state."

The main way Emerge works with batterers is through group counseling. Two Emerge therapists are present at each session, but almost more important are the support and perspective the men give each other.

A visit to a group session at Emerge changes your image of a batterer. "People think a batterer should have a tattoo on his ear," as Conway-Long puts it.

"Usually we meet Dr. Jekyll—we never get to meet Mr. Hyde." In fact, all the clients are so handsome, likable, well dressed, and articulate, you become positive that you have stumbled into the wrong pale, perhaps the Divorced Dads Workshop.

But faces tighten and smiles disappear when you mention the grimly clinical words "domestic violence."

You have to really respect people for having a problem and trying to deal with it. And deal with it head-on they did. The men were pretty hard on each other. The attitude seemed to be, "We're here to do a job, so let's get down to it."

This particular group hadn't had an incident of violence for some months, but Emerge sessions try to cope with all aspects of abusive and controlling behavior.

For instance, one man, Steve, had left his wife of many years, taken up with a girlfriend, broken off with her, and now is in couples therapy with his wife, although he doesn't want to resume the marriage. "Of course, the couples sessions are not to put our marriage back together. It's more of an autopsy," as he puts it.

The other men spend about 20 minutes telling him that this behavior is abusive. John points out, "You don't take a car to the repair shop that you're going to junk next week. You're really hurting her—giving her some false hopes." Jim describes Steve's behavior as "wishy-washy" about six times.

"I appreciate your help, guys," says Steve finally.

The topics discussed, like dealing with a partner's anger, reflect the sort of thing any couple learns to deal with. The subject of women getting angry is particularly touchy, since the men are trying to learn to control this reaction in themselves.

Adams points out that in many relationships "there's not a whole lot of room for the woman's anger. For men, there is a great tendency to translate everything into anger. You're good at expressing anger. We'd like you to be good at responding to your partner's anger."

The trap here, he says, is getting into a pattern where "you are willing to give up abuse as long as she follows the rules. If she gets angry, that gives us the 'right' to be abusive."

Jim points out that in business, men handle other people's anger very differently. For instance, in his job, if someone

points out that he has made a mistake: "I'd say, 'Wait a minute. I'm sorry. It's my fault. And I understand why you're angry.' "

He says that when he went home—"of course, now I don't have a home to go to"—he would start giving explanations and justifications.

"If you say, 'You're right. I can see why you're angry,' it defuses the whole thing. What used to be an hour argument is now four minutes. It takes the strain off . . ."

Most men who are batterers rather naturally do not want to talk about it. But some are so eager to escape from this cycle that they are willing. Some even speak up in public.

Paul, who has been going to Emerge since September, says it helps him to stand up and say, "I used to be a batterer."

He is poised, clean cut, and athletic looking, with a wide, friendly smile. In yellow tie, gray pants, and leather pilot jacket slung over a shoulder, he looks like a cover for Gentlemen's Quarterly. You believe him when he says that if you told his co-workers that he used to beat up his girlfriend, they'd say, "Oh, no—Paul's a nice guy!"

"My father was an alcoholic. I grew up watching my father come home drunk and start arguing with my mother—sometimes money, sometimes bills," he says. "He'd smack her. My brother and I, we started to protect her. I see myself as my father. I thought it was a normal kind of thing, a way of controlling women."

His face wrinkles in pain as he talks about his relationship with his girlfriend, Laura, a relationship marked by jealousy and suspicion and arguments that sometimes ended with grabbing and hitting.

"I'd feel sorry about all the thoughts that were in my head after the anger was released. I could never control it *during* the anger."

Paul would deliberately take a drink before provoking a fight, so that he could use the drink as an excuse afterward.

"I did a lot of ignoring—that's a kind of control, too. I was jealous—not trusting and not being trustworthy. I wasn't understanding anything she said or anything she talked about. I would take it in the wrong context and start an argument about that.

"I was always being negative, never positive. I did things like date other girls. I was very dishonest.

"I always felt that Laura was very

A battered wife tells her story

Not all women are completely passive in the face of violence.

Karen (not her real name) was a battered wife. She grew up in New York housing projects with her mother and three sisters.

"New York is a very fast paced life. You have to know how to protect yourself," she says.

Her husband was violent, and she defended herself: "I had weapons all over my house. If this were my kitchen I'd have a weapon under the stove and in the fridge. In the living room I'd have a weapon behind the chair and under the cushions."

Most of their fights took place at 3, 4, or 5 a.m.

"Before I left, I apologized to all the neighbors. I had holes in the wall from his punching the wall, throwing me against the wall and stuff. Particularly the way they build houses nowadays—the walls are *paper*-thin!

"I'm not a fighter. Being with him, I changed. I became a violent person. . . . I picked up a pipe. I picked up some scissors. I was going to stab him.

"To know I was capable of hurting someone—that really scared me. I said, 'It's time for me to leave.' One of us was going to die, and he's not worth going to jail for."

Her advice to other women in her situation:

"Get out before it's too late. He'll kill you and get five to 10 years, and be out two years on good behavior. You're six feet under, and *he'll* get the children.:"

Karen got up the courage to leave and to go to Boston—with $30, her small daughter, and possessions in plastic bags.

"Material things you can always buy. The emotion and respect is free, and that's what you need," she comments with conviction.

Karen is grateful to her husband for the times he was good to her, and says that she stayed with him for four years because she thought she was in love with him.

"I realize now, being here, that I wasn't. I'm a very loving person. I love a lot of people.

"But as far as a relationship, and somebody loving me back, I guess I don't know what love is." —E. S.

---

attractive. I always felt unattractive. I thought, "I'm not cute enough for her. She'll find a nicer-looking guy with a better car.' But she wasn't looking for that. She was looking for a little compassion and honesty. I didn't give her any of that."

Laura's sister was a counselor, and she told Paul about Emerge. Initially he was skeptical: "I didn't think I was getting anything. Look at these guys telling me about their problems."

Paul's worst problem had been spying on Laura when she was with other people. He made a promise to the group that he wouldn't do this anymore—a promise he wasn't always able to keep. On one 30-degree winter day, he stood freezing outside a bar where Laura was talking with her friends. "You want to do good, but you have *so much* hate and anger inside you."

The men in the group recommended another line of behavior.

"They're not only scolding me. They're comforting me, too. They want to stick by me and help me," says Paul. "Discussing my last violent act, I shed a tear, not feeling sorry for myself. It was a tear of 'look at what I am doing to this woman.' "

Ability to take criticism in the group is a key success in the program, Paul feels. He says that when a man in the "hot seat" (being critiqued by the group) "becomes totally negative and aggressive, I know he's not going to stay in the program. You can see it in a person when they change."

Batterers tend to have very traditional ideas about the relationship between men and women. Paul characterizes his old attitude: The man should be "like a god. I should be *first*," he says. "Now I look on a woman more as an equal."

At Emerge, men learn to treat women in a different way. "Walking down the street and whistling at a woman—I would never do that now. I *have* done it," Paul says. "Picking up a woman in a bar—I wouldn't do that.

"Everyone in the group has a full deep respect for women while they're sitting in that room. I think it's great that Emerge has that effect on men." Asked what about when they're not in the room, he says, "If they're lying to the group, they're only lying to themselves."

"I feel I've really progressed a lot. I'm going to stick it out at Emerge. I know it will take longer . . . I feel now as if I'm achieving something in life. I felt no good, really rotten sometimes. I was scared to face the truth. Facing the truth is the biggest obstacle to any problem."

Paul asks to have his advice to other batterers put in bold letters: "It's going to be hard [maintaining the relationship], because the woman is always going to have that question at the back of her mind: Is he going to be violent like he was before?"

Paul says he's lucky because he's only 26 and has time to resolve his problem. He wants to be married and have a family, and be "compassionate, caring, loving."

He'd like to get back together with Laura. "I want her to learn that there is good in me. The only way I can ever get married or have a relationship is by showing that the violence is gone."

Local women's shelters often have information on counseling for men. Raven, a service in St. Louis, has a national directory: Write PO Box 24159, St. Louis MO, 63130, or call (314) 725-6137. Emerge has its office at 280 Green St., Cambridge, MA 02139; telephone, (617) 547-9870.

AIDS AND RAPE

Should New York Test Sex Offenders?

Jan Hoffman

This June night is unusually still, the lawn-lined block in Yonkers is slumbering, but the house has noises of its own. The boiler rumbles, the dehumidifier purrs: rhythmic, lulling sounds to the two sleepers who live in an apartment they've fashioned in the basement. One is a five-year-old girl; in the next room is her mother, a 26-year-old unemployed construction worker named Sharon, who'd fallen thickly asleep around 11, a book she's reading about the lives of Catholic saints still open on the bed, her reading lamp still shining brightly in the window.

In the depth of Sharon's sleep, around 3 a.m., a hand clutches the back of her neck, yanking her face away from the light. As she clambers awake, a man's voice says, "Don't yell, don't say anything, don't look at me." He climbs on her bed, shoves a pillow over her head, and she feels the blade of a large knife at her throat. Sharon catches a glimpse of the knife and then she begins trembling:

"It looked exactly like our kitchen knife from upstairs," she remembered later. "My parents and my brother were up there sleeping. So was our dog, who is part German shepherd, part collie. I thought, how could this guy break into our kitchen and come down here without anyone stopping him? And I thought, they must all be dead now. And I realized no one was going to help me. I shook for the next hour. My only thought was how to keep my daughter safe." She starts sobbing, and pleads with him to close her daughter's door, so the child won't hear anything. Then the intruder flicks off the light.

She tells him she doesn't have any cash. He ransacks the room anyway but finds nothing of value. Turning back on her, he pulls down her panties, slaps the knife on her buttocks and announces, "I'm going to rape you but I'm going to put a rubber on first."

When she's scared, Sharon has a habit of chattering nervously, flippantly: "Is that so you don't catch anything from *me*?" she spits back. Then she shuts up. Her back to him, arms spread against the wall, she hears a snapping sound.

Over the next two hours he rapes her twice, ejaculating inside her both times, and tries to sodomize and rape her at least four more times. During his meandering monologues— "Don't call me bro', call me Pancho Villa"; "Don't call me Pancho Villa, call me Dude"—he talks about cocaine and alludes to the troubles that drugs have caused him. The main problem, he says, is that they are too damn expensive.

He boasts that he broke in the house by smashing a downstairs storm window, and hints that he knows about the dog and the family above. He picks up her acoustic guitar and plays some blues tunes. Badly. Loud enough to wake the dead, Sharon thinks.

He blindfolds her but then removes it, telling her she looks stupid. Later, with the knife still at her back, he demands she pour each of them a shot of Scotch. Sharon, a former bartender, turns slowly around and says almost casually, "Hey, Dude, I'm not used to sharing a drink with a guy I can't look in the face." And for a half-moment, she gets a very good look at him.

Then he rapes her again. As she lies across the sheets crying, he unhooks her phone, and tells her he has set an explosive under the bed that will disarm itself in 15 minutes as long as she doesn't move. He leaves.

Immediately she plugs in her phone and calls her next-door neighbor, a Yonkers police sergeant, and then runs upstairs. The family dog finally starts barking, and the family wakes up.

The Yonkers police catch the rapist 20 minutes later, less than a mile from her home, walking aimlessly, talking to himself. At the police station Sharon makes a positive identification. She learns that her attacker has been out on probation since January, after having spent six years in a state prison on two violent felony counts.

A police officer sits Sharon down to interview her. "Do you want a female?" he asks.

"You're a cop. Gender-wise it's the same to me," she retorts, trying to appear cocky and in control.

He begins questioning her, and she starts to cry, rambling and backtracking through her story. "I'm sorry," she sobs. "I'm acting like a girl, aren't I?"

Finally the officer asks if the rapist used a condom.

From *The Village Voice*, September 12, 1989, pp. 35–41. Reprinted by permission.

Yes, she replies, a bit unsteadily.

But the condom is never found.

Next, Sharon is driven to a hospital in Yonkers. They take blood samples, comb her pubic hairs, and find sperm in her vaginal tract and on her panties. But what was the snapping sound, then? She remembers: Her daughter had been playing with balloons that day and had left them scattered on the floor. "He lied to me!" she screams.

They do a baseline test on her blood, because, Sharon later recounted, "They wanted to see if I had already had VD or AIDS—so I couldn't claim that he'd given it to me."

By the next morning, it occurs to Sharon that the rapist should be tested for HIV, too. Her reasoning seems sound enough: He had a drug problem. He'd spent years in prison. He'd ejaculated inside her several times.

But, to this day, over a year after the attack, he has refused to be tested. Furious and frustrated, Sharon doesn't understand why, even after he was eventually convicted, he cannot be compelled to submit to the test. She has beseeched prosecutors, and rape crisis counselors have written letters on her behalf to the sentencing judge. To no avail. New York State takes his side.

TABLOID HEADLINES to the contrary, cops will not get AIDS if infected people bite or spit at them. The chances are also remote that they'll become infected from a glancing pinprick from a hypodermic needle. But the risk of HIV infection from a sexual assault can't be so readily dismissed. For preteens trapped in the sex industry, for children bound into incestuous relationships, for women caught in violent, abusive relationships—all situations where the sexual contact is ongoing—the risk of HIV transmission is acute. "In the battered women's shelters I visit, I'm finding a high number of infected women," says Rebecca Porper, an AIDS educator in the city's health department. "And I'm particularly concerned about incest victims." Susan Xenarios, who chairs the hospital committee of the New York City Task Force Against Sexual Assault, puts it bluntly: "How do you get a guy who's battering you to wear a condom?"

During a sexual assault, the victim's orifices, tense and resistant, tear easily, allowing for the seepage of blood as well as semen into the body. If there's a struggle and the victim draws blood from her attacker—or attackers, if it's a gang rape—or if the rapist turns sadistic, the risk of infection rises commensurately. There hasn't yet been a reported case of a rape victim getting AIDS from her attacker, acknowledges Porper, who has co-written a new HRA pamphlet on AIDS and sexual assault, to be made available especially to victims. Though the pamphlet emphasizes that repeated exposures to the HIV virus are usually necessary for infection, Porper is convinced cases are out there: Rape is vastly underreported, and the length of time the body takes to indicate exposure makes identifying the source of infection difficult.

If the rapist has done time in jail, the chances escalate: Since 1984, AIDS has been the leading cause of inmate deaths, responsible for more than half the mortalities in New York's state prisons. In a new study by the state health department, 17.4 per cent of the men (and 18.8 per cent of the women) entering New York state prisons tested positive; it's been estimated that 10,000 to 15,000 people who moved through the city's jail system last year were infected. As of 1987—the last date for which a five-year recidivism survey by the state's Department of Correctional Services is available—45 per cent of those with prior convictions for first-degree rape were back in prison.

Rapists and abusers are usually not the sort to volunteer for testing as a favor to their victims. But according to New York's strict AIDS confidentiality law, which went into effect on February 1, none of the offenders—in fact, nobody at all—can be tested for HIV without their informed consent. It is perhaps the toughest, most privacy-protective law in the country and hardly lacks for opponents: Legislators from pockets around the state, as well as some women's groups and victims' rights advocates, have been mounting a determined drive to alter it.

The issue has set many gays (who oppose all involuntary testing because it may encourage discrimination) against some women's groups (who see this as a matter of victims' rights). It also has divided feminists and civil libertarians: Camille F. Murphy, director of the Westchester County Office for Women, is aggressively for testing sex crime offenders because "now the law gives perpetrators greater rights than the survivor of a rape"; Judith Levin, of the ACLU AIDS Project, is dead-set against any mandatory testing, on the grounds that it defies basic Fourth Amendment guarantees against illegal search and seizure: "Even to order defendants to be tested violates the presumption of innocence."

In its extensive report to be released today on AIDS and the criminal justice system, the Association of the Bar of the City of New York takes up the ACLU position against involuntary testing of sex offenders. Catherine O'Neill of the Legal Action Center, who was on the city bar report's committee, points out that because offenders are usually apprehended so long after an attack, involuntary testing "opens a way for irrelevant and unnecessary testing to be done on defendants for a purpose that is no longer being served. We have to worry about how the information is used, whether and what information will be put into records, and the ostracism that follows a defendant when his status is made known."

A dissent to the city bar's position comes from a shocking source: noted civil liberties expert Richard Emery, who, while acknowledging that stringent measures to assure confidentiality must be made, writes that in rape cases, where a victim can elect to begin the drastic, controversial AZT treatment, "The victim's interest . . . outweighs the significant but limited threat to a defendant's rights."

The long, unpredictable period of time the antibodies take to show up in a test further complicates the debate. Bearing that in mind, last year's Presidential Commission on the HIV Epidemic reacted by recommending testing sex offenders at the "earliest possible" point in the criminal justice system.

But David Wertheimer of the New York City Gay and Lesbian Anti-Violence Project has reached the opposite conclusion: "I'm a staunch advocate of victims' rights, but knowledge of the perpetrator's HIV status is not useful to the victim"—precisely *because* of the vagaries of incubation.

The issue of testing sex offenders is so loaded that most groups who've grappled with it—legislators, jurists, public health officials, victim advocates, and AIDS activists among them—have only been able to come up with contorted, incomplete rationales for whatever stand they wind up taking. That is, if they finally take one: "It's one of the hardest and most complex issues I've had to address," says Catherine Abate, chairperson of the New York State Crime Victims Board, "and I don't have a position." And the American Bar Association, which last February released a three-page report of recommendations about AIDS and the criminal justice system, deliberately shied away from the testing issue. Even the city bar association notes that since medical technology and HIV testing might improve, "Our current position on this issue is not cast in stone."

NOWHERE HAVE THE inconsistencies and simultaneous panic attached to the issue been reflected as strongly as in the state legislatures. So far, according to the tally kept by the AIDS Policy Center in Washington, D.C., at least 18 states have adopted legislation which now mandates testing of sex offenders. Some laws mandate testing after conviction. Others insist that suspects be tested. Some specify that only sex offenders who have transmitted bodily fluids be tested. Others just leave it at all sex offenders and prostitutes. New York State Supreme Court Justice Richard Andrias, cochair of the committee that wrote the city bar's report, says that "legislators throw up their hands and say, 'We don't know what to do but we gotta do something! Let's set up camps for these lepers!'"

"I keep waiting for our own law to be challenged constitutionally," says Michael Stoy, a deputy attorney general from Idaho, a state where anyone *charged* with a sex offense is immediately tested for HIV. "But there has not yet been a definitive nationwide statement as to whether someone can be tested against their will: It's a Fourth Amendment privacy right balanced against a public health situation. The states have taken the lead and everyone is doing it differently." He pauses. "Mistakes are going to be made all along the line."

While politicians and policymakers fumble for guidelines, the country's hospitals, counseling rooms, and criminal courts confront an onslaught of tangled scenarios:

• What if: A badly traumatized rape victim is brought to a hospital emergency room, where she is met by a rape crisis advocate. Part of the counselor's responsibility is to calm the victim and help her regain a sense of control, to think of herself as a rape "survivor." Should the advocate risk panicking the victim by bringing up AIDS? Or should the advocate wait for the victim to ask about it, risking that critical early precautions (such as condoms) won't be taken?

• What if: A Kansas rapist is caught and convicted and the victim decides she wants to have him tested. Should the state take its cue from the problems inherent in the test (inaccuracy, incubation) and not let her have the results, or should it release the results and let her assume responsibility for planning her life?

• What if: An Idaho woman is raped. Six weeks later, a suspect is apprehended and, according to state law, is tested for HIV. He tests positive. Should a judge grant his attorney's demand that the victim also be tested, the results disclosed, and her sexual history introduced into court, on the chance that *she* infected him?

• What if: A gay couple in Georgia is arrested at home by police and charged with sodomy. (Georgia is one of 24 states, plus the District of Columbia, which criminalize consensual sodomy.) They are convicted. Would they be considered "sex offenders" and forced to be tested? What would prevent these states from using this application of the testing laws to persecute homosexuals?

• What if: A California man is attacked and sodomized by a gang. Two months later, he identifies one of his assailants in a lineup. According to state law, the victim can petition the court to have the defendant tested. The defendant tests positive. While he's awaiting trial, fellow inmates turn on the defendant and his wife sues for divorce. What if, during the trial, the jury concludes that the victim has misidentified him?

• What if: A Michigan woman who is six weeks pregnant is raped. The rapist is quickly apprehended: He had been paroled from prison eight months earlier, where he'd served a three-year sentence for armed robbery and may or may not have been exposed to AIDS. Under state law, he cannot be tested for HIV until after conviction, which will not be for several months, at best. She gets tested and the results are negative, but knows that antibodies may not appear for a long time. Should she have an abortion?

• What if: Exhausted and alarmed by her husband's IV-drug use, a woman finally leaves him. Even though her husband had himself tested six months ago for HIV, and swore that he was negative, the wife goes for a test. The results are positive. When confronted, her husband admits he knew he was positive but didn't tell his wife because he was terrified that she'd leave him, and besides, he figured she might have already been exposed. Should the court then be able to bring criminal sanctions for failure to disclose HIV status in a situation where the sexual contact has been consensual?

Though they often acknowledge these complexities, victims' rights advocates strenuously argue that any scrap of information about an assailant's HIV antibody status is still worth something to the victim—particularly since reports have surfaced of rapists taunting their victims by saying they had AIDS. John Stein, deputy-director of the National Organization for Victim Assistance, remarks, "It's hard to tell a rape victim that testing her rapist is a terrible invasion of his privacy."

AFTER HER HOSPITAL EXAM, Sharon goes out to lunch at a Red Lobster with her parents, her brother, an aunt, her daughter, and her grandmother. Sharon is exhausted—she's been up since 3 a.m. and it is now after noon.

It is her mother, Linda, who first mentions that her daughter should take new precautions. Linda, a nurse in a Yonkers emergency room, interviews patients about infectious diseases; she knows a great deal about AIDS. Earlier that morning she had spoken with a physician whom she considers an AIDS specialist. The treatment he urges is considered premature and even dangerous by many doctors, and has not been sanctioned by any official government agency: that Sharon begin taking AZT, which, he argues, if she's been infected might establish a hostile environment for the virus.

The doctor advises that she refrain from all sex, even safe sex, for three months. "That wasn't so bad as it sounds," she said later. "I didn't miss sex that much." For months, she feels like a pariah, even among her own family. She is afraid to kiss her daughter or share a drinking glass with her. An aunt refuses to come into the house and won't let her children visit. Every dish and plate Sharon touches, her grandmother scrubs down at least twice.

Meanwhile, Sharon tries desperately to get the rapist tested. "He has a rap sheet as long as my daughter's leg," she worries. She goes to a Victims Assistance Services office in Westchester, and counselors write letters to the court, asking for the test. She makes repeated phone calls to the prosecutors handling the case (a second one is assigned after the first goes on vacation)—but, because of incompetence, neither D.A. formally processes her request.

Nothing happens. Her family considers suing the rapist for damages. After a while, she forgets how often she has given blood, either for forensic purposes or to be repeatedly tested for HIV—10 times? 12? 15? The results, so far, have been negative. She is going for another test this month. Meanwhile, silence at the other end: The rapist, sitting in the Westchester County Jail, steadfastly refuses to be tested.

THE NEW YORK STATE AIDS confidentiality law is the latest victory in the ongoing battle between civil libertarians and victims' rights groups: Whose interests should prevail—the traumatized sexual assault victim or the defendant's? "Rape victims want to know why legislators are more sensitive to issues of confidentiality than they are to public health," says John Stein, a leading national activist for crime victims. (Others contend that the possible exposure of a single rape victim is not within the spectrum of a public health agency, which attends to infection on a large scale.) The antagonism that victims' groups have recently developed toward civil libertarians is ironic, even tragic: They now find themselves opposing the right to privacy, a cornerstone of New York's AIDS confidentiality law, even though it is also the foundation of their own hard-won rape shield laws, which protect a victim from having to disclose her sexual history in court.

Though civil liberties and civil rights are protected by the Constitution and its amendments, "victims' rights," a sympathetically understood principle, are not nationally codified.

In the early '70s, advocates, many from grassroots feminist groups, began to argue that criminal law discriminated against women and children; certain laws favored offenders at the expense of victims, and even punished them (many, for instance, point out that trials are "like being raped again"). NOVA, the National Organization for Victim Assistance, an advocacy group, was founded in 1975. Largely as a result of NOVA's efforts, and with the encouragement of the federal Office for Victims of Crime (established in 1984), 45 states have adopted some sort of "bill of rights" for crime victims, and 46 states have victim-compensation programs.

Jane Nady Burnley, director of the Office for Victims of Crime, has become the leading crusader on the national scene for testing sex offenders. A Reagan administration appointee, Burnley became interested in involuntary testing in 1987 because of a child molestation case that took place on federal lands—an Indian reservation in Arizona. A teacher was accused of sexually abusing 140 elementary school children over the course of eight years; he ultimately pled guilty to a number of the charges. Rather than placing the burden of HIV-testing on so many children from the small community, the judge ordered the defendant to be tested after he was convicted. (The results were negative.)

Last year, Burnley's recommendation that "sexual offenders be tested at the earliest possible juncture" in the criminal justice process was adopted almost verbatim by the Presidential Commission on the HIV Epidemic. Civil libertarians are dumbstruck at the imprecision of her language. Burnley, a bright, thoughtful advocate, is not exactly deaf to their concerns, but, after months of jousting at public forums, she is practiced at sidestepping specifics, preferring instead to trigger a national debate. "I'm a psychologist," she explains. "I'm not a lawyer and I'm not a medical doctor." The states will have to fine-tune their own laws, she says.

Well yes, but exactly how early is "the earliest possible juncture?" In Arkansas and Idaho, HIV tests can be required when sex offense charges are filed. From a civil liberties standpoint, as well as a pragmatic one, these statutes are fraught with problems: "Any testing prior to conviction," notes New York's Judge Andrias, "takes the presumption of innocence, which we all have to instruct to our juries, and turns it on its head."

"We're breaking ground with the testing of perpetrators and we have to be mindful of the risks," concedes Burnley. "But that doesn't mean we shouldn't proceed."

Okay. Test the sex offenders after conviction then, as do many states (including California, Florida, Michigan, Nevada, Rhode Island, and Washington). But even if that may satisfy some civil libertarians, who accept that convicted felons lose a host of rights, many public health officials and victims' advocates still think it's useless for the victim, because so much time can elapse between an attack and sentencing and the victims may not take precautions. Burnley declines to say when, from a public health perspective, it's prudent to begin testing a defendant: Immediately? And then three months later? And then in six months? In Westchester County, where a campaign is on to amend the New York State ban on involuntary testing, County Executive Andrew O'Rourke has even proposed that blood should be drawn periodically from a defendant, frozen, and then tested if he is convicted.

"The test only looks for the presence of antibodies that a person produces to respond to infection," says Rebecca Porper, of the city's health department. "The test does not look for the virus. And it can take six weeks to more than 18 months for the antibodies to be manufactured." Even if the perpetrator tests positive, Porper continues, when was he infected? Before he attacked her? Or at some point during the days, weeks, or months between the attack and his apprehension? Or in jail, awaiting trial? "So it's a waste of time to get the perpetrator tested unless the incident happened 18 months ago," she concludes. "We should concentrate on testing and retesting the *victim* and making sure she has support and counseling."

The issue turns again when the question of the *purpose* of the test is raised: Is it probative (to gather evidence for the accused crime) or nonevidentiary (in this regard, merely for the sake of the victim)?

Last year, Colorado and California responded to requests from victims' rights groups by legislating that a victim may have access to the results of an HIV test for a person charged with a sex offense. In Colorado, the test itself is ordered by the court, and is administered after a preliminary hearing—which is somewhat like New York's grand jury, and which establishes probable cause—and after the defendant is bound over for trial.

California's bill places the request for the test squarely on the victim, rather than the prosecutor or the court. A much-applauded section of its Proposition 96, passed by voters last November, allows the victim to petition the court to test a sex-offense suspect as soon as he's been charged with the crime. Critics note that the results are reportable to numerous people—including the warden, the court, the Department of Health Services, any volunteers or workers who have contact with the inmate's bodily fluids, as well as the victim—and there is no mandatory counseling for any of the recipients of the information. On the other hand, supporters point out, the results cannot be used for either criminal prosecution or civil litigation.

Burnley hails Proposition 96 as "one of the most effective approaches and legal tools" that the states have yet come up with. Even gay rights groups in California, which organized so effectively to defeat a more sweeping initiative on the ballot, were divided on 96 and many did not campaign against it.

But Judge Andrias remains highly skeptical: "There are no penalties if the victim discloses the results to anyone else. It's still a bad idea, because it's impossible to police confidentiality."

AZT COSTS SHARON about $124 a week. She is told to take two pills every four hours around the clock for six weeks after the rape. She keeps the pills in a device called a micrometer, which automatically beeps when her next dosage is due—a reminder, six times a day, that she has been raped, that she might be infected with HIV. "Sleep is so healing," she said later, "but I couldn't get a full night's worth." The micrometer beeps at 3 or 4 a.m., waking her and her boyfriend, Tom.

Tom is frightened, too; the question hangs over them for months and sometimes the tension erupts in spats. One weekend they drive to Massachusetts to relax. In the middle of the night the micrometer goes off, and to Sharon's distress, she discovers she's out of pills. The weekend is over: They immediately have to drive back to New York for a refill. Sharon worries about AZT's toxicity, is occasionally nauseous, and is always tired. Furthermore, many would tell her that taking it before she has tested positive and shown immune impairment is a dubious precaution, and even a health hazard.

One night, as she sits at the bar of a local pub, her micrometer beeps. She pulls out her pills and a guy next to her says admiringly, "Jeez, what a great way to store drugs! That's pretty neat." Then he asks her why she's taking them.

"A burglar broke into my house and raped me," she answers coolly. "There's a chance he had AIDS so I'm taking AZT as a precaution." She walks to the bathroom and, on her way back, chats with some friends. When she returns to her seat, the rest of the bar falls quiet.

THE WAY AN INMATE SEES IT, there's no good reason why he should volunteer to be tested just to do the victim a kind turn," says Susan Hendricks, deputy director of special litigation for the Legal Aid Society. "Especially if the guy is a stranger rapist or a pattern rapist, a sociopath who has no regard for women. He won't have those feelings of remorse anyway."

A fundamental reason why prisoners refuse to volunteer, says John Gresham, associate director of Prisoners' Legal Services, is that "people don't want to hear bad news." In fact, the word from prison is that an inmate is much better off *not* being tested. Even as Sharon and other victims suffer the stigma that follows the mere suspicion of infection, "There is tremendous discrimination in the jails and prisons against people who are HIV-positive, or even suspected of it," says Hendricks. "It can't be underscored enough." Prisoners' rights advocates have so far fended off initiatives to order mandatory HIV testing for all New York State prisoners.

One of their major considerations is that there is no anonymous testing available in the prisons: Once an inmate is tested, the fact of the test and the results are entered into his permanent record. And it's impossible to keep news confidential in a jail. Hendricks has handled numerous complaints of verbal harassment from guards and inmates, ostracism, threats that the prisoner had better move out of his housing unit, severe beatings. If an inmate who has conjugal visits tests positive, the visits are suspended. Prisoners with full-blown AIDS or ARC (AIDS-related complex) have told her they would even prefer to go without medical treatment to avoid detection within the jail system. David Hansell, an attorney with the Gay Men's Health Crisis, adds that sick prisoners at Riker's Island have been routinely abandoned by their court-appointed lawyers and neglected by court officers.

Some inmates have been coaxed to the point where they're willing to be tested to give the victim peace of mind, but then have ultimately refused because the confidentiality of the proceedings couldn't be ensured. There have already been many cases in which a prisoner's family has heard the bad news before the prisoner had a chance to break it to them himself.

SOME DEFENDANTS' ATTORNEYS argue that mandatory testing might also threaten the Fifth Amendment's protection against self-incrimination, a fear that is not entirely unreasonable: More and more states are introducing criminal sanctions against HIV transmission—yet another Gordian knot that has emerged from the involuntary-testing debate.

Some states have added language about risky behavior to their existing criminal code definitions of assault, attempted homicide, and reckless endangerment. The state of Washington, for example, "mandates that a person who has exposed or transmitted HIV to another person with intent to inflict bodily harm is guilty of assault in the second degree." And some states would use a positive HIV test to increase the sentences for crimes like rape and forcible sodomy.

A Boise, Idaho, case that goes to trial this month is one worst-case scenario for involuntary testing and its consequences: A 51-year-old man was charged with having "sexual contact" with children under 16. Although he resisted testing, saying that he already knew he was positive, under state law he was tested for HIV again—and was positive. Idaho had recently passed a law making willful exposure of others to HIV a felony; this case would mark the first time the state attempted to apply the new law.

In Idaho, there is no anonymous testing for HIV; if you test positive, your name is reported to the public health department. So, to prove that the man knew he'd been infected before his contact with the young boys (his verbal statement is not sufficiently convincing evidence), the prosecutor subpoenaed health department records—a step that would be illegal in states with anonymous testing, and would outrage civil libertarians nationwide. Learning that the man had indeed tested positive for HIV more than a year earlier, the prosecutor charged the man with the HIV transmission felony, which could add another 15 years to his sentence.

But what did the sexual contact consist of? So far, there have been three charges (though more may be added): that the man fondled a 12-year-old, that he kept pornographic pictures and videos of children, and that he performed fellatio on a 15-year-old boy. "There was no anal penetration," says Ada County prosecutor Bill Harrigfeld, who seems genuinely uncomfortable discussing the case. "And he didn't pass fluids. He ejaculated on the kid's stomach. But there's a question on how AIDS is passed. There's a possibility that he could have passed it through oral sex, if he had

a wound in his mouth. They're not really sure if it can be transmitted through saliva itself." The chances of this occurring are remote: the children have so far all tested negative.

In other words, Idaho tested a suspect against his will, used that information to subpoena his medical records, which then further incriminated him on charges that, on close examination, appear bogus. Moreover, all the information has been made public, damaging not only the defendant's life but the lives of the children as well.

The Idaho felony law encompasses sexual behavior that is consensual as well as forced. In the following states, it is also a felony for a person who knows he's infected to expose his sexual partner, either by not "first informing the person," or by not taking prophylactic precautions: Arkansas, Georgia, Michigan, Missouri, Oklahoma, South Carolina, and Texas (in Alabama, Florida, and Maryland, it's a misdemeanor). In Louisiana, there's a fine of up to $5000 and imprisonment with or without hard labor for 10 years for an infected person who has "sexual contact" without the informed consent of a partner.

In strong opposition to criminal sanctions for HIV transmission, the New York City bar association points out that it is extremely difficult to prove in court that a defendant had prior knowledge of infection or that he was the one who infected the victim. Criminal law solutions—whether they consist of adapting existing statutes or passing new prohibitions—divert both the attention of and the resources available to the criminal justice system away from effective actions," reads its report. "This is not to say that knowing or reckless acts that result in HIV transmission should never be punished. Where prosecution seems called for by extreme circumstances, we believe that the reckless endangerment statutes provide the appropriate framework. But . . . those [AIDS-related prosecutions] will serve more to sensationalize the problem than to educate those at risk or the public in general."

Later this fall, Jane Burnley's office will complete work on a Justice Department report considering criminal sanctions for offenders who knowingly expose their victims to HIV. But even some rape crisis counselors worry that the emphasis is being shifted to the wrong place. "Who's on trial," asks Susan Xenarios, who is also director of the rape intervention program at St. Lukes-Roosevelt Hospital, "a person with AIDS or a rapist?"

A YEAR AGO MARCH, Diane, a woman in her early forties, was woken in the middle of the night by a man who had shimmied up the scaffolding and opened the window of her third-floor brownstone apartment on the Upper West Side. A long-time feminist, a scholar, and a remarkably cool-headed woman, she managed over the next three hours to be calm and conversational with the intruder. And so he did not use his knife on her. He did, however, repeatedly rape and sodomize her, he yelled at her not to look at him and covered her head with a blanket, he slapped her and taunted her: "You'd love to call 911, wouldn't you?" Knowing she could not escape in time—her door had three locks—she did not try. Instead, convinced by her steady reassurances that she would not call the police, he eventually fell asleep in her bed.

Diane bolted out of the apartment, ran naked down the hall, and banged on the door of her landlord, who gave her a bathrobe and phoned the cops. They easily caught the rapist, who was still snoring in her bed. As the police were holding up his jacket, about to look for the jewelry that he'd taken, a hypodermic needle dropped to the floor. "I said, 'Oh, God, I hope he doesn't have AIDS,' " Diane recalled. "And the cop who didn't know very much about transmission, said, 'What do you have to worry about? He didn't stick you with the needle, did he?' "

Like Sharon, Diane went for an AIDS test, although she was not advised to take AZT. Like Sharon's, her results were negative. And like Sharon, she asked the D.A. on her case if she could get the man tested. And like the man who raped Sharon, the man who raped her also refused.

Sharon's attacker pled guilty and the case never went to trial; because it was his third felony and he had violated parole, he got 18½ years to life. But Diane's rapist pleaded not guilty, and instead accused Diane of making eyes at him on the D train and leading him on. The trial lasted a week, and her testimony was explicit, grueling, and humiliating. (Could she demonstrate to the court how loudly she screamed that night? In which position did she hold her head during oral intercourse?) After it was all over, her attacker, a parolee who had previously been imprisoned for rape, was convicted on all charges.

This March, a year after the attack, the rapist and his attorney appeared in court for sentencing. "My client is a very sick boy, your honor," pleaded the lawyer. Indeed, although no corroboration was offered, the rapist looked like he had lost at least 20 pounds. Unmoved, the judge handed down the maximum sentence.

About two weeks later, the prosecutor got word through a reliable grapevine that the prisoner had developed full-blown AIDS. The phone call and subsequent meeting she had with Diane, she says, were the most difficult things that she, a nine-year veteran in the Manhattan D.A.'s office, has faced in her career. Strictly speaking, the state's AIDS confidentiality law prohibits her from disclosing the inmate's HIV status to the victim, but the judge on the case informally gave her permission.

The prosecutor had no training in counseling, and the bad news stumbled out awkwardly. "There was no telling when he got it," Diane said dully, as she recounted her story one recent afternoon. Was it before he raped her or during his year at Riker's? As the prosecutor explained to Diane, she had almost no legal recourse to find out if he had AIDS.

Even though Diane's attack occurred before the new AIDS confidentiality law went into effect, the New York courts didn't have the power to order her assailant tested. Yes, the courts can mandate such invasive procedures as blood, sperm, and DNA testing if the information is related to the crime in question; and yes, according to Elizabeth Lederer (who is currently prosecuting the Central Park rape case), the state *can* compel testing for a sexually transmitted

disease (STD)—as in the case of a child with gonorrhea whose father is being prosecuted for sex abuse.

But in New York State, neither HIV infection nor AIDS has been classified as a sexually transmitted disease. Although, obviously, AIDS can be transmitted sexually, the state health department believes the differences between the two outweigh the similarities: unlike HIV, STDs incubate within a few weeks, are treatable, and need not be fatal. So far, the courts agree. Moreover, under public health laws, when a disease is defined as an STD, the state can exercise extraordinary powers to control its spread. It can test individuals under many conditions—especially prostitutes, upon arrest—report names to a central system, trace partners, and even place individuals in isolation (this decade's code word for quarantine).

Many activists argue vociferously that if AIDS were reclassified as an STD, these measures would cause discrimination and discourage voluntary testing. Some say that an alternative solution is to make sex offenders exceptions to the new confidentiality law; others protest that this would erode the civil liberties carefully protected by uncompromised confidentiality.

Diane remains unmoved, and remarked that: "The public doesn't realize that it's bad enough being a rape victim without the added burden of a possible death sentence hanging over your head." She recently went for another HIV test.

MANY OF THE STATES that do mandate HIV testing for sex offenders are able to do so because they've reclassified AIDS as an STD—and thus invoked decades-old public health statutes that govern the policing of epidemics. It's a decision that, especially for women, has disturbing implications.

Many of those statutes evolved around the turn of the century, as a way of curbing the spread of syphilis and gonorrhea. By the end of World War I, 32 states compelled testing of prostitutes for venereal disease. Seen as vessels of evil, poisoners of patriotic American soldiers, 30,000 prostitutes were detained in camps until the end of the war. And now 18 states specifically order prostitutes, as well as sex offenders, to be tested for HIV. Rather than supporting programs to educate (translation: time, funding) customers about risky sexual behavior with prostitutes or anyone else, legislatures have resorted to mandatory testing of prostitutes as a quick-fix method to control and punish them.

An article last year on prostitutes and AIDS in *AIDS and Public Policy Journal* analyzed 10 studies around the country in which the number of antibody-positive prostitutes in each group was almost consistently negligible. The one extreme study, which found that nearly 60 per cent of the prostitutes interviewed were HIV-positive, was conducted in a northern New Jersey methadone maintenance clinic. Drugs, more than sex, had been the key to transmission: In each of the 10 groups, almost all the infected women had been IV-drug users, or their pimps/boyfriends had been. "In terms of contact tracing," wrote authors Judith Cohen, Priscilla Alexander, and Constance Wofsy, "there have been no documented cases of men becoming infected through contact with a specific prostitute."

Yet prostitutes continue to be specifically targeted as carriers of AIDS. In a Rhode Island law which became effective last month, mandatory testing has been ordered for, among others, persons convicted of sex offenses—a term that, in Rhode Island, refers mainly to prostitutes and pimps. According to Steven Brown of the Rhode Island ACLU, legislators responded to a local state court judge who was eager to penalize a particular HIV-positive prostitute. "So far it's unclear who gets access to the test results," says Brown. "We have no idea if they'll be released to judges and affect sentencing."

In Florida, a prostitute must be tested for all STDs (including HIV) and if infected, must undergo treatment and counseling before she can be released from incarceration or "community control." If she's arrested again, in addition to the penalty for prostitution, she'll draw another sentence for first-degree misdemeanor for transmission. The U.S. Public Health Service has recommended that prostitutes be "routinely" tested for HIV and that local governing bodies find a way to stop prostitutes who are antibody-positive from practicing their trade.

"Most of the current statutes reflect sheer anger, prejudice, ignorance, and hatred in the minds of legislators," says Lawrence Gostin, an associate professor at Harvard and the executive director of the American Society of Law and Medicine, who recently reviewed 500 cases of AIDS-related litigation. "They work against the most hated groups in this country: gays, IV-drug users, and prostitutes." Gostin warns against the new involuntary testing legislations that make "laundry lists" of targeted groups.

But he concedes that sex offenses, particularly incest, make the call more difficult. Even so, he says, "Though we hate the crime, we have to follow our Constitution: The ordeal [of HIV testing and worrying] that rape victims go through may or may not be averted if the offender is tested. These [rape and incest] cases are tremendously emotional and to frame a law around them is difficult: Hard cases make bad law."

"We could be opening a Pandora's box around the testing issues," warns Veneita Porter, of the state's Office of AIDS discrimination. She urges a change in public perception: Even though sexual assault and AIDS may be intertwined during an attack, afterwards, "Rape counseling and prosecution should be handled separately from HIV counseling and testing."

Her suggestions are almost identical to those offered by every opponent of involuntary testing and criminal sanctions: widespread public education and a more concerted effort to make counseling reach the most disenfranchised, high-risk populations. Justices Richard Andrias and Robert Keating, the chief administrative judge for the city's criminal courts, have proposed making bilingual AIDS literature and counseling available in the arraignment rooms in courts throughout New York City, where so many drug users pass through daily.

None of this can be much solace to victims of sexual assault, who have to live with the additional fear of AIDS for an indeterminate length of time—though antibodies take, on the average, about six months to appear, recent studies have found that some people have tested negative three years or longer after being infected. "If I had been raped, I'd still want to know if the rapist had AIDS," says Catherine Abate, a member of Governor Cuomo's new Task Force on Rape and Sexual Assault, who is aware of the testing dilemmas. (The task force's report, which will include sections on victims and the criminal justice system, as well as discussions on HIV testing of offenders, is due in November.)

Emerging medical technology will quicken the debate over testing and its implications. "If we had a test that offered definitive knowledge of a perpetrator's HIV status, or if we get conclusive evidence that critical, early AZT treatment would make a difference, then I don't see how you can argue that the test information shouldn't be made available to the victim," says David Hansell of GMHC. (Hansell's exception is a surprise, coming from a hardline opponent of involuntary testing.)

New York State's new AIDS confidentiality law will almost certainly be contested this year, either by legislators who are now drafting amendments, or, when advocates decide to organize around a particular case, by a courtroom drama:

Last January, a month before the law went into effect, Westchester County Supreme Court Justice Nicholas Colabella faced down a coalition of feminists, victims' services groups, and ministers, who strongly urged him to order testing of a defendant accused of raping at knifepoint two women—his girlfriend and a friend of hers. "I initially refused to order him tested," says Judge Colabella, "because I felt that it was irrelevant to his sentencing and that he was already protected under existing confidentiality laws. But I also took the position that when he pled guilty, he lost that protection. He finally did consent. I never ordered him to be tested, but I would have. I also would have limited disclosure to the defendant, myself, and the victims."

Judge Colabella says he will take an offender's refusal to be tested into account for sentencing; he'd allow a consent to be tested to be used, in moderation, for plea bargaining in sentencing. This is exactly the kind of precedent that prosecutors fear but, Colabella asserts, "I have no problems with my conscience.

"AIDS is a thing unto itself," he says, before adding, as an understatement, "and the courts are in a quagmire over it."

Though Colabella remains wary about the absence of hard information and legal precedent for an epidemic of this proportion, he's perfectly willing to be the catalyst for the next firestorm over the issue in New York. "I'm going to challenge this law," he promises. "The next rape case I get, I'm going to order the test if the victim requests it."

MANY RELATIONSHIPS ARE DESTROYED AFTER A LOVED ONE BECOMES
THE VICTIM OF A VIOLENT ASSAULT. EXPERTS ARE SEEKING WAYS TO HELP.

Can A Marriage Survive Tragedy?

Sherrye Henry

AROUND MIDNIGHT on Valentine's Day in 1977, four young thugs walked into Keith and Betty Jane Spencer's Indiana farmhouse, ordered Mrs. Spencer, her son and three stepsons to lie face-down on the living-room floor and, just for the thrill of killing, shot them all. Miraculously, Mrs. Spencer survived. Bleeding from the head and back, she struggled on foot for a quarter of a mile to the nearest neighbor's house. There, she telephoned the sheriff and then her husband, who was working late at a TV station. Ten years later, the Spencers—Keith, now 58, and Betty Jane, 57, were divorced.

● On his mother's birthday in 1986, tiny T.J. Myrick of Denver slipped when the strap broke on his aging highchair. He strangled while his licensed child-care provider chatted with a neighbor. Two years later, communication between them at a standstill, the Myricks—Pam, now 36, and Steve, 41—separated after nine years of marriage.

● In 1985, Sherry Price of Forest Hills, N.Y.—then 45 and mother of a son, 18, and daughter, 20—was driving into Brooklyn one rainy day when her car broke down. A mechanic stopped his truck and offered to drive her to get an auto part. Instead, he put a knife to her throat and raped her. Several weeks later, she and the man with whom she had been involved ended a loving relationship.

● In Cincinnati, Charlotte Hullinger and her husband, Robert, a Lutheran minister, celebrated their 25th wedding anniversary in 1982 with a mutual gift of marriage counseling. Still, they separated soon afterward. Four years earlier, their daughter, Lisa Gayle, 19, had been bludgeoned to death by a fellow student in Hamburg, West Germany.

These stories reveal a highly predictable but generally unrecognized pattern for couples who face tragedies. First there's an earthquake—the unexpected, horrific attack upon or death of a loved one; then there's the aftershock—a breakup or divorce. Because the sudden tragedy is so shattering, few couples seem able to survive it.

Though there are huge numbers of couples in trouble, very few seek help. But mental-health experts and victims' organizations see the toll that disaster takes on such partners.

At least 75 percent of couples who go for treatment are on the verge of splitting up, estimates Lula Redmond, a family therapist who counsels the grieving, particularly survivors of homicide victims. She also is founder of the Center for Crime Victims and Survivors, in Clearwater, Fla. Nancy Ruhe, executive director of Parents of Murdered Children, in Cincinnati, says 80 percent of her members describe excruciating marital problems. "I would even say up to 100 percent talk about drastic changes in their lives and families," she adds. Lois Veronen, a psychologist at the Human Development Center of Winthrop College, in Rock Hill, S.C., has produced one of the few studies on partners of rape victims. She found that distress for a couple after a sexual assault is universal and that half of those relationships are destroyed within a year.

Why should couples be driven apart at the very time they might be expected to close ranks and comfort each other? The reasons are numerous and complex, but topping the list, experts say, is that a personal disaster of such proportions changes a person. "You just can't have that kind of horrible tragedy and move along as if nothing happened," says Cynthia Colean, an advocate for victims and witnesses in the Denver district attorney's office. Colean was herself raped by an intruder in 1984. She broke up a relationship soon afterward. "You have to grieve, to deal with the fears and the system and too many *other* things," she says.

"The therapeutic effort is one of inventing a new personality, adopting new values," says John Stein, deputy director of the National Organization for Victim Assistance, in Washington, D.C. He adds that many victims never recover. "The idea of constructing a new personality is easy to understand if you talk about a serious car crash and being in a wheelchair for the rest of your life. Victims of psychic injury describe themselves in the same terms." Says Betty Jane Spencer: "I really started to heal when I relinquished the person I used to be and accepted the person I am. But I can't tell you that I ever accepted the new Keith, or that he accepted the new Betty Jane."

Fear and anger seem to dominate the victims' transformations. "I woke up angry, I was angry all day, and I was terrified all the time," says Betty Jane Spencer. Six months after they buried her son, Greg Brooks, 22, and Keith's three sons—Ralph, 14, Reeve, 16, and Raymond, 18—the couple moved back into their home, site of the murders. "It was torture," she says, even though the four killers had been caught and were convicted of murder later that year. "I'd search every corner of the house with a gun in my hand until I was sure no one was there." Lula Redmond often sees such haunting fear in her patients. "There's the sense," she says, "that once this has happened, it can happen again. Experience already has *proven* the unthinkable can happen."

But partners experience fear and anger differently, and these very emotions wedge a couple apart. The psychologist Lois Veronen says of the rape victim: "She has a new set of anxieties and concerns. There has been a fundamental threat to her life. But the *partner* tends to be enraged—the victim doesn't." So, the woman victim sometimes becomes the caretaker, losing her chance to be comforted and supported. American men are socialized to be the protectors, but husbands and lovers are powerless in most rape cases. Veronen says that could explain why eventually so many men are unable to discuss the rape, and their anger then turns against the victim.

Sherry Price recalls that her relationship was on the rocks by the second week after her assault. "He was losing patience," she says. "He said I should be over this. He just didn't know what to do. Unless you've had prior experience, you don't know about the crying jags, about acting like a robot, about dependency. I wanted him around all the time, and he didn't know how to handle that." Cynthia

Colean's lover could not bear even to discuss her rape. "He needed me to be okay a week afterward," she says, "but I was not at all okay." Months later, still fearful and facing a trial, Cynthia broke off the relationship. "He just saw me as not ever getting better, not ever getting ahead," she adds. "Here I was, trying to recover, and he was worried about whether I was financially secure."

Anger toward the victim from her partner is accompanied by blame—especially for rape victims, says Ellen Brickman, project director of a continuing study for New York City's Victim Services Agency. She found that raped women often were told they should have been more careful or should have fought back more. "The same people who were being supportive were also blaming, which puts the victim in a very difficult position," says Brickman.

Steve Myrick, whose infant son died in the care of a baby sitter, says he still has problems with blame, even though he and his wife, Pam, were reunited after a four-month separation. "I just felt—maybe I still feel—that T.J. should have been with her," he says. "I know Pam loved T.J. as much as I did, if not more. But I felt that he was part of us: If you have time, you spend it *with* him." (Pam had left T.J. for two hours so her mother could treat her to a birthday lunch.)

Pam and Steve Myrick demonstrate that, in our culture, men and women experience grief differently. This is another reason so many marriages shatter after a tragedy. "My husband is not a very openly emotional person," Pam says. "I had the support of friends and family who would listen to me—I *had* to talk about it. Steve *couldn't* talk about it—for two years. I finally gave him an ultimatum: 'Get counseling or leave.' He left."

"Most American men may feel even more helpless than women, and much angrier: It's *their* job to protect the family," says Dean Kilpatrick of the Crime Victims Research and Treatment Center, in Charleston, S.C. Steve Myrick's is a typical masculine reaction in the face of this kind of family threat. "Almost everything in life you can control to some extent," he says. "This was something uncontrollable. I find it tough to talk about, because *I can't change it.*"

The Rev. Robert Hullinger, whose daughter was murdered, agrees that the male psyche, quite irrationally, may suffer more than the female psyche. "There were these feelings that I should have *known* something was going to happen," he says. "It was hard to face the fact there was *nothing* I could have done."

While men in our culture may react to tragedy by becoming aimless, grief seems to propel many women to act—

as if determined to prevent others from suffering their fate. "One could argue," says Dean Kilpatrick, "that this is one way the death can have some meaning."

In 1978, Charlotte and Robert Hullinger began organizing Parents of Murdered Children, a group that now has 18,000 members nationwide. Soon, Charlotte exchanged her housewife's role for that of crusader, while Robert eventually sought solitude. They separated for 15 months, reconciled in 1988. In 1979, Betty Jane Spencer co-founded Protect the Innocent. By the time she left the lobbyist group six years later, it had helped change 56 criminal laws in Indiana. Similarly, in 1987 Pam Myrick became a founding member of Public Awareness About Abuse in Child Care, a Denver-based group.

Robert Hullinger theorizes that because he and his wife have such different personalities, they naturally reacted differently to their daughter's death. "She couldn't understand why I didn't have a red-hot anger," he says, "and I couldn't understand why she had it *all the time*. Differences are exaggerated in any kind of grief situation and lead to further isolation."

Grief holds no less agony for the silent than it does for those able to express it. And the difficulty in male/female communication is compounded when each partner becomes so depleted by the process of mourning—tragedy is emotionally exhausting—that little consolation remains for the loved one.

As a culture, we underestimate how deeply people suffer from the emotional effects of a tragedy, suggests Dean Kilpatrick: "Friends and relatives rally, bring food, and you're excused from your usual responsibilities. Then they expect you to get back to normal, and your social support tends to fade away."

Says Charlotte Hullinger: "After my daughter's death, I reached out to friends across the country. People would tell me I should keep busy…not to think about it…life goes on. Clergy told me how fortunate I was to have my faith. I thought, '*Aren't they listening?*'"

When Sherry Price called her best friend the night of her rape, she was stunned by the response: "She had been like a sister to me—the first person I called. She listened, then said, 'I can't talk to you now, because we're going to this other friend's house. They're getting the champagne out now.' I said, '*What?*'" Today the executive director of the Victims of Crime Advocacy League, in Albany, N.Y., Sherry says she has learned to understand: "She couldn't compute this—*her* friends don't get raped. She didn't know what to do for me, and that's what happens to victims. People step back."

Those who live through a tragedy,

Kilpatrick says, "may display substantial symptoms related to the event for the rest of their lives." And as their identities and personalities change, so do values and priorities—even belief in God. Charlotte Hullinger not only left her marriage for a while but also the Lutheran Church in which her father, grandfather and great-grandfather had been ministers. "There was nothing there when I needed it," she says. She has since become an ordained minister of Community Churches. Betty Jane Spencer's faith was almost destroyed after the boys' murders. "I was mad with God," she recalls. Now the administrator of Mothers Against Drunk Driving in Florida, she says, "God and I can do anything. Sometimes it takes us a little longer than I'd like, but today God is my friend."

Value systems change too. Sherry Price restructured her friendships, her career and her priorities. "I'm much more compassionate now," she says. "When you come face to face with death, it changes your viewpoint about what's important in life."

The good news is that breakups aren't inevitable. Counseling helps. "*Know* this is going to be pervasive," Lois Veronen warns, "that it will spill out in every part of your life. Both partners will need someone to talk to, independent of the other." Lula Redmond says that, with counseling, 97 percent of the couples she helps stay together.

But more counseling services are needed. Dean Kilpatrick calls it a national shame that so few programs provide counseling to crime victims and their families. He estimates that 47 percent of all violent crimes and 90 percent of all rapes go unreported. "I'd like to see the government spend 5 percent of the money on victims that it now spends on criminals," he says.

Until then, *all* couples in crisis might heed Ellen Brickman's advice to partners of women who have been raped: "Don't make assumptions about what's the best way for her to recover, and let her talk as much as she needs. The corollary is, don't force her to talk when she's not ready but keep the channels of communication open. The second thing is to recognize that rape is a very traumatic experience, and it will take a while for her to get over it—there are no set deadlines. Sometimes just knowing this will make it easier for a partner."

As for the rest of us, who seem to become tongue-tied in the face of sorrow and despair, we must learn to ask of people we care about, over and over, "How are you?" and to say, "Tell me what you're feeling."

Prostitutes and Addicts: Special Victims of Rape

Jane Gross

Special to The New York Times

OAKLAND, Calif., Oct. 11—Prostitutes and drug addicts are being raped with increased frequency and brutality in the menacing corners of American cities and towns, but they rarely report the assaults, often disappear during an investigation or are disregarded by the criminal justice system.

There are no reliable statistics, but interviews with dozens of counselors and law enforcement officials around the nation all point to the same trend. The police and prosecutors, however, often cannot pursue the cases because of intractable problems that begin in the disordered netherworld of sex and drugs and end in courtroom debates over knotty questions of consent and coercion.

These problems came to light here last month when the Oakland police chief admitted closing rape cases without proper investigation because of cultural bias on the part of the authorities and the need to set priorities in an understaffed department. More than 200 rape cases have been reopened in Oakland, and the sexual-assault unit has been reorganized and retrained.

Advocates for rape victims say that prostitutes and addicts encounter similar problems in other cities, and cite these examples: In New Haven, faced with a prostitute dressed for work, the police have said, "What do you expect? Look at you." In Houston, officers have shut their notebooks after a victim said she was raped in a crack house. In the Atlanta suburbs, victims have been told they will be given a lie detector test and sent to jail if any part of their story is untrue.

Where Are the Villains?

But the behavior of police departments here and elsewhere is only one link in a tangled chain. "It would be easier if we could pinpoint a villain and

---

Criminal justice is rare for targets of cultural bias.

---

then get mad at that part of the system, but it isn't that simple," said Mimi Silbert, the president of the Delancy Street Foundation, a San Francisco drug-rehabilitation program.

Ms. Silbert, one of several experts who said that the spread of crack cocaine has contributed to the higher rates of rape of prostitutes and addicts, said that "everything is conspiring against" the aggressive pursuit of the rapists who prey on these women of the streets, "from their own perception of reality" to "all the other crimes that take up everyone's time."

But the stakes are enormous, she said, and the assailants likely to repeat their crimes time and again. "Even if we don't like prostitutes or addicts," she said, "the people who are raping them are raping other people too. At the basest level, we need to do something about this because it affects everybody."

Ms. Silbert, the nation's leading expert on the rape of prostitutes, many of whom are addicted to drugs, continued: "If juries were more responsive, district attorneys would be more likely to prosecute. If district attorneys were more likely to prosecute, cops would be more likely to make cases. If cops were more likely to make cases, women would be more likely to come forward."

The Most Vulnerable

Rape, in general, is an under-reported crime, its victims often blamed for their own assault. Addicts and prostitutes are the most vulnerable to rape, experts say, because of where they live and work and whom they consort with. But they are the least likely to report sexual assault, because of distrust of

the establishment, concern that they will be arrested for their own crimes and fear of retaliation by the assailant.

"I've been out of prostitution for 20 years, and I'd be hard-pressed to bring a charge of rape against anybody, even now," said Evelina Giobbe, a former prostitute who counsels prostitutes in St. Paul.

In the rare situations in which addicts or prostitutes file a complaint, experts say, they routinely lie about the circumstances of the rape, give a false name or address or disappear midway through an investigation, thwarting and sometimes infuriating overworked investigators.

"We'd rather not work these cases," said Lieut. Joe Glezman, the commander of the sex crimes unit in the Houston police department.

Investigators say that in some instances assailants seek out such victims just for that reason. Such a rapist has prowled the streets of Hollywood, Calif., for 15 years, preying on transient women. More than a dozen women have reported being raped by him, according to David Lambkin, a detective and investigator in that city's sex crime unit, but none has hung around long enough for an investigation. And for each report, Mr. Lambkin said, there are probably 10 victims who chose silence.

"He's smug when we bring him in," Mr. Lambkin said. "He says, 'You don't know where your victim is, do you?' And he's right."

In the rarest instances of all, when a rape victim is willing and able to participate in an investigation, she often faces subtle discouragement or outright hostility from police officers who do not want to invest time in a case that will be risky to prosecute because of the victim's life style.

That was the situation for June Williams, a cocaine abuser in Oakland, who told The San Francisco Examiner and local television stations a story of abuse and neglect that contributed to the police department's admission that it was improperly abandoning cases. Ms. Williams said she was raped and beaten by a cousin after a July 4 outing, then treated dismissively by investigators.

"They said I'd been partying all day, drank some wine and even smoked a rock," Ms. Williams said. "I said: 'Big deal. I didn't consent to sex.'"

The police say they dislike dealing with addicts and prostitutes, in part, because of the blurry line between consent and coercion. Exchanging sex for drugs is common in crack houses, where many of these rapes occur, and it may be difficult to distinguish an outright assault from a drug deal gone sour. Similarly, prostitutes sometime fail to get paid or agree to perform certain sex acts and then get forced into others.

Outrage Isn't Automatic

Even advocates for rape victims are confused by these cases. "It's abuse, no question about that," said Peg Ziegler, the director of a rape crisis center at Grady Memorial Hospital in Atlanta. "But legally, it's probably failure to honor a contract."

Other advocates cite situations that may be muddled, but still cry out for attention, like the prostitute recently counseled in New York City by Yolanda Serrano, who runs a drug abuse agency called Adapt. Ms. Serrano said the woman got into a car expecting to service a single client and instead was raped by five men. Two of the men were caught, but not prosecuted, Ms. Serrano said, because the police thought the victim was too disoriented by drugs to know what happened to her.

But with violent crime on the rise and police resources stretched to the limit, priorities have to be set and cases involving uncooperative or less than credible witnesses may be abandoned. Even the most sympathetic detectives said they were stymied and finally angered by women who gave an address that turned out to be an empty lot or said they were raped while visiting a sick relative when they were actually at a known prostitution location.

"It's hard enough to make a rape case with a legitimate victim," said Mr. Lambkin, the Hollywood detective, who said rapes of prostitutes and addicts were on the increase.

The drug abusers are the most difficult, here today and gone tomorrow, abusive to investigators when they are high and impatient with the process of examining sketches or answering questions when it is time to hit the streets for another fix. "They get victimized, but they are their own worst enemies," said Lieut. Vito Spano, head of the sex crimes unit in Brooklyn.

'Pending' in a Drawer

Even advocates for rape victims can lose patience with such women. "They won't let you take care of the [...] Dorothy Hicks, the medical [...] the rape crisis center at Jacks[...] rial Hospital in Miami.

Official crime statistics shed [...] on how police departments dispose of such rape cases. In Oakland last year, nearly one in four rape reports was listed as "unfounded," meaning the police believed the complainant was lying, although in many cases no interviews had been done. More commonly, these rape reports will wind up in someone's desk drawer, marked "pending" and thus not accounted for in the Federal Bureau of Investigation's Uniform Crime Report.

No matter how difficult it is to bring cases, many victim advocates and law enforcement officials say the battle is still worth fighting. Ms. Silbert said she limited her studies to assaults that did not occur on the job and nevertheless found three of four street prostitutes say they had been raped.

Linda Fairstein, the head of the sex crimes unit in the office of the Manhattan District Attorney, was just one of the experts who said that handling these cases requires uncommon patience. "You devote an inordinate amount of resources" to finding the victims and persuading them to tell the truth, she said. "But a good cop and a good prosecutor, with enough attention, can get a story and make a case."

Police

Police officers of today deal with a wide range of problems that were not the concern of the police a generation ago. Illegal drug use and trafficking is at epidemic levels, and violent crime continues to increase.

The diverse nature of policing in the United States is illustrated in "The Police in the United States." The role of women in the police ranks is still an evolving one, and the report "Women On the Move? A Report on the Status of Women in Policing" reviews some of the issues of discrimination in the hiring and promotion of women. Community-based policing is discussed in "Making Neighborhoods Safe" and "Community Policing: A Practical Guide for Police Officials." The article "Police, Hard Pressed in Drug War, Are Turning to Preventive Efforts" discusses some new methods of fighting the war against crime.

A new phenomenon facing the police is dealing with organized protestors in the issue of abortion rights. Many protestors, on either side of the issue, seek to test the system through civil disobedience. In "The Abortion Protestors and the Police," complaints of excessive police reaction to some protestors is discussed.

Looking Ahead: Challenge Questions

Is a college education a valid requirement for being a police officer?

Have women reached their full potential as police officers?

Should the police be involved in community problems not directly concerned with crime?

Unit 3

Police Response to Crime

The system responds directly to a fraction of crime

Most crime is not reported to police

. . . [O]nly about a third of all crimes are reported to police. The crimes most likely to be reported are those most serious in terms of injury and economic loss.

The criminal justice system responds to crimes brought to its attention by reports from citizens or through direct observation by law enforcement officers. Crimes are reported most often by the victim or a member of the victimized household. Police discover 3% of reported personal crimes and 2% of reported household crimes.

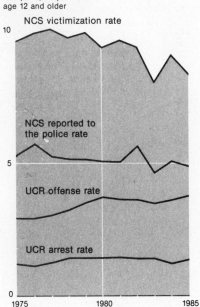

Aggravated assault rate per 1,000 persons age 12 and older

NCS victimization rate

NCS reported to the police rate

UCR offense rate

UCR arrest rate

10

5

0

1975   1980   1985

Most reported crimes are not solved by arrest. For that reason the proportion of crimes handled directly by the criminal justice system through the processing of suspects is relatively small. Indirectly, the criminal justice system may be dealing with more crime than appears from arrest data because the offenders who are processed may have committed much more crime than that for which **they are arrested.**

Fallout for the crime of aggravated assault is shown in this chart:

The first contact with the criminal justice system for most citizens is the police dispatcher

In many cities citizens can report crimes through a universal number, such as 911. In other cities the citizen must call the police directly. The dispatcher will ask for facts about the crime, such as what happened, where, when, whether or not it involved injury or loss. This information helps the police to select the most appropriate response.

Law enforcement is one of several police roles

The roles of police officers are—
• **Law enforcement**—applying legal sanctions (usually arrest) to behavior that violates a legal standard.
• **Order maintenance**—taking steps to control events and circumstances that disturb or threaten to disturb the peace. For example, a police officer may be called on to mediate a family dispute, to disperse an unruly crowd, or to quiet an overly boisterous party.

• **Information gathering**—asking routine questions at a crime scene, inspecting victimized premises, and filling out forms needed to register criminal complaints.
• **Service-related duties**—a broad range of activities, such as assisting injured persons, animal control, or fire calls.

Wilson's analysis of citizen complaints radioed to police on patrol showed that—
• 10% required enforcement of the law
• more than 30% of the calls were appeals to maintain order
• 22% were for information gathering
• 38% were service-related duties.

Most crime is not susceptible to a rapid police response

A study by the Police Executive Research Forum suggests that police response time is important in securing arrests only when they are called while the crime is in progress or within a few seconds after the crime was committed. Otherwise, the offender has plenty of time to escape.

In a study of response time in Kansas City, only about 6% of the callers reported crimes in progress. Where discovery crimes are involved (those noticed after the crime has been completed), few arrests may result even if citizen reporting immediately follows discovery; by this time the offender may be safely away. If a suspect is arrested, the length of delay between the offense and arrest may crucially affect the government's ability to prosecute the suspect successfully because of the availability of evidence and witnesses.

From *Report to the Nation on Crime and Justice,* Bureau of Justice Statistics, U.S. Department of Justice, March 1988, pp. 62-63, 66.

A variety of public agencies provide protection from crime

Today, police officers do not always respond to calls for service

Based on research and the desire for improved efficiency, many police departments now use a number of response alternatives to calls for service. The type of alternative depends on a number of factors such as whether the incident is in progress, has just occurred, or occurred some time ago and whether anyone is or could be injured. Police officers may be sent, but the call for service may also be responded to by—
• **Telephone report units** who take the crime report over the telephone. In some departments, more than a third of the calls are initially handled in this way.
• **Delayed response** if officers are not needed at once and can respond when they are available. Most departments state a maximum delay time, such as 30 to 45 minutes, after which the closest unit is assigned to respond.
• **Civilian personnel** trained to take reports; they may be evidence technicians, community service specialists, animal control officers, or parking enforcement officers.
• **Referral to other noncriminal justice agencies** such as the fire department, housing department, or social service agencies.
• **A request for a walk-in report** where the citizen comes to the police department and fills out a report.

Law enforcement evolved throughout U.S. history

In colonial times law was enforced by constables and a night watch made up of citizens who took turns watching for fires and unruly persons. By the beginning of the 19th century, most citizens who could afford it paid for someone else to take their watch.

The first publicly supported, centralized, consolidated police organization in the United States was established in New York in 1844. It was modeled after the London Metropolitan Police created in 1829 by Sir Robert Peel. Other major American cities adopted the same system soon after. Today, more than 90% of all municipalities with a population of 2,500 or more have their own police forces.

Rural policing in the United States developed from the functions of sheriffs

The office of sheriff, a direct import from 17th century England, was used primarily in the rural colonies of the South. As elected county officials, sheriffs had detention and political functions along with law enforcement responsibilities.

Originally responsible for large, sparsely populated areas, many sheriffs were faced with big city law enforcement problems because of urban growth after World War II. In some counties the sheriff's office has retained its detention functions, but law enforcement functions are handled by county police departments. In other counties the sheriff's office resembles many big city police departments. There are more than 3,000 sheriff's departments in the United States today.

Traditionally, the police function has been dominated by local governments

• In 1986 there were 11,743 municipal, 79 county, and 1,819 township general-purpose police agencies in the United States. Together, they employ 533,247 full-time equivalent employees.
• Other State and local law enforcement groups include State agencies such as the 51 State police and highway patrols and some 965 special police agencies including park rangers, harbor police, transit police, and campus security forces. Along with their independent responsibilities, these agencies often support local law enforcement on technical matters such as forensics and identification.
• The Federal Government employs 8% of all law enforcement personnel. Among the more than 50 Federal law enforcement agencies are the Federal Bureau of Investigation (FBI), the Drug Enforcement Administration (DEA), the Bureau of Alcohol, Tobacco, and Firearms (BATF), the Secret Service, and the Postal Inspection Service.

Urbanization and social change have had great impact on policing

• The dramatic shift in population to urban areas since World War II has had great impact on the demand for police service. The percentage of police officers employed in urban areas rose from 68% in 1977 to 82% in 1982.
• During the recent period of increasing concern about employment discrimination against women and minorities, mostly white, male police departments have added women and minorities to their ranks. The proportion of sworn officers who were women went from 2% in 1971 to almost 7% in 1985. The proportion of police officers and detectives who were black went from 9% in 1983 to 12% in 1985.

Professionalism and advanced technology have also transformed policing in the past half century

• In 1982, 79% of police officers in a sample survey conducted by the FBI reported that they had done some college work. 23% of the respondents had received baccalaureate degrees.[1] Basic and in-service training is now regarded as indispensable. More than 670 training academies now exist in the United States.[2]
• In 1964 only one major police department was using automated data processing.[3] More recent surveys suggest that virtually all jurisdictions of 50,000 or more population were using computers by 1981.[4]
• In 1922 less than 1,000 patrol cars were in use in the entire country.[5] At that time, only one city had radio-equipped cars. Today, the patrol car has almost replaced the "beat cop" and police communications enable the patrol officer to have access to citizen calls for service as well as data banks on a variety of critical information, including outstanding warrants and stolen property.

Private security continues to grow

After public police agencies were formed in the mid-1800s, organized pri-

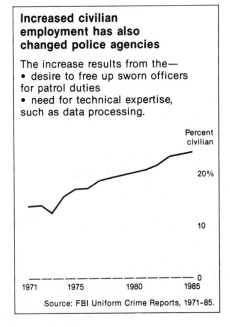

Increased civilian employment has also changed police agencies

The increase results from the—
• desire to free up sworn officers for patrol duties
• need for technical expertise, such as data processing.

Source: FBI Uniform Crime Reports, 1971–85.

Private security plays an important role in crime control

vate law enforcement developed in response to—
• the lack of public police protection in the expanding West
• problems with interstate jurisdiction
• development of the railroad
• increased industrialization.

The first private security officer, Allan Pinkerton, had a tremendous impact on private security through his work with the railroads and through his establishment of the first private security firm. Owing to the lack of a Federal law enforcement agency, Pinkerton's security agency was hired by the Federal Government in 1861. More recently there has been increased need for private security, particularly to protect defense secrets and defense supplies provided by the private sector. More recent growth in private security is in response to growth of crime and security needs in businesses.

The private security industry protects private concerns against losses from accidents, natural disasters, or crime

This for-profit industry provides—
• personnel, such as guards, investigators, couriers, bodyguards
• equipment, including safes, locks, lighting, fencing, alarm systems, closed circuit television, smoke detectors, fire extinguishers, and automatic sprinkler systems
• services, including alarm monitoring; employee background checks and drug testing; evacuation planning; computer security planning; and polygraph testing.

Private security is provided either by direct hiring (proprietary security) or by hiring specific services or equipment (contract security).

1.1 million people are estimated to be employed in private security

Proprietary security	**448,979**
Guards	346,326
Store detectives	20,106
Investigators	10,000
Other workers	12,215
Manager and staff	60,332
Contract security	**640,640**
Guards and investigators	541,600
Central alarm station	24,000
Local alarm	25,740
Armored car/courier	26,300
Security equipment	15,000
Specialized services	5,000
Security consultants	3,000
Total	1,100,000

Source: Cunningham and Taylor, *Private security and police in America: The Hallcrest report* (Portland, Oreg.: Chaneller Press, 1985).

The authority of private security personnel varies among States and localities

Many States give private security personnel authority to make felony arrests when there is "reasonable cause" to believe a crime has been committed. Unlike sworn police officers, private personnel are not obligated to tell arrestees of their rights. Private security usually cannot detain suspects or conduct searches without the suspect's consent. In some States laws give private security authority to act as "special police" within a specific jurisdiction such as a plant, a store, or university campus.

Many private security firms are licensed or regulated

In some jurisdictions both State and local requirements must be met to obtain a license to provide private security.

At the State level—
• 35 States license guard and patrol firms.
• 22 States and the District of Columbia require the registration of guards.

• 37 States license private investigators.
• Alarm companies must obtain a license in 25 States and are regulated in 10 States.
• 8 States license armored car companies and 6 States license couriers.
• In fewer than 12 States, the same agency or board regulates alarm companies and armored car firms, as well as guard, patrol, and investigative firms.
• 3 States have independent regulatory boards; 6 States have such boards in State agencies.
• Private security is regulated by the department of public safety or State police in 15 States, the department of commerce or occupational licensing agency in 7 States, and the department of state in 5 States.

Public police are often employed by private security firms

Some police officers "moonlight" as private security officers in their off-duty hours. According to the Hallcrest survey, 81% of the surveyed police departments permit moonlighting, but most estimated that 20% or less of their officers are working as private security personnel. Acting like a contract security firm, some police departments provide personnel to private concerns and use the revenue for the department.

Private security has continued to outnumber public police since the 1950s

Public police protection grew most rapidly in the late 1960s and early 1970s in response to increasing urbanization and crime rates. Public police protection has stabilized in the 1980s, but private security has continued to grow. Further growth of the private security industry is expected, particularly in relation to products using high technology, such as electronic access control and data encryption units for computer security systems.

Notes

1. FBI, *A study of factors influencing the continuing education of police officers,* LeDoux and Tully, July 1982.
2. O'Leary and Titus, *Monograph,* vols. I and II, National Association of State Directors of Law Enforcement Training (Columbia: South Carolina Criminal Justice Authority, 1986).

3. Kent Colton, "Police and computers: Use, acceptance, and impact of automation," in *The municipal yearbook, 1972* (Washington: International City Management Association, 1972).
4. *Survey of police operational and administrative practices 1978* (Washington: Police Executive Research Forum, 1978).

5. Herbert G. Locke, "The evolution of contemporary police service," in *Local government police management,* 2nd edition, Bernard L. Garmine, ed. (Washington: International City Management Association, 1982).

The Police in The United States

Beverly Sweatman and Adron Cross

Beverly R. Sweatman is public affairs assistant to the chief of INTERPOL and Adron Cross is assistant chief , Interpol /State Liasion Program. Both Sweatman and Cross work at the Interpol National Central Bureau in Washington, D.C.

The United States police system is neither as complicated nor as confusing as it might appear on the surface. It is, however, vast and complex, and involves more than 20,000 separate and distinct law enforcement agencies that employ more than half a million people. The differences between these law enforcement agencies are generated primarily by the jurisdictional authority or boundaries under which they operate and the specific laws they are empowered to enforce.

The U.S. does not have a national police force. Instead, the United States is served by a multi-layered network of police jurisdictions that include town, city, county, and state police, as well as federal law enforcement agencies.

One reason for this diverse structure lies at the foundation of the Nation's governmental system. The U.S. Constitution provides for a federal system of government, which is a two-level structure consisting of distinct and separate state governments functioning under a central national government.

Federal jurisdictions encompass crimes of interstate and international proportions, such as the illegal transporting of persons or property across state borders and crimes that endanger national security or affect the integrity of the U.S. monetary system or national borders.

At the state level, law enforcement becomes a bit more complex since each state has the right to govern itself within the parameters of the Constitution and must enforce its own law enforcement agency, which in most cases is a state police force. The states themselves are further divided into counties, metropolitan areas, cities and towns, and each of these divisions enacts its own local ordinances. Enforcing these ordinances and maintaining local law and order are thousands of county sheriffs, city and county police, and town marshals. These men and women are the first in line of law enforcement in all U.S. communities, and citizens look primarily to them for protection from criminal activity.

HISTORICAL BACKGROUND

To fully understand the police system in the United States, it is helpful to look back in colonial days in America. Many natural differences existed between the early colonies, such as size, location, population, commerce, and industry. Because of the independent nature of these colonies and the vast territory that separated them, each one developed its own system of order and authority to meet its particular needs. There was no central authority with power over all the colonies to enact or enforce laws and regulations.

The methods used to provide protection for citizens and maintain order against criminal activities varied between the colonies. For example, early in the seventieth17th century Boston established a system of nightwatchmen to supplement their military guard. New Amsterdam (later New York) and Philadelphia soon adopted a similar system. Throughout the colonies, an assortment of law enfor-

From *C.J. International*, January/February 1989, pp. 11-18. Originally appeared in *International Criminal Police Review*, official publication of Interpol. Reprinted by permission.

3. POLICE

cement officials such as constables, marshals, and sheriffs gradually developed. [1]

When the original thirteen colonies joined together to form the United States of America, they established the aforementioned federal system of government whereby power was distributed between a central national government and separate state governments. The individual states were not willing to turn over complete authority to the federal government, and they stringently guarded their rights to govern themselves within the parameters of the Constitution and to enact and enforce their own laws. Consequently, the federal government was granted jurisdiction only as set forth by the Constitution, as interpreted by the courts, and all other jurisdictions remained with the states. This action worked against the establishment of a national police force.

Development of police entities that met the specific needs of the towns and cities continued. In 1838 Boston supplemented its nightwatch with a day police force. Other cities followed, and in 1844 the New York legislature passed a law authorizing creation of "the first unified day and night police" force. Philadelphia soon followed suit and by the late nineteenth century most major American cities had municipal police forces. These forces were commanded by a chief or commissioner who was either elected or appointed. Appointments sometimes required the consent of a city council.

Thus, the mid-nineteenth century saw the emergence of the main structural elements of American policing. These

Police check on a highway in the United States.

included municipal (city or town) police, supplemented by county sheriffs in rural areas. The gradual addition of two other elements, state police and federal agencies, complete the present-day system. [3]

The Texas Rangers, created in 1835 to supplement Texas military forces, were the forerunners of today's state police forces. Other states followed after the turn of the century. Some state police agencies are restricted to enforcing traffic laws and protecting life and property on the highways. Others, however, have general policing authority in criminal matters throughout the state. [4]

In keeping with its constitutional authority to regulate international and interstate commerce and to protect U.S. property both at home and abroad, Congress enacted

federal laws against a wide range of criminal activity, and the federal government slowly expanded its police capacity.

The Revenue Cutter Service was established in 1789 to help prevent smuggling, and thirteen U.S. marshals were appointed by the president, concurrent with enactment of

Alabama State Police patrol car and helicopter

the Judiciary Act, which created the original court system for the United States. In 1836 agents responsible for investigating infringements involving postal matters were added to the staff of the Postmaster General, and in 1865, the U.S. Secret Service was formed to investigate counterfeiting that was rampant during the Civil War. Later in the century, inspectors with law enforcement powers joined the Immigration and Naturalization Service. Among the more important law enforcement responsibilities later recognized by Congress were internal revenue investigations and narcotics control. Investigators hired by the Department of Justice in late 1800 became the Bureau of Investigation in 1908, and later, in 1930, became the present day Federal Bureau of Investigation.

For some crimes, such as espionage, federal law stands alone. For others, such as arson, bank robbery, counterfeiting, or possession of illegal drugs, federal as well as state and local authorities have concurrent jurisdiction. [5]

None of the federal law enforcement agencies of today has unlimited jurisdiction over all federal laws. Each agency was created to "enforce specific laws and cope with particular situations." [6] In addition, "Federal police agencies have no particular rank order or hierarchy of command or responsibility, and each reports to the specific department or bureau to which it is responsible." [7]

Federal authority is divided primarily between two major departments of the executive branch of government - the Department of the Treasury and the Department of Justice. Other Federal organizations, such as the various inspector general offices that investigate crime within the government itself, and the U.S. Coast Guard, an agency within the Department of Transportation, which is responsible for enforcing maritime laws, all have important roles in law enforcement. The Postal Inspection Service is the law enforcement arm of the postal service and handles all postal crimes such as mail fraud and assaults upon postal employees while exercising their duties. In 1986, the State Department's Bureau of Diplomatic Security was granted law enforcement authority to investigate matters involving passport and visa fraud and special internal matters within that agency.

In addition to the civilian law enforcement authority listed above, federal statutes also grant law enforcement authority to military operations and security and crimes committed against U.S. military personnel or property or by U.S. military personnel. The three separate military investigative agencies are the Naval Investigative Service, the Air Force Office of Special Investigation, and the Army

ATF officers at the scene of a bombing

Criminal Investigation Command. Military agencies are forbidden to enforce civilian laws.

STATE LAW ENFORCEMENT (Police Agencies)

It is not possible within the scope of this article to present a description of the police structure in each of the 50 states and the District of Columbia (Washington, D.C.). Instead, we will provide an overview of the police structure of one representative state. This overview, with minor variations, is reflective of many of the police departments throughout the United States.

POLICE JURISDICTIONS IN THE STATE OF ILLINOIS

Within the state of Illinois, there are 793 town and city (municipal) police departments, employing more than 25,000 full- and part-time sworn police officers who investigate all types of crimes and enforce local ordinances of the towns and cities as well as state laws, with implicit authority to arrest for violations of federal laws. Approximately 12,000 of these sworn officers are employed by the Chicago Police Department.

The state has 102 county sheriff departments, which employ more than 3,300 sworn officers. These officers, also investigate all types of crime and have the same arrest authority as the municipal officers.

The Illinois State Police Department, which has police powers throughout the state, employs 2,168 full-time sworn

officers. There are other state agencies, such as the Secretary of State, which is responsible for driver licensing and vehicle registrations and employs 170 sworn officers who are responsible for fishing, hunting, forestry, and boating laws. These agencies, too, enforce state laws with implicit authority to arrest for violations of federal laws.

The total of 31,475 sworn officers described above does not include the officers of railroads, airports, hospitals, park districts, forest preserves, colleges, and universities that maintain law enforcement agencies of their own.

Although each of the aforementioned officers has taken an oath to enforce local ordinances as well as county, state, and federal laws, their powers of arrest are restricted to the jurisdictional boundaries of the police departments that employ them.

Illinois also has more than 700 licensed private security and detective agencies that provide guard, patrol and investigative services to businesses, corporations, and private individuals (celebrities). These private agencies must confine their services to the properties of their employers.

JURISDICTIONAL BOUNDARIES

A police officer's powers of arrest are restricted to the geographical boundaries of his employer, whether it is a town, city, state or other police department, such as airport, university, etc.

The cities of Normal, Illinois, and Bloomington, Illinois, as well as Illinois State University and Bloomington Municipal Airport, have distinct corporate and municipal boundaries. Police officers employed by these entities, therefore, are restricted to investigating crimes and enforcing laws within their respective boundaries.

The above-mentioned entities are located in the county of McLean. McLean county has a county sheriffs depart-

Arrest of a fugitive by two U.S. Marshals

ment to investigate crimes and enforce all laws in the unincorporated areas outside the jurisdiction of the cities of Normal and Bloomington, Illinois State University and the Bloomington Airport Authority. However, the sheriff's officers have full arrest powers anywhere within McLean County, including the cities of Normal and Bloomington, the university and the airport.

3. POLICE

The Illinois State Police have full arrest powers within the 102 counties that comprise the state of Illinois, including all municipal communities.

An Illinois State Supreme Court ruling has stipulated that a local police officer has no authority to make an arrest outside his jurisdiction without the aid of an arrest warrant that is valid anywhere in the state of Illinois. The various law enforcement agencies, by utilizing mutual assistance agreements, multi-jurisdictional aid compacts, and state laws, effectively assist each other in arresting criminals who have travelled from one jurisdiction to another.

Federal law enforcement agencies such as the FBI, the DEA, the U.S. Secret Service, the U.S. Customs Service, the U.S. Marshals Service, etc., have the authority to initiate arrests in any state or U.S. territory for offenses that are a violation of federal law, specifically, offenses such as bank robbery, flight to avoid prosecution, kidnapping, counterfeiting, and treason, to name a few. This is especially true when the criminal travels across a state boundary into another state jurisdiction. For example, in the case of a bank robbery, local police would respond to the initial alert and notify the FBI, subsequently releasing control of the investigation to them. Mutual assistance agreements between federal and state agencies, however, enable both agencies to join resources and collectively pursue the investigation of the bank robbery. This type of cooperation diminishes jurisdictional problems between town, city, county, state and federal police agencies.

Cooperation is further enhanced through the task force concept, a system whereby the various municipal, state and federal agencies combine information and investigative resources to address a specific criminal problem in a specific area.

FUNCTIONS OF A POLICE DEPARTMENT

Municipal police departments range in size from one- or two-man offices, such as Smithsburg, Maryland, and Ridgeway, South Carolina, to elaborate and extensive facilities, such as the cities of New York, Chicago, and Los Angeles, which, together, employ more than 46,000 police officers, according to figures reported in the 1986 *Uniform Crime Report* published by the FBI.

The departments are operationally structured to meet the needs of the town or city in which they are located. For example, larger departments generally assign squads to address specific types of crimes, while the smaller departments, which experience lower crime rates, handle whatever type of crime or investigation arises. Assistance is always available should a situation extend beyond the capability of the police entity involved.

FEDERAL LAW ENFORCEMENT AGENCIES

Division of law enforcement authority at the federal level is not only between major departments but within them as well. As indicated earlier, each federal law enforcement agency reports to the head of the specific department to which it is responsible. The heads of these departments comprise a segment of the president's cabinet.

The Department of the Treasury, for example, has four distinct law enforcement agencies: the Bureau of Alcohol, Tobacco, and Firearms, the U.S. Customs Service, the U.S. Secret Service, and the Internal Revenue Service. Each has specific duties and jurisdictions related to the mission of the U.S. Treasury.

Computerized file of missing persons in the state of Alabama

For instance, the Bureau of Alcohol, Tobacco, and Firearms, also known as ATF, enforces federal laws pertaining to the manufacture, sale, and possession of firearms and explosives and uses these laws to investigate the use of firearms or explosives to commit violent crimes. Since federal laws require that manufacturers and dealers keep records on all sales of firearms and explosives, ATF is the nation's leading agency for tracing such weapons for domestic and international law enforcement agencies.

ATF also investigates major arson cases, particularly interstate arson-for-profit schemes, and initiates joint federal, state, and local anti-arson task forces. At the same time, ATF collects federal taxes on alcohol and tobacco products, suppresses illegal traffic in these commodities, and regulates alcohol industry trade practices.

Like ATF, the U.S. Customs Service is an agency with many responsibilities. Foremost among these is the collection of import duties and taxes at more than 300 ports of entry, from both individuals and commercial carriers. At the same time, the Customs Service detects and intercepts illegal drugs, counterfeit consumer goods, and other contraband entering the United States and prevents strategic high technology from being smuggled out of the country. Recent seizures of boats, planes and other vehicles used to transport illegal drugs into the United States have received widespread media attention and are an integral part of the federal government's efforts to stem the drug trade in America.

The U.S. Secret Service is best known for its role of protecting the president and vice president and their families, as well as other elected officials and foreign heads of state visiting the United States. But, as an agency of the Treasury Department, the Secret Service also investigates crimes related to the U.S. monetary system, such as counterfeiting of currency, coins, stamps, and bonds, forgery of government checks, and credit card fraud. And, together with the FBI, the Secret Service works to stem the growing tide of computer fraud in the United States.

The Internal Revenue Service is the nation's primary revenue-collecting agency, responsible for enforcing the revenue laws and tax statutes. However, because of drug smuggling, organized crime, and other criminal operations that involve large sums of undeclared income, the Internal Revenue Service is often included in investigations in these areas.

Two officers guard a suspect

Within the Department of Justice, law enforcement also falls primarily within four agencies: the FBI, the Drug Enforcement Administration, the U.S. Marshals Service, and the Immigration and Naturalization Service. And occupying a unique category all its own is IP-Washington, the U.S. National Central Bureau for Interpol.

The FBI focuses on organized crime activities, among them racketeering, corruption, bank robbery, pornography, and prostitution. The FBI also investigates "white collar" crimes - crimes that rely on deceit and concealment rather than force or violence. As the primary agency responsible for investigating terrorist activity in the United States, the FBI also trains special antiterrorist teams to prevent and respond to terrorist attacks and tracks foreign intelligence agents and their activities within the United States. In addition, the FBI operates an extensive forensic science laboratory and a computerized fingerprint identification service that performs identifications for federal, state and local law enforcement agencies, and maintains the National Crime Information Center (NCIC), which provides investigators with data on everything from known criminals and stolen property to missing persons and unsolved violent crimes.

The Drug Enforcement Administration, or DEA, spearheads the United States' intensifying war on illegal drugs. As part of its activities, the DEA conducts surveillance operations and infiltrates drug rings. The agency also tracks illicit drug traffic, registers manufacturers and distributors of pharmaceutic drugs, tracks the movement of chemicals used to manufacture illegal drugs, and leads the nation's domestic marijuana eradication program.

The U.S. Marshals Service was created in 1789 with the appointment of thirteen federal marshals by President George Washington. Today, in addition to ensuring the security of court facilities, U.S. marshals apprehend most federal fugitives and execute federal arrest warrants. In addition, they operate the Witness Security Program, ensuring the safety of endangered witnesses. The Marshals Service has its own Air Wing to transport federal prisoners to court appearances and then to prison. At the same time, the Marshals Service is responsible for handling the seizure and disposal of property resulting from criminal activity.

The Immigration and Naturalization Service (INS) controls the entry of aliens along thousands of miles of land and sea borders, and investigates smuggling rings that bring thousands of illegal immigrants into the country each year. The INS also facilitates certification of naturalized citizens and entry of qualified aliens into the country.

IP-Washington, known in the United States as the USNCB, is also an agency within the Department of Justice. It fulfills a unique position in the U.S. police structure by coordinating investigative request for international assistance from both domestic and foreign police. Through the USNCB, state, and local police departments, as well as federal law enforcement agencies, are able to pursue international investigative leads. Conversely, foreign police seeking criminal investigative assistance anywhere in the United States can do so by contacting the USNCB through their own Interpol National Central Bureau. To meet the demands of both the domestic and foreign police communities, the USNCB makes wide use of computerization and the latest modern communications technology, effectively tying together the more than 20,000 state, local, and federal agencies and their foreign counterparts.

COOPERATION AND TRAINING

The success of American law enforcement efforts can be attributed to numerous formal and informal programs of cooperation and training. Chief among the formal cooperative programs are the special task forces mentioned earlier, such as the Organized Crime/Drug Enforcement Task Forces operating throughout the United States. These task forces bring together the expertise of state and local law enforcement authorities and federal agencies in a concentrated effort against organized crime, illicit drug operations, and other areas of mutual interest and concern. Most often, U.S. attorneys are included as important members of the task forces.

Numerous training programs offered by both federal and state agencies keep police officers current with the latest

3. POLICE

A Massachusetts State Police officer

investigative techniques and equipment. For example, the Federal Law Enforcement Training Center (FLETC) at Glynco, Georgia, is an interagency training facility serving sixty federal law enforcement organizations. The major training effort at the center is in the area of basic programs to teach common areas of law enforcement skills to police and investigative personnel. The center also conducts advanced programs and provides the facilities and support services for other agencies to conduct advanced training for their own law enforcement personnel. In addition, the center offers selective, highly specialized training programs to state and local officers.

The FBI National Academy at Quantico, Virginia, is open to senior law enforcement officers from federal, local, and state agencies as well as foreign police departments. The academy offers a wide array of course curricula covering police management, police science, firearms, forensic science, crisis management, legal problems of police administrators, fitness for police officers, and applied criminal psychology. Also, specialized courses are provided concerning death investigations, crime scenes, identification, photography, and fingerprint science. The FBI Academy also offers college credit to police officers through its affiliation with the University of Virginia.

The U.S. Secret Service offers courses to state and local police officers in the examination of questioned (forged) documents. In addition, they train firearms instructors at the James J. Rowley Training Center in Beltsville, and offer briefings in protective techniques to state and local police who are engaged in the protection of their local dig-

nitaries. These briefings better enable the state and local police to work with the Secret Service when that agency's protectees visit their areas.

On the state level, a police agency may have its own training facility for the training of officers. In addition, municipalities with a population of 100,000 or more also offer a basic training program for new officers, and this can result in a particular state having several police academies.

To ensure uniformity in the degree and quality of training given to police at the academies, most of the 50 states have local training boards that are responsible for the establishment of training standards. Course curricula to be presented to the officers must be approved by the training board prior to being offered. The basic curriculum generally consists of courses in criminal law, humanities, first aid, weapons, self defense, and investigative procedures, to name but a few. The length of the training programs varies within each state, from a minimum of 10 weeks to a maximum of 18 weeks.

Periodic inservice and specialized training is provided to all law enforcement officers by the training academies within the states. A minimum of forty hours per year has been set as a standard requirement.

Other police training institutions within the United States include the Northwestern Traffic Institute, Southern Police Traffic Institute, the Institute of Police Technology and Management, and the San Luis Obispo Training Facility, all of which provide specialized training for supervisors and managers of police agencies.

In addition to programs within agencies, professional associations, such as the International Association of Chiefs of Police and the National Sheriff's Association, offer law enforcement executives a forum for sharing ideas and provide the spark for many successful law enforcement programs.

States also form associations among themselves, such as the Association for State Criminal Investigative Agencies, which meets twice annually to share common problems and solutions and to work toward the betterment of state investigative agencies. This association's membership numbers approximately 24 states whose state police agencies have been given general policing authority throughout the state and carry out criminal investigative functions.

The states also sponsor training sessions for law enforcement personnel throughout their state that address specific types of criminal activity. For example, the Colorado Springs Police Department, in conjunction with the District Attorney's office in that district, recently hosted a seminar to address the problems of fugitives and missing persons and the law enforcement response to these problems. This seminar, with more than 200 attendees, was open to police at all levels -- municipal, county, state, and federal. In addition, the South Carolina Law Enforcement Officers Association meets annually for a retraining conference at which seminars covering various topics are held.

The Kansas Sheriffs Association, the Kansas Peace Officers Association and the Kansas Association of Chiefs of Police, recently held their second annual Joint Law Enforcement Conference for the purpose of strengthening ties between that state's various police agencies and offering workable solutions to problems of mutual interest.

A Michigan State Police Officer

Similar conferences include, to name but a few: the Western States Crime Conference, sponsored by the Arizona Department of Public Safety; the New England State Police Administrator's Conference, which is a meeting of commissioners and other representatives of six New England States, including Connecticut, Maine, Massachusetts, New Hampshire, Rhode Island, and Vermont; and the California Attorney General's Annual Criminal Intelligence Training Conference, hosted by the California Department of Justice.

These meetings, seminars, and conferences provide excellent opportunities for sharing ideas and new programs, and enhance the effectiveness of police throughout the country.

Other formal efforts include periodic crime reports that give law enforcement personnel reliable information on criminal activities and trends. For example, the Bureau of Justice Statistics (BJS) within the Department of Justice collects, analyzes, publishes, and disseminates statistical information on crime, victims of crime, criminal offenders, and the operations of justice systems at all levels of government. BJS also provides financial and technical support to state statistical agencies and analyzes national information policy on such issues as the privacy, confidentiality, and security of data and the interstate exchange of criminal records.

The National Institute of Justice (NIJ) is the primary federal sponsor of research on crime and justice. Its goal is to answer real world questions about crime control and

ensure that this new knowledge is disseminated to those who can use it. NIJ publishes *Issues and Practices* reports and research summaries to highlight findings for busy criminal justice policy makers. NIJ's National Criminal Justice Reference Service (NCJRS) gives the criminal justice community access to a data base of over 83,000 reference materials.

The Bureau of Justice Assistance (BJA) administers the Department of Justice's state and local justice assistance program to improve criminal justice operations. BJA sets priorities for and awards discretionary grants, makes block awards to the states and territories, and administers the Public Safety Officers' Benefits Program.

These and innumerable other programs provide the U.S. law enforcement community with the means to obtain their mutual objectives of enforcing laws and protecting citizens.

The activities enumerated in this article by no means include every function and activity associated with law enforcement operations in the United States. They do, however, present a brief overview of the variety and types of interaction practiced by the members of the law enforcement community, whether they represent a federal, state, or local agency.

Despite its vastness and complexity, the American police system works. It successfully serves more than 235 million people in a country that covers more than 3.5 million square miles, a monumental task by any standard.

REFERENCES

The writers gratefully acknowledge the cooperation of all those who provided them with access to the reference sources listed below and, in particular, that of the Bureau of Alcohol, Tobacco, and Firearms in granting permission to use excerpts from their video *Teamwork and the Law,* and that of Dr. David Lester of Stockton State College in Pomona, New Jersey, who provided the excerpts from **Introduction to Criminal Justice.**

Encyclopedia of Crime and Justice, McMillan & Free Press, New York, 1984 (References Nos. 1, 3 and 5).

Joseph J. Senna, L.J. Siegel, **Introduction to Criminal Justice,** West Publishing Co., St. Paul, Minn., 1981 (References Nos. 2, 4, 6 and 7).

Illinois Criminal Justice Information Authority Illinois Revised Statutes.

Illinois Department of Transportation.

Inbau, **Criminal Law for Police.**

O. Wilson, **Police Administration**.

Annual Report of the Attorney General of the U.S., 1986.

U.S. Government Manual, 1988.

WOMEN ON THE MOVE?
A Report on the Status of Women in Policing

Susan E. Martin

This report has been made possible through funding from the Ford Foundation. Its author, Dr. Susan Martin, is a project director and member of the Police Foundation research team. The Police Foundation is a public nonprofit organization devoted to improvement and innovation in policing.

Abstract

In the years following the passage of the 1972 Amendments to the Civil Rights Act, policing made significant progress in eliminating discrimination in the hiring and promotion of women. The proportion of women in both officer and supervisory ranks has increased substantially. That progress notwithstanding, there is still much to be done to correct the overall underrepresentation of women in policing.

From the entry of the first sworn female into policing in 1910 until 1972, women officers were selected according to separate criteria from men, employed as "policewomen," and limited to working with "women, children and typewriters" (Milton, 1972). The passage of the 1972 Amendments to the Civil Rights Act of 1964, however, extended the act's coverage to state and local government employees and thus guaranteed under law equal opportunity in policing. Since that date, many departments, often under the threat of a court order, have eliminated discriminatory personnel policies.

How far had these changes gone through the mid-1980s? Although most experts assumed some significant progress had been made, it was apparent that there was more to be done. Just how much, however, was unclear. The research evidence was limited.[1] The Police Foundation had completed its last research on this matter in 1978. And so, in an effort to quantify change and provide data that would guide future policies, the Police Foundation initiated in 1987 a study that included a mail survey of personnel practices in municipal and state police agencies. This report summarizes the survey findings from municipal agencies and points to some of their policy implications.

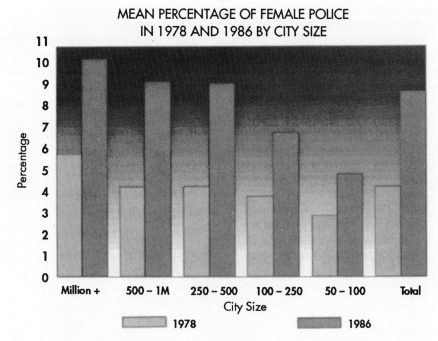

Figure 1
MEAN PERCENTAGE OF FEMALE POLICE IN 1978 AND 1986 BY CITY SIZE

Reprinted by permission from *Police Foundation Reports*, May 1989, pp. 1-8, published by the Police Foundation.

Figure 2

PERCENTAGE OF FEMALE POLICE
IN 1978 AND 1986 BY RANK

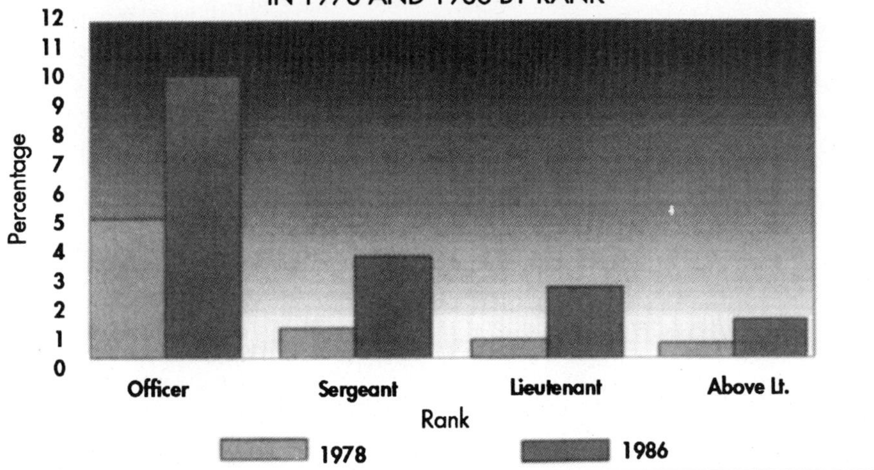

THE SURVEY

T he national mail survey of police personnel practices sought information on: (1) departmental policies and practices regarding recruitment, selection, and promotion; (2) the number and percentage of male and female officers by ethnic group, rank, and assignment; (3) male and female officer turnover rates; and (4) the existence and nature of other personnel policies related to women, including those on affirmative action, sexual harassment, and pregnancy and maternity leave.

Questionnaires were sent to all 446 municipal police departments serving populations of 50,000 and all state police agencies. This was the same sample used by the Police Foundation in its 1978 survey of women in policing.[2] Seventy-two percent of the municipal departments returned usable surveys.[3]

THE RESULTS

Representation of Women in Policing

T he proportion of women among sworn police personnel has grown steadily since 1972. In that year, a survey of cities serving populations of 250,000 or more revealed that women comprised only 2 percent of uniformed law enforcement personnel (ICMA, 1972). In 1978, women made up 4.2 percent of sworn personnel in municipal departments serving

Table 1

WOMEN'S PROMOTIONS IN MUNICIPAL DEPARTMENTS BY CITY SIZE

CITY SIZE	SERGEANT		LIEUTENANT	
	MEAN % ELIGIBLE (N=192)	MEAN % PROMOTED (N=192)	MEAN % ELIGIBLE (N=157)	MEAN % PROMOTED (N=157)
> 500,000	9.5	15.8	2.9	3.4
250,000-500,000	6.1	8.0	3.1	7.7
100,000-250,000	6.6	7.1	3.0	3.2
50,000-100,000	4.5	6.2	1.8	0.9
TOTAL	6.8	8.8	2.7	3.5

Both the proportion of women eligible for promotion and the rate at which women were promoted were directly related to size of the city served; the larger the city, the higher the percentage. The biggest gains for women came in departments serving populations of over half a million, where women made up 9.5 percent of those eligible for promotion and 15.8 percent of those achieving the rank of sergeant in 1986.

populations over 50,000 (see Figure 1). By the end of 1986, the proportion of women had risen to 8.8 percent of all sworn officers in these agencies.

Figure 1 indicates that women's representation in policing in both 1978 and 1986 was directly related to city size. Although there has been growth in the proportion of women officers in cities of all sizes, the increase has been greater in departments in the largest cities. For example, in cities over a million, women made up 5.8 percent of the officers in 1978 and 10.4 percent in 1986; in cities of 50,000 to 100,000, they made up

only 2.6 percent of the total in 1978 and 4.9 percent in 1986. In both years minority women made up a disproportionately large share of all women in policing — 38 percent in 1978 and 40 percent in 1986. In contrast, minority men constituted 10 and 21 percent of all the male officers, respectively, in 1978 and 1986. Minority female representation was closely related to city size; white female representation was not.

Regional differences in the proportion of women in policing were small but related to variations in minority representation. Women constituted 7.6 percent of all officers in the west, where the proportion of minority women is the smallest, and 9.4 percent in the south, where the proportion of minority women is largest.

How one views the representation of women in policing depends on the standard one uses to measure it. Since women make up 44.7 percent of the labor force, it can be argued that they are underrepresented in policing. In addition, in contrast to traditionally "male" professions such as law and medicine, policing appears to be lagging. According to U.S. Department of Labor data, in May 1987, women made up 21 percent of the nation's lawyers and judges; 15 percent of the health diagnosing occupations.

In comparison with other skilled "blue collar" craft occupations, however, women in policing have done well; females made up only 4 percent of mechanics and repairers and 2 percent of workers in construction trades in May 1987 (U.S. Dept. of Labor cited by Powell, 1988:76-78).

Women in Supervisory Positions

Although the proportion of women in supervisory ranks grew between 1978 and 1986, the increase was smaller than that in the rank of officer. In 1978, women made up one percent of municipal police supervisors, only 20 percent of whom were minority women. In 1986, women made up 3.3 percent of all supervisors, with 30 percent of these being minorities. While minority women continued to be under-represented in supervisory ranks, they did make gains on white female counterparts.

The size of the jurisdiction studied in

1978 made little difference because women's representation was so uniformly small. In 1986, however, a higher proportion of women supervisors were found in agencies serving populations over 250,000 (4.0 percent) than those in the smaller cities (2.1 percent).

Most of the increase in female supervisors occurred at the rank of sergeant (Figure 2). In general, the higher the rank, the smaller the percentage of women in it. For example, the proportion of women among all officers, detectives and corporals increased from 5 percent in 1978 to 10 percent in 1986. The proportion of women sergeants among all sergeants increased from 1.0 to 3.7 percent; the proportion of women lieutenants from .7 to 2.5 percent; and the proportion of those in the higher ranking command staff from .5 to 1.4 percent. These differences are attributable in part to the fact that women have not been policing in significant numbers long enough to have shown up in the highest ranks. Nonetheless, their virtual exclusion from upper level management in police departments is similar to their near absence in corporate board rooms and law partnerships.[4]

Data on the proportion of male and female officers eligible for promotion, promoted, or likely to be promoted in 1986, however, are somewhat more encouraging. As shown in Table 1, although 6.8 percent of all persons eligible for promotion to the rank of sergeant were female, 8.8 percent of those actually promoted were women; similarly, at the rank of lieutenant, women made up 2.7 percent of those eligible, but 3.5 percent of those actually promoted or likely to become lieutenants in 1986. Furthermore, across the various city size categories, with only one exception (agencies in cities with populations under 100,000), women were promoted in greater numbers than would be expected based on their representation in the eligible pools for sergeant and lieutenant.

Both the proportion of women eligible for promotion and the rate at which women were promoted were directly related to size of the city served; the larger the city, the higher the percentage. The biggest gains for women came in departments serving populations of over half a million, where women made up 9.5 percent of those eligible for promotion and 15.8 percent of those achieving the rank of sergeant in 1986.

The low proportion of women in police supervisory positions can be explained by several factors. First, a smaller proportion of women are eligible for promotion due to service requirements. Among the 226 municipal agencies providing promotion data, 41 (18 percent) indicated that no women were eligible for promotion to sergeant in 1986; men were eligible for promotion in every case. Second, promotional systems that give substantial weight to seniority beyond minimal eligibility requirements limit women's promotional opportunities and actual promotion rates. While this lack of seniority still handicaps women, it is expected that in another decade the discriminatory effects of seniority will largely disappear (one possible exception being imbalances caused by higher turnover rates for women officers).

A third factor that seems to limit promotional opportunities for women is the supervisor's evaluation—considered for final placement on promotional lists in more than half the responding departments. Although job performance is a relevant consideration in a promotion system, effective measures of police performance have not been developed, most rating systems tend to be subjective, and as such may result in subtle downgrading of women who do not fit supervisors' conscious or unconscious definition of the ideal officer.

In agencies placing greater weight on objective measures, opportunities for moving into middle management increase. In fact, the percentage of eligible women promoted to sergeant was significantly higher in agencies using an assessment center as part of the promotional process (12.2 percent) than those that did not (4.9 percent).

Sex Differences in Officer Selection and Training

It has long been known that application and selection rates are influenced by eligibility criteria and mechanisms used to recruit, screen, and select candidate officers. For many years minimum height and weight standards greatly limited the pool of female

Figure 3

IMPACT OF AFFIRMATIVE ACTION ON PROPORTION OF FEMALES AMONG APPLICANTS AND PERSONS SELECTED BY DEPARTMENTS

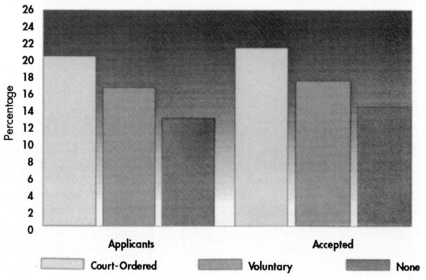

applications (Milton, 1972; Sulton and Townsey, 1981).

In the past 15 years, however, these criteria have changed dramatically, thereby enlarging the pool of eligible women. By 1986, fewer than 4 percent of municipal departments still had minimum height (mean = 5' 4") and weight (mean = 135.3) standards. Instead, the use of physical fitness tests and standards making weight proportional to height are becoming the norm (Fyfe, 1986:5). Furthermore, women applicants in the past have often been found "unsatisfactory" as a result of oral interviews in which neither questions nor responses were standardized (Gray, 1975). In 1986, the Police Foundation found that 76 percent of the responding agencies

Figure 4

1986 PERCENTAGE OF MALE AND FEMALE TURNOVER BY TYPE OF SEPARATION

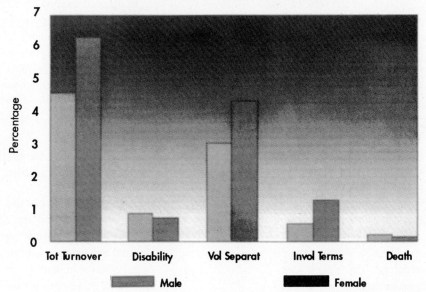

reported that they used standardized questions and 60 percent reported having predetermined acceptable answers.

Data on those who applied and were accepted for police jobs, and on those who entered and completed the training academy in municipal agencies, suggest that there is no systematic sex discrimination in the applicant selection process.

While 20 percent of the applicants were female, women comprised 20.6 percent of all those accepted by departments; 19.9 percent entering an academy; and 19.2 percent of those completing academy training. These data show that there are no significant sex differences in rates of offers of employment, or entry into and completing of the academy.[5]

A variety of actors were found to be related to the proportion of women among a department's applicants, accepted candidates, academy entrants, and new trainees. City size, for example, was directly related to each stage of selection. The proportion of women applicants in departments in cities over a million (29 percent) is more than twice the proportion in agencies in cities of 50,000 to 100,000 (13 percent). While the proportions of women accepted, entering the academy, and completing it also decreased substantially with city size, variation among departments in each size category was so great that the finding did not achieve statistical significance.

A breakdown by region suggests that there was a higher proportion of female applicants in the south and a smaller proportion in the northeast than in the north central and western states, but there were no significant regional differences in acceptance, academy entrance, or academy completion rates.

Among the selection criteria, the absence of a pre-training physical agility test was significantly associated with female application rates (19 percent versus 15 percent) and with female acceptance rates (22 percent versus 15 percent of those accepted).

A department's selection criteria and the presence and nature of its affirmative action policy also appear to have an impact on both the size of the female applicant pool and the number of female applicants accepted. Figure 3 shows that in agencies with court-ordered affirmative action plans,

21 percent of the applicants were female, in contrast to 17 percent in agencies with voluntary affirmative action plans, and 13 percent in those with no plan. Women also made up a significantly larger proportion of the applicants accepted in agencies with court-ordered affirmative action plans (21 percent), as compared to agencies with voluntary plans (18 percent) or no plans (14 percent).

Sex Differences in Turnover

Just as rates of entry into policing affect representation of women as a whole, so do turnover and separation rates. Figure 4 shows non-retirement turnover for males and females during 1986 and the four primary types of turnover, i.e., disability, voluntary separations, involuntary terminations, and death (but NOT normal retirement). During 1986, 6.3 percent of women officers and 4.6 percent of male officers separated from their departments. Although there were no sex differences in the rates of turnover due to disability or death, women had higher rates than men of both voluntary (4.3 percent versus 3.0 percent) and involuntary (1.2 versus .6 percent respectively) separations.

City size had virtually no relationship to turnover rates; women's turnover, however, was much lower in departments serving cities with populations over a million (4.2 percent) than in those serving smaller jurisdictions (7.8 percent). The factor most strongly associated with the female turnover rate was male turnover rate; where women tend to leave, men also are more likely to leave. Both male and female turnover was higher in the west than other regions.

A variety of factors related to women employees' slightly higher turnover rates may explain these findings (Kanter, 1977; O'Farrell and Harlan, 1982; Jurik, 1985). The association between male and female turnover rates suggests that departmental policies (such as willingness to eliminate trainees from the academy or during their probationary period) and local labor market conditions affect male and female officers in similar ways.

Some of the factors that probably do

contribute to higher turnover rates for women include:

• a work environment that is hostile or unpleasant for women but not for men (Martin, 1980; Hunt, 1984);

• difficulties in meshing policing with family life (particularly for a single parent on rotating shifts);

• inadequate light duty and pregnancy leave policies that make having a family and continuing to work difficult or impossible;

• an unrealistically positive picture of the work acquired from television or from recruiters seeking to meet goals; and

• the problems, e.g. performance pressures, faced by "tokens" (Kanter, 1977).

Because of the nature of police patrol, most police agencies permit or require pregnant officers to leave patrol assignments. Yet only 74 percent of the agencies reassign a pregnant officer to a light duty assignment until delivery; 14 percent force the woman to go on leave when she can no longer continue in her "normal" assignment. Twelve percent of the agencies had not yet had to deal with a pregnancy. It is likely that many of the women forced to leave policing for six to eight months in order to have a child resign temporarily or permanently from their departments.

Impact of Affirmative Action

Affirmative action policies have a major impact not only on the rates at which females apply and enter policing, but, over the long term, on women's overall representation in policing. In 1986, 15 percent of the municipal agencies responding to our survey had court-ordered affirmative action hiring policies; 42 percent had voluntary affirmative action plans in effect; and 43 percent had none.

In those agencies under court order to increase the representation of women and minorities, women made up 10.1 percent of the sworn personnel in 1986; in those with voluntary affirmative action plans, women made up 8.3 percent of the personnel, and in those without affirmative action plans women constituted only 6.1 percent of the personnel.

Affirmative action also is related to the proportion of women in supervisory positions; in departments with court-ordered affirmative action, women made up 3.5 percent of the supervisors; in those with voluntary affirmative action 2.4 percent; and in those without affirmative action 2.2 percent of the supervisory personnel.

Because the representation of women and presence of affirmative action policies were also related to other factors, the Police Foundation study used multivariate analysis to control for the effects of size, region, minority representation, and the proportion of women officers in 1978 to determine whether affirmative action policies have an independent effect. After including these variables in several regression models, we found that both court-ordered and voluntary affirmative action remained significantly associated with the proportion of women in a department in 1986 and that the presence of an affirmative action policy also was significantly associated with an increase in the representation of female officers over the 8-year period.

Because several factors also were found to be related to application and acceptance rates, researchers conducted a similar multivariate analysis to isolate the effects of affirmative action. For each test, two regression models, identical except that the second one omitted the affirmative action variables, were developed and compared (Namboodiri, Carter, and Blalock, 1975).[6]

Although we found that both court-ordered and voluntary affirmative action remained significantly associated with female application rates, after controlling for the other variables neither was found to be significantly related to the proportion of female applicants accepted for employment. This suggests that affirmative action policies make a favorable impact on recruitment, primarily in widening the applicant pool; but once that is enlarged, women are usually selected in proportion to their presence in that pool. If current selection procedures continue, women will eventually make up as much as 20 percent of police personnel. If the proportion of women is to increase beyond that, however, recruiting efforts to encourage more female applicants to enter the applicant pool may be required.

CONCLUSION AND POLICY IMPLICATIONS

The survey findings suggest that there has been some positive change in the status of women in policing in the past decade. The proportion of female officers has increased in police departments in each population category and geographic region. By the end of 1986, women made up nearly 9 percent of officers in municipal departments in cities over 50,000. This has occurred despite federal efforts to weaken affirmative action programs, which are found in more than half the agencies responding to the survey and are associated with the increased female representation.

The *pace* of change is, nonetheless, relatively slow; women still constitute less than 9 percent of all police personnel and 3.3 percent at the supervisory level. They thus continue to face the problems experienced by "tokens," e.g. performance pressures, heightened boundaries against "outsiders," and entrapment in stereotyped roles (Kanter, 1977).

Recruitment, selection, retention, and promotion rates paint an equivocal picture regarding women's status in police work. About 20 percent of both the current applicants and recruits are female, which suggests that once women apply, there does not seem to be systematic discrimination against them. There is wide variation among departments, however, in both application and acceptance rates. This points to the fact that some agencies attract women and others do not, leaving considerable room for more effective recruitment efforts. Such efforts are particularly important because women have higher turnover rates than men, and thus more women are needed to enter policing even to maintain current sex ratios.

Although women are being promoted at a rate slightly higher than might be expected based on their proportion among those eligible, current trends would indicate that women are not likely to assume departmental leadership and policymaking positions for many years in more than a handful of agencies.

What policies do these findings suggest for the next decade?

• Since affirmative action policies have substantially changed the composition of the larger departments, it is important to see that such policies are adopted where they are absent and continued where they exist.

• Voluntary affirmative action hiring policies should focus on enlargement of the pool of recruits. This will permit selection of more and more well qualified women, while avoiding imposition of court-ordered changes in hiring procedures that cause a backlash of resentment.

• To increase the rate of female promotion, departments need to alter promotion standards to eliminate criteria irrelevant to identifying supervisory ability or potential. They need to adopt policies and procedures which clearly state that promotions are based on merit.

• Increasing the number of women in recruitment and training assignments as well as in high visibility supervisory posts will create more role models for both potential recruits and women already on the job.

• Active, vigorous enforcement of existing sexual harassment policies might reduce turnover rates.

• The adoption of a pregnancy policy permitting pregnant women to remain on the job in a non-contact assignment and allowing new mothers to take leave beyond the brief period needed for physical recovery, would also have a salutary effect.

Footnotes

1. Several early studies indicated that women can perform effectively as patrol officers (Bloch and Anderson, 1974; Sherman, 1975; Sichel et al., 1978) and identified the problems and coping strategies of the first generation of women assigned to patrol work (Martin, 1980). More recent surveys of personnel practices (Fyfe, 1987; Sulton and Townsey, 1981) have found continuing changes in police agency selection criteria but lack information on changes in selection and promotion practices and turnover rates. For a critique of these early evaluations, see Morash and Greene (1986); for a discussion of the shortcomings of statistical information, see Walker (1985).

2. We subsequently discovered that the 1986 sample included all departments in Sulton and Townsey's 1978 survey, as well as 50 departments that they did not include. Forty-one of these departments were in the 50,000 to 100,000 size category in 1986 but previously had fewer than 50,000 inhabitants. The other nine were larger departments, six of which appear to have been used for a pretest.

3. Sulton and Townsey obtained usable surveys from 74 percent of the municipal agencies.

4. In 1985 only 2 percent of the top corporate executives of Fortune 500 companies were women (Powell 1988:75) and 6 percent of law firm partners were women according to a study conducted by the ABA's Commission on Women in the Profession.

5. Because in many jurisdictions, county or municipal personnel boards administer the initial entry test and "certify" qualified applicants from a list ranked by written exam score, only 60 percent of the departments were able to provide data on the number of applicants; in contrast, 72 percent provided data on academy entrance and completion. Several departments that did not provide the latter information indicated that no officers had been hired or completed training in 1986.

6. Both models included as independent variables agency size, region, percent black, percent Hispanic, percent female, whether the agency had increased its authorized sworn personnel since 1982, whether women had been assigned to patrol prior to 1974, the total percentage of applicants accepted, whether the agency uses a pre-training agility test, and whether there is either female or minority representation on the oral panel.

References

Bloch, P. and D. Anderson
1974   *Policewomen on Patrol: Final Report.* Washington: Urban Institute.

Fyfe, J.
1986   *Police Personnel Practices, 1986.* (Baseline Data Report Volume 18, Number 6). Washington, D.C.: International City Management Association.

Gray, T.C.
1975   "Selecting for a Police Subculture," pp. 46-56 in Skolnick, J.H. and T.C. Gray (eds.) *"Policing in America."* Boston: Little Brown.

Hunt, J.
1984   "The Logic of Sexism Among Police." Unpublished paper presented at the American Society of Criminology annual meeting in Cinncinati, Ohio.

International City Management Association
1972   "Personnel Practices in Municipal Police Departments" Urban Data Service 5.

Jurik, N.
1985   "An Officer and a Lady: Organizational Barriers to Women Working as Correctional Officers in Men's Prisons." *Social Problems* 32:375-388.

Kanter, R.M.
1977   *Men and Women of the Corporation.* New York: Basic Books.

Martin, S.E.
1980   *"Breaking and Entering": Policewomen on Patrol.* Berkeley: University of California Press.

Milton, C.
1972   *Women in Policing.* Washington: Police Foundation.

Morash, M. and J. Greene
1986   "Evaluating Women on Patrol: A Critique of Contemporary Wisdom." *Evaluation Review* 10:230-255.

Namboodiri, H.K., L.F. Carter, and H.M. Blalock
1975   *Applied Multivariate Analysis and Experimental Designs.* New York: McGraw Hill.

O'Farrell, B. and S. L. Harlan
1982   "Craftworkers and Clerks: The Effects of Male Coworker Hostility on Women's Satisfaction with Non-Traditional Jobs." *Social Problems* 29:252-265.

Powell, G.N.
1988   *Women and Men in Management.* Sage: Beverly Hills, CA.

Sherman, L.J.
1975   "Evaluation of policewomen on patrol in a suburban police department." *Journal of Police Science and Administration* 3:434-438.

Sichel, J.L., L.N. Friedman, J.C. Quint, and M.E. Smith
1978   *Women on Patrol: A Pilot Study of Police Performance in New York City.* Washington, DC: National Institute of Law Enforcement and Criminal Justice.

Sulton, C. and R. Townsey
1981   *A Progress Report on Women in Policing.* Washington: Police Foundation.

Walker, S.
1985   "Racial minority and female employment in policing: the implications of 'glacial' change." *Crime and Delinquency* 31:555-572.

*Sometimes "fixing broken windows" does more
to reduce crime than conventional "incident-oriented" policing*

MAKING
NEIGHBORHOODS
SAFE

JAMES Q. WILSON AND GEORGE L. KELLING

*James Q. Wilson and George L. Kelling write widely about
crime. Wilson is the Collins Professor of Management at
UCLA and the chairman of the board of directors of the Police
Foundation, a private research group in Washington, D.C.
George L. Kelling is a professor at the College of Criminal
Justice at Northeastern University, in Boston, and a fellow in
the Program in Criminal Justice at the John F. Kennedy
School of Government, at Harvard.*

NEW BRIARFIELD APARTMENTS IS AN OLD, RUN-
down collection of wooden buildings constructed
in 1942 as temporary housing for shipyard workers in Newport News, Virginia. By the mid-1980s it was
widely regarded as the worst housing project in the city.
Many of its vacant units provided hiding places for drug
users. It had the highest burglary rate in Newport News;
nearly a quarter of its apartments were broken into at least
once a year.

For decades the police had wearily answered calls for assistance and had investigated crimes in New Briarfield.
Not much came of this police attentiveness—the buildings went on deteriorating, the burglaries went on occurring, the residents went on living in terror. Then, in 1984,
Detective Tony Duke, assigned to a newly created police
task force, decided to interview the residents of New
Briarfield about their problems. Not surprisingly, he found
that they were worried about the burglaries—but they
were just as concerned about the physical deterioration of
the project. Rather than investigating only the burglaries,
Duke spent some of his time investigating the *buildings*.
Soon he learned that many city agencies—the fire department, the public-works department, the housing depart-

ment—regarded New Briarfield as a major headache. He
also discovered that its owners were in default on a federal
loan and that foreclosure was imminent.

The report he wrote to Darrel Stephens, then the police
chief, led Stephens to recommend to the city manager that
New Briarfield be demolished and its tenants relocated.
The city manager agreed. Meanwhile, Barry Haddix, the
patrol officer assigned to the area, began working with
members of other city agencies to fix up the project, pending its eventual replacement. Trash was carted away, abandoned cars were removed, potholes were filled in, the
streets were swept. According to a study recently done by
John E. Eck and William Spelman, of the Police Executive Research Forum (PERF), the burglary rate dropped by
35 percent after Duke and Haddix began their work.

Stephens, now the executive director of PERF, tells the
story of the New Briarfield project as an example of "problem-oriented policing," a concept developed by Professor
Herman Goldstein, of the University of Wisconsin Law
School, and sometimes also called community-oriented
policing. The conventional police strategy is "incident-oriented"—a citizen calls to report an incident, such as a burglary, and the police respond by recording information rel-

evant to the crime and then trying to solve it. Obviously, when a crime occurs, the victim is entitled to a rapid, effective police response. But if responding to incidents is all that the police do, the community problems that cause or explain many of these incidents will never be addressed, and so the incidents will continue and their number will perhaps increase.

This will happen for two reasons. One is that a lot of serious crime is adventitious, not the result of inexorable social forces or personal failings. A rash of burglaries may occur because drug users have found a back alley or an abandoned building in which to hang out. In their spare time, and in order to get money to buy drugs, they steal from their neighbors. If the back alleys are cleaned up and the abandoned buildings torn down, the drug users will go away. They may even use fewer drugs, because they will have difficulty finding convenient dealers and soft burglary targets. By the same token, a neglected neighborhood may become the turf of a youth gang, whose members commit more crimes together in a group than they would if they were acting alone. If the gang is broken up, former members will still commit some crimes but probably not as many as before.

Most crime in most neighborhoods is local: the offenders live near their victims. Because of this, one should not assume that changing the environmental conditions conducive to crime in one area will displace the crime to other areas. For example, when the New York City police commissioner, Ben Ward, ordered Operation Pressure Point, a crackdown on drug dealing on the Lower East Side, dealing and the criminality associated with it were reduced in that neighborhood and apparently did not immediately reappear in other, contiguous neighborhoods. Suburban customers of the local drug dealers were frightened away by the sight of dozens of police officers on the streets where these customers had once shopped openly for drugs. They could not—at least not right away—find another neighborhood in which to buy drugs as easily as they once had on the Lower East Side. At the same time, the local population included some people who were willing to aid and abet the drug dealers. When the police presence made drug dealing unattractive, the dealers could not—again, at least not for the time being—find another neighborhood that provided an equivalent social infrastructure.

The second reason that incident-oriented police work fails to discourage neighborhood crime is that law-abiding citizens who are afraid to go out onto streets filled with graffiti, winos, and loitering youths yield control of these streets to people who are not frightened by these signs of urban decay. Those not frightened turn out to be the same people who created the problem in the first place. Law-abiding citizens, already fearful, see things occurring that make them even more fearful. A vicious cycle begins of fear-induced behavior increasing the sources of that fear.

A Los Angeles police sergeant put it this way: "When people in this district see that a gang has spray-painted its initials on all the stop signs, they decide that the gang, not the people or the police, controls the streets. When they discover that the Department of Transportation needs three months to replace the stop signs, they decide that the city isn't as powerful as the gang. These people want us to help them take back the streets." Painting gang symbols on a stop sign or a storefront is not, by itself, a serious crime. As an incident, it is trivial. But as the symptom of a problem, it is very serious.

IN AN EARLIER ARTICLE IN *THE ATLANTIC* (MARCH, 1982) we called this the problem of "broken windows": If the first broken window in a building is not repaired, then people who like breaking windows will assume that no one cares about the building and more windows will be broken. Soon the building will have no windows. Likewise, when disorderly behavior—say, rude remarks by loitering youths—is left unchallenged, the signal given is that no one cares. The disorder escalates, possibly to serious crime.

The sort of police work practiced in Newport News is an effort to fix the broken windows. Similar projects are under way in cities all over America. This pattern constitutes the beginnings of the most significant redefinition of police work in the past half century. For example:

• When a gunfight occurred at Garden Village, a low-income housing project near Baltimore, the Baltimore County police responded by investigating both the shooting and the housing project. Chief Cornelius Behan directed the officers in his Community Oriented Police Enforcement (COPE) unit to find out what could be done to alleviate the fears of the project residents and the gang tensions that led to the shooting. COPE officers worked with members of other agencies to upgrade street lighting in the area, trim shrubbery, install door locks, repair the roads and alleys, and get money to build a playground. With police guidance, the tenants organized. At the same time, high-visibility patrols were started and gang members were questioned. When both a suspect in the shooting and a particularly troublesome parole violator were arrested, gang tensions eased. Crime rates dropped. In bringing about this change, the police dealt with eleven different public agencies.

• When local merchants in a New York City neighborhood complained to the police about homeless persons who created a mess on the streets and whose presence frightened away customers, the officer who responded did not roust the vagrants but instead suggested that the merchants hire them to clean the streets in front of their stores every morning. The merchants agreed, and now the streets are clean all day and the customers find the stores more attractive.

• When people in a Los Angeles neighborhood complained to the police about graffiti on walls and gang symbols on stop signs, officers assigned to the Community Mobilization Project in the Wilshire station did more than just try to catch the gang youths who were wielding the spray cans; they also organized citizens' groups and

Boy Scouts to paint over the graffiti as fast as they were put up.

• When residents of a Houston neighborhood became fearful about crime in their area, the police not only redoubled their efforts to solve the burglaries and thefts but also assigned some officers to talk with the citizens in their homes. During a nine-month period the officers visited more than a third of all the dwelling units in the area, introduced themselves, asked about any neighborhood problems, and left their business cards. When Antony Pate and Mary Ann Wycoff, researchers at the Police Foundation, evaluated the project, they found that the people in this area, unlike others living in a similar area where no citizen-contact project occurred, felt that social disorder had decreased and that the neighborhood had become a better place to live. Moreover, and quite unexpectedly, the amount of property crime was noticeably reduced.

These are all examples of community-oriented policing, whose current popularity among police chiefs is as great as the ambiguity of the idea. In a sense, the police have always been community-oriented. Every police officer knows that most crimes don't get solved if victims and witnesses do not cooperate. One way to encourage that cooperation is to cultivate the good will of both victims and witnesses. Similarly, police-citizen tensions, over racial incidents or allegations of brutality or hostility, can often be allayed, and sometimes prevented, if police officers stay in close touch with community groups. Accordingly, most departments have at least one community-relations officer, who arranges meetings between officers and citizens' groups in church basements and other neutral locales.

But these commonplace features of police work are add-ons, and rarely alter the traditional work of most patrol officers and detectives: responding to radio calls about specific incidents. The focus on incidents works against a focus on problems. If Detective Tony Duke had focused only on incidents in New Briarfield, he would still be investigating burglaries in that housing project; meanwhile, the community-relations officer would be telling outraged residents that the police were doing all they could and urging people to call in any useful leads. If a tenant at one of those meetings had complained about stopped-up drains, rotting floorboards, and abandoned refrigerators, the community-relations officer would have patiently explained that these were not "police matters."

And of course, they are not. They are the responsibility of the landlord, the tenants themselves, and city agencies other than the police. But landlords are sometimes indifferent, tenants rarely have the resources to make needed repairs, and other city agencies do not have a twenty-four-hour emergency service. Like it or not, the police are about the only city agency that makes house calls around the clock. And like it or not, the public defines broadly what it thinks of as public order, and holds the police responsible for maintaining order.

Community-oriented policing means changing the daily work of the police to include investigating problems as well as incidents. It means defining as a problem whatever a significant body of public opinion regards as a threat to community order. It means working with the good guys, and not just against the bad guys.

The link between incidents and problems can sometimes be measured. The police know from experience what research by Glenn Pierce, in Boston, and Lawrence Sherman, in Minneapolis, has established: fewer than 10 percent of the addresses from which the police receive calls account for more than 60 percent of those calls. Many of the calls involve domestic disputes. If each call is treated as a separate incident with neither a history nor a future, then each dispute will be handled by police officers anxious to pacify the complainants and get back on patrol as quickly as possible. All too often, however, the disputants move beyond shouting insults or throwing crockery at each other. A knife or a gun may be produced, and somebody may die.

A very large proportion of all killings occur in these domestic settings. A study of domestic homicides in Kansas City showed that in eight out of ten cases the police had been called to the incident address at least once before; in half the cases they had been called *five times* or more. The police are familiar with this pattern, and they have learned how best to respond to it. An experiment in Minneapolis, conducted by the Police Foundation, showed that men who were arrested after assaulting their spouses were much less likely to commit new assaults than those who were merely pacified or asked to leave the house for a few hours. Research is now under way in other cities to test this finding. Arrest may prove always to be the best disposition, or we may learn that some kind of intervention by a social agency also helps. What is indisputable is that a domestic fight—like many other events to which the police respond—is less an "incident" than a problem likely to have serious, long-term consequences.

Another such problem, familiar to New Yorkers, is graffiti on subway cars. What to some aesthetes is folk art is to most people a sign that an important public place is no longer under public control. If graffiti painters can attack cars with impunity, then muggers may feel they can attack the people in those cars with equal impunity. When we first wrote in these pages about the problem of broken windows, we dwelt on the graffiti problem as an example of a minor crime creating a major crisis.

The police seemed powerless to do much about it. They could arrest youths with cans of spray paint, but for every one arrested ten more went undetected, and of those arrested, few were punished. The New York Transit Authority, led by its chairman, Robert Kiley, and its president, David Gunn, decided that graffiti-free cars were a major management goal. New, easier-to-clean cars were bought. More important, key people in the Authority were held accountable for cleaning the cars and keeping them clean. Whereas in the early 1980s two out of every three cars were covered with graffiti, today fewer than one in six is. The Transit Police have played their part by arresting those who paint the cars, but they have been more successful at keeping cars from being defaced in the first place than they were at chasing people who were spraying already defaced ones.

WHILE THE PHRASE "COMMUNITY-ORIENTED POLICING" comes easily to the lips of police administrators, redefining the police mission is more difficult. To help the police become accustomed to fixing broken windows as well as arresting window-breakers requires doing things that are very hard for many administrators to do.

Authority over at least some patrol officers must be decentralized, so that they have a good deal of freedom to manage their time (including their paid overtime). This implies freeing them at least partly from the tyranny of the radio call. It means giving them a broad range of responsibilities: to find and understand the problems that create disorder and crime, and to deal with other public and private agencies that can help cope with these problems. It means assigning them to a neighborhood and leaving them there for an extended period of time. It means backing them up with department support and resources.

The reason these are not easy things for police chiefs to do is not simply that chiefs are slaves to tradition, though some impatient advocates of community-oriented policing like to say so. Consider for a moment how all these changes might sound to an experienced and intelligent police executive who must defend his department against media criticisms of officer misconduct, political pressure to cut budgets, and interest-group demands for more police protection everywhere. With decentralized authority, no one will know precisely how patrol officers spend their time. Moreover, decentralized authority means that patrol officers will spend time on things like schmoozing with citizens, instead of on quantifiable tasks like issuing tickets, making arrests, and clearing cases.

Making the community-oriented officers generalists means letting them deal with other city agencies, a responsibility for which few officers are well trained and which cuts across sensitive questions of turf and public expectations.

If officers are left in a neighborhood, some of them may start taking money from the dope dealers and after-hours joints. To prevent that, officers are frequently moved around. Moreover, the best people are usually kept in the detective squad that handles the really big cases. Few police executives want their best people settling into a neighborhood, walking around the bus stops and shopping malls.

The enthusiasts for community-oriented policing have answers for all these concerns, but sometimes in their zeal they forget that they are contending with more than mere bureaucratic foot-dragging—that the problems are real and require thoughtful solutions. Many police executives get in trouble not because the crime rate goes up but because cops are accused of graft, brutality, laziness, incivility, or indifference.

In short, police management is driven more by the constraints on the job than by the goals of the job. You cannot cope with those constraints without understanding them. This may be why some of the biggest changes toward community-oriented policing have occurred in cities where a new chief has come in from the outside with a mandate to shake up a moribund department. Lee Brown brought a community orientation to the Houston Police Department under precisely those circumstances—the reputation of the department was so bad that almost any change would have been regarded as an improvement.

What can we say to the worried police chief who is already running a pretty good department? Start with corruption: For decades police executives and reformers have believed that in order to prevent corruption, you have to centralize control over personnel and discourage intimacy between police officers and citizens. Maybe. But the price one pays for this is very high. For example, many neighborhoods are being destroyed by drug dealers, who hang out on every street corner. The best way to sweep them off the streets is to have patrol officers arrest them for selling drugs and intimidate their customers by parking police cars right next to suspected drug outlets. But some police chiefs forbid their patrol officers to work drug cases, for fear they will be corrupted. When the citizens in these cities see police cars drive past scenes of open drug dealing, they assume the police have been paid off. Efforts to prevent corruption have produced the appearance of corruption.

Police Commissioner Ben Ward, in New York, decided that the price of this kind of anti-corruption strategy was too high. His Operation Pressure Point put scores of police officers on the streets to break up the drug-dealing bazaar. Police corruption is no laughing matter, especially in New York, but some chiefs now believe that it will have to be fought in ways that do not require police officers to avoid contact with people.

Consider the problem of getting police resources and managing political pressures: resources can be justified with statistics, but statistics often become ends in themselves. One police captain we interviewed said that his department was preoccupied with "stacking widgets and counting beans." He asked his superior for permission to take officers out of radio cars and have them work on community problems. The superior agreed but warned that he would be watching to see what happened to "the stats." In the short run the stats—for example, calls answered, average response time—were likely to get worse, but if community problems were solved, they would get better as citizens had fewer incidents to report. The captain worried, however, that he would not be given enough time to achieve this and that the bean counters would cut off his program.

A better way to justify getting resources from the city is to stimulate popular demand for resources devoted to problem-solving. Properly handled, community-oriented policing does generate support for the department. When Newark police officers, under orders from Hubert Williams, then the police director, began stopping city buses and boarding them to enforce city ordinances against smoking, drinking, gambling, and playing loud music, the bus patrons often applauded. When Los Angeles police officers supervised the hauling away of abandoned cars, onlookers applauded. Later, when some of the officers had their time available for problem-solving work cut back, several hundred citizens attended a meeting to complain.

In Flint, Michigan, patrol officers were taken out of their cars and assigned to foot beats. Robert Trojanowicz, a professor at Michigan State University, analyzed the results and found big increases in citizen satisfaction and officer morale, and even a significant drop in crime (an earlier foot-patrol project in Newark had produced equivalent reductions in fear but no reductions in crime). Citizen support was not confined to statements made to pollsters, however. Voters in referenda twice approved tax increases to maintain the foot-patrol system, the second time by a two-to-one margin. New Briarfield tenants unquestionably found satisfaction in the role the police played in getting temporary improvements made on their housing project and getting a commitment for its ultimate replacement. Indeed, when a department experiments with a community-oriented project in one precinct, people in other precincts usually want one too.

POLITICIANS, LIKE POLICE CHIEFS, HEAR THESE VIEWS and respond. But they hear other views as well. One widespread political mandate is to keep the tax rate down. Many police departments are already stretched thin by sharp reductions in spending that occurred in the lean years of the 1970s. Putting *one* additional patrol car on the streets around the clock can cost a quarter of a million dollars or more a year.

Change may seem easier when resources are abundant. Ben Ward could start Operation Pressure Point because he had at his disposal a large number of new officers who could be thrown into a crackdown on street-level drug dealing. Things look a bit different in Los Angeles, where no big increases in personnel are on the horizon. As a result, only eight officers are assigned to the problem-solving Community Mobilization Project in the Wilshire district—an economically and ethnically diverse area of nearly 300,000 residents.

But change does not necessarily require more resources, and the availability of new resources is no guarantee that change will be attempted. One temptation is to try to sell the public on the need for more policemen and decide later how to use them. Usually when that script is followed, either the public turns down the spending increase or the extra personnel are dumped into what one LAPD captain calls the "black hole" of existing commitments, leaving no trace and producing no effects.

What may have an effect is how the police are deployed and managed. An experiment jointly conducted by the Washington, D.C., Police Department and the Police

Foundation showed that if a few experienced officers concentrate on known repeat offenders, the number of serious offenders taken off the streets grows substantially. The Flint and Newark experiences suggest that foot patrols in certain kinds of communities (but not all) can reduce fear. In Houston problem-oriented tactics seem clearly to have heightened a sense of citizen security.

The problem of interagency cooperation may, in the long run, be the most difficult of all. The police can bring problems to the attention of other city agencies, but the system is not always organized to respond. In his book *Neighborhood Services*, John Mudd calls it the "rat problem": "If a rat is found in an apartment, it is a housing inspection responsibility; if it runs into a restaurant, the health department has jurisdiction; if it goes outside and dies in an alley, public works takes over." A police officer who takes public complaints about rats seriously will go crazy trying to figure out what agency in the city has responsibility for rat control and then inducing it to kill the rats.

Matters are almost as bad if the public is complaining about abandoned houses or school-age children who are not in school. The housing department may prefer to concentrate on enforcing the housing code rather than go through the costly and time-consuming process of getting an abandoned house torn down. The school department may have expelled the truant children for making life miserable for the teachers and the other students; the last thing it wants is for the police to tell the school to take the kids back.

All city and county agencies have their own priorities and face their own pressures. Forcing them to cooperate by knocking heads together at the top rarely works; what department heads promise the mayor they will do may bear little relationship to what their rank-and-file employees actually do. From his experiences in New York City government Mudd discovered that if you want agencies to cooperate in solving neighborhood problems, you have to get the neighborhood-level supervisors from each agency together in a "district cabinet" that meets regularly and addresses common concerns. This is not an easy task (for one thing, police district lines often do not match the district boundaries of the school, housing, traffic, and public-works departments), but where it has been tried it has made solving the "rat problem" a lot easier. For example, Mudd reports, such interagency issues as park safety and refuse-laden vacant lots got handled more effectively when the field supervisors met to talk about them than when memos went up the chain of command of one agency and then down the chain of command of another.

COMMUNITY ORGANIZATIONS ALONG THE LINES OF Neighborhood Watch programs may help reduce crime, but we cannot be certain. In particular, we do not know what kinds of communities are most likely to benefit from such programs. A Police Foundation study in Minneapolis found that getting effective community organizations started in the most troubled neighborhoods was very difficult. The costs and benefits of having patrol officers and sergeants influence the delivery of services from other city agencies has never been fully assessed. No way of wresting control of a neighborhood from a street gang has yet been proved effective.

And even if these questions are answered, a police department may still have difficulty accommodating two very different working cultures: the patrol officers and detectives who handle major crimes (murders, rapes, and robberies) and the cops who work on community problems and the seemingly minor incidents they generate. In every department we visited, some of the incident-oriented officers spoke disparagingly of the problem-oriented officers as "social workers," and some of the latter responded by calling the former "ghetto blasters." If a community-service officer seems to get too close to the community, he or she may be accused of "going native." The tension between the two cultures is heightened by the fact that in many departments becoming a detective is regarded as a major promotion, and detectives are often selected from among those officers who have the best record in making major arrests—in other words, from the ranks of the incident-oriented. But this pattern need not be permanent. Promotion tracks can be changed so that a patrol officer, especially one working on community problems, is no longer regarded as somebody who "hasn't made detective." Moreover, some police executives now believe that splitting the patrol force into two units—one oriented to incidents, the other to problems—is unwise. They are searching for ways to give all patrol officers the time and resources for problem-solving activities.

Because of the gaps in our knowledge about both the results and the difficulties of community-oriented policing, no chief should be urged to accept, uncritically, the community-oriented model. But the traditional model of police professionalism—devoting resources to quick radio-car response to calls about specific crime incidents—makes little sense at a time when the principal threats to public order and safety come from *collective*, not individual, sources, and from *problems*, not incidents: from well-organized gangs and drug traffickers, from uncared-for legions of the homeless, from boisterous teenagers taking advantage of their newfound freedom and affluence in congested urban settings.

Even if community-oriented policing does not produce the dramatic gains that some of its more ardent advocates expect, it has indisputably produced one that the officers who have been involved in it immediately acknowledge: it has changed their perceptions of the community. Officer Robin Kirk, of the Houston Police Department, had to be talked into becoming part of a neighborhood fear-reduction project. Once in it, he was converted. In his words, "Traditionally, police officers after about three years get to thinking that everybody's a loser. That's the only people you're dealing with. In community policing you're dealing with the good citizens, helping them solve problems."

Community Policing:
A Practical Guide for Police Officials

Lee P. Brown

Lee P. Brown is Chief of Police in Houston, Texas, and a Research Fellow in the Program in Criminal Justice Policy and Management, John F. Kennedy School of Government, Harvard University.

Like many other social institutions, American police departments are responding to rapid social change and emerging problems by rethinking their basic strategies. In response to problems such as crime, drugs, fear, and urban decay, the police have begun experimenting with new approaches to their tasks.

Among the most prominent new approaches is the concept of community policing. Viewed from one perspective, it is not a new concept; the principles can be traced back to some of policing's oldest traditions. More recently, some of the important principles of community policing have been reflected in particular programs initiated in a variety of places within police departments.

What is new is the idea that community policing is not a particular program within a department, but instead should become the dominant philosophy throughout the department. Exactly what it means for community policing to become a department-wide philosophy and how a police executive can shift an organization from a more traditional philosophy to a community-policing philosophy has been unclear.

Our experience in Houston is beginning to clarify these issues. We are developing a clear, concrete picture of what it means to operate a police department committed to a philosophy of community policing. We have also learned how to manage the process of evolution towards a philosophy of community policing. And we are learning how the basic administrative and managerial systems of the department must be changed to accommodate and encourage community policing. The purpose of this paper is to make this experience available to the field, and to give concrete, operational content to what are otherwise mere abstractions and possibilities.

Author's Note: Special thanks are expressed to Lt. Timothy N. Oettmeier for his initial research, upon which this essay is based.

The origins of community policing

Houston's interest in community policing as an overall philosophy of policing did not spring full-blown from any particular person's mind. Instead, it has emerged from the evolution of police thought. That police leaders are challenging the assumptions they have held for several decades should not be construed as an attempt to debunk all that has worked well for many years. Rather the rethinking should be seen as a sign of police leaders' commitment to ensuring that the strategies they adopt will be viable not only now but in the future as well. Only by refining what works well and scrapping or reshaping what no longer meets the community's needs can police departments face up to the problems and deliver the services that citizens deserve and should expect.

> ❝ . . . *police leaders are challenging the assumptions they have held for several decades* . . . ❞

The evolution to community policing is not complete. What is commonly called traditional policing remains this country's dominant policing style. From its introduction in the 1930's through the 1970's, when it reached its peak of popularity, traditional policing has developed a number of identifying characteristics, such as the following:

- The police are *reactive* to incidents. The organization is driven by calls for police service.

- *Information* from and about the community is

Reprinted from *Perspectives on Policing*, U.S. Department of Justice, September 1989, pp. 1-11.

89

limited. Planning efforts focus on internally generated police data.

- *Planning* is narrow in its focus and centers on internal operations such as policies, procedures, rules, and regulations.

- *Recruitment* focuses on the spirit of adventure rather than the spirit of service.

- *Patrol officers* are restrained in their role. They are not encouraged or expected to be creative in addressing problems and are not rewarded for undertaking innovative approaches.

- *Training* is geared toward the law enforcement role of the police even though officers spend only 15 to 20 percent of their time on such activities.

- *Management* uses an authoritative style and adheres to the military model of command and control.

- *Supervision* is control-oriented as it reflects and reinforces the organization's management style.

- *Rewards* are associated with participating in daring events rather than conducting service activities.

- *Performance evaluations* are based not on outcomes but on activities. The number of arrests made and the number of citations issued are of paramount importance.

- *Agency effectiveness* is based on data—particularly crime and clearance rates—from the FBI's Uniform Crime Reports.

- *Police departments* operate as entities unto themselves, with few collaborative links to the community.

❝ *Traditional policing gave citizens a false sense of security . . . Fortunately for the police profession, the 1970's fostered a full-scale attempt to analyze a host of policing issues.* ❞

For 40 years, traditional policing ostensibly served the public well, primarily because it was seen as a marked improvement over the policing style it had replaced—one that was characterized by negative political control and widespread corruption. Traditional policing gave citizens a false

sense of security about police officers' ability to ensure the safety of the community. That the policing style might not be as effective as it seemed came into sharp focus by the middle 1960's and early 1970's when riots and protests exploded with rampant regularity across America. As citizens and police officials alike watched the scenario unfold, probing questions were raised about the apparent inability of the police to prevent—or at least control—such outbreaks.

By the time the 1960's arrived, it was increasingly clear that both elected officials and the public knew little about the police and their operations. The situation called for decisive action and led to the formation of a number of commissions to examine the events surrounding the riots and to offer recommendations for improving police operations. The commissions' discussions included topics ranging from violence in cities and on college campuses to criminal justice standards and goals.

The attempts to remedy what was seen as an intolerable situation, however, were not confined to meeting-room discussions. Massive amounts of money for police operations and research were funneled through the Federal Law Enforcement Assistance Administration as part of the Government's response to the concern.

Fortunately for the police profession, the 1970's fostered a full-scale attempt to analyze a host of policing issues. The extensive research effort, which continued into the 1980's, produced findings that prompted many thoughtful police professionals to rethink how best to use police resources. Some of the more significant findings are described below:

- *Increasing the number of police officers* does not necessarily reduce the incidence of crime nor increase the proportion of crimes that are solved. The relationship that does exist is between crime and adverse social conditions, such as poverty, illiteracy, illegal drugs, unemployment, population density, and social heterogeneity.

- *Random patrol* produces inconsistent results. It does not necessarily reduce crime nor enhance an officer's chances of apprehending a criminal suspect. It also does not bring the police closer to the public or reduce citizens' fear of crime.

The use of foot patrols (a popular tactic of community policing), on the other hand, has been shown to reduce the fear of crime though not necessarily the actual number of crimes that are committed.

- The assignment of *one officer per patrol car* is just as effective and just as safe as the assignment of two officers per car. The number of crimes committed does not rise, and the number of criminals apprehended does not fall when officers patrol solo. Nor do officers face a greater risk of injury or death when they travel alone.

- *Saturation patrol* reduces crime by temporarily suppressing the illegal activities or displacing them to other areas.

- Seldom do patrol officers encounter a *serious crime in progress.*

- *Rapid response* is not as important as previously believed because there generally is an extended delay before citizens call the police. A rapid police response is important only in the small percentage of cases where a life is being threatened or apprehension of the suspect is possible. Citizens are satisfied instead with a *predetermined response time* upon which they can depend. For incidents that are minor and do not require an officer's presence at the scene, citizens are satisfied with *alternative* methods, such as having the incident report taken over the telephone.

- *Criminal investigations* are not as successful as previously believed. Because crimes are more likely to be resolved if the suspect is apprehended immediately or a witness can supply the person's name, address, or license-plate number or recognizes him in a photograph, successful investigations occur when the suspect is known and when corroborating evidence can be obtained for arrest and prosecution. A key source of information about crimes and criminal suspects is the public.

Additional proof—beyond the reams of data generated by researchers—that time-honored policing strategies were ineffective came in the form of a widespread fear of crime among citizens, record-high crime rates, and record-high prison populations despite the availability of more officers and more funds for law enforcement efforts. As a result, progressive police administrators soon began to question the efficacy of traditional policing strategies. Their review of the situation heralded the beginning of an incremental transition to community-oriented programs and thus the beginning of Phase I of community policing.

Two phases in community policing: from programs to style

The growing awareness of the limitations of the traditional model of policing stimulated police departments across America to experiment with new approaches to reducing crime, stilling fears, improving police community relations, and restoring community confidence in the police. For the most part, these experiments were conceived and executed as discrete programs within traditional departments. That is, the

66 ... begun with fanfare, they produced important results, and then they faded ... 99

programs were typically initiated as a response to a particular problem, involved only a small fraction of the organization, were time-limited, were explicitly identified as experiments, and were subject to particularly close scrutiny by researchers. Often the programs had their own champions and command structures within the departments.

Examples of these programs include the foot patrol experiments in Newark, New Jersey, and Flint, Michigan; the problem-solving project in Newport News, Virginia; the fear reduction programs in Houston, Texas, and Newark; the Community Patrol Officer Program in New York City; the Directed Area Responsibility Team experiment in Houston; the community policing experiment in Santa Ana, California; the Basic Car Plan and Senior Lead-Officer programs in Los Angeles; and the Citizen-Oriented Police Enforcement program in Baltimore County, Maryland. Often these programs had a curious fate. They were begun with fanfare, they produced important results, and then they faded within the departments that had initiated them. These programs, and their fates, constituted Phase I of the field's experience with community policing. They taught two important lessons.

First, the programs taken together pointed toward some new frontiers for policing. They taught the field that if it viewed incidents as emerging from problems, then new avenues for contributing to the solutions of the underlying problems opened up. They taught the field that fear was an important problem in its own right, and there were things that police departments could do to reduce fear quite apart from reducing actual criminal victimization. They taught the field that the community could be an important partner in dealing with the problems of crime, fear, and drugs and that to build that partnership with the community, the police had to find more effective ways of interacting with the community and responding to their needs. These basic ideas provided the intellectual foundations for the emerging new conceptions of community policing.

Second, the ultimate demise of many of the programs showed the difficulty of trying to operate programs that embodied some of the important principles of community policing in the context of organizations whose administrative systems and managerial styles were designed for more traditional models of policing. It seemed clear that if the field as a whole or any police department within the field were to succeed in implementing community policing, it would have to be as an overall philosophy of the department.

3. POLICE

The development of community policing in Houston

Houston took these lessons to heart. We were tempted by the potential of community policing, but worried about the tendency of individual programs to collapse after they had been operating for a while. It was also hard to see how one could move from a department committed to traditional policing to a department that had adopted community policing as a philosophy. Our solution to these problems was to follow the experience of the field and to understand that the implementation of community policing in Houston would also have to have two phases.

Phase I of community policing is the implementation of programs designed to provide the public with meaningful ways to participate in policing efforts. The initial phase does *not* require a complete change in the organization's operating style. Phase II, on the other hand, *does* require the organization to make such a change.

Because Phase I involves only the implementation of individual programs, the systems that support the organization's policing style—such as recruitment, training, performance evaluation, rewards, and discipline—do not change. In other words, the individual *programs* are separate entities that do not involve the entire department or affect the entire community.

> ❝ *Phase II, however, involves more sweeping and more comprehensive changes.* ❞

Phase II, however, involves more sweeping and more comprehensive changes. It is not merely programs that are being implemented—it is the department's *style* that is being revamped. Unlike individual programs, style affects the entire department and the entire community.

The Houston Police Department evolved from Phase I to Phase II over a 5-year period starting in 1982. The department operated under a set of values that emphasized problem solving and collaboration with the community. It also redesigned its patrol beats to reflect natural neighborhood boundaries. Most important, though, were its experiments with a variety of community-oriented programs that resulted in greater community involvement with the department. At the end of the 5-year evolutionary period, the department made an organizational commitment to adopt community policing as its dominant operating style. The department's experiences during Phase I were invaluable and made the transition to Phase II much easier, for the individual programs enabled the department to accomplish the following:[2]

- Break down barriers to change.

- Educate its leaders and rank-and-file members on the merits of community policing.

- Reassure the rank-and-file that the community policing concepts being adopted had not been imported from outside the department but instead were an outgrowth of programs already in place.

- Address problems on a small scale before making the full transition to community policing.

- Reduce the likelihood that members of the department would reject the concepts of community policing as "foreign" or not appropriate for the department and the community.

- Demonstrate to the public and elected officials the benefits of community policing.

- Provide a training ground for community policing concepts and strategies.

- Create advocates among those persons who would become community-policing trainers.

- Demonstrate its willingness to experiment with new ideas.

Based on Houston's experience, it is clear that organizations that have not operated Phase I community policing programs will have to begin Phase II with a clear understanding of what community policing is and how it differs from traditional policing.

Although it is an operating style, community policing also is a *philosophy* of policing that contains several interrelated components. All are essential to the community policing concept and help distinguish it from traditional policing.

Results vs. process. The first component of the community policing philosophy is an orientation toward *problem solving*. Embracing the pioneering work of Herman Goldstein,[3] community policing focuses on *results* as well as process. Incorporated into routine operations are the techniques of problem identification, problem analysis, and problem resolution.

Values. Community policing also relies heavily on the articulation of policing values that incorporate citizen involvement in matters that directly affect the safety and quality of neighborhood life. The culture of the police department therefore becomes one that not only recognizes the merits of community involvement but also seeks to organize and manage departmental affairs in ways that are consistent with such beliefs.

Accountability. Because different neighborhoods have different concerns, desires, and priorities, it is necessary to have an adequate understanding of what is important to a particular neighborhood. To acquire such an understanding, officers must interact with residents on a routine basis and keep them informed of police efforts to fight and prevent neighborhood crime. As the communication continues, a cooperative and mutually beneficial relationship develops between the police and the community. Inherent in this relationship is the requirement that officers keep residents abreast of their activities. This ensures accountability to the community, as well as to the department.

Decentralization. The decentralization of authority and structure is another component of community policing. Roles are changed as the authority to participate in the decisionmaking process expands significantly. The expansion of such authority in turn makes it necessary to alter organizational functions throughout the department.

Power sharing. Responsibility for making decisions is shared by the police and the community after a legitimate *partnership*—one that not only enables but also encourages *active* citizen involvement in policing efforts—between the two groups has been established. *Passive* citizen involvement will not suffice. Active participation is essential because citizens possess a vast amount of information that the police can use to solve and prevent neighborhood crime. Power sharing means that the community is allowed to participate in the decisionmaking process unless the law specifically grants that authority to the police alone.

❝ *Individual neighborhoods are not placed in multiple beats.* ❞

Beat redesign. Beat boundaries are drawn to coincide with natural neighborhood boundaries rather than in an arbitrary fashion that meets the needs of the police department. Individual neighborhoods are not placed in multiple beats. If questions arise about the neighborhood to which a citizen belongs, that person is asked to help the police determine the neighborhood with which he identifies.

Permanent assignments. Under community policing, shift and beat assignments are issued on a permanent, rather than a rotating, basis. This allows the beat officer to become an integral part of the community that he has been assigned to protect. When a beat officer is reassigned to another area, his replacement is required to participate in an orientation period with the outgoing officer. During this time the outgoing officer briefs his replacement on the contacts he has made and the knowledge he has gained over the past several months or

years, thus providing a continuity of service to the community's citizens.

❝ *...beat officers ... must be given the authority to make decisions ...* ❞

Empowerment of beat officers. Rather than simply patrolling the streets, beat officers are encouraged to initiate creative responses to neighborhood problems. To do so, beat officers must become actively involved in the affairs of the community. In addition, they must be given the authority to make decisions as they see fit, based on the circumstances of the situation. This empowerment reflects the trust that police leaders have in their officers' ability to make appropriate decisions and to perform their duties in a professional, productive, and efficient manner.

Investigations. The premise that neighborhood crime is best solved with information provided by residents is an aspect of community policing that makes it necessary to decentralize the investigative function and focus on neighborhood, or area-specific, investigations. Centralized investigations, however, cannot be eliminated entirely as these are needed to conduct pattern- or suspect-specific *citywide* investigations. Both levels, despite their different focus, are responsible for developing a knowledge base about crime in their area and for developing and carrying out strategies designed to resolve crime problems. Investigations under community policing, however, are viewed from a problem-solving perspective.[4]

Supervision and management. Under community policing, the role of persons at all levels within the organization changes. For example, the patrol officer becomes the "manager" of his beat, while the first-line supervisor assumes responsibility for facilitating the problem-solving process by training, coaching, coordinating, and evaluating the officers under him. Management's role is to support the process by mobilizing the resources needed to address citizen concerns and problems. In carrying out this role, management needs to be not only flexible but also willing to allow officers to take necessary and reasonable risks in their efforts to resolve neighborhood problems and concerns.

Training. Also changed under community policing are all aspects of officer training. At the recruit level, cadets are provided information about the complexities and dynamics of the community and how the police fit into the larger picture. Cadet training also enables the future officer to develop community-organizing skills, leadership abilities, and a problem-solving perspective based on the understanding that such efforts will be more effective if departmental and community resources are used in concert.

Supervisory training, on the other hand, is designed to provide the skills needed to facilitate the problem-solving process. This is accomplished by training officers to solve problems, coordinating officers' activities, planning community-organizing activities, and mapping out criminal investigations.

Because they must be the leaders of the changed roles that characterize community policing, management personnel's training includes the further development of leadership skills, including the ability to excite people about the concept of community policing.

> **❝ . . . management personnel's training includes . . . the ability to excite people about the concept of community policing. ❞**

Performance evaluation. With the changed roles for all personnel comes the need for a revised system for evaluating officer performance. Rather than simply counting numbers (e.g., number of citations issued, number of arrests made, number of calls handled), performance quality is based on the officer's ability to solve problems and involve the community in the department's crime-fighting efforts. The criterion then becomes the *absence* of incidents such as criminal offenses, traffic accidents, and repeat calls-for-service.

Managing calls-for-service. Inherent in the community policing philosophy is the understanding that all police resources will be managed, organized, and directed in a manner that facilitates problem solving. For example, rather than directing a patrol car to each request for police service, alternative response methods are used whenever possible and appropriate. Such alternative techniques include the taking of incident reports over the telephone, by mail, or in person at police facilities; holding lower-priority calls; and having officers make appointments with an individual or a group. The result is more time available for officers to engage in problem-solving and community-organizing activities that lead to improvements in the quality of neighborhood life. Equally important, officers will be able to remain in their beats and handle those calls that require an on-scene response.

> **❝ Officers now are expected to develop innovative ways of solving neighborhood problems. ❞**

The Houston Police Department is committed to community policing and is in the process of implementing it with the name of "neighborhood-oriented policing." It is a policing *style* that is responsive to the needs of the community and involves the redesigning of roles and functions for all departmental personnel.

One significant role change is that of the beat officer. No longer is his job structured solely around random patrols and rapid response to routine calls-for-service. Officers now are expected to develop innovative ways of solving neighborhood problems. Inherent in this expanded role is the need for increased communication and interaction with the people who live or work in the officer's beat.

For more than a full year now, the department has been engaged in its version of community policing, resulting in a wealth of experience and insights that can be used to construct a definition of community policing. By definition then, community policing is *an interactive process between the police and the community to mutually identify and resolve community problems.*

Inherent in this definition is a rather dramatic change in the traditional orientation of the police toward the public. The formal separation of the police from the public no longer suffices. What is called for under community policing is the formation of a union between officers and citizens mutually committed to improving the quality of neighborhood life. The formation of such a partnership requires the police to develop appropriate management systems, use available resources more effectively, and work with the community to resolve problems and prevent and control crime.

When considered in light of the necessary reorientation of management attitudes toward the public, community policing also can be thought of as a *management philosophy.* As such, community policing provides a conceptual framework for directing an array of departmental functions and requires management personnel to do the following:

- Ensure cooperative interaction among various departmental functions.

- Ensure collaborative interaction between officers and citizens so that a consensus can be reached on what needs to be done to improve the quality of neighborhood life.

- Integrate the desires and expectations of citizens with the actions taken by the police to identify and address conditions that have a negative effect on the quality of neighborhood life.

- Ensure that all actions are designed to produce planned results.

- Begin addressing a number of organizational issues

(such as determining the exact nature of management's responsibilities, deciding which activities best enable management to carry out its responsibilities, and establishing an accountability system for monitoring progress and documenting results).

The Houston experience has shown that community policing is a better, smarter, and more cost-effective means of using police resources and that a new culture in which officers, supervisors, and managers strive to become a part *of* and not apart *from* the community is needed as well. These findings serve to illustrate the dual nature of community policing. That is, it embodies both an operational philosophy and a management philosophy, and each benefits not only the police but also the community. The benefits to the community are as follows:[5]

- *A commitment to crime prevention.* Unlike traditional policing, which focuses on the development of efficient means of *reacting* to incidents, community policing strives to reaffirm Sir Robert Peel's premise that the basic mission of the police is to *prevent* crime and disorder.

- *Public scrutiny of police operations.* Because citizens will be involved with the police, they will be exposed to the "what," "why," and "how" of police work. Such involvement is almost certain to prompt critical examinations and discussions about the responsiveness and efficiency of police operations in addressing the community's problems.

- *Accountability to the public.* Until the advent of community policing, officers were accountable for their actions only to police management. Now officers also will be accountable to the public with whom they have formed a cooperative partnership. Because citizens will be involved in activities such as strategic planning, tactic implementation, and policy development, police personnel will need to become more aware of and more concerned about the consequences of their actions.

- *Customized police service.* Because police services will be localized, officers will be required to increase their responsiveness to neighborhood problems and citizens' concerns. As police-citizen partnerships are formed and nurtured, the two groups will be better equipped to work together to identify and address problems that affect the quality of neighborhood life. For their part, police officers will develop a sense of obligation or commitment to resolving neighborhood problems. The philosophy underlying traditional policing does not provide for such a commitment.

- *Community organization.* The degree to which the community is involved in police efforts to address neighborhood problems has a significant bearing on the effectiveness of those efforts. In other words, the suc-

cess of any crime-prevention strategy or tactic depends on the police and citizens working in concert—not on one or the other carrying the entire load alone. Citizens therefore must learn what they can do to help themselves and their neighbors. The police, in turn, should take an active role in helping citizens achieve that objective.

The benefits of community policing to the police are as follows:[6]

- *Greater citizen support.* As citizens spend more time working with the police, they learn more about the police function. Experience has shown that as citizens' knowledge of the police function increases, their respect for the police increases as well. This increased respect, in turn, leads to greater support for the police. Such support is important not only because it helps officers address issues of community safety but also because it cultivates the belief that the police honestly care about the people they serve and are willing to work with all citizens in an attempt to address their concerns.

- *Shared responsibility.* Historically the police have accepted the responsibility for resolving the problem of crime in the community. Under community policing, however, citizens develop a sense of *shared* responsibility. They come to understand that the police alone cannot eradicate crime from the community—that they themselves must play an active role in the crime-fighting effort.

- *Greater job satisfaction.* Because officers are able to resolve issues and problems within a reasonable amount of time, they see the results of their efforts fairly quickly. The net result for the officer is enhanced job satisfaction.

- *Better internal relationships.* Communication problems among units and shifts have been a long-standing problem in police agencies. Because community policing focuses on problem solving and accountability, it also enhances communication and cooperation among the various segments of the department that are mutually responsible for addressing neighborhood problems. This shared responsibility facilitates interaction and cooperative relationships among the different groups.

- *Support for organizational change.* The implementation of community policing necessitates a change in traditional policing roles and in turn a change in functional responsibilities. Both modifications require a restructuring of the department's organizational structure to ensure the efficient integration of various functions, such as patrol and investigations. The changes that are needed include new management systems, new training curriculums and delivery mechanisms, a new performance-evaluation system, a new disciplinary process, a new reward system, and new ways of managing calls-for-service.

Questions asked and answered

In their book *Community Policing: Issues and Practices Around the World,* David Bayley and Jerome Skolnick urge police leaders to be cautious about the success of community policing. It is advice well taken. The process of going from a traditional style of policing to a community-oriented style is not an easy task. It therefore is essential to identify, acknowledge, and address any obstacles or legitimate concerns that might impede the transition. Some of the questions most often raised about community policing are discussed below.[7]

- *Is community policing social work?*

Community policing calls for an expansion of the role of the police in that it focuses on problems from the citizen's point of view. Experience has shown that the concerns of citizens often are different from what the police would say they are. For example, before listening to citizens' concerns became routine, officers assumed that the public worried most about major crimes such as rape, robbery, and burglary. After talking with the people who live and work in their beat, officers found that the community's main concerns were quality-of-life issues such as abandoned cars and houses, loud noises, and rowdy youngsters.

It is for this reason—the need to address citizen concerns—that the role of the police has been expanded. This is no

> 66 *Rather than being soft on crime, community policing is a more effective method . . .* 99

meant to imply, however, that the police are expected to solve the problems by themselves. On the contrary, it means that the police should be able to do at least one of two things: mobilize the community to solve the problem (e.g., organize a neighborhood clean-up program) or enlist the services of the appropriate agency to address the problem (e.g., the city Public Works Department to clean away debris).

Concerns that such activities are akin to social work are ill-founded. The police officer's expanded role does not even come close to meeting the definition of social work. As a profession, social work is an ongoing and often long-term relationship between the social worker and the client. This is

in contrast to the *usually* short-term, problem-focused relationship that develops under community policing.

- *Will community policing result in less safe neighborhoods?*

By any standard, the police working alone have been unable to control crime effectively. Experience has shown that increased citizen involvement results in more efficient crime-control efforts. The success of Neighborhood Watch groups is but one example of the effectiveness of making crime fighting a joint effort. Other programs, such as Crime Stoppers, have led to the solution of many serious offenses. Because community policing includes the public as a full partner in the provision of crime-prevention and crime-fighting services, it stands to reason that public safety will *increase* rather than decrease.

- *Will officers be reluctant to enforce the law under community policing?*

Among the tenets of community policing is the need to develop a close relationship between beat officers and the people who live and work in that area. In most neighborhoods only a small percentage of the population commits illegal acts. The goal of community policing is to become a part of the law-abiding majority and thereby develop a partnership to effectively deal with the law-violating minority.

Experience has shown that if police work closely with the "good" citizens, the "bad" ones are either displaced or driven out of the area. It therefore is incorrect to suggest that as the police develop close relationships with the citizens in their beat, law violators will not be arrested.

- *Is community policing soft on crime?*

The police always will have as one of their primary roles the enforcement of laws. Under community policing, police officers not only will have an expanded skills-base at their disposal, but they also will have access to a previously untapped resource—input from members of the community. The two resources together provide officers with a most effective means of enforcing the laws and should eliminate any concerns that community policing will weaken officers' ability to perform this task. Rather than being soft on crime, community policing is a more effective method for fighting crime.

> 66 *Will community policing result in unequal services to minority communities?* 99

Because community policing calls for the tailoring of police services to meet the unique needs of each neighborhood, minority communities can expect to receive better, rather than unequal, services. This is not to imply that one community will receive preferential treatment at the expense of another. Rather, it means that each community will receive services that are *appropriate* to its particular problems, concerns, and priorities.

● *Will community policing result in police corruption?*

Experience has not shown nor even suggested that community policing leads to corruption. For corruption to arise, there must be a culture ripe for its development, and such certainly is not the case with community policing and its emphasis on police officer professionalism, expanded discretionary decisionmaking authority, trust in officers' sound judgment and good intentions, and officers' accountability to law-abiding citizens. This does not mean, however, that the police can ignore their responsibility to detect and respond to corruptive influences and incidents should they occur.

● *Will access to community policing be distributed fairly?*

This question would be appropriate only if community policing were no more than a program; however, it is an overall operating *style* and philosophy of policing. Nowhere among the tenets of community policing is there anything that would, in and of itself, result in the unequal distribution of services between the poor and the affluent. By its very nature, community policing calls for the appropriate delivery of services to all neighborhoods.

● *Will community policing require more resources?*

Because community policing is an operating style and not a new program, no additional officers are needed. More pertinent is the issue of how the agency's resources will be used. Experience has shown that community policing is a more cost-effective means of using available resources than is traditional policing for two reasons: community participation in the crime-control function expands the amount of available resources, and the solving of problems (rather than responding again and again to the same ones) makes for a more efficient deployment of combined police and community resources.

● *Is community policing antitechnology?*

The use of high-technology equipment and applications is essential to the efficient practice of community policing. Without high technology, officers would find it difficult to provide the level and quality of services the community

deserves. Computer-aided dispatching, computers in patrol cars, automated fingerprint systems, and on-line offense-reporting systems are but a few examples of the pervasiveness of technology in agencies that practice community policing.

● *Will older officers resist community policing?*

Experience with both community-oriented *programs* and community policing as an operating *style* has shown that older officers are *more likely* to accept community policing than are younger officers. The maturation that comes with age plays a significant role in older officers' greater willingness to adopt the new policing style. Research has shown that younger officers tend to become police officers because they are looking for adventure. As officers grow older, they become less interested in action and more interested in providing services.

Conclusion

As an operating style, community policing evolves and exists in two phases. Phase I involves the implementation of community-oriented programs designed to improve the ability of the police to address problems such as crime, drugs, fear, and urban decay. These programs, however, are not intended to involve all members of the department or all members of the community. Phase I also is marked by a continuity in the organization's operating style and the systems that support it.

❝ *Because community policing becomes the dominant service-delivery style, the corresponding support systems must change as well.* ❞

Phase II involves significant changes in the police mission and the organization's operational and management philosophies. Because community policing becomes the dominant service-delivery style, the corresponding support systems must change as well.

The transition, however, is not instantaneous; rather, it is evolutionary. An institution that traditionally has delivered services on the basis of time-honored conventional wisdom cannot be expected to easily or quickly adopt a new method of operating.

The phase of community policing in which an agency finds itself should not be used as a criterion for evaluating the agency. Experience has shown, however, that implementing Phase II is easier if the agency has had experience with individual community-oriented programs.

3. POLICE

Because community policing is relatively new as a style of policing, questions have been raised about its effectiveness. Any doubts, however, should be put to rest. Experience has shown that community policing as a dominant policing style is a better, more efficient, and more cost-effective means of using police resources. In the final analysis, community policing is emerging as the most appropriate means of using police resources to improve the quality of life in neighborhoods throughout the country.

Notes

1. Jerome H. Skolnick and David H. Bayley, *The New Blue Line: Police Innovations in Six American Cities,* New York, The Free Press, 1986: 4–5.

2. See for example, Lee P. Brown et al., *Developing Neighborhood Oriented Policing in the Houston Police Department,* Arlington, Virginia, International Association of Chiefs of Police, 1988; and Timothy N. Oettmeier and William H. Bieck, *Developing a Policing Style for Neighborhood Oriented Policing:* Executive Session #1, The Houston Police Department, February 1987.

3. Herman Goldstein, "Improving Policing: A Problem-Oriented Approach," *Journal of Crime and Delinquency* 25 (April 1979): 236–258.

4. Timothy N. Oettmeier and William H. Bieck, *Integrating Investigative Operations Through Neighborhood Oriented Policing:* Executive Session #2, The Houston Police Department, January 1989.

5. Jerome H. Skolnick and David H. Bayley, *Community Policing: Issues and Practices Around the World,* Washington, D.C., National Institute of Justice, May 1988: 67–70.

6. Ibid.: 70–73.

7. Ibid.: 81–87.

Editor of this series is Susan Michaelson, Program in Criminal Justice Policy and Management, John F. Kennedy School of Government, Harvard University.

Points of view or opinions expressed in this publication are those of the author and do not necessarily represent the official position or policies of the U.S. Department of Justice or of Harvard University.

Police, Hard Pressed in Drug War, Are Turning to Preventive Efforts

ROBERT REINHOLD

Special to The New York Times

LOS ANGELES, Dec. 27 — Tactics are changing on the police lines of America's drug war. Frustrated by the overwhelming numbers of drug offenders and an almost infinite supply of illicit drugs, more and more police officers are talking like social workers, arguing that the real solution lies in preventing young people from getting involved with drugs in the first place.

"A year and a half ago we were talking about a laundry list of tough-on-crime legislation," said John B. Emerson, chief deputy city attorney of Los Angeles, who leads a legislative subcommittee of the Police Officers Association of Los Angeles County. "But the focus of our panel now is very much on preventive measures. There's been a very dramatic shift."

In one city after another, there is acknowledgment that conventional police methods have reached their limits, that on their own they cannot solve the drug problem and that the police should have a more direct role in attacking the underlying social causes of drug abuse.

"You hear police chiefs saying things they didn't say a few years ago," said Patrick V. Murphy, a former New York City Police Commissioner who is now director of police policy for the United States Conference of Mayors. "Like: 'Do I want to lose a cop in a raid on a crack house when there are 100 other crack houses in my city? Let's talk about alternatives.'"

Police Chief Isaac Fulwood of Washington said in an interview: "Our best efforts have not stemmed the flow of drugs. We have to do other things." Chief Charles A. Gruber of Shreveport, La., said in recent Congressional testimony: "For all our policing, we understand that law enforcement is not the solution to the problem of drugs in our society." And Sheriff Sherman Block of Los Angeles County, discussing what he regards as a new police role in reducing the demand for drugs, said, "We have come to the conclusion that while many responsibilities belong to

'It's time to look at the beginning of the pipeline,' a law official says.

other disciplines, if they are not being adequately carried out, at some point we'll have to deal with the failure."

The search for alternatives comes against a backdrop of growing strain on police departments, courts and prisons throughout the country.

Sharp Rise in Slayings

The number of homicides has nearly tripled in just four years in Washington, and more than half the slayings now are considered to be drug-related. In Los Angeles County, the District Attorney's Office is predicting 515 slayings by local drug gangs this year, as opposed to 212 in 1984. Forty percent of the 138 people killed in Kansas City, Mo., this year were listed as drug-related, as were 25 percent of the 96 slayings reported in Columbus, Ohio, which never bothered to record such statistics before this year.

Narcotics officers find that the people they once worked to arrest are often quickly released from overcrowded prisons. New York City jails now hold more than 14,000 drug offenders, seven times as many as in 1980. Thee were 89,112 drug arrests in New York last year, up from 18,563 in 1980.

Nationally, the Justice Department says, arrests for drug abuse violations have increased from 162,177 in 1968, or 112 per 100,000 people, to 850,034 last year, or 450 per 100,000 people. And police department overtime budgets, substantially linked to the drug problem, have increased, too. In Los Angeles, they rose from $6.8 million four years ago to $18.5 million for the current fiscal year.

It is the discouragement brought on by these kinds of statistics, along with the lack of manifest results from traditional police methods, that is causing many police officers and officials to believe they themselves have to help try to reduce the drug demand that lies behind the high drug and crime rate. Most of the alternative approaches are still experimental and in the early stages, but they are being seriously tried in thousands of cities.

A Variety of Approaches

Police officers and sheriffs are going into elementary schools in many cities to teach children how to be more assertive and to manage stress, skills needed to resist the lure of drug pushers. The Shreveport Police Department is trying to set up seven centers in poor areas to help young people find prenatal care, jobs and schooling. And in Washington, the police are working with city parks to develop after-school drug-prevention programs.

One program that is serving as a model for other urban police departments is called Drug Abuse Resistance Education, or Dare, set up by the Los Angeles Police Department and the Los Angeles Unified School District. Specially trained police officers go into fifth- and sixth-grade classrooms to give 17 lessons intended to help children learn to resist drugs.

The Dare program has now been adopted by 2,000 localities in 49 states, three foreign countries and Department of Defense schools abroad, reaching an estimated three million children this year.

New York City has a similar program, the School Program to Educate and Control Drug Abuse, in which about 100 police officers are now teaching in nearly all the community school districts.

The other day 37 police officers in Dare programs from other parts of California and from departments in Alabama and Minnesota gathered in a hotel conference room in the San Fernando Valley here for instruction in changing hardened street ways into caring teacher skills.

Police Officers as Teachers

It is hardly conventional police training. "We assist them to remove the macho image and become teachers," said Officer Harreld D. Webster, a Dare mentor, who said the program, once dismissed by many officers as the "kiddie cops," has gained respect.

The police "students" heard Officer Mario J. Valdez talk about public speaking skills and listened intently as Bernice Medinnis, a retired Los Angeles teacher, demonstrated teaching techniques that would help create what she called "very positive expectations" among all children.

The police-education programs in California cost an average of $11.94 per student annually, for officers' salaries, school coordination and materials.

Such programs, police officials say, are far cheaper than incarceration. "In Los Angeles alone last year we made over 50,000 narcotics-related arrests, more than all the jail beds in California," said Lieut. Larry Goebel, assistant commanding officer of the Dare program. "If we put them all in jail we'd fill all the beds in Califonia just from L.A. So this is a bargain. Our philosophy is pay me now or pay me later. It's cheaper to pay me now."

Some Resistance Found

Among those in the training session were two officers from Huntsville, Ala., Lonnie Stone and Thomas Dolleslager. They said that while the approach has strong support from their Police Chief, Richard V. Ottman, there was some resistance within the ranks, partly because the program diverted scarce manpower from enforcement and partly because the vice section believes the problem is best handled by more arrests. There has also been resistance from some educators, although most agree that police officers add a measure of valuable credibility.

In Washington, the Police Department is now working with the Fairline Coalition, a group of citizens that works on crime prevention and with local park workers to give children controlled supervision and drug awareness activities after school.

"We've got to expand those programs," Chief Fulwood said. "We target kids who are high risk and get them before they get into criminal activity. It's cheaper and makes more sense."

The focus on children is a theme that runs through the new police programs, and as such, coming from once-hardnosed police officers, it may carry special weight with Congress on financing social programs.

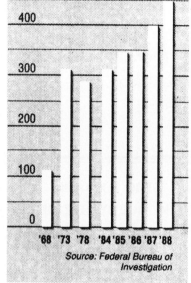

Arrested on Drug Charges

Total arrests per 100,000 population in the U.S. for the sale, manufacture or possession of drugs.

Source: Federal Bureau of Investigation

The New York Times/Dec. 28, 1989

"The most eloquent arguments for engaging on the demand-reduction front come from police officers," Senator Pete Wilson, a moderate Republican who is running for Governor of California, said in an interview.

The District Attorney's Office in Los Angeles County recently began a truancy intervention program, on the theory that truancy is an early indication of drug problems and crime. Truant children and their parents now meet with lawyers and hearing officers from the prosecutor's office, who explain the hard legal consequences of truancy.

"Our premise is that truancy is the first indication of criminal behavior," said Michael E. Tranbarger, assistant director of the bureau of special operations, which also prosecutes gang crimes. "We decided it was time to look at the beginning of the pipeline instead of concentrating all our resources on the other end, when it's too late."

But police officials say they are strapped for resources. The Shreveport Police Department, which has 358 officers, is 50 officers short. And, like many colleagues, Chief Gruber has been lobbying for more Federal aid for drug enforcement.

But he also beats the drums for what he calls "problem-oriented policing," by which the police intervene directly to mend social ills. He has applied for a $3 million Federal grant to set up seven "community action" centers in Cedar Grove and other low-income parts of the city to help young people apply for jobs and develop coping skills.

Dubious About More Work

Many departments are strapped to the limits, and some remain dubious about taking on more work.

"We don't have time for the education and rehabilitation part," said Lieut. George Gavito of the Cameron County Sheriff's Department in Brownsville, Tex., a major entry point for illicit drugs on the Mexican border. "Somebody else has to worry about that part. I don't think law enforcement should have anything to do with it. It should be handled by the schools and clinics."

Still, fewer and fewer law-enforcement officers are expressing such views; indeed, officers are speaking out philosophically about their reasons for the shifting tactics. What the police have been doing until now in the drug war, said Earl Cronin, president of the Policemen's Association in Washington, is "like trying to drain the ocean with a teaspoon."

In testifying before the House Select Committee on Narcotics Abuse and Control last month, Chief Gruber, who is president of the International Association of Chiefs of Police, said: "We can certainly add more police, make more arrests, build more jails and increase our capacity to treat addicts. However, this won't solve our problem if the inmates who come out of prison and the addicts who come out of treatment centers do not have the skills and/or the opportunities and wherewithal to lead productive lives."

Few police officers advocate legalizing illicit drugs, as Federal District Judge Robert W. Sweet urged recently in New York, but some sound similar notes in justifying their efforts to broaden police responsibility.

Chief Fulwood of Washington is representative: "We must recognize the socioeconomic side of this. We've got to have better demand-reduction programs, better treatment facilities. We must build families and communities that have values about murder — that it is not acceptable conduct. When a 13-year-old kid can murder somebody, blow his brains out, and then go home and sleep, there's something wrong."

The abortion protesters and the police

John Leo

After people from Operation Rescue invade and occupy an abortion clinic, they frequently protest about police brutality. These complaints are almost never taken seriously. Op-R is a pariah group, shunned even by the National Right to Life Committee. Its members are instructed to turn each "rescue" into a media event, so journalists, who are generally unsympathetic in the first place, tend to assume that cries about brutal treatment are just part of the show. In Pittsburgh, for instance, female protesters said they were stripped, fondled and kicked between the legs, but reporters didn't believe it, so nothing much came of the complaints.

This column is about allegations of a truly brutal police response to an Operation Rescue blitz. I interviewed 17 of the 261 arrested at the Summit Women's Center in West Hartford, Conn., on June 17, 1989. Here are three of their voices.

■ Lillian Loughlin, mother of 12, grandmother of 3, was a peaceful anti-abortion picket outside: "I noticed that the police officers had all removed their badges and name tags. I asked one, "Where are your badges?" But all I got was stony silence. A minute later, we heard a bullhorn. The police wanted us to move to an outside sidewalk farther away. We turned to walk where they wanted us to, but I guess we weren't moving fast enough. I was shoved ruthlessly from behind with a riot stick and knocked to the ground flat on my stomach. My husband came up and said, 'Hey, get off my wife.' Three policemen jumped him and put him in handcuffs. Someone straddled me from behind and took my hands, one at a time, and twisted them violently behind me. I screamed in pain. This wasn't part of handcuffing me. He did it to inflict pain. I got a glimpse of him, and it was the same policeman I had asked about the badges. It was not just him. There were other sadists, too. They were banging heads unnecessarily, getting people onto the bus, then purposely banging people against the iron seat railings as

they went down the aisle. They dragged me off the bus and threw me on the floor of the station. I was in shock and pain and trying to get myself under control. I was dragged into another room and left there face down for a half-hour or so. One of the other prisoners said, 'Your hands—they're all purple.' They had swollen to twice their normal size, and I thought they were broken. It turned out later that they weren't, but my doctor said the tissue damage was as serious as a break. I was in terrible pain, and an officer said, 'Stop faking.' Finally, the booked me and pushed me out a side door, gently this time, and I sat down on the grass trying to figure out what had happened. Finally, a stranger came along and helped me up. They never gave my husband his medicine for high blood pressure, and he never got his glasses back. That's $125, and we had to get a ride home because he couldn't see. Then I got a registered letter naming me as a conspirator in a RICO suit filed by West Hartford against Operation Rescue. Why am I a racketeer? I didn't break any laws. I gave my name, moved along when they said and cooperated in every way. I come from a police family. My father and two brothers were New York City cops. I never believed it when blacks and protesters yelled police brutality. Now, I'm inclined to listen."

■ Dean Gavaris, a born-again Christian from New Jersey, was one of those who occupied the clinic: "At the courthouse, one woman was dragged along the floor by her hair. A police officer kicked a handcuffed man hard in the ribs, for no reason, right in front of the judge, and the judge made him stop. A half-hour after the judge started, I heard terrible screaming. I remembered that sound for weeks on end. They were bringing people down some steps into the court behind the judge, and the bodies coming down sounded like basketballs thumping downstairs. These people were in bad shape. One of them was a priest. His face was totally black, with marks all over. They had roughed him up pretty good. They cut one guy's jacket open to see if he'd had a heart attack, but it was just his shoulder in agony from the pain holds. Another guy flipped out. He didn't know where he was or who he was. If he was acting, he deserved an Oscar. But he wasn't acting. His eyeballs were rolling around in his head.

"At Enfield State Prison, a guard accidentally scratched my eye. The injury was pretty serious, a torn cornea, so they sent me out of the prison three times to see an ophthalmologist. I was manacled hand and foot for 2 hours each time. The way they did it, with my arms crossed in front of my body, it hurt my shoulder more than ever. They never did treat the shoulder. A doctor said it was some sort of deep shoulder pain that would go away in three weeks. But it's still here. Thirteen months later and I still can't lift my arm without pain. I can't even throw a soccer ball to my kid."

■ Catherine Jersey, a typesetter for a weekly paper in Washingtonville, N.Y.: "I was hurt in the April 1 rescue, but it was only nerve damage to my wrists. My friend Bill Waugh has it worse. His right wrist and forearm constantly go into spasms because of what they did to him. But mine was mild. It hurts when it rains or when the air conditioning is on, and I have trouble wearing a watch, but it's nothing to complain about. But on June 17, they really hurt me. A policeman said, 'Oh, here's the one with the bad heart.' On April 1, I had told them I had a heart problem, and they remembered me. They pounced on me, cuffed me from behind and raised me up with one riot stick under my arms and another under my abdomen. I started to hemorrhage. There was severe bleeding, and I was held three days with no medical attention. In the courtroom I was going to give my name and make bail, but I got angry. I figured they should pay the medical bills. I showed the judge my clothes, all covered with blood, and demanded medical care. They took me to Niantic Prison, and I ended up having a D & C. There was gynecological damage, and I still have problems."

Genuine tones. There are many such horror stories. Diane Holland, an epileptic, says she warned police for hours that her shoulder pain and lack of sleep were likely to bring on a seizure if her husband, a minister, was not allowed in with her medication. Later, she was rushed to a hospital after apparently suffering two grand-mal seizures. One or two tales, featuring improbably time-consuming and bizarre cruelty, were hard to believe. But many of the stories I heard seemed genuine. There are internal touches that help induce belief. Loughlin says she is not a frail grandmother-martyr but a robust woman of 64. Jersey describes her April 1 damage as nothing to complain about. And the medical records of both are consistent with their accounts. Jersey's physician, Bernard Nathanson, a well-known pro-life gynecologist, confirms that she had menstrual disruption and alarming bleeding leading to a D & C within a few days after her release.

But there is another side. West Hartford Police Chief Robert McCue says Lillian Loughlin was part of a crowd that refused to move after 20 minutes of warnings and was pressing back against police at the time of the arrests. Police say that the priest with the allegedly blackened face—the Rev. Norman Weslin—simply suffered a facial bruise during arrest by flailing about, holding onto furniture and other protesters when everyone else simply went limp. The chief says he thinks Holland faked the seizures and adds that police cannot allow an unidentified man to supply unmarked medicine for a prisoner who refuses to give her name. The other stories, he says, are either false or colorfully embroidered to attract press sympathy.

In the absence of disinterested witnesses, some things are almost impossible to sort out. Take the strappado, Operation Rescue's name for a dangerous and very painful hold formed by two policemen crossing and raising their nightsticks under wrists cuffed from behind. Is this an intentional and common hold, as Op-R maintains, or is it a position rescuers slump down into for the benefit of photographers and reporters, as the police allege?

The police videotape shows officers yanking hard on plastic cuffs that seem quite tight enough, but the police say that many of the rescuers had coated their wrists with maple syrup and raw eggs to make cuffing difficult. The tape shows no instances of horrible mistreatment, but a good deal of kneeling on the backs and heads of people who were offering no resistance, simply going limp. At one point an arrested man asks, "Who is the arresting officer?" And Chief McCue responds, "One of them is the guy with his knee on your chin . . ." and then gives his name as the person to be sued. He now says that this comment was an attempt to lighten a tense situation with humor.

Police were under a good deal of pressure, dealing with rescuers out to shut down a clinic for the day and to flood and perhaps break the criminal-justice system. Many policemen clearly expressed concern about avoiding injuries. But not everything went by the book. Badges and name tags came off. Cameras of onlookers were seized and film exposed. One woman said a cop produced a clipper and cut the strap of her video camera, causing it to break on the ground. Out-of-town reporters who had no connection with the invasion were arrested. Protesters were left for hours in painful plastic cuffs that tighten with movement and tend to cut off circulation. For at least two days, those arrested were not allowed phone calls or access to attorneys. Gavaris says he was allowed his first phone call on the fifth day and used it to tell his wife where he was. When they were finally arraigned on the third day, the courtroom was closed to the public, and police were allowed to use pain holds on prisoners right in front of one judge, though another judge sharply forbade it.

Local praise. As often happens after disputed police performances, the West Hartford Town Council passed a resolution praising the police for their actions, and the local newspaper, the *Hartford Courant*, ran an editorial hailing police for their professionalism and restraint.

"Operation Rescue is not popular. Its tactics breed anger, polarization and contempt for law. But it's very much like a civil-rights sit-in."

Beyond the dispute over the facts of what happened in West Hartford, there is the policy of issue of whether pain-compliance holds should be used on nonviolent passive resisters. Operation Rescue is not popular, and I think its tactics breed anger, polarization and disrespect for law. But remember that the structure of an Op-R occupation is very much like that of a civil-rights sit-in. Would we want pain holds used on Martin Luther King, or would we shout about on-the-spot torture doled out to stop an unpopular political movement by extralegal means?

Pain holds were invented to cope with dangerous criminals resisting arrest. Under the law, going limp constitutes resistance, so police are free to twist and bend body parts painfully to get arrestees to come along. But it's a dubious technique, ignored by many departments, which simply cart protesters off or put them on stretchers.

Larry Williams, a reporter for the *Hartford Courant*, says he went to the police academy in Meriden and asked an instructor to show him a pain hold. "The holds are awesomely painful," Williams said. "The instructor put my arm behind my back and twisted it a little bit, and I was in agony. I would have walked off a cliff to avoid that kind of pain. But that was only the barest hint of what they gave people at the clinic. If my arm was sore for two days after a little demonstration twist, I can believe that those people are still feeling the effects a year later."

My own feeling is that yearlong pain should not be part of the arrest of nonviolent protesters, particularly political ones. Punishment should come from the courts, not the cops. This is not a banana republic. This is America.

The Judicial System

The courts are an equal partner in the American justice system. Just as the police have the responsibility of guarding our liberties by enforcing the law, the courts play an important role in defending these liberties by applying the law. The courts are where civilized "wars" are fought, individual rights are protected, and disputes are peacefully settled.

The articles in this unit discuss several issues concerning the judicial process. Ours is an adversary system of justice, and the protagonists, the State and the defendant, are usually represented by counsel. The articles "Public Defenders" and "The Prosecutor as a 'Minister of Justice' " discuss the roles of these participants and raise certain ethical issues.

In "Pretrial Diversion: Promises We Can't Keep," it is argued that the system of pretrial diversion is not working. In "The Myth of the General Right to Bail," it is alleged that the courts are letting too many dangerous offenders out on bail. "Convicting the Innocent" raises questions about the fairness of the judicial system.

The Supreme Court of the United States is the ultimate forum for interpreting the Constitution and guaranteeing our rights. In "When Criminal Rights Go Wrong," it is contented that the Court has gone too far in protecting the rights of the accused while in "Defendants Lose As Police Power is Broadened," decisions of the 1989–90 term are reviewed and the author feels that the Court has diminished defendants' rights.

Looking Ahead: Challenge Questions

Should bail be denied dangerous offenders?

Is the current Supreme Court of the United States too biased in favor of law enforcement?

Unit 4

The Judicial Process: Prosecutors and Courts

The courts participate in and supervise the judicial process

The courts have several functions in addition to deciding whether laws have been violated

The courts—
• settle disputes between legal entities (persons, corporations, etc.)
• invoke sanctions against law violations
• decide whether acts of the legislative and executive branches are constitutional.

In deciding about violations of the law the courts must apply the law to the facts of each case. The courts affect policy in deciding individual cases by handing down decisions about how the laws should be interpreted and carried out. Decisions of the appellate courts are the ones most likely to have policy impact.

Using an arm of the State to settle disputes is a relatively new concept

Until the Middle Ages disputes between individuals, clans, and families, including those involving criminal acts, were handled privately. Over time, acts such as murder, rape, robbery, larceny, and fraud came to be regarded as crimes against the entire community, and the State intervened on its behalf. Today in the United States the courts handle both civil actions (disputes between individuals or organizations) and criminal actions.

An independent judiciary is a basic concept of the U.S. system of government

To establish its independence and impartiality, the judiciary was created as a separate branch of government coequal to the executive and the legislative branches. Insulation of the courts from political pressure is attempted through—

• the separation of powers doctrine
• established tenure for judges
• legislative safeguards
• the canons of legal ethics.

Courts are without the power of enforcement. The executive branch must enforce their decisions. Furthermore, the courts must request that the legislature provide them with the resources needed to conduct their business.

Each State has a system of trial and appeals courts

Generally, State court systems are organized according to three basic levels of jurisdiction:

• **Courts of limited and special jurisdiction** are authorized to hear only less serious cases (misdemeanors and/or civil suits that involve small amounts of money) or to hear special types of cases such as divorce or probate suits. Such courts include traffic courts, municipal courts, family courts, small claims courts, magistrate courts, and probate courts.

• **Courts of general jurisdiction**, also called major trial courts, are unlimited in the civil or criminal cases they are authorized to hear. Almost all cases originate in the courts of limited or special jurisdiction or in courts of general jurisdiction. Most serious criminal cases are handled by courts of general jurisdiction.

• **Appellate courts** are divided into two groups, intermediate appeals courts, which hear some or all appeals that are subject to review by the court of last resort, and courts of last resort, which have jurisdiction over final appeals from courts of original jurisdiction, intermediate appeals courts, or administrative agencies. As of 1985, 36 States had intermediate appellate courts, but all States had courts of last resort.

The U.S. Constitution created the U.S. Supreme Court and authorized the Congress to establish lower courts as needed

The Federal court system now consists of various special courts, U.S. district courts (general jurisdiction courts), U.S. courts of appeals (intermediate appellate courts that receive appeals from the district courts and Federal administrative agencies), and the U.S. Supreme Court (the court of last resort). Organized on a regional basis are U.S. courts of appeals for each of 11 circuits and the District of Columbia. In Federal trial courts (the 94 U.S. district courts) more than 300,000 cases were filed in 1985; there was one criminal case for every seven civil cases. In 1985 more than half the criminal cases in district courts were for embezzlement, fraud, forgery and counterfeiting, traffic, or drug offenses.

Court organization varies greatly among the States

State courts of general jurisdiction are organized by districts, counties, dual districts, or a combination of counties and districts. In some States the courts established by the State are funded and controlled locally. In others the court of last resort may have some budgetary or administrative oversight over the entire State court system. Even within States there is considerable lack of uniformity in the roles, organization, and procedures of the courts. This has led to significant momentum among States to form "unified" court systems to provide in varying degrees, for uniform administration of the courts, and, in many cases, for the consolidation of diverse courts of limited and special jurisdiction.

From *Report to the Nation on Crime and Justice,* Bureau of Justice Statistics, U.S. Department of Justice, March 1988, pp. 81-82, 71-72, 74-75.

Most felony cases are brought in State and local courts

The traditional criminal offenses under the English common law have been adopted, in one form or another, in the criminal laws of each of the States. Most cases involving "common law" crimes are brought to trial in State or local courts. Persons charged with misdemeanors are usually tried in courts of limited jurisdiction. Those charged with felonies (more serious crimes) are tried in courts of general jurisdiction.

In all States criminal defendants may appeal most decisions of criminal courts of limited jurisdiction; the avenue of appeal usually ends with the State supreme court. However, the U.S. Supreme Court may elect to hear the case if the appeal is based on an alleged violation of the Constitutional rights of the defendant.

State courts process a large volume of cases, many of them minor

In 1983, 46 States and the District of Columbia reported more than 80 million cases filed in State and local courts. About 70% were traffic-related cases, 16% were civil cases (torts, contracts, small claims, etc.), 13% were criminal cases, and 1% were juvenile cases. Civil and criminal cases both appear to be increasing. Of 39 States that reported civil filings for 1978 and 1983, 32 had increases. Of the 36 States that reported criminal filings for both years, 33 showed an increase in the volume of criminal filings.

In the 24 States that could report, felony filings comprised from 5% to 32% of total criminal filings with a median of 9%.

Victims and witnesses are taking a more significant part in the prosecution of felons

Recent attention to crime victims has spurred the development of legislation and services that are more responsive to victims.
• Some States have raised witness fees from $5–10 per day in trial to $20–30 per day, established procedures for victim and witness notification of court proceedings, and guaranteed the right to speedy disposition of cases
• 9 States and the Federal Government have comprehensive bills of rights for victims
• 39 States and the Federal Government have laws or guidelines requiring that victims and witnesses be notified of the scheduling and cancellation of criminal proceedings
• 33 States and the Federal Government allow victims to participate in criminal proceedings via oral or written testimony.

Courts at various levels of government interact in many ways

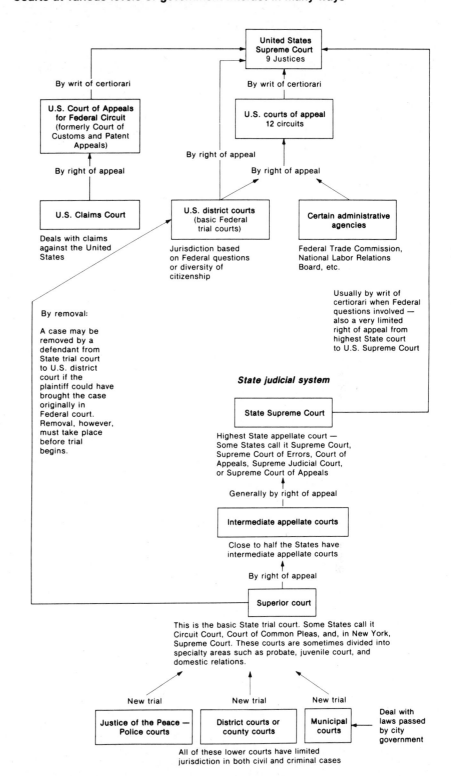

Updated and reprinted by permission from *The American Legal Environment* by William T. Schantz. Copyright © 1976 by West Publishing Company. All rights reserved.

The prosecutor provides the link between the law enforcement and adjudicatory processes

The separate system of justice for juveniles often operates within the existing court organization

Jurisdiction over juvenile delinquency, dependent or neglected children, and related matters is vested in various types of courts. In many States the juvenile court is a division of the court of general jurisdiction. A few States have statewide systems of juvenile or family courts. Juvenile jurisdiction is vested in the courts of general jurisdiction in some counties and in separate juvenile courts or courts of limited jurisdiction in others.

The American prosecutor is unique in the world

First, the American prosecutor is a public prosecutor representing the people in matters of criminal law. Historically, European societies viewed crimes as wrongs against an individual whose claims could be pressed through private prosecution. Second, the American prosecutor is usually a local official, reflecting the development of autonomous local governments in the colonies. Finally, as an elected official, the local American prosecutor is responsible to the voters.

Prosecution is the function of representing the people in criminal cases

After the police arrest a suspect, the prosecutor coordinates the government's response to crime—from the initial screening, when the prosecutor decides whether or not to press charges, through trial. In some instances, it continues through sentencing with the presentation of sentencing recommendations.

Prosecutors have been accorded much discretion in carrying out their responsibilities. They make many of the decisions that determine whether a case will proceed through the criminal justice process.

Prosecution is predominantly a State and local function

Prosecuting officials include State, district, county, prosecuting, and commonwealth attorneys; corporation counsels; circuit solicitors; attorneys general; and U.S. attorneys. Prosecution is carried out

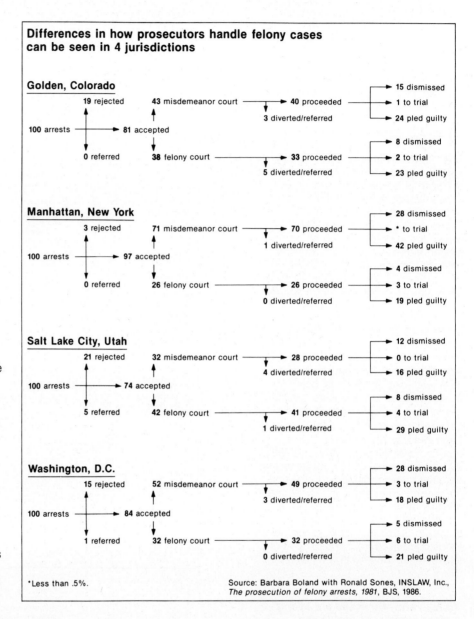

Differences in how prosecutors handle felony cases can be seen in 4 jurisdictions

Golden, Colorado

100 arrests → 81 accepted; 19 rejected; 0 referred
43 misdemeanor court → 40 proceeded; 3 diverted/referred → 15 dismissed; 1 to trial; 24 pled guilty
38 felony court → 33 proceeded; 5 diverted/referred → 8 dismissed; 2 to trial; 23 pled guilty

Manhattan, New York

100 arrests → 97 accepted; 3 rejected; 0 referred
71 misdemeanor court → 70 proceeded; 1 diverted/referred → 28 dismissed; * to trial; 42 pled guilty
26 felony court → 26 proceeded; 0 diverted/referred → 4 dismissed; 3 to trial; 19 pled guilty

Salt Lake City, Utah

100 arrests → 74 accepted; 21 rejected; 5 referred
32 misdemeanor court → 28 proceeded; 4 diverted/referred → 12 dismissed; 0 to trial; 16 pled guilty
42 felony court → 41 proceeded; 1 diverted/referred → 8 dismissed; 4 to trial; 29 pled guilty

Washington, D.C.

100 arrests → 84 accepted; 15 rejected; 1 referred
52 misdemeanor court → 49 proceeded; 3 diverted/referred → 28 dismissed; 3 to trial; 18 pled guilty
32 felony court → 32 proceeded; 0 diverted/referred → 5 dismissed; 6 to trial; 21 pled guilty

*Less than .5%.

Source: Barbara Boland with Ronald Sones, INSLAW, Inc., *The prosecution of felony arrests, 1981*, BJS, 1986.

by more than 8,000 State, county, municipal, and township prosecution agencies.[1] In all but five States, local prosecutors are elected officials. Many small jurisdictions engage a part-time prosecutor who also maintains a private law practice. In some areas police share the charging responsibility of local prosecutors. Prosecutors in urban jurisdictions often have offices staffed by many full-time assistants. Each State has an office of the attorney general, which has jurisdiction over all matters involving State law but generally, unless specifically requested, is not involved in local prosecution. Federal prosecution is the responsibility of 93 U.S. attorneys who

are appointed by the President subject to confirmation by the Senate.

The decision to charge is generally a function of the prosecutor

Results of a 1981 survey of police and prosecution agencies in localities of over 100,000 indicate that police file initial charges in half the jurisdictions surveyed. This arrangement, sometimes referred to as the police court, is not commonly found in the larger urban areas that account for most of the UCR Index crime. Usually, once an arrest is made and the case is referred to the prosecutor, most prosecutors screen cases to see if they merit prosecution. The prosecutor can refuse to prosecute, for example, because of insufficient evidence. The decision to charge is not usually reviewable by any other branch of government.

Some prosecutors accept almost all cases for prosecution; others screen out many cases

Some prosecutors have screening units designed to reject cases at the earliest possible point. Others tend to accept most arrests, more of which are dismissed by judges later in the adjudication process. Most prosecutor offices fall somewhere between these two extremes.

Arrest disposition patterns in 16 jurisdictions range from 0 to 47% of arrests rejected for prosecution. Jurisdictions with high rejection rates generally were found to have lower rates of dismissal at later stages of the criminal process. Conversely, jurisdictions that accepted most or all arrests usually had high dismissal rates.

Prosecutorial screening practices are of several distinct types

Several studies conclude that screening decisions consider—
• evidentiary factors
• the views of the prosecutor on key criminal justice issues
• the political and social environment in which the prosecutor functions
• the resource constraints and organization of prosecutorial operations.

Jacoby's study confirmed the presence of at least three policies that affect the screening decision:
• Legal sufficiency—an arrest is accepted for prosecution if, on routine review of the arrest, the minimum legal elements of a case are present.
• System efficiency—arrests are disposed as quickly as possible by the fastest means possible, which are rejections, dismissals, and pleas.
• Trial sufficiency—the prosecutor accepts only those arrests for which, in his or her view, there is sufficient evidence to convict in court.

The official accusation in felony cases is a grand jury indictment or a prosecutor's bill of information

According to Jacoby, the accusatory process usually follows one of four paths:
• arrest to preliminary hearing for bindover to grand jury for indictment

• arrest to grand jury for indictment
• arrest to preliminary hearing to a bill of information
• a combination of the above at the prosecutor's discretion.

Whatever the method of accusation, the State must demonstrate only that there is probable cause to support the charge.

The preliminary hearing is used in some jurisdictions to determine probable cause

The purpose of the hearing is to see if there is probable cause to believe a crime has been committed and that the defendant committed it. Evidence may be presented by both the prosecution and the defense. On a finding of probable cause the defendant is held to answer in the next stage of a felony proceeding.

The grand jury emerged from the American Revolution as the people's protection against oppressive prosecution by the State

Today, the grand jury is a group of ordinary citizens, usually no more than 23, which has both accusatory and investigative functions. The jury's proceedings are secret and not adversarial so that most rules of evidence for trials do not apply. Usually, evidence is presented by the prosecutor who brings a case to the grand jury's attention. However, in some States the grand jury is used primarily to investigate issues of public corruption and organized crime.

Some States do not require a grand jury indictment to initiate prosecutions

Grand jury indictment required	Grand jury indictment optional
All crimes	Arizona
New Jersey	Arkansas
South Carolina	California
Tennessee	Colorado
Virginia	Idaho
	Illinois
All felonies	Indiana
Alabama	Iowa
Alaska	Kansas
Delaware	Maryland
District of Columbia	Michigan
Georgia	Missouri
Hawaii	Montana
Kentucky	Nebraska
Maine	Nevada
Mississippi	New Mexico
New Hampshire	North Dakota
New York	Oklahoma
North Carolina	Oregon
Ohio	South Dakota
Texas	Utah

West Virginia	Vermont
	Washington
Capital crimes only	Wisconsin
Connecticut	Wyoming
Florida	
Louisiana	**Grand jury lacks**
Massachusetts	**authority to indict**
Minnesota	
Rhode Island	Pennsylvania

Note: With the exception of capital cases a defendant can always waive the right to an indictment. Thus, the requirement for an indictment to initiate prosecution exists only in the absence of a waiver.

Source: Deborah Day Emerson, *Grand jury reform: A review of key issues,* National Institute of Justice, U.S. Department of Justice, January 1983.

The secrecy of the grand jury is a matter of controversy

Critics of the grand jury process suggest it denies due process and equal protection under the law and exists only to serve the prosecutor. Recent criticisms have fostered a number of reforms requiring due process protections for persons under investigation and for witnesses; requiring improvements in the quality and quantity of evidence presented; and opening the proceeding to outside review. While there is much variation in the nature and implementation of reforms, 15 States have enacted laws affording the right to counsel, and 10 States require evidentiary standards approaching the requirements imposed at trial.

The defense attorney's function is to protect the defendant's legal rights and to be the defendant's advocate in the adversary process

Defendants have the right to defend themselves, but most prefer to be represented by a specialist in the law. Relatively few members of the legal profession specialize in criminal law, but lawyers who normally handle other types of legal matters may take criminal cases.

The right to the assistance of counsel is more than the right to hire a lawyer

Supreme Court decisions in *Gideon* v. *Wainwright* (1963) and *Argersinger* v. *Hamlin* (1972) established that the right to an attorney may not be frustrated by lack of means. For both felonies and misdemeanors for which jail or prison can be the penalty, the State must provide an attorney to any accused person who is indigent.

The institutional response to this Constitutional mandate is still evolving as States experiment with various ways to provide legal counsel for indigent defendants.

Public Defenders

AGNES A. SERPE

Agnes A. Serpe is a student at Creighton University in Omaha, Nebraska. She is pursuing Creighton's Three Plus Three program, a combination Business Administration/Law program.

They [public defenders] are a fraternity of righteous, these low-paid lawyers, dogmatists of the criminal justice system, who often find themselves lining up on the sides of rapists, murderers, child-molesters, and drug dealers.[1]

A public defender is an attorney appointed to aid indigent persons, usually in cases involving possible imprisonment. Because the Supreme Court guarantees that all persons accused of felonies, regardless of their ability to pay for counsel, have the right to a publicly provided defense lawyer during police questioning, pretrial hearings, the trial, and appeal, the public defender is a busy attorney.[2]

With the rate of crime in the United States continuing to rise, the demand for defense counsel increases. Public defenders are expected to begin research and representation early on in their cases, and they are expected to follow through to the appeals stages and probation revocation hearings.[3] The problem is that there are more cases in need of public defense counsel than there are attorneys with the time, money, and expertise to handle such cases. The result is that cases involving indigent clients are often delayed or expedited, hampering the public defender in effectively representing his client.[4]

Although the problems facing public defense counsel in the United States today are severe ones, the present judicial system has a strong foundation. The U.S. bases its whole judicial system on the fundamental principle ". . . laid down by the greatest English judges . . ."[5] The system holds that it is better to let many guilty persons escape than it is to let one innocent person be imprisoned.[6]

Since the primary goal of the judicial system is to protect the innocent, the system holds that every individual has the right to counsel. In 1791, Congress passed the Sixth Amendment to the Constitution, guaranteeing in all criminal prosecutions, the accused person has the right to a ". . . speedy and public trial, by an impartial jury of the state and district wherein the crime shall have been committed. . . and to have the assistance of counsel for his defense."[7] According to the Sixth Amendment, 'counsel' does not include lay persons, but rather refers only to persons authorized to practice law.[8]

Despite the amendment, flaws still remained in the system. Only until after 1961 did the Supreme Court rule that the guarantees found in the Sixth Amendment apply to the state trial courts as well as the federal trial courts.[9] Also, court-appointed attorneys were expected to serve the public without compensation, burdening the practicing bar of attorneys and forcing the judges to appoint young, inexperienced counsel.[10] Moreover, a public defender program was not established until the early 1920's.[11]

History

At first, public defenders were part of the legal aid societies that were supported by charities. The society handled both civil and criminal cases and had the authority to accept or reject cases. The earliest legal aid society was Der Deutsche Rechtsshutz

Verein (the German Legal Defense Society) which was organized in 1876 to help German immigrants. Later, in 1888, New York City created the New York Legal Aid Society, and Chicago established the Chicago Bureau of Justice.[12]

Early legal aid societies, such as the ones in New York and Chicago, did not take many criminal cases because they lacked the time, money, and personnel to conduct criminal investigations and absorb the trial work.[13] By 1962, the burden of criminal caseloads shifted from the legal aid societies to the 110 newly established public defender offices across America. The number of public defender offices was very few in proportion to the population of the country, but enough to provide minimal service in some major cities. Accordingly, the offices were noted for being understaffed.[14]

Furthermore, up until 1963, any legal assistance providing defense services for indigent criminals had been a matter left up to the judge to decide, depending heavily upon the charitable time and money contributions from the bar association. The demand for sufficient funding resulted in the Ford Foundation's decision to create the National Defender Project in 1964. Donating $6,000,000 to the National Legal Aid and Defender Association over a five-year period, the foundation provided the funds that were needed to improve and establish organized defense systems in over sixty cities across the nation.[15]

The Ford Foundation's sudden display of generosity occurred immediately after the landmark court case Gideon v Wainwright in 1963. In this case, Clarence Earl Gideon, the defendant, who was tried and convicted in a Florida state court, committed the felony of breaking and entering (a poolroom) with the intent to commit a misdemeanor theft. When he requested an attorney for his trial, the judge refused him. The judge claimed that he could not assign an attorney to Gideon because Gideon was not charged with a capital offense (that is, one punishable by death). Since the judge did have the power to appoint counsel, the judge had made an obvious mistake.[16] As a result, the Supreme Court ruled that Gideon's quality of defense was inadequate

and "about as well as could be expected from a layman."[17]

Therefore, the outcome of Gideon v Wainwright was an emphasis on what the Sixth Amendment is all about. "The right to legal representation must be granted to all indigent defendants in all felonies."[18]

"This noble idea [right to counsel] cannot be realized if the poor man charged with crime has to face his accusers without a lawyer to defend him," stated Mr. Justice Black, who was in harmony with the majority opinion in Gideon v Wainwright.[19]

> *Although there was a time when public defenders were paid a great deal less than the state's prosecuting attorney, today the difference between the public defender's salary and the state's prosecuting attorney's salary has decreased.*

Thus, the Gideon v Wainwright decision came at the right time, prompting the Ford Foundation to donate money. Also, the case proved that ". . . lawyers in criminal courts are necessities, not luxuries."[20] The foundation had heard the pleas for the funding and had solved some problems for the time being.

Later, in 1964, The Criminal Justice Act was passed, making the federal government provide funds for judges to pay attorneys to represent indigent defendants. At first, however, these funds were available only to attorneys who defended federal crimes, not state crimes. The earliest response was from the state of New Jersey which enacted a state-wide public defender program.[21]

Public Defenders Today

Generally, there are two main means of appointing defense counsel in the U.S. One is the ad hoc, or random, appointment of counsel, and the other is the coordinated assigned counsel program.[22] With ad hoc appointments, the more predominant of the two methods, attorneys are appointed case by case rather than in accordance with an organized plan. The attorneys who are appointed to a case are often the ones who just happen to be in the courtroom at the time of the client's arraignment. As a result the allocation of the burdens placed on defense attorneys is often unfair, and often denies the accused person competent and prepared defense counsel.[23]

On the other hand, the coordinated assigned counsel programs have systematic methods and procedures for the assignment of defense counsel. Some of the programs have loosely structured control over appointments; whereas, others maintain a strict level of control.[24] The coordinated assigned counsel system may be administered by the organized bar, as in San Mateo County, California;[25] a defender office, as in the state of New Jersey;[26] the county, as in King County, Washington;[27] an independent agency, as in the state of Wisconsin;[28] a judge or other court official who provides a rotating list of attorneys;[29] or a client who selects his own attorney, as in Ontario, Canada.[30]

It seems clear that lawyers join the public defender's office to gain trial experience and to make a positive contribution to society through public service.[31] However, the number of attorneys interested in this type of work is declining because of low salaries, and also due to the attraction of big law firms and corporate law,[32] and the extensive and specialized expertise needed for public defender work.[33] As a result, all too often the poor accused of crimes in our country do not receive the fair trial and the full attention to which they are entitled.

Problems and Solutions

Nowadays, the public defender's problem with money is not so much related to salary as it is the lack of sufficient funding for research provided by the federal government. Although there was a time when public defenders were paid a great deal less than the state's prosecuting attorney, today the difference between the public defender's salary and the state's prosecuting attorney's salary has decreased.[34] For example, in 1931, the public defender's salary was $300 per year; whereas, the state's attorney's salary was $1,000 per year. However, in 1984, public defenders were paid approximately $29,863 per year; and the state's attorneys were paid approximately $30,680

per year—a difference of only $817.[35] That is to say that public defenders no longer are justified to complain about the major salary difference between themselves and the state's attorneys.

On the other hand, public defenders are justified in complaining about the difference between their salaries and the salaries of young lawyers who enter legal aid groups. An entry level attorney at a legal aid group will be guaranteed a salary of at least $32,500 per year, along with some extra help with paying back student loans. Although the entry level attorney's pay at legal aid groups is under one-half of what entry level attorneys at major law firms earn, it is still higher than the public defender's salary.[36]

Furthermore, many salaried public defenders, like the ones in New York City and St. Louis, Missouri,[37] have valid reasons to complain about heavy caseloads because the federal government does not provide the necessary funds required for the adequate defense of indigents.[38] Even though public defenders are tireless and dedicated workers, they lack the resources and government funding needed for their overwhelming caseload.[39] For example, in 1983 in St. Louis, Missouri, twenty-two public defenders handled 12.000 cases on a budget of $695,000. At the same time, forty-five attorneys in the state prosecutor's office had a budget of $2.4 million.[40] Therefore, all too often, the public defender does not or cannot find the time and the money to spend researching and preparing a client's case to the best of his ability. Accordingly, indigent clients often do not receive adequate representation.

A second problem that hinders a public defender from effectively defending his client is the lack of manpower. Even though about one-half of all criminal cases in New York City and St. Louis, Missouri, involved defendants who were too poor to pay for their counsel, state and federal levels failed to support the proposed increase in the staff of the public defender office in both these cities.[41]

Furthermore, the problems stem from the attorneys themselves who do not want to become public defenders. The American Bar Association reports that 17.7% of our nation's 659,000 private attorneys practice pro bono work. In Los Angeles, Public Counsel—a group that provides the poor with legal assistance—has lost its participation from outside law firms. The total drop in participation from outside law firms is 30% since 1986.[42] The point is that not enought attorneys are willing to spend their time and money representing the poor free of charge, even though a held belief of the profession is that all lawyers should devote part of their time to pro bono work in either a public defender's office or legal aid society.[43]

Accordingly, Circuit Court Judge, Byron Kinder of Jefferson City, Missouri, subpoenaed 100 lawyers who work for Missouri agencies based in Jefferson City—the state's capital—to press them into service as public defenders for indigent criminal defendants. The U.S. Constitution guarantees a lawyer to all poor defendants. However, Cole County—the county in which Jefferson City is located—has only one public defender. Also, the county has run out of money to pay private attorneys to help out.[44]

One solution to the lack of attorneys is to make pro bono work mandatory for all private attorneys. The proposed system would allow courts, legislatures, and bar associations to force attorneys into donating their time to public defense. However, in some cases, attorneys may avoid their service obligation by paying a fee. Recently, a mandatory pro bono program has been imposed in Westchester County, New York, and El Paso, Texas.[45]

The problem with mandatory pro bono work is that its requirements are not fair to small law practices. Solo practitioners and small law firms, unlike large law firms with many young associates who can be assigned to meet pro bono requirements, will find it nearly impossible to meet pro bono quotas.[46]

Moreover, mandatory pro bono work is a problem for the indigent defendant as well as the solo practitioner. For example, some legal aid attorneys testify that 'drafting' attorneys is not the answer because it may lead to the attorney's lack of conviction and/or his lack of legal skills needed to defend the poor.[47]

The third and final problem contributing to ineffective defense counsel in the U.S. is that few attorneys possess the expertise needed to defend the poor and carry out the functions of a public defender. All public defenders need special skills and knowledge, an unorthodox philosophy, and patience. All too often, the defense counsel in the U.S. is lacking in one or more of the aspects of expertise, resulting in ineffective public counsel for the poor.[48]

To begin with, law school students gain practical trial experience working for public defender organizations and legal aid departments. As a result, clients may be getting help from students rather than professional counsel who have acquired skill through past experience.[49] Also, the past few years, younger lawyers tend to serve people who are too poor to afford their own lawyers—especially poor persons accused of narcotics law violations. The accused person's defense in drug-related crimes requires technical statutes and procedures that many lawyers are not familiar with. Therefore, young attorneys are the ones who tend to handle the bulk of these cases, resulting in questionable representation.[50]

Furthermore, effective defense counsel need skills and knowledge to deal with the problems of the indigent. As one attorney explains, "Your clients have no funds. . . no witnesses. . . only have one name. . . hang out on the streets. . . don't have phones. . . don't have a life like the rest of us."[51]

Adding to the problem, most of the accused are not articulate and tend to be less intelligent and more sociopathic than the general population.[52] Thus, the public defender needs special skills for dealing with the poor.

Second, the problem with the lack of expertise is the lack of attorneys who are capable of having an unconventional philosophy. Since the basis of legal ethics is loyalty to the client, public defenders have ethics which are practically opposite of what is commonly understood to be ethical. If, in fact, the client did commit a crime, the defense attorney is supposed to prevent the "coming out" of the crime and the jury's recognition of the crime.[53] In other words, it would be legally unethical for a defense attorney to refrain from doing everything in his power to protect his client. For example, even when a lawyer knows that his client is a thief, the public defender must attempt to prevent the search for the victim's stolen property.[54] Because justice under the law is not always the same as true justice, public defenders often find it difficult to uphold and believe in their legal ethics. James S. Kunen, a former public defender who found it difficult to believe in legal ethics, stated the following:

. . . my job was to get what my client wanted. . . [Judge Ugast] flew into one of his daily earnest, rages, upbraiding me for being 'an idealist' with abstract notions of legal duty and no contact with reality, adding that I typified everything that was wrong with the Public Defender Service. I was pleased . . . because. . . I shared the judge's preference for doing what you think is right, as opposed to what you are supposed to do . . . .[55]

If public defenders find it difficult to believe in legal ethics, then what are their motives to defend the indigent criminal? Aside from striving "to legitimize themselves as professionals," the public defenders' motives stem from the belief that a person is innocent until proven guilty beyond reasonable doubt. Also, they believe that it is right to defend the guilty client because—although he is guilty—he needs protection from police, prosecutorial, and judicial abuse.[56]

Finally, the third essential to defense expertise is patience. The rest of the judicial system—that is, the police, the prosecuting attorney, and the judges—along with the clients and the general public, all test the patience of the public defender.

For instance, not only must a public defender accept that he will probably not win his cases,[57] but also, he must deal with the habitual postponements of his cases. Public defenders' cases get postponed more often than cases involving private defense attorneys.[58] Some judges act as if they are being considerate of private attorneys by calling their cases before public defenders' cases because "time is money for the private attorney."[59]

In reality, some of these judges lack respect for the public defender. All too often judges are "prosecution-minded and. . . generally tougher on the defense attorney."[60] They tend to treat public defenders as "second-class lawyers."[61] One public

defender explains just how some judges treat public defenders:

[Judges] view the public defenders very similar to how they view court clerks. We are gophers, we run for things. Whenever there's something the judge needs done, if there is not a clerk available, the judge gives it to the public defender and has him do it. They would never think of having the state's attorney do it. But public defenders have to do the silly stuff.[62]

> *Not only do public defenders need patience with the judicial system, but they need to have patience with their clients.*

Not only do public defenders need patience with the judicial system, but they need to have patience with their clients. Clients often doubt the public defender's ability as a trial lawyer. As a result, public defenders are continually swallowing their pride for their clients—most of whom lack faith in the legal profession. One public defender protested, "I am a real lawyer, I went to a real law school, I passed a real bar exam!"[63]

Because of unappreciative clients, public defenders believe, and have the right to believe, that the people in their community do not appreciate them as competent attorneys.[64] Even though a small portion of the population does respect public defenders, the profession has clearly been degraded time and time again:

Public defenders in America have been both maligned and idealized. Some [people] view them as champions of individual rights, the defenders of the poor and down trodden. Others see them as 'cop-out' artists who are too quick to bargain away the precious rights of their underprivileged clients.[65]

Furthermore, the public defender has the problem of developing the expertise of patience with a judicial system that delays cases to the point where witnesses disappear, and expedites trials so that the defense is at a disadvantage.[66]

Conclusion

The search for an improved public defender program continues. The ideal program would have adequate staffing and more than enough funding to assign cases to attorneys according to their experience and workload. The primary goals of the program would be efficiency, effectiveness, and productivity.[67]

The productivity measurement would include a high quality of service, which will be the most difficult to render.[68] However, despite the rocky history and recent beginning of the public defender program, the level of expertise that exists among attorneys now is much better than it was a few years ago. Therefore, the office of the public defender—although it has major problems—is improving, and will continue to improve as long as it attempts to solve its problems.

> Thirty years ago the public defender office seemed to be little more than a beneficient (though ultimately benign) gesture, on the part of a few county governments, toward poor people in trouble with the law. . . But. . . public defenders today play such an important role in the administration of criminal justice that without them, the work of our urban criminal courts especially would come to a standstill.[69]

---

[1] Lisa McIntyre, *The Public Defender* (Chicago, Illinois: The University of Chicago Press, 1987), p. 86.

[2] "Public Defenders," *Funk and Wagnalls New World Encyclopedia,* 1983.

[3] William McDonald, *The Defense Counsel* (Beverly Hills, California: Sage Publications, 1983), p. 79.

[4] "Public Defenders Assail Felony Judges' New Rules to Speed Court Cases," *Milwaukee Journal,* October 28, 1988, p. A1, Col. 1–6.

[5] James Kunen, *How Can You Defend Those People?* (New York: Random House, 1983), p. vii.

[6] *Ibid.,* p. vii.

[7] United States Constitution, Amendment 6.

[8] *Ibid.,* p. 314.

[9] McIntyre, p. 21.

[10] McDonald, p. 76.

[11] Robert Janosik, *Encyclopedia of the American Judicial System* (New York: Charles Scribner's Sons, 1972), p. 645.

[12] *Ibid.,* p. 645.

[13] *Ibid.,* p. 645.

[14] *Ibid.,* p. 646.

[15] McDonald, p. 81.

[16] McIntyre, p. 21.

[17] *Ibid.,* p. 21.

[18] *Ibid.,* p. 21.

[19] McDonald, p. 76.

[20] McIntyre, p. 21.

[21] Janosik, p. 645.

[22] McDonald, p. 85.

[23] *Ibid.,* p. 86.

[24] *Ibid.,* p. 87.

[25] *Ibid.,* p. 87.

[26] *Ibid.,* p. 88.

[27] *Ibid.,* p. 88.

[28] Richard J. Phelps, *Office of the State Public Defender Biennial Report* (Madison, Wisconsin: 1987), p. 5.

[29] McDonald, p. 89.

[30] *Ibid.,* p. 89.

[31] McIntyre, p. 86.

[32] R. Lacayo, "The Sad Fate of Legal Aid," *Time,* June 20, 1988, p. 59.

[33] B. Kinder, "Lawyer Round-up in Jeff City," *Time,* May 4, 1981, p. 44.

[34] McIntyre, p. 90.

[35] *Ibid.,* p. 90.

[36] Lacayo, p. 59.

[37] Janosik, p. 645.

[38] Denise Shekerjian, *Competent Counsel: Working With Lawyers* (New York: Dodd, Mead, and Co., 1985), p. 55.

[39] *Ibid.,* p. 55.

[40] Janosik, p. 645.

[41] *Ibid.,* p. 645.

[42] Lacayo, p. 59.

[43] *Ibid.,* p. 59.

[44] Kinder, p. 44.

[45] Lacayo, p. 59.

[46] *Ibid.,* p. 59.

[47] *Ibid.,* p. 59.

[48] Kinder, p. 44.

[49] Henry Poor, *You and the Law* (New York: Reader's Digest, 1984), p. 733.

[50] *Ibid.,* p. 736.

[51] McIntyre, p. 144.

[52] *Ibid.,* p. 144.

[53] James Kunen, "How Can You Defend Those People?" *Harper's,* April, 1982, p. 83.

[54] *Ibid.,* p. 86.

[55] *Ibid.,* p. 82.

[56] McIntyre, p. 169.

[57] *Ibid.,* p. 162.

[58] Kunen, p. 83.

[59] McIntyre, . 87.

[60] *Ibid.,* p. 87.

[61] *Ibid.,* p. 87.

[62] *Ibid.,* p. 88.

[63] *Ibid.,* p. 89.

[64] *Ibid.,* p. 87.

[65] McDonald, p. 67.

[66] Kunen, p. 83.

[67] McDonald, p. 299.

[68] *Ibid.,* p. 299.

[69] McIntyre, p. 1.

The Prosecutor as a "Minister of Justice"

BENNETT L. GERSHMAN

The author is an Adjunct Professor of Law at Pace University School of Law, and practices law in White Plains, New York. He was a prosecutor for ten years in the offices of Frank S. Hogan and Maurice H. Nadjari, and has written extensively about prosecutorial and police conduct.

These are heady times for prosecutors. Gone are the days when the Supreme Court every other week, it seemed, would invoke a new due process right for criminal defendants; when prosecutors would frantically prepare for strange new hearings labeled "Mapp", "Huntley", and "Wade"; would be embroiled in sensational, political trials—Harlem 6; Chicago 7; Harrisburg 8; Boston 5; Panther 21—only to be rebuked by defense counsel, the press, the public, and juries. Prosecutors were often on the defensive in those days.

Times have changed. Today, prosecutors are on top of the world. Their powers are enormous, and constantly reinforced by sympathetic legislatures and courts. The "awful instruments of the criminal law," as Justice Frankfurter described the system,[1] are today supplemented with broad new crimes,[2] easier proof requirements,[3] heavier sentencing laws,[4] and an extremely cooperative judiciary, from district and state judges, to the highest Court in the land.

Indeed, Supreme Court watchers, and I am one of them, carefully analyze the oracles from our Nation's legal equivalent of Mt. Olympus, and try to discern trends. Some trends are easy to decipher, such as the Death of the Fourth Amendment; the continuing drift from adjudicative fair play, symbolized by the Due Process Revolution of the Nineteen-Sixties, to crime control, epitomized by what I have termed the Counter-Revolution of Harmless Error;[5] and the increasing availability and use of draconian forms of punishment, whether labeled preventive detention,[6] consecutive jail sentences for overlapping criminal acts,[7] and more and more executions.[8]

Another trend, more subtle, perhaps, has been a change in the role of the prosecutor. Twenty-five years ago, in one of the great cases of this or any generation — Brady v. Maryland[9] — the Supreme Court could write this about the prosecutor's duty: "Society wins not only when the guilty are convicted but when criminal trials are fair; our system of the administration of justice suffers when any accused is treated unfairly."[10]

This statement was a kind of banner under which enthusiastic young men and women began legal careers in prosecutors offices, particularly in the office of New York County District Attorney Frank S. Hogan. Indeed, the cover story of one issue of the New York Times Magazine profiled that office, under the title: "Hogan's Office Is a Kind of Ministry of Justice."[11] For a long time it has been an accepted part of the conventional legal wisdom, translated into one of the principal Standards of Criminal Justice of the American Bar Association, that it is the duty of the prosecutor "to seek justice, not merely to convict."[12]

There are, however, serious practical and conceptual difficulties in squaring the prosecutor's function with that of a "Minister of Justice." The concept was seriously eroded in two important decisions of the Supreme Court —Coolidge v. New Hampshire[13] and Gerstein v. Pugh[14]—in which the Court recognized that it is realistically impossible for a prosecutor to play the dual roles of vigorous advocate and protector of public justice. In Coolidge, the Court said that the prosecutor is too heavily involved in the "competitive enterprise of ferreting out crime" to pass on the sufficiency of a search warrant in a case being investigated under his supervision. Only a judge is neutral and impartial enough to do so. And in Gerstein, the Court held that an information drafted by a prosecutor is not "judicial" enough to provide an objective guarantee of probable cause comparable to that furnished by a grand jury, because the prosecutor is inherently partisan, while the grand jury is an arm of the court.

From New York State Bar Journal, Vol. 60, No. 4, May 1988, pp. 8-12, 63-64. Copyright © 1988 by the New York State Bar Association.

Furthermore, anybody who has carefully followed recent developments in criminal justice, and particularly the Supreme Court's treatment of prosecutorial behavior, must view such references to the prosecutor's purported justice function with considerable skepticism. This is not to suggest that prosecutors by and large behave unfairly. They do not. However, the prosecutor's role is not that of a justice-giver, but of an advocate, a "Champion of the People," in the same way that defense counsel's role is not a defender of abstract justice, but, rather, a Champion of the Defendant. Frequent ceremonial language about the prosecutor's quasi-judicial function[15] is not only misleading, but may be detrimental. It places the prosecutor in an untenable conflict, forcing him constantly to walk a tightrope, and it invites the judiciary to display a kind of obeisance towards the prosecutor, suggesting that he or she stands above the fray, omnipotent and infallible.

To be sure, the prosecutor has a fundamental commitment to fair dealing, not foul play.[16] The respect, and success, of any prosecutor's office depends on a high degree of skill, good judgment, and fairness. If the prosecutor plays fairly and by the rules, justice probably will work itself out under our system of adversarial testing. However, to the extent that some courts, particularly the Supreme Court, continue to evince a consistent and unyielding philosophy of judicial permissiveness in the face of prosecutorial excesses, many prosecutors will get the wrong message, namely, that misconduct pays.[17] And to the extent that bar disciplinary committees wink at prosecutorial excesses, the message is reinforced.[18]

Clearly, prosecutors have legal and ethical obligations different from their defense counterparts. Prosecutors are guided by stricter rules, many of which are embodied in the constitution. Moreover, in contrast to defense counsel, prosecutors wield tremendous power and tremendous discretion. The juxtaposition of such power and discretion can be dangerous, especially if courts display restraint, passivity, and even withdrawal in the face of prosecutorial misbehavior. Indeed, such combination can be lethal. For example, in the recent capital case of *Darden* v. *Wainwright*,[19] the prosecutor, among other things, characterized the defendant as an "animal;" told the jury that the only guarantee against his future crimes would be to execute him; that he should have "a leash on him;" and that he should have "his face blown away by a shotgun." Darden's trial was "not perfect," said the Supreme Court in upholding his conviction and death sentence. "Few are." "But neither was it fundamentally unfair."[19a]

Obviously, we can never know to what extent the jury in finding guilt and imposing death, was influenced by the prosecutor's outrageous remarks. Was Darden treated unfairly? The answer depends, in part, on where one sits. One of the major problems with the Supreme Court's prosecutorial jurisprudence — and that of appellate courts generally — is that these courts look at trial proceedings retrospectively, and can only guess, quantitatively or qualitatively, at the prejudicial impact of such misconduct, or its influence on the fairness of the trial.[20]

To be sure, the Supreme Court has not tolerated every form of prosecutorial misconduct. In one case — *Batson* v. *Kentucky*[21] — the Court at long last outlawed the pernicious prosecutorial practice of peremptorily challenging minority jurors from jury service. *Batson*, as well as *Vasquez* v. *Hillery*,[22] which dealt with grand jury discrimination, are clearly long overdue and are to be applauded. However, they involve equal protection concerns to which the Court has displayed far greater sensitivity than to due process concerns. Indeed, virtually every important decision of the Supreme Court over the past several terms addressing the prosecutor's conduct involved a lower court judgment — state or federal — which had sustained the defendant's claim of improper prosecutorial behavior. In virtually every case, the Supreme Court reversed. It also should be noted that among the dozens of summary reversals by the Court — done without briefs or oral argument — well over 90% were decided in the prosecutor's favor.[23]

Any lingering notion that the prosecutor is obligated to dispense justice has been dispelled by recent decisions of the Supreme Court. For example, the increasingly expansive use of the harmless error doctrine is one of the principal themes in the Court's treatment of prosecutorial misconduct. Thus, in *United States* v. *Mechanik*,[24] the Court for the first time held that prosecutorial misconduct in the grand jury, reviewed on appeal following a conviction, could be harmless error. Similarly, in *United States* v. *Lane*,[25] the Court held for the first time that improper conduct in mischarging crimes, reviewed on appeal following a conviction, could be harmless error. Further, in *United States* v. *Hasting*,[26] the Court held that lower federal courts could not use their supervisory powers to discipline errant prosecutors who had consistently violated that circuit's rules. These courts were ordered to apply the harmless error test instead.

It is in the area of nondisclosure of exculpatory evidence, however, that the Supreme Court has rendered most meaningless notions of fundamental fairness and constitutional protections afforded criminal defendants. This is the one area above all else that depends on the integrity and good faith of the prosecutor. If the prosecutor hides evidence, it will probably never be known. Moreover, as an advocate, the prosecutor, if candid, will concede that his or her inclination is not to disclose. By way of rough analogy, we do not enjoy paying taxes. Since the government's auditing powers are severly limited, the tax system depends largely on the integrity of the individual taxpayer. Many evaders are not apprehended. But if a tax cheat is caught, the chances are good that the courts will impose severe sanctions, mostly for deterrent purposes.

So, it seems, should it be with prosecutorial suppression of evidence. But in this one area, where the prosecutor's fairness is so dramatically put to the test, the Supreme Court has continued to default. First, according to the Court, the prosecutor's good or bad faith in secreting evidence is irrelevant.[27] But surely if one seeks to deter prosecutors from hiding exculpatory evidence, willful violations should be severely punished. Not so, according to the Court. The hidden evidence has to be "material," that is, as the Court wrote recently in United States v. Bagley,[28] a case involving a prosecutor's false representations to defense counsel about monetary inducements to government witnesses, it has to be shown that but for the nondisclosure, the verdict would have been different.

Examples of this quagmire spawned by the Court are numerous. In Smith v. Phillips,[29] the prosecutor suppressed information that a juror in a murder trial had sought employment with the same prosecutor's office. The Supreme Court reversed the Second Circuit, which had granted the habeas corpus petition. The Court said first, that there was no showing of actual bias, nor, secondly, any showing that the defendant was prejudiced by the nondisclosure. Ethical standards may be overlooked, said Justice Rehnquist for the majority, because the "touchstone of due process analysis is the fairness of the trial, not the culpability of the prosecutor." But, quaere, how does one demonstrate prejudice if the juror swears: "I was not prejudiced"? Similarly, in United States v. Valenzuela-Bernal,[30] the prosecutor

ordered the deportation of illegal-alien eyewitnesses to the defendant's crime before they could be interviewed by defense counsel. The Supreme Court reversed the Ninth Circuit, which had reversed the conviction. The prompt deportation of illegal-aliens is an overriding duty of the Executive Branch, the Court said, to which the Court will defer absent a plausible showing that the lost evidence would be material and favorable to the defense. Of course, as the dissent correctly pointed out, showing the importance of evidence without an opportunity to examine that evidence can be exceedingly difficult. And in California v. Trombetta,[31] the Court reversed the state court which had reversed the defendant's intoxicated driving conviction because the prosecutor had failed to preserve as evidence the contents of a breathilyzer test. The evidence was not sufficiently material, said the Court. To be material, a defendant is required to show that the evidence possessed an exculpatory quality that was apparent before the evidence was destroyed, and was of such nature that the defendant would be unable to obtain comparable evidence. Again, how does a defendant show the importance of evidence that is no longer available?

Moreover, the Supreme Court's undue deference to the prosecutor, as noted above, can result in wholesale abdication of traditional judicial functions. With due respect to the judiciary, the prosecutor is the most dominant and powerful official in the criminal justice system. The prosecutor runs the show. The prosecutor decides whether or not to bring criminal charges; who to charge; what charges to bring; whether a defendant will stand trial, plead guilty, or be conferred with immunity. The prosecutor even possesses broad sentencing powers, as the New York Court of Appeals' decision in People v. Farrar illustrates.[32] The prosecutor enjoys virtual independence. He has no superiors. He cannot be compelled to bring charges or to terminate

them. Moreover, in using these vast powers, the prosecutor is presumed to act in good faith. The Supreme Court wrote a few months ago in a case involving the use of a private prosecutor: "Between the private life of the citizen and the public glare of criminal accusation stands the prosecutor, with the power to employ the full machinery of the state in scrutinizing any given individual."[33] And, one might add, to stigmatize that person for life. To be sure, the prosecutor's vast charging discretion is constrained by a few modest doctrines: the prosecutor must not be unfairly selective, vindictive, or demagogic in using his charging powers. These doctrines, however, are rarely invoked, and hardly ever successful.

No area of criminal justice is more complex and controversial than that of the prosecutor's discretion, particularly as it relates to charging, plea bargaining, dismissing, and granting immunity. It is here, in my judgment, that the courts should exercise more vigilance and control. Yet here, more than any other area, the courts have withdrawn more than ever.[34] Several recent cases illustrate the ineffectiveness of doctrine as it relates to the prosecutor's discretion. In Wayte v. United States,[35] for example, the defendant, a vocal opponent of the Selective Service system, was one of a handful of nonregistrants who was prosecuted, out of nearly a million non-vocal nonregistrants. Wayte made a colorable showing that he was impermissibly targeted for prosecution based on his exercise of First Amendment rights. He sought to discover information in the prosecutor's files. When the prosecutor resisted, the district court dismissed the indictment. The Supreme Court treated the case not as a discovery problem. The Court found that there was no showing that the defendant was selected "because of his protest activities," a showing of prosecutorial motivation that seems almost impossible to prove. Given the presumption of prosecutorial good faith, the prosecutor's expertise, and the prosecutor's law enforcement plans and priorities, matters which are ill-suited to judicial review, said the Court, there would be no interference with the prosecutor's discretion, even in this obvious instance of a prima facie case of selective prosecution.

Unfair selectivity is matched by prosecutorial retaliation in the form of increased charges after defendants raise statutory or constitutional claims. Prosecutors, however, may not be vindictive in response to a defendant's exercise of rights. Proving prosecutorial vindictiveness, however, is another matter. The courts have indulged the prosecutor in this area as well. Thus, prosecutorial retaliation by increasing charges after a plea offer is refused is not legally vindictive, said the Supreme Court in *United States* v. *Goodwin*,[36] reaffirming *Bordenkircher* v. *Hayes*,[37] even though such tactics may demonstrate actual vindictiveness. The concerns are purely pragmatic. Prosecutors need this leverage to run the system. If prosecutors could not threaten defendants by "upping the ante," they would obtain fewer pleas. Further, in virtually every pretrial context in which prosecutors have increased charges after defendants have exercised rights, courts uniformly have found no vindictiveness. This can result in some patently unfair decisions. In one recent New York case,[38] the prosecutor charged the defendant with perjury after his motion to suppress evidence was granted. The hearing court found that the defendant was a credible witness, and the police witnesses were not. This is a blatant instance of prosecutorial vindictiveness, or alternatively, of prosecutorial bad faith, particularly after a judge already had made a credibility determination in the defendant's favor.

Prosecutorial behavior in plea bargaining is standardless and often highly coercive. A plea bargain is a constitutional contract. The prosecutor must keep his promise.

However, the prosecutor's decisions usually are deferred to by the Courts, and the prosecutor's interpretation of the bargain usually controls. A good example of this is *Ricketts* v. *Adamson*,[39] decided by the Supreme Court last June. The case arose out of the murder of Arizona newspaper reporter Don Bolles. The prosecutor and Adamson agreed that Adamson would testify fully and completely in return for a plea to a reduced murder charge and a reduced sentence. Adamson testified at the murder trial of two other co-defendants and was sentenced. All told, Adamson made 14 court appearances in 5 separate cases — 31 days of testimony and over 200 interview sessions with the prosecutor — but balked at testifying at a retrial after the above murder convictions were reversed. He claimed that his plea agreement, reasonably construed, did not require such additional testimony. The prosecutor disagreed, claimed that Adamson breached his agreement, and notwithstanding Adamson's willingness to accede to the prosecutor's interpretation, nonetheless indicted and convicted Adamson of first degree murder, and obtained a death sentence. A majority of the Court upheld the prosecutor's interpretation of the agreement, and found there was no double jeopardy bar to Adamson's conviction. The four dissenting Justices, on the other hand, said that Adamson had not breached, that there was a reasonable basis for his interpretation, and that the matter should have been submitted to the courts for resolution. Overzealousness may be an appropriate characterization of the prosecutor's conduct here. He behaved more like an "Avenging Angel" than a "Minister of Justice."

Although prosecutors may need "leverage" in plea bargaining, they do not need leverage when seeking a defendant's agreement to release the police or municipality from civil liability following an arrest, and using the dismissal of charges as a

weapon to compel such agreement. In *Newton* v. *Rumery*,[40] the First Circuit, as had several other circuits, found such release-dismissal agreements invalid as contravening public policy. The Supreme Court reversed, finding that the agreement was voluntarily and knowingly entered into, as in the case of plea bargains. But as the dissent pointed out, the release-dismissal agreement is inherently coercive and unfair, there being no mutuality of advantage, as there is in plea bargaining. Moreover, there is a conflict of interest between the prosecutor's interest in furthering legitimate law enforcement objectives, and at the same time protecting the town, police, or other public officials, from civil liability.

Finally, as noted above, the standards applied by the courts to prosecutors often are unrealistic. Clearly, the search for a prosecutorial *mens rea*, or guilty mind, is hazardous at best. Prosecutors do not confess their misdeeds, and presumptions are rarely invoked. Thus, in *Oregon* v. *Kennedy*,[41] a case in which a prosecutor's misconduct provoked the defendant to ask for a mistrial, the Supreme Court was asked to decide whether retrial should be barred on double jeopardy grounds. Several courts, including some New York courts, looked to the seriousness of the misconduct in deciding whether to bar retrial.[42] The Supreme Court, however, adopted the most restrictive approach possible, requiring proof that the prosecutor's specific intention was to goad the defendant into seeking a mistrial, rather than prejudicing the defendant generally. Proving such specific intent, said the four dissenting justices, is "almost inconceivable."[43]

For some prosecutors, the temptation to cross over the allowable ethical line often must be irresistible, particularly because misconduct frequently creates distinct advantages to prosecutors in helping to win their case. It takes a steadfast effort on the part of prosecutors to maintain high moral and professional standards necessary to avoid such temptations. Regrettably, many courts, notably the Supreme Court, have provided few incentives to prosecutors to avoid misconduct. As with punishment generally, deterring misconduct requires the imposition of realistic sanctions. Such sanctions are either nonexistent or not used. Prosecutors are generally immune from civil liability.[44] Imposition of discipline by bar committees is virtually unheard of.[45] Contempt rulings by trial judges are rare.[46] Appellate reversals may punish society more than the prosecutor.[47] And although appellate courts occasionally issue stinging rebukes, the decisions rarely if ever identify the offending prosecutor by name. Perhaps if the prosecutor were forced to appear before the appellate tribunal to defend his or her conduct, the incidence of courtroom misconduct might diminish.

Although not a Minister of Justice, the prosecutor's role may well be the most exacting of any public official. But by the same token, the public has a right to require of that official the highest measure of responsibility, professionalism, and integrity. Prosecutors who use their prodigious powers gracefully and fairly are no less effective as Champions of the People, and will be far worthier of respect and admiration. Courts and bar associations have to send out better messages, and provide stronger incentives for prosecutors to behave fairly.

---

[1] *McNabb* v. *United States*, 318 U.S. 332, 343 (1943).

[2] *See, e.g.* 18 U.S.C. §§ 1961 *et. seq.* (Racketeer and Corrupt Organizations Act); 18 U.S.C. § 1952 (A) (murder for hire); 18 U.S.C. § 1952 (B) (commission of violent crimes in aid of racketeering activity).

[3] *See* 18 U.S.C. § 1623 (lessening proof requirements in perjury prosecutions); Fed.R.Evid. 801 (d)(2)(E) (lessening proof requirements in conspiracy prosecutions, as interpreted in *Bourjaily* v. *United States,* 107 S.Ct. 2775 (1987).

[4] *See* 21 U.S.C. § 841 (b)(1) (increasing penalties for drug trafficking); 18 U.S.C. § 924 (c) (imposing mandatory penalty for use of firearms during commission of violent crime).

[5] Gershman, "The Harmless Error Rule: Overlooking Violations of Constitutional Rights," 14 West.B.J. 3 (1987).

[6] *United States* v. *Salerno,* 107 S.Ct. 2095 (1987) (upholding 18 U.S.C. § 3142 (e) of Bail Reform Act of 1984).

[7] *Albernaz* v. *United States,* 450 U.S. 333 (1981); *United States* v. *Blocker,* 802 F.2d 1102 (9th Cir. 1986).

[8] *See* "Rise in Executions Widening Debate," *N.Y. Times,* Nov. 1, 1987, p. 30. In *McCleskey* v. *Kemp,* 107 S.Ct. 1756 (1987), the Supreme Court upheld the imposition of the death penalty over claims that the penalty was imposed disproportionately against racial minorities. This decision may have involved the last major challenge to the death penalty as violative of the Eighth Amendment's proscription against "cruel and unusual punishments."

[9] 373 U.S. 83 (1963).

[10] *Id.* at 87.

[11] Mayer, "Hogan's Office is a kind of Ministry of Justice," *N.Y. Times Magazine,* July 23, 1967, p. 7.

[12] ABA, Standards for Criminal Justice, 3-1.1(c) (1980).

[13] 403 U.S. 443 (1971).

[14] 420 U.S. 103 (1975).

[15] *United States* v. *Young,* 470 U.S. 1, 7 (1985), quoting *Berger* v. *United States,* 295 U.S. 78, 88 (1935).

[16] *Berger* v. *United States, supra.*

[17] *See Rose* v. *Clark,* 106 Sup.Ct. 3101, 3112 (1986) (Stevens, J., concurring). *See also* Gershman, "Why Prosecutors Misbehave," 22 *Crim. L. Bull.* 131 (1986).

[18] Bar Committees rarely impose discipline on offending prosecutors. *But see In re Rook,* 276 Ore. 695, 556 P.2d 1351 (1976) (misconduct in plea bargaining). It is virtually unheard of for disciplinary sanctions to be imposed for misconduct in the courtroom.

[19] 106 Sup.Ct. 2464, 2471-73 (1986).

[19a] On March 15, 1988, Willie Darden was executed in Florida's electric chair. *N.Y. Times,* March 16, 1988, p. A15.

[20] *See* R. Traynor, THE RIDDLE OF HARMLESS ERROR (1969); Note, "Prosecutor Indiscretion: A Result of Political Influence" 34 Ind. L. J. 477, 486 (1959).

[21] 106 S.Ct. 1712 (1986).

[22] 106 S.Ct. 617 (1986).

[23] *See United States* v. *Benchimol,* 471 U.S. 453, 458 (1985) (dissenting opinion).

[24] 475 U.S. 66 (1986).

[25] 474 U.S. 438 (1986).

[26] 461 U.S. 499 (1983).

[27] *United States* v. *Agurs,* 427 U.S. 97 (1976); *Giglio* v. *United States,* 405 U.S. 150 (1972).

[28] 473 U.S. 667, 682 (1985).

[29] 455 U.S. 209 (1982).

[30] 458 U.S. 858 (1982).

[31] 467 U.S. 479 (1984).

[32] 52 N.Y.2d 304, 419 N.E.2d 864, 437 N.Y.S.2d 961. (1981).

[33] *Young* v. *United States ex rel. Vuitton et Fils S.A.,* 107 S.Ct. 2124, 2141 (1987).

[34] *See* A. Goldstein, THE PASSIVE JUDICIARY: PROSECUTORIAL DISCRETION AND THE GUILTY PLEA (1981).

[35] 470 U.S. 598 (1985).

[36] 457 U.S. 368 (1982).

[37] 434 U.S. 357 (1978).

[38] *People* v. *Stephens,* 122 A.D.2d 608, 505 N.Y.S.2d 393 (4th Dept. 1986).

[39] 107 S.Ct. 2680 (1987).

[40] 107 S.Ct. 1187 (1987).

[41] 456 U.S. 667 (1982).

[42] *See People* v. *Cavallerio,* 104 Misc.2d 436, 428 N.Y.S.2d 585 (1980). *See also Petrucelli* v. *Smith,* 544 F.Supp. 627 (W.D.N.Y. 1982).

[43] 456 U.S. at 688.

[44] *Imbler* v. *Pachtman.* 424 U.S. 409 (1976).

[45] *See* B. Gershman, PROSECUTORIAL MISCONDUCT § 13.6 (1985).

[46] *See* B. Gershman, PROSECUTORIAL MISCONDUCT § 13.3 (1985).

[47] *See United States* v. *Modica,* 663 F.2d 1173, 1182-86 (2d Cir. 1981), *cert. denied,* 456 U.S. 989 (1982).

Pretrial Diversion: Promises We Can't Keep

William G. Matthews

Mr. Matthews is Director of the Ingham County Prosecutor's Diversion Program, 303 W. Kalamazoo, Lansing, MI 48933.

ABSTRACT. The pretrial diversion movement was spawned in the wake of 1960s reforms and represented a major departure from current criminological practice. The thinking was that diversion would shift the focus from a punitive orientation to a client-centered or "helping" approach. Simultaneously, diversion offered a panacea to the system's aging aches and pains. In the final analysis, the diversion movement has not achieved many (if any) of the reforms or goals that were originally formulated. Its survival today is based almost exclusively in terms of how well it serves the political interests of the jurisdiction in which it is located. Helping the offender is no longer what the diversion movement is all about.

In 1965, Genesee County Prosecutor Robert Leonard introduced the first operational adult diversion program in the United States in the city of Flint, Michigan. Called the Citizens' Probation Authority[1] (CPA), it represented a radical departure from current criminological practice. It questioned the traditional wisdom and the conventional response to criminality by emphasizing a nonpunitive route to the delivery of rehabilitative services. The thinking was that such a response would shift the focus from a "punitive" orientation to a client-centered "helping" approach, thus eliminating the criminogenic stigma associated with lengthy adversarial proceedings and the ensuing conviction.

In this model, "clients" were offered a "voluntary" probation with expanded rehabilitative services (e.g., employment counseling and training, individual counseling, etc.) by professional counselors and social workers—services not considered readily available in most probation departments. Successful participants were allowed to have the criminal charge dismissed and the record "cleared," providing the participant " . . . with an alternative to a permanently recorded label of 'delinquent' or 'criminal,' as well as an avenue through which to gain a foothold in the legitimate opportunity structure of society" (Pieczenik, 1970, p. 2).

Within a few short years, the concept of diversion was greeted with messianic enthusiasm by a host of prestigious commissions and organizations, including the American Bar Association, the U.S. Department of Justice, and the National Council on Crime and Delinquency, to name just a few. Although the actual practice[2] was far from new, the introduction of *formalized* models of diversion promised a "visible" form of discretion that would not only rehabilitate the offender, but relieve congested court and prosecutorial dockets, reduce incarceration rates, expedite the delivery of services, and generally cure the system's many infirmities.

In 1967, the President's Crime Commission recommended that " . . . alternatives to pretrial incarceration be developed for the non-criminal disposition . . ." of defendants charged with criminal violations. Shortly thereafter, the Department of Labor Manpower Administration, and later the Law Enforcement Assistance Administration provided the seed money for diversion programs around the United States. Grants for diversion generally consisted of three-year projects, reducing the federal share with each successive year.

The movement spread quickly, if haphazardly, in spite of the fact that there was little formal analysis or research to determine its impact or effectiveness. The possibility of infringement of rights in the process was given only scant attention—with some exceptions.[3] By 1980, according to the National Association of Pretrial Services Directory, some two-hundred adult diversion programs had been introduced. But the practice and the theory of diversion were immediately irreconcilable. Crohn (1980) states that "a partial explanation for these diverse and contrasting practices can be found in the lack of preexisting statutory or constitutional bases for their development" (p. 23). She contrasts this

From *Journal of Offender Counseling Services & Rehabilitation*, Vol. 12, No. 2, Spring 1988, pp. 191-202. Copyright © 1988 by The Haworth Press, Inc., 10 Alice Street, Binghampton, NY 13904.

sharply with the Bail Reform Act of 1966 that serves as the reference document for the pretrial release movement.

In 1978, following several years of debate, the National Association of Pretrial Services adopted a handbook of performance standards and goals. Today, the *Handbook* still embodies the "ideals" of diversion, although there is little agreement among practitioners as to what constitutes normative practice. Currently, only a few states have enacted a statutory mandate for diversion, and many of these were accomplished only after the programs were substantially developed.

Many programs today continue to divert cases on an ad hoc basis[4] or use vague screening procedures that keep out those defendants considered "bad risks" by police and prosecutors. Diversion also provided prosecutors with a new tool: "diversion bargaining." Defendants who were not otherwise considered eligible for diversion under established guidelines, often had charges against them reduced to meet referral criteria in exchange for testimony or for turning informant. Conversely, defendants who satisfied the initial screening criteria often received additional charges in order to contravene admission criteria.[5] The worst models combined surveillance techniques with polygraphs and interrogation.

In the process, the practice of diversion almost immediately violated one of the basic tenets of the movement by obfuscating the decision making process. The discretion was shifted from prosecutor to screening attorney to program administrator without the possibility of administrative review or appeal. This issue was compounded and further confused by the wide array of organizational structures that operated diversion programs: police, prosecutorial, private, and judicial. Admission criteria, as well as requirements for participation, were determined more by the local political climate than by statute or by law.

Today, the national *Standards* chief use seems to rest in chronologing a dying reform movement (Pryor, 1980). Few, if any, programs come close to realizing the *Standards* in practice. Most programs are particularly vulnerable in the areas of admission and eligibility criteria, confidentiality, and revocations.

The societal context of the first diversion programs is of no small significance in assessing the development of the movement. These were troubled and tumultuous times characterized by civil disorder and confrontation between the socially and economically disenfranchised and the major institutions of our society. It was equally clear that " . . . the conventional techniques of the criminal justice agencies were not aiding their involvement . . . and often resulted in increased hostility and bitterness" (Vera, 1972, p. 78).

Consequently, the first models of diversion were concerned primarily with the needs of the individual defendant. The criminal justice system was viewed as

the criminogenic enemy, and to be effective meant operating outside of the system.[6] Spawned in the wake of Keynesian economics and Johnsonian "Great Society" social experimentation, diversion programs were in the vanguard of the new evangelism. The diversion position was supported by the work of Martinson (1974) whose analysis of correctional programs claimed that the system itself was self-perpetuating and criminogenic.

Borrowing generously from the principles of labeling theory (Becker, 1964; Schur, 1969, 1971; Lemert, 1976), diversion programs claimed that they could be more successful than their adversarial counterparts because of the absence of a "societal reaction" dimension.[7] In this model the deviant's behavior is of far less importance than the stigmatizing effects of the criminal justice response in perpetuating antisocial behavior. "Furthermore, formal dispositions are likely to entail both coercion, by threatening sanctions in response to any lack of cooperation with officials, and social control, through placing the individual under strict rules of behavior" (Osgood and Weichselbaum, 1984, p. 35).

Although diversion programs viewed the entire adversarial system as part of the problem, they quickly adopted their own set of rules and procedures which paralleled the coercive and controlling features of the system they were designed to replace. Noncompliance with the terms of a "voluntary" probation produced consequences no less significant for the individual than a similar court ordered revocation proceeding. In fact, it is highly likely that an unsuccessful termination from a diversion program may actually produce a more harsh reaction from the system; tantamount to a court ordered revocation. This is based on the notion that diversion programs are still considered to be more service oriented than traditional probation. Consequently, a failure at this point is an additional negative label that the defendant must carry, not to mention the implicit assumption of guilt that stems from such participation. This is particularly alarming when one considers that prior to the diversion participation, "most . . . would receive little or no sanction from the system" (Baker, 1977).

At least part of the apparent disparity between theory and practice can also be explained by the constantly shifting societal focus. Just as the liberal affluence of the 1960s produced a generation critical of institutional authority, the 1970s gave way to Proposition-13 inflation fighting approaches that forced critical decisions at all levels of government. The new buzz words were "efficiency" and "effectiveness." As federal and state grants expired, local jurisdictions were forced to either absorb operating budgets of diversion programs, or abandon them altogether. To survive, diversion programs were encouraged to once again overstate and overpromise what they could do, not for the defendant, but for the system. Crohn (1980) again observes correctly that it was at this point that pretrial diversion switched from being an alternative to the criminal justice system to one *within* the criminal justice system " . . . dominated by the priorities of the system under which it functions" (p. 33).

The issues of "social justice" quickly became submerged in a new mood and a new lexicon that demanded harsher measures and declared "war on crime." The image of diversion as a criminal justice welfare program was no longer an asset. However, diversion programs demonstrated their versatility and resourcefulness, by realigning their operating procedures and shifting their underlying rationale more consistent with the current national mood, and the system's goals of effectiveness and efficiency. In some instances this meant eliminating all but a skeletal structure of staff, relying heavily on volunteers, and, sadly, forfeiting the human services emphasis. Eventually, most diversion programs were reduced drastically in size, or were reconstituted under the aegis of probation departments, and became diversionary in name only. As the mood of the country shifted, diversion programs stepped to the front of the class and proved that they could be as tough, or tougher, than their adversarial competition. But the new measure of success had less to do with client success than it did with meeting the political demands of the immediate environment. This translated into diverting only low-risk cases and then extracting high penalties in the form of probation fees, restitution, and community service—penalties substantially harsher than would have normally accrued from a conviction on the crime.

Relieved of much of the bureaucratic and legal encumbrance of the traditional system, diversion programs were able to compensate victims more quickly, and often at a higher dollar return. Restitution formulas often included a modified punitive damages formula, or assessed liability based purely on *acknowledged* crimes. Defendants, in some jurisdictions, were occasionally held accountable for the lost wages of victims, and/or the wages of police and security personnel involved in the crime.

Faced with diminishing operating budgets, diversion programs assessed probation costs to participants as well. Many programs have, in fact, received considerable popular support by adjusting their probation fee rate to reflect actual dollar funding, targeting economic self-sufficiency as a system goal. Fees assessed frequently reached the three-hundred dollar range on even the most minor offense.[8]

The diversion programs that survived into the 1980s emerged with finely honed political and survival skills, and quickly adapted to the prevailing Zeitgeist. Just as "efficiency" and "effectiveness" were the buzz words of the 1970s, "networking" "self-help," and "accountability" peppered the language of the 1980s. "Community service," now standard practice in diversion programs and probation departments, as well, became part of the new order. It provided diversion programs with a measure of increased control, and gave the respective officeholder a tactical means for addressing local political interests that was both potent and highly visible. As local service agencies felt the inflationary crunch of reduced staff and smaller operating budgets, they frequently turned to community diversion programs to supplement their losses. Unlike probation departments operated by the courts, diversion programs were able to respond quickly to these community demands. Consequently, the diversion participant emerged as the "new volunteer" for the 1980s. Through "networking," the continued vitality of both programs (or agencies) was assured, with divertees being required to perform as many as two-hundred hours of volunteer work on the most minor offense. Today it is axiomatic that diversion programs are synonymous with the community service condition in many jurisdictions, and the steady proliferation of municipal diversion programs across the country seems to be based almost entirely on this sanction for their existence.[9]

Finally, to ensure further public support, screening categories were restricted to low-risk, low priority prosecution cases. This typically meant misdemeanor larcenies, malicious destruction, domestic crimes, or minor (drug) possession offenses: cases that were frequently dismissed outright, or which resulted in summary probation only. The intent was to target a population of offenders that was mainstream America: middle-class kids charged with shoplifting or possession of marijuana.

Needless to say, the diversion programs that survived into the 1980s were only shadows of their former selves. The underlying rationale and philosophy had been altered beyond recognition. The rights and the needs of the individual defendant held little or no consideration in many program operations.

Today in fact, it is axiomatic of diversion programs across America, that they tend to be harsher, more restrictive, and more controlling that the court imposed sanction. But the promises still linger.

PROMISE: CLEAN RECORDS

One of the primary assumptions inherent in diversion models is that of providing the defendant with an alternative, so that he might avoid the stigma of being branded "criminal." Defendants who successfully participate in diversion are promised that their records will be wiped clean. The theory is that by avoiding the criminal label, they will also avoid the societal reaction that might deprive them of legitimate opportunity.

Few programs today, however, can keep their promise of a clean record. In some jurisdictions, the record is marked "expunged," but the original record is easily detectable. Other jurisdictions enter the criminal offense data as they normally would in the law enforcement computer (LEIN), reporting the disposition status as simply "unknown," or "referred to diversion." This, of course, is frequently tantamount to a conviction, especially where the defendant comes into contact with the authorities again. Additionally, many jurisdictions have a friendly relationship with the court probation department and the police, and allow open access to closed diversion files even where the record is one of successful completion. Where the referral occurs at the pre-arrest stage, there is still the possibility of an "informal" record being maintained by police. Finally, an arrest record often results in the creation of an FBI computer file. Even where successful completion earns the defendant the right to have a clean record with local and state authorities, the same guarantee cannot be made with respect to the FBI file, since this is outside of the jurisdictional authority of local programs.

PROMISE: FORMALIZED DISCRETION

Traditionally, the prosecutor had been granted the statutory authority to decide when to charge and what to charge. This is extended to the administration of diversion programs which operate under the prosecutor's broad powers of discretion. Consequently, the prosecutor may decide whether a defendant will receive diversion consideration, or be charged in the criminal justice system. In *State v. Leonardis* (1977) the Supreme Court of New Jersey affirmed the prosecutor's right to exercise control in the decision to divert unless the defendant could demonstrate arbitrariness and capriciousness on the prosecutor's part.

Most diversion programs today have distilled the diversion decision into written policies and guidelines. Decisions to divert are generally based on offense category, criminal record, and occasionally residence status, with a wide variation between programs as to which offense categories are divertible. Once the initial decision to refer a case has been made, however, the final decision is generally made by program staff. Consequently, while the guidelines are "formalized," the decision to divert is an administrative one that is unchecked and unreviewed in most program operations. For example, a defendant in some jurisdictions may be declined because of vague attitudinal or motivational characteristics. Others are rejected as "excessive risk" which can imply almost anything from a belief on the part of the investigator that the person is involved in ongoing criminal activity, to the presence of a chronic drug problem. It is not unusual for a prosecutorial diversion program to reject fifty percent of all cases referred for one reason or another.

Equally troublesome is the issue of program revoca-

tion. Two categories are recognized for termination: (1) violation of the terms of the probation through acts of omission or commission, or (2) violation of the criminal statutes. In the first instance, failure to keep appointments or participate in some aspect of the rehabilitative process is recognized as grounds for revocation. Almost all diversion programs recognize the commission of a new offense as automatic grounds for revocation.[10] The decision to divert, as well as the final decision to terminate, is usually an administrative function by program staff with only scant attention to due process.[11]

PROMISE: A SYSTEM ALTERNATIVE

Early on in its development diversion programs sold criminal justice rainbows, promising relief from jail overcrowding, spiraling court dockets, runaway recidivism rates, and burgeoning prosecutorial caseloads. Diversion held out the promise to defendants that they would be saved the needless expense, humiliation, punishment, and ultimately, the record, resulting from the adversarial process. Unfortunately, in most cases the defendants "volunteered" for sanctions that were harsher and more restrictive than would have normally accrued if convicted on the original charge.

Fueled by domestic spending cuts and legislative initiatives that demanded more accountability in social programs, plus a new public attitude that was less sympathetic to the plight of the offender, the diversion movement began to wane almost immediately. The offense instead of the offender was targeted for diversion. This meant that only low-priority, low-risk cases—cases which could not possibly demonstrate either cost-effectiveness or system impact were diverted. Substantial research supported the claim that defendants would receive little or no sanction from the system (Baker, 1977). Further, many cases in the absence of a diversion mechanism, would automatically be dismissed.

Even as this phenomenon was becoming understood, however, many programs continued to make rehabilitative claims that bordered on the ridiculous. Statistical reports on recidivism rates constituted a gross misrepresentation of program impact. In New Jersey, one report stated that they were successful " . . . in achieving rehabilitation in nineteen out of twenty cases (SCCPI)." Not infrequently, diversion programs advertised rehabilitative success in ninety-five percent of their cases. Very little recognition was given to the more important qualitative factors involved in that computation. Regrettably, program administrators refused to acknowledge that the low recidivism rate was just another measure that diversion, as an alternative, was clearly off the mark.

SUMMARY AND CONCLUSION

Diversion, as originally conceived, was designed to reform some of the old notions about crime and punishment. Theoretically, it was supposed to serve the defendant by assisting him to obtain needed rehabilitative services, while avoiding the labeling and dehumanizing aspect of the traditional system.[12] The focus, however, soon shifted as the national climate shifted from an emphasis on offender rehabilitative programs to victim compensation programs. This shift was accompanied by a "hardening" of attitudes towards the criminal justice system in general, as well as a more conservative economic outlook. The offender, increasingly unpopular among funding sources, was quickly abandoned in the shuffle, except where he could be used to benefit the system. Diversion annual reports stressed their achievements almost exclusively in terms of the criminal justice economy: community service hours, restitution and service fee collections, and recidivism rates. Increasingly, diversion came to resemble the system it was designed to replace.

The survival of diversion today is based almost exclusively in terms of how well it serves the political and community interests of the jurisdiction in which it is located. This translates plainly into increased revenues, and political clout through public work projects. If defendants are counseled, or employed, or assisted in the process that is, presumably, a laudable act of the second order. But *helping* the offender is no longer what diversion is all about. Unfortunately, diversion programs are still sold to the public based on the premises and the promises of the 1960s.

In the final analysis, the diversion movement has not achieved many (if any) of the reforms or goals that were originally formulated. It has not significantly reduced either court or prosecutorial caseloads. It has not impacted incarceration rates. It has not produced a more effective service delivery system for offenders, or eliminated the labeling process. Neither has it reduced financial costs. In fact, evidence seems to suggest that just the opposite may be true: diversion is associated with higher costs due to the fact that it creates a separate system for cases normally targeted either for dismissal or summary probation. Given the prevailing mood, there is no indication that this will change in the foreseeable future. As long as the shoplifter remains the "rehabilitative focus" of diversion, alternatives will be a luxury we can scarcely afford.

NOTES

1. Diversion programs are variously known as Citizens' Probation Authority, deferred prosecution programs, or, simply, diversion programs. The focus of the present analysis is on the prosecutorial model of diversion.

2. The practice of diversion is as old as the criminal justice system itself. The model of diversion that emerged was conceived as a visible and formal model, distinct from the informal practice of diversion.

3. The National Association of Pretrial Services (NAPSA) was one of the first organizations to recognize the peril to citizen rights.

4. Although most diversion programs recognize an objective screen and have promulgated offense categories and referral criteria, there is considerable latitude in terms of which cases get referred. Additionally, most police agencies have become adept at avoiding the diversion screen when it suits their purposes.

5. For example, an individual charged with non-sufficient funds might be denied diversion based on a report of additional "outstanding" checks, even where no other charges are sought which would disqualify the defendant. Similarly, a defendant might be charged with two or more offenses, any one of which might disqualify the individual for diversion.

6. Operating outside of the system actually translated into operating "in the wings" of the system, because most programs were attached umbilically to a particular office.

7. This was probably naive thinking. Defendants referred to diversion were frequently arrested and arraigned beforehand. Later, the process of participating in various referrals or programs as part of the rehabilitative regimen constituted a "societal reaction" under any definition.

8. Most programs offer a waiver of indigency on all or part of the fee for those who cannot afford to pay.

9. In municipal diversion programs, participants are often referred to the local voluntary action program for screening to other community agencies, and lack the casework component.

10. Diversion participants are generally revoked for a new charge, not a conviction.

11. New Jersey was one of the first states to incorporate procedural safeguards into the termination process of defendants who did not complete the program. Their procedures are similar to *Morrissey v. Brewer* and *Gagnon v. Scarpelli*.

12. In practice, diversion participants are no more "voluntary" clients than those convicted and placed on a court ordered probation.

REFERENCES

Baker, S. *Court Employment Project Evaluation.* Vera Institute of Justice, New York, New York, 1977.

Becker, H. S. *The other side.* New York: Free Press, 1964.

Becker, H. S. Outsiders. In E. Rubington and M. Weinberg (Eds.), *Deviance: The interactionist perspective.* New York: Macmillan, 1978.

Gagnon v. Scarpelli 411 *U.S.* 778, 93 *S. Ct.* 1756, 36 *L. Ed.* 2d 656 (1973).

Irwin, J. *Prisons in turmoil.* Boston: Little, Brown and Company, 1980.

Lemert, E. M. Instead of court: Diversion in juvenile justice. In Carter & Klein (Eds.), *Back on the street.* New York: Prentice-Hall, 1976.

Martinson, R. What works? Questions and answers about prison reform. *The Public Interest,* 1974, *35,* 22–54.

Morrissey v. Brewer 408 *U.S.* 471, 92 *S. Ct.* 2593, *L. Ed.* 2d 484 (1972).

Performance Standards and Goals for Pretrial Release and Diversion, National Association of Pretrial Services Agencies (NAPSA), Washington, DC, 1978.

Pryor, D. E. and Smith, W. F. *Pretrial Issues: Significant Findings Concerning Pretrial Release,* 1982. Pretrial Resource Center, Washington, DC.

Schur, E. Reactions to deviance: A critical assessment. *American Journal of Sociology,* 1969, *75,* 309–322.

Schur, E. *Labeling deviant behavior,* New York: Harper and Row, 1971.

State v. Leonardis, II, 73 N.J. 360 (1977).

The Myth of the General Right to Bail

Robert F. Nagel

Machine-gun fire on city streets in broad daylight, pushers arrested in schoolyard playgrounds, commando operations against drug lords in South American jungles—such are the images that in recent years have frightened the public and galvanized it to declare a war on drugs. Proposals for coping with drug-related crimes range from executing "kingpins" to banning beepers from public schools. Legislation enacted in 1988 provides more federal money for drug treatment and education, and denies certain benefits (including public housing) to drug felons. Former Mayor Koch called for using the military to arrest drug offenders and for incarcerating them in tents in the Nevada desert. Others urge legalization of narcotic use. The nation now has a drug "czar," who has proposed an elaborate national strategy that includes expanding drug-testing programs, sending offenders to boot camps, and publicizing the names of first-time users.

As serious as the spread of drug-related crime is, the alarm and dismay that it has precipitated are connected to even deeper reservoirs of fear. The prevalence of illegal drug use and its associated street crime raises doubts about the capacity of government to maintain minimal order. This underlying anxiety over the precariousness of civil life may seem paranoid in a stable, wealthy democracy. But short confrontations with anarchy are realistic threats for everyone. The possibility of sudden violence has always been with us, especially for the elderly, the urban poor, and women. The drug crisis has intensified and spread the fears that have long been felt by these vulnerable groups. It has engendered a broad array of policy proposals because it has given all groups a sharper sense of the possibility of violent disorder and civil breakdown.

Despite our concern about violence, however, we continue to allow those who have been arrested for serious crimes to return to society on bail. Sometimes we even release felons convicted of violent offenses pending the completion of their appeals. Already in-

jured and frightened by what cannot be controlled, why do we release suspects who have been identified, captured, and safely detained?

The answer is not that those awaiting trial or appeal are harmless. As one would expect, there are many reported instances of bailed suspects repeating the crime for which they had been arrested. In one California case, for instance, a man posted bond after being arrested for two murders; he then murdered a seventeen-year-old, only to be released on bail *again*. Rearrest rates for bailees have been found to be as high as 35 percent, and in one study almost 30 percent of those rearrested were arrested two or more times while on bail. Such findings are only suggestive because arrests do not always lead to convictions and because crimes do not always result in arrests. Statistical studies of "bail crime," moreover, yield varying results and are the subject of considerable debate. But it is surely not necessary to wait for definitive numbers before concluding that a significant portion of those charged with violent crimes are dangerous. This common-sense view has shaped bail laws throughout Western Europe, Australia, and elsewhere. In the United States it influenced the federal Bail Reform Act of 1984, which provides for preventive detention when there is convincing evidence that the arrestee is dangerous, and it is implicit in the common (though illicit) American practice of setting prohibitively high bail for serious crimes.

Still, in this country we often turn suspects loose despite strong evidence that they have sold narcotics, burgled, robbed, shot, maimed, or raped. Even under the federal preventive-detention law, only 17 percent of drug defendants are denied bail under the "dangerousness" provisions; 68 percent are released. While we cannot eliminate crime completely, we can take the obvious and direct step of denying bail for serious felonies. The reason that we do not is a textbook illustration of the way in which extravagant claims about constitutional rights work themselves into our thinking, eventually converting costly, even bizarre, policies into unassailable moral imperatives.

Inflated Rhetoric

The language used even in informed discourse about the Constitution betrays how strong is the appeal of certainty and simplicity. Through the years, academic commentary on the right to bail has often referred to "our absolute right to bail" in noncapital cases. Supreme Court justices have intoned that without an "unequivocal" right to freedom before conviction, "the presumption of innocence, secured only after centuries of struggle, would lose its meaning." In bemoaning the preventive-detention provisions of the 1984 Bail Reform Act, the *New York Times* editorialized that "America's very sense of justice turns on the noble presumption of innocence."

Carried along by such heady rhetoric, a conscientious citizen might conclude that the Constitution requires the government to treat people who have been seen committing vicious crimes as if they were innocent. Presumably even violent felons are entitled to walk out of jail after arrest, at least if they can show that they have appeared punctually when tried for their previous crimes. If such an inference seems too strange to warrant serious attention, consider the words of Harvard Law School's Laurence Tribe:

> [The presumption of innocence] represents a commitment to the proposition that a man who stands accused of crime is no less entitled than his accuser to freedom and respect as an innocent member of the community. Only those deprivations necessary to assure the progress of the proceedings against him . . . may be squared with this basic postulate of dignity and equality.

Elevated and simplistic rhetoric of this kind comes naturally to the elites who are immersed in constitutional law, in part because their subject matter is supposed to represent our fundamental, abiding political morality. Those who write about our deepest values can be expected to indulge some inspirational and exaggerated notions. The Constitution, however, is neither absolute nor clear on the issue of pretrial release; rhetoric about "the presumption of innocence" is not true to the limited and ambiguous values that are actually part of our fundamental charter.

The Fifth and Fourteenth Amendments provide, not that those arrested must be presumed innocent, but that government may not deprive any person of liberty "without due process of law." To require that legal process be followed is not at all the same as to specify that only a full criminal trial can justify detaining those accused of crimes. Indeed, we know the Framers did not mean the latter because their practice was to deprive the accused of at least some liberty after those limited procedures incident to lawful arrest.

Similarly, the Eighth Amendment provides, not that there is a right to bail, but that "excessive" bail shall not be required. To demand that judges set reasonable bail where legislatures have indicated that bail is appropriate is not at all the same as to require that legislatures authorize bail for all offenses. Indeed, we know the Framers did not mean the latter because their practice was to deny bail in capital cases. In the face of a long English and colonial history of statutory specification of the offenses for which bail was available, the Framers addressed the Eighth Amendment primarily to judges. The Framers did not require that "bail shall be admitted," although they certainly knew how to use such language; not only did the Judiciary Act of 1789, which was enacted by the same Congress that proposed the Bill of Rights, make this provision with respect to noncapital crimes, but other constitutional rights—for example, that "the accused shall enjoy the right to a speedy and public trial"—were plainly worded to create substantive protections. Against all this evidence, many constitutional scholars have nevertheless concluded that the Framers intended to create a right to bail. The main reason for ascribing this astonishing intention to the Framers is Professor Caleb Foote's suggestion that George Mason (who drafted the language of the bail clause) did not know what he was doing because he was not a lawyer.

Bail and Legal Traditions

Perhaps recognizing that attributing important constitutional meaning to a drafting mistake is a bit weak, much of the bail commentary also relies on assertions about "our" traditions and practices. Thus Daniel Freed and Patricia Wald write in their influential *Bail in the United States* that "bail in America has developed for a single lawful purpose: to release the accused with assurance he will return at trial." According to Tribe, "we have traditionally detained individuals likely to flee or otherwise avoid prosecution," and indeed "we have accepted some risk of crime as the inevitable price of a system that promises to punish no man until it is shown beyond a reasonable doubt that he has committed a specific illegal act."

These descriptions of what "we" have done are no more accurate than the farfetched arguments about what our forefathers supposedly did. It is true, as most writings emphasize, that ever since the Judiciary Act of 1789 there has been a federal statutory right to bail in noncapital cases, and that a long history of colonial laws provided for bail "unless for capital offenses, where the proof is evident, or the presumption great." As Albert Alschuler has demonstrated, this legal tradition extends both backward and forward in time. It extends back to thirteenth-century England, were statutes created a right to bail if the punishment did not involve loss of "life or member" or if there was only "light suspicion." It extends forward to the constitutions of some forty states, where bail is provided for except in capital cases where "the proof is evident."

But this impressively long history gives little support to a general right to bail. In thirteenth-century England, bail could be denied for robbery, rape, burglary, manslaughter, and other felonies if the defendant was caught in the act. During the American colonial period, bail could be denied in capital cases, which included such crimes as murder, idolatry, witchcraft, bestiality, adultery, rape, treason, arson, and burglary. At the time that the Eighth Amendment and the Judiciary Act of 1789 were being framed, most serious felonies were capital offenses. It was well into the nineteenth century before the federal government reduced the dozens of crimes punishable by death to a few that included murder, treason, and rape. In this century, states dropped and added crimes to the list of capital offenses in response to public mood; at one time or another, train wrecking, kidnapping, armed robbery, espionage, rape, arson, treason, and providing narcotics to minors have each been punishable by death.

In short, for almost all of our history both the federal government and state governments made the death penalty available for those crimes thought to be especially heinous or threatening. A secondary effect of classifying a crime as "capital" was to permit the denial of bail for that offense. "We" have long followed the sensible path of using legislation to reflect the public's sense of repugnance to particular crimes, at once determining the severity of the punishment and allowing for an adequate sense of community safety.

But imposition of the death penalty can no longer be used as a shorthand method for making decisions about the availability of bail. In recent years the Supreme Court has declared capital punishment to be unconstitutional "cruel and unusual punishment" when imposed for offenses—like rape—that do not involve murder, and it has greatly restricted the availability of capital punishment even in murder cases. Moreover, attitudes on the morality of the death penalty have changed since the framing of our Constitution, and some states do not permit capital punishment even for first-degree murder. Despite the fact that these decisions are not directly relevant either legally or morally to the issue of pretrial detention, their consequence has been to make a range of reprehensible and dangerous crimes not only exempt from the death penalty but also bailable.

The decision to link capital punishment and the denial of bail, however, was always a matter of federal statute and state law. Now that the Court has strictly limited the availability of the death penalty, Congress and the states can exercise the discretion that the drafters of the Constitution wisely left them. They can decide whether the availability of bail should be determined on a different basis than the availability of the death penalty.

Already there are some legislative initiatives that permit or require the denial of bail for certain noncapital crimes. The District of Columbia Council recently approved emergency rules permitting pretrial detention for crimes involving firearms and drugs, and Senators Brock Adams and Phil Gramm have suggested a parallel congressional enactment. Michigan has classified serious sexual offenses and certain other violent crimes as nonbailable. Nebraska similarly classifies first-degree sexual assault, and several jurisdictions limit bail for multiple offenders. As Alschuler has pointed out, these state laws continue the legal tradition dating back to the thirteenth century of permitting the denial of bail for serious crimes, if the proof is "evident or the presumption great."

So far, however, the reassertion of traditional decisionmaking prerogatives on bail has been *ad hoc* and scattered. One reason is the influence over public opinion of the "presumption of innocence" mythology. The elite groups that propagate this exaggerated and simplistic mythology are clinging to a position that no ordinary sensible person (let alone the rigorously realistic Framers of our Constitution) would take seriously. The influence of these groups has helped to keep us from coming to grips with the tragic consequences and dilemmas associated with pretrial release.

One-Way Compassion

Constitutional opinion-leaders tend to focus their concern on those against whom the government is acting. Our actual Constitution, of course, was designed not only to protect individuals from government power but also to authorize the collective use of power to insure, among other things, domestic tranquillity. Everyone knows this, but those immersed in constitutional law are inclined to emphasize what courts normally concern themselves with—the adjudication of claims about rights. Thus the great bulk of influential writing about bail has centered on the various injustices that can surround the denial of bail: the racial and economic discrimination that can be involved in setting high bail, the availability of alternate mechanisms to assure appearance at trial, the difficulty of predicting dangerousness, and so on. These are all serious problems, but for the most part the literature emphasizes the costs to individuals of denying bail to such an extent that it ignores or minimizes the costs to society of granting bail.

Again, Professor Tribe illustrates the deficiency. Writing in 1970, he described the offenses committed by persons awaiting trial as "only a small component of the total crime problem." Indeed, "only 5.9% of all persons indicted in the United States District Court for the District of Columbia in 1968 allegedly committed an offense while on bail." He described another study as showing that "less than 9.2%" of those released were charged with new offenses, and in yet another study "only 4.5%" were arrested for violent crimes. Masked by all those "only"s is the reality of suffering and fear felt by the victims unlucky enough to be asserting a simple need for governmental protection rather than a constitutional right against government. If there is any doubt about how far one-sided attention to rights can drive sophisticated constitutionalists, Tribe resolves it: "Indeed, it is difficult to imagine any governmental interest unrelated to the integrity of pending proceedings that might justify singling out for special disabilities those persons charged with crime."

Such hyperconcern for rights not only obscures the importance of social interests, but also magnifies the harms that might result from limiting rights. When the *New York Times* editorialized against the preventive-detention reforms of 1984, it acknowledged that some pretrial detainees present a threat of violence to the public, but concluded: "The sharper danger is that tomorrow's prosecutor will find it easier to 'regulate' other defendants who harbor unpopular ideas." While there are real problems with preventive detention, surely it is strained to paint the immediate threat of violence by accused criminals as less real than the remote possibility that the government will misuse pretrial detention to trample freedom of speech. Nonetheless, in making dire predictions about the consequences of restricting bail, the *Times* was just echoing constitutional experts. Justice Jackson (quoted with approval by Freed and Wald) wrote that "imprisonment to protect society from predicted . . . offenses is . . . fraught with danger of excesses and injustice. . . ." And Tribe, concerned that continuing pressure to broaden preventive detention is "inevitable," has concluded ominously: "What begins as an ounce of detention . . . may well become the first step of a profound shift in our system of criminal justice." In the topsy-turvy world of what is called "constitutional" law, real dangers and immediate injuries that could be prevented by collective action are unimportant, while hypothetical and often fanciful fears about future violations of rights have grave significance.

In normal discourse, anyone asserting this peculiar combination of positions would bear a strong burden of persuasion. Ordinary reactions and common-sense beliefs can, of course, be wrong, but usually those asserting strongly counterintuitive claims shoulder a responsibility of justification. The elites who expound the Constitution, however, do not rely on their own authority; they purport to be reaffirming basic decisions already made, extraordinary wisdom already applied. Indeed, the mythic status of the Constitution is actually consistent with decisions that seem unwise and beyond common understanding. The essential idea of constitutional rights, says the legal philosopher Ronald Dworkin, is "that an individual is entitled to protection . . . even at the cost of the general interest." Under this view, to persist stoically in guarding rights in ways that have unfortunate consequences is actually one sign that the rights being vindicated are "constitutional."

It is always possible that original constitutional understandings or our deep political traditions require the protection of particular rights that have turned out to be unwise and socially harmful. But it is fairly clear that the right to bail does not fall into this category. Nevertheless, realistic bail reform is as precarious as it is limited. Not only do many conscientious decision-makers assume that it would be somehow un-American to deny bail in noncapital cases, but the habits of thought that underlie bail mythology find their purest expression in judicial interpretations. It is distinctly possible that the Supreme Court might invalidate some of the sensible bail reforms that have arisen so hesitantly from the ashes of the Court's death-penalty case law. It is important, therefore, to ask whether our real Constitution—the Constitution of the Founding Fathers and of our sustained political traditions—can be vindicated in the courts, where too often common sense is the first casualty.

Prospects in the Courts

"Sophisticated" thinking about the right to bail has not given expression to our underlying constitutional agreements, but rather has diverted attention from solid evidence about the nature and extent of those agreements. This diversion is not necessarily cynical or dishonest; it is primarily the result of earnest efforts to cope with facts that contradict the overwrought moralistic claims that are the starting place for so much of the discourse on the Constitution. As the Court's record in such areas as free speech, equal protection, and due process fully demonstrates, our jurists can be as subject as the rest of us to the allure of uncomplicated moralism.

Judges, moreover, have a special temptation to simplify the complex constitutional values relating to bail because they have the very real difficulty of applying a contradictory set of principles in concrete circumstances. Consider the problem that the courts face: We have a long legal tradition of permitting the denial of bail where there is compelling evidence of a serious crime, and this practice is consistent with the limited constitutional protection against "excessive bail" in the Eighth Amendment. We also have a strong tradition of allowing punishment only after the procedural protections afforded in a trial, and this tradition is manifest in the due-process clauses of the Fifth and Fourteenth Amendments. How can a principle that permits pretrial detention be squared with the principle of due process? Although it would surely be an enticing solution, a serious judge cannot ignore either principle. A mature understanding of the Constitution requires coming to terms with its limitations and inconsistencies. The best that courts can do is to try to accommodate the conflicting standards that coexist in our fundamental law.

The Supreme Court has tried to do just this by insisting that pretrial detention is not "punishment" if its objective is "regulatory" rather than "punitive." If the purpose behind incarceration is moral condemnation and punishment, the detention is considered punitive. But if the motive is to protect society (for example, from predicted criminal acts), the purpose is said to be regulatory. It was on the basis of this distinction that the Court upheld federal preventive-detention provisions in the 1987 case of *United States v. Salerno.*

The virtue of this distinction is that it permits symbolic affirmation of both constitutional principles. The distinction, however, is not realistic; "punishment" and "regulation" simply are not separate categories. The Court's distinction is cold comfort to the untried defendant who sits behind bars in a county jail, for the effect of incarceration is to punish no matter what the purpose may be. A civilized society, moreover, would not protect itself from a defendant's predicted behavior ("regulate") unless it also condemned what the defendant was thought to have done already. Preventive detention, viewed realistically, is therefore not purely regulatory. Nor are criminal sentences purely punitive; their traditional purposes include deterrence and rehabilitation, both of which are regulatory objectives in the sense that they forestall anticipated harms to society. Civilized societies normally do not act for solely punitive purposes any more than they act for solely regulatory ones.

There are sound reasons for basing pretrial detention on the seriousness of the crime and on the substantiality of the evidence, rather than on predictions about future conduct. The problem with preventive detention is that it requires an open-ended, potentially difficult hearing about something that need not be an issue. What ought to matter is the strength of the evidence that the suspect has committed a serious crime, not speculations about what the suspect might do in the future. After all, if the proof is clear that a heinous crime has been committed, dangerousness need not be predicted. It has been demonstrated.

The Supreme Court, however, may see in such a system too much moral condemnation and not enough regulation. As forthright analysts like Mickey Kaus have noted, the truth is that a useful system of pretrial detention would be broadly "punitive." Like the historic practice of detaining those accused of capital offenses, a sensible list of offenses eligible for pretrial detention would be inextricably tied to moral repugnance at the seriousness of the crimes. Pretrial deten-

tion, moreover, would serve other purposes of criminal punishment besides condemnation. By making incarceration (if only for a relatively short term) more certain, it would act as a powerful deterrent, especially for those in the criminal culture whose time perspective is too short to be influenced by remote and contingent punishment after trial.

Nonetheless, other "regulatory" programs, including preventive detention, inevitably act as deterrents as well. The fact that policymakers recognize how pretrial detention can serve many of the same purposes as criminal punishment ought not to serve as a basis for invalidating pretrial detention. It is realistic, not invidious, to see the necessary overlap between punishment and regulation.

While a pretrial detention system would be partly punitive, it would also be regulatory in important respects. Behind any system of legitimate laws lies the public's sense that the coercive power of government will be used in serious and reliable ways. To arrest someone for a violent crime, to possess solid and convincing evidence of that person's guilt, and then to release him is to undermine the implicit pact between government and citizen. It is to diminish the importance of what has happened to the victim and what could happen to others. It makes the criminal-justice system seem frivolous, an arena for a game rather than for a morally significant enterprise. The victim of a rape or burglary who sees the bailed suspect out on the street is harmed even if the suspect does not repeat his crime. The victim need not feel any need for vengeance (although such a need will certainly be felt) to have a justifiable sense of outrage and betrayal. The victim's claim—and by extension the claims of those who sympathize and identify with the victim—is not purely punitive, and it is more than a demand for protection. It is a demand that government take what happened seriously, that the law deserve the respect that it demands. The release of suspects against whom there is strong proof of a significant crime is, for society, a self-inflicted wound. It undermines the social compact and aggravates deep fears of social disintegration. In preventing this injury, pretrial detention would serve some of the most fundamental regulatory purposes.

Would the Court accept such interests as being both "regulatory" and sufficiently important to justify pretrial detention? The *Salerno* decision does not foreclose this possibility but suggests some impediments. The purpose of the Bail Reform Act of 1984 was to prevent "danger to the community." The Court noted that under the Act the government must provide "convincing proof that the arrestee, already indicted . . . for a serious crime, presents a demonstrable danger to the community." It concluded that "under these narrow circumstances, society's interest in crime prevention is at its greatest." The governmental interests promoted by classifying some crimes as nonbailable would not be so concrete. Although the objectives would include preventing the repetition of especially frightening and harmful crimes, this would not be tied to individualized determinations of dangerousness. More importantly, the government's interest would not be limited to crime prevention; its interests would extend to the more generalized purpose of communicating respect and concern for alleged victims and potential victims, thereby promoting the legitimacy of the criminal-justice system itself. No court could question the importance of such objectives. But in many areas of constitutional law, the judiciary displays a reflexive preference for purposes that are specific and tangible. (Recall, for example, the Court's recent dismissive treatment of the social interests behind flag-desecration laws.) *Salerno* is at least consistent with the judicial bias against diffuse public purposes.

The Court may believe there is a special reason for rejecting broad government interests as justifications for restricting bail. In *Salerno*, the justices said: "In our society liberty is the norm, and detention prior to trial or without trial is the carefully limited exception." Accordingly, they emphasized that the preventive-detention statute not only carefully itemizes those few crimes dangerous enough to warrant holding the suspect but also requires a finding that "no condition of release" can dispel the danger. In contrast, it might be thought that regard for victim and governmental legitimacy would be such general justifications as to permit pretrial detention to become the norm.

It would be a partial answer to this objection to define very carefully those crimes that are to be nonbailable. The stronger the indications that the selected crimes are in fact tied to physical danger and public fear, the more credible the claim that bail is still available except where special justifications exist for denial. Nevertheless, there is a difference between case-by-case and categorical determinations. On this point, the exaggerations of constitutional rhetoric must be met head on. The fact is that under our written Constitution and our political traditions, the question of how exceptional the denial of bail should be is, in the first instance, the province of the legislatures. Before, during, and after the framing of the Constitution, the political branches had discretion to respond to the public's sense of outrage by classifying crimes as capital and thus authorizing the denial of bail. At times this meant that many serious crimes were nonbailable, and at other times it meant that few were. Grand claims about how the availability of bail is normal should not be permitted to obscure the real discretion tradi-

tionally allowed our legislatures to categorize crimes as nonbailable.

This legislative authority has been constrained by one crucial limitation that, oddly, is missing from the preventive-detention statute that the Court has already approved. Not only the Judiciary Act of 1789 but virtually all state enactments have required an individualized determination that the proof is "evident, or the presumption great." This requirement echoes the ancient English practice of limiting bail denial to circumstances where the accused was caught red-handed. The Bail Reform Act of 1984 contains no such heightened demand for proof of guilt. In this important respect, categorical pretrial detention would be more exceptional than the limits on bail that the Court validated in *Salerno* and far more in keeping with the sustained consensus that our Constitution is supposed to represent.

Pretrial detention represents a grievous loss of liberty for the defendant. Nevertheless, it is not inconsistent with the core of the principle of due process. The full force of the law's punishment still would not be inflicted until after a fair trial. And the harm to the suspect would not be inflicted without an adequate hearing that established clear and convincing proof that the suspect committed a serious, dangerous crime. This is not perfect due process of law, and it is full of risks. Some innocent people will be incarcerated. But there is risk under the present system, where judges often either pretend bond is appropriate but purposely set it too high or base their decisions on predictions rather than on fact-finding.

Mythical thinking about constitutional "rights" should not prevent us from recognizing the risks that arise from releasing suspects as a matter of course or when proof of future dangerousness is impractical. Those suspects do commit new crimes and their presence in the community does frighten people and devalue the legal system. The Constitution, read as a complex and contradictory document, could not and does not require perfect procedural protection before incarceration. As the movement to enact pretrial-detention statutes spreads, elite commentators and jurists should recognize that popular grievances are justified. The Constitution that we would have under a system of pretrial detention for noncapital crimes would be fairly close to the one we have always had. It might seem somewhat less perfect than the idealized and simplified "constitution" that so beguiles and distorts our discourse. But the Constitution that is based on our collective good sense is both morally balanced and politically secure.

Convicting the Innocent

JAMES MCCLOSKEY

James McCloskey is Director of Centurion Ministries, Inc, Princeton, N.J.

On most occasions when it has been discovered that the wrong person was convicted for another's crime, the local law enforcement community, if it has commented at all, has assured the public that such instances are indeed rare and isolated aberrations of a criminal justice system that bats nearly 1,000 percent in convicting the guilty and acquitting the innocent. And this view is shared, I think, not only by the vast majority of the public but also by almost all of the professionals (lawyers and judges) whose work comes together to produce the results.

I realize that I am a voice crying in the wilderness, but I believe that the innocent are convicted far more frequently than the public cares to believe, and far more frequently than those who operate the system dare to believe. An innocent person in prison, in my view, is about as rare as a pigeon in the park. The primary purpose of this article is to delineate why and how I have come to believe that this phenomenon of the "convicted innocent" is so alarmingly widespread in the United States. Although no one has any real idea of what proportion it has reached, it is my perception that at least 10 percent of those convicted of serious and violent crimes are completely innocent. Those whose business it is to convict or to defend would more than likely concede to such mistakes occurring in only 1 percent of cases, if that. Regardless of where the reader places his estimate, these percentages, when converted into absolute numbers, tell us that thousands and even tens of thousands of innocent people languish in prisons across the nation.

Allow me to outline briefly the ground of experience on which I stand and speak. For the past eight years I have been working full time on behalf of the innocent in prison. To date, the nonprofit organization I founded to do this work has freed and vindicated three innocent lifers in New Jersey. Another, on Texas's death row, has been declared "innocent" by a specially appointed evidentiary hearing judge, who has recommended a new trial to Texas's highest court. Currently we are working on ten cases across the country (New Jersey, Pennsylvania, Virginia, Louisiana, Texas, and California). We have received well over 1,000 requests for assistance and have developed extensive files on more than 500 of these requests, which come to us daily from every state of the nation from those who have been convicted, or from their advocates, proclaiming their innocence. We serve as active advisors on many of those cases.

Besides being innocent and serving life or death sentences, our beneficiaries have lost their legal appeals. Their freedom can be secured only by developing new evidence sufficient to earn a retrial. This new evidence must materially demonstrate either that the person is not guilty or that the key state witnesses lied in critical areas of their testimony. We are not lawyers. We are concerned only with whether the person is in fact completely not guilty in that he or she had

nothing whatsoever to do with the crime. When we enter the case it is usually five to fifteen years after the conviction. Our sole focus is to reexamine the factual foundation of the conviction -- to conduct an exhaustive investigation of the cast of characters and the circumstances in the case, however long that might take.

We find and interview as often as necessary anyone who has knowledge about the case and/or the people who are related to the case. We search for documentation and employ whatever forensic scientific tests are available that in any way shed light on, point to, or establish the truth of the matter. While developing this new information, we retain and work with the most suitable attorney in seeking judicial relief for our clients. We raise and disburse whatever funds are required to meet the legal, investigative, and administrative costs of seeking justice for these otherwise forgotten and forsaken souls buried in our prisons all across the land.

Appellate Relief for the Convicted Innocent

As all lawyers and jurists know, but most lay people do not, innocence or guilt is irrelevant when seeking redress in the appellate courts. As the noted attorney F. Lee Bailey observed, "Appellate courts have only one function, and that is to correct legal mistakes of a serious nature made by a judge at a lower level. Should a jury have erred by believing a lying witness, or by drawing an

Reprinted from *Criminal Justice Ethics*, Vol. 8, No. 1 (Winter/Spring 1989), pp. 2, 54-59. Reprinted by permission.

attractive but misleading inference, there is nothing to appeal." So, if the imprisoned innocent person is unable to persuade the appellate judges of any legal errors at trial, and generally he cannot, even though he suffered the ultimate trial error, he has no recourse. Nothing can be done legally to free him unless new evidence somehow surfaces that impeaches the validity of the conviction. Commonly, the incarcerated innocent are rubber-stamped into oblivion throughout the appeals process, both at the state and at the federal level.

So where does that leave the innocent person once he is convicted? Dead in the water, that's where! He is screaming his head off that he is innocent, but no one believes him. One of our beneficiaries standing before his sentencing judge told him, "Your Honor . . . I will eat a stone, I will eat dust, I will eat anything worse in the world for me to prove my innocence. I am not the man. I am innocent. I am not the man." The jury didn't believe him. The judge didn't. Certainly the prosecutor didn't, and more important than all of these put together, neither did his trial attorney nor his appellate lawyer. And so it goes for the convicted innocent. Their cries of innocence will forever fall on deaf ears and cynical minds.

Once he is convicted, no one in whose hands his life is placed (his lawyer and the appellate judges) either believes him or is concerned about his innocence or guilt. It is no longer an issue of relevance. The only question remaining that is important or material is whether he "legally" received a fair trial, not whether the trial yielded a result that was factually accurate. Appellate attorneys are not expected to, nor do they have the time, inclination, and resources to, initiate an investigation designed to unearth new evidence that goes to the question of a false conviction. Such an effort is simply beyond the scope of their thinking and beyond the realm of their professional responsibility. It is a rare attorney indeed who would dare go before any American appellate court and attempt to win a retrial for his client based on his innocence. That's like asking an actor in a Shakespearian tragedy to go on stage and pretend it's a comedy. It is simply not done.

Causes of Wrongful Conviction

But enough of this post-conviction appellate talk. That's putting the cart before the horse. Let's return to the trial and discuss those elements that commonly combine to convict the innocent. Let me state at the outset that each of these ingredients is systemic and not peculiar to one part of the country or one type of case. We see these elements as constant themes or patterns informing the cases that cross our desks. They are the seeds that sow wrongful convictions. After one has reflected on them individually and as a whole, it becomes readily apparent, I think, how easy it is and how real the potential is in every courthouse in America for wrongful convictions to take place.

(a) *Presumption of Guilt* The first factor I would like to consider is the "presumption-of-innocence" principle. Although we would all like to believe that a defendant is truly considered innocent by those who represent and judge him, this is just not so. Once accusations have matured through the system to the point at which the accused is actually brought to trial, is it not the tendency of human nature to suspect deep down or even believe that the defendant probably did it? Most people are inclined to believe that where there is smoke, there is fire. This applies to professional and lay people alike albeit for different reasons perhaps.

The innate inclinations of the average American law-abiding citizen whose jury experience is that person's first

---

Most people are inclined to believe that where there is smoke, there is fire.

---

exposure to the criminal justice system is to think that law enforcement people have earnestly investigated the case and surely would not bring someone to trial unless they had bona fide evidence against the person. That is a strong barrier and a heavy burden for the defense to overcome. And how about judges and defense lawyers? These professionals, like members of any profession, have a natural tendency to become somewhat cynical and callous with time. After all, isn't it true that the great majority of the defendants who have paraded before them

in the past have been guilty? Why should this case be any different? As far as defense attorneys are concerned, if they really believe in their clients' innocence, why is it that in so many instances they are quick to urge them to take a plea for a lesser sentence than they would get with a trial conviction? So, by the time a person is in the trial docket, the system (including the media) has already tarnished him with its multitude of prejudices, which, of course, would all be denied by those who entertain such prejudices.

(b) *Perjury by Police* Another reason for widespread perversions of justice is the pervasiveness of perjury. The recent District Attorney of Philadelphia once said, "In almost any factual hearing or trial, someone is committing perjury; and if we investigate all of those things, literally we would be doing nothing but prosecuting perjury cases." If he is guilty, the defendant and his supporters would lie to save his skin and keep him from going to prison. That is assumed and even expected by the jury and the judge. But what would surprise and even shock most jury members is the extent to which police officers lie on the stand to reinforce the prosecution and not jeopardize their own standing within their own particular law enforcement community. The words of one twenty-five-year veteran senior officer of a northern New Jersey police force still ring in my ears: "They [the defense] lie, so we [police] lie. I don't know one of my fellow officers who hasn't lied under oath." Not too long ago a prominent New York judge, when asked if perjury by police was a problem, responded, "Oh, sure, cops often lie on the stand."

(c) *False Witnesses for the Prosecution* What is more, not only do law officers frequently lie, but the primary witnesses for the prosecution often commit perjury for the state, and do so under the subtle guidance of the prosecutor. Inveterately, common criminals who are in deep trouble themselves with the same prosecutor's office or local police authority are employed as star state witnesses. In exchange for their false testimony, their own charges are dismissed, or they are given non-custodial or greatly reduced prison sentences. In other words a secret deal is struck whereby the witness is paid for his fabricated testimony with that most precious of all commodities -- freedom!

Such witnesses are usually brought forward by the state to say either that the defendant confessed the crime to them

---

Jailhouse confessions are a total perversion of the truth-seeking process.

---

or that they saw the defendant near the crime scene shortly before it happened, or they saw him flee the scene of the crime as it was occurring. If I have seen one, I have seen a hundred "jailhouse confessions" spring open the prison doors for the witness who will tell a jury on behalf of the state that the defendant confessed the crime to him while they shared the same cell or tier. When the state needs important help, it goes to its bullpen, the local county jail, and brings in one of the many ace relievers housed there to put out the fire. As several of these "jailhouse priests" have told me, "It's a matter of survival: either I go away or he [the defendant] goes away, and I'm not goin'." Jailhouse confessions are a total perversion of the truth-seeking process. Amazingly enough, they are a highly effective prosecutorial means to a conviction. Part and parcel of a jailhouse confession is the witness lying to the jury when he assures them that he expects nothing in return for his testimony, that he is willing to swallow whatever pill he must for his own crimes.

(d) *Prosecutorial Misconduct* The right decision by a jury depends largely on prosecutorial integrity and proper use of prosecutorial power. If law enforcement officers, in their zeal to win and convict, manipulate or intimidate witnesses into false testimony, or suppress evidence that impeaches the prosecution's own witnesses or even goes to the defendant's innocence, then the chances of an accurate jury verdict are greatly diminished. Sadly, we see this far too often. It is frightening how easily people respond to pressure or threats of trouble by the authorities of the law. Our insecurities and fears as well as our desires to please those who can punish us allow all of us to be far more malleable than we like to think.

Few of us have the inner strength we

think we have to resist such overreaching by the law. This applies to mainline citizenry as well as to those living on the margins. However, the underclasses are particularly vulnerable and susceptible to police pressure because they are powerless; and both they and the police know it. A few examples will illustrate.

In 1981 three white high school janitors were threatened by the Texas Rangers into testifying that they had seen Clarence Brandley, their black custodial supervisor, walking into the restroom area of the high school where the victim had entered only minutes before she had disappeared. Brandley was convicted and sentenced to death based on the inferential testimony that since he was the last person seen near her, then he must have killed her. Eight years later Brandley was exonerated by the judge who conducted his evidentiary hearing when one of these janitors came forward and told how they had lied in implicating Brandley because of coercion by the investigating law officer.

On the eve of the Rene Santana trial in Newark, New Jersey, which was a year and a half after the crime, the prosecutors produced a surprise "eyewitness" who said he saw Mr. Santana flee the scene of the crime. A decade later that same witness visited Mr. Santana at New Jersey's Rahway State Prison and asked for his forgiveness after admitting to him that he had concocted the "eyewitness" testimony in response to intense pressure from the prosecutor's investigator. Since this "eyewitness" was from Trujillo's Dominican Republic police state, his innate fear of the police made him vulnerable to such police coercion.

Or how about the Wingo case in white, rural northwestern Louisiana? Wingo's common-law wife came forward on the eve of his execution and admitted that she had lied at his trial five years earlier because the deputy sheriff had threatened to put her in jail and forever separate her from her children unless she regurgitated at trial what he wanted her to say.

And in the Terry McCracken case in the suburbs of Philadelphia, a fellow high school student of the caucasian McCracken testified that he saw McCracken flee the convenience store moments after a customer was shot to death during the course of a robbery.

The teenager was induced to manufacture this false eyewitness account after three visits to the police station. Among the evidence that vindicates McCracken are the confessions by the real robber/killers. So, you see, it not only can happen anywhere, it does happen everywhere; and it does happen to all different people, regardless of race and background.

Another common trait of wrongful convictions is the prosecutor's habit of suppressing or withholding evidence which he is obliged to provide to the defendant in the interests of justice and fairness. Clarence Darrow was right when he said, "A courtroom is not a place where truth and innocence inevitably triumph; it is only an arena where contending lawyers fight not for justice but to win." And so many times this hidden information is not only "favorable" to the defendant but it clears him. In Philadelphia's Miguel Rivera case the district attorney withheld the fact that two shopkeepers had seen the defendant outside their shop when the art museum murder was actually in progress. And in the Gordon Marsh case near Baltimore, Maryland, the state failed to tell the defendant that its main witness against him was in jail when she said she saw him running from the murder scene. One has to wonder what the primary objective of prosecutors is. Is it to convict, regardless of the factual truth, or is it to pursue justice?

The prosecution is the "house" in the criminal justice system's game of poker. The cards are his, and he deals them. He decides whom and what to charge for

---

The prosecution is the "house" in the criminal justice system's game of poker.

---

crimes, and if there will be a trial or whether a plea is acceptable. He dominates. Unfortunately, his power is virtually unchecked because he is practically immune from punishment for offenses, no matter how flagrant or miscreant. According to many state and federal courts, prosecutorial misbehavior occurs with "disturbing frequency." When the "house" cheats, the innocent lose. Lamentably, we see prosecutors throughout the nation continually violating the standards set for them by the U.S. Supreme Court in 1935 when it said that the prosecutor's

interest in a criminal prosecution is not that it shall win a case, but that justice shall be done. . . . He is in a peculiar and very definite sense the servant of the law, the twofold arm of which is that guilt shall not escape or innocence suffer. . . . While he may strike hard blows, he is not at liberty to strike foul ones. It is as much his duty to refrain from improper methods calculated to produce a wrongful conviction as it is to use every legitimate means to bring about a just one.

It is human nature to resist any information that indicates that we have made a grievous mistake. This is particularly true of prosecutors when presented with new evidence that impeaches a conviction and goes to the innocence of a person convicted by their office at a prior time, whether it occurred four months or forty years before. Not only are they coldly unresponsive to such indications but they quickly act to suppress or stamp them out. New evidence usually comes in the form of a state witness who, plagued with a guilty conscience, admits that he lied at the trial; or from a person completely new to the case who comes forward with his exculpatory knowledge. Without exception, in my experience, the prosecutor's office will treat that person with total contempt in its usually successful attempt to force the person to retreat into silence. If that doesn't work, it will dismiss such testimony as somehow undeserving of any credibility and blithely ignore it. This prosecutorial impishness reminds me of a little boy holding his hands to his ears on hearing an unpleasant sound.

The Joyce Ann Brown case is a poignant illustration of this kind of prosecutorial posturing. One year after Joyce's 1980 conviction for being one of two black women who had robbed a Dallas, Texas furrier and killed one of the proprietors, the admitted shooter was captured and pleaded guilty while accepting a life sentence. She also told her attorney that the district attorney had convicted the wrong woman (Joyce Brown) as her partner in the crime. She had never known or even heard of that Joyce Brown. With the district attorney fighting her with all of his might, Joyce

sits in prison to this day trying to win a retrial as we try to develop new evidence on her behalf.

(e) *Shoddy Police Work* The police work of investigating crimes, when done correctly and thoroughly, is indeed a noble profession. Law and order are essential to a cohesive and just society. Because police work is fraught with so many different kinds of pressures, it is rather easy for an investigation to go awry. The high volume of violent crime plagues every urban police department. Skilled detectives are few, and their caseloads are overwhelming. The "burnout" syndrome is a well-documented reality within police ranks. Interdepartmental politics and the bureaucracy stifle initiative and energy. The pressure to "solve" a case is intensely felt by the line detective and comes both from his superiors and the

---

If today's climate of "burn or bury them" puts more pressure on the detective to resolve, it also gives him more license to do so by whatever means.

---

community and from his own ambitious need for recognition and advancement. If today's climate of "burn or bury" them puts more pressure on the detective to resolve, it also gives him more license to do so by whatever means.

Too often, as a result of the above factors, police officers take the easy way out. Once they come to suspect someone as the culprit, and this often occurs early within the investigation and is based on rather flimsy circumstantial information, then the investigation blindly focuses in on that adopted "target." Crucial pieces of evidence are overlooked and disregarded. Some witnesses are not interviewed who should be, while others are seduced or coerced into telling the police what they want to hear. Evidence or information that does not fit the suspect or the prevailing theory of the crime is dismissed as not material or is changed to implicate the suspect. Good old-fashioned legwork is replaced by expediency and shortcuts. Coercive confessions are extracted and solid leads are ignored.

Before too long, momentum has gathered, and the "project" now is to put it on the suspect. Any information that points

to the suspect, no matter how spuriously secured, is somehow obtained; and anything that points away from him is ridiculed and twisted into nothingness. The task is made much easier if the suspect has a police record because he should be "taken off the streets" anyhow. That kind of person is not only a prime suspect but also a prime scapegoat. An example of this is Clarence Brandley, who was mentioned earlier. He was arrested in late August four days after the crime and on the weekend before school was to begin. The high school where the rape and murder took place was flooded with telephone calls by scared parents who refused to send their children to school until the murderer was caught. The arrest of Brandley calmed the community, and school started as scheduled. It was after Brandley's arrest that the investigation then spent five hundred hours building the case against him.

(f) *Incompetent Defense Counsel* The wrongly convicted invariably find themselves between the rock of police/prosecutorial misconduct and the hard place of an incompetent and irresponsible defense attorney. While the correct decision by a jury hinges on a fair prosecution, it also depends on dedicated and skilled defendant lawyering. And there is such a paucity of the latter. Not only are there very few highly competent defense lawyers but there are very few criminal defense lawyers, period. They are rapidly becoming an extinct species.

The current Attorney General of New Jersey not too long ago told the New Jersey State Bar Association that finding quality private defense attorneys "may be the most crying need that we have." He also told this same assemblage that unless there is an adequate number of well-trained private defense lawyers, there will be little hope for justice. Of the 30,000 lawyers in New Jersey, the number of those doing primarily criminal defense work is only in the hundreds. At this same conference the First Assistant Attorney General pointed out that 85 percent of New Jersey's criminal cases are handled by the public defender system; and he wondered if there would be a private defense bar by the year 2000.

This means, of course, that 85 percent of those charged with a crime cannot afford an attorney, so they are forced to use the public defender system. As competent as New Jersey's full-time salaried public defenders generally are, their resources (budget and people) are vastly inadequate and are dwarfed by those of their adversaries (the local prosecutor's office). Moreover, they are so overwhelmed by the sheer volume of caseload that no defender can give quality attention to any one of his cases, let alone all of them. So, in response to this shortage, public defender cases are farmed out to "pooled" attorneys, who are paid a pittance relative to what they earn from other clients who retain them privately.

The experience of these pooled attorneys in criminal matters is often limited and scanty. In addition, they do not bring to their new-found indigent client the desired level of heart and enthusiasm for their cases. All of these conditions leave the defendant with an attorney somewhat lacking in will, effort, resources, and experience. Thus, the defendant goes to trial with two strikes against him.

What we have discovered as a common theme among those whose cases we have studied from all over the country is that their trial attorney, whether from the public domain or privately retained, undertakes his work with an appalling lack of assiduity. Communication with the defendant is almost nonexistent. When

---

Eighty-five percent of those charged with a crime cannot afford an attorney.

---

it does take place, it is carried on in a hurried, callous, and dismissive manner. Attempts at discovery are made perfunctorily. Prosecutors are not pressed for this material. Investigation is shallow and narrow, if conducted at all. Preparation meets minimal standards. And advocacy at trial is weak. Cross-examination is superficial and tentative.

Physical evidence is left untested, and forensic experts are not called to rebut whatever scientific evidence the state introduces through its criminalists. I cannot help thinking of the Nate Walker case, where, at Nate's 1976 trial for rape and kidnapping, the doctor who examined the victim the night of her ordeal testified that he found semen in her vaginal cavity. Walker's privately retained attorney had no questions for the doctor when it came time for cross-examination, nor

did he even ask anyone to test the vaginal semen for blood type. Twelve years later, that test was peformed at our request, and Walker was exonerated and immediately freed.

This is not to say, however, that we have not encountered some outstanding examples of vigorous and thorough defense lawyering that left no stones unturned. What a rare but inspiring sight! We could not do our work without the critically important services of the extremely able and dedicated attorneys with whom we team up. If only the preponderance of attorneys would heed the admonition of Herbert Stern, a former U.S. Attorney and U.S. District Court judge in Newark, New Jersey, when he addressed a new crop of attorneys who had just been sworn in. He told them that they were free to choose their own clients. "But," he continued, "once that choice is made, once a representation is undertaken, then that responsibility is as sacred to us as the one assumed by a surgeon in the operating room. You must be as committed and as selfless as any surgeon." He further challenged them to "be an advocate. Represent your clients -- all of them -- fearlessly, diligently, unflinchingly. . . . Withhold no proper legal assistance from any client. And when you do that, you thereby preserve, protect, and defend the Constitution of the United States, just as you have this day sworn to."

(g) *Nature of Convicting Evidence* The unschooled public largely and erroneously believes that convictions are mostly obtained through the use of one form of tangible evidence or another. This naive impression is shaped by watching too many TV shows like Perry Mason or Matlock. The reality is that in most criminal trials the verdict more often than not hinges on whose witnesses -- the state's or defendant's -- the jury chooses to believe. It boils down to a matter of credibility. There is no "smoking gun" scientific evidence that clearly points to the defendant. This puts an extremely heavy burden on the jury. It must somehow ferret out and piece together the truth from substantially inconsistent and contradictory testimony between and within each side. The jury is forced to make one subjective call after another in deciding whom to believe and what inferences to draw from conflicting statements.

For example, how can a jury accept a victim's positive identification at trial of the defendant as her assailant when she had previously described her attacker in physical terms that were very different from the actual physical characteristics of the defendant, or when the defense has presented documented information that precludes the defendant from being the assaulter? Several cases come to mind. Boy was convicted of robbing a convenience store in Georgia. The clerk initially told the police that since she was 5 feet 3 inches, was standing on a 3-inch platform, and had direct eye contact with the robber, he must have been about 5 feet 6 inches tall. Boy is 6 feet 5 inches tall. Four teenage girls identified Russell Burton as their rapist on a particular day in Arkansas. Burton introduced evidence that on that day his penis was badly blistered from an operation two days before for removal of a wart. And a Virginia woman was certain that Edward Honaker was her rapist even though her rapist had left semen within her, and Honaker had had a vasectomy well in advance of the assault.

Criminal prosecutions that primarily or exclusively depend on the victim's identification of the defendant as the perpetrator must be viewed with some skepticism unless solid corroborating evidence is also introduced. Traumatized by a crime as it occurs, the victim frequently is looking but not seeing. Victims are extremely vulnerable and can easily be led by the police, through unduly suggestive techniques, into identifying a particular person. The victim in Nate Walker's case, for example, was with her abductor/rapist for two and a half hours with ample opportunity to clearly view him. She told the jury without hestitation eighteen months later that "he's the man." Nate had an ironclad alibi. The jury struggled for several days but in the end came in with a guilty verdict. As mentioned earlier, he was scientifically vindicated twelve years later.

When juries are confronted with a choice between a victim's ringing declaration that "that's the man" and solid evidence that "it couldn't be him," they usually cast their lot with the victim. I suggest that this can be a very dangerous tendency and practice. And this is particularly so when identification crosses racial lines, that is, when a white victim says it was that black person. Future jurors should be aware that identifications can be very unreliable forms of evidence.

Another type of evidence that can be misleading and even confusing to jurors is that offered by laboratory scientists. Results of laboratory tests that are presented by the forensic scientists are not always what they appear to be, although they strongly influence jury decisions. A recent New York Times article pointed out that there is a "growing concern about the professionalism and impartiality of the laboratory scientists whose testimony in court can often mean conviction or acquittal." This article went

---

The reality is that in most criminal trials the verdict more often than not hinges on whose witnesses -- the state's or defendant's -- the jury chooses to believe.

---

on to say that the work of forensic technicians in police crime laboratories is plagued by uneven training and questionable objectivity.

We share this mounting concern because we see instance after instance where the prosecutor's crime laboratory experts cross the line from science to advocacy. They exaggerate the results of their analysis of hairs, fibers, blood, or semen in such a manner that it is absolutely devastating to the defendant. To put the defendants at a further disadvantage, the defense attorneys do not educate themselves in the forensic science in question, and therefore conduct a weak cross-examination. Also, in many cases, the defense does not call in its own forensic experts, whose testimony in numerous instances could severely damage the state's scientific analysis.

One case profoundly reflects this common cause of numerous unjust convictions. Roger Coleman sits on Virginia's death row today primarily because the Commonwealth's Bureau of Forensic Science expert testified that the two foreign pubic hairs found on the murdered victim were "consistent" with Mr. Coleman's, and that it was "unlikely" that these hairs came from someone other than Mr. Coleman. The defense offered nothing in rebuttal, so this testimony stood unchallenged. In a post-convic-

tion hearing Mr. Coleman's new lawyer introduced the testimony of a forensic hair specialist who had twenty-five years of experience with the F.B.I. He testified that "it is improper to conclude that it is likely that hairs came from a particular person simply because they are consistent with that person's hair because hairs belonging to different people are often consistent with each other, especially pubic hairs."

Another problem that we continually observe within the realm of forensic evidence is the phenomenon of lost and untested physical evidence. Often, especially in cases up to the early 1980s, the specimens that have the potential to exclude the defendant have not been tested and eventually get misplaced. At best this is gross negligence on the part of both the police technician and the defense attorney in not ensuring that the tests be done.

Conclusion

We agree with a past president of the New Jersey Division of the Association of Trial Lawyers of America who said that "juries are strange creatures. Even after taking part in many, many trials, I still find them to be unpredictable. The jury system isn't perfect, but it does represent the best system to mete out justice. They're right in their decisions more often than not." Remember when I quoted a former District Attorney who said that "in almost any factual hearing or trial someone is committing perjury." So, a wide margin of error exists when earnest but all too fallible juries are only right "more often than not" and when trial testimony is so frequently and pervasively perjurious. My contention is that at least 10 percent of those convicted for serious, violent crimes are incorrectly convicted because some combination of the trial infirmities described in this article results in mistaken jury determinations.

Everyone will agree that the system is not perfect, but the real question is this: To what extent do its imperfections prevail? I contend that for all the reasons detailed above the system is a far leakier cistern than any among us has ever imagined. Untold numbers of innocents have tumbled into the dark pit of prison. Some of them have eventually gained their freedom, but a majority remain

buried in prison, completely forsaken and forgotten by the outside world.

Other than my own wholly inadequate organization, no person or agency, private or public, exists anywhere that works full time and serves exclusively as an advocate and arm for the innocent in prison. The body of justice that has evolved over the centuries has many members. But not one part that functions within this whole has been created or is properly equipped specifically to secure the freedom of the incarcerated innocent.

Publications Received

Timo Airaksinen, *Ethics of Coercion and Authority: A Philosophical Study of Social Life* (Pittsburgh, PA: University of Pittsburgh Press, 1988), ix + 219 pp.

George F. Cole, *The American System of Criminal Justice* (5th ed) (Pacific Grove, CA: Brooks/Cole Publishing Co., 1989), xxiv + 706 pp.

Joshua Dressler, *Understanding Criminal Law* (New York: Mathew Bender & Co., 1987), xli + 540 pp.

Franco Ferracuti, ed. *Trattato Di Criminologia, Medicina Criminologia E Psichiatria Forense* (Milano: Dott. A. Guiffre Editore, 1988) IX. *Forme di Organizzazioni Criminali e terrorismo* xiii + 403 pp.

Mark S. Gaylord & John F. Galliher, *The Criminology of Edwin Sutherland* (New Brunswick: Transaction Inc., 1988) xiv + 183 pp.

Jean Harris, *"They Always Call Us LADIES": Stories from Prison* (New York: Charles Scribner's Sons, 1988), vii + 276 pp.

Geoffrey C. Hazard, Jr. & Deborah L. Rhode, *The Legal Profession: Responsibility and Regulation* (2nd ed) (Westbury, NY: The Foundation Press, Inc., 1988), viii + 505 pp.

Jack Katz, *Seductions of Crime: Moral and Sensual Attractions in Doing Evil* (New

4. THE JUDICIAL SYSTEM

York: Basic Books, Inc., 1988), viii + 367 pp.

Kelsey Kauffman, *Prison Officers and their World* (Cambridge: Harvard University Press, 1988), ix + 290 pp.

Robert Klitgaard, *Controlling Corruption* (Berkeley & Los Angeles: University of California Press, 1988), xiii + 220 pp.

Richard A. Myren & Carol Henderson Garcia, *Investigation for Determination of Fact: A Primer on Proof* (Pacific Grove, CA: Brooks/Cole Publishing Co., 1988), xv + 240 pp.

David W. Neubauer, *America's Courts and the Criminal Justice System* (3rd ed) (Pacific Grove, CA: Brooks/Cole Publishing Co., 1988), xvi + 464 pp.

Andrew Oldenquist, *The Non-Suicidal So-ciety* (Bloomington & Indianapolis: Indiana University Press, 1986), viii + 263 pp.

Richard Polenberg, *Fighting Faiths: The Abrams Case, the SupremeCourt, and Free Speech* (New York: Viking Penguin Inc., 1987), xiv + 431 pp.

Joycelyn M. Pollock-Byrne, *Ethics in Crime & Justice: Dilemmas and Decisions* (Pacific Grove, CA: Brooks/Cole Publishing Co., 1989), xiii + 169 pp.

Curtis Prout & Robert N. Ross, *Care and Punishment: The Dilemmas of Prison Medicine* (Pittsburgh, PA: University of Pittsburgh Press, 1988), x + 276 pp.

Lionel Tiger, *The Manufacture of Evil -- Ethics, Evolution and the Industrial System* (New York: Harper & Row, 1987), 345 pp.

Michael Tonry & Norval Morris, eds. *Crime and Justice: A Review of Research* (Vol. 10) (Chicago: The University of Chicago Press, 1988), x + 343 pp.

UMI, ed. *Criminal Justice Periodical Index* (Vol. 13) (Ann Arbor: University Microfilms Inc., 1988), xi + 391 pp.

H. Richard Uviller, *Tempered Zeal -- A Columbia Law Professor's Year on the Streets with the New York City Police* (Chicago & New York: Contemporary Books, 1988, xvii + 234 pp.

Samuel Walker, *Sense and Nonsense about Crime: A Policy Guide* (2nd ed) (Pacific Grove, CA: Brooks/Cole Publishing Co., 1989), xvi + 276 pp.

Stanton Wheeler, Kenneth Mann, & Austin Sarat, *Sitting in Judgement: The Sentencing of White-Collar Criminals* (New York: Yale University Press, 1988), xii + 199 pp.

When Criminal Rights Go Wrong

Forget liberal. Forget conservative. Think common sense.

Paul Savoy

Paul Savoy, a former prosecutor and law professor, is working on a book about the Supreme Court.

It has become one of those commonplaces of bicentennial speeches and Fourth of July orations to cite reports by pollsters that if the Bill of Rights were put to a vote today, a surprisingly large number of citizens would fail to ratify some of our most fundamental freedoms. A 1989 survey conducted by *The National Law Journal* showed that Americans are so fearful about the drug-driven crime epidemic that more than half of those polled who expressed an opinion favored cutting back the constitutional rights of criminal defendants and overruling Supreme Court decisions that limit police conduct in gathering evidence.

When Americans reject the ideals of one of our founding documents, we are urged to believe, as Garry Wills observed on the occasion of the 200th anniversary of the Declaration of Independence, that something has gone wrong with America; that somehow, in failing to subscribe to the Supreme Court's interpretation of certain 18th-century ideals, America "has ceased in part to be itself." What we have failed to consider is the possibility that what may be misguided are the orthodox teachings of the American legal establishment, not the majority opinions of the American people.

The approach of the 200th anniversary of the ratification of the Bill of Rights provides a timely opportunity for the legal profession to consider an unsettling idea: There may be considerable validity to the profound, though poorly articulated, intuition of the public at large that the procedural guarantees of the Constitution are not to be used to undermine a defendant's responsibility for his criminal acts. Because readers will be (and should be) extremely skeptical of the claim that much of what law schools have been teaching and courts have been espousing since the advent of the Warren Court era may be fundamentally flawed, a heavy burden rests with those who would challenge the prevailing orthodoxy.

Taking rights too seriously?

Having provided the framework for what was surely the most ambitious and idealistic effort in the history of the Supreme Court to bring the Constitution to bear upon flagrant abuses in the administration of criminal justice, liberals have become willing to accept the assumptions and principles of that 1960s revolution as dogma beyond accountability to serious moral or intellectual inquiry. Deeper and more mature reflection on the history and purpose of the procedural guarantees of the Constitution—including most prominently the Fourth Amendment prohibition of unreasonable searches and seizures and the Fifth Amendment privilege against compul-

"Don't ask me why I did it," Edgar Smith, a convicted murderer, later wrote from San Quentin Prison. "Ask those self-righteous public servants why they gave me the opportunity to do it."

sory self-incrimination—will show that these fundamental rights were not intended, and should not be construed, to protect the guilty.

In 1957, Edgar Smith was convicted of murdering a 15-year-old girl and sentenced to die in the electric chair. High school sophomore Vickie Zielinski had disappeared on her way home from visiting a friend, and her battered body was found the next day in a sand pit on the outskirts of the small New Jersey town where she lived. Her skull had been crushed with a 44-pound boulder, leaving a gaping hole in her head and her brains scattered along the bank.

In 1969, the Supreme Court ordered a hearing to determine if incriminating statements Smith made to police had been obtained in violation of his constitutional rights. Although Smith acknowledged that he had not been mistreated by the police officer who conducted the interrogation, and three psychiatrists testified that the statements were "the result of his free will and rational choice," a federal court in New Jersey ruled the statements were inadmissible because they were obtained under "coercive" circumstances: Smith had not been advised of his right to remain silent or his right to counsel, and his interrogation had extended over a period of more than 10 hours. After 14 years on Death Row, Smith, who continued to assert his innocence, was released from prison because, without his statements, there was insufficient evidence to retry him for first-degree murder.

Five years after his release, in 1976, Smith finally did confess to killing Vickie Zielinski—at a trial in San Diego in which he was convicted of kidnapping and attempted murder after abducting another woman and stabbing her with a six-inch butcher knife as she struggled to escape. "Don't ask me why I did it," Smith later wrote from San Quentin Prison regarding the San Diego attack. "Ask those self-righteous public servants why they gave me the opportunity to do it."

No constitutional controversy has generated as much public furor, nor elicited a more unsatisfying response from the legal profession, than the debate over the rights of people accused of crimes. The notion that criminals have constitutional rights may of-

fend the average citizen concerned about the increase in drug-related crime and gang violence, but every law student soon learns that the common sense of the common man is wrong. The basic premise of our constitutional system of criminal justice is that a defense attorney has the duty to raise every available legal defense without regard to the actual guilt or innocence of his client. If cross-examination can be used to discredit a nervous and easily confused witness, use it, even though you know he is telling the truth. If the evidence has been illegally seized, move to suppress it, even though it establishes incontrovertible proof of your client's guilt. If the eyewitness's identification is tainted by an improperly conducted lineup, challenge it, even if the witness has correctly identified your client as her assailant. If the police interrogated your client without advising him of his right to remain silent, move to exclude his confession, without regard to whether it is truthful or whether your client is actually guilty of the kidnapping and murder with which he is charged.

"Defense counsel has no obligation to ascertain or present the truth," explains Justice Byron White in a classic statement of the criminal lawyer's role. "Our system assigns him a different mission. . . . [and] permits counsel to put the State's case in the worst possible light, regardless of what he thinks or knows to be the truth." If an injustice results, in the sense that a guilty person escapes a punishment he deserves, it results because the Constitution, according to the received view, not only permits it, but requires it. "The constitutional rights of criminal defendants are granted to the innocent and the guilty alike," Justice William Brennan reminds us in a recent affirmation of this fundamental principle of constitutional jurisprudence. Beginning in the early sixties, the constitutional rights of criminal defendants came to be defended in such eloquent and eminently reasonable terms that no one with a modicum of civic virtue could disagree. That all people, without regard to guilt or innocence, are entitled to claim the procedural decencies of the Constitution in resisting the power of government to invade their freedom and privacy—who would dispute such a ringing affirmation of human dignity and the rule of law? Few statements about the Bill of Rights seem so obvious from the text or sound so seductive. And yet few are so deeply and grievously flawed.

In the 1980s, the perception that there is something radically wrong with the prevailing liberal view of the rights of people accused of crimes became widespread. Outrage about the extent to which victims are sacrificed to the rights of criminals is evident in the wave of films in the last several years that depart from the Perry Mason school of criminal law, in which all clients are innocent. The outrage is there in *The Jagged Edge*, the story of a defense lawyer portrayed by Glenn Close, who skillfully wins an acquittal for her client in a murder trial, only to discover that she is about to become his next victim. It is there in *Star Chamber*, in which a group of trial judges, fed up with having to dismiss cases against guilty defen-

> *A long line of distinguished authorities confirm the conclusion that in common law, an arrest violated no right of the accused if he was actually guilty.*

dants on technicalities, deputize themselves to try the culprits *in absentia* and order their execution by hired hit men. And in *True Believer,* James Woods portrays San Francisco attorney Tony Serra, a sixties defender of political activists turned eighties drug lawyer, who is berated by a disenchanted young associate for "using exalted principles to get off scumbags," until he gets a chance to redeem himself by defending an innocent man.

By the end of the 1988 presidential campaign, drugs and violent crime had vaulted to the top of the American political agenda. The defeat of Michael Dukakis became the most visible symbol of the deep fissures and contradictions in "liberal" that have made it synonymous with "soft-on-crime."

There is considerable irony in the extent to which liberalism has taken the heat for coddling criminals. Despite its rhetoric of liberty and human dignity, the due process school of criminal procedure is not a legitimate child of classical liberal thought. John Stuart Mill, the founding father of liberal legal theory, actually denounced as "sophistry" and as "palpably untenable and absurd" those arguments invoked by barristers in early 19th-century England to rationalize the use of procedural rules to defeat the prosecution of clients they knew were guilty of the crimes with which they were charged. "The benefit which would arise from the abolition of the exclusionary rule," Mill wrote in a postscript to Jeremy Bentham's classic treatise on the law of evidence, "would consist rather in the higher tone of morality that would be introduced into the profession itself." The exclusionary rule to which Mill was referring was the attorney-client privilege, which, in the context of criminal defense practice, "gives an express license to that willful concealment of the criminal's guilt, which would have constituted any person [besides the criminal's lawyer] an accessory to the crime." With Bentham, Mill called for a reform of legal ethics:

"We should not then hear an advocate boasting of the artifices by which he had [manipulated]. . . a deluded jury into a verdict in direct opposition to the strongest evidence; or of the effrontery with which he had, by repeated insults, thrown the faculties of a bona fide witness into a state of confusion, which had caused him to be taken for a perjurer, and as such,

disbelieved. Nor would an Old Bailey counsel any longer plume himself upon the number of pickpockets whom, in the course of a long career, he had succeeded in rescuing from the arms of the law. The professional lawyer would be a minister of justice, not an abettor of crime; a guardian of truth, not a suborner of mendacity."

The so-called "liberal" model of criminal procedure that prevails in the United States today is actually an odd coupling of free-market theory with a particularly interventionist form of governmental regulation—not regulation of the private sector, but regulation of government by government: regulation of the police by the courts. It is governmental regulation in the name of individualism, not the traditional individualism of Jefferson or John Stuart Mill, but the free-enterprise individualism of modern libertarianism decked out in the pious rhetoric of the founding fathers.

Staples of injustice

In the early morning hours of May 5, 1979, the badly burned body of Sandra Boulware was discovered in a vacant lot in the Roxbury section of Boston. An autopsy revealed that she had died of multiple compound skull fractures caused by repeated blows to the head. After an investigation, police linked the homicide to one of the victim's boyfriends, Osborne Sheppard, and obtained a warrant authorizing a search of Sheppard's house. Police officers found several pieces of incriminating evidence there, including a pair of bloodstained boots, a hairpiece belonging to the murdered woman, and strands of wire similar to wire fragments found on the victim's body.

Sheppard was found guilty of first-degree murder after a trial in which these items were received in evidence. Two years later, the Massachusetts Supreme Judicial Court overturned the conviction on the ground that the evidence had been illegally seized. Because Detective Peter O'Malley had applied for a search warrant on a Sunday, the local courthouse was closed, and he could not find an application form for the warrant. O'Malley finally obtained a warrant form designed for narcotics cases, but he failed to delete the reference to "controlled substances" in the part describing the evidence to be seized. O'Malley had included a detailed description of the evidence in an affidavit that accompanied the warrant application, and the warrant would have been valid if the judge had written "see attached affidavit" on the form and stapled the affidavit to the warrant. But the judge issued the warrant without making the necessary changes. The mistake proved fatal, insofar as the Fourth Amendment requires that a warrant "particularly describe" the evidence to be seized. Because of a failure to staple two pieces of paper together, the state's highest court reversed Sheppard's murder conviction.

In 1984, the U.S. Supreme Court agreed to hear the case. By then, the Burger Court had already be-

The right to remain silent reflects our unwillingness as a society to permit an innocent person to become the instrument of his own conviction.

gun whittling away at the 1961 Warren Court decision in *Mapp v. Ohio*, which established the principle that evidence seized in violation of the Fourth Amendment is inadmissible in state as well as federal prosecutions. In an opinion written by Justice White and joined by five other members of the Court, Sheppard's conviction was reinstated and the exclusionary rule was modified to incorporate a "good faith" exception. This exception permits illegally seized evidence to be used against a defendant if the police officer who conducted the search reasonably believed that it was authorized by a valid warrant. Affirming earlier indications of the Burger court that the exclusionary rule is not to be regarded as a "personal constitutional right of the person aggrieved," the conservative majority in *Sheppard* concluded that illegally seized evidence should not be excluded when the benefits of the rule in deterring police misconduct are outweighed by its costs in freeing guilty defendants.

Civil libertarians denounced the Court's decision as tantamount to repealing the Fourth Amendment. Liberal defenders of the exclusionary rule, including Justices William Brennan and Thurgood Marshall, who both dissented from the Court's ruling in the Sheppard case, maintained that the exclusionary rule is not a discretionary remedy that the Court is free to balance against the costs of letting guilty defendants off, but rather, "a direct constitutional command." In a widely quoted speech delivered the following year, Justice Brennan, one of the two remaining members of the Warren Court majority, lamented the Court's failure in the post-Warren years to fulfill its historic mission "as a protector of the individual's constitutional rights."

The debate between liberals and conservatives over the good-faith exception to the exclusionary rule has manifested itself in the form of a question that captures the constitutional crisis in a more compelling way than might at first appear—as a kind of Zen koan for our times: *Does a police officer's reasonable belief in the reasonableness of an unreasonable search make the search reasonable?* The cabalistic nature of such constitutional conundrums is not so much a function of some profound legal mystery as it is a symptom of the breakdown of the ruling doctrines that have shaped the Court's thinking about

them. Behind the smoke and mirrors of the constitutional arguments is one simple and fundamental disagreement between liberals and conservatives that everyone could understand if candid explanations were not ruled out by the legal profession's allegiance to the cult of complexity: Liberals believe that everyone is entitled to claim the protection of the Fourth Amendment, without regard to their guilt or innocence; conservatives, while they pay lip service to this constitutional canon, do not actually believe it—and with good reason. That a person driving a car with a corpse in the trunk and a five-year-old kidnap victim on the floor has some legitimate expectation of privacy is about as ludicrous a proposition as one could imagine. But back on the record, Everyman's car is his castle.

More than 30 years ago, before *Mapp* was decided and the ideological silos had hardened, Edward Barrett, former dean and professor emeritus of the University of California at Davis, posed the commonsense question in an article in the *California Law Review*: "If one were to look only to the rights of the defendants, why would it not be reasonable to take the position that by engaging in [criminal activity] within their houses, they have waived their constitutional right to privacy and could in no event complain of the police entries?" A closer reading of certain celebrated 18th-century cases, frequently cited by liberal jurists and commentators as "landmarks of English liberty," supports Professor Barrett's suggestion that criminals should not have any right to use their privacy to conceal criminal activity. It appears that the original purpose of the Fourth Amendment was not to create a personal sanctuary where even the criminal might claim a legitimate expectation of privacy, as modern authorities assert, but rather to protect law-abiding citizens from invasions of privacy by overzealous law enforcement officers.

Common law, common sense

In 1763, the Chief Justice of the English Court of Common Pleas, later elevated to the peerage as Lord Camden, authored an opinion which would immortalize him, in the words of Samuel Johnson, as the "zealous supporter of English liberty by law." John Wilkes, a member of Parliament, and 49 other individuals had been arrested the preceding year and charged with seditious libel in connection with their publication of one of a series of political pamphlets that contained an unusually bitter attack both on Charles II and on the use of general warrants to search for evidence of violations of an unpopular tax on cider. A general warrant was issued by the secretary of state, pursuant to which Wilkes' house was ransacked and all his private papers seized. Wilkes brought a civil suit against the governmental official responsible for the execution of the warrant and won a judgment of 1,000 pounds.

Although Lord Camden roundly condemned the use of general warrants as "totally subversive of the liberty of the subject," a careful reading of his opinion makes it clear that the guilt or innocence of the householder was far more relevant to the validity of the search than the standard liberal accounts suggest. The chief justice declared that although the warrant was unsupported by probable cause, "If upon the whole, they [the jury] should esteem Mr. Wilkes to be the author and publisher [of the pamphlet], the justification [for the search] would be fully proved."

A long line of distinguished authorities, from Sir Matthew Hale's classic 18th-century work on the English common law of liberty to the American Law Institute's modern *Restatement of Torts*, confirm the conclusion that under common law, an arrest, even though made without a warrant or probable cause, violated no right of the accused *if he was actually guilty of the crime for which he was arrested*. It was the common sense of the common law that the criminal had no standing to complain of being caught.

This is not to say that in acting without probable cause or in failing to obtain a valid warrant, the police have not violated the Fourth Amendment, but only that in so acting, *they have violated no personal right of a felon*. On this revisionist view of the Fourth Amendment, the function of the exclusionary rule, when invoked by a factually guilty defendant to object to illegally seized evidence, is not to vindicate any personal right of the accused but actually enables him as a representative of the public interest to enlist the judiciary in protecting the collective security of the rest of us. The defendant, in effect, is "asserting that he must be recognized as a private attorney general, protecting the Fourth Amendment rights of the public at large," explains Columbia University Professor of Constitutional Law Henry Monaghan.

The public debate over the exclusionary rule has proceeded as if the issue were "the rights of the suspect" versus "the rights of society." Formulating the problem in such terms misapprehends the true nature of the rights asserted by the criminal defendant. When a defense attorney moves to suppress the 400 pounds of cocaine with which his client was caught red-handed, what is actually being defended is not a personal right of the defendant, but the right of drug traffickers to defend the rights of the rest of us without our consent—a prerogative that leading constitutional scholars are beginning to recognize has no basis in the Bill of Rights.

The Court has no power per se to reverse a conviction because the police have violated the Constitution. The rights guaranteed by the Constitution normally may be enforced only by someone whose own personal protection was infringed by the violation. In the rare instance when individuals are permitted to assert the rights of third parties or of the public at large, the Court has held that some relationship must exist that makes the individual asserting the right an adequate representative of the members of the public in whose behalf the right is claimed.

We have done something strange and almost incomprehensible in our constitutional system of criminal justice. On the one hand, the justices have closed the federal courthouse door to law-abiding citizens seeking to protect their own rights with public interest lawsuits and have refused to issue injunctions against police misconduct even when individuals have been seriously injured as a result of those abuses. (In a lawsuit challenging the use of choke-holds by the Los Angeles Police Department, the plaintiff, who had been strangled into unconsciousness by a police officer during the course of a stop for a traffic infraction, was denied injunctive relief against the use of the holds, even though by the time the Court heard the case in 1983, 16 deaths had occurred as a result of the departmental practice.) On the other hand, the Supreme Court has deputized criminals to protect the constitutional rights of law-abiding citizens. The factually guilty defendant, however, insofar as he seeks to enforce the public interest by obtaining exemption from punishment, is a most improbable and inadequate representative of the public interest.

The real objection to using illegally seized evidence against a factually guilty defendant is not that such use is contrary to the Constitution, but that a court is normally unable to determine whether a defendant is guilty of using his privacy for criminal purposes without considering the very evidence that has been unlawfully seized. The Supreme Court has declared that "an arrest is not justified by what the subsequent search discloses." Perhaps it is time for the Court to reconsider this doctrine and permit the fruits of the search to be used, not to justify the search, but to determine whether the defendant was using his privacy for criminal purposes, thereby reserving the exclusionary rule for people who maintain a legitimate expectation of privacy.

A dubious privilege

After being arrested at his home in Phoenix, Arizona, Ernesto Miranda was picked out of a lineup by an 18-year-old victim as the man who had kidnapped and brutally raped her. Two officers then took Miranda into a separate room to question him. At first he denied his guilt, but after two hours of interrogation, he gave a detailed oral confession and then wrote out and signed a brief statement in which he admitted and described the crime. Although unmarked by any of the traditional indicia of coercion, Miranda's oral and written confessions were held inadmissible because the police had failed to advise him of his right to remain silent and his right to a lawyer. As Justice John Harlan suggested, in dissenting with three other members of the Warren Court from the majority's ruling almost 25 years ago in *Miranda v. Arizona* "one is entitled to feel astonished" that the Constitution can be read to create such a dubious privilege: *a right of criminals to conceal their crimes.*

To be sure, the law has long regarded torture and other blatant forms of coercion as unlawful means of obtaining a confession, for the reasons that a coerced confession is likely to be untrustworthy and that the use of physical brutality offends civilized standards of fair play and decency. But when a confession is indisputably true, and the police have not used the blackjack or the third-degree, the reason for the privilege is more difficult to fathom. This is not to dispute the wisdom of the Court's decision in *Miranda* requiring that, before questioning, people in police custody be advised of their rights under the Fifth and Sixth Amendments. A decision about whether to invoke a constitutional right should be the product of an informed and independent choice, and advising a person that he has such a right contributes to his freedom to choose.

The more obvious question, but one that is rarely asked about *Miranda*, is why a criminal suspect should have a right to remain silent in the first place. Even as conservative a critic of *Miranda* as former Attorney General Edwin Meese conceded that "if a person doesn't want to answer, that's [his] right." However, as Judge Henry Friendly once observed, "no parent would teach such a doctrine to his children." The guilty, according to the moral standards that prevail outside the courtroom, should own up to their guilt, while the innocent, one would think, have nothing to fear by telling the truth.

Carvin' Miranda

Describing the complex of values embodied in the Fifth Amendment privilege against compulsory self-incrimination, Chief Justice Warren, in his opinion for the Court in *Miranda*, explained that the privilege has come to be recognized in part as an individual's "right to a private enclave where he may lead a private life." Elsewhere, the Court has said of the privilege that it is "intended to shield the guilty and imprudent as well as the innocent."

Despite the Court's confident pronouncements, however, the conclusion that a person who has committed a rape or any other crime has a privacy interest in not answering a police officer's questions is supported neither by the historical record nor by evolving standards of fair play and decency. The story of the historic struggle for the privilege as a protest in behalf of the guilty and the innocent alike against the abuses of inquisitorial methods of interrogation is largely a fairy tale.

The privilege traces its roots in Anglo-American history to early 17th-century England, when the infamous Star Chamber and the ecclesiastical courts prosecuted various religious and political offenses by requiring Puritan dissenters to take an oath and answer questions regarding deviations from the established faith. The resistance of dissident preachers and pamphleteers to these proceedings took the form of the defense that "no man is bound to accuse himself," and received its most articulate exposition from the Levellers, whose ideas furnished the intellectual bulwark of the Puritan Revolution. This much about the history of the Fifth Amendment is generally known and agreed upon by constitutional scholars and jurists.

What is not generally known is that the Levellers articulated the privilege not as a right of the guilty

and the innocent alike, but as a protection for those who sincerely believed they were innocent—either in the sense that they had not committed the acts with which they were charged, or more commonly, that they had a conscientious belief that the crimes of which they were accused were beyond the power of government to punish (heresy, seditious libel, and treason were the usual offenses). According to John Lilburne, the most prominent and prolific of the Leveller leaders, the right to remain silent was a right "that no man be questioned, or molested, or put to answer for anything, *but wherein he materially violates the person, goods, or good name of another.*" [Emphasis added.]

The opposition in England to compulsory self-incrimination, although related to resistance to torture and other physically abusive forms of interrogation, went far beyond those concerns. The privilege proceeded primarily from the objection to the moral compulsion associated with the oath and the dilemma it created for *people of conscience* either to lie under oath or to tell the truth and thereby risk conviction for offenses they believed the state was without power to punish. A petition circulated in 1648 by the Levellers contained what was perhaps the first formal declaration of the privilege in language clarifying its relation to the oath and leaving no doubt that its roots were planted in the soil of conscience: "That all Statutes for all kinds of Oaths, whether in Corporations, Cities, or other, which ensnare conscientious people. . .be forthwith repealed and nulled, *and that nothing be imposed upon the consciences of any to compel them to sin against their own consciences.*" [Emphasis added.]

The privilege against self-incrimination was thus originally conceived as an essentially spiritual principle that permitted a person who had a conscientious belief in his innocence to assert what was tantamount to a right of passive resistance against an unjust law or a false accusation. The modern use of the privilege that best exemplifies its original purpose was the exercise of the Fifth Amendment during the McCarthy era. Given the Cold War climate of the fifties, a Supreme Court that could not quite bring itself to declare that active membership in the Communist Party was protected by the First Amendment could nevertheless find in the procedural guarantee of the Fifth Amendment a politically safe way of permitting people of conscience to resist legislative inquisitions into left-wing departures from the established democratic faith.

Even when freedom of conscience is not at stake, the privilege operates to protect the innocent. Contrary to popular belief, an innocent person may have a great deal to lose by telling the truth. For example, an innocent person, by admitting certain elements missing from the prosecution's case, such as his presence at the scene of the crime, or that he owned the murder weapon, or even that it was he who fatally stabbed the victim (though in self-defense), has a legitimate concern that by telling the truth he may contribute to his being convicted of a crime he did not in fact commit or for which he had sufficient justification. The right to remain silent thus reflects our unwillingness as a society to permit an *innocent* person to become the instrument of his own conviction.

Given the purpose of the privilege to protect the innocent and those who hold a conscientious belief in their innocence, a revised set of *Miranda* warnings that would be more consistent with the history of the privilege, as well as contemporary standards of fairness and justice, should include, in addition to the existing admonitions regarding the right to consult with an attorney, the following: 1) If you believe you are innocent, you are not required to make a statement, or to answer any questions; 2) If you are guilty, you have a legal duty to answer questions and to state truthfully the circumstances concerning your commission of the offense with which you are charged.

The implications of this revisionist interpretation of the Fifth Amendment may have applications beyond the administration of *Miranda* warnings. Two years before *Miranda* was decided, in *Murphy vs. Waterfront Commission*, the Supreme Court made it clear that "by requiring the government in its contest with the individual to shoulder the entire load," the privilege against self-incrimination provides the constitutional core of the presumption of innocence. Rethinking the Fifth Amendment may thus ultimately require rethinking the presumption of innocence as well as Justice White's classic statement of the criminal lawyer's role—"to put the State's case in the worst possible light, regardless of what he thinks or knows to be the truth." In a subsequent article, I will explore this most troubling and difficult aspect of the defense of criminal cases.

Defendants Lose As Police Power Is Broadened

IRA MICKENBERG
Special to The National Law Journal

Mr. Mickenberg is an attorney specializing in criminal appeals in New York.

PLACING THE decisions of a single Supreme Court term in their proper historical context can be a tricky business. A case that seems significant when decided may be overruled or simply made irrelevant the following term. Today's minor ruling may provide the basis for tomorrow's landmark decision. Only the passage of time gives us the perspective to recognize larger trends the court may be setting.

When a right-wing majority began to solidify on the court in the mid-1970s, many commentators were called alarmists for predicting an immediate dismemberment of the Warren Court's criminal procedure precedents. With more than a decade to look back on, it now seems that the alarmists may have been wrong in their timing but on the mark as to the court's ultimate direction.

During the past decade, the scope of *Miranda* has been drastically narrowed, the class of persons able to assert Fourth Amendment protections has been limited and the substance of those protections shrunk. Virtually every law passed by Congress to increase penalties, forfeit assets and create new classes of inchoate crimes has been upheld. A morbid joke circulating among defense lawyers is that the only reason to buy advance sheets is to find out what rights we had yesterday that no longer exist today.

IN THE 1989-'90 term, the court consistently followed up on its earlier efforts to increase the power of police and prosecutors. Although there was no single, dominant issue uniting its opinions, the court once again resolved virtually every case against the defense. In many situations, the court took the opportunity to expand upon its own decisions of the past few years and carve out new areas in which the government may act in criminal cases.

One of the most significant expansions of police power occurred in *Alabama v. White,*[1] a case that received little national publicity, but which will have significant impact on future search-and-seizure litigation. This case also provides a very clear example of how the court has built upon its own prior decisions to cut deeper and deeper into the rights afforded criminal suspects. *White* involved one of the most problematic Fourth Amendment questions: When can a tip from an anonymous caller be sufficient to provide the police with the reasonable suspicion needed to conduct a stop and frisk someone?

In 1964, the Supreme Court first adopted a definitive test for determining when an informer's tip is sufficiently reliable to permit the police to conduct a search. In *Aguilar v. Texas,*[2] the court held that before the government could conduct a search it must establish the reliability of both the informant and the information. This "two-prong" test later was confirmed in *Spinelli v. United States.*[3]

To many, the *Aguilar/Spinelli* test seemed to be no more than simple common sense; before acting on a tip the police should have some reason to

believe that both the source of the information and the information itself are reliable. The test also was not difficult to satisfy. Reliability of the informant could be established if his or her identity was known to the police, or if he or she previously had provided accurate information. The information itself would be deemed reliable if corroborated by police observation of important details.

The primary restriction *Aguilar/Spinelli* imposed on the police was that it prevented them from making searches and seizures based on anonymous, uncorroborated tips.

In 1983, however, the Burger Court decided to give the police even more leeway. In *Illinois v. Gates,*[4] the court held that instead of requiring the government to prove both prongs of *Aguilar/Spinelli*, trial courts need look only at the "totality of the circumstances"

During the past decade, the scope of *Miranda* has been narrowed drastically.

to determine whether probable cause or reasonable suspicion has been established.

Under this new standard, searches could be justified even if the reliability of the informant and/or the information was not specifically determined. Although many searches that would have been condemned under *Aguilar/ Spinelli* were now upheld, the worst abuses — where police acted on anonymous and uncorroborated tips — still were often overturned.

In *Alabama v. White*, however, the Rehnquist Court expanded on *Gates* to permit police action based on virtually any kind of anonymous information. In that case, officers received an anonymous call stating that Vanessa White would be leaving a particular apartment at a particular time in a brown Plymouth station wagon with a broken right taillight. She would be carrying a brown attache case containing an ounce of cocaine, and would go to a specified motel.

In response to this tip, officers went to the apartment complex and observed a woman, later identified as Vanessa White, enter a brown Plymouth station wagon with a broken right taillight. She was not carrying an attache case. The officers followed the car and stopped it about 300 yards from the motel. A search of the car turned up an attache case containing some marijuana, but no cocaine. Ms. White was arrested, and a later search at the police station turned up a trace amount of cocaine in her purse.

The majority held that this was "a close case," in which the police found sufficient "indicia of reliability" for the anonymous tip to justify stopping the car. The dissenters noted, however, that an anonymous tip "is anything but a reliable basis for assuming that the commuter is in possession of an illegal substance — particularly when the person is not even carrying the attache case described by the tipster."

The majority position in *White* creates two dangers. First, as the dissent recognized, "every citizen is [now] subject to being seized and questioned by an officer who is prepared to testify that...[he or she received]...an anonymous tip predicting whatever conduct the officer just observed."

Second, and even more dangerous, *White* sends a signal to trial court judges that virtually any denial of a motion to suppress will be upheld when an anonymous tip is involved.

TWO OTHER decisions also made significant inroads into suspects' protections against illegal searches and seizures. In *Maryland v. Buie*,[5] the court addressed the question of how far afield the police may search after arresting a defendant in his home.

It is well established that after making a lawful arrest, officers may search anywhere within the immediate area from which the suspect could possibly grab a weapon.[6] Moreover, when someone is arrested inside his or her home, the police may conduct a "protective sweep" if they believe that another suspect or some other dangerous condition is concealed on the premises.

In *Buie*, the police obtained warrants to arrest Jerome Buie and one other man on robbery charges. The officers were aware that during the crime, one of the robbers had worn a red running suit. Mr. Buie was lawfully arrested as he emerged from the basement of his house. He was subsequently searched and handcuffed. The arresting officer then went down into the basement, "in case there was someone else" there. Although he did not find any other suspects, he did observe a red running suit in "plain view," which he seized.

The Maryland Court of Appeals ruled that the running suit must be suppressed because the officers had no right to search the basement without a warrant. The authority to search Buie's "grabbable area" pursuant to the arrest did not extend to the basement, since there was no real possibility that the suspect could reach downstairs for a weapon. The search could not be upheld as a "protective sweep" because the police did not have probable cause to believe that the other suspect might be in the house.

The U.S. Supreme Court reversed, holding that the search was justified as a "protective sweep." Writing for the majority, Justice Byron R. White dealt with the absence of probable cause by holding that probable cause is not required. Instead, the police merely need to possess "a reasonable belief based on specific and articulable facts that the area to be swept harbors an individual posing a danger to those on the arrest scene."

As Justice William J. Brennan Jr. noted in dissent, this is the first time the court has extended the "stop and frisk" rationale of the 1968 case of *Terry v. Ohio*[7] into the home. *Terry* originally was viewed as a narrow exception to the probable cause requirement, only to be used when a police officer is confronted with a street situation he reasonably suspects poses a danger to him or others. In such cases, *Terry* allowed the officer to "frisk," or pat down, the exterior of the suspect's clothing for weapons. Because it could be justified by less than probable cause, the frisk was limited to protecting the officer from weapons, as opposed to being a general search for contraband.

More recently, the court has used *Terry* as the basis for permitting a wide range of searches where the police admittedly do not have probable cause. Notable among these cases was *Michigan v. Long*,[8] in which the majority permitted the "frisk" of a car when the officers lacked probable cause to search the vehicle.

Until *Buie*, however, an individual's home always has been afforded greater Fourth Amendment protection than any other area. This latest expansion of police power apparently has ended even that tradition. As Justice Brennan remarked in his dissent, *Buie* is but the latest in a series of decisions that demonstrate an "emerging tendency on the part of the court to convert the *Terry* decision from a narrow exception into one that swallows the general rule that searches are reasonable only if based on probable cause."

Those with a sense of irony also will note that the majority, which prides itself on exercising "judicial restraint," used *Buie* to expand police authority in a direction that had nothing at all to do with the facts before the court. The majority admitted that *Buie* did not involve the *Chimel v. California* situation of a search incident to an arrest. Nonetheless, Justice White wrote that "as an incident to the arrest the officers could, without probable cause or reasonable suspicion, look in closets and other spaces immediately adjoining the place of arrest from which an attack could be immediately launched."

This is a significant expansion of the police authority granted by *Chimel*. No longer are the officers limited to searching an area from which the suspect could grab a weapon. Now the police may search "closets and spaces" adjoining the place of arrest, even if they have no cause at all to believe that anyone is hiding there and even if they are certain the defendant is alone and could not possibly get a weapon. Of course, the officers are then free to seize whatever evidence they find "in plain view" while searching for a non-existent co-defendant or gun.

Although it is not surprising that the court chose to expand the scope of *Chimel* searches, it is odd that Justice White chose to do so in a case that did not involve a search incident to arrest or any "adjoining closets or spaces." One's definition of judicial activism seems to depend in large part on whose judicial ox is being gored.

Until *Buie*, the home always had more Fourth Amendment protections than any other area.

THE COURT, in *Maryland v. Buie*, relaxed the standards for police officers to conduct searches once inside a suspect's home. In *Illinois v. Rodriguez*,[9] the court made it easier for the police to get into the home in the first place. In general, officers must obtain a warrant before entering a house to make an arrest or search. One of the exceptions to the warrant requirement permits entry if the police were given consent to enter. In most such cases, consent is given by the defendant himself. In others, police obtain the consent of a third party, such as a spouse, who has common authority over the premises.[10]

In *Rodriguez*, the police received consent to search the defendant's home from a woman who claimed to have common access to the apartment. The Illinois courts suppressed the fruits of the search because the woman actually did not have any right to enter the home. Although she had once lived with the defendant, they had separated several weeks earlier and she no longer lived in the apartment or had authority to enter.

The U.S. Supreme Court reversed. Despite the fact that the police were afforded entry by someone who had no right to consent, the search was upheld. The court reasoned that as long as the officers reasonably believed the woman had authority to consent, they were justified in entering the home. Writing for the majority, Justice Scalia held that when police officers conduct "a search or seizure under one of the exceptions to the warrant requirement, [the Fourth Amendment demands]...not that they always be correct, but that they always be reasonable."

The dissent noted that this opinion runs contrary to the very reason for which warrantless searches are allowed on the consent of authorized third parties. The Fourth Amendment is intended to protect the privacy rights of individuals. When a person grants common authority over an area to a third party, he has, in effect, surrendered part of his privacy in that area. He cannot then be heard to complain if the third party exercises her authority by allowing the police to enter.

The majority in *Rodriguez*, however, permits the police to search even when the suspect has not surrendered any of his privacy interest to a third party. Justice Thurgood Marshall's closing remarks in dissent could well serve as a commentary on the entire series of Fourth Amendment cases decided by the court this term:

"Where this free-floating creation of 'reasonable' exceptions to the warrant requirement will end...is unclear. But by allowing a person to be subjected to a warrantless search in his home without his consent and without exigency, the majority has taken away some of the liberty that the Fourth Amendment was designed to protect."

IN ADDITION to the search and seizure cases, the court took the opportunity to decide a trio of matters that will facilitate the prosecution of child abuse cases. In *Baltimore City Department of Social Services v. Bouknight*,[11] a juvenile court held that Jacqueline Bouknight had abused her son. It was ordered that she could retain custody only by agreeing to extensive conditions.

After she violated the conditions, Ms. Bouknight was ordered to produce the child in court. She refused and was held in contempt. In response to the contempt charge, the defendant asserted her Fifth Amendment right against self-incrimination. The Maryland Court of Appeals agreed, holding that the order required Ms. Bouknight to admit, through the act of producing the child, that she still exercised control over him. Moreover, she was ordered to do so in circumstances where it was reasonable to believe she would be prosecuted.

The Supreme Court reversed, citing two grounds. First, the court noted that the right against self-incrimination applies only when one is forced to give evidence that is "testimonial" in nature. The act of producing the child, although possibly incriminating, is not testimonial; thus, it is not protected by the Fifth Amendment. Second, the court ruled that even if producing the child was an act covered by the privilege against self-incrimination, Ms. Bouknight, by agreeing to the court's initial custody conditions, had agreed to care for the boy in a manner consis-tent with standards established by the state. This included implicit consent to permit inspection of the child.

Bouknight provided the government with an additional means of determining whether a child abuse prosecution should be initiated. *Idaho v. Wright* and *Maryland v. Craig*[12] clarified some of the limits to government action once a case gets to trial.

In *Wright*, the defendant was charged with sexually abusing her two daughters, aged 5½ and 2½. All parties agreed that the younger child did not meet the legal standard for testifying before a jury. The trial court, however, permitted a pediatrician to testify to several statements the child had made to him, describing the abuse of herself and her sister. This evidence was admitted under the state's "residual hearsay" rule — a catchall provision allowing the introduction of statements that do not fall under any recognized exception to the hearsay rule, but are deemed reliable enough to be admissible at trial.

The Idaho Supreme Court reversed, finding that the defendant's right to confrontation was violated because the hearsay was not subject to cross-examination, did not fall within any exception to the hearsay rule and was based on an interview that lacked any procedural safeguards that might guarantee its reliability.

The Idaho court particularly noted that the doctor's interview with the child was not recorded on videotape, employed blatantly leading questions and was conducted by someone who obviously had a preconceived belief that the child had been abused. The court then established a series of procedural safeguards to ensure the reliability of the child's statements that must be satisfied before the hearsay will be admitted at trial.

The U.S. Supreme Court agreed with the conclusion of the Idaho Supreme Court, but did so in a manner that relaxes the burden placed by the state court on future prosecutions.

It ruled that admission of the child's statements was error, because they lacked sufficient indicia of reliability to avoid the need for cross-examination. The court further held, however, that the Idaho court erred by imposing strict procedural requirements on the introduction of such testimony in the future. Instead, the U.S. Supreme Court ruled that the prosecution need only show that the hearsay is reliable "given the totality of the circumstances that surround the making of the statement."

Thus, the hearsay may be admissible even if not videotaped or spoken to an objective listener, as long as "the totality of the circumstances" indicates that it is reliable. Like other "totality" tests adopted by the court (e.g., for informants and search warrants), this one permits a trial court to admit damaging evidence even if the government has not been overly careful about its source.

AS IN Fourth Amendment cases, this approach to child hearsay conveys a message to trial courts that virtually any decision will be upheld, as long as it is accompanied by a sufficiently murky finding about "the totality of the circumstances."

Ever since the 1988 decision in *Coy v. Iowa*,[13] state courts have grappled with the problem of affording defendants in child abuse cases the right to confront their accusers, while simultaneously protecting vulnerable young witnesses from the potentially traumatic effects of testifying.

In *Coy*, the U.S. Supreme Court ruled that it was not proper to place a screen between the defendant and the witness stand that prevented the parties from seeing each other. The court left open, however, the question of whether any exceptions may exist to a defendant's right to a face-to-face confrontation at trial.

In *Craig*, that question was answered in the affirmative.

The court began its analysis by determining that the confrontation clause does not guarantee defendants an absolute right to a face-to-face meeting with witnesses at trial. That right may be abrogated, but only where it is necessary to further an important public policy, and the procedure used to protect the witness also assures the reliability of the testimony.

The court held that Maryland's interest in protecting child witnesses is an important enough policy to allow restrictions on the right to confrontation.

The key question, then, is whether the arrangements made by the trial court are sufficient to assure the reliability of the testimony, absent a face-to-face confrontation. As in *Wright*, the court held that this determination must be made on a case-by-case basis. No specific protections would be required.

In *Craig*, the witness, prosecutor and defense lawyer were stationed in one room, where the child was examined and cross-examined. The defendant, judge and jury remained in the courtroom where they watched a live, closed-circuit transmission of the testimony. This scheme is similar to that adopted by many state legislatures in the past two years.

The Supreme Court in *Craig* ruled that the scheme satisfies constitutional scrutiny. The procedure will now be upheld as long as the trial court finds first, that it is necessary to protect the child's welfare, and second, that the defendant was still able to cross-examine and observe the witness during her testimony, which was given under oath. Given the ruling in *Craig*, it should be expected that most jurisdictions will adopt this kind of scheme for child-abuse trials. We should anticipate that closed-circuit video testimony will soon become the norm when child-abuse victims take the stand.

NOTES

(1) 58 U.S.L.W. 4747 (1990).
(2) 378 U.S. 108 (1964).
(3) 393 U.S. 410 (1969).
(4) 462 U.S. 213 (1983).
(5) 58 U.S.L.W. 4281 (1990).
(6) Chimel v. California, 395 U.S. 752 (1969).
(7) 392 U.S. 1 (1968).
(8) 463 U.S. 1032 (1983).
(9) 58 U.S.L.W. 4892 (1990).
(10) United States v. Matlock, 415 U.S. 164 (1974).
(11) 58 U.S.L.W. 4184 (1990).
(12) 58 U.S.L.W. 5036 (1990); 58 U.S.L.W. 5044 (1990).
(13) 487 U.S. 1012 (1988).

Juvenile Justice

A century ago children found guilty of committing crimes were punished as if they were adults. Since there were few specialized juvenile detention institutions, children were thrown into jails and prisons with murderers, thieves, drunks, tramps, and prostitutes, with no protection and no programs for rehabilitation.

The establishment of a special criminal justice system for the handling of juvenile offenders was hailed in the 1920s by humanitarians, reformers, and social scientists, and accepted, somewhat reluctantly, by the legal profession and the police. Only recently has the cry of dissent been heard.

Judge Ben Lindsay and others who pioneered the juvenile court movement believed that juveniles sinned out of ignorance, because of the growing pains of adolescence, or because they were corrupted by adults. They believed that a juvenile court should concern itself with finding out why a juvenile was in trouble and what society could do to help him or her. They saw the juvenile judge as parental, concerned, and sympathetic, rather than judgmental. They viewed the juvenile justice process as diagnostic and therapeutic, rather than prosecutive and punitive.

The proponents of this system were, of course, thinking of the delinquents of their time—the runaway, the truant, the petty thief, the beggar, the sexual experimenter, and the insubordinate. Now, however, the juvenile in court is more likely to be on trial for murder, gang rape, arson, or mugging. The 1990s also differ from the 1920s in other ways. Juvenile courts are everywhere, as are juvenile police, juvenile probation officers, and juvenile prisons. Literally hundreds of thousands of American juveniles enter this system annually.

It is clear at this time that the winds of change are blowing across the nation's juvenile justice system. Traditional reforms are being replaced by a new and more conservative agenda. This new reform movement emphasizes the welfare of victims, a punitive approach toward serious juvenile offenders, and protection of children from physical and sexual exploitation. Policies that favor diversion and deinstitutionalization are less popular. After many years of attempting to remove status offenders from the juvenile justice system, there are increasing calls for returning truants, runaways, and other troubled youth to juvenile court jurisdiction. In spite of these developments, however, there are many juvenile justice reformers who remain dedicated to advancing due process rights for children and reducing reliance on incarceration.

Clearly, there is conflict and tension between the old and new juvenile justice reform agendas. The articles in this section evaluate problems with the current juvenile justice system and present some possible solutions.

The first essay, "Handling of Juvenile Cases," draws distinctions between juvenile cases and adult cases, explains the circumstances under which juveniles may be tried in criminal courts, and reveals that juveniles receive dispositions rather than sentences.

In "The Evolution of the Juvenile Justice System," Barry Krisberg explains how the original purpose for the juvenile system when it was first conceived has been altered rather dramatically.

Are existing delinquency causation theories adequate to the task of explaining female delinquency and official reactions to girls' deviance? The answer is clearly no, according to the author of the next essay, "Girls' Crime and Woman's Place." She maintains that the academic study of delinquent behavior usually focuses on male delinquency alone.

Should parents be held responsible for the crimes of their children? This is one of the proposals under discussion in "Juvenile Crime: Who Is Responsible?" The section closes by exploring information about drug abuse among teenagers, in "Teenage Addiction."

Looking Ahead: Challenge Questions

When the juvenile court was first conceived, what convictions did its pioneers hold about juvenile offenders?

Some argue that the failure of the juvenile court to fulfill its rehabilitative and preventive promise stems from a grossly oversimplistic view of the phenomenon of juvenile criminality. Do you agree? Why or why not?

Do you believe the departure of the juvenile justice system from its original purpose is warranted?

Unit 5

Handling of Juvenile Cases

Cases involving juveniles are handled much differently than adult cases

The juvenile court and a separate process for handling juveniles resulted from reform movements of the late 19th century

Until that time juveniles who committed crimes were processed through the criminal courts. In 1899 Illinois established the first juvenile court based on the concepts that a juvenile was a salvageable human being who needed treatment rather than punishment and that the juvenile court was to protect the child from the stigma of criminal proceedings. Delinquency and other situations such as neglect and adoption were deemed to warrant the court's intervention on the child's behalf. The juvenile court also handled "status offenses" (such as truancy, running away, and incorrigibility), which are not applicable to adults.

While the juvenile courts and the handling of juveniles remain separated from criminal processing, the concepts on which they are based have changed. Today, juvenile courts usually consider an element of personal responsibility when making decisions about juvenile offenders.

Juvenile courts may retain jurisdiction until a juvenile becomes legally an adult (at age 21 or less in most States). This limit sets a cap on the length of time juveniles may be institutionalized that is often much less than that for adults who commit similar offenses. Some jurisdictions transfer the cases of juveniles accused of serious offenses or with long criminal histories to criminal court so that the length of the sanction cannot be abridged.

Juvenile courts are very different from criminal courts

The language used in juvenile courts is less harsh. For example, juvenile courts—

• accept "petitions" of "delinquency" rather than criminal complaints
• conduct "hearings," not trials
• "adjudicate" juveniles to be "delinquent" rather than find them guilty of a crime
• order one of a number of available "dispositions" rather than sentences.

Despite the wide discretion and informality associated with juvenile court proceedings, juveniles are protected by most of the due process safeguards associated with adult criminal trials.

Most referrals to juvenile court are for property crimes, but 17% are for status offenses

Reasons for referrals to juvenile courts

11%	**Crimes against persons**	
	Criminal homicide	1%
	Forcible rape	2
	Robbery	17
	Aggravated assault	20
	Simple assault	59
		100%
46%	**Crimes against property**	
	Burglary	25%
	Larceny	47
	Motor vehicle theft	5
	Arson	1
	Vandalism and trespassing	19
	Stolen property offenses	3
		100%
5%	**Drug offenses**	100%
21%	**Offenses against public order**	
	Weapons offenses	6%
	Sex offenses	6
	Drunkenness and disorderly conduct	23
	Contempt, probation, and parole violations	21
	Other	44
		100%
17%	**Status offenses**	
	Running away	28%
	Truancy and curfew violations	21
	Ungovernability	28
	Liquor violations	23
		100%
100%	Total all offenses	

Note: Percents may not add to 100 because of rounding.

Source: *Delinquency in the United States 1983*, National Center for Juvenile Justice, July 1986.

Arrest is not the only means of referring juveniles to the courts

While adults may begin criminal justice processing only through arrest, summons, or citation, juveniles may be referred to court by law enforcement agencies, parents, schools, victims, probation officers, or other sources.

Law enforcement agencies refer three-quarters of the juvenile cases, and they are most likely to be the referral source in cases involving curfew violations, drug offenses, and property crimes. Other referral sources are most likely in cases involving status offenses (truancy, ungovernability, and running away).

"Intake" is the first step in the processing of juveniles

At intake, decisions are made about whether to begin formal proceedings. Intake is most frequently performed by the juvenile court or an executive branch intake unit, but increasingly prosecutors are becoming involved. In addition to beginning formal court proceedings, officials at intake may refer the juvenile for psychiatric evaluation, informal probation, or counseling, or, if appropriate, they may close the case altogether.

For a case involving a juvenile to proceed to a court adjudication, the intake unit must file a petition with the court

Intake units handle most cases informally without a petition. The National Center for Juvenile Justice estimates that more than half of all juvenile cases disposed of at intake are handled informally without a petition and are dismissed and/or referred to a social service agency.

From *Report to the Nation on Crime and Justice*, Bureau of Justice Statistics, U.S. Department of Justice, March 1988, pp. 78-79, 95.

Initial juvenile detention decisions are usually made by the intake staff

Prior to holding an adjudicatory hearing, juveniles may be released in the custody of their parents, put in protective custody (usually in foster homes or runaway shelters), or admitted to detention facilities. In most States juveniles are not eligible for bail, unlike adults.

Relatively few juveniles are detained prior

to court appearance

One juvenile case in five involved secure detention prior to adjudication in 1983. Status offenders were least likely to be detained. The proportion of status offenders detained has declined from 40% in 1975 to 11% in 1983.

Under certain circumstances, juveniles may be tried in criminal courts

Age at which criminal courts gain jurisdiction of young offenders ranges from 16 to 19

Age of offender when under criminal court jurisdiction	States
16 years	Connecticut, New York, North Carolina
17	Georgia, Illinois, Louisiana, Massachusetts, Missouri, South Carolina, Texas
18	Alabama, Alaska, Arizona, Arkansas, California, Colorado, Delaware, District of Columbia, Florida, Hawaii, Idaho, Indiana, Iowa, Kansas, Kentucky, Maine, Maryland, Michigan, Minnesota, Mississippi, Montana, Nebraska, Nevada, New Hampshire, New Jersey, New Mexico, North Dakota, Ohio, Oklahoma, Oregon, Pennsylvania, Rhode Island, South Dakota, Tennessee, Utah, Vermont, Virginia, Washington, West Virginia, Wisconsin, Federal districts
19	Wyoming

Source: "Upper age of juvenile court jurisdiction statutes analysis," Linda A. Szymanski, National Center for Juvenile Justice, March 1987.

All States allow juveniles to be tried as adults in criminal courts

Juveniles are referred to criminal courts in one of three ways—
• **Concurrent jurisdiction**—the prosecutor has the discretion of filing charges for certain offenses in either juvenile or criminal courts
• **Excluded offenses**—the legislature excludes from juvenile court jurisdiction certain offenses usually either very minor, such as traffic or fishing violations, or very serious, such as murder or rape
• **Judicial waiver**—the juvenile court waives its jurisdiction and transfers the case to criminal court (the procedure is

also known as "binding over" or "certifying" juvenile cases to criminal courts).

12 States authorize prosecutors to file cases in the juvenile or criminal courts at their discretion

This procedure, known as concurrent jurisdiction, may be limited to certain offenses or to juveniles of a certain age. Four States provide concurrent jurisdiction over juveniles charged with traffic violations. Georgia, Nebraska, and Wyoming have concurrent criminal jurisdiction statutes.

As of 1987, 36 States excluded certain offenses from juvenile court jurisdictions

Eighteen States excluded only traffic, watercraft, fish, or game violations. Another 13 States excluded serious offenses; the other 5 excluded serious offenses and some minor offenses. The serious offenses most often excluded are capital crimes such as murder, but several States exclude juveniles previously convicted in criminal courts.

48 States, the District of Columbia, and the Federal Government have judicial waiver provisions

Youngest age at which juvenile may be transferred to criminal court by judicial waiver	States
No specific age	Alaska, Arizona, Arkansas, Delaware, Florida, Indiana, Kentucky, Maine, Maryland, New Hampshire, New Jersey, Oklahoma, South Dakota, West Virginia, Wyoming, Federal districts
10 years	Vermont
12	Montana
13	Georgia, Illinois, Mississippi
14	Alabama, Colorado, Connecticut, Idaho, Iowa, Massachusetts, Minnesota, Missouri, North Carolina, North Dakota, Pennsylvania, South Carolina, Tennessee, Utah
15	District of Columbia, Louisiana, Michigan, New Mexico, Ohio, Oregon, Texas, Virginia
16	California, Hawaii, Kansas, Nevada, Rhode Island, Washington, Wisconsin

Note: Many judicial waiver statutes also specify offenses that are waivable. This chart lists the States by the youngest age for which judicial waiver may be sought without regard to offense.

Source: "Waiver/transfer/certification of juveniles to criminal court: Age restrictions: Crime restrictions," Linda A. Szymanski, National Center for Juvenile Justice, February 1987.

A small proportion of juvenile cases are referred to criminal court

Recent studies found that most juveniles referred to criminal court were age 17 and were charged with property offenses. However, juveniles charged with violent offenses or with serious prior offense histories were more likely to be adjudicated in criminal court. Waiver of juveniles to criminal court is less likely where court jurisdiction extends for several years beyond the juvenile's 18th birthday.

Juveniles tried as adults have a very high conviction rate, but most receive sentences of probation or fines

More than 90% of the judicial waiver or concurrent jurisdiction cases in Hamparian's study resulted in guilty verdicts, and more than half the convictions led to fines or probation. Sentences to probation often occur because the criminal

5. JUVENILE JUSTICE

courts view juveniles as first offenders regardless of their prior juvenile record. However, serious violent juvenile offenders are more likely to be institutionalized. In a study of 12 jurisdictions with Habitual Serious or Violent Juvenile Offender Programs, 63% of those convicted were sentenced to prison and 14% to jail. The average prison sentence was 6.8 years.

Correctional activities for juveniles tried as adults in most States occur within the criminal justice system

In 1978, in more than half the States, youths convicted as adults and given an incarcerative sentence could only be placed in adult corrections facilities. In 18 jurisdictions, youths convicted as adults could be placed in either adult or juvenile corrections facilities, but sometimes this discretion was limited by special circumstances. Only 6 jurisdictions restricted placements of juveniles convicted as adults to State juvenile corrections institutions. Generally, youths sentenced in this manner will be transferred to adult facilities to serve the remainder of their sentence on reaching majority.

Juveniles receive dispositions rather than sentences

Juvenile court dispositions tend to be indeterminate

The dispositions of juveniles adjudicated to be delinquent extend until the juvenile legally becomes an adult (21 years of age in most States) or until the offending behavior has been corrected, whichever is sooner.

Of the 45 States and the District of Columbia that authorize indeterminate periods of confinement—
• 32 grant releasing authority to the State juvenile corrections agency
• 6 delegate it to juvenile paroling agencies
• 5 place such authority with the committing judges
• 3 have dual or overlapping jurisdiction.

Most juvenile cases are disposed of informally

In 1982 about 54% of all cases referred to juvenile courts by the police and other agencies were handled informally without the filing of a petition. About 20% of all cases involved some detention prior to disposition.

Of about 600,000 cases in which petitions were filed, 64% resulted in formal adjudication. Of these, 61% resulted in some form of probation, and 29% resulted in an out-of-home placement.

The juvenile justice system is also undergoing changes in the degree of discretion permitted in confinement decisions

Determinate dispositions are now used in six States, but they do not apply to all offenses or offenders. In most cases they apply only to specified felony cases or to the juveniles with prior adjudications for serious delinquencies.

California imposes determinate periods of confinement for delinquents committed to State agencies based on the standards and guidelines of its paroling agency. Four States have similar procedures, administered by the State agencies responsible for operating their juvenile corrections facilities.

As of 1981 eight States had serious-delinquent statutes requiring that juveniles who are either serious, violent, repeat, or habitual offenders be adjudicated and committed in a manner that differs from the adjudication of other delinquents. Such laws require minimum lengths of commitment, prescribe a fixed range of time for commitment, or mandate a minimum length of stay in a type of placement, such as a secure institution.

Dispositions for serious juvenile offenders tend to look like those for adults

Aggregate statistics on juvenile court dispositions do not provide an accurate picture of what happens to the more serious offenders because many of the cases coming before juvenile courts involve minor criminal or status offenses. These minor cases are more likely to be handled informally by the juvenile court.

An analysis of California cases involving older juveniles and young adults charged by the police with robbery or burglary revealed more similarities in their disposition patterns than the aggregate juvenile court statistics would suggest. For both types of offenses, juvenile petitions were filed and settled formally in court about as often as were complaints filed and convictions obtained in the cases against adults. The juveniles charged with the more serious offenses and those with the more extensive prior records were the most likely to have their cases reach adjudication. At the upper limits of

offense and prior record severity, juveniles were committed to secure institutions about as frequently as were young adults with comparable records.

The outcomes of juvenile and adult proceedings are similar, but some options are not available in juvenile court

For example, juvenile courts cannot order the death penalty, life terms, or terms that could exceed the maximum jurisdiction of the court itself. In Arizona the State Supreme Court held that, despite statutory jurisdiction of the juvenile courts to age 21, delinquents could not be held in State juvenile corrections facilities beyond age 18.[3]

Yet, juvenile courts may go further than criminal courts in regulating the lifestyles of juvenile offenders placed in the community under probation supervision. For example, the court may order them to—
• live in certain locations
• attend school
• participate in programs intended to improve their behavior.

The National Center for Juvenile Justice estimates that almost 70% of the juveniles whose cases are not waived or dismissed are put on probation; about 10% are committed to an institution.

Most juveniles committed to juvenile facilities are delinquents

	Percent of juveniles
Total	100%
Delinquents	74
Nondelinquents	
Status offenders	12
Nonoffenders (dependency, neglect, abuse, etc.)	14

Source: BJS Children in Custody, 1985, unpublished data.

THE EVOLUTION OF THE JUVENILE JUSTICE SYSTEM

Barry Krisberg

Barry Krisberg is president of the National Council on Crime and Delinquency. He has written extensively on the subject of juvenile delinquency.

This article is an adaptation of an earlier version published by the National Council on Crime and Delinquency.

In part, perhaps, due to sensational accounts of youth crime which have been highlighted by the media in recent years, a public sentiment that is less than sympathetic to young offenders has become prevalent. Yet, many of the juveniles caught in the wave of "get tough" legislation and calls for sterner measures against young criminals may be losing the opportunity to redeem their lives and their futures. The juvenile justice system has evolved into a system quite removed from the original purpose for which it was conceived—the protection of young people from unwarranted punishment. In what follows, three revolutions in the history of the juvenile justice system will be described, showing how the gap between theory and reality emerged.

The first revolution in juvenile justice culminated in the creation of the juvenile court. As early as 1817, the founding of the Society for the Prevention of Pauperism began a new era in the care of troubled youngsters. This group, which in 1824 was renamed the Society for the Reformation of Juvenile Delinquents, consisted of philanthropists who were committed to religious charity in a secular world. These reformers were philosophically close to the Federalists

in that they rejected the concept of popular democracy and viewed themselves as the moral stewards of their community.[1] The Society for the Prevention of Pauperism conducted investigations into methods of dealing with the poor and ultimately recommended changes in policy and legislation. It led campaigns against the corrupting influences of taverns and theatres. Of special importance was its focus on the linkages between poverty and delinquency.

These early reformers, like those of later generations, decried the housing of children in adult jails. The Society's members believed that harsh jail conditions did not result in the rehabilitation of delinquents. In fact, many of them feared that deplorable jail conditions led juries and judges to acquit young criminals rather than send them to these places. Fundamentally, these early reformers believed that the available penal institutions could not solve the underlying problems of pauperism. They envisioned a special prison for wayward youth that would emphasize education, industry and moral training.[2] The first of these youth prisons, the New York City House of Refuge, was opened in 1825. Within a few years other houses of refuge were established in Philadelphia, Boston and other major cities, and accepted children convicted of crimes as well as destitute youth. These new facilities were preventive institutions designed to accept the children of unfit parents. This new concept immediately brought judicial review to define the limits of the houses of refuge to supercede parental authority. The Pennsylvania Supreme Court carefully examined this matter in *Ex Parte*

Crouse (1838), holding that parental control was not an inalienable right.

> The object of charity is reformation by training of inmates; by imbuing their minds with principles of morality and religion; by furnishing them with a means to earn a living; and, above all, by separating them from the corrupting influences of improper associates. To this end, may not the natural parents, when unequal to the task of education, or unworthy of it, be superceded by the *parens patriae* or common guardian of the community?[3]

The *Crouse* case elaborated the key legal doctrine of *parens patriae* that supported the virtually unrestrained powers of later juvenile courts.

While the houses of refuge had many prominent supporters, the new youth prisons also suffered the problems that would plague later juvenile correctional facilities. For example, there is ample evidence of the use of solitary confinement, whipping and other forms of corporal punishment. The labor system within the houses of refuge was managed by outside contractors who sometimes abused the children. There was rarely enough work to keep all of the inmates busy and that which was available was mostly menial in nature. Violence was commonplace in these prisons, and one historian estimates that 40 percent of the children escaped from the institutions or from their post-release placements.[4]

Throughout the nineteenth century, the practice of incarcerating wayward youth expanded. Over the next several decades the houses of refuge, which were established by private philanthropic groups, were taken over by state and local governments. The shift from private to public operation was stimulated by the scandals and abuses aforementioned and the growing influence of government in the management of welfare programs. By 1890, every state outside the South had a refuge or reform school and many jurisdictions had separate facilities for males and females.

This rapidly growing youth corrections system also had its critics. Nineteenth century child advocates, including Samuel Gridley Howe and Charles Loring Brace, founded children's aid societies to rescue youth from lives of depravity and crime. The societies emphasized missionary work in urban neighborhoods. Members' personal experiences convinced them that urban poverty was too widespread to be contained by expanding the number of correctional facilities. In particular, Brace asserted that houses of refuge were breeding grounds for crime. To replace them, he advocated solving delinquency by placing urban poor children with families in the West. Brace had traveled to Europe and was impressed with the values and strength of the German farm family. To Brace and his followers, the family was "God's reformatory" and the American farm families of the West seemed to possess the same qualities he found in Germany.

Partly in response to Brace and his followers, many juvenile facilities attempted to reorganize their routines around a "cottage" or "family" system, placing youth in smaller living units of 40 or less with live-in house parents. Corrections officials responded to the claims about the rehabilitative values of farm life by locating new institutions in rural areas and expanding inmate participation in agricultural labor.

Probation was a parallel development during the mid-nineteenth century. In 1841, a Boston shoemaker, John Augustus, began putting up bail money for public inebriates. Although he possessed no formal court position, Augustus soon expanded his efforts to young offenders. He supervised wayward youngsters on bail and provided them with clothing and shelter, in addition to helping them find jobs and often paying their court expenses. As word of Augustus' good works spread, several children's aid societies took up similar activities. By 1869, Massachusetts had

Early reformers envisioned a special prison for wayward youth that would emphasize education, industry, and moral training.

established a system in which representatives of the Board of State Charities assumed responsibility for youths before they appeared in court. Youngsters placed under the custody of the Board of Charities were then released on probation subject to their maintaining proper behavior in the future.

Proponents of correctional facilities and those who stressed the need for community-based services were often engaged in intensely ideological debates, fueled by regular reports of arson and violence in the juvenile prisons, along with continuous accounts of physical abuse of incarcerated children. Moreover, the labor unions objected to the system of contract labor in the reform schools. The rumors of scandal and abuse led to a series of well-publicized investigations. Many states formed special boards and commissions to inspect the youth facilities and to make recommendations for reform. While some hoped that the new state boards would find alternatives to reform schools, the number of incarcerated young people continued to increase.

These historical forces culminated in the Illinois Juvenile Court Law of 1899 —the first comprehensive child welfare legislation in American history. The state of Illinois possessed virtually no specialized institutions for children, for its earlier reform schools had been destroyed by fires. Juvenile justice advocates, who were joined by powerful allies such as the Chicago Bar Association and Chicago Women's Club, decried the practice of holding large numbers of youngsters in the Cook County jail.

The new Illinois juvenile court was mandated to handle delinquent, dependent and neglected children. Court jurisdiction was intentionally made broad and the new "children's court" inherited much of the legal thinking that surrounded the houses of refuge. Juveniles who violated any state law or municipal ordinance could be brought before the court, which was also responsible for controlling youth charged with truancy, running away and chronic disobedience. The Illinois law gave the court enormous discretion to remove youngsters from their homes or to supervise them in the community. Interestingly, the new law recognized the role of unpaid probation officers to assist the court in its work.

The concept of a separate children's court was quickly adopted by many states. By 1925, all but two states had specialized legal proceedings for young people. Child advocates believed they had ushered in a new model for dealing with wayward youth. The Pennsylvania Supreme Court echoed the earlier sentiments of the *Crouse* case in defending the state's new juvenile court law.

To save a child from becoming a criminal, or continuing a career of crime . . . the legislatures surely may provide for the salvation of such a child, if its parents or guardians be unwilling or unable to do so, by bringing it into one of the courts of the state *without any process at all*, for the purpose of subjecting it to the state's guardianship and protection.[5]

The juvenile court did have its early detractors, many of whom pointed to the large number of children that continued to languish in adult jails. Some legal scholars, including Roscoe Pound and Judge Ben Lindsey, worried about the seemingly unlimited discretion of the children's court. Moreover, many observers noted that urban courts were virtually swamped with children and families whose needs greatly outstripped available court resources. The promise of individualized treatment and close supervision quickly came apart under staggering court dockets that often permitted less than ten minutes per case for hearings.

The founders of the juvenile court movement sought to solve some of these problems by employing the emerging technologies suggested by the new behavioral sciences. Influential reformers such as Julia Lathrop and Jane Addams raised funds to sponsor comprehensive studies of children going through the juvenile courts. The child advocates commissioned Dr. William A. Healy to examine thousands of youngsters using social, psychological and even anthropometric measures. It was Healy's hope that these detailed studies would lead to highly individualized treatment plans for each youth. This early scientific work was heavily influenced by the theories of Freudian psychology and emphasized the importance of the family as the key to delinquent behavior.

Healy's work helped establish child guidance clinics that were attached to most urban juvenile courts. By 1931, there were 232 clinics across the nation, including a traveling child guidance clinic that visited Western rural communities. Most important, the new clinics provided a rationale for the extremely flexible and discretionary operations of the court. The clinic movement led to a de-emphasis on legal principles and increased reliance on "experts" trained in social work and the behavioral sciences. The basic model of the children's court and the child guidance clinic dominated juvenile justice for the next three decades.

JUVENILE JUSTICE

Whereas the first revolution in juvenile justice culminated in a new children's court with expansive powers, the second revolution aimed at reducing the intrusion of the juvenile court into children's lives. Sociologist LaMar Empey[6] has characterized this second transformation of juvenile justice in terms of the "Four D's"—decriminalization, due process, diversion and deinstitutionalization. Before discussing the specific components of the second revolution, it is important to examine the forces that motivated these reform efforts.

During the two decades after World War II, the juvenile justice system faced many intractable problems, including the spread of adolescent drug use and the emergence of violent youth gangs. The court's clients were increasingly minority children and their families, whose cultural backgrounds and experiences differed greatly from those of court staff. The ex-

Throughout the nineteenth century, the practice of incarcerating wayward youth expanded.

tent of urban poverty and social deprivation increased, placing further burdens on the juvenile court's already strained resources.

Critics of the juvenile court became more vocal and more organized. The most politically potent attack on the court charged that judges were overly lenient with violent and serious offenders. Some critics questioned the court's practice of mixing dependent and neglected youth with serious criminal offenders, while others alleged that the court was particularly punitive in handling female status offenders. The mounting attacks on the court were fueled by periodic reports of scandals and child abuse in juvenile correctional facilities.

During the 1960s, growing doubts about the juvenile court led to a series of major U.S. Supreme Court decisions that fundamentally changed the court's character. For example, in *Kent v. U.S.* (1966) the Supreme Court warned juvenile courts against arbitrariness in detention procedures. One year later in *In re Gault* (1967) the Supreme Court specified a detailed list of rights that must be accorded juveniles in court hearings. The *Gault* decision focused on notification of charges, protections against self-incrimination, the right to confront witnesses and the right to have a written transcript of the proceedings. Many juvenile court personnel were opposed to these new rights, claiming that the informal humanitarian juvenile court would be supplanted by an impersonal junior criminal court. Nonetheless, communities across the nation struggled to find methods of providing legal representation for indigent youth and virtually every state was required to redraft its juvenile court codes to conform with the Supreme Court's dictates.

Concurrent with the judicial review of court practices, a professional and political consensus emerged on behalf of limiting formal court intervention in children's lives. The President's Commission

on Law Enforcement and the Administration of Justice (1967), established by President Lyndon Johnson, advocated the expansion of programs to divert youth from the court system and reduce the number of youngsters housed in detention centers and training schools. In 1974 the Congress enacted, by an overwhelming majority, the Juvenile Justice and Delinquency Prevention Act (JJDPA) which provided federal judges to states which agreed to remove status offenders from secure confinement and to separate children from adults in jails.[7] These new federal funds were earmarked for programs of diversion, deinstitutionalization, delinquency prevention and other "advanced practices." Almost immediately, all but a few states voluntarily joined the new federal juvenile justice policies.

Child advocates and federal lawmakers were also strongly influenced by dramatic developments occurring in Massachusetts during the early 1970s. Led by Commissioner Jerome Miller, the Massachusetts Department of Youth Services closed all of the state's training schools —moving nearly 1000 youngsters into a diverse array of small, community-based programs. Encouraged by the apparent successes in Massachusetts and the availability of substantial federal grant funds, juvenile justice reformers hoped to usher in a new age of enlightened juvenile justice practices.

Decriminalization. As states moved to revise their juvenile codes pursuant to the *Gault* decision, the separate status offender category was often included in new statutes. Suddenly there were Children in Need of Supervision (CHINS), Minors in Need of Supervision (MINS) and Unruly Children (UC). A national task force on juvenile justice even recommended the category of Families in Need of Supervision (FINS). Yet many youth advocates were unhappy with the new legal labels. Concerns were voiced that People in Need of Supervision (PINS) were not treated substantially differently than delinquents. For example, there was continued mixing of delinquents and status offenders in secure detention centers. Other critics questioned the logic of moving status offenders into the child welfare systems which were already overloaded with dependency and neglect cases. Also, courts employed their contempt powers to incarcerate status offenders who defied court orders or who ran away from placements.

The National Council on Crime and Delinquency called for the complete elimination of court jurisdiction over status offenders, arguing that community-based programs rather than court services were more relevant to solving the personal and family problems of status offenders.[8]

Despite the impressive array of groups seeking to end court jurisdiction over status offenses, very few states moved in this direction.

Diversion. The 1967 President's Crime Commission had strongly endorsed diversion as a new method of handling status offenders and petty delinquents. Youth were to be diverted from formal juvenile justice processing into community-based services. Diversion could be accomplished either by police agencies or by court intake personnel. The Crime Commission recommended that communities create youth services bureaus that would assist the police and courts in making diversion decisions as well as providing a range of voluntary services. Funding from the United States Department of Justice helped launch hundreds of youth services bureaus across the nation.

The diversion movement soon encountered several problems. As federal funding ended, the community-based youth services bureaus were replaced by diversion programs operated by juvenile justice agencies. Observers expressed the concern that diversion programs were dominated by the interests of law enforcement agencies—who controlled intake into diversion programs, thereby defining which clients they would serve. Diversion programs have been criticized as discriminatory towards female offenders. Some research showed that diversion programs often "widened the net" of social control —drawing clients from youth who previously would have had their cases dismissed or would not even have been referred. Further, other studies indicated that diversion programs that emphasized individual and family counseling produced worse outcomes across several measures

During the 1960s, a series of major U.S. Supreme Court decisions fundamentally changed the Court's character.

than programs which diverted youth to no services.

The aggregate data on the impact of diversion is mixed. The *Uniform Crime Reports* data on juvenile arrests showed a major drop in the volume of juvenile arrests from 1971 to 1981, including a decline in arrests for status offenses. But of those arrested, a higher proportion of youth were taken into custody. The proportion of youngsters referred to noncourt agencies declined. Thus, it appears that the police were not arresting status offenders at the same levels as previously. It is less clear whether this drop in status offense arrests was attributable to diversion programs. During this period there was a significant decline in the overall size of the youth population that could partially explain the drop in status offense arrests. Moreover, some have argued that the movement to decriminalize status offenses may have produced the unanticipated consequence of status offenders being relabeled as delinquents.

During this same period, juvenile court caseloads remained relatively constant. The proportions of court referrals handled via formal versus informal dispositions were largely unchanged—suggesting a minimal impact of diversion at the court level. In the 1980s, fiscal constraints and major retrenchments in federal funding led to the demise of most diversion programs. Diversion programs could not withstand the increasingly shrill political rhetoric to "get tough" with juvenile offenders.

Deinstitutionalization. If youngsters could not be diverted from the juvenile court, at least they could be treated in smaller community-based programs. Developments in Massachusetts and California's Probation Subsidy program had shown the way and the federal Office of Juvenile Justice and Delinquency Prevention (OJJDP) provided funds to encourage the deinstitutionalization process. This juvenile justice reform movement resonated with similar system change efforts in the

treatment of the mentally ill, the dependent and the disabled.[9] The key concepts of this period were "mainstreaming," "normalization" and "community-based care." Advocates of deinstitutionalization asserted that these new programs would avert the many abuses that were regularly occurring in large state-run institutions and that the smaller, localized treatment environments would produce better outcomes for clients.

The deinstitutionalization movement initially produced promising results. For example, admissions to public juvenile correctional facilities declined by 12 percent between 1974 and 1979; the number of confined youth as measured by a series of one day counts also declined slightly. The drop in admissions was largely due to fewer status offenders being sent to detention centers. Admissions to training schools remained fairly constant during this period.

Data on admissions to private juvenile facilities suggest that youth, particularly females, were shifted from public to private facilities, raising questions about the real impact of the deinstitutionalization process. However, it must be recalled that the advocates of deinstitutionalization sought to increase placements in private and community-based programs. In general, private facilities were more likely to be small group homes and half-way houses, whereas public placements mostly consisted of large secure detention centers and training schools. Some critics raised important questions about (1) the quality of care in private programs, (2) the longer average stays in private facilities and (3) the apparent discriminatory tendency to place white youth in private programs and minority youngsters in public facilities.

After 1979, the data on children in juvenile facilities revealed growing numbers of young people in public and private facilities.[10] These increases were primarily caused by lengthening institutional stays. In the late 1970s, most states enacted new legislation designed to harshen the penalties for serious juvenile offenders. States passed laws making it easier to transfer juveniles to adult criminal courts and mandated stiffer penalties in juvenile courts. The policy of the OJJDP urged the passage of tougher sentencing laws and openly questioned the wisdom of deinstitutionalization policies.

Despite the new "get tough" policies of the U.S. Department of Justice and in statehouses across the nation, several states made substantial progress in removing juveniles from large, congregate institutions. In states as diverse as Utah, Pennsylvania, Louisiana, Oklahoma, Colorado, Oregon and Texas, juvenile officials closed down or "down-sized" antiquated juvenile training schools and initiated community-based programs for youthful offenders. These reforms were energized by litigation or the credible threat of court intervention and were stewarded by progressive juvenile justice professionals in these jurisdictions.

As with diversion and decriminalization, the deinstitutionalization movement failed to meet all of its optimistic goals. Overall, the numbers of incarcerated youth continued to rise despite declining rates of juvenile crime. As noted earlier, some observers have raised important concerns about the quality of care in privately-run alternative programs.

Due Process. The final "D" of the second revolution in juvenile stands for due process. The *Gault* case motivated many state legislatures to revamp their juvenile court practices. Later U.S. Supreme Court and other federal appellate court decisions expanded and specified the rights enunciated in *In re Gault*.

In the late 1970s and 1980s, the U.S. Supreme Court began redefining the boundaries of how far legal rights for juveniles extended. These judicial reforms stopped short of key rights accorded adult offenders: (1) the right to jury trials, (2) the right to public proceedings and (3) the right to bail. Some observers have criticized the adequacy of legal counsel for juveniles. The appellate courts have let stand statutory provisions governing juvenile status offenders and have approved the exercise of broad discretion in the preventive detention of children.

In the view of retired Supreme Court Chief Justice Warren Burger:

What the juvenile court system needs is less, not more, of the trappings of legal procedure and judicial formalism; the juvenile court needs breathing room and flexibility to survive the repeated assaults on the court. The real problem is not the deprivation of constitutional rights but inadequate juvenile court staffs and facilities.[11]

Former juvenile judge H. Ted Rubin believes the *Gault* case brought about significant advancements. However, he also enumerated a litany of abuses still occurring in the juvenile court. He observed:

The foregoing cases are but a smattering of the abuses of juvenile rights which have occurred in our courts and the juvenile justice agencies in the years since *Gault*. From the defense point of view, actualization of due process and uniformly executed legal safeguards remain, today, more rhetoric than reality.[12]

The divergent opinions expressed by Justice Burger and Judge Rubin exemplify the contemporary debate on how much success the due process movement has achieved.

From the late 1970s into the 1980s, a very different and more conservative political agenda dominated the juvenile justice policy arena. For instance, in 1984 the National Advisory Committee for Juvenile Justice and Delinquency Prevention (NAC) stated that "the time has come for a major departure from the existing philosophy and activity of the federal government in the juvenile justice field."[13] The NAC sharply attacked the previous policy thrust toward deinstitutionalization and diversion. The liberal agenda of reform was pejoratively described as "ideas whose vogue has run far ahead of solid knowledge."[14] The NAC argued for a new federal focus on serious juvenile offenders —with an emphasis on deterrence, just deserts and incarceration of youth. Moreover, new doubts were expressed about the federal government's role in regulating local practices concerning status offenders and children in adult jails.

Conservatives called for (1) vigorous prosecution of serious and violent juvenile offenders, (2) a new focus on the plight of "missing children," (3) mandatory and harsher sentencing laws for young offenders, (4) national crusades against drugs and pornography and (5) programs to reduce school violence. These themes defined the federal funding priorities throughout the Reagan administration.

Changes in federal policy were also reflected in actions at the state level. Since 1976, legislation was enacted in nearly half of the states which makes it easier to transfer juveniles to adult courts. State lawmakers have moved to lower the age of transfer (Tennessee, Kentucky and South Carolina), have excluded certain serious offenses from juvenile court jurisdiction (Illinois, Indiana, Oklahoma and Louisiana) and have made it easier to prosecute children as adult offenders (Florida and California). In addition, several jurisdictions have stiffened juvenile court responses to serious offenders via mandatory minimum terms of incarceration (Colorado, New York and Idaho) and comprehensive sentencing guidelines (Washington).

In addition to the wave of "get tough" legislation and political calls for sterner measures against young criminals, conservative policies are also reflected in significant state and federal court decisions. For example, the U.S. Supreme Court's majority opinion in *Schall v. Martin* (1984) is a clear indicator of the High Court's more restrictive attitude toward children's rights.

Plaintiffs in *Schall v. Martin* challenged the constitutionality of New York's Family Court Act as it pertained to the preventive detention of juveniles. It was alleged that the law was too vague and that juveniles were denied due process. A federal District Court struck down the statute and its decision was affirmed by the U.S. Court of Appeals. However, the U.S. Supreme Court reversed the lower courts, holding that preventive detention of juveniles for their own protection and to prevent pretrial crimes was a legitimate state action.

A consensus emerged on behalf of limiting formal court intervention in children's lives.

159

DISARRAY IN JUVENILE
CORRECTIONS

Although the conservative revolution in juvenile justice was motivated by the concepts of deterrence and deserts, the emergence of a "get tough" philosophy also produced another "D" in the world of juvenile justice—disarray. The juvenile corrections system is confronted with (1) growing levels of overcrowding, (2) increased litigation challenging the abuse of children in training schools and detention centers and (3) increased rates of minority youth incarceration.

These results have occurred despite a declining youth population and a corresponding decline in juvenile arrests. For example, between 1976 and 1985, juvenile arrests for serious crime dropped by 21 percent. While juvenile arrests were declining, police were referring a higher proportion of these cases to juvenile and adult courts. Judges were sentencing a larger share of convicted juvenile offenders to correctional facilities for longer periods of confinement. Because of these new policies, the number of incarcerated youth increased dramatically: between 1974 and 1985, the numbers of children in juvenile facilities rose by almost 10 percent. Other data show that during the 1979 to 1985 period, the number of persons under 18 years residing in prisons rose from approximately 2700 to nearly 4000—an increase of 48 percent.

By 1985, the BJS reported that nearly two-thirds of youth residing in the larger juvenile institutions (those with more than 100 beds) were living in chronically overcrowded facilities. While there was a modest increase in the operating budgets of detention centers, expenditures for training schools barely kept pace with the rate of inflation and seldom have provided resources for increased populations.

Another ominous sign was the growing proportion of minority youths confined in public juvenile correctional facilities. In 1982, more than half (53 percent) of those in public facilities were minority youths, while approximately two-thirds of those confined in private juvenile correctional facilities were white. Between 1979 and 1982 when the number of incarcerated youngsters grew by 6,178, minority youth accounted for 93 percent of this increase. The rise in minority youth incarceration cannot be explained in terms of higher rates of minority youth crime.

Many juvenile correctional agencies

From the late 1970s, a very different and more conservative political agenda dominated the juvenile justice policy arena.

have been unable to secure the funding for facility maintenance, increased populations or the provision of basic inmate needs. These pressures have resulted in extensive litigation against juvenile correctional facilities challenging the constitutionality of conditions of confinement.

It is worth recalling that the mounting problems of the juvenile justice system occurred despite declines in the general youth population and juvenile arrests. The demographic trends that produced these declines are now reversing. In the coming decade, there will be a new surge of adolescents going through their high-risk years in terms of criminal behavior. Unless our approach to juvenile justice is restructured now, this new wave of youth will produce even higher future rates of incarceration. It is unrealistic to believe that enough juvenile facilities can be built to stay ahead of this problem.

JUVENILE JUSTICE: POSSIBLE FUTURES

The future of the juvenile court is fraught with uncertainty. Some would question whether it has any future. There have been several calls for the abolition of the children's court. Moreover, criticism of the children's court from both liberal and conservative quarters remains strong. With the reduced caseload of status offenders, the juvenile court has lost its traditional preventive mission. It must now deal with youth who are typically repetitive property offenders, drug offenders and those who have failed in child welfare placements. These youth have very high recidivism rates—making the juvenile court's effectiveness look quite bad. Within this policy environment the court needs a revitalized mission to bolster its image and public support.

One potentially negative future direction would be to reintroduce status offenders into the court's mainstream.

Those who wish to control status offenders allege that the deinstitutionalization movement has failed. They assert that many youth are being victimized and exploited due to lack of proper supervision. Public awareness campaigns have already stimulated great concern over missing children and the sexual abuse of young people. Much has also been heard about the exploitation of children by the pornography industry and the involvement of teenage runaways in prostitution. We are just beginning to hear claims that runaways are at great risk of contracting and transmitting AIDS—although the scientific evidence to support these assertions is absent. The "child as victim" provides a seemingly powerful justification for the court to return to its previous rule as regulator of family life.

State legislatures are considering expanding the court's authority to incarcerate status offenders. Even where state laws limit the confinement of status offenders, growing numbers of runaways and truants are showing up in detention centers. Judges are using the contempt powers of the court to lock up chronic status offenders. The sentence of 30 days in detention is the preferred sanction of many juvenile court judges for female status offenders.

Service gaps do exist for severely troubled youth. Many communities have failed to fund the alternative community-based programs called for by the deinstitutionalization movement. Yet, returning status offenders to detention centers is an inappropriate response to their real needs.

Any proposal to return status offenders to the juvenile justice system must answer serious policy concerns about (1) the commingling of status offenders with serious offenders, (2) the traditional over-reliance on institutional placements versus home-based services and (3) the dangers that status offenders will be unnecessarily drawn further into the juvenile justice process.

As the juvenile court moves toward a punishment model, more attention must be paid to issues of due process, equal protection, and proportionality of sanctions.

Those who seek a more punishment-oriented juvenile court argue that juveniles must be held accountable for their criminal behavior. Even the National Council of Juvenile and Family Court Judges, an advocate of the traditional juvenile court philosophy, has proposed that punishment and just deserts play a larger role in juvenile justice practice.

The emphasis on enhancing punishment has led to an exploration of determinate sentencing for juveniles. As the juvenile court moves toward a punishment model, more attention must be paid to issues of due process, equal protection and proportionality of sanctions. The comprehensive reform of Washington State's juvenile code in 1979 represents a most significant movement toward a determinate sentencing model for juveniles. Soon after the Washington code was implemented, the number of youth in detention and in training schools rose dramatically. The state quickly implemented early release policies to avert severe crowding in its juvenile facilities.

The political environment supporting harsher juvenile court policies and penalties exists in several jurisdictions. These "get tough" policies are popular with politicians who are responsive to persistent public fears about crime. But, the most immediate results of "get tough" policies are overcrowded facilities and demands for increased funding for corrections agencies. There is no evidence that tougher penalties actually reduce youth crime. Until recently, the true costs of enhancing punishments for juvenile offenders have been hidden by the enormous expenditures required by skyrocketing prison and jail populations. The severe problems of the juvenile system have not successfully competed for public attention in most jurisdictions. Even more troubling, the ethos of punishment may have blunted the response of public officials to the continuing legacy of abuses within juvenile facilities. Some juvenile justice officials claim that the public actually supports these abusive practices. While litigation by itself has rarely been sufficient to achieve major juvenile justice reforms, increased legal challenges are crucial in order to hold public officials accountable for minimum standards of decency in the care of troubled youngsters.

RECLAIMING THE JUVENILE COURT'S VISION

A more promising future for the juvenile court would entail the rediscovery and updating of its historic vision. Reforms should pursue the "best interests of the children" by truly implementing individualized treatment plans and expanding the range of dispositional options available to the court. Incarceration should be used as a last resort. Large-scale training schools must be replaced with a continuum of placements and services, including small, service-intensive secure programs for the few violent youth and community-based placements for other offenders. Lower caseloads make possible correctional programming geared to meeting individual youth needs.

Innovative correctional programs emphasize aftercare and preparation for community reentry. In fact, planning for the offender's eventual return to community living starts soon after admission. Upon release from secure programs, violent and chronic offenders should enter highly structured community programs. Those offenders placed in community settings should be supervised very closely. Many of these youth should also attend educationally-based day treatment programs and pay restitution or perform community service.

States as diverse as Massachusetts and Utah have shown that this neo-traditional view of juvenile justice can be actualized. In these states, less than 25 percent of youth committed to state corrections agencies are housed in secure facilities. Research results from these states strongly indicate that their more community-based response to youthful offenders does not endanger public safety.[15]

Massachusetts and Utah are not alone in reducing the over-reliance on incarceration. States such as Maryland, Georgia, Louisiana, Oklahoma, Oregon, Pennsylvania, Texas, Florida and Delaware have adopted similar juvenile justice policy goals. However, only a few states, most notably California, Michigan and Arizona, have embarked on massive programs to build new training schools.

Individualized treatment and "the best interests of the child" do not require a return to the arbitrary and often capricious decision-making that has plagued the juvenile court. It is time to recognize that the values of due process, equal protection and proportionality are in the best interests of children. First and foremost, the juvenile court must be a full-fledged justice court. The excellent work of the American Bar Association and the Institute for Judicial Administration provides a blueprint for court proceedings that are completely consistent with a humane vision of justice for youth. Indeed, it is worth noting that jurisdictions possessing the widest assortment of treatment resources for children are often those that also pay careful attention to protecting the legal rights of young people.

Winning support for an individualized, treatment-oriented future for the juvenile court will be very difficult. The public is frustrated and angry about unacceptably high levels of youth violence and drug abuse. It is the challenge of modern day reformers to garner influential and powerful support for progressive policies that benefit disadvantaged youth. While juvenile justice reform can be justified on humanitarian grounds alone, it will be crucial to demonstrate the societal utility of more enlightened policies.

Besides reforming the juvenile court, the reclaimed vision of justice for youth must confront stark economic and social trends. Nearly 25 percent of all children under the age of 18 are growing up in poverty. The number of homeless families has skyrocketed: In New York City alone, 10,000 children reside in "welfare hotels" on a given day. School dropout rates are at obscenely high levels in urban areas. Job prospects for those at the bottom of the social system have worsened because of basic economic transformations. Our cities contain neighborhoods more disorganized and chaotic than in recent memory. These social trends portend even higher rates of youth crime in the future.

5. JUVENILE JUSTICE

According to criminologists Alden Miller and Lloyd Ohlin:

Delinquency is a community problem. In the final analysis the means for its prevention and control must be built into the fabric of community life. This can only happen if the community accepts its share of responsibility for having generated and perpetuated paths of socialization that lead to sporadic criminal episodes for some youth and careers in crime for others.[16]

A new generation of childsavers may be required to advance the principles of social justice and community reconstruction called for by Miller and Ohlin.

Whether an enlightened concept of juvenile justice will be limited to a few jurisdictions or whether it can achieve wider public acceptance is difficult to predict. In too many communities, abusive and inferior care of troubled and disadvantaged youngsters is still the norm. Now more than ever the redemptive vision of justice symbolized by the juvenile court must be rekindled.

---

1. Pickett, 1969.
2. Mennel, 1973.
3. *Ex Parte Crouse*, 4 Wharton PA 9 (1838).
4. Mennel, 1973.
5. *Commonwealth v. Fisher*, 213 Pennsylvania 48 (1905) (emphasis added).
6. Empey, 1978.
7. In 1980, the JJDPA was amended to require the complete removal of children from jails.
8. NCCD, 1975.
9. Lerman, 1982.
10. BJS, 1986.
11. *In re Winship*, 397 U.S. 358 (1970).
12. Rubin, 1979:211.
13. NAC, 1984:iii.
14. NAC, 1984:8.
15. NCCD, 1987, 1988.
16. Miller and Ohlin, 1985.

CASES CITED

Commonwealth v. Fisher, 213 P.A. 48 (1905)
Ex Parte Crouse, 4 Wharton PA 9 (1838)
In re Gault, 387 U.S. 1 (1967)
In re Winship, 397 U.S. 358 (1970)
Kent v. U.S., 383 U.S. 541 (1966)
Schall v. Martin, 467 U.S. 253

REFERENCES

Bureau of Justice Statistics
1986   *1984 Census of State Adult Correctional Facilities*. Washington, D.C.: Bureau of Statistics.

Empey, LaMar
1978   *American Delinquency: Its Meaning and Construction*. Homewood, IL: Dorsey Press.

Lerman, Paul
1982   *Deinstitutionalization and the Welfare State*. New Jersey: Rutgers University Press.

Mennel, Robert
1973   *Thorns and Thistles*. Hanover, NH: The University of New Hampshire.

Miller, Alden and Lloyd Ohlin
1985   *Delinquency and Community*. Beverly Hills, CA: Sage Publications.

National Advisory Committee for Juvenile Justice and Delinquency Prevention
1984   *Serious Juvenile Crime: A Redirected Federal Effort*. Washington, D.C.: Office of Juvenile Justice and Delinquency Prevention.

National Council on Crime and Delinquency
1988   *Study of the Massachusetts Division of Youth Services: Basic Data Tables*. San Francisco: NCCD.
1987   *The Impact of Juvenile Court Sanctions*. San Francisco: NCCD.

National Council on Crime and Delinquency, Board of Directors
1975   "Jurisdiction Over Status Offenders Should be Removed from the Juvenile Court." *Crime and Delinquency*. Vol. 21, pp. 97-99.

National Probation and Parole Association
1957   *Guides for Juvenile Court Judges*. New York: National Probation and Parole Association.

Pickett, Robert
1969   *House of Refuge: Origins of Juvenile Justice Reform in New York*. Syracuse: Syracuse University Press. pp. 1815-1857.

Rubin, H. Ted
1979   *Juvenile Justice Policy, Practice and Law*. Santa Monica, CA: Goodyear.

Girls' Crime and Woman's Place: Toward a Feminist Model of Female Delinquency

This article argues that existing delinquency theories are fundamentally inadequate to the task of explaining female delinquency and official reactions to girls' deviance. To establish this, the article first reviews the degree of the androcentric bias in the major theories of delinquent behavior. Then the need for a feminist model of female delinquency is explored by reviewing the available evidence on girls' offending. This review shows that the extensive focus on disadvantaged males in public settings has meant that girls' victimization and the relationship between that experience and girls' crime has been systematically ignored. Also missed has been the central role played by the juvenile justice system in the sexualization of female delinquency and the criminalization of girls' survival strategies. Finally, it will be suggested that the official actions of the juvenile justice system should be understood as major forces in women's oppression as they have historically served to reinforce the obedience of all young women to the demands of patriarchal authority no matter how abusive and arbitrary.

Meda Chesney-Lind

Meda Chesney-Lind: Associate Professor of Women's Studies and an Associate Researcher with the Center for Youth Research at the University of Hawaii, Manoa.

I ran away so many times. I tried anything man, and they wouldn't believe me. . . . As far as they are concerned they think I'm the problem. You know, runaway, bad label. (Statement of a 16-year-old girl who, after having been physically and sexually assaulted, started running away from home and was arrested as a "runaway" in Hawaii.)

You know, one of these days I'm going to have to kill myself before you guys are gonna listen to me. I can't stay at home. (Statement of a 16-year-old Tucson runaway with a long history of physical abuse [Davidson, 1982, p. 26].)

Who is the typical female delinquent? What causes her to get into trouble? What happens to her if she is caught? These are questions that few members of the general public could answer quickly. By contrast, almost every citizen can talk about "delinquency," by which they generally mean male delinquency, and can even generate some fairly specific complaints about, for ex-

ample, the failure of the juvenile justice system to deal with such problems as "the alarming increase in the rate of serious juvenile crime" and the fact that the juvenile courts are too lenient on juveniles found guilty of these offenses (Opinion Research Corporation, 1982).

This situation should come as no surprise since even the academic study of delinquent behavior has, for all intents and purposes, been the study of male delinquency. "The delinquent is a rogue male" declared Albert Cohen (1955, p. 140) in his influential book on gang delinquency. More than a decade later, Travis Hirschi, in his equally important book entitled *The Causes of Delinquency,* relegated women to a footnote that suggested, somewhat apologetically, that "in the analysis that follows, the 'non-Negro' becomes 'white,' and the girls disappear."

This pattern of neglect is not all that unusual. All areas of social inquiry have been notoriously gender blind. What is

perhaps less well understood is that theories developed to describe the misbehavior of working- or lower-class male youth fail to capture the full nature of delinquency in America; and, more to the point, are woefully inadequate when it comes to explaining female misbehavior and official reactions to girls' deviance.

To be specific, delinquent behavior involves a range of activities far broader than those committed by the stereotypical street gang. Moreover, many more young people than the small visible group of "troublemakers" that exist on every intermediate and high school campus commit some sort of juvenile offense and many of these youth have brushes with the law. One study revealed, for example, that 33% of all the boys and 14% of the girls born in 1958 had at least one contact with the police before reaching their eighteenth birthday (Tracy, Wolfgang, and Figlio, 1985, p. 5). Indeed, some forms of serious

Reprinted from *Crime & Delinquency*, Vol. 35, No. 1, January 1989, pp. 5-29. Copyright © 1989 by The National Council on Crime and Delinquency, Sage Publications.

delinquent behavior, such as drug and alcohol abuse, are far more frequent than the stereotypical delinquent behavior of gang fighting and vandalism and appear to cut across class and gender lines.

Studies that solicit from youth themselves the volume of their delinquent behavior consistently confirm that large numbers of adolescents engage in at least some form of misbehavior that could result in their arrest. As a consequence, it is largely trivial misconduct, rather than the commission of serious crime, that shapes the actual nature of juvenile delinquency. One national study of youth aged 15-21, for example, noted that only 5% reported involvement in a serious assault, and only 6% reported having participated in a gang fight. In contrast, 81% admitted to having used alcohol, 44% admitted to having used marijuana, 37% admitted to having been publicly drunk, 42% admitted to having skipped classes (truancy), 44% admitted having had sexual intercourse, and 15% admitted to having stolen from the family (McGarrell and Flanagan, 1985, p. 363). Clearly, not all of these activities are as serious as the others. It is important to remember that young people can be arrested for all of these behaviors.

Indeed, one of the most important points to understand about the nature of delinquency, and particularly female delinquency, is that youth can be taken into custody for both criminal acts and a wide variety of what are often called "status offenses." These offenses, in contrast to criminal violations, permit the arrest of youth for a wide range of behaviors that are violations of parental authority: "running away from home," "being a person in need of supervision," "minor in need of supervision," being "incorrigible," "beyond control," truant, in need of "care and protection," and so on. Juvenile delinquents, then, are youths arrested for either criminal or noncriminal status offenses; and, as this discussion will establish, the role played by uniquely juvenile offenses is by no means insignificant, particularly when considering the character of female delinquency.

Examining the types of offenses for which youth are actually arrested, it is clear that again most are arrested for the less serious criminal acts and status offenses. Of the one and a half million youth arrested in 1983, for example, only 4.5% of these arrests were for such serious violent offenses as murder, rape, robbery, or aggravated assault (McGarrell and Flanagan, 1985, p. 479). In contrast, 21% were arrested for a single offense (larceny, theft) much of

which, particularly for girls, is shoplifting (Sheldon and Horvath, 1986).

Table 1 presents the five most frequent offenses for which male and female youth are arrested and from this it can be seen that while trivial offenses dominate both male and female delinquency, trivial offenses, particularly status offenses, are more significant in the case of girls' arrests; for example the five offenses listed in Table 1 account for nearly three-quarters of female offenses and only slightly more than half of male offenses.

More to the point, it is clear that, though routinely neglected in most delinquency research, status offenses play a significant role in girls' official delinquency. Status offenses accounted for about 25.2% of all girls' arrests in 1986 (as compared to 26.9% in 1977) and only about 8.3% of boys' arrests (compared to 8.8% in 1977). These figures are somewhat surprising since dramatic declines in arrests of youth for these offenses might have been expected as a result of the passage of the Juvenile Justice and Delinquency Prevention Act in 1974, which, among other things, encouraged jurisdictions to divert and deinstitutionalize youth charged with noncriminal offenses. While the figures in Table 1 do show a decline in these arrests, virtually all of this decline occurred in the 1970s. Between 1982 and 1986 girls' curfew arrests increased by 5.1% and runaway arrests increased by a striking 24.5%. And the upward trend continues; arrests of girls for running away increased by 3% between 1985 and 1986 and arrests of girls for curfew violations increased by 12.4% (Federal Bureau of Investigation, 1987, p. 171).

Looking at girls who find their way into juvenile court populations, it is apparent that status offenses continue to play an important role in the character of girls' official delinquency. In total, 34% of the girls, but only 12% of the boys, were referred to court in 1983 for these offenses (Snyder and Finnegan, 1987, pp. 6–20). Stating these figures differently, they mean that while males constituted about 81% of all delinquency referrals, females constituted 46% of all status offenders in courts (Snyder and Finnegan, 1987, p. 20). Similar figures were reported for 1977 by Black and Smith (1981). Fifteen years earlier, about half of the girls and about 20% of the boys were referred to court for these offenses (Children's Bureau, 1965). These data do seem to signal a drop in female status offense referrals, though not as dramatic a decline as might have been expected.

For many years statistics showing

large numbers of girls arrested and referred for status offenses were taken to be representative of the different types of male and female delinquency. However, self-report studies of male and female delinquency do not reflect the dramatic differences in misbehavior found in official statistics. Specifically, it appears that girls charged with these noncriminal status offenses have been and continue to be significantly overrepresented in court populations.

Teilmann and Landry (1981) compared girls' contribution to arrests for runaway and incorrigibility with girls' self-reports of these two activities, and found a 10.4% overrepresentation of females among those arrested for runaway and a 30.9% overrepresentation in arrests for incorrigibility. From these data they concluded that girls are "arrested for status offenses at a higher rate than boys, when contrasted to their self-reported delinquency rates" (Teilmann and Landry, 1981, pp. 74–75). These findings were confirmed in another recent self-report study. Figueira-McDonough (1985, p. 277) analyzed the delinquent conduct of 2,000 youths and found "no evidence of greater involvement of females in status offenses." Similarly, Canter (1982) found in the National Youth Survey that there was no evidence of greater female involvement, compared to males, in any category of delinquent behavior. Indeed, in this sample, males were significantly more likely than females to report status offenses.

Utilizing Canter's national data on the extensiveness of girls self-reported delinquency and comparing these figures to official arrests of girls (see Table 2) reveals that girls are underrepresented in every arrest category with the exception of status offenses and larceny theft. These figures strongly suggest that official practices tend to exaggerate the role played by status offenses in girls' delinquency.

Delinquency theory, because it has virtually ignored female delinquency, failed to pursue anomalies such as these found in the few early studies examining gender differences in delinquent behavior. Indeed, most delinquency theories have ignored status offenses. As a consequence, there is considerable question as to whether existing theories that were admittedly developed to explain male delinquency can adequately explain female delinquency. Clearly, these theories were much influenced by the notion that class and protest masculinity were at the core of delinquency. Will the "add women and stir approach" be sufficient? Are these really theories of delin-

TABLE 1: Rank Order of Adolescent Male and Female Arrests for Specific Offenses, 1977 and 1986

Male				Female			
1977	% of Total Arrests	1986	% of Total Arrests	1977	% of Total Arrests	1986	% of Total Arrests
(1) Larceny-Theft	18.4	(1) Larceny-Theft	20.4	(1) Larceny-Theft	27.0	(1) Larceny-Theft	25.7
(2) Other Offenses	14.5	(2) Other Offenses	16.5	(2) Runaway	22.9	(2) Runaway	20.5
(3) Burglary	13.0	(3) Burglary	9.1	(3) Other Offenses	14.2	(3) Other Offenses	14.8
(4) Drug Abuse Violations	6.5	(4) Vandalism	7.0	(4) Liquor Laws	5.5	(4) Liquor Laws	8.4
(5) Vandalism	6.4	(5) Vandalism	6.3	(5) Curfew & Loitering Violations	4.0	(5) Curfew & Loitering Violations	4.7

	1977	1986	% N Change		1977	1986	% N Change
Arrests for Serious Violent Offenses[a]	4.2%	4.7%	2.3	Arrests for Serious Violent Offenses	1.8%	2.0%	+1.7
Arrests of All Violent Offenses[b]	7.6%	9.6%	+10.3	Arrests of All Violent Offenses	5.1%	7.1%	+26.0
Arrests for Status Offenses[c]	8.8%	8.3%	−17.8	Arrests for Status Offenses	26.9%	25.2%	−14.7

SOURCE: Compiled from Federal Bureau of Investigation (1987, p. 169).
a. Arrests for murder and nonnegligent manslaughter, robbery, forcible rape, and aggravated assault.
b. Also includes arrests for other assaults.
c. Arrests for curfew and loitering law violation and runaway.

quent behavior as some (Simons, Miller, and Aigner, 1980) have argued?

This article will suggest that they are not. The extensive focus on male delinquency and the inattention the role played by patriarchal arrangements in the generation of adolescent delinquency and conformity has rendered the major delinquency theories fundamentally inadequate to the task of explaining female behavior. There is, in short, an urgent need to rethink current models in light of girls' situation in patriarchal society.

To understand why such work must occur, it is first necessary to explore briefly the dimensions of the androcentric bias found in the dominant and influential delinquency theories. Then the need for a feminist model of female delinquency will be explored by reviewing the available evidence on girls' offending. This discussion will also establish that the proposed overhaul of delinquency theory is not, as some might think, solely an academic exercise. Specifically, it is incorrect to assume that because girls are charged with less serious offenses, they actually have few problems and are treated gently when they are drawn into the juvenile justice system. Indeed, the extensive focus on disadvantaged males in public settings has meant that girls' victimization and the relationship between that experience and girls' crime has been systematically ignored. Also missed has been the central role played by the juvenile justice system in the sexualization of girls' delinquency and the criminalization of girls' survival strategies. Finally, it will be suggested that the

official actions of the juvenile justice system should be understood as major forces in girls' oppression as they have historically served to reinforce the obedience of all young women to demands of patriarchal authority no matter how abusive and arbitrary.

THE ROMANCE OF THE GANG OR THE *WEST SIDE STORY* SYNDROME

From the start, the field of delinquency research focused on visible lower-class male delinquency, often justifying the neglect of girls in the most cavalier of terms. Take, for example, the extremely important and influential work of Clifford R. Shaw and Henry D. McKay who beginning in 1929, utilized an ecological approach to the study of juvenile delinquency. Their impressive work, particularly *Juvenile Delinquency in Urban Areas* (1942) and intensive biographical case studies such as Shaw's *Brothers in Crime* (1938) and *The Jackroller* (1930), set the stage for much of the subcultural research on gang delinquency. In their ecological work, however, Shaw and McKay analyzed only the official arrest data on male delinquents in Chicago and repeatedly referred to these rates as "delinquency rates" (though they occasionally made parenthetical reference to data on female delinquency) (see Shaw and McKay, 1942, p. 356). Similarly, their biographical work traced only male experiences with the law; in *Brothers in Crime,* for example, the delinquent and criminal careers of five brothers were followed for fifteen years. In none of these works was any justification given for the equation of male delinquency with delinquency.

Early fieldwork on delinquent gangs in Chicago set the stage for another style of delinquency research. Yet here too researchers were interested only in talking to and following the boys. Thrasher studied over a thousand juvenile gangs in Chicago during roughly the same period as Shaw and McKay's more quantitative work was being done. He spent approximately one page out of 600 on the five of six female gangs he encountered in his field observation of juvenile gangs. Thrasher (1927, p. 228) did mention, in passing, two factors he felt accounted for the lower number of girl gangs: "First, the social patterns for the behavior of girls, powerfully backed by the great weight of tradition and custom, are contrary to the gang and its activities; and secondly, girls, even in urban disorganized areas, are much more closely supervised and guarded than boys and usually well incorporated into the family groups or some other social structure."

Another major theoretical approach to delinquency focuses on the subculture of lower-class communities as a generating milieu for delinquent behavior. Here again, noted delinquency researchers concentrated either exclusively or nearly exclusively on male lower-class culture. For example, Cohen's work on the subculture of delinquent gangs, which was written nearly twenty years after Thrasher's, deliberately considers only boys' delinquency. His justification for the exclusion of the girls is quite illuminating:

My skin has nothing of the quality of down or silk, there is nothing limpid or flute-like about my voice, I am a total

TABLE 2: Comparison of Sex Differences in Self-Reported
and Official Delinquency for Selected Offenses

	Self-Report[a] M/F Ratios (1976)	Official Statistics[b] M/F Arrest Ratio	
		1976	1986
Theft	3.5:1 (Felony Theft) 3.4:1 (Minor Theft)	2.5:1	2.7:1
Drug Violation	1:1 (Hard Drug Use)	5.1:1	6.0:1 (Drug Abuse Violations)
Vandalism	5.1:1	12.3:1	10.0:1
Disorderly Conduct	2.8:1	4.5:1	4.4:1
Serious Assault	3.5:1 (Felony Assault)	5.6:1	5.5:1 (Aggravated Assault)
Minor Assault	3.4:1	3.8:1	3.4:1
Status Offenses	1.6:1	1.3:1	1.1:1 (Runaway, Curfew)

a. Extracted from Rachelle Canter (1982, p. 383).
b. Compiled from Federal Bureau of Investigation (1986, p. 173).

loss with needle and thread, my posture and carriage are wholly lacking in grace. These imperfections cause me no distress—if anything, they are gratifying—because I conceive myself to be a man and want people to recognize me as a full-fledged, unequivocal representative of my sex. My wife, on the other hand, is not greatly embarrassed by her inability to tinker with or talk about the internal organs of a car, by her modest attainments in arithmetic or by her inability to lift heavy objects. Indeed, I am reliably informed that many women—I do not suggest that my wife is among them—often affect ignorance, frailty and emotional instability because to do otherwise would be out of keeping with a reputation for indubitable femininity. In short, people do not simply want to excel; they want to excel as a man or as a woman [Cohen, 1955, p. 138.]

From this Cohen (1955, p. 140) concludes that the delinquent response "however it may be condemned by others on moral grounds has least one virtue; it incontestably confirms, in the eyes of all concerned, his essential masculinity." Much the same line of argument appears in Miller's influential paper on the "focal concerns" of lower-class life with its emphasis on importance of trouble, toughness, excitement, and so on. These, the author concludes, predispose poor youth (particularly male youth) to criminal misconduct. However, Cohen's comments are notable in their candor and probably capture both the allure that male delinquency has had for at least some male theorists as well as the fact that sexism has rendered the female delinquent as irrelevant to their work.

Emphasis on blocked opportunities (sometimes the "strain" theories)

emerged out of the work of Robert K. Merton (1938) who stressed the need to consider how some social structures exert a definite pressure upon certain persons in the society to engage in nonconformist rather than conformist conduct. His work influenced research largely through the efforts of Cloward and Ohlin who discussed access to "legitimate" and "illegitimate" opportunities for male youth. No mention of female delinquency can be found in their *Delinquency and Opportunity* except that women are blamed for male delinquency. Here, the familiar notion is that boys, "engulfed by a feminine world and uncertain of their own identification . . . tend to 'protest' against femininity" (Cloward and Ohlin, 1960, p. 49). Early efforts by Ruth Morris to test this hypothesis utilizing different definitions of success based on the gender of respondents met with mixed success. Attempting to assess boys' perceptions about access to economic power status while for girls the variable concerned itself with the ability or inability of girls to maintain effective relationships, Morris was unable to find a clear relationship between "female" goals and delinquency (Morris, 1964).

The work of Edwin Sutherland emphasized the fact that criminal behavior was learned in intimate personal groups. His work, particularly the notion of differential association, which also influenced Cloward and Ohlin's work, was similarly male oriented as much of his work was affected by case studies he conducted of male criminals. Indeed, in describing his notion of how differential association works, he utilized male examples (e.g., "In an area where the delinquency rate is high a boy who is

sociable, gregarious, active, and athletic is very likely to come in contact with the other boys, in the neighborhood, learn delinquent behavior from them, and become a gangster" [Sutherland, 1978, p. 131]). Finally, the work of Travis Hirschi on the social bonds that control delinquency ("social control theiry") was, as was stated earlier, derived out of research on male delinquents (though he, at least, studied delinquent behavior as reported by youth themselves rather than studying only those who were arrested).

Such a persistent focus on social class and such an absence of interest in gender in delinquency is ironic for two reasons. As even the work of Hirschi demonstrated, and as later studies would validate, a clear relationship between social class position and delinquency is problematic, while it is clear that gender has a dramatic and consistent effect on delinquency causation (Hagan, Gillis, and Simpson, 1985). The second irony, and one that consistently eludes even contemporary delinquency theorists, is the fact that while the academics had little interest in female delinquents, the same could not be said for the juvenile justice system. Indeed, work on the early history of the separate system for youth, reveals that concerns about girls' immoral conduct were really at the center of what some have called the "childsaving movement" (Platt, 1969) that set up the juvenile justice system.

"THE BEST PLACE TO CONQUER GIRLS"

The movement to establish separate institutions for youthful offenders was part of the larger Progressive movement, which among other things was keenly concerned about prostitution and other "social evils" (white slavery and the like) (Schlossman and Wallach, 1978; Rafter, 1985, p. 54). Childsaving was also a celebration of women's domesticity, though ironically women were influential in the movement (Platt, 1969; Rafter, 1985). In a sense, privileged women found, in the moral purity crusades and the establishment of family courts, a safe outlet for their energies. As the legitimate guardians of the moral sphere, women were seen as uniquely suited to patrol the normative boundaries of the social order. Embracing rather than challenging these stereotypes, women carved out for themselves a role in the policing of women and girls (Feinman, 1980; Freedman, 1981; Messerschmidt, 1987). Ultimately, many of the early childsavers' activities revolved around the monitoring of young girls', particularly immigrant girls', behavior to prevent their straying from the path.

This state of affairs was the direct consequence of a disturbing coalition between some feminists and the more conservative social purity movement. Concerned about female victimization and distrustful of male (and to some degree female) sexuality, notable women leaders, including Susan B. Anthony, found common cause with the social purists around such issues as opposing the regulation of prostitution and raising the age of consent (see Messerschmidt, 1987). The consequences of such a partnership are an important lesson for contemporary feminist movements that are, to some extent, faced with the same possible coalitions.

Girls were the clear losers in this reform effort. Studies of early family court activity reveal that virtually all the girls who appeared in these courts were charged for immorality or waywardness (Chesney-Lind, 1971; Schlossman and Wallach, 1978; Shelden, 1981). More to the point, the sanctions for such misbehavior were extremely severe. For example, in Chicago (where the first family court was founded), one-half of the girl delinquents, but only one-fifth of the boy delinquents, were sent to reformatories between 1899–1909. In Milwaukee, twice as many girls as boys were committed to training schools (Schlossman and Wallach, 1978, p. 72); and in Memphis females were twice as likely as males to be committed to training schools (Shelden, 1981, p. 70).

In Honolulu, during the period 1929–1930, over half of the girls referred to court were charged with "immorality," which meant evidence of sexual intercourse. In addition, another 30% were charged with "waywardness." Evidence of immorality was vigorously pursued by both arresting officers and social workers through lengthy questioning of the girl and, if possible, males with whom she was suspected of having sex. Other evidence of "exposure" was provided by gynecological examinations that were routinely ordered in virtually all girls' cases. Doctors, who understood the purpose of such examinations, would routinely note the condition of the hymen: "admits intercourse hymen rupture," "no laceration," "hymen ruptured" are typical of the notations on the forms. Girls during this period were also twice as likely as males to be detained where they spent five times as long on the average as their male counterparts. They were also nearly three times more likely to be sentenced to the training school (Chesney-Lind, 1971). Indeed, girls were half of those commit-

ted to training schools in Honolulu well into the 1950s (Chesney-Lind, 1973).

Not surprisingly, large numbers of girls'reformatories and training schools were established during this period as well as places of "rescue and reform." For example, Schlossman and Wallach note that 23 facilities for girls were opened during the 1910–1920 decade (in contrast to the 1850–1910 period where the average was 5 reformatories per decade [Schlossman and Wallach, 1985, p. 70]), and these institutions did much to set the tone of official response to female delinquency. Obsessed with precocious female sexuality, the institutions set about to isolate the females from all contact with males while housing them in bucolic settings. The intention was to hold the girls until marriageable age and to occupy them in domestic pursuits during their sometimes lengthy incarceration.

The links between these attitudes and those of juvenile courts some decades later are, of course, arguable; but an examination of the record of the court does not inspire confidence. A few examples of the persistence of what might be called a double standard of juvenile justice will suffice here.

A study conducted in the early 1970s in a Connecticut training school revealed large numbers of girls incarcerated "for their own protection." Explaining this pattern, one judge explained, "Why most of the girls I commit are for status offenses, I figure if a girl is about to get pregnant, we'll keep her until she's sixteen and then ADC (Aid to Dependent Children) will pick her up" (Rogers, 1972). For more evidence of official concern with adolescent sexual misconduct, consider Linda Hancock's (1981) content analysis of police referrals in Australia. She noted that 40% of the referrals of girls to court made specific mention of sexual and moral conduct compared to only 5% of the referrals of boys. These sorts of results suggest that all youthful female misbehavior has traditionally been subject to surveillance for evidence of sexual misconduct.

Gelsthorpe's (1986) field research on an English police station also revealed how everyday police decision making resulted in disregard of complaints about male problem behavior in contrast to active concern about the "problem behavior" of girls. Notable, here, was the concern about the girls' sexual behavior. In one case, she describes police persistence in pursuing a "moral danger" order for a 14-year-old picked up in a truancy run. Over the objections of both the girl's parents and the Social Services Department and in the face of a written confirmation from a surgeon

that the girl was still premenstrual, the officers pursued the application because, in one officer's words, "I know her sort . . . free and easy. I'm still suspicious that she might be pregnant. Anyway, if the doctor can't provide evidence we'll do her for being beyond the care and control of her parents, no one can dispute that. Running away is proof" (Gelsthorpe, 1986, p. 136). This sexualization of female deviance is highly significant and explains why criminal activities by girls (particularly in past years) were overlooked so long as they did not appear to signal defiance of parental control (see Smith, 1978).

In their historic obsession about precocious female sexuality, juvenile justice workers rarely reflected on the broader nature of female misbehavior or on the sources of this misbehavior. It was enough for them that girls' parents reported them out of control. Indeed, court personnel tended to "sexualize" virtually all female defiance that lent itself to that construction and ignore other misbehavior (Chesney-Lind, 1973, 1977; Smith, 1978). For their part, academic students of delinquency were so entranced with the notion of the delinquent as a romantic rogue male challenging a rigid and unequal class structure, that they spent little time on middle-class delinquency, trivial offenders, or status offenders. Yet it is clear that the vast bulk of delinquent behavior is of this type.

Some have argued that such an imbalance in theoretical work is appropriate as minor misconduct, while troublesome, is not a threat to the safety and well-being of the community. This argument might be persuasive if two additional points could be established. One, that some small number of youth "specialize" in serious criminal behavior while the rest commit only minor acts, and, two, that the juvenile court rapidly releases those youth that come into its purview for these minor offenses, thus reserving resources for the most serious youthful offenders.

The evidence is mixed on both of these points. Determined efforts to locate the "serious juvenile offender" have failed to locate a group of offenders who specialize only in serious violent offenses. For example, in a recent analysis of a national self-report data set, Elliott and his associates noted "there is little evidence for specialization in serious violent offending; to the contrary, serious violent offending appears to be embedded in a more general involvement in a wide range of serious and non-serious offenses" (Elliott, Huizinga, and Morse, 1987). Indeed, they went so far as to speculate that arrest histories that tend to high-light particular types of offenders reflect variations in police policy, practices, and processes of uncovering crime as well as underlying offending patterns.

More to the point, police and court personnel are, it turns out, far more interested in youth they charge with trivial or status offenses than anyone imagined. Efforts to deinstitutionalize "status offenders," for example, ran afoul of juvenile justice personnel who had little interest in releasing youth guilty of noncriminal offenses (Chesney-Lind, 1988). As has been established, much of this is a product of the system's history that encouraged court officers to involve themselves in the noncriminal behavior of youth in order to "save" them from a variety of social ills.

Indeed, parallels can be found between the earlier Progressive period and current national efforts to challenge the deinstitutionalization components of the Juvenile Justice and Delinquency Prevention Act of 1974. These come complete with their celebration of family values and concerns about youthful independence. One of the arguments against the act has been that it allegedly gave children the "freedom to run away" (Office of Juvenile Justice and Delinquency Prevention, 1985) and that it has hampered "reunions" of "missing" children with their parents (Office of Juvenile Justice, 1986). Suspicions about teen sexuality are reflected in excessive concern about the control of teen prostitution and child pornography.

Opponents have also attempted to justify continued intervention into the lives of status offenders by suggesting that without such intervention, the youth would "escalate" to criminal behavior. Yet there is little evidence that status offenders escalate to criminal offenses, and the evidence is particularly weak when considering female delinquents (particularly white female delinquents) (Datesman and Aickin, 1984). Finally, if escalation is occurring, it is likely the product of the justice system's insistence on enforcing status offense laws, thereby forcing youth in crisis to live lives of escaped criminals.

The most influential delinquency theories, however, have largely ducked the issue of status and trivial offenses and, as a consequence, neglected the role played by the agencies of official control (police, probation officers, juvenile court judges, detention home workers, and training school personnel) in the shaping of the "delinquency problem." When confronting the less than distinct picture that emerges from the actual distribution of delinquent behavior, how-ever, the conclusion that agents of social control have considerable discretion in labeling or choosing not to label particular behavior as "delinquent" is inescapable. This symbiotic relationship between delinquent behavior and the official response to that behavior is particularly critical when the question of female delinquency is considered.

TOWARD A FEMINIST THEORY OF DELINQUENCY

To sketch out completely a feminist theory of delinquency is a task beyond the scope of this article. It may be sufficient, at this point, simply to identify a few of the most obvious problems with attempts to adapt male-oriented theory to explain female conformity and deviance. Most significant of these is the fact that all existing theories were developed with no concern about gender stratification.

Note that this is not simply an observation about the power of gender roles (though this power is undeniable). It is increasingly clear that gender stratification in patriarchal society is as powerful a system as is class. A feminist approach to delinquency means construction of explanations of female behavior that are sensitive to its patriarchal context. Feminist analysis of delinquency would also examine ways in which agencies of social control—the police, the courts, and the prisons—act in ways to reinforce woman's place in male society (Harris, 1977; Chesney-Lind, 1986). Efforts to construct a feminist model of delinquency must first and foremost be sensitive to the situations of girls. Failure to consider the existing empirical evidence on girls' lives and behavior can quickly lead to stereotypical thinking and theoretical dead ends.

An example of this sort of flawed theory building was the early fascination with the notion that the women's movement was causing an increase in women's crime; a notion that is now more or less discredited (Steffensmeier, 1980; Gora, 1982). A more recent example of the same sort of thinking can be found in recent work on the "power-control" model of delinquency (Hagan, Simpson, and Gillis, 1987). Here, the authors speculate that girls commit less delinquency in part because their behavior is more closely controlled by the patriarchal family. The authors' promising beginning quickly gets bogged down in a very limited definition of patriarchal control (focusing on parental supervision and variations in power within the family). Ultimately, the authors' narrow formulation of patriarchal control results in their arguing that mother's work force participation (particularly in high status occupations) leads to increases in daughters' delinquency since these girls find themselves in more "egalitarian families."

This is essentially a not-too-subtle variation on the earlier "liberation" hypothesis. Now, mother's liberation causes daughter's crime. Aside from the methodological problems with the study (e.g., the authors argue that female-headed households are equivalent to upper-status "egalitarian" families where both parents work, and they measure delinquency using a six-item scale that contains no status offense items), there is a more fundamental problem with the hypothesis. There is no evidence to suggest that as women's labor force participation accelerated and the number of female-headed households soared, aggregate female delinquency measured both by self-report and official statistics either declined or remained stable (Ageton, 1983; Chilton and Datesman, 1987; Federal Bureau of Investigation, 1987).

By contrast, a feminist model of delinquency would focus more extensively on the few pieces of information about girls' actual lives and the role played by girls' problems, including those caused by racism and poverty, in their delinquency behavior. Fortunately, a considerable literature is now developing on girls' lives and much of it bears directly on girls' crime.

CRIMINALIZING GIRLS' SURVIVAL

It has long been understood that a major reason for girls' presence in juvenile courts was the fact that their parents insisted on their arrest. In the early years, conflicts with parents were by far the most significant referral source; in Honolulu 44% of the girls who appeared in court in 1929 through 1930 were referred by parents.

Recent national data, while slightly less explicit, also show that girls are more likely to be referred to court by "sources other than law enforcement agencies" (which would include parents). In 1983, nearly a quarter (23%) of all girls but only 16% of boys charged with delinquent offenses were referred to court by non-law enforcement agencies. The pattern among youth referred for status offenses (for which girls are overrepresented) was even more pronounced. Well over half (56%) of the girls charged with these offenses and 45% of the boys were referred by sources other than law enforcement (Snyder and Finnegan, 1987, p. 21; see also Pope and Feyerherm, 1982).

The fact that parents are often committed to two standards of adolescent behavior is one explanation for such a disparity—and one that should not be discounted as a major source of tension even in modern families. Despite expectations to the contrary, gender-specific socialization patterns have not changed very much and this is especially true for parents' relationships with their daughters (Katz, 1979). It appears that even parents who oppose sexism in general feel "uncomfortable tampering with existing traditions" and "do not want to risk their children becoming misfits" (Katz, 1979, p. 24). Clearly, parental attempts to adhere to and enforce these traditional notions will continue to be a source of conflict between girls and their elders. Another important explanation for girls' problems with their parents, which has received attention only in more recent years, is the problem of physical and sexual abuse. Looking specifically at the problem of childhood sexual abuse, it is increasingly clear that this form of abuse is a particular problem for girls.

Girls are, for example, much more likely to be the victims of child sexual abuse than are boys. Finkelhor and Baron estimate from a review of community studies that roughly 70% of the victims of sexual abuse are female (Finkelhor and Baron, 1986, p. 45). Girls' sexual abuse also tends to start earlier than boys (Finkelhor and Baron, 1986, p. 48); they are more likely than boys to be assaulted by a family member (often a stepfather)(DeJong, Hervada, and Emmett, 1983; Russell, 1986), and as a consequence, their abuse tends to last longer than male sexual abuse (De-Jong,Hervada, and Emmett, 1983). All of these factors are associated with more severe trauma—causing dramatic short- and long-term effects in victims (Adams-Tucker, 1982). The effects noted by researchers in this area move from the more well known "fear, anxiety, depression, anger and hostility, and inappropriate sexual behavior" (Browne and Finkelhor, 1986, p. 69) to behaviors of greater familiarity to criminologists, including running away from home, difficulties in school, truancy, and early marriage (Browne and Finkelhor, 1986). Herman's study of incest survivors in therapy found that they were more likely to have run away from home than a matched sample of women whose fathers were "seductive" (33% compared to 5%). Another study of women patients found that 50% of the victims of child sexual abuse, but only 20% of the nonvictim group, had left home before the age of 19 (Meiselman, 1978).

Not surprisingly, then, studies of girls on the streets or in court populations are showing high rates of both physical and sexual abuse. Silbert and Pines (1981, p. 409) found, for example, that 60% of the street prostitutes they interviewed had been sexually abused as juveniles. Girls at an Arkansas diagnostic unit and school who had been adjudicated for either status or delinquent offenses reported similarly high levels of sexual abuse as well as high levels of physical abuse; 53% indicated they had been sexually abused, 25% recalled scars, 38% recalled bleeding from abuse, and 51% recalled bruises (Mouzakitas, 1981).

A sample survey of girls in the juvenile justice system in Wisconsin (Phelps et al., 1982) revealed that 79% had been subjected to physical abuse that resulted in some form of injury, and 32% had been sexually abused by parents or other persons who were closely connected to their families. Moreover, 50% had been sexually assaulted ("raped" or forced to participate in sexual acts)(Phelps et al., 1982, p. 66). Even higher figures were reported by McCormack and her associates (McCormack, Janus, and Burgess, 1986) in their study of youth in a runaway shelter in Toronto. They found that 73% of the females and 38% of the males had been sexually abused. Finally, a study of youth charged with running away, truancy, or listed as missing persons in Arizona found that 55% were incest victims (Reich and Gutierres, 1979).

Many young women, then, are running away from profound sexual victimization at home, and once on the streets they are forced further into crime in order to survive. Interviews with girls who have run away from home show, very clearly, that they do not have a lot of attachment to their delinquent activities. In fact, they are angry about being labeled as delinquent, yet all engaged in illegal acts (Koroki and Chesney-Lind, 1985). The Wisconsin study found that 54% of the girls who ran away found it necessary to steal money, food, and clothing in order to survive. A few exchanged sexual contact for money, food, and/or shelter (Phelps et al., 1982, p. 67). In their study of runaway youth, McCormack, Janus, and Burgess (1986, pp. 392–393) found that sexually abused female runaways were significantly more likely than their nonabused counterparts to engage in delinquent or criminal activities such as substance abuse, petty theft, and prostitution. No such pattern was found among male runaways.

Research (Chesney-Lind and Rodriguez, 1983) on the backgrounds of adult women in prison underscores the important links between women's childhood victimizations and their later criminal careers. The interviews revealed that virtually all of this sample were the victims of physical and/or sexual abuse as youngsters; over 60% had been sexually abused and about half had been raped as young women. This situation prompted these women to run away from home (three-quarters had been arrested for status offenses) where once on the streets they began engaging in prostitution and other forms of petty property crime. They also begin what becomes a lifetime problem with drugs. As adults, the women continue in these activities since they possess truncated educational backgrounds and virtually no marketable occupational skills (see also Miller, 1986).

Confirmation of the consequences of childhood sexual and physical abuse on adult female criminal behavior has also recently come from a large quantitative study of 908 individuals with substantiated and validated histories of these victimizations. Widom (1988) found that abused or neglected females were twice as likely as a matched group of controls to have an adult record (16% compared to 7.5). The difference was also found among men, but it was not as dramatic (42% compared to 33%). Men with abuse backgrounds were also more likely to contribute to the "cycle of violence" with more arrests for violent offenses as adult offenders than the control group. In contrast, when women with abuse backgrounds did become involved with the criminal justice system, their arrests tended to involve property and order offenses (such as disorderly conduct, curfew, and loitering violations) (Widon, 1988, p. 17).

Given this information, a brief example of how a feminist perspective on the causes of female delinquency might look seems appropriate. First, like young men, girls are frequently the recipients of violence and sexual abuse. But unlike boys, girls' victimization and their response to that victimization is specifically shaped by their status as young women. Perhaps because of the gender and sexual scripts found in patriarchal families, girls are much more likely than boys to be victim of family-related sexual abuse. Men, particularly men with traditional attitudes toward women, are likely to define their daughters or stepdaughters as their sexual property (Finkelhor, 1982). In a society that idealizes inequality in male/female relationships and venerates youth in women, girls are easily defined as sexually attractive by older men (Bell, 1984). In addition, girls' vulnerability to both physical and sexual abuse is heightened by norms that require that they stay at home where their victimizers have access to them.

Moreover, their victimizers (usually males) have the ability to invoke official agencies of social control in their efforts to keep young women at home and vulnerable. That is to say, abusers have traditionally been able to utilize the uncritical commitment of the juvenile justice system toward parental authority to force girls to obey them. Girls' complaints about abuse were, until recently, routinely ignored. For this reason, statutes that were originally placed in law to "protect" young people have, in the case of girls' delinquency, criminalized their survival strategies. As they run away from abusive homes, parents have been able to employ agencies to enforce their return. If they persisted in their refusal to stay in that home, however intolerable, they were incarcerated.

Young women, a large number of whom are on the run from homes characterized by sexual abuse and parental neglect, are forced by the very statutes designed to protect them into the lives of escaped convicts. Unable to enroll in school or take a job to support themselves because they fear detection, young female runaways are forced into the streets. Here they engage in panhandling, petty theft, and occasional prostitution in order to survive. Young women in conflict with their parents (often for very legitimate reasons) may actually be forced by present laws into petty criminal activity, prostitution, and drug use.

In addition, the fact that young girls (but not necessarily young boys) are defined as sexually desirable and, in fact, more desirable than their older sisters due to the double standard of aging means that their lives on the streets (and their survival strategies) take on unique shape—one again shaped by patriarchal values. It is no accident that girls on the run from abusive homes, or on the streets because of profound poverty, get involved in criminal activities that exploit their sexual object status. American society has defined as desirable youthful, physically perfect women. This means that girls on the streets, who have little else of value to trade, are encouraged to utilize this "resource" (Campagna and Poffenberger, 1988). It also means that the criminal subculture views them from this perspective (Miller, 1986).

FEMALE DELINQUENCY, PATRIARCHAL AUTHORITY, AND FAMILY COURTS

The early insights into male delinquency were largely gleaned by intensive field observation of delinquent boys. Very little of this sort of work has been done in the case of girls' delinquency, though it is vital to an understanding of girls' definitions of their own situations, choices, and behavior (for exceptions to this see Campbell, 1984; Peacock, 1981; Miller, 1986; Rosenberg and Zimmerman, 1977). Time must be spent listening to girls. Fuller research on the settings, such as families and schools, that girls find themselves in and the impact of variations in those settings should also be undertaken (see Figueira-McDonough, 1986). A more complete understanding of how poverty and racism shape girls' lives is also vital (see Messerschmidt, 1986; Campbell, 1984). Finally, current qualitative research on the reaction of official agencies to girls' delinquency must be conducted. This latter task, admittedly more difficult, is particularly critical to the development of delinquency theory that is as sensitive to gender as it is to race and class.

It is clear that throughout most of the court's history, virtually all female delinquency has been placed within the larger context of girls' sexual behavior. One explanation for this pattern is that familial control over girls' sexual capital has historically been central to the maintenance of patriarchy (Lerner, 1986). The fact that young women have relatively more of this capital has been one reason for the excessive concern that both families and official agencies of social control have expressed about youthful female defiance (otherwise much of the behavior of criminal justice personnel makes virtually no sense). Only if one considers the role of women's control over their sexuality at the point in their lives that their value to patriarchal society is so pronounced, does the historic pattern of jailing of huge numbers of girls guilty of minor misconduct make sense.

This framework also explains the enormous resistance that the movement to curb the juvenile justice system's authority over status offenders encountered. Supporters of the change were not really prepared for the political significance of giving youth the freedom to run. Horror stories told by the opponents of deinstitutionalization about victimized youth, youthful prostitution, and youthful involvement in pornography (Office of Juvenile Justice and Delinquency Prevention, 1985) all neglect the unpleasant reality that most of these behaviors were often in direct response to earlier victimization, frequently by parents, that officials had, for years, routinely ignored. What may be at stake in efforts to roll back deinstitutionaliza-

tion efforts is not so much "protection" of youth as it is curbing the right of young women to defy patriarchy.

In sum, research in both the dynamics of girls' delinquency and official reactions to that behavior is essential to the development of theories of delinquency that are sensitive to its patriarchal as well as class and racial context.

REFERENCES

Adams-Tucker, Christine. 1982. "Proximate Effects of Sexual Abuse in Childhood." *American Journal of Psychiatry* 193: 1252–1256.

Ageton, Suzanne S. 1983. "The Dynamics of Female Delinquency, 1976–1980.," *Criminology* 21:555–584.

Bell, Inge Powell. 1984. "The Double Standard: Age." in *Women: A Feminist Perspective,* edited by Jo Freeman. Palo Alto, CA: Mayfield.

Black, T. Edwin and Charles P. Smith, 1981. *A Preliminary National Assessment of the Number and Characteristics of Juveniles Processed in the Juvenile Justice System.* Washington, DC: Government Printing Office.

Browne, Angela and David Finkelhor, 1986. "Impact of Child Sexual Abuse: A Review of Research," *Psychological Bulletin* 99:66–77.

Campagna, Daniel S. and Donald I. Poffenberger, 1988. *The Sexual Trafficking in Children,* Dover, DE; Auburn House.

Campbell, Ann. 1984. *The Girls in the Gang.* Oxford: Basil Blackwell.

Canter, Rachelle J. 1982. "Sex Differences in Self-Report Delinquency," *Criminology* 20:373–393.

Chesney-Lind, Meda. 1971, *Female Juvenile Delinquency in Hawaii,* Master's thesis, University of Hawaii.

———1973. "Judicial Enforcement of the Female Sex Role," *Issues in Criminology* 3:51–71.

———1978. "Young Women in the Arms of the Law," In *Women, Crime and the Criminal Justice System,* edited by Lee H. Bowker, Boston: Lexington.

———1986. "Women and Crime: The Female Offender," *Signs* 12:78–96.

———1988. "Girls and Deinstitutionalization: Is Juvenile Justice Still Sexist?" *Journal of Criminal Justice Abstracts* 20:144–165.

———and Noelie Rodriguez 1983. "Women Under Lock and Key," *Prison Journal* 63:47–65.

Children's Bureau, Department of Health, Education and Welfare, 1965. *1964 Statistics on Public Institutions for Delinquent Children.* Washington, DC; Government Printing Office.

Chilton, Roland and Susan K. Datesman, 1987, "Gender, Race and Crime: An Analysis of Urban Arrest Trends, 1960–1980," *Gender and Society* 1:152–171.

Cloward, Richard A. and Lloyd E. Ohlin, 1960. *Delinquency and Opportunity,* New York: Free Press.

Cohen, Albert K., 1955. *Delinquent Boys: The Culture of the Gang,* New York: Free Press.

Datesman, Susan and Mikel Aickin, 1984, "Offense Specialization and Escalation Among Status Offenders," *Journal of Criminal Law and Criminology*, 75:1246–1275.

Davidson, Sue, ed. 1982. *Justice for Young Women.* Tucson, AZ; New Directions for Young Women.

DeJong, Allan R., Arturo R. Hervada, and Gary A. Emmett, 1983. "Epidemiologic Variations in Childhood Sexual Abuse," *Child Abuse and Neglect* 7:155–162.

Elliott, Delbert, David Huizinga, and Barbara Morse, 1987, "A Career Analysis of Serious Violent Offenders," In *Violent Juvenile Crime: What Can We Do About It?* edited by Ira Schwartz, Minneapolis, MN: Hubert Humphrey Institute.

Federal Bureau of Investigation, 1987. *Crime in the United States 1986,* Washington, DC; Government Printing Office.

Feinman, Clarice, 1980. *Women in the Criminal Justice System,* New York; Praeger.

Figueira-McDonough, Josefina, 1985. "Are Girls Different? Gender Discrepancies Between Delinquent Behavior and Control," *Child Welfare* 64:273–289.

_____1986, "School Context, Gender, and Delinquency," *Journal of Youth and Adolescence* 15:79–98.

Finkelhor, David, 1982. "Sexual Abuse: A Sociological Perspective," *Child Abuse and Neglect* 6:95–102.

_____and Larry Baron. 1986. "Risk Factors for Child Sexual Abuse," *Journal of Interpersonal Violence* 1:43–71.

Freedman, Estelle, 1981. *Their Sisters' Keepers,* Ann Arbor; University of Michigan Press.

Geltshorpe, Loraine, 1986. "Towards a Sceptical Look at Sexism," *International Journal of the Sociology of Law* 14:125–152.

Gora, JoAnn, 1982. *The New Female Criminal: Empirical Reality or Social Myth,* New York: Praeger.

Hagan, John, A. R. Gillis, and John Simpson, 1985. "The Class Structure of Gender and Delinquency: Toward a Power-Control Theory of Common Delinquent Behavior," *American Journal of Sociology* 90:1151–1178.

Hagan, John, John Simpson, and A. R. Gillis, 1987. "Class in the Household: A Power-Control Theory of Gender and Delinquency," *American Journal of Sociology* 92:788–816.

Hancock, Linda. 1981. "The Myth that Females are Treated More Leniently than Males in the Juvenile Justice System." *Australian and New Zealand Journal of Criminology* 16:4–14.

Harris, Anthony, 1977. "Sex and Theories of Deviance," *American Sociological Review* 42:3–16.

Herman, Jullia L. 1981. *Father-Daughter Incest.* Cambridge, MA; Harvard University Press.

Katz, Phyllis A. 1979. "The Development of Female Identity," In *Becoming Female: Perspectives on Development,* edited by Claire B. Kopp, New York; Plenum.

Koroki, Jan and Meda Chesney-Lind. 1985, *Everything Just Going Down the Drain.* Hawaii; Youth Development and Research Center.

Lerner, Gerda. 1986. *The Creation of Patriarchy.* New York: Oxford.

McCormack, Arlene, Mark-David Janus, and Ann Wolbert Burgess, 1986. "Runaway Youths and Sexual Victimization: Gender Differences In an Adolescent Runaway Population," *Child Abuse and Neglect* 10:387–395.

McGarrell, Edmund F. and Timothy J. Flanagan, eds. 1985. *Sourcebook of Criminal Justice Statistics—1984.* Washington, DC; Government Printing Office.

Meiselman, Karen. 1978. *Incest.* San Francisco: Jossey-Bass.

Merton, Robert K. 1938. "Social Structure and Anomie." *American Sociological Review* 3(October):672–782.

Messerschmidt, James, 1986. *Capitalism, Patriarchy, and Crime: Toward a Socialist Feminist Criminology,* Totowa, NJ: Rowman & Littlefield.

_____1987. "Feminism, Criminology, and the Rise of the Female Sex Delinquent, 1880–1930," *Contemporary Crises* 11: 243–263.

Miller, Eleanor, 1986. *Street Woman,* Philadelphia: Temple University Press.

Miller, Walter B. 1958, "Lower Class Culture as the Generating Milieu of Gang Delinquency," *Journal of Social Issues* 14:5–19.

Morris, Ruth, 1964, "Female Delinquency and Relational Problems," *Social Forces* 43:82–89.

Mouzakitas, C. M. 1981, "An Inquiry into the Problem of Child Abuse and Juvenile Delinquency," In *Exploring the Relationship Between Child Abuse and Delinquency,* edited by R. J. Hunner and Y. E. Walkers, Montclair, NJ: Allanheld, Osmun.

National Female Advocacy Project, 1981. *Young Women and the Justice System: Basic Facts and Issues.* Tucson, AZ; New Directions for Young Women.

Office of Juvenile Justice and Delinquency Prevention, 1985. *Runaway Children and the Juvenile Justice and Delinquency Prevention Act: What is the Impact?* Washington, DC; Government Printing Office.

Opinion Research Corporation, 1982, "Public Attitudes Toward Youth Crime: National Public Opinion Poll." Mimeographed. Minnesota; Hubert Humphrey Institute of Public Affairs, University of Minnesota.

Peacock, Carol, 1981. *Hand Me Down Dreams.* New York: Shocken.

Phelps, R. J. et al. 1982. *Wisconsin Female Juvenile Offender Study Project Summary Report,* Wisconsin: Youth Policy and Law Center, Wisconsin Council of Juvenile Justice.

Platt, Anthony M. 1969. *The Childsavers,* Chicago: University of Chicago Press.

Pope, Carl and William H. Feyerherm. 1982. "Gender Bias in Juvenile Court Dispositions," *Social Service Review* 6:1–17.

Rafter, Nicole Hahn, 1985. *Partial Justice.* Boston: Northeastern University Press.

Reich, J. W. And S. E. Gutierres, 1979, "Escape/Aggression Incidence in Sexually Abused Juvenile Delinquents," *Criminal Justice and Behavior* 6:239–243.

Rogers, Kristine, 1972. "For Her Own Protection. . . . Conditions of Incarceration for Female Juvenile Offenders in the State of Connecticut," *Law and Society Review* (Winter):223–246.

Rosenberg, Debby and Carol Zimmerman, 1977. *Are My Dreams Too Much To Ask For?* Tucson, A. Z: New Directions for Young Women.

Russell, Diana E. 1986. *The Secret Trauma: Incest in the Lives of Girls and Women,* New York: Basic Books.

Schlossman, Steven and Stephanie Wallach, 1978. "The Crime of Precocious Sexuality: Female Juvenile Delinquency in the Progressive Era," *Harvard Educational Review* 48:65–94.

Shaw, Clifford R. 1930. *The Jack-Roller,* Chicago: University of Chicago Press.

_____1938. *Brothers in Crime,* Chicago: University of Chicago Press.

_____and Henry D. McKay, 1942. *Juvenile Delinquency in Urban Areas,* Chicago: University of Chicago Press.

Shelden, Randall, 1981. "Sex Discrimination in the Juvenile Justice System: Memphis, Tennessee, 1900–1917." In *Comparing Female and Male Offenders,* edited by Marguerite Q. Warren. Beverly Hills, CA: Sage.

_____and John Horvath, 1986. "Processing Offenders in a Juvenile Court: A Comparison of Males and Females." Paper presented at the annual meeting of the Western Society of Criminology, Newport Beach, CA, February 27–March 2.

Silbert, Mimi and Ayala M. Pines, 1981. "Sexual Child Abuse as an Antecedent to Prostitution," *Child Abuse and Neglect* 5:407–411.

Simons, Ronald L., Martin G. Miller, and Stephen M. Aigner, 1980. "Contemporary Theories of Deviance and Female Delinquency: An Empirical Test," *Journal of Research in Crime and Delinquency* 17:42–57.

Smith, Lesley Shacklady, 1978. "Sexist Assumptions and Female Delinquency," In *Women, Sexuality and Social Control,* edited by Carol Smart and Barry Smart, London: Routledge & Kegan Paul.

Snyder, Howard N. and Terrence A. Finnegan, 1987. *Delinquency in the United States.* Washington, DC: Department of Justice.

Steffensmeier, Darrell J. 1980 "Sex Differences in Patterns of Adult Crime, 1965–1977," *Social Forces* 58:1080–1109.

Sutherland, Edwin, 1978. "Differential Association." in *Children of Ishmael: Critical Perspectives on Juvenile Justice,* edited by Barry Krisberg and James Austin. Palo Alto, CA: Mayfield.

Teilmann, Katherine S. and Pierre H. Landry, Jr. 1981. "Gender Bias in Juvenile Justice." *Journal of Research in Crime and Delinquency* 18:47–80.

Thrasher, Frederic M. 1927. *The Gang.* Chicago: University of Chicago Press.

Tracy, Paul E., Marvin E. Wolfgang, and Robert M. Figlio. 1985. *Delinquency in Two Birth Cohorts: Executive Summary.* Washington, DC: Department of Justice.

Widom, Cathy Spatz. 1988. "Child Abuse, Neglect, and Violent Criminal Behavior." Unpublished manuscript.

JUVENILE CRIME: WHO IS RESPONSIBLE?

Robert E. Shepherd, Jr.

Robert E. Shepherd, Jr., is professor of law at the University of Richmond Law School in Richmond, Virginia. He is a former chairperson of the Juvenile Justice Committee of the American Bar Association and chairs the Commission on the Needs of Children of the Virginia Bar Association.

At a time when a "get tough" stance toward juvenile crime prevails, a focus of concern has been the issue of responsibility for minors' criminal actions. In one arena, this has translated into efforts to make young people more accountable for their acts by transferring the cases of young offenders from juvenile to adult courts. A second, and just as controversial, topic regarding juvenile criminal responsibility is the proposal that parents be held responsible for the crimes of their children. The consequence of this latter focus has been a curious patchwork quilt of court decisions, regulations, and statutes grouped around the issues of parental criminal responsibility for delinquent acts or truancy, parental civil liability for delinquency or noncriminal misbehavior, such as truancy, and reduction of welfare benefits, or eviction from public housing for acts committed by family juveniles.

Historically, parents were not civilly liable to victims for the intentional or negligent acts of their children unless the child was an employee or acted under the direction of the parents or there was some actual negligence on the parents' part, as where an automobile or other dangerous object was entrusted to

an unlicensed or underage child and an accident resulted. Despite the inherent limitations in these common law rules, there is a growing body of court decisions that follow the American Law Institute's *Restatement of Torts, Second*'s more liberal rule that a parent is obligated to exercise reasonable care to control his or her child if the parent has the ability to do so and knows of the necessity and opportunity to exercise that control.[1] Thus, as a hypothetical example appended to the rule illustrates, if a parent is informed that his six-year-old child is shooting with a .22 rifle at a target on a residential street in a dangerous manner and fails to take any action prior to the injury of a pedestrian, the parent will be liable for damages to the wounded victim.

as where an automobile or other dangerous object was entrusted to an unlicensed or underage child and an accident resulted. Despite the inherent limitations in these common law rules, there is a growing body of court decisions that follow the American Law Institute's *Restatement of Torts, Second*'s more liberal rule that a parent is obligated to exercise reasonable care to control his or her child if the parent has the ability to do so and knows of the necessity and opportunity to exercise that control.[1] Thus, as a hypothetical example appended to the rule illustrates, if a parent is informed that his six-year-old child is shooting with a .22 rifle at a target on a residential street in a dangerous manner and fails to take any action prior to the injury of a pedestrian, the parent will be liable for damages to the wounded victim.

Despite the prestige of *Restatement*, courts have not universally embraced the rule, preferring to defer to legislators the decision to adopt such a departure from common law rule. In a Virginia case, for example, the state supreme court declined to hold parents responsible for failing to control their sixteen-year-old emotionally disturbed son, who committed an assault on a hotel desk clerk with a knife in the course of a rape attempt. The court was unwilling to "impose civil liability upon parents who fail to control their minor child's criminal behavior" without legislative direction. The court also pointed to the numerous public policy issues presented by such a rule, including the possible extension of such a rule to other family relationships, such as spouses. This raised questions as to whether the rule would apply equally to children of all ages, even though parental control may diminish as the child matured; and the implications of such a liability holding on "the mental health system, the judicial system, and traditional family relationships." In the absence of evidence of actual control or direction of a youth at the time of the intentional criminal activity, courts are reluctant to embrace the *Restatement* rule, although a growing number have.

However, every state has adopted some type of statute imposing financial liability on parents, typically with a defined dollar limit, for acts of vandalism by their children to either public or private property, or to persons. Twenty of the fifty states allow compensation for property damage only, while the rest permit recovery for personal injury as well. A few of the states establish a minimum age and all of them set a maximum age, typically the age of majority (eighteen in practically all states). Most states also require that the child's actions be willful, malicious, criminal, intentional, unlawful, reckless, purposeful, or the like before liability is imposed on the parents. The broadest statute appears to be one of the oldest, Louisiana's, derived from the state's civil law heritage (based on the Napoleonic Code), which places no limitation on the amount of damages and which ignores the child's ability to distinguish between right or wrong.

There have been a number of constitutionally based attacks on these statutes for imposing vicarious liability on parents for the acts of their children, but they have failed for the most part. The attacks have generally been made on due process grounds—that the law allowed for the taking of property without a finding of fault —but the courts have concluded that legitimate goals were served: the compensation of persons damaged by the wrongful acts of the child, and the deterrence of youthful vandalism by penalizing parental inaction. A federal court upheld a Hawaii statute, saying that the law provided "an incentive to parents to exercise greater supervision over the activities of their children." The ceiling provided on damages in most states also induces the courts to focus on the delinquency-curbing purpose for the statute rather than on the vicarious liability element.

A 1977 Ohio case illustrates how far a court may go under such a statute when the court there imposed liability in damages on a father, up to the statutory maximum, for the minor son's rape and kidnaping of a woman even though the son was married, employed, and living away from home. Few cases have been willing to go this far, preferring to apply such statutes in a conservative fashion, limiting liability to instances where the parents have actual custody and control over the child.

CRIMINAL LIABILITY OF PARENTS FOR THEIR CHILDREN'S ACTS

A more recent tentative trend which has been highly publicized is the attempted imposition of criminal liability on parents for the delinquent acts or truancy of their children.[2] For some time most states

One judge sentenced the parents of chronically truant children to 180 days in jail.

have had statutes punishing adults for contributing to the delinquency of a minor, but few prosecutions under these laws have been directed at parents, and there is even some doubt as to whether they apply to parental conduct. It has been far more common for a parent to be prosecuted under a state compulsory school attendance law, or even for "education neglect" under an abuse or neglect statute, for the child's truancy where some parental responsibility is found. However, such prosecutions have generally resulted in nothing more than a fine, or an admonition to get the child to school enforced by the threat of contempt.

Recently, states and localities have gotten tougher in applying the truancy laws to parents. A Bloomington, Indiana, judge sentenced the parents of chronically truant children to 180 days in jail, not coincidentally the length of the school year, and an Indianapolis judge has imposed a similar jail sentence on parents. A Baltimore judge recently sentenced the mother of a truant teenager to the maximum ten days in jail when her son had missed 101 days of the school year. The Arkansas legislature has passed bills authorizing civil fines for parents who refuse to show up for parent-teacher conferences or whose children are excessively absent. The bills also allow a court to order the parents to attend parenting classes or to participate in community service. Wisconsin is now linking child welfare benefits to school attendance, so that the benefits could be withheld if the youth drops out of school.

States are now going even farther. Since 1985, Wisconsin has made grandparents financially responsible for a baby born to their unmarried minor children, and Florida's new gun law makes parents liable for a possible prison term or fine if a child uses a loaded gun that is not secured in the home. California has taken a quantum leap beyond these laws. The California Street Terrorism Enforcement and Prevention Act, enacted in 1988,

amended section 272 of the Penal Code, the law punishing persons for contributing to the delinquency of a child, to provide explicitly that "a parent or legal guardian to any person under the age of 18 years shall have the duty to exercise reasonable care, supervision, protection, and control over their minor child." The amendment was intended to help address the growing tide of street gang violence in the state, and the offense is punishable by a $2,500 fine and one year in jail. The first prosecution in that state was of the mother of a gang member who was involved in a gang rape begun in his mother's yard. The mother had had her picture taken with gang members at gang functions, and her home displayed gang-related graffiti. The charges were dropped when the mother enrolled in a parenting class, and there have been few prosecutions since. The parents in those subsequent cases have likewise attended courses to enhance their parenting skills, and the charges were withdrawn. A constitutional attack on the statute has been mounted by the ACLU in Los Angeles.

None of the new criminally oriented statutes directed at parents have resulted in many prosecutions, and they have had questionable effectiveness in reducing the evil perceived. For example, the Wisconsin grandparent responsibility law has been invoked in fewer than twenty cases since its enactment in 1985, and the teenage pregnancy rate in the state has continued to mount. Child advocates in California have charged that the law in that state was proposed by Los Angeles District Attorney Ira Reiner to advance his campaign for state attorney general.

The history of the juvenile system in America, much like that of the criminal justice system, has been marked by a desire for quick fixes, a wish for easy answers to complex problems. The current emphasis on transferring more juveniles for trial as adults or for increasing the number and the length of juvenile placements in secure institutions, and on enacting laws holding parents responsible for their children's crimes, appears to be another example of such a quest.

However, the solution to juvenile crime is not within the easy reach of a few efforts to fine-tune the juvenile justice system. Although increasing the percentage of juvenile cases handled formally within the juvenile court may focus more attention on delinquent behavior, it may also serve to dilute the time the court can devote to individual cases and spread limited resources over a greater number of matters, and it may also allow inappropriate cases to penetrate more deeply into the system. Committing more juveniles to state institutions for longer stays may re-

move risky youth from society and may deter other juveniles, but it may result in higher recidivism rates as the California data shows and it may necessitate the creation of more beds in more institutions, thus spreading the limited resources even thinner. The deterrent effect is even more controversial where juveniles are concerned than with adults because of the impulsivity of adolescents. Increasing the categories of juveniles who may be transferred to the adult court may enhance accountability, but may also result in shorter periods of incarceration and greater numbers of brutalized young adults released from prisons into society.

Similarly, although parental responsibility laws may serve to motivate par-

ents to exercise greater control over their children and may cause parents charged to become involved in parenting classes, undue reliance on such statutes may ignore the facts that peers increasingly have more influence over the behavior of adolescents than parents do. More importantly, a quest for panaceas and easy answers causes society to ignore far more pressing and significant problems such as poverty, inadequate housing, the disruption of families, poor schools, the lack of prenatal and early childhood health care, and other societal problems that place children at risk for delinquent behavior.

---

1. *Restatement of Torts, Second* 316.
2. See "Now, Parents on Trial," *Newsweek*, October 2, 1989, p. 54.

TEENAGE ADDICTION

Chemical dependency is a problem that discriminates against no one, old, young, rich or poor, black or white. Yet, the tragedy of addiction seems more acute when it afflicts our adolescents, those whose bright futures seem threatened by drugs alcohol. In this section, we present three reports: one on the differences in treating teenage and adult chemical dependents; another on a successful school-based program on helping adolescent addicts; and finally, summaries of recent research on adolescent drug and alcohol abuse.

DON'T TREAT CHEMICALLY DEPENDENT TEENAGERS AS ADULTS

Martin N. Buxton, M.D., F.A.A.C.P.

Martin Buxton is director of the Chemical Dependency Program at Carter Westbrook Hospital, Richmond, Virginia and a member of the Editorial Advisory Board of The Addiction Letter.

Despite what they think, teenagers are not adults. Unfortunately, many of us treating chemically dependent adolescents forget that truism and use expertise we developed with adults on teenaged clients. It's not our fault; most training programs use adults as prototype patients, and while there has been an increasing reflection on the child-oriented family as part of the alcoholic system, there is still a dearth of literature on the chemically dependent adolescent patient.

In my experience in treating both adults and teenagers, I have found there are both subtle and not-so-subtle differences between the two groups. Dealing with adolescents requires the use of certain techniques that would be unsuccessful, if not extremely provoca-tive, if tried on adults. Here are five techniques that I have found successful:

1. Don't treat the adolescent as an adult. This may be obvious, but it is vitally important. I would guess that 98% of the adolescents entering our treatment program are co-dependent, having at least one parent who is either chemically dependent and/or co-dependent themselves. Most come from at least a three-generational chemically dependent family system. Their age-expected developmental denial lulls them into taking risks in using chemicals, thinking "damage can't happen to me." The denial is exacerbated by the fact that as co-dependent, pseudo-adult, pseudo-precocious, omnipotent-thinking adolescents, they and

From *When Children Need Help*, Manisses Communications Group, 1987, pp. 15-27. Published with permission of The Brown University Child Behavior and Development Letter, Manisses Communications Group, Inc., Three Governor Street, P.O. Box 3357, Wayland Square, Providence, RI 02906-0357.

the world often see themselves as being older than they really are. If you aren't careful, you'll be lulled into the same attitude that enables their addiction. You must subtly recognize co-dependent adolescents' need to be friendly in an adult-to-adult fashion and deal with them in a way that does not reject them. At the same time, however, you must softly but realistically identify the fact that there is an age difference and that they are not adults.

2. Encourage them to develop relationships. Alcoholics Anonymous wisely teaches adults not to have a relationship within the first year of recovery, or else they risk an impulsive and ill-timed marriage or commitment. And adolescents, too, during their active co-dependency, may be prone to making serious but unhealthy commitments at a young age. Once this issue is worked out sufficiently, however, adolescents, as part of their healthy identity formation as heterosexual beings, should be encouraged to have involvement in relationships. Your need to see adolescence as a developmental entity distinct from adults requires you to encourage them to have healthy relationships that are not compulsively rife with sexuality or co-dependent caretaking.

3. Intervene more to keep adolescents in therapy. As caregivers, we are very aware of the concept of "parens patriae" which implies that we, who work in an institution or other treatment facility, often function as surrogate parents. But we also recognize the importance of the "Serenity Prayer," accepting the things we cannot change. These notions lead to a "laissez-faire" approach to treating adults, who may need to face more consequences of their addiction before they can be treated successfully.

The nature of chemically dependent adolescents, however, requires a different approach, at least at the beginning of treatment. More often than with adults, chemically dependent adolescents enter treatment not of their own volition but because they either attempted suicide, showed other self-destructive tendencies, or because of trouble with the law. As a result, more heroics and activism must be used by the therapist in order to keep a teenager in treatment, at least until the adolescent becomes enlisted in the therapeutic process.

You cannot go overboard, however, and seduce the adolescent into oppositional resistance. Evoking opposition is one of the dangers of working with adolescents, who often are contrary in order to establish their identity and autonomy. So you must be careful not to let the issues of staying sober and sticking with recovery become involved in the adolescent autonomy struggle, while trying to intervene assertively and clarify identity confusions.

4. Hold marathon sessions. We use this technique in our inpatient unit where we try to undo the alcoholic family types of communication and replace it with healthy family communication. Often, we'll find that a number of the youngsters have know that another has been using drugs or is planning on going AWOL. Yet they did not speak up despite the fact that they themselves are doing well in recovery. As we track this down, we come to understand that the youngsters are recapitulating the unrecovered alcoholic system's communications in that there are coalitions and alliances that do not address the truth of what is happening. We'll "close" the unit and keep the youngsters in a marathon intervention session, perhaps for hours at a time. The enabling denial of the process is addressed and resistance wears down, setting the stage for the reunification of healthy family lines of communication.

5. Use paradoxical intervention. Pioneered by the family systems people in Philadelphia, this technique is invaluable if used delicately. I have found it most helpful, given my personality style, when a youngster is entrenched in a co-dependent position and cannot see it objectively. In such cases, I'll have the co-dependent youngster be in charge of all ashtrays or being responsible for seeing that another youngster is on time for group therapy. It helps show the co-dependent adolescent their tendency to try to take care of people and control things as a way of avoiding their own issues. You must be careful that the patient has enough insight to be able to understand the abstract nature of what is being said and does not take it literally. If a tone of humor, without sarcasm is used, paradox can be a very successful intervention technique.

These aren't the only techniques that are helpful with adolescents. But they should stimulate more ideas in your own practice in dealing with the unique characteristics of adolescents. Certainly, both in a transferential and counter-transferential sense, you may find yourself more of a parent than a friend or counselor. But, as long as you are aware of the complications, you can use it in helping your teenaged patient attain recovery.

SCHOOL: AN AVENUE FOR CHANGE FOR DRUG-USING TEENAGERS

Matthew C. Green, M. Ed., C.A.C.

Matthew C. Green is co-director of the Newton Youth Drug/ Alcohol Program, 100 Walnut Street, Newtonville, MA 02160 (617–552–7679).

Alcohol, drugs, and teenagers have been a troublesome problem for high schools since the 1960's. Whether they used pot, LSD, or cocaine—not to mention the ever-present alcohol—adolescents using chemicals have been a problem for two decades and most communities are frustrated in their inability to stem the tide of drug use on a broad scale.

Since teenagers, by law in most states, are required to participate in some kind of formal education process through the age of 16, schools have a large stake in the drug issue. In most cases, teens bring their drug problems to the schoolhouse door, forcing the school as well as communities and parents to have equal responsibility in dealing with the problem.

In recent years, there has also been an increase in the number of teenagers appearing in courts throughout the country for drug and alcohol-related violations. Most courts send the teenagers to correctional facilities or put them on probation, completely ignoring what created the problem: drugs and alcohol. In addition, physicians, social workers and teachers have seen increasing numbers of adolescents with drug problems. These professionals rarely have adequate training or experience in substance abuse to enable them to feel comfortable and competent in helping teens who abuse drugs.

In Newton, Massachusetts, we have formed an unusual alliance between schools and the courts, the two institutions most important in the life of the drug-abusing teenager. Now in its eighth year, the Newton Youth Drug/Alcohol Program has worked together with court probation departments and public school staff to meet the needs of about 40 adolescents in trouble with drugs each year.

I should note that, in Massachusetts anyway, school administrators are cool towards the concept of alcohol and drug treatment operated through public school. Schools are for education, they believe, not for medical or mental health treatment. School does not own the responsibility for the students' emotional and physical problems, they say.

The Newton community, however, believes that when school is the only constant in an adolescent's life and when children bring their drug and alcohol problems into the school environment, then the educational system is obligated to implement change.

At Least a Year
Students enter the Newton Youth Drug/Alcohol Program either as a condition of probation or as a school requirement. Court-referred teens remain in the program for the duration of their probation, usually one to three years or until they fail to comply with the program's requirements. School-referred students commit themselves for a least one year.

Satisfactory completion of the program means earned high school credit for all participants. Unsatisfactory performance means denial of credit for those

referred from school and surrender and final disposition for those on probation.

Participants must attend either Alcoholics Anonymous and/or Narcotics Anonymous as well as group therapy and individual counseling. Vocational assistance, court liaison and interpretation of events are available to each student. Students are required to attend all meetings on time. Absence and tardiness are not tolerated and result in termination from the program. Furthermore, students must attend meetings sober and free of any mind-altering chemical.

Lack of Limits
The program's philosophy is based on the premise that the lack of limits in an adolescent's life promotes the drug abusing life-style. Adolescents are frightened of the decisions they are forced to make in their teenage years—on values, and life goals—so they respond to firm guidance and strict limits. Program workers are available to students 24 hours per day, seven days per week, and 52 weeks a year in case of crisis.

The program has grown during the past five years. In the 1980–81 school year, the courts referred eight youngsters, seven of whom completed the program and remained in school. None was referred by school officials. During 1984–85, 53 were enrolled in the program, 46 referred by the courts and 7 by the schools. Completing the program last year were 30 of the 46 on probation (40 are still in school) and 5 of the 7 school-referred youths. (All 7 are still in school). Of the 46, 24 were new enrollees while the remainder had continued from the previous year.

The program is designed to provide:
- A framework to help students understand their drug-using behavior.
- Skills for self-awareness.
- A non-threatening environment for discussion.
- Experiences which encapsulate various life situations (through AA, NA, and discussion).
- High school credits as an added incentive for success and a road back for those who dropped out of school.
- A mechanism for the schools and courts to monitor the student/offenders' behavior.

Successful Completion
A student will have successfully completed the program if he or she is able to state thoughts and feelings which lead to abusive drinking and/or drug use; identify moments when the student is beginning to feel out of control concerning alcohol or drugs; list alternatives to use at such moments; and practice skills or alternatives (ways of handling arguments, conflict, tension and boredom) which take control of his or her future, by describing specific actions in his or her personal plan for future development.

Individuals with drug and alcohol problems continually suffer from unrealistic aspirations. Our students learn through discussion the type of risks they usually take. The effect of consistently taking high risks is discussed in our groups, in the context of resolving family disputes, work, recreational activities, driving and abusive drinking and drug use. Our students are encouraged to seek help from other professionals, and to view it as a way of using resources rather than as a weakness or character defect. We emphasize seeking personal change that is realistic and have benchmarks for testing the program periodically. For many students, plans for maintaining sobriety and continued treatment become an essential part of their future plans. The program has had extensive contact with inpatient detoxification and treatment/rehabilitation facilities throughout the Northeast, making referrals as well as being used as an aftercare placement for students coming back from these facilities.

Treatment and prevention are closely allied, and the Newton program combines the two effectively. Once a student is "straight," he or she becomes a staunch advocate of abstinence and an evangelist in approaching their drug-using friends. We have young people—ages 17 to 22—who are teachers by example to their peers. One such group of young people started an NA and AA group of their own in Newton and are speaking to other young adults about alcohol and drug dependency.

The program is broader than the cooperation between schools and courts implies. Students are not only referred by school officials and probation departments but by police and city human services departments. It provides support services to adolescents returning to school from residential chemical dependency programs and to parents and staff who are being trained in the identification of potential problems in adolescence.

All referrals coming from the various community agencies are the same adolescents who are also having difficulties in school. Therefore the Newton program is able to coordinate these groups to provide appropriate services for the adolescent with difficulties, avoiding outside placement and providing early identification of special needs.

Attitudes of disbelief and denial are often found in communities. We are finding kids coming to school either hungover, stoned or tripping; some are even coming to school drunk. For the most part, our students are ingesting their drugs outside of the school building, but are playing out their trip either in the classrooms, the corridors, the washrooms, or the cafeteria. Most often when questioned about their drug problem, these kids don't see it as a problem at all.

One 17-year-old we interviewed provides a stark example. He said he began using drugs and alcohol at the age of 10 and identified his use of illegal substances as "moderate" by the time he reached the age of 12. At that time, he smoked an ounce of marijuana and drank a six-pack of beer daily. He used LSD weekly. He was identified in school and in the community as delinquent because of his occasional criminal behavior and was remanded to the State Department of Youth Services for a two-year period. It was upon incarceration, that he stated, "My drug use then began to get bad."

This case simply exemplifies the attitude of individuals as well as the community surrounding a teenager's use of drugs and alcohol. The outward behavior, criminal activity, is punished, and the root of the problem continues to grow. In addition, teens are often unaware that their drug use or their friends' drug use is dangerous, life-threatening, and producing negative consequences.

The Newton program is set up on the premise that education is the primary tool to break through this denial. Legal controls have proved largely ineffective in controlling alcohol and drug use by youth. Preaching and scare tactics generally have also met with failure.

If the problem of alcoholism and drug abuse is to be managed in the future, it will be because young people have adopted a responsible attitude. They gain this through adult examples of responsible behavior as well as learning all the facts, positive and negative. Programs like the Newton Youth Drug/Alcohol Program, which link education, adjudication and rehabilitation, accomplish this task.

INDIRECT INDICATORS OF CHEMICAL ABUSE

How can we tell whether children are abusing chemicals?

Abusive use itself (being drunk at school, using drugs to get high, etc.) is, of course, a direct indicator of a problem with chemicals. But the Johnson Institute, a Minneapolis training center for addiction professionals, found in a 1984 survey of Minnesota teenagers several other indicators—some related to chemical use, some lacking any apparent connection—that correlated with chemical abuse by teenagers.

The presence of one or two of the following indicators hardly suggests chemical abuse, but the presence of several, perhaps five or more, should at least raise the question of chemical abuse:

- Low grades—a consistent pattern of below average grades or a recent drop in grades. Low grades are three times as likely among heavy users (11%) as among abstainers (4%).
- Absenteeism from school. Heavy users are four times more likely than abstainers to miss school (37% vs. 10%).
- A negative opinion of school. Heavy users are much more likely than abstainers to complain that they don't like school (37% vs. 16%) or to complain that they don't get along with their teachers (18% vs. 6%).

- Cigarette smoking. Two-thirds of heavy users smoke tobacco vs. 6% of infrequent users vs. 3% of abstainers.
- Drinking hard liquor (as opposed to beer or wine).
- Using marijuana.
- Avoiding parties where no chemicals are available or attending parties where drugs other than alcohol are available.
- Drinking in cars (86% of heavy users vs. 13% of infrequent users vs.—of course—0% abstainers).
- Lack of involvement in community activities, organized sports or other school activities. (Heavy users are less likely to have a part-time job or be involved in organized sports. They are much less likely than infrequent users or abstainers to be involved in other school activities (21% vs. 72% vs. 63%).
- The student is a male in grades 10–12.

***

RECENT STUDIES PROVIDE INSIGHT INTO DRUG USE AMONG TEENS

Reflecting the general public's increasing concern about teenagers' use of drugs and alcohol, numerous recent studies attempt to shed light on why adolescents experiment with alcohol and drugs, how use and experiment progress to dependency, and which teenagers are more at risk of developing chemical dependency. Here are several of the more significant recent studies:

The Role of Personality

Does a teenager's personality predict whether he or she will use drugs or alcohol? A recent study by Erich W. Labouvie and Connel R. McGee at Rutgers' Center of Alcohol studies says yes, strongly suggesting that personality may cause later use of alcohol and drugs. The study was published in Journal of Consulting and Clinical Psychology (1986, 54:289–293).

The researchers randomly selected 882 adolescents in three waves in 1979, 1980 and 1981. Initially tested at the ages of 12, 15 and 18, participants in the first two waves were retested after three years at the ages of 15, 18 and 21 years. The researchers asked the teenagers how often and how much they used alcohol, cigarettes, marijuana and cocaine. They also measured whether they used alcohol, cigarettes and illicit drugs as a coping device; their personality attributes; and, finally, their self-esteem.

After testing, researchers divided the sample into three groups, light, moderate and heavy users of substances. They found that male adolescents used marijuana and alcohol more than females, but that females smoke cigarettes more.

Light users in early adolescence tend to use only alcohol by age 21 and to maintain limited usage. Moderate users, by age 15, exhibit fairly regular use of alcohol and cigarettes, and by age 18, regular use of marijuana. Heavy users indulge in marijuana, cigarettes and alcohol by age 15 and use cocaine occasionally by age 21. The heavy users are involved with multiple drugs.

Heavy users scored high on the personality test on autonomy, exhibitionism, impulsivity, and play. They scored low on achievement, cognitive structure and harm avoidance. Light users scored the opposite. The authors suggest strongly that personality causes later alcohol and drug use. Personality changes were not significant over time, they said, indicating that use did not cause the personality characteristics. They found, however, that self-esteem did not correlate with use levels, suggesting that use among today's adolescents may no longer represent deviance or self-rejection. They note that adolescents who scored lower in achievement, cognitive structure and harm avoidance are not only more likely to use substances, but also to underdevelop those characteristics over time.

They caution, however, against concluding that heavy adolescent use predicts adult alcoholism. They hypothesize that the heavy using teenager find the substances as instant gratification for needs of play and impulsivity with little effort or skill expended. Second, the researchers suggest that alcohol and drug use may help the teens express needs for affiliation, autonomy, and exhibitionism. Finally, adolescents with risk-taking attributes are likely to be at odds with their environment and alcohol and drug use would relieve that stress via rebellion and expression of individuality.

Drug Use Begins in Sixth Grade

A longitudinal study of more than 1,100 children in two New England towns, published in the Journal of Drug Education (1986, 16: 203–220), shows that drug use begins as early as sixth grade and that there are critical periods for onset of use that may be helpful in designing effective prevention strategies.

The researchers, Katherine Grady, David L. Snow, and Marion Kessen of Yale University, and Kelin E. Gersick of the California School of Professional Psychology at Los Angeles, first studied the youngsters during their sixth grade and re-evaluated them in their seventh and eighth grades.

They had noted that other studies showed patterns of use that include significant experimentation and use in increasingly early grades. Youths typically move from initial experimentation to increasing experimentation and that they move from beer and wine, then tobacco and hard liquor, then to marijuana and other illicit drugs.

For their study, the authors divided use into four stages: none-use, experimental use (less than once monthly), regular use (one to two times monthly) and heavy use (once a week or more).

The study used a two-part questionnaire: the first asked them how often they had been offered any of ten listed drugs: tobacco, LSD, marijuana, alcohol, amphetamines, barbiturates, heroin, inhalants, cocaine, and other drugs. The second asked them if and how often they had used the drugs.

The study confirmed that alcohol, tobacco, and marijuana are gateway drugs. Sixty-five percent of the sixth graders had at least experimented with alcohol. That increased to 68% in seventh grade, and 74% in eighth grade. Experimentation or use of tobacco increased from 36% in sixth grade to 59% in the eighth. Experimentation and use of marijuana increased from 11% in sixth grade to 38% in the eighth. For other drugs, the study indicated sizable increases in experimentation but not in regular or heavy use over the three years.

Males used more alcohol, marijuana and other substances in the sixth grade, but by the eighth grade, there were no gender differences. Females used tobacco more in seventh and eighth grades. Whites used more than blacks in all grades. Rates of use were higher in the town having a middle school structure than in the town having a K–6, 7–8, and 9–12 system.

Family situations also affected use rates. Students from broken homes used tobacco and marijuana more in all three grades and higher use of alcohol in sixth grade. Students with remarried parents had slightly lower use rates than students reporting separated or divorced parents. Religious background showed little correlation, except for seventh grade tobacco use. Protestants used more than Catholics.

Offer rates were higher than use rates by the eighth grades. By then, 78% had been offered alcohol, 77% tobacco, 58% marijuana, 18% inhalants, 20% amphetamines, 19% barbiturates, and 16% cocaine.

Few students rejected alcohol in all three years, while rejection rates were moderate for tobacco and high for marijuana. Over the three years, the percentage of students rejecting decreases.

The authors concluded that prevention programs in the younger grades may need to focus on boys' use of alcohol and drugs and girls' use of tobacco. Students from broken homes need programs to meet their special needs.

The critical period for initiation into alcohol use occurs prior to the middle school years, they conclude, requiring earlier prevention programs and intensive parent and school involvement. Prevention programs should aim at preventing experimentation and increasing rejection of alcohol when offered.

The critical period for tobacco use seems to be the sixth grade. Prevention programs should include earlier grades with the middle school focus being on increasing the capacity to reject offers of tobacco.

For marijuana the researchers suggest sixth grade as the best time for prevention programs since use is most evident in seventh and eighth grades. Prevention programs for non-gateway drugs need to build on these programs when experimentation with such drugs as amphetamines and cocaine are just beginning.

Polydrug Abusers Seek Pleasure or Escape Pain
A study of 433 high school students, published in Adolescence (1985, 20: 853–861) found that 12% were polydrug users or abusers and that the reason they used drugs was to seek pleasure or escape pain.

Polydrug use, in this case, means that the users used more than one drug at the same time or in close sequence to produce different effects. They researcher, Loyd S. Wright, a psychologist at Southwest Texas State University, noted the dangers of the synergistic effects that polydrug use pose to users and abusers. In his study, seniors at two Texas high schools filled out confidential questionnaires on their drug using habits as well as how they perceived their parents and themselves.

Polydrug users and abusers more likely:
• Were physically abused or in conflict with their parents;
• Rated themselves as lazy, bored, rejected and unhealthy;
• Have serious suicidal thoughts, delinquent behavior, early use of marijuana and alcohol and the tendency to drink more than six alcoholic drinks at a sitting; and
• Agreed with the statements "If something feels good, I usually do it and don't worry about the consequences" and "I try to play as much as possible and work as little as possible."

Wright concluded that the results confirmed the notion that polydrug users seek either relief or pleasure and, therefore, do not see their drug use as a problem. He writes, "a variety of treatment and prevention strategies are necessary. Any drug abuse treatment program that hopes to have an impact on the pleasure seekers must get them to reexamine their basic philosophy, remove their peer support, and provide alternatives that will meet their needs for excitement and adventure."

Model College Drug and Alcohol Treatment Program
A model program to treat drug and alcohol abusers in college was proposed by three researchers after a national study of currently available university-based programs.

James Dean, DMIN, Hannah Dean, RN, Ph.D., and Donna Kleiner, MA, writing in the Journal of Substance Abuse Treatment (1986, 3 95–101), maintain that current use levels and accompanying problems require greater involvement than currently exists.

They propose that each institution form a planning committee to set attainable goals for the institution. Variables would include the extent of alcohol and drug problems, campus and community political climate, available resources and the financial capacity of the school. These factors will dictate the degree of involvement possible on a continuum ranging from no response to crisis intervention, identification and assessment only, or identification, assessment, and treatment. Most universities have counseling services for career, academic and personal needs. Only half have alcohol and drug services, they said.

The structural style of a program will reflect campus size, location, affiliation, student age, financial resources, state and local laws. Off-campus referral might be most applicable for some, while others might better utilize on-campus treatment. On-campus treatment would need to be offered through the counseling center. Friction with traditional psychological counseling service providers can be minimized by considering the chemical problem as central with psychological services potentially available, the authors suggest.

Physical services need to be available in support of alcohol and drug abuse crisis situations. Campus police, residence hall and dean of students' staffs, and crisis response team members need special training.

Treatment philosophy in the national survey was found by the authors to reflect a variety of models including AA/NA, psychoanalytical, behavioral, cognitive, family systems, Gestalt, religious, disease and eclectic approaches. The authors urge avoid use of labels in any model such as "alcoholic" or "drug addict," but rather to focus on the specific problems behavior associated with chemical use.

They note the need for trained staff with alcohol and drug treatment approach as most useful with attention focused on chemical use, on environmental and intrapsychic factors that influence use. They cite the University of North Dakota assessment as most helpful. They collect family and personal history, history of previous treatment, arrests, and psychological disorders. This data is supplemented with tests such as the MMPI and Beck Depression Inventory.

Referral to counseling comes via word of mouth, radio and TV publicity campaigns, and linkage to housing and resident hall disciplinary systems. They note the North Dakota system as most effective. It involves observing the problem behavior, encountering the problem by presenting facts to the student and referral. The student has the choice of accepting assistance or facing disciplinary action. A similar model is used by the Greek system and is run as a peer intervention system.

The authors stress the need for high-level administrative support and financial budgeting. Primary and secondary prevention are both the legitimate concerns of academic institutions to prevent problems before they occur, and to arrest them before they become serious and disabling, they conclude.

Youth 'Heavy Involvements' in Drugs and Alcohol

More than one-quarter of all senior high school students use marijuana, and one in ten 12th graders used cocaine during the 1985–86 school year, according to the results of a survey conducted for the Parents' Resource Institute for Drug Education (PRIDE) of Atlanta, Georgia.

The survey also reported that, based on interviews with 40,000 students in 17 states in grades 6 through 12, few students use drugs or alcohol during school hours. Only 1% of all students used alcohol, and 2% marijuana, during school hours.

"However, this does not suggest that drug and alcohol abuse is not a school problem. Students who have smoked marijuana while waiting for the bus or who have a hangover from too much alcohol the night before will be less receptive to instruction during the school day," PRIDE said.

PRIDE also reported that alcohol abuse among students was high, with more than one quarter of students in grades 6–8 reporting some use of liquor during the past year, a figure that jumps to 60% for ninth through 12th graders.

Students reported an even higher incidence of beer or wine use, with just under half of all junior high school students, and nearly three quarters of all senior high students admitting to some experience with those products.

Although the incidence of alcohol abuse far outpaced that of drug abuse, PRIDE officials reserved their direst warnings for parents of students using drugs, particularly cocaine.

"Only 1.6% of the junior high students reported any cocaine use while 6.4% of the senior high school students reported cocaine use," the survey's summary reported. Cocaine use increased with age, with 10.4% of 12th grade students admitting to some experience with the drug," the report stated.

Worse, PRIDE reported, cocaine users admitted that, when they used alcohol or marijuana, they did so expressly to get "bombed" or "very high."

Almost half of all students who have used cocaine report that they become intoxicated when using any drug or alcohol products. By comparison, only 4.5% of students who use only beer or wine reported intoxication.

Finally, the report concluded that students—particularly older high school students—abuse drugs and alcohol outside of parents' purview, and, alarmingly, continue to do so while driving. Nine percent of beer and wine drinkers, and 6% of marijuana abusers, are combining substance use with driving.

"This use of alcohol and marijuana outside the home and the reported direct use of these substances in a car suggest a serious problem with teenagers driving under the influence," PRIDE concluded.

(Parents Resource Institute for Drug Education, 100 Edgewood Ave., #1002, Atlanta, GA 30303, 800–241–7946.)

Teens Concerned About
Health Consequences of Drinking

A new study sponsored by the Alcoholism Council of Greater New York, suggests that teenagers are as concerned about the personal health problems associated with heavy drinking as about the social consequences.

The study, by an Albert Einstein College of Medicine researcher, involved 108 adolescents, ages 12 through 18, in three New York City community centers of the Children's Aid Society.

In a questionnaire which never mentions alcohol, the youths were asked to indicate their level of concern about specific health problems (such as acne, cancer, diabetes, and obesity) and behavior problems (peer acceptance, relationship with parents, and so on).

On 34 health issues, 19 represented problems that can be associated with heavy drinking, and 15 were not alcohol-related. All of the 19 behavioral items could be alcohol-related.

In an analysis of the responses, Thomas Ashby Wills, an assistant professor of psychology and epidemiology in Albert Einstein's Department of Epidemiology and Social Medicine, found the youths' concern about health problems "comparable to, and possibly greater than, their level of concern about behavioral problems."

"Concern about health consequences of alcohol may be an effective component of educational programs to reduce rates of alcohol abuse, in addition to the social consequences approach used in current alcohol education," he said.

The study was part of the Alcoholism Council's current Health Awareness Campaign designed to inform the public of alcohol's hidden effects on health, fitness and appearance.

(Alcoholism Council of Greater New York, 133 East 62nd St., New York, NY 10021; 212–935–7075)

Reasons for Drug Use

For teenagers, drugs: serve as rationalization vehicles for otherwise unacceptable behavior, enhance identity states, enable users to find companionship, and fulfill expectations of effects, as a hostility releaser, as a deepening of consciousness, or as an expression of civil disobedience.

These are the conclusions of Craig R. Thorne and Richard R. DeBlassie, who surveyed numerous recent studies and published their findings in Adolescence (1985, 78: 335–347).

According to the researchers, onset of use involves

opportunity. At first, the teenager does not use at the first opportunity, but if his or her peer group uses drugs or alcohol, he or she, gradually, will follow suit. Young adults 18–25 years of age are most likely to use illicit drugs—especially if living away from family, alone or with peers. Perceived availability of drugs also influences use, with marijuana being seen as the universally most available, followed, in order, by psychotherapeutic drugs, barbiturates, cocaine, hallucinogens, opiates and heroin.

Marijuana is the most widely used illicit drug among high school seniors with 60% having used it, but alcohol and tobacco are the most widespread with 93% having tried alcohol and 71% having tried tobacco.

Use of illicit drugs occurs in the last three years of high school. Marijuana, alcohol, and tobacco are tried prior to high school. Inhalant use occurs typically prior to 10th grade while illicit drugs excluding inhalant and marijuana use begin after 10th grade. Marijuana use is increasing in all grade levels down to 8th grade, but on a declining curve.

Males and females exhibited difference in frequency of use with males using more of all substances except tobacco. Early aggressiveness and shyness correlate to later substance abuse in males only. Males rank peer and school bonds as primary. Females ranked family and school bonds as most important for them. Strong peer bonds correlates with use. College aspirations correlate with lower rates of illicit drug use. Northeastern American residents have highest rates of use, the Southern, the lowest. Urban areas outscore rural areas on use, except for tranquilizers, sedatives, stimulants, and tobacco which show no association to setting.

Family influence in this report involves older siblings' examples, mothers who smoke and drink moderately. Fathers' use does not appear, according to the authors, to be a significant factor.

Virtually all students perceived parental attitudes to be disapproving of drug use. Peer attitude is closest to the student's attitude toward use.

Prevention programs surveyed have largely focused on the individual, take place in an institutional setting rather than in the community, are directed at the middle-class, white population, aim at prevention of all drug use, and are presented to rather large audiences.

Four models of treatment are prevalent—legal, medical, traditional (AA, abstinence), and emergent (learned behavior/controlled use outcome). Increased opportunity for use relates with gradual increase in use. There is much cause of continuing concern and continued prevention efforts, work in the legal, research, and treatment areas.

The authors cite recognition of our individual and collective attitudes and beliefs as primary elements in overcoming substance abuse worldwide.

Self-image and Alcohol Use

Teenagers' self-images and social images were found to be factors as to whether they drank alcohol, according to researchers Laurie Chassin, Christine Tetzloff, and Miriam Hershey, who published the results of their study in the Journal of Studies on Alcohol (1985, 46: 39–47). They hypothesized that adolescents would drink if their self-concepts were consistent with a drinking image (consistency theory), or if their peers admired a drinking image (impression management theory).

They studied 266 students in a southwestern suburban high school, 51% male, 49% female and 92.5% white, 4.7% Hispanic, 2.4% Indian. The average age was 15 years old.

They were shown slides of youths holding beverage cans—beer or soft drinks—in pairs. Questions were asked on the desirability of the model as a friend, and how much like the model the student was. The Adolescent Alcohol Involvement Scale was given, testing frequency and quantity of use, and social and psychological problems resulting. Finally, adolescents gave intentions for future use.

The social image associated with alcohol use was ambivalent. They saw the adolescent drinker as projecting an image of toughness and precocity—a perceived social asset. It also conveys the association of rebellion against authority. On the negative side, they associated users with being less happy and honest, and more socially rejected regardless of sex of model. Drinking alcohol was noted by the authors as having significantly more social acceptability to adolescents than smoking. The authors suggest that the distress associated with use may be seen as teens viewing drinkers as more likely to bear dysphoric symptoms. They may see use as increasing positive mood states.

Adolescent boys tend to aspire to the drinking image and to believe that the drinker attributes are valued by their peers (toughness and precocity).

Girls who did not misuse alcohol followed this pattern. Significantly, girls who did misuse alcohol had ideal self-images that were less like the drinker image than their actual self-descriptions. The authors infer that these girls may be using alcohol to control mood or reduce stress.

Adolescents of both sexes who saw themselves as similar to a drinking image were more involved with alcohol (consistency hypothesis). Seeing peers as admiring the drinking image correlates with intent to use in the future (impression management hypothesis). Males who saw their ideal self-image as similar to the drinking image used more (self enhancement hypothesis).

The precise mechanics of causes of use by adolescents is unclear. Peer influence, modeling, opportunities, and social reinforcement are all cited as being involved by the authors. More work is needed to provide adequate programs for prevention. Finding ways to work around the social image associated with drug use—finding alternatives—is the course they suggest.

Punishment and Corrections

In the American system of criminal justice, the term "corrections" has a special meaning. It designates programs and agencies that have legal authority over the custody or supervision of persons who have been convicted of a criminal act by the courts.

The correctional process begins with the sentencing of the convicted offender. The predominant sentencing pattern in the United States encourages maximum judicial discretion and offers a range of alternatives from probation (supervised conditional freedom within the community), through imprisonment, to the death penalty. Selections in this unit focus on the current condition of the penal system in the United States, and the effects that sentencing, probation, imprisonment, and parole have on the rehabilitation of criminals.

"Sentencing and Corrections" illustrates how society, through sentencing, expresses its objectives for the correctional process. The objectives are deterrence, incapacitation, rehabilitation, retribution, and restitution.

Some 60 percent of inmates released from state and federal lockups return to prison. Recidivism contributes greatly to the overcrowding that plagues prisons throughout the United States. Crowded, tense conditions make survival the principal goal. Rehabilitation is pushed into the background in the effort to manage incipient chaos.

Other issues and aspects of the correctional system—house arrest, AIDS, women in prison, female corrections officers, probation and parole, the influence of Cesare Beccaria, a prison family violence project, turning the jailhouse into a schoolhouse, and the death penalty are other topics in this unit.

The article "Women in Jail: Unequal Justice" asserts that women have been subjected to greater restrictions than their crimes warrant. Are women corrections officers effective workers in men's prisons? "Some Observations of the Status and Performance of Female Corrections Officers in Men's Prisons" says that they are.

Fred Scaglione discusses a new high-tech, yet age-old approach to confinement in "You're Under Arrest—AT HOME." American probation and parole systems are not keeping pace with the challenge presented by rising caseloads of very troubled clients, according to "Difficult Clients, Large Caseloads Plague Probation, Parole Agencies."

"Learning to Live With AIDS in Prison" examines more enlightened attitudes and policies toward convicts with AIDS. Cesare Beccaria, the "father of criminology" is the subject of Dominic Massaro's article, "Of Crime and Punishment." A former inmate offers his views about making jails more productive in "Turn the Jailhouse Into a Schoolhouse."

Take a glimpse at the progressive prison program titled "Family Violence Program at Bedford Hills . . . Feeling 'Free and Safe' in Prison." The most controversial punishment of all is under discussion in the concluding article, " 'This Man Has Expired.' "

Looking Ahead: Challenge Questions

If you were to argue the pathology of imprisonment, what points would you make? On the other hand, if you were to justify continued imprisonment of offenders, what would you stress?

Some authorities would have us believe that probation and parole are ineffective correctional strategies, and should be abandoned. Others maintain that they have yet to really be tried. What is your view?

If you were a high-level correctional administrator and had the luxury of designing a "humane" prison, what would it be like? What aspects of a traditional prison would you keep? What would you eliminate? What new strategies or programs would you introduce?

What are your feelings about the death penalty? Do you think it is an effective deterrent to murder?

Sentencing and Corrections

Through sentencing, society attempts to express its goals for the correctional process

The sentencing of criminals often reflects conflicting social goals

These objectives are—
• **Retribution**—giving offenders their "just deserts" and expressing society's disapproval of criminal behavior
• **Incapacitation**—separating offenders from the community to reduce the opportunity for further crime while they are incarcerated
• **Deterrence**—demonstrating the certainty and severity of punishment to discourage future crime by the offender (specific deterrence) and by others (general deterrence)
• **Rehabilitation**—providing psychological or educational assistance or job training to offenders to make them less likely to engage in future criminality
• **Restitution**—having the offender repay the victim or the community in money or services.

Attitudes about sentencing reflect multiple goals and other factors

Research on judicial attitudes and practices in sentencing revealed that judges vary greatly in their commitment to various goals when imposing sentences. Public opinion also has shown much diversity about the goals of sentencing, and public attitudes have changed over the years. In fashioning criminal penalties, legislators have tended to reflect this lack of public consensus.

Sentencing laws are further complicated by concerns for—
• **Proportionality**—severity of punishment should be commensurate with the seriousness of the crime
• **Equity**—similar crimes and similar criminals should be treated alike
• **Social debt**—the severity of punishment should take into account the offender's prior criminal behavior.

Judges usually have a great deal of discretion in sentencing offenders

The different sentencing laws give various amounts of discretion to the judge in setting the length of a prison or jail term. In a more fundamental respect, however, the judge often has a high degree of discretion in deciding whether or not to incarcerate the offender at all. Alternatives to imprisonment include—
• probation
• fines
• forfeiture of the proceeds of criminal activity
• restitution to victims
• community service
• split sentences, consisting of a short period of incarceration followed by probation in the community.

Often, before a sentence is imposed a presentence investigation is conducted to provide the judge with information about the offender's characteristics and prior criminal record.

Disparity and uncertainty arose from a lack of consensus over sentencing goals

By the early 1970s researchers and critics of the justice system had begun to note that trying to achieve the mixed goals of the justice system without new limits on the discretionary options given to judges had—
• reduced the *certainty* of sanctions, presumably eroding the deterrent effect of corrections
• resulted in *disparity* in the severity of punishment, with differences in the sentences imposed for similar cases and offenders
• failed to validate the effectiveness of various rehabilitation programs in changing offender behavior or predicting future criminality.

Recent sentencing reforms reflect more severe attitudes and seek to reduce disparity and uncertainty

Reforms in recent years have used statutory and administrative changes to—
• clarify the aims of sentencing
• reduce disparity by limiting judicial and parole discretion
• provide a system of penalties that is more consistent and predictable
• provide sanctions consistent with the concept of "just deserts."

The changes have included—
• making prison mandatory for certain crimes and for recidivists
• specifying presumptive sentence lengths
• requiring sentence enhancements for offenders with prior felony convictions
• introducing sentencing guidelines
• limiting parole discretion through the use of parole guidelines
• total elimination of discretionary parole release (determinate sentencing).

States use a variety of strategies for sentencing

Sentencing is perhaps the most diversified part of the Nation's criminal justice process. Each State has a unique set of sentencing laws, and frequent and substantial changes have been made in recent years. This diversity complicates the classification of sentencing systems. For nearly any criterion that may be considered, there will be some States with hybrid systems that straddle the boundary between categories.

From *Report to the Nation on Crime and Justice,* Bureau of Justice Statistics, U.S. Department of Justice, March 1988, pp. 90-93.

The basic difference in sentencing systems is the apportioning of discretion between the judge and parole authorities

Indeterminate sentencing—the judge specifies minimum and maximum sentence lengths. These set upper and lower bounds on the time to be served. The actual release date (and therefore the time actually served) is determined later by parole authorities within those limits.

Partially indeterminate sentencing—a variation of indeterminate sentencing in which the judge specifies only the maximum sentence length. An associated minimum automatically is implied, but is not within the judge's discretion. The implied minimum may be a fixed time (such as 1 year) for all sentences or a fixed proportion of the maximum. In some States the implied minimum is zero; thus the parole board is empowered to release the prisoner at any time.

Determinate sentencing—the judge specifies a fixed term of incarceration, which must be served in full (less any "goodtime" earned in prison). There is no discretionary parole release.

Since 1975 many States have adopted determinate sentencing, but most still use indeterminate sentencing

In 1976 Maine was the first State to adopt determinate sentencing. The sentencing system is entirely or predominantly determinate in these 10 States:

California	Maine
Connecticut	Minnesota
Florida	New Mexico
Illinois	North Carolina
Indiana	Washington

The other States and the District of Columbia use indeterminate sentencing in its various forms. One State, Colorado, after changing to determinate sentencing in 1979, went back to indeterminate sentencing in 1985. The Federal justice system has adopted determinate sentencing through a system of sentencing guidelines.

States employ other sentencing features in conjunction with their basic strategies

Mandatory sentencing—Law requires the judge to impose a sentence of incarceration, often of specified length, for certain crimes or certain categories of offenders. There is no option of probation or a suspended sentence.

Mandatory sentencing laws are in force in 46 States (all except Maine, Minnesota, Nebraska, and Rhode Island) and the District of Columbia. In 25 States imprisonment is mandatory for certain repeat felony offenders. In 30 States imprisonment is mandatory if a firearm was involved in the commission of a crime. In 45 States conviction for certain offenses or classes of offenses leads to mandatory imprisonment; most such offenses are serious, violent crimes, and drug trafficking is included in 18 of the States. Many States have recently made drunk driving an offense for which incarceration is mandated (usually for relatively short periods in a local jail rather than a State prison).

Presumptive sentencing—The discretion of a judge who imposes a prison sentence is constrained by a specific sentence length set by law for each offense or class of offense. That sentence must be imposed in all unexceptional cases. In response to mitigating or aggravating circumstances, the judge may shorten or lengthen the sentence within specified boundaries, usually with written justification being required.

Presumptive sentencing is used, at least to some degree, in about 12 States.

Sentencing guidelines—Explicit policies and procedures are specified for deciding on individual sentences. The decision is usually based on the nature of the offense and the offender's criminal record. For example, the prescribed sentence for a certain offense might be probation if the offender has no previous felony convictions, a short term of incarceration if the offender has one prior conviction, and progressively longer prison terms if the offender's criminal history is more extensive.

Sentencing guidelines came into use in the late 1970s. They are—
• used in 13 States and the Federal criminal justice system
• written into statute in the Federal system and in Florida, Louisiana, Maryland, Minnesota, New Jersey, Ohio, Pennsylvania, and Tennessee
• used systemwide, but not mandated by law, in Utah
• applied selectively in Massachusetts, Michigan, Rhode Island, and Wisconsin
• being considered for adoption in other States and the District of Columbia.

Sentence enhancements—In nearly all States, the judge may lengthen the prison term for an offender with prior felony convictions. The lengths of such enhancements and the criteria for imposing them vary among the States.

In some States that group felonies according to their seriousness, the repeat offender may be given a sentence ordinarily imposed for a higher seriousness category. Some States prescribe lengthening the sentences of habitual offenders by specified amounts or imposing a mandatory minimum term that must be served before parole can be considered. In other States the guidelines provide for sentences that reflect the offender's criminal history as well as the seriousness of the offense. Many States prescribe conditions under which parole eligibility is limited or eliminated. For example, a person with three or more prior felony convictions, if convicted of a serious violent offense, might be sentenced to life imprisonment without parole.

Sources: Surveys conducted for the Bureau of Justice Statistics by the U.S. Bureau of the Census in 1985 and by the Pennsylvania Commission on Crime and Delinquency in 1986.

Sentencing guidelines usually are developed by a separate sentencing commission

Such a commission may be appointed by the legislative, executive, or judicial branch of State government. This is a departure from traditional practice in that sentences are prescribed through an administrative procedure rather than by explicit legislation.

In some States the guidelines are prescriptive in that they specify whether or not the judge must impose a prison sentence and the presumptive sentence length. In other States the guidelines are advisory in that they provide information to the judge but do not mandate sentencing decisions.

To determine whether a prison sentence should be imposed, the guidelines usually consider offense severity and the offender's prior criminal record. A matrix that relates these two factors may be used.

6. PUNISHMENT AND CORRECTIONS

Sentencing matrix

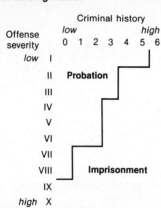

Adapted from *Preliminary report on the development and impact of the Minnesota sentencing guidelines*, Minnesota Sentencing Guidelines Commission, July 1982.

Sentencing guidelines used in the Federal justice system were developed by the United States Sentencing Commission. The guidelines provide for determinate sentencing and the abolition of parole. Ranges of sentence length are specified for various offense classifications and offender characteristics. The judge must provide written justification for any sentence that deviates from the guideline range; sentences that are less severe can be appealed by the prosecution, and sentences that are more severe can be appealed by the defense.

Changes in sentencing have brought changes in correctional practices

Many sentencing reforms have led to changes in the way correctional systems operate:

The proliferation of determinate and mandatory sentences during the past decade, together with dissatisfaction about the uncertainties of indeterminate sentencing (especially the linking of release decisions to rehabilitative progress or predictions of future behavior), have led to modifications in parole decisionmaking. Many States now use parole guidelines, and many have modified their use of "goodtime" and other incentives for controlling inmate behavior and determining release dates.

New administrative requirements, such as collection of victim restitution funds, operation of community service programs, and levying fees for probation supervision, room and board, and other services, have been added to traditional correctional practices.

Changes in sentencing laws and prac-

tices may be affecting the size of the correctional clientele. Such changes include—
• using determinate and mandatory sentencing
• limiting or abolishing parole discretion

• lowering the age at which youthful offenders become subject to the adult criminal justice system
• enacting in a few jurisdictions laws providing for life imprisonment without the possibility of parole.

Forfeiture is a relatively new sanction

What is forfeiture?

Forfeiture is government seizure of property derived from or used in criminal activity. Its use as a sanction aims to strip racketeers and drug traffickers of their economic power because the traditional sanctions of imprisonment and fines have been found inadequate to deter or punish enormously profitable crimes. Seizure of assets aims not only to reduce the profitability of illegal activity but to curtail the financial ability of criminal organizations to continue illegal operations.

There are two types of forfeiture: civil and criminal

• **Civil forfeiture**—a proceeding against property used in criminal activity. Property subject to civil forfeiture often includes vehicles used to transport contraband, equipment used to manufacture illegal drugs, cash used in illegal transactions, and property purchased with the proceeds of the crime. No finding of criminal guilt is required in such proceedings. The government is required to post notice of the proceedings so that any party who has an interest in the property may contest the forfeiture.

• **Criminal forfeiture**—a part of the criminal action taken against a defendant accused of racketeering or drug trafficking. The forfeiture is a sanction imposed on conviction that requires the defendant to forfeit various property rights and interests related to the violation. In 1970 Congress revived this sanction that had been dormant in American law since the Revolution.

The use of forfeiture varies greatly among jurisdictions

The Federal Government originally provided for criminal forfeiture in the Racketeer Influenced and Corrupt Organization (RICO) statute and the

Comprehensive Drug Prevention and Control Act, both enacted in 1970. Before that time civil forfeiture had been provided in Federal laws on some narcotics, customs, and revenue infractions. More recently, language on forfeiture has been included in the Comprehensive Crime Control Act of 1984, the Money Laundering Act of 1986, and the Anti-drug Abuse Act of 1986.

Most State forfeiture procedures appear in controlled substances or RICO laws. A few States provide for forfeiture of property connected with the commission of any felony. Most State forfeiture provisions allow for civil rather than criminal forfeiture. A recent survey responded to by 44 States and territories found that under the controlled substances laws most States provide only for civil forfeiture. Eight States (Arizona, Kentucky, Nevada, New Mexico, North Carolina, Utah, Vermont, and West Virginia), however, have criminal forfeiture provisions.[1] Of the 19 States with RICO statutes, all but 8 include the criminal forfeiture sanction.[2]

What is forfeitable?

Originally most forfeiture provisions aimed to cover the seizure of contraband or modes of transporting or facilitating distribution of such materials. The types of property that may be forfeited have been expanded since the 1970s to include assets, cash, securities, negotiable instruments, real property including houses or other real estate, and proceeds traceable directly or indirectly to violations of certain laws. Common provisions permit seizure of conveyances such as airplanes, boats, or cars; raw materials, products, and equipment used in manufacturing, trafficking, or cultivation of illegal drugs; and drug paraphernalia.

How long does it take to determine if property can be forfeited?

In most cases some time is provided before the actual forfeiture to allow persons with an interest in seized property to make a claim. Seized property is normally kept for 6 months to 1 year before being declared forfeit and disposed of. Contraband or materials that are illegal *per se*, such as drugs, are disposed of relatively quickly. Cars, airplanes, boats, and other forms of transportation are usually kept for about 6 months before disposal. Real property is often kept for longer periods. Administrative forfeitures usually take less time than ones that require judicial determination.

Because of the depreciation in value of many assets over time and the cost of storing or caring for such assets, forfeiture may result in a cost rather than revenue to the prosecuting jurisdiction.

What happens to forfeited property?

The disposition of forfeited property is controlled by statute or in some States by their constitutions. In many cases, the seizing agency is permitted to place an asset in official use once it has been declared forfeit by a court. Such assets are usually cars, trucks, boats, or planes used during the crime or proceeds of the crime.

For assets that are sold, the proceeds are usually used first to pay any outstanding liens. The costs of storing, maintaining, and selling the property are reimbursed next. Some States require that, after administrative costs are reimbursed, the costs of law enforcement and prosecution must be paid. More than half the States provide that any outstanding balance go to the State or local treasury, or a part to both.

In eight States law enforcement agencies can keep all property, cash, or sales proceeds. If the State constitution governs distribution, the receiving agency is usually the State or local school system. Some States have specified the recipients to be special programs for drug abuse prevention and rehabilitation.

In 1984 the Federal Government established the Department of Justice Assets Forfeiture Fund to collect proceeds from forfeitures and defray the costs of forfeitures under the Comprehensive Drug Abuse Prevention and Control Act and the Customs Forfeiture Fund for forfeitures under customs laws. These acts also require that the property and proceeds of forfeiture be shared equitably with State and local law enforcement commensurate with their participation in the investigations leading to forfeiture.

Women in Jail: Unequal Justice

An unprecedented influx of female inmates leaves prisons overcrowded and overwhelmed

Californians call it The Campus, and with its low-lying, red-brick buildings set against 120 acres of dairy land, the California Institution for Women at Frontera looks deceptively civilized. The illusion ends inside. Constructed in the early 1950s as a repository for 800 or so wayward ladies, Frontera today holds more than 2,500 women at any given moment. The convicts complain that guards spy on them while they're showering or using the toilet. Inspectors have found rodent droppings and roaches in the food. In a lawsuit against the state, inmates charged that shower drains get so backed up, they have to stand on crates to avoid the slime.

A continent away, New York City's Rose M. Singer jail stands as a testimony to penal enlightenment. Because most inmates are young and sometimes high-spirited, the jail can feel a bit like a boarding school for girls. But the starkly lit hallways and pervasive smell of disinfectant are constant reminders of the true purpose of the place. And even though it was completed only two years ago, it is already seriously overcrowded—a dining room has been turned into a dorm. Above all, the inmates hate the lack of privacy. Says Carmen Gonzalez, who is serving nine months for selling crack, "I wish I was in a cell."

Stiff penalties: For years, the ranks of convicted criminals have been swelling steadily, bringing the nation's prison system perilously close to an overload. The vast majority—94.4 percent—of those inmates are men. But even in jail, women are breaking down the barriers to equal achievement. The Bureau of Justice Statistics reported last week that the female prison population jumped 21.8 percent from 1988 to 1989—the ninth consecutive year that

the rate of increase at women's institutions far outstripped the men's. The number of women doing time has doubled to 40,000 in the last five years (chart). The main reason is drugs. Stiffer penalties are on the books throughout the country and women, who have turned to crack in a way they never embraced other narcotics, have been caught in the sweep. Judges have also shown a greater willingness to incarcerate women than in the past, when chivalry extended even to lawbreakers. "Courts used to look at it as if they were sentencing a mother," says Gary Maynard, Oklahoma's corrections director. "Now they look at it as if they are sentencing a criminal."

Prisons have been largely unprepared to handle the unique problems of their growing female populations. "We assumed that they could benefit from the same programs as men," says Dan Russell, administrator of Montana's division of corrections. "But women have a lot of psychological and medical needs" that men do not. Often, children are at the heart of the matter. Three quarters of the women are mothers, and many of them single parents. In recent years, a number of prisons have created programs to provide greater contact between kids and inmate moms (box). And public officials have begun to acknowledge—sometimes nudged along by lawsuits—that prisons do not provide women with the same rehabilitation or educational programs as men. Inequities in the correctional system, says Washington, D.C., Superior Court Associate Judge Gladys Kessler, "are a mirror of the sex discrimination that occurs in the nonprison population."

Fed by steamy, seamy '50s movies like "Reform School Girl," Americans have had a long fascination with women behind bars. The reality is a good deal more disturb-

ing—and pathetic. The typical offender, according to a 1988 national study conducted for the American Correctional Association, is a young minority mother. In general, she is slightly better educated and less violent than her male counterpart. Many inmates were victims themselves—of poverty, physical violence or sexual abuse. Though most poor people are obviously law abiding, some analysts say more

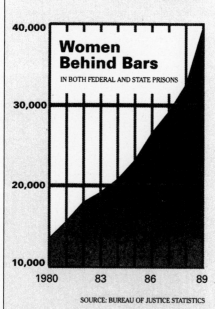

Filling Prisons

The number of women inmates has almost tripled in the last 10 years.

Women Behind Bars
IN BOTH FEDERAL AND STATE PRISONS

SOURCE: BUREAU OF JUSTICE STATISTICS

'Dear Mommy, How Are You Doing?'

It is Mother's Day at the Lorton Correctional Complex outside Washington, D.C., and Michael, 10, is waiting impatiently as the women in camouflage pants file into the gym. Finally, Jennifer Nimmons, who is serving 18 months on a drug charge, arrives and Michael rushes into her arms. He has brought his mother a present: a cutout of a dancing bear with a letter on its stomach, which he reads aloud. "Dear Mommy, How are you doing in the hospital? Have a happy mother's day, this is a poem for you. 'Roses are red, Violets are blue, You are the best mother, I ever wrote to'." Then he asks: "Is this a hospital?"

Confused, enraged, hurt—children like Michael are innocent victims of their mothers' crimes. Until recently, prison officials didn't recognize that a child's emotional dependence doesn't stop just because his mother lands behind bars. Now attitudes are changing: institutions around the country have put programs in place to foster that vital relationship.

Some of the most innovative begin at birth. Federal prisons separate mothers and newborns after 24 hours, and few state pens allow inmates to spend time with infants. The Rose M. Singer Center on Rikers Island is a heartening contrast. The mothers' cells surround the glass-walled nursery on three sides, and an intercom system keeps them in constant touch. If kids cry, moms can rush to their aid—the cells are never locked. Because a female federal prisoner is likely to do time far from home, a program called PACT (Parents and Children Together) is designed to improve long-distance parenting. "We counsel inmates to get as involved as possible by calling teachers on a regular basis," says Jaretta Jones, an instructor at the federal penitentiary in Lexington, Ky.

Psychic costs: Penal authorities have also become more sensitive about the psychic costs to kids. Some children feel guilty about their parents' predicaments—imagining, for example, if they hadn't opened the door for the cops, Mom would be free. The Huron Valley Women's Facility in Ypsilanti, Mich., provides kids with therapy after visits. "If we are going to lock up these mothers, we have to take some responsibility for those children," says Marilyn Marshall, a vocational counselor at the prison. "They will certainly be our next generation of prisoners unless we pay attention now."

---

women have taken to crime to support their families as economic conditions have worsened. In Florida last year, more than two thirds of the men were working at the time of their arrest, while 73.8 percent of the women were jobless.

New Breed: Women prisoners have always been easier to manage than the men—they're more prone to verbal than physical abuse. But that may be changing. Some penologists worry that the lack of space will not only exacerbate existing problems—for example, fights stemming from lesbian jealousies—but provoke the women into new forms of aggression. "The recidivism, as well as the level of violence, seems to be directly linked to the amount of overcrowding," says Rebecca Jurado, an attorney with the ACLU of southern California.

Drugs, in particular, have stimulated violent outbreaks. More than half the women in the federal system were convicted on drug charges. And the problem doesn't stop at the prison gate. Mary Vermeer, a deputy warden in Perryville, Ariz., says new inmates are delighted to discover that, despite efforts to stem the flow, the drug pipeline makes it almost as easy to get a fix inside as out. At Frontera, crack houses and shooting galleries operate in portable toilets in the yard. Old-timers complain about the new breed of "druggie." "They don't care about nothing," says Delores Lee, 37, who is doing 25 years in Florida on a murder conviction. "They steal; they break things."

AIDS also contributes to the crisis atmosphere in American prisons. So far, there are no national figures measuring the disease among the convict population. An official Massachusetts study based on 400 inmates who volunteered to be tested found that 35 percent of the women were HIV-positive, compared with 13 percent of the men. In California, any woman who tested positive was put into a segregated AIDS unit—whether or not she was actually ill. As a result of a discrimination lawsuit, many HIV inmates at Frontera have been mainstreamed during the day—but must return to their separate quarters to sleep.

Though few would argue that male convicts are socially well adjusted, penal experts tend to agree that female inmates require—and desire—more psychological counseling. Many women feel enormous guilt about their kids. "When men get arrested, they ask for a lawyer," says Brenda Smith, an attorney at the National Women's Law Center in Washington, D.C. "When women get arrested, they ask about their children." The children effectively serve as hostages on the outside, ensuring that the women make few demands. "The No. 1 issue for women is getting their kids back," says Sarah Buel, a battered-women's advocate in Massachusetts. "The unwritten rule is, don't make a fuss and we'll help you get [them] back."

Prison officials have begun to acknowledge the enormous disparity in the treatment of men and women. In a number of recent lawsuits, women plaintiffs have accused the system of gender bias. A major problem is "overincarceration." Because of a lack of facilities, many low-security inmates have landed in medium-security penitentiaries. Many of the women have been subjected to greater restrictions, such as strip searches, than their crimes warrant—and which their male counterparts are largely spared.

Some social critics believe the states should help inmates break the cycle of abuse and poverty that led many of them into crime in the first place. They also argue that the system should recognize that women generally pose less of a threat to public safety than men and deserve more lenient sentences. "Assuming that we want to help offenders, the best place to do this is not in prison," says Nicole Hahn Rafter, author of "Partial Justice," a history of women's prisons. That attitude is unlikely to win much support, particularly now that public opinion favors strict penalties. But it is clear that the overcrowded conditions and lack of rehabilitation programs doubly punish women—and do little to advance the society's interests.

ELOISE SALHOLZ with LYNDA WRIGHT in Los Angeles, CLARA BINGHAM in Washington, TONY CLIFTON in New York, GINNY CARROLL in Houston, SPENCER REISS in Miami, FARAI CHIDEYA in Boston and bureau reports

Some Observations of the Status and Performance of Female Corrections Officers in Men's Prisons

Judith D. Simon and Rita J. Simon

The observations of a young female officer about the role of female guards in men's prisons and the interaction between male and female guards in those prisons are the major foci of this article. The conclusions reached are that women officers carry their weight in men's prisons and that most of the inmates like having female officers around. They humanize the institution.

INTRODUCTION

This article focuses on two controversial issues concerning female roles in the criminal justice system: the quality of the interaction between male and female corrections officers: and the relationships between inmates and female officers. It examines such issues as the reported resentment on the part of male officers at having to work with women. There is the feelings on their part that women officers could not hold their own in difficult or tense situations. There exist the additional feeling in the prison, men would not only have to protect themselves, and get the situation under control, but would have the additional worry of looking after their women colleagues. Male guards have been quoted as saying, "Rather than having the protection of a buddy working along side me, we have an extra burden--that of looking after the women officers."[1]

The data for this article stems primarily from the observations of a young, middle class, white woman who worked in a men's medium security prison for 13 months as a corrections officer. Altogether there were 150 corrections officers in this prison, about 40 of whom were women; only two of whom were white. The administrative staff consisted of the warden, two assistant deputy wardens, the inspector, three captains, six lieutenants, and 10 sergeants. With the exception of two female lieutenants and one sergeant, the rest were males. The first woman corrections officer had been hired about a decade earlier in the late 1970s. Prior to that, women had worked in the prison as teachers, secretaries, nurses, and in social service capacities.

Built originally as a city house of corrections, the state took over the facility in 1985. The state retained all the city employees but required they undergo an extensive training program the same as any new state corrections officer (or non-custody workers) would undergo. Of the city employees, more than half left the facility and took other positions in civil service.

Of those who chose to remain and work for the state, half quit within several months after the state took over. The few that did not quit report that those who left did not like the more restrictive rules and regulations imposed by the state. They felt that they were stripped of much of their power and authority over prisoners, leaving them in a dangerous situation. For example, under the city rules, the guards were permitted to carry weapons with them inside the facility, but under the state rules, no weapons were permitted inside the perimeters other than during riot conditions. The city guards were also upset at the loss of many services that the prisoners used to provide them free of charge such as haircuts, shoe shines, and car washes. When the facility was run by the city there were no women guards. There was one woman sergeant, a former city police officer, and there were a number of women who worked in a social service capacity.

The inmate population in the fall of 1986 was 650; a year later the number had been reduced to 500, the maximum permitted under state regulations. Under the state classification system, the facility is a medium security prison which specializes in parole violators. That means that most of the inmates have served time earlier and were somewhat older than the typical state prisoner. The offenses for which they violated their parole are primarily drug related property crimes. There was also a fairly large group of violent offenders who had been found guilty of murder, manslaughter, armed robbery, and aggravated assault. At least 80 percent of the inmates were black, there was a small group of Hispanics, and all the others were white males.

From *Issues in Justice*, Chapter 11, pp. 140-148, edited with contributions by Roslyn Muraskin, 1990. Reprinted by permission of Wyndham Hall Press, Inc., Bristol, IN.

The Tasks Assigned Male and Female Guards

There was no difference between the duties and responsibilities of the male and female commanding officers. They included scheduling the custody staff, reviewing and updating employee personnel files, insuring that the daily operations of the prison ran smoothly, and filing reports on all critical incidents. Additionally, the commanders reviewed disciplinary "tickets" (reports) that officers wrote on the prisoners, occasionally heard prisoners' complaints, and monitored the on-the-job training of new officers. One member of the command staff was required to monitor each meal in the dining hall, and at least once during their eight hour shift, they made rounds, and inspected all the housing units. There was one commander in the control center at all times.

According to Department of Corrections policy, commanding officers were supposed to assign staff to positions without consideration of the officer's sex. The extent to which this policy was followed depended on which commander was doing the scheduling. At the beginning of one of the author's employ in the prison, she observed that women were assigned either to the information desk, the control center or the front gate; men were always assigned to the arsenal, the alert response vehicles, and the yard. After a few months, a change was men as well as women were regularly assigned to the information desk and the control center. Women were just as likely to be assigned to the arsenal and to the alert response vehicles as were the male officers. The changes seemed to be the result of an influx of new officers and other changes in the command staff that are described below.

There was a dramatic difference between the attitudes of the men who had recently completed the training academy and those who had either been with the state for many years or had worked for the city. The men who were newer to the system generally accepted women as equals and respected the women officers and commanders. There was a sense of camaraderie and teamwork between the young officers (in experience, not necessarily in years) who completed the academy. But since the academy had only been in existence for a few years there were only a limited number of officers who shared that experience. These men exhibited almost no animosity toward their female colleagues nor did they complain that they were incompetent. That is to not to say that they did not complain about a particular woman, but the complaints did not stem from the officer being a woman. The male guards who had either worked for the city or had been with the state for many years were more likely to resent women generally and many of these officers indicated that they would have preferred that women not work inside the prison at all.

Many of the women were housing unit officers. They were in charge of running a unit of 40-55 men for eight hours. The yard crew, frequently all male officers, were in charge of relieving these unit officers for their restroom breaks as well as their regular meal breaks. Often times the yard crew would complain that the women officers would demand many more restroom reliefs than the male officers. These men would accuse the women of demanding these breaks even when they did not need to use the restroom. It is possible that the women did abuse the system however, it is important to note that the male officers often did not ask for restroom reliefs because they were able to use the restrooms in the housing units since the prisoners and the guards were all men. The only women's restrooms were located in the kitchen and in the administration building.

Situations occurred several times a week when an officer would call the control center asking for assistance or com-

plaining that he/she was having difficulty managing the unit. Other times a member of the yard crew who arrived at a housing unit to relieve a regular officer would notify the control center that the unit was out of control. These problems occurred more frequently with male officers than with female officers. There were several men and women who had problems controlling their units on a regular basis and there seemed to be no solution for these officers other than to assign them to posts with less inmate contact. Additionally, there were some officers who could not carry out their duties properly whatever their assignment. Here too the problems occurred more often with men than with women officers. The commanders were well aware of these problems and of the problem officers. But the commanders rarely made generalized statements indicating one gender of officers was preferable over another. The shift commander occasionally remarked that women officers had a better overall record of reporting for work on time than men officers did. One explanation offered was that the woman officers were less likely "to stay out drinking until late at night." The occasions when women officers failed to report to work were usually because their children were sick or other family problems presented themselves.

Occasionally, there were disturbances in the yard or in the housing units that required several officers to respond immediately. All officers who were in a position to do so were expected to respond: men and women alike. As a general rule, officers were anxious to come to the aid of their fellow officers and responded quickly. However, there were some officers who were notorious for disappearing during emergencies. There were several men and women who enjoyed this reputation. There were also men and women officers whom their fellow officers preferred not to have on the scene. Generally the male officers who were not welcomed were feared because they tended to get the prisoners riled up and to escalate the situation. The unwelcomed women officers were not desired because they were ineffective. The prisoners made fun of these women; and thus, it was more difficult to quell the disturbance.

The Reactions of the Inmates to Female Guards

In general, the prisoners tended to relate to each officer as an individual. They tried to play on the officer's weaknesses in the hops of receiving favorable treatment, or of getting the officer to do favors for them, or of allowing them to get away with prohibited acts. The prisoners played on women officers' appearance or sex appeal by complimenting them, by making suggestive remarks, and by asking a lot of personal questions. They would try to make all new officers, and in particular the woman officer feel uncomfortable and frightened, hoping that these feelings would prompt the officer to seek out friendships with the prisoners. The prisoners would then use these friendships to their benefit, starting out perhaps with extra portions at meals, or extra phone time and leading to sexual favors, or even complicity in escape. For the first several weeks the prisoners seem to pull out all the stops to try and "set up" a new officer, be it a man or a woman. They tried hard to treat the officer as a "special" person.

But a prisoner's primary concern is his personal safety and the safety of his belongings. Any other preferences or desires are secondary to these concerns for survival and safety. Thus, any consideration a prisoner might give to liking a male or female officer is secondary to his concern that the officer be able and willing to protect him and his property.

6. PUNISHMENT AND CORRECTIONS

Protecting the prisoners does not necessarily involve great physical strength or size; rather it involves the guard's ability to maintain order and enforce the prison's rules. Initially, prisoners are skeptical of any officer's ability to maintain order. Once an officer proves him or herself, most prisoners are ready to accept that officer. Some prisoners do not like women in general; and they may especially resent women in positions of authority. Some think all women officers are reformed prostitutes (once the state did hire many ex-prostitutes). Still others dislike women officers because they claim that some women purposely set out to tease them and thus are a source of great frustration e.g., women who wear their clothes too tight, use too much make-up, have on too much jewelry. Finally, there are those who dislike certain women officers because they think they are too "manly", indicating they are lesbians. These inmates are unwilling to concede that a woman officer is able to maintain order and they cause trouble whenever a woman is in charge. But they are a small minority of the inmates.

Once a woman officer establishes her competency, many of the prisoners are pleased to have her in place of a man. Many of the inmates believe that women treat them with more respect and more care than the male guards. They believe that the women guards do not need to constantly affirm their power over the prisoners, as opposed to the male officers who see power and control as symbols of their manhood. Many of the prisoners are also more anxious to talk to women officers about their personal situation; once they are past their initial "wooing" stage.

The Authority Wielded by Prison Gurards

In his account of social interactions and patterns of authority in total institutions Erving Goffman observed that any staff member, no matter how lowly his or her status, can exercise power over any inmate/patient in the institution irrespective of the inmate's or patient's prior role in the larger society (Goffman, 1961). As observed in the prison, this authority is particularly evident in one-on-one confrontations between a prisoner and an officer. An officer may lose a particular battle. He may not, for example, succeed in forcing a prisoner to turn over a piece of contraband at a particular moment but he always wins the war, because in the end it is the officer's word against the inmate's word. He will get the contraband from the prisoner.

Each officer usually comes up with his/her own standards, about how much discretion to exercise. Some believe that the best way to do their job, is to be nice to the prisoners, to do little extras. After all, if you are nice to them, they will be nice to you. In the training academy, instructors try to discourage this approach because they believe it is dangerous.

Some prisoners become angry that others are getting special treatment, just by asking. Those who become angry will not ask; it is against their prison code. Prisoners are frightened and feel insecure if the rules are not enforced strictly. Their fear also makes them angry. Other officers try to cultivate a few friendships, hoping that these prisoners will come to their aid if there is trouble. This, too, is discouraged by the training staff because it is rare for a prisoner to openly protect an officer at the expense of another prisoner since this is likely to lead to retaliation by "friends" of the injured prisoner.

Still other officers adopt the style of enforcing the rules to the fullest extent such as writing a ticket when a violation occurs, not negotiating with the prisoner once a violation has taken place, and treating all prisoners the same. It is often the case that these officers write the fewest tickets; after their brief initial period when they have established control by writing lots of tickets and have gained the prisoners' respect for their authority. The prisoners are more likely to respond to these officers' requests and demands and they are more likely to adhere to prison rules when these officers are in charge.

Concluding Remarks

In sum, our overall assessment about whether women correction's officers carry their weight in a men's prison and whether they are accepted by their male colleagues and the male inmates is positive. A male officer's position is neither threatened nor endangered by having to work along side a female officer. Female officers are as likely to assume their responsibilities, stand up to the prisoners, and enforce the rules as male officers are; and for the most part the male and female officers recognize the absence of differences. As for the prisoners, most of them like having women around; it humanizes the institution.

ENDNOTE

1. For further discussion of these issues see: Lynn Zimmer, 1986, WOMEN GUARDING MEN, Chicago: University of Chicago Press; Clarice Feinman, 1980, WOMEN IN THE CRIMINAL JUSTICE SYSTEM, New York: Praeger; Nicole Hahn Rafter and Elizabeth A. Stanko, 1982, WOMEN, GENDER ROLES AND CRIMINAL JUSTICE, Boston: Northeastern University Press.

REFERENCE

Goffman, Erving. 1961. **Asylum: Essays on the Social Situations of Mental Patients and Other Inmates.** Garden City, New York: Anchor Books.

You're Under Arrest—AT HOME

With a jail's daily operating costs of $35-$125 per prisoner, home detention represents big savings for hard-pressed correction officials.

Fred Scaglione

Mr. Scaglione is a New York free-lance writer.

NOBODY wants a prison in his or her neighborhood, but don't be surprised if that split level next door is already a jail cell. As the nation's penal system staggers under the weight of an ever-rising inmate population, corrections officials are taking a new, high-tech look at an age-old technique—house arrest. Jurisdictions in 32 states now are sending almost 2,000 offenders to their homes, rather than to traditional lock-ups, and outfitting them with an array of electronic equipment to ensure they stay there. "We believe this is an important enhancement to a criminal justice system that is already overburdened," says James K. Stewart, director of the National Institute of Justice (NIJ).

Offenders accepted into these programs are given a daily schedule, allowing them to leave the house for work, approved counseling sessions, and religious services. Some are fitted with continuously signaling anklets or wristlets which broadcast to a second unit attached to their home telephone lines. If the offender leaves the house and takes the transmitter out of the broadcast range, the telephone-based receiver automatically calls the program's central monitoring station. There, a computer programmed with the offender's daily schedule determines if the absence is au-

thorized or if a violation report is warranted.

Other jurisdictions use a computer-generated random calling system, requiring the offender to verify his presence in a variety of ways each time the phone rings. The central schedule monitoring station works the same in both cases. Neither system eavesdrops on the offender's conversations or activities, nor can they track him if he leaves the house. "The monitor is the baby sitter and I'm your mom," explains In-House Arrest Officer Trish Dosset to new program participants in Palm Beach County, Fla. "For the next 30 days, you don't go anywhere without asking me first."

The programs also require regular face-to-face meetings, verification of employment and hours worked, telephone checks, and occasional site visits at the offender's home and workplace. Clients with drug and alcohol problems may be required to attend counseling sessions and undergo randomly scheduled urine tests.

Inmates may be the nation's fastest growing community group. By June, 1986, there were over 750,000 residents of Federal, state, and local penal institutions, twice the number of 10 years earlier. The American Correctional Association ex-

pects the population to double again by soon after the year 2000, as legislators continue to demand longer sentences generally and mandatory imprisonment for specific offenses.

Law enforcement officials have been unable to accommodate their burgeoning clientele. Prisons in Connecticut, California, and Ohio, for example, were 83%, 76%, and 69%, respectively, above their designed capacities in 1986. Almost one-quarter of all city and county jails now have court orders limiting their populations.

Efforts to expand the prison system have been devastatingly expensive. The average construction cost of a new jail cell is estimated at $75,000. Jurisdictions then go on to pay operating costs ranging from $35 to $125 per night. It's not surprising that correctional expenses are now the fastest growing segment of state government spending.

Electronic monitors, on the other hand, cost anywhere from $2 to $10 per day for each offender, depending on the type of equipment and the size of the program. Staff costs will vary according to the level of personal supervision a program specifies. Clackamas County, Ore., estimates

A continuously signaling device is installed on the ankle of a man under house arrest. A telephone-based receiver will call authorities if his body transmitter is taken out of broadcast range.

to visit him. He gets to know his wife and kids, stops drinking or doing drugs, saves his money, and works around the house. Nine months later, they take off the monitor and he still comes home at night. He's got a job, a bank account, and a whole new relationship with his family. The monitor and house arrest have made him healthy, wealthy, and wise.

If it sounds like a law-enforcement fairy tale, it is. However, for certain offenders it's also true. "I now own my own deli," says a 25-year-old man after five years on cocaine, six months in prison, and 10 months on the New Jersey ISP program. "I do not do drugs and I will not go back to doing drugs. This program was a life-saver for me."

An auto mechanic, also in his mid-20's and convicted on drug charges, stands in the service station where he works, talking about his wife, baby, and the five-year sentence he started serving in state prison. "I'm going to make it," he asserts, explaining how he's regained much of the weight he lost to drugs. "That cost me $2,800," he adds, pointing to a large metal tool cabinet. "I never could save up to buy decent tools before."

"We've had people who, for the first time in their lives, are working. They're going home and they're providing some kind of support for their family," says Ingrid Lewis, administrator of the house arrest program in Clackamas County. "They're at home and they have to take care of responsibilities at home," explains Capt. Ken Lane of the Fairfax County, Va., Sheriff's Office. However, corrections officials, perhaps out of experience, are quick to burst their own bubble. They are cautious about predicting success or prescribing monitoring programs for too many offenders.

Many of the plans which have sprung up in recent years mirror the two original Palm Beach County models established in 1984. Approximately one-third of all participants throughout the county are traffic offenders, predominately drunk-drivers. Some jurisdictions extend participation to work-release inmates and to those convicted of low-level property crimes. A history of violence, drug abuse, or sexual misconduct often will disqualify an applicant. White-collar criminals also make appearances in many of the local programs. In July, 1987, for example, a Los Angeles court sentenced a local slumlord to house arrest in one of his rat-infested buildings.

Growth also has come through monitoring a wide range of offenders with varying,

total costs at $12 per day; Utah officials quote $17.

No matter how you add it up, home detention represents big savings for hard-pressed corrections officials. "We're buying additional jail beds for $10," says Marie Whittington as Orange County, Calif., prepares to expand its house arrest program from 25 to 75 slots.

New Jersey, with 400 felons on pre-release from its overcrowded prison system, estimates that its Intensive Supervision Probation (ISP) program is saving approximately $6,700,000 in direct expenditures annually. In addition, working program participants usually make a wide range of payments that further offset the costs of supervision; most programs collect a fee from participants to cover the cost of monitoring equipment. Palm Beach County's PRIDE, Inc., for example, charges the fairly typical amount of $7 per day. Of-

fenders also pay taxes, fines, and restitution as required. They often are obligated to work on community service projects as well. New Jersey estimates that these payments and activities add up to an additional $1,400,000.

Life-saving programs

Yet, these programs may be saving more than money. They may be saving lives. Success stories are depressingly rare in the world of correction, but many administrators of home detention programs like to tell one—the same one. It's about the offender who comes to their program near the end of his personal rope. He's sick—busted in more ways than one. He gets a monitor and a curfew, and goes to work every morning and comes home every night. He stops seeing his friends on the corner or at the bar and they don't bother

and more serious, backgrounds. Clackamas County, for example, assigns offenders convicted of violent felonies like armed robbery and manslaughter. They are also one of the few programs to accept sex offenders. "We look at the individual, not just the crime," says Ingrid Lewis.

As the technology has grown more reliable, a number of states have incorporated monitoring into pre-release programs aimed at freeing up bed space in crowded prisons. Inmates agree to a variety of conditions, including monitoring and curfews, in exchange for the chance to get out of prison early. Michigan, for example, began providing monitors to convicted felons in its Extended Furlough Program in April, 1987. It now monitors nearly 1,000 offenders.

About 90% of all participants successfully complete home-monitoring programs. "I'm continuously amazed with the level of compliance that prisoners give us," states Jim Putnam of the Michigan Department of Correction. However, there still is relatively little hard data to support the gut feelings of administrators that these successful graduates go on to live crime-free lives. A recent survey of 327 offenders who completed the New Jersey ISP program since 1984 did find that only four percent had been rearrested in the state, an excellent result compared with typical studies of recidivism. The National Institute of Justice is funding a series of tests to follow offenders randomly assigned to electronic monitoring as opposed to other programs.

Of the 10% who fail to complete the programs, the majority are sent back to jail for violating in-house rules—missed curfews, refusal to attend counseling sessions, or failed urine tests. A small fraction are sent back because of new arrests. In county-run programs, these tend to be relatively infrequent and for minor offenses.

State-run pre-release programs generally have a greater return rate with more serious rearrests despite screening out 70-80% of all potential candidates. The New Jersey ISP program, for example, has returned approximately seven percent of its participants to prison because of new charges, with approximately two-thirds of those for felonies. Michigan's program recently suffered a murder/suicide by one of its participants, the most serious crime committed by a monitored offender to date. Incidents such as these appear inevit-

able when offenders are sent back into the community. Yet, so far, electronically monitored home detention seems to have drawn high marks in protecting the public safety.

If anything, administrators, particularly on the local level, have been criticized for being too cautious in their selection of offenders. "Judges are gun shy," says Joan Petersilia of the Rand Corporation, a research/consulting firm in Santa Monica, Calif. "They're picking people who they are fairly sure won't embarrass the program." If this means that monitoring is used for offenders who wouldn't normally draw jail time and pose little risk to the public safety, she argues that the program is self-defeating. "It's costly. It's intrusive. I don't think we can afford to do those symbolic punishments anymore."

Monitoring probation

However, there is a group now walking the streets of society for which electronic monitoring is appropriate, Petersilia believes. The nation's overflowing prisons have swelled the probation caseload to over 1,800,000, more than twice the number incarcerated. At the same time, dwindling resources have reduced routine probation supervision to an exercise in paper-shuffling. "Half of all people now on probation are convicted felons," she states, "and a quarter of them are convicted of violent crimes." A recent Rand study found that 65% of California probationers are rearrested within 40 months, 75% for serious crimes. This population, she feels, is much too dangerous to be receiving nominal probation supervision. "The system must develop intermediate forms of punishment more restrictive than routine probation, but not as severe or expensive as prison."

Electronic monitoring may be at least part of the answer. Some officials worry, however, that monitoring will become a popular and counterproductive crutch. "I'm concerned about programs that put too much emphasis on the equipment and not enough emphasis on a balanced program of equipment and personal supervision," says Marie Whittington, director of Orange County's Work Furlough Program. "The monitors are only a back-up," agrees New Jersey ISP officer Mike McCree. "What makes this program work is close personal contact."

In fact, New Jersey puts electronic mon-

itors on only 20 problem cases out of its total of 400 participants. Another 200 receive computer-generated nightly telephone calls, but are not required to wear a bracelet to verify their identities. Unlike many jurisdictions which require only one office visit per week, New Jersey's program averages 27 contacts per month, many of them face to face in the offender's home. Participants attend weekly rap sessions, special ISP-sponsored drug counseling sessions, and 16 hours per month of community service. They also must maintain an up-to-date diary and personal budget.

"We get involved in every aspect of their lives," McCree says, adding with a smile, "I've been to two or three weddings and we've got a wall full of baby pictures."

Although offenders with monitors may certainly feel that Big Brother is watching, the American Civil Liberties Union (ACLU) has yet to take issue with any of the house arrest programs. "The overarching problem in correction is overcrowding," says Ed Koren, an attorney with the ACLU's National Prison Project. "We'd like to see this happen if it can get people out of prison." Therefore, while it remains sensitive to the threat of abuse through overutilization and to possibilities of discrimination in selection and offender contribution requirements, the ACLU basically is watching as the strategy continues to develop.

While programs similar to those already in existence are likely to continue to grow rapidly, new technological developments are offering the possibility of even more comprehensive electronic surveillance. One manufacturer has added a blood alcohol-level monitoring system to its house arrest equipment. At least two others are developing methods to track an offender's position geographically as he travels throughout a metropolitan area and report it back to a computerized central control station for comparison with his approved daily schedule.

Some corrections officials respond favorably to this prospect of expanded surveillance. Others, however, are skeptical. "I think the technology is a long way off," says Joan Petersilia, "but I think the public acceptance of that is an even longer way off." Nevertheless, electronic monitoring and house arrest clearly are here to stay as correctional strategies. "The future of this is very bright," concludes the NIJ's Stewart.

Difficult clients, large caseloads plague probation, parole agencies

Randall Guynes

American probation and parole systems now face an increasingly difficult clientele despite less adequate resources. Despite greater financial resources, personnel increases are not keeping pace with rising caseloads of clients with serious problems. These are some of the major findings of a survey of State and local probation and parole officers conducted as part of the National Assessment Program (NAP) sponsored by the National Institute of Justice.

This *Research in Action* describes survey results from 49 State probation and parole directors and 339 local offices. Of the local offices, 43 percent provide probation services only, and 21 percent are parole field offices. The remaining 36 percent are responsible for both probation and parole and are referred to as "combined" agencies throughout this publication.

The primary aim of the National Assessment Program is to identify key needs and problems of local and State criminal justice practitioners. To accomplish this, the National Institute of Justice (NIJ) contracted with the Institute for Law and Justice, Inc., to conduct a national survey of approximately 2,500 practitioners from a

The Institute for Law and Justice, Inc., Alexandria, Virginia, conducted the 1986 National Assessment Program for the National Institute of Justice. Under a subcontract, the Institute for Economic and Policy Studies, Inc., conducted the surveys of correctional officials, including this report by Randall Guynes on the survey of probation and parole agency directors.

sample of 375 counties across the Nation. Included were all 175 counties with populations greater than 250,000 and a sample of 200 counties having less than that number.[1] Persons receiving surveys in each sampled county included the police chief of the largest city, sheriff, jail administrator, prosecutor, chief judge, trial court administrator (where applicable), and probation and parole agency heads. In addition, surveys were also sent to State probation and parole agencies to obtain their viewpoints.

The survey covered five general areas: agency background, criminal justice problems, caseload, staffing, and operations. The results for each of these areas are discussed in detail in the following sections.

Background

Organizational Units. Using political subdivisions to sample probation and parole agencies obviously results in a diverse set of respondents including directors of county probation departments, heads of branch offices for State agencies, and agencies responsible for several counties. Yet this reflects the diversity of organizational arrangements in probation and parole generally (see Exhibit 1).

In about 25 percent of the States, probation is primarily a local responsibility, with the State accountable only for functions such as providing financial support, setting standards, and arranging training courses. This locally based approach accounts for about two-thirds of all persons under probation supervision in the United States.[2]

The governmental branch responsible also varies. A State or local department may be in the judicial or the executive branch of government, and supervision of probationers may cross branches or levels within branches. Despite these variations, agency functions are similar: supervising and monitoring persons; collecting and analyzing information for decisionmakers; and performing other duties such as collecting fees, fines, restitution, and child support payments.

Staffing and budgets. For the agencies responding, the median numbers of employees are 32 for combined agencies, 47 for probation, and 62 for parole. The respective medians of cases monthly are 934, 1,225, and 885. Probation directors indicate a median of 129 presentence, revocation, diversion, or other investigations monthly, compared to 75 for parole and 94 for combined agencies.

As expected, parole cases are generally classified at higher supervision levels than cases handled by either probation or combined agencies. Parole reports the highest proportion of intensive (11 percent) and maximum (35 percent) cases and the lowest median caseload (65 cases per officer). The other two groups indicated from 22 to less than 4 percent in intensive and maximum supervision categories and had correspondingly higher median caseloads (probation 109, combined 99). However, 27 percent of the parole caseload is classified as "unsupervised."

A larger proportion of parole agencies (29 percent) report budget increases in excess of 30 percent over the last 3

Difficult clients, large caseloads plague probation, parole agenices

Exhibit 1

Exhibit 1
Probation structures, National Assessment Project

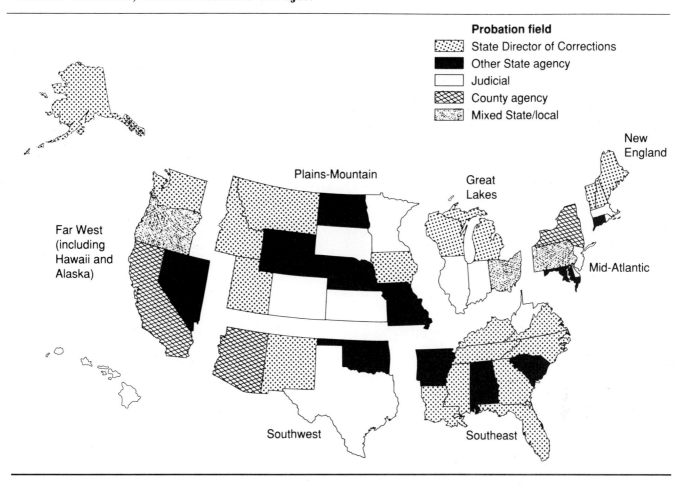

Probation field
State Director of Corrections
Other State agency
Judicial
County agency
Mixed State/local

years than did probation (22 percent) and combined agencies (16 percent). More than two-thirds of the directors of combined offices rate their financial resources as inadequate, while 55 percent of probation respondents and 48 percent of parole respondents rate their resources as inadequate.

Criminal justice problems

Based on the previous National Assessment Survey in 1983,[3] the current survey asked respondents to rank the severity of seven criminal justice problems within their systems: lack of staff skills, prison crowding, agency management, staff shortages, jail crowding, coordination among agencies, and the public's lack of understanding of criminal justice agencies. Respondents ranked these items from most serious (1) to least serious (7). Exhibit 2 shows the average ranking for each issue by type of agency. The percentage of "number 1" responses appears in parentheses.

Staff shortage is clearly the dominant problem for all agencies. It has the highest average rank for probation and combined agencies and second highest for parole. Prison crowding also rates high among parole agencies and combined agencies. Similarly, State

probation and parole directors (not shown in Exhibit 2) rank prison crowding and staff shortages as the most significant issues.

After staff shortage, probation respondents see the criminal justice system as being troubled almost equally by coordination problems, a lack of understanding by the public, and both jail and prison crowding. Coordination is significant to probation officers because the regular performance of their duties requires them to work with judges, law enforcement personnel, jail managers, and sometimes prison officials. As for crowding, probation

6. PUNISHMENT AND CORRECTIONS

officers are affected by both jail crowding, as local governments attempt to control jail populations with probation supervision, and prison crowding, as courts and legislatures attempt to control prison populations through increased probation.

In most of the remainder of the survey, respondents were asked to rate problems and needs on a scale of 1 to 4 with a rating of 1 representing "Not at all" and 4 representing "Major" problem or need. In the discussion that follows, the ratings of 3 and 4 combine to indicate a significant problem or need.

Agencies were asked to rate the degree to which eight factors had contributed to increased caseloads over the past 3 years (see Exhibit 3). All respondent groups identified increased supervision needs of offenders as the first or second greatest reason for caseload increases. Other significant contributors to caseloads were jail and prison crowding, slow growth in residential options, and time required for investigations and reporting. Increased supervision terms were rated low by all groups. In general, directors of parole field offices rated all contributing factors higher than did directors of other agencies. Parole and combined agencies reported prison crowding and early parole release as important contributors to caseloads—a result in agreement with their views on significant criminal justice problems.

Reflecting their different perspectives, 63 percent of parole directors, but only 28 percent of probation directors, gave a high rating to the related issue of early parole release. State agency directors considered slow growth in community residential beds as less significant than did directors of local offices. However, State directors gave more emphasis than other respondents to investigation and reporting time as a contributor to caseloads.

There were significant regional variations in how much crowding, early parole release, and increased supervision terms affect caseload. From 80 to 100 percent of probation or parole directors in the Southeast and Plains-Mountain regions considered prison crowding an important factor in increasing caseloads. They were joined

by parole agencies from New England and probation agencies from the Southwest. The greatest concern with early parole release was expressed by Southeast (93 percent) and Southwest (78 percent) parole directors.

Exhibit 2

Most serious criminal justice problem (average ranking by type of agency)

Average rank	Probation only agencies	Probation and parole agencies	Parole only agencies
1.0			
2.3			
2.4			Prison crowding(41%)
2.5			
2.6			
2.7	Staff shortage(48%)		
2.8		Staff shortage(38%)	
2.9			
3.0			Staff shortage(30%)
3.1		Prison crowding(25%)	
3.2			
3.3			
3.4			
3.5	Coordination(9%)		Jail crowding(6%)
3.6	Jail crowding(16%)	Jail crowding(10%)	
3.7	Lack of public understanding(13%)		
3.8	Prison crowding (11%)	Lack of public understanding(11%)	
3.9			
4.0			
4.1			
4.2		Lack coordination(10%)	
4.3			Lack of public understanding(10%)
4.4			Lack coordination(1%)
4.5			
4.6			
4.7			
4.8		Management(8%)	Management(10%)
4.9			
5.0			
5.1			
5.2	Lack staff skill(4%)		
5.3			
5.4	Management(1%)	Lack staff skills(3%)	
5.5			Lack staff skills(3%)
5.6			
7.0			

Note: The number in parentheses is the percentage of persons assigning rank of 1 to the problem.

For example, among probation and parole agencies, "staff shortages" was given an average seriousness of 2.8 on a scale of 1 down to 7, but 38 percent ranked it as a number 1 problem.

As shown in Exhibit 3, increased supervision terms is rated lowest as a contributor by all groups of respondents. However, an interesting regional variation is that respondents from the Southeast and Southwest consider

Difficult clients, large caseloads plague probation, parole agenices

Exhibit 3
Caseload contributors

Reason	State agencies	Probation agencies	Parole agencies	Combined agencies
Increased supervision needs	75%	82%	80%	79%
Staff increases not keeping pace	73	79	74	73
Prison crowding	79	68	86	79
Local jail crowding	63	62	61	63
Time for reports and investigations	60	59	57	64
Early parole release	55	28	63	61
Residential options not keeping pace	53	57	64	52
Increased supervision terms	42	37	51	35

longer supervision terms as a very significant contributor to caseload increases (93 and 100 percent respectively). Generally, respondents from the Southeast and Southwest express greater concern on more items affecting caseloads than those from other regions.

Responses to caseload management problems

Respondents were asked to list projects in their jurisdictions that have improved personnel and operational problems. Projects listed to improve caseload management speak to changing times in probation and parole. Responding agencies exhibited creativity in managing increased and more difficult caseloads with little or no increases in human resources. Almost one-third of the projects mentioned involve differential supervision, including intensive, minimum, and unsupervised. Another third were examining their workloads or developing liaisons with other key criminal justice system actors (usually court officers) as precursors to reducing supervision levels.

About 10 percent of the respondents who listed projects used early terminations and about 25 percent relied on

alternative program assignments (e.g., pretrial diversion and drug treatment programs). Other approaches included streamlining paperwork assignments while acknowledging that presentence investigations consumed considerable time. Interestingly, only one respondent cited reduction in service levels as a solution.

The two major reasons for increased caseloads were disproportionate growth in increased supervision needs of offenders and staffing levels. These reasons imply that personnel and case management issues will continue to be major operational concerns for probation and parole agencies.

Operations and procedures

Agencies were asked questions about their needs to improve operations and procedures in five general categories: classification, community resources, scheduling, management information systems, and private sector contracting. As explained in the sections that follow, the last three are the most salient concerns for the respondents.

Classification. When asked to list projects that have improved classification, almost half the respondents stated that they had developed an evaluative

technique incorporating risk. Less than 40 percent of each respondent group indicated a need to improve initial and subsequent classification of offenders' risks or needs.

Scheduling. Since field services organizations are dependent on others to complete many of their tasks, it was hypothesized that scheduling with other criminal justice agencies might be a problem. Respondents were asked to rate the degree to which scheduling is a problem for each of the following groups or activities:

- Court hearings (sentence and revocation hearings).
- Prison officials (investigations).
- Timing for sentence investigations.
- Clerk of court (fines and fees).

From this list, only scheduling problems with regard to sentencing and revocation hearings were rated high. More than 50 percent of local directors and 47 percent of State directors noted this as a problem. Combined agencies indicated this was a more severe problem (68 percent) than the other agencies.

Management information systems. The analysis of the questions on management information systems suggests that the use of these systems is limited. Only about 15 percent of the agencies have automated systems to support classification. The overwhelming majority of respondents either (1) did not have a system in place, (2) were just in the process of developing such a capability, or (3) limited the use of their system to minor applications such as word processing.

Respondents generally wanted historical data, such as criminal record and substance abuse information on their clients, to be computerized. The computerized system would further enhance the classification procedures and make the client information readily available for other uses. A need was also expressed for information on referrals for service to be used in the ongoing management of cases. Greater concern for referral information was reported by probation offices in the New England, Mid-Atlantic, and Far West areas. Interestingly, most groups did not place a priority on improving information on management supervision assignments and levels.

The needs expressed for management information reflected different collection strategies. Historical data on criminal records and substance abuse generally depended on information from other criminal agencies and the clients, supplemented by information from families and friends. In contrast, referrals for service and associated dates could generally be found within the agency—at least during the supervision period—and were easier to maintain within a system.

Community resources. Probation and parole rely on public and private resources outside their agencies to supply many services to offenders. Directors were asked to rate the degree to which they see the need to improve or create nine types of community services (Exhibit 4). In general, parole agencies rated the items as more significant needs than the other groups.

One-half or more of the directors reported that the number of residential options were not keeping pace with offenders' needs, and at least three out of four believed increased supervision requirements were contributing to caseload management problems. Given the higher levels of supervision now required, one respondent from the Northeast argued that halfway houses and other options were needed to "restore probation and parole as legitimate sanctions." In addition to current needs for residential programs, one director noted that the challenge of the next 3 years will be "development of new programs to divert those currently in jails awaiting transfer to prison custody—to the extent that the community is not jeopardized."

Other differences appeared to reflect the stage of the criminal justice process at which offenders were referred. For example, 80 percent of parole agencies reported a need for housing referral services, compared to about 62 percent of other field offices. In contrast, there were few differences among agencies regarding the need for job readiness training, which was cited by 65 to 73 percent of the field offices. Vocational education services were reported as a need by 74 percent of parole and 61 percent of probation agencies, and 56 percent of combined agencies.

Exhibit 4
Needs for new or improved community resources

Community resources	State agencies	Probation agencies	Parole agencies	Combined agencies
Residential programs	80%	72%	83%	73%
Housing referral services	57	63	80	62
Job readiness training	65	68	73	69
Mental health services	72	60	71	67
Drug programs	81	63	79	62
Employment referral services	50	70	66	61
Alcohol programs	62	50	73	54
Vocational education	62	61	74	56
Adult basic education	31	33	60	33

There were several regional variations in perceived need for improved or expanded community resources. Although adult basic education was the lowest priority for everyone, directors in the Great Lakes, Mid-Atlantic, and Southwest rated the problem considerably higher than their colleagues. Drug programs were of more concern to parole directors in the Mid-Atlantic, Southwest, and Far West than in other parts of the country. Probation offices in New England (83 percent) and the Far West (91 percent) reported a greater need for mental health services than probation offices overall (60 percent).

Contracted services. Residential, drug, job readiness, and mental health programs can be provided internally or through arrangements with public or private service providers. Recent attention given to contracting in corrections and the reduction in government-supported social service programs suggests that the demand for privately sponsored arrangements may increase. Probation and parole officials were asked to indicate whether they currently purchase none, some, most, or all of eight specific services.

The most prevalent service currently provided under contract is staff training. At least four-fifths of the respondents contract for some or all of their staff training. In contrast, emergency food is provided under contract to fewer than one-third of parole agencies and in less than 15 percent of other field offices.

The private sector is used less overall in the Southeast than in other regions. All local directors in the Southeast report fewer purchases of drug testing and medical services. Single-function agencies contract for staff training less frequently than combined agencies. Only 7 percent of local parole offices and a lower percentage of combined agencies use the private sector for residential centers or emergency housing.

Fewer than 35 percent of Great Lakes parole directors contract for any staff training, urinalysis, mental health services, emergency food, or housing. Approximately the same percentage of probation agencies in the Great Lakes, Mid-Atlantic, and Plains-Mountain regions contract for medical services. Only about two-fifths of the Far West offices responsible for both probation and parole purchase any medical or halfway house services.

Staff recruitment and retention

As reflected in Exhibit 2, staff shortages were rated high as a problem by all three groups of agencies. The results from the recruitment and retention sections of the survey provided insights into this problem.

Recruitment. Among the most significant recruitment problems are low salaries, locating qualified professional staff, shortages of qualified minority applicants, hiring freezes, and poor image of corrections work.

In general, State directors saw fewer recruitment problems than did local officers and considered a shortage of minority applicants the most important

Difficult clients, large caseloads plague probation, parole agenices

Exhibit 5
Recruitment problems

Issue	State agencies	Probation agencies	Parole agencies	Combined agencies
Low salaries	33%	50%	53%	68%
Shortage of minority applicants	48	44	41	50
Locating qualified staff	31	46	52	49
Hiring freeze	29	47	38	40
Poor image of corrections	21	27	43	37
Entrance requirements too high	17	22	28	19

recruitment issue (Exhibit 5). In contrast, 50 percent of the local probation directors, 53 percent of the parole directors, and 68 percent of the combined agency directors considered low salaries an important recruitment problem. Approximately 45 percent of local agencies reported problems recruiting minorities.

Restrictions on hiring significantly affect recruitment for more than 47 percent of local probation directors, but only 38 percent of their counterparts in parole. In contrast, the poor image of corrections work was a significant problem for 43 percent of local parole agencies.

Retention. Agency directors were asked to rate the degree to which seven items contribute to staff turnover: salary increases, burnout, inability to use leave time, poor image of corrections work, substance abuse, inadequate career incentives, and excessive overtime. Career incentives were considered the number one staff retention issue by State directors (58 percent), local parole (70 percent), probation (60 percent), and combined agencies (71 percent). Salary increases and burnout were cited as serious by 40 percent or more of all four groups, with the remaining problems receiving substantially lower

ratings. The salary problem was considered a major issue by 68 percent of the combined agencies.

Forty-seven percent of the probation offices and 67 percent of both parole field offices and combined agency directors rated burnout as a serious retention problem. "Burnout" is used to encompass a variety of situations, from personal crises unrelated to occupation, through systemic dysfunctions in organizations, to uncertain environmental conditions. Its causes may be personal, organizational, environmental, or (more frequently) a combination. Within the limits of this survey, it was not possible to determine the specific causes of burnout at the local level. Interestingly, from other survey responses, burnout is apparently not being caused by excessive overtime (rated as a problem by only one respondent in five) or employee substance abuse (rated as a problem by less than 2 percent of all respondents).

Responses. It is clear that compensation, including "career incentives," is perceived as essential for both attracting and holding probation and parole staff. What is unclear is whether salaries are considered inadequate relative to similar occupations and other public service jobs in terms of skill levels

required and risks involved. Addressing these staffing issues tests the ingenuity of agencies facing increased demands with constrained resources. Few agencies, for example, cite new funding as the way they are trying to solve their personnel problems. Instead, evaluation and reorganization of workload are used as the major way of alleviating staffing burdens. Frequently cited recruitment methods (reported by over one-half of all those responding) included special minority recruiters and outreach in the community and at colleges.

Training. Respondents were asked to rate their agencies' interest in several training topics (Exhibit 6). Consistent with the finding that "increased supervision needs" increased caseload problems, at least 76 percent of all groups reported they need to upgrade staff skills to handle special problem offenders. Six other topics interested at least half of all local agencies: offender monitoring techniques, counseling, stress management, legal liability, report writing, and caseload management.

While overall training needs were high (with parole reporting the highest overall), responses varied substantially by agency function. Consistent with high burnout, stress management training was a greater need in parole and combined agencies, with almost 70 percent of agencies significantly interested. Probation agencies rank handling special offenders highest (80 percent), followed by case management (63 percent), offender monitoring (57 percent), and liability (57 percent).

There were also interesting differences between State and local perceptions of training needs. State directors reported a somewhat greater degree of interest in training in counseling techniques (61 percent) than did local offices (about 50 percent). Forty-one percent of State directors favored training in report writing, compared to 53 percent of local directors. Caseload management skills were among the most wanted training for local respondents, but among the least significant for State directors. If training policy and resource allocation were influenced primarily by State officials, these results suggested a need to reconcile local and State perspectives.

6. PUNISHMENT AND CORRECTIONS

Exhibit 6
Training needs

Training area	State agencies	Probation agencies	Parole agencies	Combined agencies
Handling special problem offenders	79%	80%	86%	76%
Caseload management	49	63	71	61
Offender monitoring	57	57	58	58
Liability issues	53	57	67	55
Report writing	41	54	63	53
Stress management	54	52	68	69
Counseling techniques	61	52	56	57

There are also some notable regional variations. Report writing was considered significant by parole in the Mid-Atlantic region and by parole and combined agencies in the Plains-Mountain States. Sixty-seven percent of directors responsible for both probation and parole in the Great Lakes region considered training in investigative techniques a significant need.

Legal liability training was deemed more serious by both probation and parole in the Plains-Mountain, Southwest, and Far West, where from 83 to 100 percent of agency directors considered this an important training topic.

What makes these results more striking is that monitoring, counseling, and report writing are fundamental to probation and parole functions. Along with investigations (a high priority only for parole respondents), there are the set of activities generally labeled "case management." Yet, probation and parole officials generally reported a significant need for training in these basic skills areas.

When acute basic skills deficiencies are considered along with workload, recruitment, and retention problems, they make a gloomy scenario for probation and parole. Staffing levels are not keeping pace with a growing caseload. At the same time, supervision needs are increasing. Recruitment is made difficult by low salaries that will not attract enough qualified applicants, and, once hired, employees are discouraged by poor career incentives, small salary increases, and burnout.

Conclusion

In broad strokes, the NAP survey painted a picture of America's probation and parole systems as facing unprecedented challenges. Despite recent budget increases of more than 20 percent for many agencies and major improvements in risk management, more than 75 percent of all agencies said staff increases are not keeping pace with the number of offenders.

Compounding this increase in staff-to-client ratio is the fact that at least three-fourths of the respondents believe offenders' supervision needs are greater now than in the past. Thus, not only are the numbers larger, the offenders are also a more difficult group to manage.

Fifty to sixty-eight percent of all local probation and parole offices report that salaries are too low to attract qualified applicants. Once hired, personnel did not find financial and other incentives sufficient to stay in positions where burnout is a major problem.

Employees in general have extremely high training needs, even in such basic skills as counseling, report writing, offender monitoring, and caseload management. Fifty-five to seventy-five percent of all local directors rate one or more of these as a significant need. In addition to training in basic skills, training in handling special problem offenders, stress management, and legal liabilities are also needed by the majority of respondents.

Unlike institutions, probation and parole agencies depend on a supply of community resources to carry out their core responsibilities. Today, over half the local offices report a need to expand or improve all types of community resource efforts, including drug programs, residential programs, housing referral services, vocational education, job readiness training, and mental health services.

Over the last 15 years, probation and parole agencies have expanded their domain from primarily presentence investigations and offender supervision to pretrial diversion, halfway houses, alleviating institutional crowding, and a host of other activities. "Dealing with an increased number and variety of alternative programs in an effective manner" was cited by one director as the most serious management problem over the next few years.

Data submitted by these 388 professionals suggested that not only must this type of growth stop or slow dramatically, but also that serious questions must be raised about the system's present capacity to absorb additional offenders. Large and difficult caseloads coupled with a lack of staff and a shortage of community resources reflect a criminal justice subsystem strained to its limits.

Notes

1. The random sample was drawn from counties with populations greater than 50,000 and less than 200,000.

2. *Juvenile and Adult Correctional Departments, Institutions, Agencies, and Paroling Authorities*, College Park, Maryland, American Correctional Association, 1987.

3. The 1983 National Assessment Survey was conducted for the National Institute of Justice by Abt Associates, Inc., Cambridge, Massachusetts.

NCJ 113768

Learning to Live With AIDS in Prison

Behind bars, there is a new death row, but its inmates are being dealt with in enlightened ways

Inside the walls of American prisons, convicts call it "the package." AIDS, an agonizing, protracted form of execution, has created a new death row, more dreaded than the old. Over the years, cellblock grapevines buzzed with tales of prisoners who were beaten and stabbed by other inmates, or thrown into solitary confinement by guards—just for having AIDS. But now prisons, sometimes prodded by lawsuits filed by prisoner-rights organizations, are beginning to adopt enlightened policies toward convicts with AIDS. In New York state, for example, inmates who are not currently hospitalized with an AIDS-related illness can return to the "mainstream" prison population. To reduce fear among staff and inmates, many prison systems have set up AIDS-education programs. Guards no longer automatically wear masks and gloves when escorting inmates with AIDS. Some states even allow inmates to go home to die.

When the AIDS epidemic hit in 1981, doomsayers predicted prison hospitals would overflow with junkies, homosexual rapists and cellblock "queens." "We're going to see a whopping epidemic," complained one Maryland prison official a few years ago. But to date, this grievous scenario has proved exaggerated. According to a study funded by the Justice Department, there have been only 3,136 confirmed cases of AIDS behind bars, less than 4 percent of the national total. The number of prison AIDS cases increased by 60 percent last year, but on the outside, the rate of increase was 76 percent. Of the 49,414 federal prisoners tested for AIDS antibodies since 1987, only 1,417 inmates tested positive. In 1988 less than 3 percent of new federal inmates coming in from the outside were found to be HIV positive. Says James Riley of the Texas Department of Corrections, "It's a myth that prisons are breeding grounds."

One reason that the AIDS rate in prison may be lower than expected is caution on the part of the prisoners. Some inmates say that high-risk behavior—unsafe sex in which body fluids are exchanged, sharing smuggled drugs and needles, even tattooing—has dropped off substantially. "It's gone down to a minimum," says AIDS patient Robert DeMaio, 36, who is serving time for second-degree murder in New York's Sing Sing prison.

While the stigma of AIDS has eased, reports of serious abuse continue. In a well-publicized case last year, guards in a federal prison in Richmond, Va., allegedly handcuffed Michael Henson, 33, and tossed him into "the hole" after he tested positive for AIDS antibodies. (The prison denies Henson's charges.) In Nocatee, Fla., Scott Brewer—who later tested negative—told a jailer that he might have been exposed to the virus. "They stuck me in an isolation cell with an AIDS patient," Brewer said. "The officer yelled, 'I've got one with AIDS here'." A bigger problem than abuse is unreliable medical treatment. At the U.S. Medical Center for Federal Prisoners in Springfield, Mo., Michael Lingard had to sue for the right to take regular doses of AZT, the drug that appears to prolong the lives of people with AIDS. Around the country, numerous inmates have died prematurely because prison doctors misdiagnosed their symptoms. A New York state study made last year found the mean survival of AIDS inmates was 128 days—about eight months less than on the outside.

Home to die: But even the most critical AIDS activists concede that some progress has been made. One of the most welcome reforms has been the "compassionate release" parole. California has had the policy for three years, but only two patients have gone home. New York's plan is little more than a year old, and 46 parolees have taken advantage. "Most families accept them," says Ann Quinlan, nurse adminis-

trator at Sing Sing. "They see how we deal with patients, and learn by osmosis." Some families still say no. "No one wants to die in jail," said "Lucky," 39, a Georgia convict, "but that's the way it is sometimes." (Last month Lucky died in a prison hospital.)

Allowing prisoners access to condoms for "safe sex" in prison has been the most controversial new policy. Prisons in Vermont and Mississippi, as well as New York City jails, make prophylactics available. But in Bible-belt Mississippi, where sodomy laws are still on the books, church groups protested loudly. Nationwide, prison officials are largely opposed on the ground that free condoms might encourage sexual activity, even rape, as well as create other problems. "Our security people are concerned about this," says Texas administrator Riley. "These things can be turned into slingshots. They can be filled up with a variety of items, and turned into bombs."

Several states, including California, cite the threat of homosexual rape and needle sharing to justify quarantine policies. At the California Medical Facility at Vacaville, healthy HIV-positive inmates are segregated alongside AIDS patients. Some officials fear the situation could erupt into violence. "Parole violators are living with lifers and murderers," says physician Jan Diamond who treats AIDS patients at Vacaville, "and that creates stress." David Wayne Smith, 33, a petty thief housed in the unit, agrees: "Something's not clicking and the tension is mounting all the time," he says. In a recent incident at an AIDS unit in the California Institution for Men in Chino, 15 HIV-positive inmates broke 220 windows to protest their segregation. Elsewhere, even in states that allow AIDS inmates to live in the general population, anyone with a potentially violent nature is isolated: in 1987 a Florida convict laced a

For Women: Education and Mutual Support

They tell a parable about "Blackie" at the Bedford Hills Correctional Facility, New York's maximum-security prison for women. Blackie, an inmate who died of AIDS last year, used to say she could always leave her things lying around because she knew no one would dare touch them for fear of being exposed to the virus. Then in 1985 the prison had its first AIDS Counseling and Education program (ACE), and attitudes started to change. "Eventually everyone started stealing [Blackie's things]," an ACE participant recalls. "That was a good sign."

Around the country, some of the most innovative AIDS-education programs have been developed for women be-

hind bars. In San Francisco, Sean Reynolds, an AIDS counselor for the county public-health department, uses tough talk to teach women in the tanks. "Think of condoms as your American Express card, honey," she says. "Don't leave home without it." In Boston, an activist organization called Social Justice for Women developed "AIDS 101" that features "speak outs" where inmates can go to an open mike and say what's on their minds about the disease. "Before, if women tested positive, [inmates] would call them 'AIDS-carrying bitches'," says Francine Melanson, a former drug addict who runs AIDS 101 at the Massachusetts Correctional Institute at Framingham.

"Now they're knocking down my door, asking how they can help."

The programs often inspire women to take the antibody test. "I'm going to get tested when I get out," said Michelle Thompson, 23, after one of Reynolds's seminars. "I've been on the streets since I was 11 . . . doing heroin." ACE has stayed in touch with a number of parolees and hopes to set up counseling groups on the outside. But the biggest benefit may be to prisoners who are dying of AIDS. Says Sonya, a frail Bedford Hills inmate who can remember what it was like to be harassed for having AIDS, "These people take care of you."

guard's coffee with his own AIDS-infected blood.

But at the federal medical center in Springfield, AIDS patients find a potentially positive advantage in being forced to live on a rigid schedule: they welcome being guinea pigs for experimental drugs such as CD-4, which impedes the virus's destruction of the immune system. "You've got inmates in a controlled environment," says Michael Miller, 43, who is HIV positive. "I, for one, would be standing in line for any test."

Prisons sometimes actually involve AIDS activists in policymaking, bringing them in to develop education programs. "We do role playing," says John Egan of the Mid-Hudson AIDS Task Force in White Plains, N.Y. "Inmates act out scenes like

being tested or being told they're antibody positive." But some activists say prison officials, reluctant to concede that sex and drug use cannot be controlled, provide too little education. And even when programs exist, the critics say, institutions do not require attendance, rarely offer follow-up sessions and rely on printed material for people with a high illiteracy rate.

If ignorance is one obstacle, complacency is another. Many prison officials are encouraged by the low number of AIDS cases in federal prisons, but they know that most inmates are in state facilities. Only 13 states, largely in areas where AIDS is relatively rare, screen for antibodies. Moreover, the full force of the epidemic may not have hit prisons yet. "There's no hotbed now," says Dr. C. E. Alexander,

medical director of Texas prisons. "But what's going to happen in 1995?" Indeed, on the outside, AIDS continues to spread rapidly among i.v.-drug addicts, and in New York state alone, the Department of Correctional Services estimates that between 60 and 70 percent of all inmates have a history of i.v.-drug abuse. Epidemiologists now believe the incubation period for the virus can be more than eight years, maybe as high as 20. Prison officials have to stay vigilant: if the numbers start to climb in the 1990s, the new death row may yet become as overcrowded as was originally feared.

JAMES N. BAKER with SUE HUTCHISON in Boston, NADINE JOSEPH in Vacaville, HOWARD MANLY in Atlanta, DANIEL PEDERSEN in Houston, KAREN SPRINGEN in Springfield and NED ZEMAN in New York

Of Crimes and Punishment

DOMINIC R. MASSARO

New York City

The author was named by the Governor as a Judge of the State Court of Claims in December, 1986; he is currently on assignment as a Justice of the Supreme Court, Criminal Branch, Bronx County.

This article is excerpted from a thesis now in preparation.

The name of Cesare Bonesara, the Marquis de Beccaria, is hardly known in the United States today. Yet, as much as any other, it is he who inspired our attitudes on the subject of criminal justice.

Clearly, there is a unanimity in the scholarship of criminal jurisprudence that "the glory of having expelled the use of torture from every tribunal throughout Christendom" belongs primarily to Beccaria.[1] And the overall influence of his treatise, *On Crimes and Punishments,* is generally acknowledged to have had more practical effect than any other ever written in the long campaign to reform criminal law and procedure.[2]

Beccaria's importance to America is not new, but his perceptive vision again looms large at a time when the classical approach to viewing crime and criminality is in serious revival. This revival reflects, at least in part, dissatisfaction with the positivist orientation of searching for the causes and cures of crime, which has dominated the field for the past century. Those who favor abandoning the use of the criminal law as an instrument of social reform (i.e., positivism) and emphasizing the more modest objectives of humane punishment that affords societal self-protection (i.e., classicism) argue that such a move would be quite effective in reducing crime rates.[3] Indeed, there is at present a sharp disagreement not only on alternatives to incarceration, but on the purpose of punishment itself; in particular, a pervasive anxiety continues over the ultimate punishment, the penalty of death.

Beccaria, of course, was the most forceful early opponent of capital punishment. In holding it unconstitutional in 1972, the Supreme Court, *inter alia,* spoke to his view of social inutility.[4] But his enlightened reasoning also presents for our review a philosophy of criminal law based on balanced retributive principles rooted in secure philosophic foundations.

Thus, the biennium should not pass, especially for those involved with the criminal law, without a word of appreciation for this scholar, a man once famous on both sides of the Atlantic; 1988 is the two hundred and fiftieth anniversary of his birth; 1989 the two hundred and twenty-fifth of his far-reaching publication.

Early Acclaim

Beccaria was born at Milan, in 1738. One seeks in vain for clues in his formative years which would suggest the renowned essay on criminal law and penal reform that he would later write—an essay for which he was deservedly lauded, and whose underlying concepts of human rights and individual dignity were to find expression in what is perhaps the most celebrated document of the Enlightenment, the **United States Constitution.** Likewise, it is not an exaggeration to regard his work as foreseeing all of the important reforms in the administration of criminal justice which the civilized world today considers commonplace. A re-reading of his ideas reveals them as fresh and timely as when they were penned.

The son of aristocratic parents, he received his schooling at the Jesuit College in Parma, and was graduated in law from the University of Pavia in 1758. Within six years, at 26, he would be famous. His publication, *Dei dilitti e elle pene* (Liviono, 1764), later published under the title, *An Essay on Crimes and Punishments* (London, 1767), was enthusiastically received and widely acclaimed. Sixty editions would issue in a score of languages.

Chief amongst his admirers was Voltaire, the most popular writer of the century. In his *Commentary*, Voltaire endorsed almost all of Beccaria's ideas and stressed the urgency of penal reforms.[5] Many of the principles contained in that celebrated French document, the Declaration of the Rights of Man, are taken almost word for word from Beccaria's treatise.

Frederick II of Prussia expressed his admiration by complaining, in a letter to Voltaire, that Beccaria "had left hardly anything to be gleaned after him; we need only follow what he has so wisely indicated."[6] Marie Teresa of Austria and Grand Duke Leopold of Tuscany, publicly declared their intentions to be guided by the book in the reformation of their laws. Catherine the Great of Russia called upon its author to reside at her court and attend to the necessary reforms in person.[7]

In England, it was Beccaria's treatise, as Sir William Holdsworth states, that "helped Blackstone to crystallize his ideas and it was Beccaria's influence which helped to give a more critical tone to his treatment of the English criminal law than to his treatment of any other part of English law."[8] Across the Atlantic, America's Founding Fathers took inspiration.

While the book was being received with great enthusiasm in enlightened circles, tradition jurists and the inquisitional Council of Venice were quick to attack. In 1776, the treatise was placed on the index of condemned books by the Church of Rome.[9] But this adverse criticism proved of little consequence; and Beccaria was saved from further difficulty when the head of Milan adminstration, Count Carlo Firmian, both praised the book to his Austrian overlord and intervened personally to end attempts at persecution. The Austrian government itself was moved to assign Beccaria a professorial chair in law at the Palatine College of Milan.[10]

State of the Criminal Law

Beccaria dealt with the state of the criminal law. His was a tightly reasoned attack designed to undermine inequity. That his book gave rise to hostility, it did so only from those who stood to gain by the perpetuation of the prevailing system. The fact that the essay was at first published anonymously suggests the author's fear of retaliation. But the Patriotic Society of Berne, even before knowing who the author was, decided to award a gold medal to "a citizen who dared to raise his voice in favor of humanity against the most deeply ingrained prejudices."[11] Once it was clear the Milanese political authorities welcomed the treatise, anonymity was discarded.

To fully appreciate Beccaria, it is important to remember that he wrote in a period when Church theology of the Fall from Grace and the doctrine of the divine right of kings were pitted against the intellectualism and nationalism of contemporary thought. The conventional wisdom held that individuals come together by way of social contract; that societal control of aberrant behavior is best exercised by way of fear; and that the right of punishment for criminal acts was ceded by the individual to the state.

To understand the reason Beccaria's brief essay created such excitement, one need only to recall the criminal law in Europe. As for the characteristic of cruelty, it was considered dutiful — on the basis of narrowly interpreted divine law — to apply literally the biblical retaliation, the *lex talionis* of "an eye for an eye."[12] Moreover, the supposed divine origin of this principle precluded any mitigation.

> The criminal law of eighteenth century Europe was . . . repressive, uncertain and barbaric. Its administration permitted . . . incredibly arbitrary and abusive practices. The agents of the criminal law . . . were allowed tremendous latitude in dealing with persons accused and convicted . . . and corruption was rampant. . . .
>
> Fantastic as it may now seem . . . the criminal law vested in officials the power to deprive persons of their freedom, property and life without regard for any of the principles which are now embodied in the phrase 'due process of law.' Secret accusations were in vogue and persons were imprisoned on the flimsiest of evidence. Torture, ingenious and horrible, was employed to wrench confessions . . . Judges were permitted to exercise unlimited discretion in punishing . . . The sentences imposed were arbitrary, inconsistent and depended upon the status and power of the convicted. Punishments inflicted upon the more unfortunate of the offenders were extremely severe. A great array of crimes were punished by death not infrequently preceded by inhuman atrocities. Equality before the law as a principle of justice was practically non-existent . . . [N]o distinction was made between the accused and the convicted. Both were detained in the same institution and subjected to the same horrors . . . This practice prevailed in regard to the convicted young and old, the murderer and the bankrupt, first offenders and hardened criminals, men and women. All such categories of persons were promiscuously thrown together free to intermingle and interact.[13]

England was the only European country which had resisted the inquisitorial system. And while the procedure there was more advanced — open accusations, public trials, the institution of the jury — its corporal punishments were just as cruel. Death by hanging was inflicted with incredible frequency, even for small thefts.[14] By the time George III ascended the throne in 1760, 86 crimes were so punishable.[15]

Most of England's laws were still underwritten. And trial by jury had to be expressly accepted by the accused. The silent could not be tried. Recourse to the torment of iron weights to break one's body and lead to death was inflicted; a man would suffer it to avoid conviction. In this way his lands and goods were not confiscated and preserved for his family. This absurd practice was not abolished until 1772.

Imprisonment as a penalty was thought a mitigation of the harshness of the *lex talionis*.[16] Early prisons, as noted, were notoriously disagreeable places, as horrible and as frightening as the corporal and capital sentences they were replacing! Whipping the inmate upon reception, at stated intervals, and again upon release was commonplace. The view was that imprisonment constituted a severe form of punishment, and the business of institutional discipline was to make life so dehumanizing that men would be afraid to commit crime again.

Root of Thought

A review of the highlights of Beccaria's thin volume is now in order: The social contract theory is the root of its intellectual orientation. "Laws are the conditions under which men unite to form a society," Beccaria writes.[17]

> [T]he sum of all . . . liberty of each individual constitutes the sovereignty of a nation . . . deposited in and administered by a legitimate sovereign. But merely to have established this deposit was not enough; it had to be defended against private usurpation . . . . It is because of this that punishments were established . . .

Beccaria warns, however, that every punishment which is not founded upon the absolute necessity to defend the liberty and rights of all the people is tyrannical.

He then states the principle which should guide all legislation. The enactment of law has but one purpose: "the greatest happiness shared by the greatest number."[18] While recognizing progress in many fields, he points to the deplorable state of the criminal law and the irregularities found in criminal procedure.

"The immortal Montesquieu has . . . touched upon this subject [and] truth . . . has obligated me to follow . . .," he notes. "If by defending the rights of man and of . . . truth I should help to save from the agonies of death some wretched victim of tyranny and ignorance . . . [his] thanks and tears . . . would console

me for the contempt of all mankind."

Having set forth his basic principle, Beccaria declares the source of law to be the legislature, not the judiciary.

> [T]he authority of making penal law can reside only with the legislator, who represents the whole society. No magistrate can, with justice, inflict punishments upon another . . . that exceeds the limits fixed by the laws . . . [nor] under any pretext, augment the punishment already established . . . .

Beccaria holds that there can be no crime and no punishment without a law, and that no law can have a retroactive effect.

He states that law should apply equally to all, regardless of station; and that courts are needed to resolve issues of fact. Likewise, he holds that while the right to punish has been ceded by the individual, if severe punishment is useless in the prevention of crime, such cruelty is contrary to enlightened reason and justice.

Further, since judges are not legislators, they have no right or authority to interpret penal laws, but simply to apply them; their task is to determine whether a person has or has not acted contrary to law. And in so doing, judges should conduct the inquiry with strict adherence to rules. The inequities that may arise from a policy of formal application of penal laws, according to Beccaria, cannot be compared in their deleterious effect with the inequities that may flow from judicial discretion in consulting "the spirit of the laws," then a popular axiom. The power to remedy any such inequity should be vested in legislators that life, property and freedom be maximized.

"In this way citizens acquire that sense of security for their own persons which is just . . . because it enables them to calculate accurately the inconveniences of a misdeed," he notes.

Beccaria now proceeds to an exposition of the practical implica-

tions of dealing with the shortcomings and inconsistencies of the criminal law and justice system of the day.

Logical Implications

1. *Obscurity of the Laws.* Beccaria calls for the law to be written in clear language and widely published, not a feature of the period. "We can thus see how useful the art of printing, which makes the public, and not some few individuals, the guardians of the laws."

"When the number of those who can understand the sacred code of laws and hold it in their hands increases, the frequency of crimes will . . . decrease, for undoubtedly ignorance of punishments add much to the eloquence of the passion."

2. *Detention Pending Trial.* Completely arbitrary at the time, a judge was "free to imprison a citizen at his own pleasure . . . to deprive an enemy of liberty on frivolous pretexts, and to leave a friend unpunished notwithstanding the clearest evidence of his guilt."

Admitting the sometimes necessity to imprison before trial, Beccaria holds that detention must be determined by the law, the law must indicate what evidence should be required to justify it. He suggests "[a] man's notoriety, his flight, his nonjudicial confession, the confession of an accomplice, threats . . . the manifest fact of the crime . . . are proofs sufficient to justify imprisonment of a citizen." He makes it clear, however, that an accused should not be put in the same jail with convicted criminals, and that "he who has been imprisoned and acquitted, ought not to be branded with infamy."

3. *Evidence.* Beccaria is opposed to the system, then widespread, whereby a full proof of guilt is determined by two half-proofs or a number of minor proofs dependent one upon another. "When the proofs are independent of each other, that is, when the evidence is

proved otherwise than through itself, the greater the certainty of the fact." Only proof of the crime, "that exclude(s) the possibility of innocence." he says, "can authorize conviction." Where the laws are clear and precise, a judge's duty merely is to ascertain the facts.

Moreover, Beccaria is in favor of everything open, nothing secret: "Let the verdicts be made public so that opinion, the best social restraint, may serve to restrain passions."

4. *Jury System.* "Happy is the nation where the laws need not be a science!," Beccaria tells us. The jury system is to him preferable.

> Most useful is the law that each man ought to be judged by his peers . . . [N]either the superiority with which the prosperous man regards the unfortunate, nor the disdain with which the inferior regards his superior, can have any place in judgment . . . . It also accords with justice to permit the accused to refuse on suspicion, and without opposition, a certain number of his judges.

5. *Witnesses.* Here Beccaria argues that the true measure of credibility of a witness is nothing other than his interest in telling or not telling the truth; therefore, no testimony should be rejected beforehand. "For this reason it is frivolous to insist that women are too weak [to testify] . . . and meaningless to insist on the infamy of the infamous when they have no interest in lying."

According to him, "the credibility of a witness must diminish in proportion to the hatred, or friendship, or close connections between him and the accused"; and he calls attention to "the tone, the gesture, all that precedes or follows the different ideas men attach to the same words" in determining credibility.

6. *Secret Accusations.* The weakness of government is found here, Beccaria argues. To accuse in this manner "makes men feel false and deceptive" because "whoever can suspect another of being an informer beholds in him an enemy." "Who," he asks, "can defend himself

against calumny when it comes armed with tyranny's strongest shield, secrecy?"

Admitting that "this evil practice [is] deeply ingrained in nations," he adds "were I called upon to dictate new laws . . . before authorizing such a practice, my hand would tremble. . . . "

Beccaria tells us that "public accusations are more suited to a republic, in which the principal passion ought to be for the public good . . . but every government, republican as well as monarchic, ought to inflict [punishment] upon the false accuser . . . . "

7. *Oaths.* "The affairs of heaven are regulated by laws altogether different from those that regulate human affairs," Beccaria asserts in dealing with self incrimination. "Why compromise one with the other? Why confront a man with the terrible alternative of either sinning against God or concurring in his own ruin? The law that requires such an oath commands one to be either a bad Christian or a martyr?"

8. *Torture.* Here Beccaria reaffirms with great strength the enlightened viewpoint, adding his own eloquence based on the principle that a man is innocent unless proven guilty.

> A cruelty consecrated by the practice of most nations is torture of the accused, either to make him confess the crime or to clear up contradictory statements, or to discover accomplices, or to purge him of infamy in some incomprehensible way or, finally, to discover other crimes of which he might be guilty but of which he is not accused.

He continues, "Crime is either certain or uncertain: if certain, no punishment should be inflicted other than the one established by law; if uncertain, it is wrong to torture an innocent man, since he must be considered innocent as long as his guilt has not been proven."

"What right is it . . . which empowers a judge to inflict punishment on a citizen while doubt still remains as to his guilt or innocence?" Beccaria asks.

"This infamous crucible of truth is a still-standing memorial to the ancient and barbarous . . . time when trials by fire and boiling water, as well as the uncertain outcomes of duels, were called judgments of God . . .," he notes.

> A strange consequence that necessarily follows from the use of torture is that the innocent is placed in a condition worse than the guilty . . . the circumstances are all against the former. Either he confesses the crime and is condemned, or he is declared innocent and has suffered a punishment he did not deserve.

"This abuse should not be tolerated in the eighteenth century," he intones.

9. *Prosecution and Prescriptions.*[19] Trials, Beccaria says, should be held with the least possible delay because promptness of punishment is "one of the principal checks against crime." Of course, the accused "must be allowed opportune time and means for his defense . . . the laws should fix a definite length of time both for the defense of the accused and for the proof of crimes; the judge would become a legislator were he to decide the time necessary for the latter." But, he adds, "[a]trocious crimes which are long remembered do not, when they have been proved, merit any prescription in favor of the criminal who has spared himself by flight."

10. *Attempts, Accomplices, Impunity.* "Laws do not punish intent; but surely an act undertaken with the manifest intention of committing a crime deserves punishment, though less than that which is due upon the actual execution of the crime," Beccaria tells us.

As regards accomplices and favorable treatment accorded those who reveal his companions, he sees disadvantages as well as advantages. One disadvantage is that "the nation authorizes treachery"; another is that the tribunal "simply reveals its own uncertainty and weakness of its law" when it has to seek the aid of those who break it. On the other hand, such concession makes possible "the prevention of greater crimes which intimidate the populace" by the prosecution of criminals who otherwise remain free.

While hesitant on the subject, Beccaria states: "It would seem to me that a general law promising impunity to the accomplice who reveals a crime would be preferable . . . for the mutual fear that each accomplice would then have of being alone in his risk would prevent [criminal] associations."

11. *Punishment.* A fundamental chapter, Beccaria sets forth the principle "that the purpose of punishment is neither to torment and afflict . . . nor to undo a crime already committed." Primarily, he holds, punishment is to insure the continued existence of society; it is an educative process. "The purpose can only be to prevent the criminal from inflicting new injuries on citizens and to deter others from similar acts. Always keeping due proportions," he importunes,

> [s]uch punishments ought to be chosen which will make the strongest and most lasting impression on the minds of men, and inflict the least torment on the body of the criminal.
>
> For punishment to attain its end . . . [it] has only to exceed the advantage derivable from the crime; in this one should include the certainty of punishment and the loss of the good which the crime might have produced. All beyond this is superfluous and for that reason tyrannical.

The author relates directly the state of a nation to its scales of punishment.

12. *Death Penalty.* In considering the death penalty, Beccaria argues that it is neither legitimate nor necessary. "[I am] prompted to examine whether death is really useful and just in a well organized government," he asks.

He proposes that men in forming the social contract did not cede their right to life. To have done so would have been illogical since the primary reason for the creation of society was to better insure the right of men

to live. "What manner of right can men attribute to themselves to kill their fellow human being? Was there ever a man who can have wished to leave to other men the choice of killing him?"

Beccaria advances two possible reasons where the death penalty may be just and necessary: threat to the national security and "if death were the only real way of restraining others from crime." But, he explains,

> [i]t is not the intensity of punishment that has the greatest effect on the human spirit, but its duration . . . . It is not the terrible yet momentary spectacle of the death . . . but the long and painful example of a man deprived of liberty . . . which is the strongest curb against crimes.

Thus, Beccaria is in favor of imprisonment as a civilized alternative, and for the more serious crimes, he prescribes a life sentence.

This is perhaps his most daring proposal: he challenges the right of men to kill other men for any reason; he equates execution, though it may be authorized by law, with an act of barbarity. "[A] life sentence in place of the death penalty has in it what suffices to deter any determined spirit," he asserts. "It seems to me absurd that the laws, which are an expression of the public will, which detest and punish homicide, should themselves commit it."

Penalties and Crimes

The subsequent chapters of Beccaria's book deal with other types of penalties, types of crimes and their classification. He stresses again the importance of swiftness in the conviction of criminals.

> The more promptly and more closely punishment follows upon the commission of a crime, the more just and useful . . . so much stronger and more lasting in the human mind is the association of these two ideas, crime and punishment; they then become inseparable, one to be considered as the cause, the other as the necessary inevitable effect.

Therefore, together with urging a milder system of laws than then in effect, Beccaria says must go the certainty of punishment. A pardon, in his view, "is the tacit disapprobation for a code." Showing men that crimes may be forgiven encourages the hope of impunity. "Let the laws be inexorable, but let the legislators be humane."

The same reason that makes Beccaria oppose the granting of pardons makes him oppose asylum. Referring to the ecclesiastical privilege of the day, he says: "Within the confines of a country there should be no place independent of the laws."[20] He is firm for the proposition that one cannot be subject to two contradictory codes of law. Likewise where a criminal escapes to another country; Beccaria is for the principle of extradition, that justice be rendered in the country of the misdeed(s). However, he sets forth the prerequisite that all participating nations to such a pact must have moderate and just laws. As long as in some countries absurd and cruel punishments exist, deportation may itself be a cruel act.

Beccaria then goes on to detail the necessity of a just proportion between crimes and punishments. "It is in the common interest," he says, "not only that crimes not be committed, but also that they be less frequent in proportion to the harm they cause." Therefore, he concludes, obstacles that deter men from committing crimes should be stronger when the crimes are more harmful to the public good.

"Whoever sees the same death penalty, for instance, decreed for the killing of a pheasant and for the assasination of a man . . . will make no distinction between such crimes," he maintains. Moral feelings will be numbed. "It is enough for the wise legislator to mark the principal points of division [between types of crimes] without disturbing the order [of classes of crime], not assigning to crimes of the first grade the punishment of the last."

Having made it clear that the only true measure of crime is the harm done to society, Beccaria states that the law should apply equally. It will be recalled that in his time equality before the law was more often a theoretical right with special privileges in favor of the nobility and the clergy.

"The great and the rich," he says, "should not have [advantage over] the weak and the poor. There is no liberty whenever the laws permit . . . a man [to] cease to be a person and become a thing." He asserts that punishments should be the same for "the first and least citizen."

Turning to the types of crimes, he makes clear that there should be no attempt to confuse human and divine justice. Men cannot judge or punish those who sin against God. "[This is] a relation of dependence on a perfect Being who has reserved to himself alone the right to be legislator and judge . . . ." With reference to the forces of the Inquisition, Becarria says, "If God has established eternal punishment for anyone who disobeys his omnipotence, what insect is it that shall dare to take the place of divine justice."

He then treats with crimes against the security of the citizen. "Some crimes are attempts against the person, others against property. The penalties for the first should always be corporeal punishments," he states. He makes a clear distinction between simple thefts and those accompanied by assault. For the former, fines or short prison terms are thought proper; for the latter, severer punishment, since the sacredness of human life is imperiled.

Suicide he considers a crime, probably under a rubic that would otherwise weaken his opposition to the death penalty. In any event, he is quick to add that no punishment should follow because it would fall either to the innocent relatives of the deceased or else upon a cold and in-sensitive body. "If the latter is apt to impress the living no more than would the flaying of a statute, the former is unjust and tyrannical for political liberty in men requires of necessity that punishments be purely personal."

There is one class of crimes that Beccaria tells us he does not wish to treat, "a class of crimes that has covered Europe with human blood and has raised those awful piles where living human bodies are used to serve as food for flames." These are the so-called crimes of heresy, whereby people were prosecuted for expressing thoughts contrary to prevailing belief.

By his words Beccaria shows that he is in favor of freedom of conscience and against authoritarian mind control. While it cannot be overlooked that fear of persecution that might otherwise have followed hedge his expression, the author's indirect criticism is, nonetheless, clear: "[R]easonable men will see that the place, the age, and the matters at hand do not permit me to examine the nature of such a crime."

In a dual meaning, he sarcastically refers to them as "well beyond the capacity of mortals."

In the final chapter, Beccaria examines ways of preventing crime. "It is better to prevent crimes than to punish them," he writes. "This is the ultimate end of good legislation." Several ways are suggested in addition to his already mentioned code of just, clearly stated laws, known and understood by the citizenry, for "enlightenment accompanies liberty." Included are an honest judiciary, a sufficient number of judges, and the rewarding of virtuous deeds upholding of the law. Finally, Beccaria says, "the surest but most difficult way to prevent crimes is by perfecting education" through a selection of creative ideas to lead youth.

In a short concluding paragraph, the author sets forth a theorem:

"In order for punishment not to be an act of violence of one or of many against a private citizen, it must be essentially public, prompt, necessary, the least possible in the given circumstances, proportionate to the crimes and dictated by the law."

Thus closes the first work that sets down uniformly applied principles for reforming the criminal law. Because Beccaria expressed himself in a systematic and concise way, with human rights clearly defined and buttressed with logical argument, his book quickly became the classic that it is.

American Legacy

In his *Commentaries on the Laws of England*, Blackstone referred to the criminal laws of other nations and said that their inhumanity and mistaken policy had already been pointed out by writers such as Beccaria. "But even with us in England," continued Blackstone, "where our crown law is with justice suppose to be more nearly advanced to perfection . . . even here we shall occasionally find room to remake some particulars that seem to want revision and amendment.[21]

The Lord Chancellor was the first author in England to follow Beccaria in some of the most progressive ideas and principles.

A young jurist, Jeremy Bentham, began to be active at this time and was soon to show his enthusiasm and dedication in the battle for reform. A disciple of Beccaria, Bentham could not refrain from addressing his mentor: "Oh, my master, first evangelist of reason, you who have raised your Italy so far above England . . . .[22]

In his judicial essays Bentham made clear that Beccaria was the principal source of his penal theories. The English reformer Samual Romilly would join the battle for humane legislation,[23] but reform of the English criminal code would not follow until the next century.

Benjamin Franklin, then serving as American minister to France, spoke often of the cruelty and absurdity in existing legal systems. He wrote discussing those aspects of English law that seemed to him most reprehensible, namely, the disproportion between offenses and punishments. "To put a man to death for an offense which does not deserve death, is it not murder?" In referencing the execution of a woman convicted at Old Bailey for stealing gauze from a shop, he exclaims,

[m]ight not that woman, by her labour, have made reparation . . . . Is not all punishment inflicted beyond the merit of the offense, so much punishment of innocence. In this light, how vast is the annual quantity of not only injured, but the suffering innocence, in almost all the civilized states of Europe![24]

Franklin did not follow Beccaria in his opposition to the death penalty as a question of principle however he shared the view that crime flourishes in a climate of cruelty and violence.

But Franklin was not the first to see the light. Beccaria's great popularity in America was already significant. English editions of his work were available, and an American edition was advertised in *Livingston's New York Gazetteer* as early as October 28, 1773. An edition appeared in Charleston in 1777.[25]

John Adams, when he took up the defense of the British soldiers implicated in "The Boston Massacre," paraphrased Beccaria's Introduction to an unfriendly 1770 court:

I am for the prisoners at the bar, and shall apologize for it only in the words of the marquis Beccaria: 'If I can be the instrument of preserving one life, his blessings and tears of transport shall be a sufficient consolation to me for the contempt of all mankind.'[26]

None were found guilty of murder, the trial a great success for Adams.[27] So highly prized was Beccaria's book that Adams willed it to his son.

The criminal law in America underwent significant changes immediately following the Revolution.

Punishments were reduced in severity and "cruel and unusual punishments," so common in the colonial administration(s), were abolished.[28] These changes came at different periods, in the different states, but the trend definitely began in Pennsylvania.

Robert J. Turnbull, in a series of articles which appeared during February, 1796 in the *Charleston Daily Gazette* wrote of penal law reform on a visit to that state:

[s]everal circumstances combined to make . . . alteration expedient, and among others the small and valuable gift of the immortal Beccaria to the world had its due influence . . . for on the framing of the new constitution of the state, in 1776, the legislature were directed to proceed . . . to the reformation of the penal laws and to invent punishments less sanguinary and better proportional to the various degrees of criminality.[29]

Thus, after a seris of legislative acts, death was reserved for "murder in the first degree."[30] At the same time, hard labor was first introduced as the penalty for other major offenses.

The exemplary administration of the Pennsylvania penitentiaries, which likewise were to serve as a model in other states, are described by Turnbull in a classic report[31] on a Philadelphia institution he called a "wonder of the world." "[O]f all the . . . penitentiaries I ever read or heard of, I have met with none founded on similar principles, or which could in any manner boast of an administration so extensively useful and humane."

The influence of Beccaria's ideas in Pennsylvania was so great that several prominent men went so far as to follow him for the complete abolition of the death penalty. In 1792, Dr. Benjamin Rush, a signer of the Declaration of Independence and drafter of America's first reasoned argument against capital punishment, proclaimed that "the marquis of Beccaria has established a connexion between the abolition of capital punishment and the order and the happiness of society."[32]

In neighboring Virginia, we find yet another proof of Beccaria's early acclaim. Thomas Jefferson's *Commonplace Book* extracts him no less than twenty-six times. Written between 1774 and 1776, Jefferson was then serving on the Virginia Committee of Revisors for the reform of the legal system. By 1778, Jefferson's "Bill for Proportioning Crimes and Punishments in Cases hertofore Capital" footnotes Beccaria four times.

In his autobiography, Jefferson credits the Pennsylvania example and writes: "Beccaria . . . had satisfied the reasonable world of the unrightfulness and inefficacy of the punishment of crimes by death; and hard labor on roads, canals and other public works, had been suggested as a proper substitute. The Revisors had adopted these opinions . . . ."[33] When adopted, the law limited the death penalty to the crimes of treason and murder.

Likewise, Jefferson agreed with Beccaria on the subject of restricting pardons: "When laws are made as mild as they should be . . . pardons are absurd. The principle of Beccarria is sound."[34]

Thus, it may be said with confidence that we owe it in great measure to Beccaria if laws were enacted which reduced considerably the number of executions in the newly established American states.[35] Indeed, the Northwest Ordinance of 1787, enacted under the Articles of Confederation and laying the foundation by which new states might seek admission to the Union, included a prohibition against cruel and unusual punishment.

The Founding Fathers, quite naturally, identified oppression with abuse of the criminal law, and identified the rights of man with the basic right to a fair trial. The first laws of the Federal government thus show Beccaria's influence. The document promulgated at Philadelphia provides for trial by jury; it prohibits ex post facto laws and bills of attainder. Other provisions were added in the amendments to the

Constitution in 1791.[36] While the English tradition is clearly visible, there is no doubt that the writings of Beccaria are responsible for an attitude that prevailed throughout America's period of constitution-making.

William Bradford, who was later to serve as Attorney General of the United States, wrote:

[w]e perceive . . . that the severity of our [English] criminal law is an exotic plant, and not native growth . . . It has endured but, I believe, has never been a favorite. . . . and as soon as the principles of Beccaria were disseminated, they found a soil that was prepared to receive them. During our connection with Great Britian no reform was attempted; but as soon as we separated from her the public sentiment disclosed itself and this benevolent undertaking was enjoyed by the constitution. This was one of the first fruits of liberty . . . .[37]

Bradford's pamphlet is significant for it gives a review of the operation of the criminal law in colonial America as is unavailable in any other source. Crediting Beccaria as having "led the way," Bradford singles out the constitutions of New Hampshire, Vermont and Maryland as enjoying the fruits of Beccaria's "march" whose principles "serve to protect the rights of humanity and to prevent the abuses of government [and] are so important that they deserve a place among the fundamental laws of every free country."[38]

He concluded that it was doubtful whether capital punishment was at all necessary, advice, as we have noted, largely adopted.

Dean Santoro is instructive:

[M]uch of Beccaria's thoughts have found their way directly into the American Constitution. He believed in fundamental rights and 'the pursuit of happiness' — a phrase so familiar to us. Beccaria argued that punishment should fit the crime . . . .
• Beccaria attacked the arbitrary detention of persons pending trial. Our Fifth Amendment requires an indictment. Our Sixth Amendment requires a speedy trial. Our Constitution provides for bail.
• Beccaria railed against torture and cruel punishments. Our Eighth Amendment prohibits cruel and unusual punishment.
• Baccaria believed the laws of heaven were conducted by laws absolutely different from those governing human affairs. Our Fifth Amendment provides that no one need incriminate himself.
• Beccaria thought there should be no secret accusations. Our Sixth Amendment gives the accused the right to confront witnesses against him.

I do not think America would have been vastly different without [Beccaria], but clearly it is better because of [his] contribution to our freedom.[39]

Notes

[1] See, generally, Radzinowicz, Leon, *A History of English Criminal Law* (1948), I, 277-83.

[2] Barnes, Harry E. and Becker, Howard, *Social Thought from Lore to Science* (1952), I, 551.

[3] See, generally, Wilson, James Q., *Thinking About Crime* (1975); van den Haag, Ernest, *Punishing Criminals* (1975).

[4] *Furman v. Georgia*, 408 U.S. 238, 33 L. (1972). In a condemnation of punishment as simply retributive, and contrasting it with the adoption of Eighth Amendment, the court references Beccaria at Note 85, Marshall, J., concurring.
But, see, *Gregg v. Georgia*, 428 U.S. 153, (1976), 50 L. Ed. 2d 158, 97 S. Ct. 197, 97 S. Ct. 198. Although unable to agree on an opinion, seven members of the Court did find that the imposition of the death penalty for the crime of murder did not under all circumstances violate the prohibition against the infliction of cruel and unusual punishment.

[5] Maestro, Marcello, *Cesare Beccaria and the Origins of Penal Reform* (1973), 45.

[6] Voltaire, Francois-Marie Arouet, *Oeuvres Completes*, L. Ed. Moland (1877-85), L, 265.

[7] Phillipson, Coleman, *Three Criminal Law Reformers: Beccaria, Benthan, Romilly* (1923), 83 ff.

[8] Radzinowicz, *supra*, I, 346.

[9] Nicci, Savini, *Encyclopedia Cattolico*: "Beccaria, Cesare" (1949), II, 1126. *On Crimes and Punishments* remained on the list until the Index itself was abolished by the Ecumenical Council convoked by Pope John XXIII in 1962.

[10] Phillipson, *supra*, 14 ff.

[11] Maestro, *supra*, 20.

[12] One of the more quotable formulations of this general principle may be found in the Mosaic Code, the Book of Exodus 21:23:25 (King James Version of the Holy Bible): "And if any mischief follow, thou shalt give life for life, eye for eye, tooth for tooth, hand for hand, foot for foot, burning for burning, wound for wound, stripe for stripe."

[13] Monachesi, Elio, *Journal of Criminal Law and Criminology*: "Pioneers in Criminology: Cesare Beccaria (1738-1794), (Nov./Dec. 1955), 46(4), 441-42.

[14] "Once it was a capital offense to steal from the person something 'above the value of a shilling'." *McGauthu v. California*, 402 U.S. 183, 241 [1971], Douglas, J., dissenting, quoting I.J. Stephen, *History of the Criminal Law of England* 467 (1883).

[15] Bedau, H., *The Death Penalty in America* (1967 rev. ed.), Introduction. George III (1760-1820) increased the number by 60.

[16] Though used occasionally in ancient Greece and Rome, imprisonment appears first as a systematic penalty utilized by the Church for mild transgressions dealt with during the course of the Inquisition.

[17] For the quotations from Beccaria's 100-page treatise *On Crimes and Punishments* the English translation by Paolucci, Henry (1963) has been used. Specific notes referring to the test have been omitted, the translation of the contents following the sequence of chapters in the printed order of the Bobbs-Merrill edition.

[18] [Translator's Note: Many approximations of this celebrated formula are no doubt to be found in the extensive literature . . . which originated with the ancient Greeks, but there is no question that Jeremy Bentham, who made the formula famous, first encountered it here.]

[19] [Translator's Note: "As used by Beccaria, the term 'prescription' must be understood to mean 'limitation of criminal prosecution'."]

[20] The "right of sanctuary," for instance, avoided severe penalty by seeking refuge in a church, to be dealt with in accordance with the milder precept of canon law. The barbarism of treating with the "crimes" of heresy and witchcraft aside, prisoners were frequently released on commutation of sentence, in recognition of what was assumed to be evidence of restoration to the faith.

[21] Blackstone, William, *Commentaries on the Laws of England* (1769) IV, 1426.

[22] Halevy, Elie, *The Growth of the Philosophical Radicalism* (1928), 21.

[23] Maestro, *supra*, 131.

[24] Franklin to Benjamin Vaughan, March 14, 1785: *The Writings of Benjamin Franklin*, Ed. Smyth, Albert H. (1907) IX, 291 ff.

[25] Maestro, *supra*, 43.

[26] Kidder, Frederick, *History of the Boston Massacre* (1870), 232.

[27] Interestingly, two were found guilty of manslaughter, but were discharged after being burnt on the hand.

[28] In the average colony there were 12 capital crimes. This was far fewer than existed in England; yet there were many executions because "[w]ith county jails inadequate and insecure, the criminal population seemed best controlled by death . . . ." Filler, "Movements to Abolish the Death Penalty in the United States," 284, *Annals Am. Acad. Pol. & Soc. Sci.*, 124 (1952).

[29] Turnbull, Robert J., *A Visit to the Philadelphia Prison* (1796), 6.

[30] See *Pennsylvania Statutes:* An Act for the Better Preventing of Crimes, March 25, 1794.

[31] Turnbull, *supra,* 3.

[32] See Rush, Dr. Benjamin, *Consideration of the Injustice and Impolicy of Punishing Murder By Death* (1792), 3.

[33] See Jefferson, Thomas, *Writings* (1903), I, 67. It should be noted that the Pennsylvania experiment of hard labor as a public spectacle did not prove successful; in secluded penitentiaries it worked well, and this system was soon initiated in Virginia and elsewhere.

[34] See *The Complete Jefferson,* Ed. Padover, Saul Kussiel, (1943), 61.

[35] See, generally, Maestro, *supra,* 138 ff.

[36] *E.g.,* the Eighth Amendment. "[T]here is evidence in the debates of the various state conventions that were called upon to ratify the Constitution of great concern for the omission of any prohibition against torture or other cruel punishments." Furman, *supra, at 396, quoting 2 J. Elliot's Debates* 111 (2d Ed. 1876), at 447-481.

It should be noted that while the precise language of the Eighth Amendment was drawn verbatim from the English Bill of Rights of 1689, scholarship is divided as to whether the prohibition is properly read as a response to illegal punishment or as a reaction to barbaric and objectional modes of punishment, or both. The legislative history has led most historians to conclude it as a reaction to inhumane punishments. From every indication, it would appear that the framers intended to give the phrase a meaning far different from that of its English precursor. See, generally, Granucci, Anthony F., "Nor Cruel and Unusual Punishments Inflicted: The Original Meaning," 57 Calif. L. Rev. 839 (1969). It is also clear that prior to the adoption of the Amendment there was feeling in the colonies that a safeguard against cruelty was needed. See, generally, Schwartz, B., 7 *The Bill of Rights: A Documentary History,* 71 (1971).

[37] *American Journal of Legal History:* "An Enquiry How Far the Punishment of Death is Necessary in Pennsylvania" (1793), 122, 137, reprinted 1968.

[38] *Id.,* Introduction, at 127.

[39] Banquet address of Anthony J. Santoro, Dean, Delaware Law School, Order Sons of Italy in America (Pennsylvania), The Hershey Hotel, Philadelphia, October 10, 1987.

Turn the Jailhouse Into a Schoolhouse

Young inmates need an incentive to change their lives,

not go on wasting them.

Andrew James

Andrew James (a pseudonym) has spent time in a New York correctional facility. He is currently a free-lance writer completing a Master's degree in Human Resource Management.

WHAT IF INSTEAD of sending young people to jail for nonviolent offenses we sent them to school? What if we kept the fences, cameras and guards, but changed the standard inside from vegetation to education?

What if we rejected the mindless passage of time as an acceptable standard for incarcerated youth? What if we structured the young offender's time: Replaced watching "Wheel of Fortune" with English composition, replaced Penthouse and Hustler with Shakespeare and Whitman, replaced "The Price Is Right" with algebra? What if we built correctional schools where young inmates passed tests, not time?

Crazy? Impossible? A waste? Perhaps, but by what standard? The fact that our prison population is exploding and that the rate of repeat offenders tops 75 percent indicates that we are achieving very little correction with our current approach. Which, then, is crazier? Locking youths in a cage with adult criminals and expecting them to see the error of their ways, or locking them in school and offering them a chance to change their ways?

Skeptics will argue that while teaching underachievers to read and write is admirable, it hardly solves the crime problem. And they are right. Correctional schools will not make crime disappear — but is that a realistic standard? A trusted business axiom suggests that when a problem is too large, too complex, or too diverse to attack in its entirety, then break it down, identify key pieces and target goals whose accomplishment moves you in the right direction. Correctional schools offer such a constructive alternative.

Targeting youth recognizes the clinical reality that the earlier problems are addressed, the greater the chance of rehabilitation. The sooner we reach young offenders, the fewer appearances they will make in backlogged courtrooms, the fewer trips they will make to overcrowded jails and the less damage they will do to society and themselves.

Youths who succeed in correctional schools will provide a valuable pool of role models for other youth. The "Just Say No" and "Stay In School" messages are more potent when delivered by young people who know firsthand the price of doing otherwise.

Most states have laws designed to bring education into jails. New York, for example, mandates that incarcerated youths 16 to 21 years old be given the opportunity to work toward a General Equivalency Diploma (GED). The degree to which jailhouse education fails may vary with the facility, but a look at one county correctional installation in New York — which I won't name but will call one of the state's best — illustrates the magnitude of the problem.

The jail's staff includes an education coordinator, a teacher and a teacher's assistant. Once a week, a social worker visits. The classroom can accommodate 15 students, is equipped with several IBM PC computers and uses excellent IBM learning software. While taking nothing away from the dedicated efforts of the education staff, several factors dilute the effectiveness of their efforts.

First, participation in the GED program is strictly voluntary — a youth decides on a day-to-day basis whether or not he will attend class. However, no incentive exists for enrollment or attendance. The inmate's sentence will not be reduced if he obtains a GED; he will not receive an extra hour of family visitation for enrolling in the program. Nor will he be allowed an extra phone call, or be moved from a cell block where older inmates harass him to nicer open-bay quarters with windows instead of bars. He will even have to buy his own paper and pens.

On the other hand, if he volunteers to wash the sheriff's patrol cars, he will be made a trustee and given those visitation, phone and living perks. In fact, if he volunteers for any detail from peeling potatoes to mopping floors, he will improve his living conditions and trustee perks. In this present system, what attraction does education offer?

Second, the jail was designed to incarcerate, not educate. Inefficiency in moving inmates from cells to class, mandatory "lock-in" periods and unscheduled interruptions reduce classroom time for inmates to an average of just two hours a day. The jail's library can accommodate only 10 of the nearly 300 inmates and is open just six hours a day. Its shelves are lined with legal books, case studies and dockets that would stump a first-year law student much less a high school dropout. A smattering of paperback mysteries, romances and religious books completes the inadequate inventory.

Female inmates are at an even greater disadvantage when it comes to education in this facility. While understandably housed in a separate part of the jail, state law provides for co-ed classroom instruction to permit equal access to educational services. The sheriff's policy, however, prohibits such instruction for "security reasons." As a result, women are not able to use the computers. Their instruction hinges on copied pages of material shuttled back and forth by the teacher's assistant. The reduction in quality of education afforded women is significant.

Environment, however, deals the death blow to jailhouse education. Outside the classroom there is not the thinnest veil of rehabilitative concern. Guards and inmates alike are engulfed in an atmosphere of despair and hostility. What reinforcement is there for self-improvement when intimidation, coercion and cynicism are the tools of daily survival? It is hard enough to survive the racial tensions, cramped quarters and constant harassment — especially for younger inmates — let alone try to get an education. We hand youthful prisoners buried alive in a human landfill a spoon and tell them to dig themselves out. Who are we kidding?

The operating budget of this county jail will ap-proach two **$2 million this year, a sizable investment for any small community. Are we getting an** acceptable return on those tax dollars? Statistics from this facility suggest we are not.

The percentage of persons passing the GED exam has fallen steadily the past three years from 56 percent in 1987, to 44 percent in 1988, to just 28 percent in 1989.

While the average passing score has moved little— 244 in 1987, 254 in 1988 and 248 in 1989. The average failing score has plummeted from 201 in 1987 to 182 in 1989. Even more discouraging, not one person who failed a GED exam and took a remake exam ever passed the remake; not one person in three years.

What's behind these dismal statistics is a blind allegiance to a "lock 'em up and throw away the key" mentality. But is it really in our best interests to pay $50-plus per day over three months while a 16-year-old just sits in jail waiting for the legal machinery to process his disorderly conduct charge? Are we really being tough on crime by sending a 17-year-old shoplifter to jail for six months—or just tough on our wallets?

What correction is taking place while we pay for an 18-year-old drug user to sit in jail for a year? Should we then be surprised when his first instinct after release is to get high? Does sending a 20-year-old illiterate to jail for writing a bad check teach him to balance a checkbook? Spending millions of dollars on "correctional facilities" that do not correct constitutes fraud.

It is pointless to continue expecting correction from a system where failure is assumed and accepted. We can change direction. We must change direction. When mountains of garbage filled our landfills to capacity and threatened to pollute our drinking water, we turned to recycling as a constructive step in the right direction. We must now apply that same wisdom to managing the human landfills we call "correctional facilities." If we understand the value of recycling garbage, can we be any less willing to recycle young minds?

Family Violence Program at Bedford Hills...

Feeling 'Free and Safe' in Prison

There is a group of women in prison who say that for the first time in their lives they feel "free and safe."

They are women participating in a unique Family Violence Program at the Bedford Hills Correctional Facility.

Many of them are in prison because they struck back, killing the men who had brutalized them.

Program Coordinator Sharon Smolick, herself the survivor of an abusive childhood, calls it a "sad commentary about our society" that the women had to go to prison to find safety and freedom. However, she stresses the importance of understanding that "prisons are not the solution to the problem."

Bedford's program grew out of an unprecedented hearing at the prison in 1985, during which 12 incarcerated women testified before a panel of top state officials.

The components that made the Bedford program possible are rare, Ms. Smolick said:

- A willingness on the part of the Commissioner of the New York State Department of Correctional Services and his staff to have the first public hearing ever held in a maximum security prison and to address some of the broader issues of incarcerated women.

- A humane superintendent and institutional staff that supported both the women and the process.

- A concerned director of the NYS Division for Women.

- The time and commitment of the staffs of the Governor's Office on Domestic Violence and the NYS Coalition Against Domestic Violence.

After the hearing, a support group was maintained for the 12 women who testified.

Ms. Smolick became involved as a social worker and was named program coordinator in November 1987.

Jean Kwartler, who was on the staff of the Division for Women working in the field of domestic violence, was loaned to the program. She now is on Bedford's staff.

There are 127 women in the program, with another 60 on a waiting list. There are support groups for battered women, adult survivors of child abuse and women with child-related crimes, as well as a therapy group for incest survivors.

Through the support of the Women's Resource Center in Mahopec, formerly battered women from the outside community are matched with seasoned women at Bedford and trained as co-facilitators for support groups.

Recently, a grant was obtained to fund a graduate student internship program with the Child Abuse Center of Fordham University's School of Social Work.

This will provide approximately 100 hours of clinical services for the program.

An Educational and Public Awareness Campaign Committee is working with ODN productions, a contract agency funded by the Children's and Family

From *DOCS Today*, Spring 1990, pp. 6-7, 10. *DOCS Today*, published by the New York State Department of Correctional Services.

Bedford Women Describe Experiences

The women in Bedford Hills' Family Violence Program have many different stories to tell about the experiences that led them to seek help and what the program has meant to them.

"When I was growing up I felt very unloved, very detached. I always felt it was my fault. I thought I had this disease inside of me."

Kathy S., an adult survivor of childhood abuse, heard about the Family Violence Program when she was taking part in other programs at the prison. She decided to give it a try.

"It was hard going at first," she says. "Now I look forward to it."

Joining one of the support groups in the program is strictly voluntary. While each group has trained facilitators, themselves survivors of some form of family violence, it is the members themselves who decide what they want to discuss.

Talking about what happened to them is painful.

When Connie first entered the program she didn't even realize she was a battered woman.

"I didn't know there was a name for what happened to me, that I was not the only one who felt the isolation and the fear. ... I was so closed down I never talked about my experiences of being abused."

The program has given Connie the confidence to talk about what she has gone through.

"I know that if I don't break the silence I'm not going to be able to heal," she says.

Viniece has found it reassuring to have a place to go where she is not different.

Trust Fund, NYS Department of Social Services, to conduct a four-year statewide public education media campaign for family violence prevention.

In her frequent speaking engagements, Ms. Smolick shares what the women in the Bedford program want others to know.

First she relates some horrifying statistics that show the pervasiveness of family violence in our society.

- Every 15 seconds in this country a woman is reported beaten (that is 5,760 women a day).

- Every three minutes a rape is reported (only 10 to 25 percent of all rapes are estimated to be reported.

- Twenty percent of all murders in the U.S. are committed within the family, 13 percent of them by spouses or boyfriends.

- Forty percent of female homicide victims in the U.S. are killed by family members or boyfriends.

- Alleged deaths from child abuse and maltreatment increased 21 percent from 1984 through 1986.

- Although child sexual assault and incest are among the most under-reported crimes, one in three girls and possibly one in four boys will be sexually molested in the U.S. before the age of 18.

- Every four days a woman is beaten to death by a man she knows well.

- One in every 30 elderly experience an incidence of violence (physical, verbal or deprivation of basic needs) by their family.

Ms. Smolick stresses that family violence "is not just an issue for women in prison, it is not just an issue for battered and abused women in poor communities, it is not just a women's issue.

"It is, in fact and experience, a societal problem ... and it affects all of us."

The women in the program at Bedford Hills call it a "blessing in disguise."

For the first time in their lives they feel safe and free. They are bonding together and learning that they are not alone, and need no longer be afraid. They are becoming stronger and wiser.

Their motto, Ms. Smolick says, is simple: "Stop the silence, no more violence."

Abusers as well as the abused need help and the only way to end the violence is for those being abused, and those who are aware of abuse, to speak out.

The Family Violence Program coordinator tells her own story as an example of what can happen.

"For as many years as I can remember as a child, I went to school with black and blue marks all over my body, chunks of hair ripped out of my head. I was withdrawn and angry. I fit nowhere, rarely laughed and told no one what I was living through.

"At age 12 I was raped by a neighborhood 18-year-old under knife point. Afterward I scalded 2/3 of my body in hot water trying to wash away the shame."

She started drinking boilermakers, continuing until she discovered heroin.

"By the age of 16 I was a heroin user. The very first time I used heroin, I remember clearly thinking that no one would ever be able to hurt me again. And for the next 10 years I anesthetized my pain, victimizing myself and others."

Through all that time, even when she needed medical care for a stab wound she received during the rape, "no one, not one single person, ever stopped and asked me if I was being abused."

Ms. Smolick survived her traumatic childhood and was able to turn her life around. Now she is helping others.

"It is not an easy task to untangle the years of abuse in people's lives, but it is possible," she says. "It is possible because the survivors work hard on their healing ... I have never seen the courage of the women at Bedford fail. Regardless of the difficulties they face in their lives, they come together weekly and roll up their sleeves and go to work in their groups."

Twice a month the program has open community meetings where the women discuss common themes, problems and concerns.

"We are clear within our community that there are no step-children, no bad or good crimes. We come together to support and heal," Ms. Smolick said.

"It is an arena for women to work through their differences and better understand their commonalties."

It also is a time for interaction with the outside.

For example, Dr. Julie Blackman, a court expert on battered women's defense, met with the women to learn their views for a presentation to the New York State Family Court Judges.

In her own talks, Ms. Smolick urges placing priorities on the family.

"We have to educate ourselves and others about the extent of family violence, the impact of family violence. We have to recognize that men and women who have grown up in violent families have no other frame of reference."

She recalls the story of a woman who had been a severely abused child—beaten with sticks and iron cords—growing up to marry a violent, alcoholic man and, in a fit of anger, causing the death of one of her children.

During a Being a Better Parent class, she told the program coordinator that she knew a lot about what was wrong with parents, but very little about what constituted a good parent.

"We have to teach the skills and stop taking them for granted," Ms. Smolick says ...

"We have to, as a society, begin to find our humanity, our kindness, our gentleness and our love of children."

Ms. Smolick finds it sad that many women who have left Bedford want to return because they have found no support on the outside.

"We have a lot of work to do," she said.

"We're all the same. If I say something I don't have to worry about them throwing it in my face."

Virginia is one of the original 12 who testified at the 1985 hearing. They are called Sister-Sisters.

Virginia co-facilitates a support group, helps with training and is involved in one-on-one counseling.

Program staff member Jean Kwartler notes that it was Sister-Sisters who "made the program possible."

Karen, another of the Sister-Sisters, said the "original focus was to bring attention to the problem. Most of us tried like crazy to do something legally. It was a matter of the system letting us down."

Karen tries to get the message across to battered women that no matter how bad the situation gets, "striking back is not the answer.

"It creates a whole new set of problems. It didn't set me free physically or emotionally ... My husband has been dead eight years and he's still hitting and kicking me."

Being abused by a family member, someone who is supposed to love and protect you, is much worse than having a stranger do it, the women say.

"Only people who have lived through it can feel it," says Suzette, a member of the Mothers Anonymous Group.

"I am here for taking the life of my own son," she said.

The stigma attached to mothers who have killed their children makes it especially difficult for them to achieve a feeling of self worth.

"They don't have a place where they can talk openly and freely," Suzette said.

The group has ground rules of confidentiality and membership. Members choose the issues they want to deal with, such as taking responsibility for the crime, and the overwhelming guilt they feel.

"Right now we are working on anger. Most of us have a tremendous amount of trouble dealing with it. (The group provides) a safe place for us to recover and deal with it," Suzette said.

Johnnie spoke about the overwhelming anger and frustration she felt from years of abuse, that sent her out of control and led to the death of her baby son.

"I was emotionally ill when I came here," she says.

"You think to yourself, 'How could I do something like that?' ... You are harder on yourself than the outside forces."

For Hannah, the Family Violence Program has meant being able to trust people once again.

At Bedford since 1987 for killing an abusive husband, she was unable to talk at all because of the four years of torture she had endured.

"I was scared to talk to people," she says.

Group meetings and one-on-one counseling have brought her to the point where she has no difficulty in sharing her experiences.

The women have found that hugs, even more than words, can lift them out of low moments and reassure them that they are not alone, that somebody cares.

Outside the meetings, in the routine of prison life, they find themselves sensitive to the feelings of others. They don't hesitate to reach out to someone they realize is hurting inside.

The women end each session with a group hug, making a circle, arms around each other, and spontaneously sharing thoughts and messages.

"We are a family," Ms. Kwartler says. "We are more than a family because what happens to one, happens to all."

'THIS MAN HAS EXPIRED'

WITNESS TO AN EXECUTION

ROBERT JOHNSON

ROBERT JOHNSON *is professor of justice, law, and society at The American University, Washington, D.C. This article is drawn from a Distinguished Faculty Lecture, given under the auspices of the university's senate last spring.*

The death penalty has made a comeback in recent years. In the late sixties and through most of the seventies, such a thing seemed impossible. There was a moratorium on executions in the U.S., backed by the authority of the Supreme Court. The hiatus lasted roughly a decade. Coming on the heels of a gradual but persistent decline in the use of the death penalty in the Western world, it appeared to some that executions would pass from the American scene [cf. *Commonweal*, January 15, 1988]. Nothing could have been further from the truth.

Beginning with the execution of Gary Gilmore in 1977, over 100 people have been put to death, most of them in the last few years. Some 2,200 prisoners are presently confined on death rows across the nation. The majority of these prisoners have lived under sentence of death for years, in some cases a decade or more, and are running out of legal appeals. It is fair to say that the death penalty is alive and well in America, and that executions will be with us for the foreseeable future.

Gilmore's execution marked the resurrection of the modern death penalty and was big news. It was commemorated in a best-selling tome by Norman Mailer, *The Executioner's Song*. The title was deceptive. Like others who have examined the death penalty, Mailer told us a great deal about the condemned but very little about the executioners. Indeed, if we dwell on Mailer's account, the executioner's story is not only unsung; it is distorted.

Gilmore's execution was quite atypical. His was an instance of state-assisted suicide accompanied by an element of romance and played out against a backdrop of media fanfare. Unrepentant and unafraid, Gilmore refused to appeal his conviction. He dared the state of Utah to take his life, and the media repeated the challenge until it became a taunt that may well have goaded officials to action. A failed suicide pact with his lover staged only days before the execution, using drugs she delivered to him in a visit marked by unusual intimacy, added a hint of melodrama to the proceedings. Gilmore's final words, "Let's do it," seemed to invite the lethal hail of bullets from the firing squad. The nonchalant phrase, at once fatalistic and brazenly rebellious, became Gilmore's epitaph. It clinched his outlaw-hero image, and found its way onto tee shirts that confirmed his celebrity status.

Befitting a celebrity, Gilmore was treated with unusual leniency by prison officials during his confinement on death row. He was, for example, allowed to hold a party the night before his execution, during which he was free to eat, drink, and make merry with his guests until the early morning hours. This is not entirely unprecedented. Notorious English convicts of centuries past would throw farewell balls in prison on the eve of their executions. News accounts of such affairs sometimes included a commentary on the richness of the table and the quality of the dancing. For the record, Gilmore served Tang, Kool-Aid, cookies, and coffee, later supplemented by contraband pizza and an unidentified liquor. Periodically, he gobbled drugs obligingly provided by the prison pharmacy. He played a modest arrangement of rock music albums but refrained from dancing.

Gilmore's execution generally, like his parting fete, was decidedly out of step with the tenor of the modern death penalty. Most condemned prisoners fight to save their lives, not to have them taken. They do not see their fate in romantic terms; there are no farewell parties. Nor are they given medication to ease their anxiety or win their compliance. The subjects of typical executions remain anonymous to the public and even to their keepers. They are very much alone at the end.

In contrast to Mailer's account, the focus of the research I have conducted is on the executioners themselves as they carry out typical executions. In my experience executioners—not unlike Mailer himself—can be quite voluble, and sometimes quite moving, in expressing themselves. I shall draw upon their words to describe the death work they carry out in our name.

DEATH WORK AND DEATH WORKERS

Executioners are not a popular subject of social research, let alone conversation at the dinner table or cocktail party. We simply don't give the subject much thought. When we think of executioners at all, the imagery runs to individual men of disreputable, or at least questionable, character who work stealthily behind the scenes to carry out their grim labors. We picture hooded men hiding in the shadow of the gallows, or anonymous figures lurking out of sight behind electric chairs, gas chambers, firing blinds, or, more recently, hospital gurneys. We wonder who would do such grisly work and how they sleep at night.

This image of the executioner as a sinister and often solitary character is today misleading. To be sure, a few states hire free-lance executioners and traffic in macabre theatrics. Executioners may be picked up under cover of darkness and some may still wear black hoods. But today, executions are generally the work of a highly disciplined and efficient team of correctional officers.

Broadly speaking, the execution process as it is now practiced starts with the prisoner's confinement on death row, an oppressive prison-within-a-prison where the condemned are housed, sometimes for years, awaiting execution. Death work gains momentum when an execution date draws near and the prisoner is moved to the death house, a short walk from the death chamber. Finally, the process culminates in the death watch, a twenty-four-hour period that ends when the prisoner has been executed.

This final period, the death watch, is generally undertaken by correctional officers who work as a team and report directly to the prison warden. The warden or his representative, in turn, must by law preside over the execution. In many states, it is a member of the death watch or execution team, acting under the warden's authority, who in fact plays the formal role of executioner. Though this officer may technically work alone, his teammates view the execution as a shared responsibility. As one officer on the death watch told me in no uncertain terms: "We all take part in it; we all play 100 percent in it, too. That takes the load off this one individual [who pulls the switch]." The formal executioner concurred. "Everyone on the team can do it, and nobody will tell you I did it. I know my team." I found nothing in my research to dispute these claims.

The officers of these death watch teams are our modern executioners. As part of a larger study of the death work process, I studied one such group. This team, comprised of nine seasoned officers of varying ranks, had carried out five electrocutions at the time I began my research. I interviewed each officer on the team after the fifth execution, then served as an official witness at a sixth electrocution. Later, I served as a behind-the-scenes observer during their seventh execution.

The results of this phase of my research form the substance of this essay.

THE DEATH WATCH TEAM

The death watch or execution team members refer to themselves, with evident pride, as simply "the team." This pride is shared by other correctional officials. The warden at the institution I was observing praised members of the team as solid citizens—in his words, country boys. These country boys, he assured me, could be counted on to do the job and do it well. As a fellow administrator put it, "an execution is something [that] needs to be done and good people, dedicated people who believe in the American system, should do it. And there's a certain amount of feeling, probably one to another, that they're part of that—that when they have to hang tough, they can do it, and they can do it right. And that it's just the right thing to do."

The official view is that an execution is a job that has to be done, and done right. The death penalty is, after all, the law of the land. In this context, the phrase "done right" means that an execution should be a proper, professional, dignified undertaking. In the words of a prison administrator, "We had to be sure that we did it properly, professionally, and [that] we gave as much dignity to the person as we possibly could in the process....If you've gotta do it, it might just as well be done the way it's supposed to be done—without any sensation."

In the language of the prison officials, "proper" refers to procedures that go off smoothly; "professional" means without personal feelings that intrude on the procedures in any way. The desire for executions that take place "without any sensation" no doubt refers to the absence of media sensationalism, particularly if there should be an embarrassing and undignified hitch in the procedures, for example, a prisoner who breaks down or becomes violent and must be forcibly placed in the electric chair as witnesses, some from the media, look on in horror. Still, I can't help but note that this may be a revealing slip of the tongue. For executions are indeed meant to go off without any human feeling, without any sensation. A profound absence of feeling would seem to capture the bureaucratic ideal embodied in the modern execution.

The view of executions held by the execution team members parallels that of correctional administrators but is somewhat more restrained. The officers of the team are closer to the killing and dying, and are less apt to wax abstract or eloquent in describing the process. Listen to one man's observations:

It's a job. I don't take it personally. You know, I don't take it like I'm having a grudge against this person and this person has done something to me. I'm just carrying out a job, doing what I was asked to do....This man has been sentenced to death in the courts. This is the law and he broke this law, and he has to suffer the consequences. And one of the consequences is to put him to death.

I found that few members of the execution team support the death penalty outright or without reservation. Having seen executions close up, many of them have lingering doubts about the justice or wisdom of this sanction. As one officer put it:

I'm not sure the death penalty is the right way. I don't know if there is a right answer. So I look at it like this: if it's gotta be done, at least it can be done in a humane way, if there is such a word for it. . . . The only way it should be done, I feel, is the way we do it. It's done professionally; it's not no horseplaying. Everything is done by documentation. On time. By the book.

Arranging executions that occur "without any sensation" and that go "by the book" is no mean task, but it is a task that is undertaken in earnest by the execution team. The tone of the enterprise is set by the team leader, a man who takes a hard-boiled, no-nonsense approach to correctional work in general and death work in particular. "My style," he says, "is this: if it's a job to do, get it done. Do it and that's it." He seeks out kindred spirits, men who see killing condemned prisoners as a job—a dirty job one does reluctantly, perhaps, but above all a job one carries out dispassionately and in the line of duty.

To make sure that line of duty is a straight and accurate one, the death watch team has been carefully drilled by the team leader in the mechanics of execution. The process has been broken down into simple, discrete tasks and practiced repeatedly. The team leader describes the division of labor in the following exchange:

the execution team is a nine-officer team and each one has certain things to do. When I would train you, maybe you'd buckle a belt, that might be all you'd have to do. . . . And you'd be expected to do one thing and that's all you'd be expected to do. And if everybody does what they were taught, or what they were trained to do, at the end the man would be put in the chair and everything would be complete. It's all come together now.

So it's broken down into very small steps. . . .

Very small, yes. Each person has *one* thing to do.

I see. What's the purpose of breaking it down into such small steps?

So people won't get confused. I've learned it's kind of a tense time. When you're executin' a person, killing a person—you call it killin', executin', whatever you want—the man dies anyway. I find the less you got on your mind, why, the better you'll carry it out. So it's just very simple things. And so far, you know, it's all come together, we haven't had any problems.

This division of labor allows each man on the execution team to become a specialist, a technician with a sense of pride in his work. Said one man,

My assignment is the leg piece. Right leg. I roll his pants leg up, place a piece [electrode] on his leg, strap his leg in. . . . I've got all the moves down pat. We train from different posts; I can do any of them. But that's my main post.

The implication is not that the officers are incapable of performing multiple or complex tasks, but simply that it is more efficient to focus each officer's efforts on one easy task.

An essential part of the training is practice. Practice is meant to produce a confident group, capable of fast and accurate performance under pressure. The rewards of practice are reaped in improved performance. Executions take place with increasing efficiency, and eventually occur with precision. "The first one was grisly," a team member confided to me. He explained that there was a certain amount of fumbling, which made the execution seem interminable. There were technical problems as well: The generator was set too high so the body was badly burned. But that is the past, the officer assured me. "The ones now, we know what we're doing. It's just like clockwork."

THE DEATH WATCH

The death-watch team is deployed during the last twenty-four hours before an execution. In the state under study, the death watch starts at 11 o'clock the night before the execution and ends at 11 o'clock the next night when the execution takes place. At least two officers would be with the prisoner at any given time during that period. Their objective is to keep the prisoner alive and "on schedule." That is, to move him through a series of critical and cumulatively demoralizing junctures that begin with his last meal and end with his last walk. When the time comes, they must deliver the prisoner up for execution as quickly and unobtrusively as possible.

Broadly speaking, the job of the death watch officer, as one man put it, "is to sit and keep the inmate calm for the last twenty-four hours—and get the man ready to go." Keeping a condemned prisoner calm means, in part, serving his immediate needs. It seems paradoxical to think of the death watch officers as providing services to the condemned, but the logistics of the job make service a central obligation of the officers. Here's how one officer made this point:

Well, you can't help but be involved with many of the things that he's involved with. Because if he wants to make a call to his family, well, you'll have to dial the number. And you keep records of whatever calls he makes. If he wants a cigarette, well he's not allowed to keep matches so you light it for him. You've got to pour his coffee, too. So you're aware what he's doing. It's not like you can just ignore him. You've gotta just be with him whether he wants it or not, and cater to his needs.

Officers cater to the condemned because contented inmates are easier to keep under control. To a man, the officers say this is so. But one can never trust even a contented, condemned prisoner.

The death-watch officers see condemned prisoners as men with explosive personalities. "You don't know what, what a man's gonna do," noted one officer. "He's liable to snap, he's liable to pass out. We watch him all the time to prevent him from committing suicide. You've got to be ready—he's liable to do anything." The prisoner is never out of at least one officer's sight. Thus surveillance is constant, and control, for all intents and purposes, is total.

Relations between the officers and their charges during the death watch can be quite intense. Watching and being watched are central to this enterprise, and these are always engaging activities, particularly when the stakes are life and death. These relations are, nevertheless, utterly impersonal; there are no grudges but neither is there compassion or fellow-feeling. Officers are civil but cool; they keep an emotional distance from the men they are about to kill. To do otherwise, they maintain, would make it harder to execute condemned prisoners. The attitude of the officers is that the prisoners arrive as strangers and are easier to kill if they stay that way.

During the last five or six hours, two specific team officers are assigned to guard the prisoner. Unlike their more taciturn and aloof colleagues on earlier shifts, these officers make a conscious effort to talk with the prisoner. In one officer's words, "We keep them right there and keep talking to them—about anything except the chair." The point of these conversations is not merely to pass time; it is to keep tabs on the prisoner's state of mind, and to steer him away from subjects that might depress, anger, or otherwise upset him. Sociability, in other words, quite explicitly serves as a source of social control. Relationships, such as they are, serve purely manipulative ends. This is impersonality at its worst, masquerading as concern for the strangers one hopes to execute with as little trouble as possible.

Generally speaking, as the execution moves closer, the mood becomes more somber and subdued. There is a last meal. Prisoners can order pretty much what they want, but most eat little or nothing at all. At this point, the prisoners may steadfastly maintain that their executions will be stayed. Such bravado is belied by their loss of appetite. "You can see them going down," said one officer. "Food is the last thing they got on their minds."

Next the prisoners must box their meager worldly goods. These are inventoried by the staff, recorded on a one-page checklist form, and marked for disposition to family or friends. Prisoners are visibly saddened, even moved to tears, by this procedure, which at once summarizes their lives and highlights the imminence of death. At this point, said one of the officers, "I really get into him; I watch him real close." The execution schedule, the officer pointed out, is "picking up momentum, and we don't want to lose control of the situation."

This momentum is not lost on the condemned prisoner. Critical milestones have been passed. The prisoner moves in a limbo existence devoid of food or possessions; he has seen the last of such things, unless he receives a stay of execution and rejoins the living. His identity is expropriated as well. The critical juncture in this regard is the shaving of the man's head (including facial hair) and right leg. Hair is shaved to facilitate the electrocution; it reduces physical resistance to electricity and minimizes singeing and burning. But the process has obvious psychological significance as well, adding greatly to the momentum of the execution.

The shaving procedure is quite public and intimidating. The condemned man is taken from his cell and seated in the middle of the tier. His hands and feet are cuffed, and he is dressed only in undershorts. The entire death watch team is

assembled around him. They stay at a discrete distance, but it is obvious that they are there to maintain control should he resist in any way or make any untoward move. As a rule, the man is overwhelmed. As one officer told me in blunt terms, "Come eight o'clock, we've got a dead man. Eight o'clock is when we shave the man. We take his identity; it goes with the hair." This taking of identity is indeed a collective process—the team makes a forceful "we," the prisoner their helpless object. The staff is confident that the prisoner's capacity to resist is now compromised. What is left of the man erodes gradually and, according the officers, perceptibly over the remaining three hours before the execution.

After the prisoner has been shaved, he is then made to shower and don a fresh set of clothes for the execution. The clothes are unremarkable in appearance, except that velcro replaces buttons and zippers, to reduce the chance of burning the body. The main significance of the clothes is symbolic: they mark the prisoner as a man who is ready for execution. Now physically "prepped," to quote one team member, the prisoner is placed in an empty tomblike cell, the death cell. All that is left is the wait. During this fateful period, the prisoner is more like an object "without any sensation" than like a flesh-and-blood person on the threshold of death.

For condemned prisoners, like Gilmore, who come to accept and even to relish their impending deaths, a genuine calm seems to prevail. It is as if they can transcend the dehumanizing forces at work around them and go to their deaths in peace. For most condemned prisoners, however, numb resignation rather than peaceful acceptance is the norm. By the account of the death-watch officers, these more typical prisoners are beaten men. Listen to the officers' accounts:

A lot of 'em die in their minds before they go to that chair. I've never known of one or heard of one putting up a fight. . . . By the time they walk to the chair, they've completely faced it. Such a reality most people can't understand. Cause they don't fight it. They don't seem to have anything to say. It's just something like "Get it over with." They may be numb, sort of in a trance.

They go through stages. And, at this stage, they're real humble. Humblest bunch of people I ever seen. Most all of 'em is real, real weak. Most of the time you'd only need one or two people to carry out an execution, as weak and as humble as they are.

These men seem barely human and alive to their keepers. They wait meekly to be escorted to their deaths. The people who come for them are the warden and the remainder of the death watch team, flanked by high-ranking correctional officials. The warden reads the court order, known popularly as a death warrant. This is, as one officer said, "the real deal," and nobody misses its significance. The condemned prisoners then go to their deaths compliantly, captives of the inexorable, irresistible momentum of the situation. As one officer put it, "There's no struggle. . . . They just walk right on in there." So too, do the staff "just walk right on in there," following a routine they have come to know well. Both the condemned and the executioners, it would seem, find a relief of sorts in mindless mechanical conformity to the modern execution drill.

WITNESS TO AN EXECUTION

As the team and administrators prepare to commence the good fight, as they might say, another group, the official witnesses, are also preparing themselves for their role in the execution. Numbering between six and twelve for any given execution, the official witnesses are disinterested citizens in good standing drawn from a cross-section of the state's population. If you will, they are every good or decent person, called upon to represent the community and use their good offices to testify to the propriety of the execution. I served as an official witness at the execution of an inmate.

At eight in the evening, about the time the prisoner is shaved in preparation for the execution, the witnesses are assembled. Eleven in all, we included three newspaper and two television reporters, a state trooper, two police officers, a magistrate, a businessman, and myself. We were picked up in the parking lot behind the main office of the corrections department. There was nothing unusual or even memorable about any of this. Gothic touches were notable by their absence. It wasn't a dark and stormy night; no one emerged from the shadows to lead us to the prison gates.

Mundane considerations prevailed. The van sent for us was missing a few rows of seats so there wasn't enough room for all of us. Obliging prison officials volunteered their cars. Our rather ordinary cavalcade reached the prison but only after getting lost. Once within the prison's walls, we were sequestered for some two hours in a bare and almost shabby administrative conference room. A public information officer was assigned to accompany us and answer our questions. We grilled this official about the prisoner and the execution procedure he would undergo shortly, but little information was to be had. The man confessed ignorance on the most basic points. Disgruntled at this and increasingly anxious, we made small talk and drank coffee.

At 10:40 P.M., roughly two-and-a-half hours after we were assembled and only twenty minutes before the execution was scheduled to occur, the witnesses were taken to the basement of the prison's administrative building, frisked, then led down an alleyway that ran along the exterior of the building. We entered a neighboring cell block and were admitted to a vestibule adjoining the death chamber. Each of us signed a log, and was then led off to the witness area. To our left, around a corner some thirty feet away, the prisoner sat in the condemned cell. He couldn't see us, but I'm quite certain he could hear us. It occurred to me that our arrival was a fateful reminder for the prisoner. The next group would be led by the warden, and it would be coming for him.

We entered the witness area, a room within the death chamber, and took our seats. A picture window covering the front wall of the witness room offered a clear view of the electric chair, which was about twelve feet away from us and well illuminated. The chair, a large, high-back solid oak structure with imposing black straps, dominated the death chamber. Behind it, on the back wall, was an open panel full of coils and lights. Peeling paint hung from the ceiling and walls; water stains from persistent leaks were everywhere in evidence.

Two officers, one a hulking figure weighing some 400 pounds, stood alongside the electric chair. Each had his hands crossed at the lap and wore a forbidding, blank expression on his face. The witnesses gazed at them and the chair, most of us scribbling notes furiously. We did this, I suppose, as much to record the experience as to have a distraction from the growing tension. A correctional officer entered the witness room and announced that a trial run of the machinery would be undertaken. Seconds later, lights flashed on the control panel behind the chair indicating that the chair was in working order. A white curtain, opened for the test, separated the chair and the witness area. After the test, the curtain was drawn. More tests were performed behind the curtain. Afterwards, the curtain was reopened, and would be left open until the execution was over. Then it would be closed to allow the officers to remove the body.

A handful of high-level correctional officials were present in the death chamber, standing just outside the witness area. There were two regional administrators, the director of the Department of Corrections, and the prison warden. The prisoner's chaplain and lawyer were also present. Other than the chaplain's black religious garb, subdued grey pinstripes and bland correctional uniforms prevailed. All parties were quite solemn.

At 10:58 the prisoner entered the death chamber. He was, I knew from my research, a man with a checkered, tragic past. He had been grossly abused as a child, and went on to become grossly abusive of others. I was told he could not describe his life, from childhood on, without talking about confrontations in defense of a precarious sense of self—at home, in school, on the streets, in the prison yard. Belittled by life and choking with rage, he was hungry to be noticed. Paradoxically, he had found his moment in the spotlight, but it was a dim and unflattering light cast before a small and unappreciative audience. "He'd pose for cameras in the chair—for the attention," his counselor had told me earlier in the day. But the truth was that the prisoner wasn't smiling, and there were no cameras.

The prisoner walked quickly and silently toward the chair, an escort of officers in tow. His eyes were turned downward, his expression a bit glazed. Like many before him, the prisoner had threatened to stage a last stand. But that was lifetimes ago, on death row. In the death house, he joined the humble bunch and kept to the executioner's schedule. He appeared to have given up on life before he died in the chair.

En route to the chair, the prisoner stumbled slightly, as if the momentum of the event had overtaken him. Were he not held securely by two officers, one at each elbow, he might have fallen. Were the routine to be broken in this or indeed any other way, the officers believe, the prisoner might faint or panic or become violent, and have to be forcibly placed in the chair. Perhaps as a precaution, when the prisoner reached the chair he did not turn on his own but rather was turned, firmly but without malice, by the officers in his escort. These included the two men at his elbows, and four others who followed behind him. Once the prisoner was seated, again with help, the officers strapped him into the chair.

The execution team worked with machine precision. Like a disciplined swarm, they enveloped him. Arms, legs, stomach, chest, and head were secured in a matter of seconds. Electrodes were attached to the cap holding his head and to the strap holding his exposed right leg. A leather mask was placed over his face. The last officer mopped the prisoner's brow, then touched his hand in a gesture of farewell.

During the brief procession to the electric chair, the prisoner was attended by a chaplain. As the execution team worked feverishly to secure the condemned man's body, the chaplain, who appeared to be upset, leaned over him and placed his forehead in contact with the prisoner's, whispering urgently. The priest might have been praying, but I had the impression he was consoling the man, perhaps assuring him that a forgiving God awaited him in the next life. If he heard the chaplain, I doubt the man comprehended his message. He didn't seem comforted. Rather, he looked stricken and appeared to be in shock. Perhaps the priest's urgent ministrations betrayed his doubts that the prisoner could hold himself together. The chaplain then withdrew at the warden's request, allowing the officers to affix the death mask.

The strapped and masked figure sat before us, utterly alone, waiting to be killed. The cap and mask dominated his face. The cap was nothing more than a sponge encased in a leather shell with a metal piece at the top to accept an electrode. It looked decrepit and resembled a cheap, ill-fitting toupee. The mask, made entirely of leather, appeared soiled and worn. It had two parts. The bottom part covered the chin and mouth, the top the eyes and lower forehead. Only the nose was exposed. The effect of a rigidly restrained body, together with the bizarre cap and the protruding nose, was nothing short of grotesque. A faceless man breathed before us in a tragicomic trance, waiting for a blast of electricity that would extinguish his life. Endless seconds passed. His last act was to swallow, nervously, pathetically, with his Adam's apple bobbing. I was struck by that simple movement then, and can't forget it even now. It told me, as nothing else did, that in the prisoner's restrained body, behind that mask, lurked a fellow human being who, at some level, however primitive, knew or sensed himself to be moments from death.

The condemned man sat perfectly still for what seemed an eternity but was in fact no more than thirty seconds. Finally the electricity hit him. His body stiffened spasmodically, though only briefly. A thin swirl of smoke trailed away from his head and then dissipated quickly. The body remained taut, with the right foot raised slightly at the heel, seemingly frozen

there. A brief pause, then another minute of shock. When it was over, the body was flaccid and inert.

Three minutes passed while the officials let the body cool. (Immediately after the execution, I'm told, the body would be too hot to touch and would blister anyone who did.) All eyes were riveted to the chair; I felt trapped in my witness seat, at once transfixed and yet eager for release. I can't recall any clear thoughts from that moment. One of the death watch officers later volunteered that he shared this experience of staring blankly at the execution scene. Had the prisoner's mind been mercifully blank before the end? I hoped so.

An officer walked up to the body, opened the shirt at chest level, then continued on to get the physician from an adjoining room. The physician listened for a heartbeat. Hearing none, he turned to the warden and said, "This man has expired." The warden, speaking to the director, solemnly intoned: "Mr. Director, the court order has been fulfilled." The curtain was then drawn and the witnesses filed out.

THE MORNING AFTER

As the team prepared the body for the morgue, the witnesses were led to the front door of the prison. On the way, we passed a number of cell blocks. We could hear the normal sounds of prison life, including the occasional catcall and lewd comment hurled at uninvited guests like ourselves. But no trouble came in the wake of the execution. Small protests were going on outside the walls, we were told, but we could not hear them. Soon the media would be gone; the protestors would disperse and head for their homes. The prisoners, already home, had been indifferent to the proceedings, as they always are unless the condemned prisoner had been a figure of some consequence in the convict community. Then there might be tension and maybe even a modest disturbance on a prison tier or two. But few convict luminaries are executed, and the dead man had not been one of them. Our escort officer offered a sad tribute to the prisoner: "The inmates, they didn't care about this guy."

I couldn't help but think they weren't alone in this. The executioners went home and set about their lives. Having taken life, they would savor a bit of life themselves. They showered, ate, made love, slept, then took a day or two off. For some, the prisoner's image would linger for that night. The men who strapped him in remembered what it was like to touch him; they showered as soon as they got home to wash off the feel and smell of death. One official sat up picturing how the prisoner looked at the end. (I had a few drinks myself that night with that same image for company.) There was some talk about delayed reactions to the stress of carrying out executions. Though such concerns seemed remote that evening, I learned later that problems would surface for some of the officers. But no one on the team, then or later, was haunted by the executed man's memory, nor would anyone grieve for him. "When I go home after one of these things," said one man, "I sleep like a rock." His may or may not be the sleep of the just, but one can only marvel at such a thing, and perhaps envy such a man.

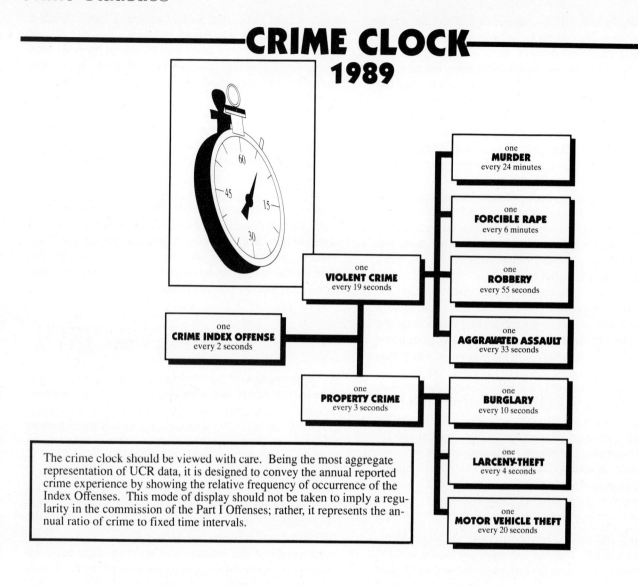

CRIME CLOCK
1989

one
MURDER
every 24 minutes

one
FORCIBLE RAPE
every 6 minutes

one
VIOLENT CRIME
every 19 seconds

one
ROBBERY
every 55 seconds

one
CRIME INDEX OFFENSE
every 2 seconds

one
AGGRAVATED ASSAULT
every 33 seconds

one
PROPERTY CRIME
every 3 seconds

one
BURGLARY
every 10 seconds

one
LARCENY-THEFT
every 4 seconds

one
MOTOR VEHICLE THEFT
every 20 seconds

The crime clock should be viewed with care. Being the most aggregate representation of UCR data, it is designed to convey the annual reported crime experience by showing the relative frequency of occurrence of the Index Offenses. This mode of display should not be taken to imply a regularity in the commission of the Part I Offenses; rather, it represents the annual ratio of crime to fixed time intervals.

Crime in the United States 1989

The Crime Index total rose 2 percent to 14.3 million offenses in 1989. Five- and 10-year percent changes showed the 1989 total was 15 percent above the 1985 level and 6 percent higher than in 1980.

From 1988 to 1989, overall violent crime showed a 5-percent increase. The number of property crimes increased 2 percent for the 2-year period.

The largest volume of Crime Index offenses occurred in the Southern States which accounted for 37 percent of the total. Following were the Western States with 24 percent, the Midwestern States with 21 percent, and the Northeastern States with 18 percent.

Crime rates relate the incidence of crime to population.

In 1989, there were an estimated 5,741 Crime Index offenses for each 100,000 in population nationwide. The violent crime rate was 663, and for property crime, it was 5,078 per 100,000.

Regionally, the Crime Index rates per 100,000 inhabitants ranged from 6,550 in the West to 4,949 in the Midwest. The South registered a rate of 6,205 per 100,000 inhabitants, and the Northeast, 5,072.

National estimates of volume and rate per 100,000 inhabitants for all Crime Index offenses covering the past decade are set forth in Table 1, "Index of Crime, United States, 1980-1989."

Table 1.—Index of Crime, United States, 1980-1989

Population[1]	Crime Index total[2]	Modified Crime Index total[3]	Violent crime[4]	Property crime[4]	Murder and non-negligent man-slaughter	Forcible rape	Robbery	Aggra-vated assault	Burglary	Larceny-theft	Motor vehicle theft	Arson[3]
					Number of Offenses							
Population by year:												
1980-225,349,264	13,408,300		1,344,520	12,063,700	23,040	82,990	565,840	672,650	3,795,200	7,136,900	1,131,700	
1981-229,146,000	13,423,800		1,361,820	12,061,900	22,520	82,500	592,910	663,900	3,779,700	7,194,400	1,087,800	
1982-231,534,000	12,974,400		1,322,390	11,652,000	21,010	78,770	553,130	669,480	3,447,100	7,142,500	1,062,400	
1983-233,981,000	12,108,600		1,258,090	10,850,500	19,310	78,920	506,570	653,290	3,129,900	6,712,800	1,007,900	
1984-236,158,000	11,881,800		1,273,280	10,608,500	18,690	84,230	485,010	685,350	2,984,400	6,591,900	1,032,200	
1985-238,740,000	12,431,400		1,328,800	11,102,600	18,980	88,670	497,870	723,250	3,073,300	6,926,400	1,102,900	
1986-241,077,000	13,211,900		1,489,170	11,722,700	20,610	91,460	542,780	834,320	3,241,400	7,257,200	1,224,100	
1987-243,400,000	13,508,700		1,484,000	12,024,700	20,100	91,110	517,700	855,090	3,236,200	7,499,900	1,288,700	
1988-245,807,000	13,923,100		1,566,220	12,356,900	20,680	92,490	542,970	910,090	3,218,100	7,705,900	1,432,900	
1989-248,239,000	14,251,400		1,646,040	12,605,400	21,500	94,500	578,330	951,710	3,168,200	7,872,400	1,564,800	
Percent change: number of offenses:												
1989/1988	+2.4		+5.1	+2.0	+4.0	+2.2	+6.5	+4.6	−1.6	+2.2	+9.2	
1989/1985	+14.6		+23.9	+13.5	+13.3	+6.6	+16.2	+31.6	+3.1	+13.7	+41.9	
1989/1980	+6.3		+22.4	+4.5	−6.7	+13.9	+2.2	+41.5	−16.5	+10.3	+38.3	
					Rate per 100,000 Inhabitants							
Year:												
1980	5,950.0		596.6	5,353.3	10.2	36.8	251.1	298.5	1,684.1	3,167.0	502.2	
1981	5,858.2		594.3	5,263.9	9.8	36.0	258.7	289.7	1,649.5	3,139.7	474.7	
1982	5,603.6		571.1	5,032.5	9.1	34.0	238.9	289.2	1,488.8	3,084.8	458.8	
1983	5,175.0		537.7	4,637.4	8.3	33.7	216.5	279.2	1,337.7	2,868.9	430.8	
1984	5,031.3		539.2	4,492.1	7.9	35.7	205.4	290.2	1,263.7	2,791.3	437.1	
1985	5,207.1		556.6	4,650.5	7.9	37.1	208.5	302.9	1,287.3	2,901.2	462.0	
1986	5,480.4		617.7	4,862.6	8.6	37.9	225.1	346.1	1,344.6	3,010.3	507.8	
1987	5,550.0		609.7	4,940.3	8.3	37.4	212.7	351.3	1,329.6	3,081.3	529.4	
1988	5,664.2		637.2	5,027.1	8.4	37.6	220.9	370.2	1,309.2	3,134.9	582.9	
1989	5,741.0		663.1	5,077.9	8.7	38.1	233.0	383.4	1,276.3	3,171.3	630.4	
Percent change: rate per 100,000 inhabitants:												
1989/1988	+1.4		+4.1	+1.0	+3.6	+1.3	+5.5	+3.6	−2.5	+1.2	+8.1	
1989/1985	+10.3		+19.1	+9.2	+10.1	+2.7	+11.8	+26.6	−.9	+9.3	+36.5	
1989/1980	−3.5		+11.1	−5.1	−14.7	+3.5	−7.2	+28.4	−24.2	+.1	+25.5	

[1]Populations are Bureau of the Census provisional estimates as of July 1, except April 1, 1980, preliminary census counts, and are subject to change.
[2]Because of rounding, the offenses may not add to totals.
[3]Although arson data are included in the trend and clearance tables, sufficient data are not available to estimate totals for this offense.
[4]Violent crimes are offenses of murder, forcible rape, robbery, and aggravated assault. Property crimes are offenses of burglary, larceny–theft, and motor vehicle theft. Data are not included for the property crime of arson.
All rates were calculated on the offenses before rounding.
Data for 1988 were not available for the States of Florida and Kentucky; therefore, it was necessary that their crime counts be estimated. See "Offense Estimation", page 3 for details.

CRIME INDEX OFFENSES REPORTED

MURDER AND NONNEGLIGENT MANSLAUGHTER

DEFINITION

Murder and nonnegligent manslaughter, as defined in the Uniform Crime Reporting Program, is the willful (nonnegligent) killing of one human being by another.

TREND

Year	Number of offenses	Rate per 100,000 inhabitants
1988	20,675	8.4
1989	21,500	8.7
Percent change ..	+4.0	+3.6

Volume

The total number of murders in the United States during 1989 was estimated at 21,500 or 1 percent of the violent crimes reported. More persons were murdered in July than any other month, while the fewest were killed during February.

Murder by Month, 1985-1989

[Percent of annual total]

Months	1985	1986	1987	1988	1989
January	8.1	7.7	7.7	8.2	8.1
February	7.9	7.0	7.9	7.2	7.1
March	8.1	8.3	8.2	7.7	7.8
April	7.6	8.0	7.6	7.7	7.9
May	7.6	8.2	8.6	7.8	7.8
June	8.2	8.3	7.8	7.7	8.2
July	9.3	9.4	8.6	8.9	9.1
August	9.1	9.4	8.9	9.5	9.0
September	8.1	9.1	8.3	8.9	8.8
October	8.4	8.3	8.8	8.9	8.9
November	8.2	8.0	8.3	8.2	8.5
December	9.4	8.4	9.1	9.2	8.7

When viewing the four regions of the Nation, the Southern States the most populous, accounted for 43 percent of the murders. The Western States reported 20 percent; the Midwestern States, 19 percent; and the Northeastern States, 18 percent.

Trend

The murder volume was up 4 percent nationwide in 1989 over 1988. The Nation's cities overall experienced an increase of 6 percent, with upward trends recorded in all but two city population groupings. Of the cities, those with populations of 25,000 to 49,999 registered the greatest increase, 14 percent. Suburban counties recorded a 1-percent rise, while the rural counties registered a 3-percent decline.

All regions experienced more murders during 1989 than in 1988. The number of murders was up 6 percent in the South; 4 percent in both the Northeast and Midwest; and 1 percent in the West.

The accompanying chart reveals a 13-percent rise nationally in the murder counts from 1985 to 1989. The 10-year trend showed the 1989 total 7 percent below the 1980 level, when the national murder total was at an all-time high.

Rate

Up 4 percent from 1988, the 1989 United States murder rate was 9 per 100,000 inhabitants. On a regional basis, the Southern States averaged 11 murders per 100,000 people; both the Western and Northeastern States, 8 per 100,000; and the Midwestern States, 7 per 100,000. Compared to 1988, murder rates in 1989 increased 5 percent in the South; 4 percent in the Northeast; and 3 percent in the Midwest. The murder rate in the West was down 2 percent.

The Nation's metropolitan areas reported a 1989 murder rate of 10 victims per 100,000 inhabitants. The rural counties, as well as cities outside metropolitan areas, registered a lower rate of 5 per 100,000.

Nature

Supplemental data provided by contributing agencies recorded information for 18,954 of the estimated 21,500 murders in 1989. Submitted monthly, the data consist of the age, sex, and race of both victims and offenders; the types of weapons used; the relationships of victims to the offenders; and the circumstances surrounding the murders.

Based on this information, 76 percent of the murder victims in 1989 were males; and 90 percent were persons 18 years of age or older. Forty-nine percent were aged 20 through 34 years. Considering victims for whom race was known, an average of 50 of every 100 were black, 49 were white, and the remainder were persons of other races.

FORCIBLE RAPE

DEFINITION

Forcible rape, as defined in the Program, is the carnal knowledge of a female forcibly and against her will. Assaults or attempts to commit rape by force or threat of force are also included; however, statutory rape (without force) and other sex offenses are excluded.

TREND

Year	Number of offenses	Rate per 100,000 inhabitants
1988	92,486	37.6
1989	94,504	38.1
Percent change	+2.2	+1.3

Volume

During 1989, there were an estimated 94,504 forcible rapes in the Nation. Rape offenses comprised 6 percent of the total violent crimes. Geographically, the Southern States, the region with the largest population, accounted for 37 percent of the forcible rapes reported to law enforcement. Following were the Midwest with 25 percent, the West with 23 percent, and the Northeast with 15 percent.

Monthly totals showed the greatest number of forcible rapes was reported during the summer, with July recording the highest frequency. The lowest total was registered in February.

Forcible Rape by Month, 1985-1989

[Percent of annual total]

Months	1985	1986	1987	1988	1989
January	7.2	7.1	7.2	7.4	7.4
February	6.6	6.7	6.8	7.3	6.3
March	8.2	7.9	8.1	8.0	7.7
April	8.3	8.1	8.2	8.0	8.3
May	8.9	8.8	8.9	9.0	8.6
June	9.0	9.2	9.3	8.7	8.9
July	10.1	9.8	9.7	9.9	10.0
August	9.9	10.2	9.8	9.8	9.5
September	8.8	9.1	8.9	9.0	8.8
October	8.5	8.4	8.1	8.4	8.9
November	7.7	7.8	7.7	7.6	8.3
December	6.9	7.0	7.3	6.8	7.3

Trend

Compared to the previous year, the 1989 forcible rape volume increased 2 percent nationwide. In the cities collectively, the total was up 1 percent. The rural counties recorded a 12-percent increase and the suburban counties, a 5-percent rise. City trends ranged from 6-percent increases in those with populations of 10,000 to 24,999 and 50,000 to 99,999 to a 4-percent decline in cities with 500,000 or more inhabitants.

Geographically, three of the four regions reported higher forcible rape volumes in 1989 as compared to 1988. The increases were 4 percent in the Western States, 3 percent in the Southern States, and 2 percent in the Midwestern States. The Northeastern States recorded the only decrease, 2 percent.

National trends for 5 and 10 years show that the forcible rape total rose 7 percent over 1985 and 14 percent above 1980.

Rate

By Uniform Crime Reporting definition, the victims of forcible rape are always female. In 1989, an estimated 75 of every 100,000 females in the country were reported rape victims, an increase of 2 percent from the 1988 rate. Since 1985, the female forcible rape rate has risen 3 percent.

Female forcible rape rates for 1989 showed there were 83 victims per 100,000 females in MSAs, 53 per 100,000 females in cities outside metropolitan areas, and 41 per 100,000 females in rural counties.

Regionally, the highest female rape rate was in the Western States, which recorded 83 victims per 100,000 females. Following were the Southern States with a rate of 80, the Midwestern States with 76, and the Northeastern States with 55.

Nature

Of all reported forcible rapes during 1989, 83 percent were rapes by force. The remainder were attempts or assaults to commit forcible rape. A 4-percent increase was registered in the number of rapes by force, while attempts to commit rape decreased 5 percent from the 1988 figure.

Clearances

Nationwide and in the cities, 52 percent of the forcible rapes reported to law enforcement were cleared by arrest or exceptional means in 1989. Rural county law enforcement agencies cleared 55 percent of the offenses brought to their attention, while suburban county agencies cleared 51 percent.

Clearance rates for the regions ranged from 46 percent in the Midwestern States to 59 percent in the Southern States. In the Northeastern States, the clearance rate for forcible rape was 54 percent, and in the Western States, it was 49 percent.

Of the total clearances for forcible rape in the country as a whole, 10 percent involved only persons under 18 years of age. The rural and suburban counties also recorded a 10-percent involvement of this age group, while in the Nation's cities, only persons under 18 accounted for 9 percent of the forcible rape clearances.

Persons Arrested

The number of arrests for forcible rape rose 1 percent nationwide from 1988 to 1989. Arrests for this offense rose 8 percent in the rural counties and 6 percent in the suburban counties. The Nation's cities experienced a 1-percent decline in forcible rape arrests. For the 5-year period, 1985 to 1989, the total forcible rape arrests, those of adults, and of persons under 18 years of age showed virtually no change.

Of the forcible rape arrestees in 1989, 44 percent were persons under the age of 25, with 28 percent of the total being in the 18- to 24-year age group. Fifty-two percent of those arrested were white, 47 percent were black, and the remainder, other races.

ROBBERY

DEFINITION

Robbery is the taking or attempting to take anything of value from the care, custody, or control of a person or persons by force or threat of force or violence and/or by putting the victim in fear.

TREND

Year	Number of offenses	Rate per 100,000 inhabitants
1988	542,968	220.9
1989	578,326	233.0
Percent change ..	+ 6.5	+ 5.5

Volume

Estimated at 578,326 offenses in 1989, robbery accounted for 4 percent of all Index crimes and 35 percent of the crimes of violence. During the year, robberies occurred most frequently in December and least often in April.

Robbery by Month, 1985-1989
[Percent of annual total]

Months	1985	1986	1987	1988	1989
January	8.6	8.7	8.9	8.6	8.8
February	7.4	7.7	8.1	7.9	7.4
March	7.9	8.2	8.2	8.0	8.0
April	7.3	7.6	7.5	7.3	7.3
May	7.5	7.7	7.5	7.6	7.6
June	7.7	8.0	7.6	7.6	7.6
July	8.6	8.4	8.3	8.4	8.4
August	8.9	9.3	8.7	8.7	8.6
September	8.4	8.6	8.5	8.7	8.6
October	9.1	8.7	8.8	9.1	9.2
November	8.8	8.3	8.5	9.0	9.0
December	9.7	9.0	9.2	9.2	9.3

Distribution figures for the regions showed that the most populous Southern States registered 32 percent of all reported robberies. Following were the Northeastern States with 28 percent, the Western States with 21 percent, and the Midwestern States with the remainder.

Trend

Upward trends in robbery were evident nationwide and throughout all population groups in 1989. Nationally and in cities overall, the 1989 robbery volume was 7 percent higher than the 1988 level. The suburban counties experienced a 6-percent increase in robberies, and the rural counties, a 2-percent rise. Of the cities, those with populations of 250,000 to 499,999 registered the greatest increase, 9 percent.

Two-year trends show the number of robberies in 1989 was up in all four regions as compared to 1988. The increases were 8 percent in both the Northeast and the West and 5 percent in the South and the Midwest.

The accompanying chart depicts the trend in the robbery volume, as well as the robbery rate, for the years 1985-1989. In 1989, the number of robbery offenses was 16 percent higher than in 1985 and 2 percent above the 1980 total.

Rate

The national robbery rate in 1989 was 233 per 100,000 people, 5 percent higher than in 1988. In metropolitan areas, the robbery rate was 293; in cities outside metropolitan areas, it was 58; and in the rural areas, it was 16. With 992 robberies per 100,000 inhabitants, the highest rate was recorded in cities with a million or more inhabitants.

A comparison of 1988 and 1989 regional rates showed an 8-percent increase in the Northeast, which had a rate of 323 per 100,000 population. The rates of 236 in the West and 177 in the Midwest were each up 5 percent, and the South's rate of 217 was 4 percent higher.

Nature

In 1989, a total estimated national loss of $405 million was due to robberies. The value of property stolen during robberies averaged $701 per incident. Average dollar losses ranged from $364 taken during robberies of convenience stores to $3,591 per bank robbery. The impact of this violent crime on its victims cannot be measured in terms of monetary loss alone. While the object of a robbery is to obtain money or property, the crime always involves force or threat of force, and many victims suffer serious personal injury.

As in previous years, robberies on streets or highways accounted for more than half (55 percent) of the offenses in this category. Robberies of commercial and financial establishments accounted for an additional 22 percent, and those occurring at residences, 10 percent. The remainder were miscellaneous types. By type, all categories of robbery showed increases from 1988 to 1989. The increases ranged from 1 percent for residential robberies to 9 percent for street/highway robberies.

Robbery, Percent Distribution, 1989

[By region]

	United States Total	North-eastern States	Mid-western States	Southern States	Western States
Total[1]	100.0	100.0	100.0	100.0	100.0
Street/highway	54.9	64.5	56.5	45.6	51.8
Commercial house	11.8	8.0	10.7	14.7	14.3
Gas or service station ...	2.8	2.1	3.8	3.0	2.7
Convenience store	6.3	2.0	4.0	13.0	6.4
Residence	9.8	10.3	9.7	11.0	8.2
Bank	1.4	.8	1.0	1.1	2.7
Miscellaneous	12.9	12.3	14.4	11.6	13.9

[1]Because of rounding, percentages may not add to totals.

AGGRAVATED ASSAULT

DEFINITION

Aggravated assault is an unlawful attack by one person upon another for the purpose of inflicting severe or aggravated bodily injury. This type of assault is usually accompanied by the use of a weapon or by means likely to produce death or great bodily harm.

TREND

Year	Number of offenses	Rate per 100,000 inhabitants
1988	910,092	370.2
1989	951,707	383.4
Percent change ..	+4.6	+3.6

Volume

Totaling an estimated 951,707 offenses nationally, aggravated assaults in 1989 accounted for 58 percent of the violent crimes. Geographic distribution figures show that 37 percent of the aggravated assault volume was accounted for by the South, 25 percent by the West, and 19 percent each by the Northeast and Midwest.

The 1989 monthly figures show that the greatest number of aggravated assaults was recorded during July, while the lowest volume occurred in February.

Aggravated Assault by Month, 1985-1989

[Percent of annual total]

Months	1985	1986	1987	1988	1989
January	7.0	6.8	7.3	7.2	7.5
February	6.8	6.3	7.0	7.0	6.6
March	8.2	8.0	7.8	7.9	7.9
April	8.2	8.1	8.1	8.1	8.1
May	8.8	9.1	8.9	8.9	8.9
June	9.0	9.7	8.9	9.0	8.9
July	9.5	10.0	9.5	9.8	9.6
August	9.5	10.0	9.5	9.8	9.2
September	8.9	8.8	8.7	9.0	8.8
October	8.8	8.3	8.5	8.4	9.1
November	7.9	7.6	7.9	7.5	7.9
December	7.4	7.4	7.8	7.5	7.5

Trend

In 1989, aggravated assaults were up nationwide, as well as in all regions and population groups, as compared to 1988. The Nation and all cities collectively each recorded 5-percent increases, while the suburban and rural counties experienced 4-percent jumps for the 2-year period. By population grouping, cities with 100,000 to 249,999 inhabitants recorded the greatest rise, 8 percent. During the same time period, the South and West registered 6-percent upswings in their aggravated assault volumes, while increases of 3 and 2 percent were recorded in the Midwest and Northeast, respectively.

Five- and 10-year trends show aggravated assaults up 32 percent above the 1985 level and 41 percent over the 1980 experience.

Rate

Up 4 percent above the 1988 rate, there were 383 reported victims of aggravated assault for every 100,000 people nationwide in 1989. The rate was 27 percent higher than in 1985 and 28 percent above the 1980 rate.

Higher than the national average, the rate in metropolitan areas was 435 per 100,000 in 1989. Cities outside metropolitan areas experienced a rate of 304, and rural counties, a rate of 147.

Regionally, the aggravated assault rates ranged from 468 per 100,000 people in the West to 306 per 100,000 in the Midwest. The rate in the South for 1989 was 406, and in the Northeast, 351. In the South, the rate was up 5 percent in 1989 over 1988. The Midwest and the West each showed rate increases of 3 percent, while the rate in the Northeast rose 2 percent.

Nature

In 1989, 32 percent of the aggravated assaults were committed with blunt objects or other dangerous weapons. Of the remaining weapon categories, personal weapons such as hands, fists, and feet were used in 27 percent of the offenses; firearms in 22 percent; and knives or cutting instruments in the remainder.

Assaults with firearms showed the greatest increase from 1988 to 1989, 8 percent. Those committed with knives or cutting instruments were up 1 percent, those involving blunt objects or other dangerous weapons increased 6 percent, and those in which personal weapons were used rose 4 percent.

Aggravated Assault, Type of Weapons Used, 1989

[Percent distribution by region]

Region	Total all weapons[1]	Fire-arms	Knives or cutting instruments	Other weapons (clubs, blunt objects, etc.)	Personal weapons
Total	100.0	21.5	19.9	31.9	26.8
Northeastern States	100.0	16.3	22.5	34.9	26.3
Midwestern States	100.0	23.6	20.5	32.9	23.1
Southern States	100.0	25.3	22.0	30.7	22.0
Western States	100.0	19.5	15.4	30.1	34.9

[1]Because of rounding, percentages may not add to totals.

BURGLARY

DEFINITION

The Uniform Crime Reporting Program defines burglary as the unlawful entry of a structure to commit a felony or theft. The use of force to gain entry is not required to classify an offense as burglary.

———— TREND ————

Year	Number of offenses	Rate per 100,000 inhabitants
1988	3,218,077	1,309.2
1989	3,168,170	1,276.3
Percent change ..	−1.6	−2.5

Volume

An estimated 3,168,170 burglaries occurred in the United States during 1989. These offenses accounted for 22 percent of the total Crime Index and 25 percent of the property crimes.

Distribution figures for the regions showed that the highest burglary volume occurred in the most populous Southern States, accounting for 42 percent of the total. The Western States followed with 23 percent, the Midwestern States with 19 percent, and the Northeastern States with 16 percent.

Like the previous year, more burglaries occurred in August than any other month. The lowest number was reported in February.

Burglary by Month, 1985-1989

[Percent of annual total]

Months	1985	1986	1987	1988	1989
January	8.2	8.4	8.4	8.4	8.8
February	7.2	7.5	7.8	7.8	7.3
March	8.2	8.3	8.3	8.1	8.2
April	7.8	7.9	7.6	7.5	7.7
May	8.0	8.1	8.0	8.1	8.4
June	7.9	8.1	8.0	8.0	8.3
July	9.0	8.9	8.8	8.8	9.2
August	9.1	9.0	9.1	9.3	9.3
September	8.5	8.5	8.4	8.6	8.6
October	9.0	8.4	8.4	8.5	8.5
November	8.5	8.1	8.4	8.4	8.1
December	8.8	8.8	8.8	8.5	7.8

Trend

Nationwide, the burglary volume decreased 2 percent in 1989 from the 1988 total. By population groupings, the only increases were registered in cities under 10,000 in population, with a rise of less than one-half of 1 percent, and in the rural counties, 1 percent.

Geographically, all four regions of the United States reported decreases in burglaries during 1989 as compared to 1988. The declines were 2 percent in the Western and Midwestern States, and 1 percent in the Northeastern and Southern States.

Rate

A burglary rate of 1,276 per 100,000 inhabitants was registered nationwide in 1989. The rate fell 3 percent from 1988 and was 24 percent below the 1980 rate, the highest in history. In 1989, for every 100,000 in population, the rate was 1,412 in the metropolitan areas, 1,040 in the cities outside metropolitan areas, and 673 in the rural counties.

Regionally, the burglary rate was 1,554 in the Southern States, 1,388 in the Western States, 1,013 in the Midwestern States, and 1,007 in the Northeastern States. A comparison of 1988 and 1989 rates showed decreases of 5 percent in the West, 3 percent in the Midwest, 2 percent in the South, and 1 percent in the Northeast.

Nature

Two of every 3 burglaries in 1989 were residential in nature. Seventy percent of all burglaries involved forcible entry, 22 percent were unlawful entries (without force), and the remainder were forcible entry attempts. Offenses for which time of occurrence was reported showed that 49 percent happened during the daytime hours and 51 percent during the nighttime hours.

Burglary victims suffered losses estimated at $3.4 billion in 1989, and the average dollar loss per burglary was $1,060. The average loss for residential offenses was $1,080, while for nonresidential property, it was $1,023.

Residential burglary showed a 3-percent decline from 1988 to 1989; nonresidential offenses showed a 2-percent increase during the same period.

Clearances

Geographically, 14 percent of the burglaries brought to the attention of law enforcement agencies across the country and in the Northeast were cleared in 1989. In the South, the clearance rate was 16 percent; in the West, 13 percent; and in the Midwest, 12 percent.

Rural county law enforcement cleared 16 percent of the burglaries in their jurisdictions. Equivalent to the national experience, 14-percent clearance rates were recorded by agencies in cities and suburban counties.

Adults were involved in 83 percent of all burglary offenses cleared, and only young people under 18 years of age were offenders in the remaining 17 percent. Similar to the national experience, persons under age 18 accounted for 17 percent of the burglary clearances in cities. Suburban and rural county law enforcement agencies reported 18 and 19 percent, respectively, of their burglary clearances involved only juveniles. The highest degree of juvenile involvement was recorded in the Nation's smallest cities (under 10,000 in population) where young persons under 18 years of age accounted for 23 percent of the clearances.

LARCENY-THEFT

DEFINITION

Larceny-theft is the unlawful taking, carrying, leading, or riding away of property from the possession or constructive possession of another. It includes crimes such as shoplifting, pocket-picking, purse-snatching, thefts from motor vehicles, thefts of motor vehicle parts and accessories, bicycle thefts, etc., in which no use of force, violence, or fraud occurs.

TREND

Year	Number of offenses	Rate per 100,000 inhabitants
1988	7,705,872	3,134.9
1989	7,872,442	3,171.3
Percent change ..	+ 2.2	+ 1.2

Volume

Estimated at nearly 7.9 million offenses during 1989, larceny-thefts comprised 55 percent of the Crime Index total and 62 percent of the property crimes. Similar to the experience in previous years, larceny-thefts were recorded most often during August and least frequently in February. When viewed geographically, the most populous Southern States recorded 37 percent of the larceny-theft total. The Western States registered 24 percent; the Midwestern States, 22 percent; and the Northeastern States, 17 percent.

Larceny-Theft by Month, 1985-1989

[Percent of annual total]

Months	1985	1986	1987	1988	1989
January	7.4	7.8	7.6	7.6	8.0
February	7.0	7.2	7.5	7.5	7.2
March	8.2	8.3	8.3	8.2	8.2
April	8.1	8.2	8.0	7.8	8.0
May	8.4	8.4	8.2	8.3	8.6
June	8.5	8.6	8.5	8.5	8.7
July	9.3	9.1	9.1	9.0	9.2
August	9.5	9.3	9.2	9.5	9.5
September	8.4	8.4	8.4	8.5	8.3
October	8.9	8.5	8.6	8.7	8.6
November	8.2	7.9	8.1	8.2	8.0
December	8.1	8.3	8.4	8.3	7.7

Trend

Upward trends in the 1989 volume of larceny-thefts were evident nationwide and in all population groups when compared to 1988. The Nation, all cities collectively, and the suburban and rural counties each showed 2-percent increases. Regionally, volume upswings of 3 percent were recorded in both the Midwestern and the Southern States. The Western States registered a 2-percent increase, while the Northeastern States showed virtually no change.

The 5- and 10-year national trends indicated larceny was up 14 percent over the 1985 total and rose 10 percent above the 1980 level.

Rate

The 1989 larceny-theft rate was 3,171 per 100,000 United States inhabitants. While the 1989 rate was 1 percent higher than in 1988 and 9 percent above the 1985 level, it showed no change from 1980. The 1989 rate was 3,534 per 100,000 inhabitants of metropolitan areas; 3,380 per 100,000 population in cities outside metropolitan areas; and 995 per 100,000 people in the rural counties.

Regionally, the rates of 3,404 in the South and 2,936 in the Midwest were up 2 percent over 1988 levels. Showing no change from 1988, the 1989 rates per 100,000 inhabitants in the West and the Northeast were 3,633 and 2,586, respectively.

Nature

During 1989, the average value of property stolen due to larceny-theft was $462, up from $426 in 1988. When the average value was applied to the estimated number of larceny-thefts, the loss to victims nationally was $3.6 billion for the year. This estimated dollar loss is considered conservative since many offenses in the larceny category, particularly if the value of the stolen goods is small, never come to law enforcement attention. Losses in 24 percent of the thefts reported to law enforcement in 1989 ranged from $50 to $200, while in 35 percent, they were over $200.

Losses of goods and property reported stolen as a result of pocket-picking averaged $303; purse-snatching, $244; and shoplifting, $102. Thefts from buildings resulted in an average loss of $747; from motor vehicles, $502; and from coin-operated machines, $153. The average value loss due to thefts of motor vehicle accessories was $315 and for thefts of bicycles, $204.

Thefts of motor vehicle parts, accessories, and contents made up the largest portion of reported larcenies–38 percent. Also contributing to the high volume of thefts were shoplifting, accounting for 16 percent; thefts from buildings, 15 percent; and bicycle thefts, 5 percent. The remainder were distributed among pocket-picking, purse-snatching, thefts from coin-operated machines, and all other types of larceny-thefts. The accompanying table presents the distribution of larceny-theft by type and geographic region.

Larceny Analysis by Region, 1989

[Percent distribution]

	United States Total	North-eastern States	Mid-western States	Southern States	Western States
Total[1]	100.0	100.0	100.0	100.0	100.0
Pocket-picking	1.0	3.5	.6	.3	.4
Purse-snatching	1.1	2.1	1.1	.9	.7
Shoplifting	15.6	13.0	13.3	15.9	19.1
From motor vehicles (except accessories)	22.0	22.5	18.8	19.3	27.6
Motor vehicle accessories	15.6	16.5	15.4	17.4	12.9
Bicycles	5.5	5.4	5.6	4.0	7.2
From buildings	14.7	18.5	19.0	11.7	11.9
From coin-operated machines	.8	1.2	.6	.9	.6
All others	23.7	17.2	25.5	29.6	19.4

[1]Because of rounding, percentages may not add to totals.

MOTOR VEHICLE THEFT

DEFINITION
Defined as the theft or attempted theft of a motor vehicle, this offense category includes the stealing of automobiles, trucks, buses, motorcycles, motorscooters, snowmobiles, etc.

TREND

Year	Number of offenses	Rate per 100,000 inhabitants
1988	1,432,916	582.9
1989	1,564,800	630.4
Percent change ..	+9.2	+8.1

Volume

An estimated total of 1,564,800 thefts of motor vehicles occurred in the United States during 1989. These offenses comprised 12 percent of all property crimes. The regional distribution of motor vehicle thefts showed 31 percent of the volume was in the Southern States, 26 percent in the Western States, 25 percent in the Northeastern States, and 18 percent in the Midwestern States.

The 1989 monthly figures show that the greatest numbers of motor vehicle thefts were recorded during August and October, while the lowest count was in February.

Motor Vehicle Theft by Month, 1985-1989

[Percent of annual total]

Months	1985	1986	1987	1988	1989
January	7.8	7.9	7.9	8.0	8.3
February	7.1	7.1	7.5	7.6	7.3
March	8.1	8.1	8.4	7.9	8.1
April	7.8	7.8	7.9	7.4	7.5
May	8.0	8.0	8.0	7.8	8.0
June	8.2	8.2	8.1	8.0	8.2
July	8.9	8.9	8.8	8.8	8.8
August	9.1	9.5	9.0	9.4	9.0
September	8.7	8.7	8.4	8.7	8.5
October	9.1	9.0	8.8	9.0	9.0
November	8.6	8.5	8.5	8.7	8.7
December	8.7	8.3	8.7	8.7	8.5

Trend

The number of motor vehicle thefts increased 9 percent nationally from 1988 to 1989. This upward trend was evident in all population groups with cities having populations of 100,000 to 249,999 showing the largest increase, 13 percent. Suburban and rural counties showed increases of 8 percent and 3 percent, respectively.

Geographically, all four regions experienced motor vehicle theft increases. The increases were 12 percent in the Western Region, 10 percent in the Southern Region, 8 percent in the Northeastern Region, and 6 percent in the Midwestern Region.

The accompanying chart shows that the volume of motor vehicle thefts in 1989 increased 42 percent over the 1985 volume.

Rate

The 1989 national motor vehicle theft rate—630 per 100,000 people—was 8 percent higher than the rate in 1988. The rate was 36 percent higher than in 1985 and 26 percent above the 1980 rate.

For every 100,000 inhabitants living in MSAs, there were 771 motor vehicle thefts reported in 1989. The rate in cities outside metropolitan areas (other cities) was 221 and in rural counties, 117. As in previous years, the highest rates were in the Nation's most heavily populated municipalities, indicating that this offense is primarily a large-city problem. For every 100,000 inhabitants in cities with populations over 250,000, the 1989 motor vehicle theft rate was 1,602. The Nation's smallest cities, those with fewer than 10,000 inhabitants, recorded a rate of 251 per 100,000.

Among the regions, the motor vehicle theft rates ranged from 775 per 100,000 people in the Western States to 471 in the Midwestern States. The Northeastern States' rate was 769 and the Southern States' rate, 572. All regions registered rate increases from 1988 to 1989. In both the Western and Southern States, the increase was 9 percent; in the Northeastern States, 8 percent; and in the Midwestern States, 6 percent.

An estimated average of 1 of every 121 registered motor vehicles was stolen nationwide during 1989. Regionally, this rate was greatest in the Northeast where 1 of every 86 motor vehicles registered was stolen. The other three regions reported lesser rates—1 per 102 in the West, 1 per 137 in the South, and 1 per 168 in the Midwest.

Nature

During 1989, the estimated value of motor vehicles stolen nationwide was over $8 billion. At the time of theft, the average value per vehicle stolen was $5,222.

Seventy-nine percent of all motor vehicles reported stolen during the year were automobiles, 15 percent were trucks or buses, and the remainder were other types.

Motor Vehicle Theft, 1989

[Percent distribution by region]

Region	Total[1]	Autos	Trucks and buses	Other vehicles
Total	100.0	78.8	14.8	6.4
Northeastern States	100.0	92.4	4.6	3.0
Midwestern States	100.0	82.4	10.7	6.9
Southern States	100.0	73.5	18.9	7.6
Western States	100.0	68.5	23.3	8.1

[1]Because of rounding, percentages may not add to totals.

Bibliography

Abraham, H., *The Judicial Process,* Oxford University Press, 1968.

Adler, F., *Sisters in Crime,* McGraw-Hill, 1975.

Allen, H. and C. Simonsen, *Corrections in America,* Glencoe Press, 1978.

Amos, W., *Delinquent Children in Juvenile Correctional Institutions,* C.C. Thomas, 1966.

Atkins, B. and M. Pogrebin, *The Invisible Justice System,* W.H. Anderson, 1978.

Balton, M., *European Policing,* John Jay Press, 1978.

Bartollas, C., S. Miller, and S. Dinitz, *Juvenile Victimization,* Sage Publications, Inc., 1976.

Bartollas, C. and S.J. Miller, *Correctional Administration: Theory and Practice,* McGraw-Hill, 1978.

Bartollas, C. and S.J. Miller, *The Juvenile Offender: Control, Correction and Treatment,* Allyn & Bacon, Inc., 1978.

Bayley, D., *Police and Society,* Sage Publications, Inc., 1978.

Beigel, H., *Beneath the Badge,* Harper and Row Publishers, Inc., 1977.

Bell, J.B., *Time of Terror: How Democratic Societies Respond to Revolutionary Violence,* Basic Books Inc., 1978.

Bequai, A., *Organized Crime,* Lexington Books, 1979.

Bequai, A., *White Collar Crime,* Lexington Books, 1979.

Berkeley, G., *The Democratic Policeman,* Beacon Press, 1969.

Berkley, G., *Introduction to Criminal Justice,* Holbrook, 1980.

Berns, W., *For Capital Punishment: Crime and the Morality of the Death Penalty,* Basic Books, Inc., 1979.

Best, A., *The Politics of Law Enforcement,* Lexington Books, 1974.

Bittner, E., *The Functions of Police in Modern Society,* U.S. Government Printing Office, 1970.

Bittner, E., and S. Krantz, *Standards Relating to Police Handling of Juvenile Problems,* Ballinger Publishing Co., 1978.

Blumberg, A.S., *Criminal Justice: Issues and Ironies,* New Viewpoints, 1979.

Bond, J., *Plea-Bargaining and Guilty Pleas,* Clark Boardman Co., 1975.

Bouza, A., *Police Administration,* Pergamon Press, Inc., 1979.

Bowker, L., *Women, Crime, and the Criminal Justice System,* Lexington Books, 1978.

Bowker, L., *Prison Victimization,* Elsevier, 1980.

Bracey, D.H., *"Baby-Pros"—Preliminary Profiles of Juvenile Prostitutes,* John Jay Press, 1978.

Butler, A., *The Law Enforcement Process,* Alfred Publishing Co., Inc., 1976.

Carlson, D.L., *Criminal Justice Procedure,* W.H. Anderson, 1979.

Carrington, F., *The Victims,* Arlington House, Inc., 1975.

Carte, G., *Police Reform in the United States,* University of California Press, 1975.

Carter, R. and L. Wilkins, *Probation, Parole and Community Corrections,* Wiley, 1976.

Challenge of Crime in a Free Society, The, Presidential Commission on Law Enforcement and Administration of Justice, 1967.

Chambliss, W., *Law, Order, and Power,* Addison-Wesley Publishing Co., 1971.

Chevigny, P., *Cops and Rebels: A Study of Provocation,* Random House, Inc., 1972.

Clinard, M.B., *Cities with Little Crime,* Cambridge University Press, 1978.

Cole, G., *The American System of Criminal Justice,* Duxbury, 1976.

Collins, M.C., *The Child-Abuser,* Publishing Sciences Group, 1978.

Conklin, J.,, *"Illegal But Not Criminal": Business Crime in America,* Prentice-Hall, Inc., 1977.

Conley, J.A., *Theory and Research in Criminal Justice,* W.H. Anderson, 1979.

Conrad, J., *Crime and Its Correction,* University of California Press, 1965.

Conrad, J., *The Dangerous and the Endangered,* Lexington Books, 1978.

Conrad, J. and S. Dinitz, *In Fear of Each Other: Studies of Dangerousness in America,* Lexington Books, 1977.

Cook, J.G., *Constitutional Rights of the Accused, The,* Lawyers Co-Operative Publishing Co., 1972.

Cotte, T.J., *Children in Jail,* Beacon Press, 1978.

Creamer, J., *The Law of Arrest, Search and Seizure,* W.B. Saunders Co., 1975.

Cressey, D., *Criminal Organization,* Harper & Row Publishers, Inc., 1972.

Davis, K., *Discretionary Justice,* University of Illinois Press, 1971.

Delin, B., *The Sex Offender,* Beacon Press, 1978.

Devine, P.E., *The Ethics of Homicide,* Cornell University Press, 1979.

Dowling, J., *Criminal Procedure,* West, 1976.

Drapkin, I. and E. Viano, *Victimology,* Lexington Books, 1974.

Empey, L.T., *American Delinquency: Its Meaning and Construction,* Dorsey, 1978.

Falkin, G.R., *Reducing Delinquency,* Lexington Books, 1978.

Felkenes, G., *Constitutional Law for Criminal Justice,* Prentice-Hall, Inc., 1977.

Felkenes, G., *The Criminal Justice System,* Prentice-Hall, Inc., 1973.

Felkenes, G., *Criminal Law and Procedure,* Prentice-Hall, Inc., 1976.

Felt, M., *The FBI Pyramid,* G.P. Putnam's Sons, 1979.

Field, H.S. and N.J. Barnett, *Jurors and Rape,* Lexington Books, 1978.

Folley, V.L., *American Law Enforcement,* Allyn & Bacon, Inc., 1980.

Fogel, D., *The Justice Model for Corrections,* W.H. Anderson, 1979.

Foucault, M., *Discipline and Punish,* Pantheon Books, Inc., 1978.

Fox, J.A., *Forecasting Crime Data,* Lexington Books, 1979.

Fox, J.G., *Women in Cages,* Ballinger Publishing Co., 1979.

Frankel, M., *Criminal Sentences,* Hill & Wang, 1972.

Freeman, J.C., *Prisons Past and Future,* Heinemann, 1979.

Gardiner, J. and M. Mulkey, *Crime and Criminal Justice,* Heath, 1975.

Gaylin, W., *Partial Justice,* Knopf, Inc., 1974.

Geis, G., *Not the Law's Business,* NIMH, 1972.

Geis, G. and R. Meier, *White Collar Crime,* Free Press, 1977.

Gerber, R., *Contemporary Punishment,* University of Notre Dame Press, 1972.

Germann, A., et al., *Introduction to Law Enforcement,* C.C. Thomas, 1973.

Gibbs, J., *Crime, Punishment, and Deterrence,* Elsevier North-Holland, Inc., 1975.

Gifis, S.H., *Law Dictionary,* Barron's, 1975.

Glaser, D., *Adult Crime and Social Policy,* Prentice-Hall, Inc., 1972.

Glaser, D., *Crime in Our Changing Society,* Holt, Rinehart & Winston, Inc., 1978.

Goldsmith, J. and S.S. Goldsmith, *Crime and the Elderly,* D.C. Heath, 1976.

Goldstein, A., et al., *Police Crisis Intervention,* Pergamon Press, Inc., 1979.

Goldstein, H., *Policing a Free Society,* Ballinger Publishing Co., 1977.

Gottfredson, M.R. and D.M. Gottfredson, *Decision-Making in Criminal Justice,* Ballinger Publishing Co., 1979.

Greenberg, D., *Corrections and Punishment,* Sage, 1977.

Greenwood, P., *The Criminal Investigation Process,* Rand McNally Co., 1975.

Grosman, B., *New Directions in Sentencing,* Butterworths, 1980.

Gross, Hyman, *A Theory of Criminal Justice,* Oxford University Press, 1978.

Guide to Criminal Justice Information Sources, National Council on Crime and Delinquency, 1977.

Hahn, P.H., *Crimes Against the Elderly,* Davis, 1976.

Hahn, P.H., *The Juvenile Offender and the Law,* W.H. Anderson, 1978.

Haskell, M.R. and L. Yablonsky, *Crime and Delinquency,* Rand-McNally Co., 1978.

Hemphill, C.F., *Criminal Procedure: The Administration of Justice,* Goodyear Publishing Co., Inc., 1978.

Heumann, M., *Plea-Bargaining,* University of Chicago Press, 1978.

Hills, S., *Crime, Power and Morality,* Chandler, 1971.

Jahnige, T., *The Federal Judicial System,* Holt, Rinehart and Winston, Inc., 1978.

James, H., *Crisis in the Courts,* McKay, 1971.

Johnson, N., *The Human Cage: A Brief History of Prison Architecture,* Walker, 1973.

Johnson, R.E., *Juvenile Delinquency and Its Origins,* Cambridge University Press, 1979.

Johnson, T.A., G. Mizner, and L.P. Brown, *The Police and Society,* Prentice-Hall, 1981.

Jones, D.A., *Crime and Criminal Responsibility,* Nelson-Hall Publishers, 1978.

Jones, D.A., *Crime Without Punishment,* Lexington Books, 1979.

Kalven, H. and H. Zeisel, *The American Jury,* Little, Brown and Co., 1966.

Kamisar, Y., et al., *Criminal Law and Procedure,* West, 1974.

Kassebaum, G., *Prison Treatment and Parole Survival,* Wiley, 1972.

Killinger, G. and P. Cromwell, *Penology,* West, 1973.

Killinger, G.G. and P.F. Cromwell, *Corrections in the Community,* West, 1978.

Klein, I., *Law of Evidence for Police,* West, 1973.

Klein, M., *The Juvenile Justice System,* Sage Publications, Inc., 1976.

Klotter, J. and J. Kanovitz, *Constitutional Law for Police,* Anderson, 1977.

Kratcoski, P. and D. Walker, *Criminal Justice in America,* Scott, Foresman and Co., 1978.

Kratcoski, P.C. and L.D. Kratcoski, *Juvenile Delinquency,* Prentice-Hall, Inc., 1979.

LaFave, W.R., *Principles of Criminal Law,* West, 1979.

LaPatra, J.W., *Analyzing the Criminal Justice System,* Lexington Books, 1978.

Levin, M., *Urban Politics and the Criminal Courts,* University of Chicago Press, 1977.

Lewis, P.W. and K.D. Peoples, *The Supreme Court and the Criminal Process,* W.B. Saunders Co., 1978.

Lipton, D., R. Martinson, and J. Wilks, *The Effectiveness of Correctional Treatment,* Praeger Publishers, Inc., 1975.

Loeb, R.H., *Crime and Capital Punishment,* Franklin-Watts, 1978.

MacNamara, D. and F. Montanino, *Incarceration,* Sage Publications, 1978.

MacNamara, D. and E. Sagarin, *Perspectives on Correction,* Thomas Y. Crowell Co., 1971.

MacNamara, D. and E. Sagarin, *Sex, Crime, and the Law,* Macmillan-Free Press, 1977.

MacNamara, D. and M. Riedel, *Police: Problems and Prospects,* Praeger Publishers, Inc., 1974.

MacNamara, D. and E. Sagarin, *Corrections, Punishment and Rehabilitation,* Praeger, 1972.

MacNamara, D.E.J. and L.W. McCorkle, *Crime, Criminals and Corrections,* John Jay Press, 1982.

Marmor, J., *Homosexual Behavior: A Modern Reappraisal,* Basic Books, 1979.

Mathias, W., *Foundations of Criminal Justice,* Prentice-Hall, 1980.

McDonald, W., *Criminal Justice and the Victim,* Sage Publications, 1976.

Menninger, K., *The Crime of Punishment,* Viking Press, 1968.

Miller, F., *The Correctional Process,* The Foundation Press, 1971.

Miller, F., *Prosecution,* Little, Brown and Co., 1970.

Mitford, J., *Kind and Usual Punishment,* Knopf, Inc., 1973.

More, H., *Effective Police Administration,* West, 1979.

Morris, N., *The Honest Politician's Guide to Crime Control,* The University of Chicago Press, 1970.

Morris, N., *The Future of Imprisonment,* The University of Chicago Press, 1974.

Munro, J., *Administrative Behavior and Police Organization,* W.H. Anderson, 1974.

Nagel, S., *Modeling the Criminal Justice System,* Sage Publications, 1977.

Nagel, S., *The Rights of the Accused,* Sage Publications, 1972.

Nagel, S. and H.G. Neef, *Decision Theory and the Legal Process,* Lexington Books, 1979.

Navasky, V. and D. Paster, *Law Enforcement: The Federal Role,* McGraw-Hill Book Co., 1976.

Neary, M., *Corruption and Its Management,* American Academy for Professional Law Enforcement, 1977.

Netter, G., *Explaining Crime,* McGraw-Hill Book Co., 1978.

Neubauer, D., *Criminal Justice in Middle America,* General Learning Press, 1974.

Newman, C., *Probation, Parole and Pardons,* C.C. Thomas, 1970.

Newman, G., *The Punishment Response,* J.P. Lippincott Co., 1978.

Niederhoffer, A., *The Ambivalent Force,* Ginn and Co., 1970.

Niederhoffer, A., *The Police Family,* Lexington Books, 1978.

O'Brien, J.T. and M. Marcus, *Crime and Justice in America,* Pergamon Press Inc., 1979.

Ohlin, L.E., *et al., Reforming Juvenile Corrections,* Ballinger Publishing Co., 1979.

Packer, H., *The Limits of the Criminal Sanction,* Stanford University Press, 1968.

Platt, A., *The Child Savers: The Invention of Delinquency,* The University of Chicago Press, 1977.

Platt, T. and P. Takagi, *Punishment and Penal Discipline,* Crime and Social Justice Press, 1979.

Price, B., *Police Professionalism,* Lexington Books, 1977.

Quinney, R., *Critique of the Legal Order,* Little, Brown and Co., 1974.

Rawls, J., *A Theory of Justice,* Harvard University Press, 1971.

Reid, S.T., *Crime and Criminology,* Holt, Rinehart, & Winston, Inc., 1979.

Reiss, A., *The Police and the Public,* Yale University Press, 1971.

Reppetto, T., *Residential Crime,* Ballinger Publishing Co., 1974.

Reppetto, T., *The Blue Parade,* The Free Press, 1978.

Rich, V., *Law and the Administration of Justice,* Wiley, 1979.

Rieber, R.W. and H.J. Vetter, *The Psychological Foundations of Criminal Justice,* John Jay Press, 1979.

Rifai, M.A., *Justice and Older Americans,* D.C. Heath and Co., 1977.

Ross, R. and P. Gendreau, *Effective Correctional Treatment,* Butterworths, 1980.

Rossett, A. and D. Cressey, *Justice by Consent,* J.P. Lippincott Co., 1976.

Rothman, D., *The Discovery of Asylum,* Little, Brown and Co., 1971.

Rubin, S., *Law of Criminal Correction,* West, 1973.

Rush, G.E., *Dictionary of Criminal Justice,* Holbrook Press Inc., 1977.

Sagarin, E., *Deviants and Deviance,* Praeger Publishers, Inc., 1976.

Sagarin, E., *Criminology: New Concerns,* Sage, 1979.

Saks, M.J., *Jury Verdicts,* D.C. Heath and Co., 1977.

Sanders, W., *Detective Work,* The Free Press, 1977.

Saunders, C., *Upgrading the American Police,* The Brookings Institution, 1970.

Schultz, D.D., *Modern Police Administration,* Gulf Publishing Co., 1979.

Schur, E., *Crimes Without Victims,* Prentice-Hall, Inc., 1965.

Senna, J. and L. Siegel, *Introduction to Criminal Justice,* West, 1978.

Shanahan, D.T. and Whisenand, P.M., *Dimensions of Criminal Justice Planning,* Allyn & Bacon, Inc., 1980.

Sheehan, S., *A Prison and a Prisoner,* Houghton Mifflin Co., 1978.

Sherman, L.W., *The Quality of Police Education,* Jossey-Bass, Inc., 1978.

Sherman, L.W., *Scandal and Reform: Controlling Police Corruption,* University of California Press, 1978.

Silberman, C., *Criminal Violence—Criminal Justice,* Random House, Inc., 1978.

Simon, R., *Women and Crime,* Lexington Books, 1975.

Simon, R., *The Jury System in America,* Lexington Books, 1979.

Simonsen, C.E. and M.S. Gordon, *Juvenile Justice in America,* Glencoe Press, 1979.

Skolnick, J. and T. Gray, *Police in America,* Little, Brown, 1975.

Snortum, J. and I. Hadar, *Criminal Justice,* Palisades Publishers, 1976.

Stanley, D., *Prisoners Among Us: The Problem of Parole,* The Brookings Institution, 1975.

Stead, P.J., *Pioneers in Policing,* Patterson Smith, 1977.

Strasburg, P., *Violent Delinquents,* Monarch Books, 1978.

Strickland, K.G., *Correctional Institutions for Women in the United States,* Lexington Books, 1978.

Stuckey, G.B., *Evidence for the Law Enforcement Officer,* McGraw-Hill Book Co., 1979.

Szasz, T., *Psychiatric Justice,* Macmillan, 1965.

Toch, H., *Living in Prison,* The Free Press, 1977.

Turk, A., *Legal Sanctions and Social Control,* NIMH, 1972.

Ungar, S., *F.B.I.,* Little-Brown and Co., 1976.

Ulviller, H., *Adjudication,* West, 1975.

Van Dyke, J.M., *Jury Selection,* Ballinger Publishing Co., 1977.

Vetter, H. and C. Simonsen, *Criminal Justice in America,* W.B. Saunders Co., 1976.

Viano, E.C., *Victims and Society,* Visage Press, 1976.

Von Grimme, T.L., *Your Career in Law Enforcement,* ARCO, 1979.

Von Hirsch, A., *Doing Justice: The Choice of Punishments,* Hill and Wang, 1976.

Walker, A., *A Critical History of Police Reform,* Lexington Books, 1977.

Warren, E., *The Memoirs of Chief Justice Warren,* Doubleday, 1977.

Weaver, S., *Decisions to Prosecute,* M.I.T. Press, 1977.

Weinreb, L., *Leading Constitutional Cases on Criminal Justice,* Foundation Press, 1978.

Wheeler, R. and H. Whitcomb, *Judicial Administration,* Prentice-Hall, 1977.

Whisenand, P., *Crime Prevention,* Holbrook Press, 1977.

Weiss, J.A., *Law of the Elderly,* Practicing Law Institute, 1977.

Wice, R., *Bail and Its Reform,* National Institute of Law Enforcement and Criminal Law, 1974.

Wilkins, L., *Evaluation of Penal Measures,* Random House, 1969.

Wilson, J., *Varieties of Police Behavior,* Harvard University Press, 1968.

Wilson, J., *Thinking About Crime,* Basic Books, 1975.

Wilson, J., *The Investigators: Managing the FBI and Narcotics Agents,* Basic Books, 1978.

Witt, J.W., *The Police, the Courts and the Minority Community,* Lexington Books, 1978.

Wolf, J.B., *The Police Intelligence System,* John Jay Press, 1978.

Wolfgang, M.E., *Prisons: Success and Failure,* Lexington Books, 1978.

Wolfgang, M.E. and F. Ferracuti, *Diagnosis in Criminal Justice Systems,* Lexington Books, 1978.

Wootton, B., *Crime and Penal Policy,* Allen & Unwin, 1978.

Wright, E., *The Politics of Punishment,* Harper & Row, 1973.

Zimring, F. and G. Hawkins, *Deterrence,* University of Chicago Press, 1973.

Glossary

Abet To encourage another to commit a crime. This encouragement may be by advice, inducement, command, etc. The abettor of a crime is equally guilty with the one who actually commits the crime.

Accessory after the Fact One who harbors, assists, or protects another person, although he knows that person has committed a crime.

Accessory before the Fact One who helps another to commit a crime, even though he is absent when the crime is committed.

Accomplice One who is involved in the commission of a crime with others, whether he actually commits the crime or abets the same. The term *principal* means the same thing, except that one may be a principal if he commits a crime without the aid of others.

Acquit To free a person from an accusation of criminal guilt; to find "not guilty."

Affidavit A written declaration or statement sworn to and affirmed by an officer having authority to administer an oath.

Affirmation To swear on one's conscience that what he says is true. An *oath* means that one calls upon God to witness the truth of what he says.

Alias Any name by which one is known other than his true name. *Alias dictus* is the more technically correct term but it is rarely used.

Alibi A claim that one was in a place different from that charged. If the person proves his alibi, he proves that he could not have committed the crime charged.

Allegation The declaration of a party to a lawsuit made in a pleading, that states what he expects to prove.

Amnesty A class or group pardon (e.g., all political prisoners).

Appeal A case carried to a higher court to ask that the decision of the lower court, in which the case originated, be altered or overruled completely.

Appellate Court A court that has jurisdiction to hear cases on appeal; not a trial court.

Arraignment The appearance before the court of a person charged with a crime. He or she is advised of the charges, bail is set, and a plea of "guilty" or "not guilty" is entered.

Arrest To take a person into custody so that he may be held to answer for a crime.

Autopsy A post-mortem examination of a human body to determine the cause of death.

Bail Property (usually money) deposited with a court in exchange for the release of a person in custody to assure later appearance.

Bail Bond An obligation signed by the accused and his sureties, that insures his presence in court.

Bailiff A court attendant whose duties are to keep order in the courtroom and to have custody of the jury.

Bench Warrant An order by the court for the apprehension and arrest of a defendant or other person who has failed to appear when so ordered.

Bill of Rights The first ten amendments to the Constitution of the United States which define such rights as: due process of law, immunity from illegal search and seizure, the ban on cruel and unusual punishment, unreasonably high bail, indictment by a grand jury, and speedy trial.

Bind Over To hold for trial.

"Blue" Laws Laws in some jurisdictions prohibiting sales of merchandise, athletic contests, and the sale of alcoholic beverages on Sundays.

Booking The procedure at a police station of entering the name and identifying particulars relating to an arrested person, the charges filed against him, and the name of the arresting officer.

Burden of Proof The duty of affirmatively proving the guilt of the defendant "beyond a reasonable doubt."

Calendar A list of cases to be heard in a trial court, on a specific day, and containing the title of the case, the lawyers involved, and the index number.

Capital Crime Any crime that may be punishable by death or imprisonment for life.

Caseload The number of cases actively being investigated by a police detective or being supervised by a probation or parole officer.

Change of Venue The removal of a trial from one jurisdiction to another in order to avoid local prejudice.

Charge In criminal law, the accusation made against a person. It also refers to the judge's instruction to the jury on legal points.

Circumstantial Evidence Indirect evidence; evidence from which the principal fact can be proved or disproved by inference. Example: a finger-print found at the crime scene.

Citizen's Arrest A taking into custody of an alleged offender by a person not a law enforcement officer. Such an arrest is lawful if the crime was attempted or committed in his presence.

Code A compilation, compendium, or revision of laws, arranged into chapters, having a table of contents and index, and promulgated by legislative authority. Criminal code; penal code.

Coercion The compelling of a person to do that which he is not obliged to do, or to omit doing what he may legally do, by some illegal threat, force, or intimidation. For example: a forced confession.

Commit To place a person in custody in a prison or other institution by lawful order.

Common Law Law that derives its authority from usage and custom or court decisions.

Commutation To change the punishment meted out to a criminal to one less severe. Executive clemency.

Complainant The victim of a crime who brings the facts to the attention of the authorities.

Complaint A sworn written allegation stating that a specified person committed a crime. Sometimes called an *information*. When issued from a *Grand Jury*, it is called an *indictment*.

Compulsion An irresistible impulse to commit some act, such as stealing, setting a fire, or an illegal sexual act.

Confession An admission by the accused of his guilt; a partial admission (e.g., that he was at the crime scene; that he had a motive) is referred to as "an admission against interest."

Confinement Deprivation of liberty in a jail or prison either as punishment for a crime or as detention while guilt or innocence is being determined.

Consensual Crime A crime without a victim; one in which both parties voluntarily participate (e.g., adultery, sodomy, etc.).

Conspiracy A secret combination of two or more persons who plan for the purpose of committing a crime or any unlawful act or a lawful act by unlawful or criminal means.

Contempt of Court Behavior that impugns the authority of a court or obstructs the execution of court orders.

Continuance A delay in trial granted by the judge on request of either the prosecutor or defense counsel; an adjournment.

Conviction A finding by the jury (or by the trial judge in cases tried without a jury) that the accused is guilty of a crime.

Corporal Corporal punishment is pain inflicted on the body of another. Flogging.

Corpus Delicti The objective proof that a crime has been committed as distinguished from an accidental death, injury or loss.

Corrections Area of criminal justice dealing with convicted offenders in jails, prisons; on probation or parole.

Corroborating Evidence Supplementary evidence that tends to strengthen or confirm other evidence given previously.

Crime An act or omission prohibited and punishable by law. Crimes are divided into *felonies* and *misdemeanors;* and recorded as "crimes against the person" (murder, rape, assault, robbery) and "crimes against property" (burglary, larceny, auto theft). There are also crimes against public morality and against public order.

Criminal Insanity Lack of mental capacity to do or refrain from doing a criminal act; inability to distinguish right from wrong.

Criminalistics Crime laboratory procedures (e.g., ballistics, analysis of stains, etc.).

Criminology The scientific study of crime and criminals.

Cross-Examination The questioning of a witness by the party who did not produce the witness.

Culpability Guilt; *see also mens rea.*

Defendant The person who is being prosecuted.

Delinquency Criminality by a boy or girl who has not as yet reached the age set by the state for trial as an adult (the age varies from jurisdiction to jurisdiction and from crime to crime).

Demurrer In court procedure, a statement that the charge that a crime has been committed has no sufficient basis in law, despite the truth of the facts alleged.

Deposition The testimony of a witness not taken in open court but taken in pursuance of authority to take such testimony elsewhere.

Detention To hold a person in confinement while awaiting trial or sentence, or as a material witness.

Deterrence To prevent criminality by fear of the consequences; one of the rationalizations for punishing offenders.

Directed Verdict An instruction by the judge to the jury to return a specific verdict. A judge may not direct a guilty verdict.

Direct Evidence Proof of facts by witnesses who actually saw acts or heard words, as distinguished from *Circumstantial Evidence.*

Direct Examination The first questioning of a witness by the party who produced him.

Discretion The decision-making powers of officers of the criminal justice system (e.g., to arrest or not, to prosecute or not, to plea-bargain, to grant probation, or to sentence to a penal institution).

District Attorney Prosecutor; sometimes County Attorney, (U.S. Attorney in Federal practice).

Docket The formal record maintained by the court clerk, listing all cases heard. It contains the defendant's name, index number, date of arrest, and the outcome of the case.

Double Jeopardy To be prosecuted twice for the same offense.

Due Process Law in its regular course of administration through the courts of justice. Guaranteed by the 5th and 14th Amendments.

Embracery An attempt to influence a jury, or a member thereof, in their verdict by any improper means.

Entrapment The instigation of a crime by officers or agents of a government who induce a person to commit a crime that he did not originally contemplate in order to institute a criminal prosecution against him.

Evidence All the means used to prove or disprove the fact at issue.

Examination An investigation of a witness by counsel in the form of questions for the purpose of bringing before the court knowledge possessed by the witness.

Exception A formal objection to the action of the court during a trial. The indication is that the excepting party will seek to reverse the court's action at some future proceeding. *Objection.*

Exclusionary Rule Rule of evidence which makes illegally acquired evidence inadmissible; *see* Mapp vs. Ohio.

Expert Evidence Testimony by one qualified to speak authoritatively on technical matters because of his special training or skill.

Ex Post Facto After the fact. An ex post facto law is a criminal law that makes an act unlawful although it was committed prior to the passage of that law.

Extradition The surrender by one state to another of an individual accused of a crime.

False Arrest Any unlawful physical restraint of another's freedom of movement. Unlawful arrest.

Felonious Evil, malicious, or criminal. A felonious act is not necessarily a felony, but is criminal in some degree.

Felony Generally, an offense punishable by death or imprisonment in a penitentiary.

Forensic Relating to the court. Thus, forensic medicine would refer to medicine in relation to court proceedings and the law in general.

Grand Jury A group of 16 to 23 citizens of a county who examine evidence against the person suspected of a crime, and hand down an indictment if there is sufficient evidence to warrant one.

Habeas Corpus (Writ of) An order that requires a jailor, warden, police chief, or other public official to produce a person being held in custody before a court in order to show that they have a legal right to hold him in custody.

Hearsay Evidence not originating from the witness' personal knowledge.

Homicide The killing of a human being; may be murder, negligent or non-negligent manslaughter, or excusable or justifiable homicide.

Impeach To discredit. To question the truthfulness of a witness. Also: to charge a president or governor with criminal misconduct.

Imprisonment The act of confining a convicted felon in a federal or state prison.

In Camera In the judge's private chambers; in secrecy; the general public and press are excluded.

Indictment The document prepared by a prosecutor and approved by the grand jury which charges a certain person with a specific crime or crimes for which that person is later to be tried in court. Truebill.

Inference A conclusion one draws about something based on proof of certain other facts.

Injunction An order by a court prohibiting a defendant from committing an act.

Intent A design or determination of the mind to do or not do a certain thing. Intent may be determined from the nature of one's acts. Mens Rea.

Interpol International Criminal Police Commission.

Jail A short-term confinement institution for the detention of persons awaiting trial and the serving of sentences by those convicted of misdemeanors and offenses.

Jeopardy The danger of conviction and punishment that a defendant faces in a criminal trial. *Double Jeopardy.*

Judicial Notice The rule that a court will accept certain things as common knowledge without proof.

Jurisdiction The power of a court to hear and determine a criminal case.

Jury A certain number of persons who are sworn to examine the evidence and determine the truth on the basis of that evidence. Grand jury; trial jury.

Juvenile Delinquent A boy or girl who has not reached the age of criminal liability (varies from state to state) and who commits an act which would be a misdemeanor or felony if he were an adult. Delinquents are tried in *Juvenile Court* and confined to separate facilities.

L.E.A.A. Law Enforcement Assistance Administration, U.S. Dept. of Justice.

Leniency An unusually mild sentence imposed on a convicted offender; clemency granted by the President or a state governor; early release by a parole board.

Lie Detector An instrument which measures certain physiological reactions of the human body from which a trained operator may determine whether the subject is telling the truth or lies; polygraph; psychological stress evaluator.

Mala In Se Evil in itself. Acts that are made crimes because they are, by their nature, evil and morally wrong.

Mala Prohibita Evil because they are prohibited. Acts that are not wrong in themselves but which, to protect the general welfare, are made crimes by statute.

Malfeasance The act of a public officer in committing a crime relating to his official duties or powers. Accepting or demanding a bribe.

Malice An evil intent to vex, annoy, or injure another; intentional evil.

Malicious Prosecution An action instituted in bad faith with the intention of injuring the defendant.

Mandamus A writ that issues from a superior court, directed to any person, corporation, or inferior court, requiring it to do some particular thing.

Mens Rea A guilty intent.

Miranda Warning A police officer when taking a suspect into custody must warn him of his right to remain silent and of his right to an attorney.

Misdemeanor Any crime not a *Felony.* Usually, a crime punishable by a fine or imprisonment in the county or other local jail.

Misprision Failing to reveal a crime.

Mistrial A trial discontinued before reaching a verdict because of some procedural defect or impediment.

Modus Operandi Method of operation by criminals.

Motions Procedural moves made by either defense attorney or prosecutor and submitted to the court, helping to define and set the ground rules for the proceedings of a particular case. For example: to suppress illegally seized evidence or to seek a change of venue.

Motive The reason for committing a crime.

N.C.C.D. National Council on Crime and Delinquency.

No Bill A phrase used by a *Grand Jury* when they fail to indict.

Nolle Prosequi A declaration to a court, by the prosecutor that he does not wish to further prosecute the case.

Nolo Contendre A pleading, usually used by a defendant in a criminal case, that literally means "I will not contest."

Objection The act of taking exception to some statement or procedure in a trial. Used to call the court's attention to some improper evidence or procedure.

Opinion Evidence A witness' belief or opinion about a fact in dispute, as distinguished from personal knowledge of the fact. Expert testimony.

Ordinance A statute enacted by the city or municipal government.

Organized Crime The crime syndicate; cosa nostra; Mafia; an organized, continuing criminal conspiracy which engages in crime as a business (e.g., loan sharking, illegal gambling, prostitution, extortion, etc.).

Original Jurisdiction Trial jurisdiction.

Over Act An open or physical act, as opposed to a thought or mere intention.

Pardon Executive clemency setting aside a conviction and penalty.

Parole A conditional release from prison, under supervision.

Penal Code The criminal law of a jurisdiction, (sometimes the criminal procedure law is included but in other states it is codified separately).

Penology The study of punishment and corrections.

Peremptory Challenge The act of objecting to a certain number of jurors without assigning a cause for their dismissal. Used during the *voir dire* examination.

Perjury The legal offense of deliberately testifying falsely under oath about a material fact.

Petit Jury The ordinary jury composed of 12 persons who hear criminal cases. Determines guilt or innocence of the accused.

Plea-Bargaining A negotiation between the defense attorney and the prosecutor in which defendant receives a reduced penalty in return for a plea of "guilty."

Police Power The authority of the legislation to make laws in the interest of the general public, even at the risk of placing some hardship on individuals.

Post Mortem After death. Commonly applied to examination of a dead body. An autopsy is a post mortem examination to determine the cause of death.

Preliminary Hearing A proceeding in front of a lower court to determine if there is sufficient evidence for submitting a felony case to the grand jury.

Presumption of Fact An inference as to the truth or falsity of any proposition or fact, made in the absence of actual certainty of its truth or falsity or until such certainty can be attained.

Presumption of Law A rule of law that courts and judges must draw a particular inference from a particular fact or evidence, unless the inference can be disproved.

Prima Facie So far as can be judged from the first appearance or at first sight.

Prison Federal or state penal institution for the confinement of convicted felons. Penitentiary.

Probation A penalty placing a convicted person under the supervision of a probation officer for a stated time, instead of being confined.

Prosecutor One who initiates a criminal prosecution against an accused. One who acts as a trial attorney for the government as the representative of the people.

Provost Marshal Military police officer in charge of discipline, crime control and traffic law enforcement at a military post.

Public Defender An appointed or elected public official charged with providing legal representation for indigent persons accused of crimes.

Reasonable Doubt That state of mind of jurors when they do not feel a moral certainty about the truth of the charge and when the evidence does not exclude every other reasonable hypothesis except that the defendant is guilty as charged.

Rebuttal The introduction of contradicting testimony; the showing that statements made by a witness are not true; the point in the trial at which such evidence may be introduced.

Recidivist A repeater in crime; a habitual offender.

Recognizance When a person binds himself to do a certain act or else suffer a penalty, as, for example, with a recognizance bond. Release on recognizance is release without posting bail or bond.

Relevant Applying to the issue in question; related to the issue; useful in determining the truth or falsity of an alleged fact.

Remand To send back. To remand a case for new trial or sentencing.

Reprieve A stay of execution or sentence.

Search Warrant A written order, issued by judicial authority in the name of the state, directing a law enforcement officer to search for personal property and, if found, to bring it before the court.

Sentence The punishment (harsh or lenient) imposed by the trial judge on a convicted offender; major options include: fines, probation, indeterminate sentencing (e.g., three to ten years), indefinite sentencing (e.g., not more than three years), and capital punishment (death).

Stare Decisis To abide by decided cases. The doctrine that once a court has laid down a principle of law as applicable to certain facts, it will apply it to all future cases when the facts are substantially the same.

State's Evidence Testimony given by an accomplice or participant in a crime, tending to convict others.

Status Offense An act which is punishable only because the offender has not as yet reached a statutorily prescribed age (e.g., truancy, running away, drinking alcoholic beverages by a minor, etc.).

Statute A law.

Stay A stopping of a judicial proceeding by a court order.

Subpoena A court order requiring a witness to attend and testify in a court proceeding.

Subpoena Duces Tecum A court order requiring a witness to testify and to bring all books, documents, and papers that might affect the outcome of the proceedings.

Summons An order to appear in court on a particular date, which is issued by a police officer after or instead of arrest. It may also be a notification to a witness or a juror to appear in court.

Suspect One whom the police have determined as very likely to be the guilty perpetrator of an offense. Once the police identify a person as a suspect, they must warn him of his rights (Miranda warning) to remain silent and to have legal advice.

Testimony Evidence given by a competent witness, under oath, as distinguished from evidence from writings and other sources.

Tort A legal wrong committed against a person or property for which compensation may be obtained by a civil action.

Uniform Crime Reports (U.C.R.) Annual statistical tabulation of "crimes known to the police" and "crimes cleared by arrest" published by the Federal Bureau of Investigation.

Venue The geographical area in which a court with jurisdiction sits. The power of a court to compel the presence of the parties to a litigation. See also *Change of Venue*.

Verdict The decision of a court.

Victimology Sub-discipline of criminology which emphasizes the study of victims; includes *victim compensation*.

Voir Dire The examination or questioning of prospective jurors.

Waive To give up a personal right. For example: to testify before the grand jury.

Warrant A court order directing a police officer to arrest a named person or search a specific premise.

Witness One who has seen, heard, acquired knowledge about some element in a crime. An *expert witness* is one who, though he has no direct knowledge of the crime for which the defendant is being tried, may testify as to the defendant's sanity, the amount of alcohol in the deceased's blood, whether a signature is genuine, that a fingerprint is or is not that of the accused, etc.

Index

Credits/
Acknowledgments

Cover design by Charles Vitelli

1. Crime and Justice in America
Facing overview—Courtesy of Pamela Carley Petersen.

2. Victimology
Facing overview—EPA Documerica.

3. Police
Facing overview—Insurance Institute for Highway Safety.

4. The Judicial System
Facing overview—EPA Documerica.

5. Juvenile Justice
Facing overview—United Nations photo by John Robaton.

6. Punishment and Corrections
Facing overview—Federal Bureau of Prisons.

ANNUAL EDITIONS ARTICLE REVIEW FORM

■ NAME: _____ DATE: _____

■ TITLE AND NUMBER OF ARTICLE: _____

■ BRIEFLY STATE THE MAIN IDEA OF THIS ARTICLE: _____

_____

_____

_____

_____

■ LIST THREE IMPORTANT FACTS THAT THE AUTHOR USES TO SUPPORT THE MAIN IDEA:

_____

_____

_____

_____

_____

_____

■ WHAT INFORMATION OR IDEAS DISCUSSED IN THIS ARTICLE ARE ALSO DISCUSSED IN YOUR
TEXTBOOK OR OTHER READING YOU HAVE DONE? LIST THE TEXTBOOK CHAPTERS AND PAGE
NUMBERS:

_____

_____

_____

_____

_____

_____

■ LIST ANY EXAMPLES OF BIAS OR FAULTY REASONING THAT YOU FOUND IN THE ARTICLE:

_____

_____

_____

_____

■ LIST ANY NEW TERMS/CONCEPTS THAT WERE DISCUSSED IN THE ARTICLE AND WRITE A
SHORT DEFINITION:

_____

_____

_____

_____

*Your instructor may require you to use this Annual Editions Article Review Form in any number of ways:
for articles that are assigned, for extra credit, as a tool to assist in developing assigned papers, or simply
for your own reference. Even if it is not required, we encourage you to photocopy and use this page:
you'll find that reflecting on the articles will greatly enhance the information from your text.

ANNUAL EDITIONS: CRIMINAL JUSTICE 91/92

Article Rating Form

Here is an opportunity for you to have direct input into the next revision of this volume. We would like you to rate each of the 44 articles listed below, using the following scale:

1. **Excellent: should definitely be retained**
2. **Above average: should probably be retained**
3. **Below average: should probably be deleted**
4. **Poor: should definitely be deleted**

Your ratings will play a vital part in the next revision. So please mail this prepaid form to us just as soon as you complete it.
Thanks for your help!

We Want Your Advice

Annual Editions revisions depend on two major opinion sources: one is our Advisory Board, listed in the front of this volume, which works with us in scanning the thousands of articles published in the public press each year; the other is you—the person actually using the book. Please help us and the users of the next edition by completing the prepaid article rating form on this page and returning it to us. Thank you.

Rating	Article	Rating	Article
	1. An Overview of the Criminal Justice System		23. Public Defenders
	2. What Is Crime?		24. The Prosecutor as a 'Minister of Justice'
	3. Are Criminals Made or Born?		25. Pretrial Diversion: Promises We Can't Keep
	4. Number of Killings Soars In Big Cities Across the U.S.		26. The Myth of the General Right to Bail
	5. New Faces of Organized Crime		27. Convicting the Innocent
	6. New Strategies to Fight Crime Go Far Beyond Stiffer Terms and More Cells		28. When Criminal Rights Go Wrong
	7. RICO: A Racketeering Law Run Amok		29. Defendants Lose As Police Power Is Broadened
	8. Radical Right vs. Radical Left		30. Handling of Juvenile Cases
	9. The Fear of Crime		31. The Evolution of the Juvenile Justice System
	10. The Implementation of Victims' Rights: A Challenge for Criminal Justice Professionals		32. Girls' Crime and Woman's Place: Toward a Feminist Model of Female Delinquency
	11. Battered Families: Voices of the Abused; Voices of the Abusers		33. Juvenile Crime: Who Is Responsible?
	12. AIDS and Rape: Should New York Test Sex Offenders?		34. Teenage Addiction
	13. Can a Marriage Survive Tragedy?		35. Sentencing and Corrections
	14. Prostitutes and Addicts: Special Victims of Rape		36. Women in Jail: Unequal Justice
	15. Police Response to Crime		37. Some Observations of the Status and Performance of Female Corrections Officers in Men's Prisons
	16. The Police in the United States		38. You're Under Arrest—AT HOME
	17. Women On the Move? A Report on the Status of Women in Policing		39. Difficult Clients, Large Caseloads Plague Probation, Parole Agencies
	18. Making Neighborhoods Safe		40. Learning to Live With AIDS in Prison
	19. Community Policing: A Practical Guide for Police Officials		41. Of Crimes and Punishment
	20. Police, Hard Pressed in Drug War, Are Turning to Preventive Efforts		42. Turn the Jailhouse Into a Schoolhouse
	21. The Abortion Protesters and the Police		43. Family Violence Program at Bedford Hills . . . Feeling 'Free and Safe' in Prison
	22. The Judicial Process: Prosecutors and Courts		44. 'This Man Has Expired'

(Continued on next page)

ABOUT YOU

Name_____ Date_____

Are you a teacher? ☐ Or student? ☐

Your School Name _____

Department _____

Address _____

City _____ State _____ Zip _____

School Telephone # _____

YOUR COMMENTS ARE IMPORTANT TO US!

Please fill in the following information:

For which course did you use this book? _____

Did you use a text with this Annual Edition? ☐ yes ☐ no

The title of the text? _____

What are your general reactions to the Annual Editions concept?

Have you read any particular articles recently that you think should be included in the next edition?

Are there any articles you feel should be replaced in the next edition? Why?

Are there other areas that you feel would utilize an Annual Edition?

May we contact you for editorial input?

May we quote you from above?

ANNUAL EDITIONS: CRIMINAL JUSTICE 91/92